A
BLACK BYZANTIUM

THE *ETSU* NUPE

A
BLACK BYZANTIUM

THE KINGDOM OF NUPE
IN NIGERIA

BY

S. F. NADEL, PH.D.

Professor of Anthropology in the
National University of Australia, Canberra

WITH A FOREWORD BY
THE RIGHT HON. LORD LUGARD
G.C.M.G., D.S.O., O.B.E.
Formerly Governor General of Nigeria

Published for the
INTERNATIONAL AFRICAN INSTITUTE
by the
OXFORD UNIVERSITY PRESS
LONDON   NEW YORK   TORONTO

1942

Oxford University Press, Ely House, London W. 1

GLASGOW NEW YORK TORONTO MELBOURNE WELLINGTON
CAPE TOWN IBADAN NAIROBI DAR ES SALAAM LUSAKA ADDIS ABABA
DELHI BOMBAY CALCUTTA MADRAS KARACHI LAHORE DACCA
KUALA LUMPUR SINGAPORE HONG KONG TOKYO

ISBN 0 19 724123 9

First edition 1942
Reprinted 1946, 1951, 1961, 1965, 1969, and 1973

*Printed in Great Britain
at the University Press, Oxford
by Vivian Ridler
Printer to the University*

TO

MY WIFE

WHOSE BOOK THIS IS

AS MUCH AS MINE

FOREWORD

By LORD LUGARD

THIS exhaustive treatise on one of the most important communities in Nigeria owes its inception to the generosity of the Rockefeller Foundation of New York, which placed a large sum at the disposal of the International Institute for the Study of African Languages and Cultures. Fellowships were instituted to enable specially trained students to undertake scientific research into the social organization of a selected unit of African society, the factors of social cohesion which operate to prevent its disintegration by contact with European civilization, the openings for co-operation, and the tendencies towards new groupings. Others were specially concerned with linguistic studies.

Dr. Nadel, of the University of Vienna, was one of the original Fellows, and he selected the Nupe of the middle Niger for his field of research. He brought to his task not only a thorough mastery of the technique of scientific investigation, but an original mind, and a sympathy with and understanding of the African, which won the confidence and friendship without which scientific qualifications can effect little.

His exceptional talents as a linguist enabled him not only to converse, at first in the *lingua franca* (Hausa), but in less than six months to acquire, and speak with fluency the very difficult 'tone' language of the Nupe. Many an English reader of this book may even envy his command of idiomatic English. The Nupe seem to have regarded him as an unusual phenomenon and conferred upon him a high title of tribal rank.

As an 'Anthropologist' he is concerned at the outset to explain that the term—whether 'functional', 'practical', or 'applied'—is ill adapted to the research he had undertaken. But surely the study of 'a native society in all its complexity', and the factors which had affected its social evolution are better described as 'Sociology' than as 'Anthropology'—which is defined as 'the study of man as an animal'? A clear understanding on the other hand of the connotation of the term 'Culture' as used by a highly qualified sociologist is essential to the appreciation of his work.

'Culture (he says) varies with environment and . . . expresses the changing dominant interests involved in social, political, and economic conditions. . . . It is not a sum total of discrete traits (but) . . . a conscious unity created by and embodied in a common group life (by) . . . the people who form the group, . . . specific to it and only to it irrespective of variations within, or similarities with groups outside, the tribal boundaries.' (pp. 14–15.)

The distinctive individuality of the 'tribe' depends in turn on the presumption that it is a 'group possessing more or less the same culture' and language.

The 'social and economic complexity' of the Nupe State as it exists to-day is epitomized in the comparison he has chosen as the title for his book. Affiliations with neighbouring tribes, migrations to found new settlements, and above all the influence of foreign rulers have introduced modifications, but without radical change in the traditional culture. The complete absence of any written records, and the reticence of the people until complete confidence had been established, accentuate the difficulty of elucidating the origin of the tribe before and up to the death of Tsoede, the mythical founder of the kingdom. From the end of the sixteenth century, however, the history can claim comparative accuracy. Comparison of the Nupe language with those of neighbouring tribes is complicated by the existence of five distinct dialects.

Dr. Nadel's first object was to discriminate between the essential characteristics of Nupe culture, and the variations from the typical pattern in 'a heterogeneous society divided by gulfs of culture, ethnic extraction, community, and class'. For this purpose he considered that what he calls 'the anthropological quadrivium—kinship, political organization, economics and religion'—was unsuitable, and decided to base his research on 'the two inseparable aspects of culture, political and economic organization', with special reference to religion and law.

This involved in the first place an examination of 'the factors of social cohesion' upon which the claim of a community to rank as a unit of self-government is based, and in the second place the effect of changes brought about, *inter alia*, by contact with Europeans and especially by the British Administration—the two main objectives in his 'terms of reference'.

Since it is the declared policy of the British Government to help the different units of native society to govern themselves in accordance with civilized canons of justice, and of impartiality between rival claims arising from 'the interpenetration of essentially different social systems', such as Islam and paganism, it goes without the saying how valuable such an objective study would be to the Administration. We find that, in fact, it has been utilized in conjunction with the researches of District Officers.

Among the binding forces which constitute the state, kinship, says Dr. Nadel, has no part. Its influence is limited to component groups only. Nor can economic interdependence exert a binding influence. It is more likely to be disruptive. He finds that the factors which have contributed to the solidarity of the Nupe State are primarily the attachment of the people to the principle of Kingship, of which the *Etsu* (king) and the holders of the important Offices of State are the symbol.

The *Etsu* personifies the heroic achievements of the mythical Founders of the Kingdom whose glories are enshrined in legend and song, and in which the people take pride as citizens of the state. A second and potent centripetal force was the acceptance of the brotherhood of Islam, the creed of the ruling race, and the avenue to title and dignity.

The annual festival of the *Sallah* (*Id el Kebir*), attended by immense crowds, became a day of national ceremonial and national unity. To these influences may be added the common participation in a uniform system of law and justice. It is surprising that the cohesive effect of a language radically different from the *lingua franca* is not mentioned in this connexion, since it is surely one of the most important of the characteristics which confer a distinct individuality upon the Nupe State and a common bond among its people?

The two view-points of political and of economic organization inevitably involved research into 'urban and rural culture, Mohammedanism and paganism, the organization of the state, and the organization of the village community'. It is only possible here to name a few of the varied aspects of native life, of which the reader will find a very full analysis in these pages. They include the modifications of traditional law and custom brought about by the advent of Islam and later by the British Administration and the abolition of slavery.

The tenure of land; the place of women in the body politic; the relation of the ruling classes to the peasantry; the psychological effect of the multiplicity of titles of rank in every class and every vocation (not wholly peculiar to Nupe), are all exhaustively described. The comparatively advanced methods adopted in agriculture include manuring and rotation of crops, and Dr. Nadel has some shrewd comments on the system of 'mixed farming' introduced by the Government.

We learn how completely this African State has accustomed itself to a 'money-economy'—the extent of its trade, the contrasts between urban and rural economy, the system of collective assistance (*egbe*) and 'labour-units', and of financial expedients such as *dashi*, with careful estimates of the cost of living and of the family budgets of different classes. The account of the different Guilds—of blacksmiths, glass-makers, weavers and the rest, including the 'luxury-crafts' of bead-workers, and of artistic ornaments, is specially interesting.

The book is an exhaustive and meticulous picture of the life of an African community which has maintained its individuality through many cycles of change. It will be a very valuable addition to the parallel researches by other Fellows of the Institute. We may congratulate the Sudan on having secured the services of so competent a sociologist.

ABINGER COMMON
September 1941

INTRODUCTION

THIS book has been conceived, written, and published under the shadow that darkens the face of the world to-day. We have long believed that the furtherance of knowledge carries its own justification. But in recent years the legitimacy of pure, self-contained, detached science has become more and more dubious.[1] For no field of science is this more true than for the science of society, which has been pressed into the service of ruthless political aims, persecution, and suppression. Historical falsifications, racial doctrines, distorted dogmas of social necessities, have produced weapons no less deadly than those manufactured in factories and laboratories. A science that could be thus abused must no longer hope to recover its spurious detachment. It will find redemption only in closeness to the problems of our existence as society and civilization.

A student of society professing this belief in the social mission of science could not wish for more congenial material than the African society described in these pages. Indeed, I have not been satisfied with the bare description of a remote and strange social existence. I have tried, on a modest scale, to contribute to our understanding of the forces that shape the fate of societies—of our own society to-day as of that West African polity. Wars, suppression, persecution, and the reactions against these forces—you will find them all in this book. And you will find them so presented that their relation to the problems of our own social existence is never obscured. I believe that some lessons might be read from these facts: at least, I have tried to write them out as legibly as I could.

And another thing. Large parts of this book are dedicated to what has become known as 'practical' or 'applied' anthropology. It has been said that modern anthropology is destined to be of great assistance to colonial governments in providing the knowledge of the social structure of native groups upon which a sound and harmonious Native Administration, as envisaged in Indirect Rule, should be built. Let me say that I for one firmly believe in the possibility of such co-operation between anthropologist and administrator. Indeed I hope that this book will bring evidence of the fruitfulness of the co-operation. The form which it should take in the concrete case is perhaps not as yet well defined or universally accepted, and a few words must be said about the view taken in this book.

Obviously, the description of a native society as it might appear if it had never been touched by modern changes, even a mere compilation of facts to which the administrator could turn as to a dictionary or gazetteer, would be misleading because artificially simplified. It must be the duty of the anthropologist to demonstrate the native society in all its complexity, fashioned as it is by a multitude of social causes and effects, in which the efforts of administration represent causes and effects

[1] See J. D. Bernal, *The Social Function of Science*, 1939.

among others. It may be debatable how far the anthropologist can go in
this demonstration without introducing values of his own, without
venturing criticisms or committing himself to concrete suggestions, and
thus going outside his domain. But there can be no doubt about the
legitimacy of his task to demonstrate alternative developments that have
arisen, or are likely to arise, from administrative measures or their
omission, from a new extraneous change or the unbroken continuance of
an indigenous institution. If such a view is called implied or indirect
criticism, I shall bear the blame lightly. For this 'indirect criticism' is
nothing but a legitimate scientific device (used throughout the book) to
assess the effectiveness of social forces—internal or extraneous, historical
or modern. Moreover, all criticism stands or falls with the conception of
principles and necessities of which it is an expression. Anthropologists
and administrators may differ about these principles and necessities—
we anthropologists are the first to realize this. But we feel that this
divergence of view—if divergence there be—should be placed in the full
light of knowledge; if our 'criticisms' are discounted, as indeed they
may well be, the final decision should yet be inspired by them, and take
the form of conscious choice.

Modern anthropologists will not lightly surrender their claim to the
name 'explorer'. True, their work no longer takes them to peoples
whom no traveller has yet encountered, and to countries which no white
man's eye has yet seen. But they probe more deeply into the society of
primitive man than any of the early explorers. They have set themselves the task of lifting the knowledge of primitive cultures beyond
casual acquaintance, on to the plane of true scientific insight. They are
explorers, not of the surface of the globe, but of an unknown social realm.
As an explorer, the anthropologist is faced with the difficulties of
method and technique that beset all pioneer work. Anthropology in this
new intensive sense is a young science, which is still evolving its
methods of approach and has to find its instruments of research as it
goes along. It has not yet been able even to map out with sufficient
exactitude all the possible forms of society which its field-workers might
encounter. Every new field-work may mean the discovery of unknown
social structures unapproachable with the techniques hitherto used.
This is indeed the plea that this book makes: a plea for understanding—
and consideration—of its nature as a pioneer work, and for the difficulties and shortcomings inherent in such work.
The present book can claim to be regarded as a pioneer work in more
than one respect. The technique of modern anthropology ('functional'
anthropology as it is called by some) has been evolved on small islands
in the Pacific, and in the study of small groups and cultures infinitely
simpler than our historical civilizations. The West African society dealt
with in this book is half a million strong. It is far from 'simple' or
'primitive'. Its social and economic complexity is comparable only with
the civilizations of Imperial Rome, of Byzantium, of medieval Europe.
Yet if the technique of anthropological field-work in the accepted sense
must thus prove inadequate, the method of approach normally applied

in the study of these historical cultures is equally barred. Very few historical records exist, and they are hardly informative from the sociological point of view. The people of Nupe have not yet risen to the stage of education producing written records and accounts of important events or institutions. With the exception of a few educated Mohammedan scholars whose co-operation I was able to enlist in the recording of folk-lore and historical traditions, I have been unable to use a single literate informant, for example, to keep diaries of important events, or to handle questionnaires. Lastly, the most essential evidence in the study of complex societies, namely statistics, scarcely exists. The statistics in this book were, with few exceptions, compiled single-handed and on a scale of the inadequacy of which no one can be more aware than the author.

I have described elsewhere the technique of inquiry which I applied, and need say nothing on that point here.[1] But it is necessary to describe the general plan of research I pursued, for it illustrates the methods by which I attempted to circumvent some of the difficulties just mentioned. I spent two years in the field, in the course of two expeditions in 1934 and 1935–6. From the outset I was confronted with the problem how to cover, in intensive study, the vast area inhabited by the Nupe people. The political configuration forbade the selection of one section to the disregard of others. The widespread political system had clearly to be studied at different points, in its centre as well as on its periphery. Moreover, a short preliminary survey already revealed the existence of considerable cultural differences within the tribe. The further my studies proceeded the more manifest became the significance of these differences as variations of a common pattern, the study of which was essential to the understanding of the forces that moulded the culture of the people. The investigation thus became perforce a comparative study within the framework of one tribe and one culture. At a certain stage of my investigation I even had to go outside this framework and devote some study to neighbouring groups—the Kakanda, Gbari, and Bassa—which, closely akin to the Nupe and partly their fellow citizens in the Nupe kingdom, might throw light on certain aspects of Nupe culture.

The main problem was to discover representative sections and centres for the study of this widely spread social system and its varying culture. I will not speak of the difficulties which I encountered in this task, helped as I was only by records and information which soon proved superficial and inexact. In the first six or seven months I was reduced almost to the method of trial and error: a very short stay in a new place would have been useless even merely to discover whether or not this place might prove a useful centre; and once I decided on a long stay the time was gone and could not be recovered even if the place turned out to be less profitable than I had expected. Let me admit that this did indeed happen in two villages (Mokwa and Sakpe) which I had made my centres upon the advice of various informants and which, as I discovered later, were not as significant or essential as certain other places would have been. However, certain general facts about the culture and the

[1] See 'The Interview Technique in Social Anthropology', in *The Study of Society*, chapter xiii, 1939.

people could be obtained there as well as anywhere, and on my second expedition I could to some extent correct the mistakes of the first. On the other hand, I was unable to study one or two villages (e.g. Yeti, in the oil-palm area, and Kutiwengi, where an interesting variety of a certain religious cult is reported to exist), because I had discovered their significance too late and my time did not allow the inclusion of further centres and communities.

The main centres on which I based my investigation were: Bida town, with its surrounding belt of hamlets and small villages; the large villages of Kutigi, in the centre of Nupe country, and Mokwa, in the west; and finally Jebba Island on the Niger, which commands an important stretch of the river area. Each of these centres I visited several times. The repeated periods of study enabled me to check my material and to remedy oversights; often they led to the discovery of new points of view which only emerged from the comparison of the cultural variations typical of different areas and local communities. In addition I stayed for shorter periods in certain other communities in order to study a specific question or to collect certain comparative evidence. Thus, for example, I paid several short visits to the village Lemu, twenty miles north of Bida, because a new commercial crop had been adopted that year by the people of Lemu; and once I spent two weeks in Patigi (a quite uninteresting visit, by the way), because there the last descendants of the old dynasty of Nupe kings hold court.

Bida, the large capital of the country, required the longest time. Here also I began my studies of the Nupe language with the help of the English- and Hausa-speaking teachers of Bida Middle School. During these first months I carried out my anthropological work through the medium of Hausa, which I had studied before going to the field, and which is widely understood among the people of Bida, but from the fifth or sixth month of my stay I used Nupe exclusively. During the first expedition I spent altogether six months in Bida and the Bida area, in the course of three visits; three months in Kutigi, in the course of two visits; and one month each in Mokwa, Agaie, and Jebba Island. During the second expedition I spent five months in Bida, in the course of two visits, two months in Kutigi, in the course of two visits, three months, in one visit, in Jebba and on the river, and two months on travels to the neighbouring area of Gbari country and to Ilorin, Ibadan, and Lokoja, where I made a special study of the large Nupe colonies in these towns.

The difficulty of discovering in this large and complex culture representative areas and group sections, and of distinguishing them from others whose cultural life must be regarded as a variation of the main pattern, arises in a different form with regard to documentation. The problem here is how to prove with scientific exactitude the typical or non-typical nature of cultural facts and events, and how to present them convincingly as representative or as in some degree deviating from the norm. The distinction between typical and non-typical facts is primarily a question of frequency, and the ideal method of documentation would be one in which all descriptions and analyses were backed by statistical evidence. For obvious reasons such a method of documentation is rarely applicable. So far as it was possible I have made efforts to supplement all descriptions with quantitative evidence to show the frequency and regularity of social facts and events. It must be understood that where I limited myself to a few descriptions or single instances these are presented (unless stated otherwise) as typical instances, and that there exists sufficient evidence of their representative nature. But I must admit that in certain cases no such evidence could be adduced: if I record the absence of a certain cultural fact or its occurrence in a certain degree of frequency, this may only mean that the fact did not occur at all, or did not occur in any higher degree of frequency, in the areas and groups with which I was mainly dealing, and during the time of my investigation. Unhappily, the orbit of the anthropologist is limited by time and space. The larger and more complex the group which he studies, the more strongly he feels his dependence upon that treacherous purveyor of facts, chance. It was chance that brought to my knowledge the fact that in one small and unimportant Nupe village succession to chieftainship is matrilineal—an isolated occurrence in that otherwise conspicuously patrilineal society. And it was chance that led me to the discovery, in a small riverain village, of a certain ritual which amounted to a symbolic 'king-killing'—again a usage for which there seems to be no parallel in other parts of Nupe. I could discover no evidence that would allow me to explain these anomalies, and I have put them down as such, well aware of the possibility (slight though it may be) of such evidence existing, undiscovered, in the villages and group sections of Nupe to which my studies did not extend. The general knowledge of the cultural constellation gained from the available material allows us to a certain extent to formulate theories, to predict, as it were, whether or not a certain cultural fact is likely to occur, or to occur in this or that frequency. But we can predict only a likelihood; we can delimit the possible sources of error: we can eliminate them as little as we can eliminate chance itself.

The presentation of the material involves also difficulties of a more technical nature. Its very quantity forbade treatment in the form of a comprehensive monograph. Nor did the material lend itself to a neat division into a number of separate treatises each dealing with a different aspect of the anthropological quadrivium—kinship, political organization, economics, religion. The solution could only be found in a compromise. My original intention was to build the book round the relation between the two paramount group configurations, political association and family—'Kingdom and Kinship'. But this would still have meant a very unwieldy book. The final result, then, is a 'rump' monograph, dealing with the culture of Nupe viewed from the two angles of political and economic organization—two aspects of culture which must be regarded as inseparable. Even so, I had to leave out, or to reduce to a short quasi-preliminary outline, the description of two domains of culture the bearing of which upon the problems of the book I will not minimize: religion and law.

I must anticipate two further criticisms. One may be provoked by the rather unusual dichotomous arrangement of certain chapters. It was necessitated by the nature of the material, by the contrasting configurations which dominate the cultural life of Nupe—urban and rural culture, Mohammedanism and paganism, the organization of the state and the organization of the village community. One dichotomous formulation I have made almost the *leitmotif* of this analysis, namely, the twofold classification of social systems, formulated most clearly by MacIver, into *Communities* and *Associations*. Let me quote his definition: Community is a 'circle of people who live together, who belong together, so that they share, not this or that particular interest, but a whole set of interests wide enough and comprehensive enough to include their lives'. And Association: 'a group specifically organized for the purpose of an interest or group of interests which its members have in common.'[1] These two categories are used in this book consistently in MacIver's sense, that is, as descriptive categories defining, not rigidly separated social entities, but rather two poles of a more fluid social reality of many shades and grades.

Again, it might be objected that the descriptive accounts in this book are frequently interspersed with theoretical discussions. I shall offer no apology. Description is meaningless and misleading unless supplemented by a clarification of the concepts and categories with which it operates, and by an assessment in terms of theoretical generalizations of the concrete data which it produces. This is doubly true of the complex and, from the viewpoint of traditional anthropology, unusual culture described in this book. Thus I was forced to devote comparatively long theoretical discussions to the examination of such concepts as 'tribe' (in Chapter II) and 'state' (in Chapter VI), to the analysis of social class in Nupe (Chapter VIII), and to an inquiry into the relation between economics and sociology (Chapter XX).

In the research programme of the International Institute of African Languages and Cultures, under whose auspices the present investigation was carried out, the study of culture change under the impact of modern Western civilization is assigned a prominent place. Culture contact in Nupe is not restricted to this most recent historical phase; nor does it affect only certain well-defined domains of social life—it pervades the whole history and the whole living culture of the people. Nor can it be said (with some anthropologists) that the study of modern culture contact entails specific methods of approach, applicable only to this one aspect of social development. It did not therefore seem feasible to concentrate its examination in special chapters. Every description and analysis contained in this book bears to lesser or greater extent also on the problems of culture contact and culture change, ancient or modern. Only in a few instances did the material lend itself to a separate treatment of modern culture contact. They will be found in Chapter X, under the heading 'Problems of Adaptation', in Chapter XVII, which is entitled 'Industrial Labour', and in Chapter XIX, in the section on 'Modern Business Methods'.

[1] R. M. MacIver, *Society, Its Structure and Changes*, 1931, pp. 9, 12, 13.

A minor technical point, in conclusion. In the orthography of vernacular words I have used the phonetic script generally accepted to-day by students of African languages, which, in the case of Nupe, contains only two not very common symbols: ~ for nasalized vowels, and ẓ for the fricative sound (like s in 'lesion'). I have not distinguished open and closed e and o vowels since this distinction is not of great importance in Nupe. And, for the sake of simplicity, I have not marked tones, although Nupe is a pure tone language; or rather, I have reduced the symbols for the five tones of Nupe (low, medium, high, rising, and falling tone) to a single accent (') indicating the relative higher tone—a mark which the reader unfamiliar with tone languages can interpret as accent indicating stress. In words where no accents are marked, the different syllables are of equal tone or stress. I have marked the low tone only in the case of the negation, which consists of the suffix a pronounced on the low tone (à). In the spelling of geographical names I have kept largely to the spelling used in official maps (e.g. Kacha instead of Kaca). Only where the official spelling is at variance with the correct pronunciation have I corrected the spelling (e.g. Gbako river for Bako river, Eggã for Eggan, &c.).

There remains the last task of Introductions—acknowledgements. The first acknowledgements are due to my teachers and friends, to whom I owe most of my scientific equipment, the late Professors Malinowski and Seligman; to the International Institute of African Languages and Cultures, as whose research fellow I went to the field and whose subsidy rendered the publication of this book possible; and to the Government of Nigeria and to the many officers with whom my work has brought me into contact for the generous help in many forms which they extended to me throughout my stay in Nigeria. I am greatly indebted to Professor Radcliffe-Brown for many fruitful suggestions and criticisms. I owe special gratitude to Sir Gordon Lethem, Governor of the Leeward Islands, late Lieutenant-Governor of Northern Nigeria, who first drew my attention to the Nupe tribe, and to the Rev. Dr. G. P. Bargery, who initiated me into the secrets of Hausa and the world of Nigeria. Mr. T. E. Alvarez of the Church Missionary Society in Bida and Rev. Ira W. Sherk of the United Sudan Mission in Mokwa have been most kind friends and helpers to the new-comer in a country of which they had lifelong knowledge. Last but not least I owe deep gratitude to all my native friends without whose freely given help my work would not have succeeded: *Etsu* Ndayako, the Emir of Bida; Mallam Aliyu, the Headmaster of Bida Middle School, who was my teacher in Nupe and my first guide through Bida life; Mallam Ndayako, whom I was proud to call my friend; old Ndakotsu, who is dead now, and who was so close a friend of mine that the Bida people knew me as the *nasara* Ndakotsu—Ndakotsu's European; and many others whose words and opinions are quoted in these pages.

CONTENTS

LIST OF ILLUSTRATIONS

MAPS

CHAPTER I

ENVIRONMENT

THE COUNTRY

THE people who call themselves Nupe live in the heart of Nigeria, in the low basin that is formed by the valleys of the two rivers Niger and Kaduna, between 9° 30' and 8° 30' N.L. A line drawn from Leaba, on the Niger, eastward to Kataeregi marks the northern boundary of Nupe land, another line drawn eastward from Shari (or Tsaragi) to Abugi and on to the Niger south of Baro the southern boundary. The Niger, flowing almost straight north–south between Leaba and Jebba, divides Nupe country from Yoruba in the west; the slowly rising country, east of Lapai and Gidi, sloping upward towards the hills of Gbari country, forms the eastern boundary of Nupe.

It is a low-lying, softly undulating country, not more than 200 feet above sea-level in most parts. A few low ridges of broken, rocky hills stretch out, rib-like, from the river valleys, and curiously symmetrical flat-topped hillocks rise abruptly here and there from the plain. The highest points are no more than 800 feet above sea-level. At Jebba the Niger forces its way through a narrow passage formed by rocks, the ragged end of a short, broken chain of hills. Farther south, at Kpatagbā and Baro, and above Yankyedya in the north, hills and rocks close in upon the river. Rabá, the ancient river capital of Nupe kingdom, stands on high cliffs of red sandstone. Between cliffs and rocks the river bed is bordered by low banks on which stretches of thick rain-forest alternate with shrub and low bush. During the rains both forest-covered banks and open bush are flooded far inland and turned into vast swamps; the level of the Kaduna at Wuya rises by 30 feet; and in the Niger valley villages which lie on high ground in the dry season have the water of the river washing the threshold of their houses. Part of Jebba Island is flooded every year; and Nupeko, near the confluence of Niger and Kaduna, about two miles from the river in the dry season, can be reached only by canoe in the rains.

The big rivers Niger and Kaduna form the two axes of the country, an efficient, natural system of communication. It is no accident that the early Nupe kingdom grew in the area near the confluence of the two rivers, which were its first high-roads as well as its natural boundaries. A net of smaller rivers and creeks, rich in fish, covers the country, providing an efficient system of natural irrigation. In most parts of Nupe land the soil is rich and fertile, especially in the thinly inhabited districts west of the Kaduna, the only part of Nupe which still possesses large areas of virgin forest. East of the Kaduna, especially round Bida, a dense population and intensive cultivation have reduced the fertility of the land. It is the typical soil of Northern Nigeria, red earth mixed with laterite and rich in silicates—a fact which becomes important for the native glass industry in Bida. In a few districts, round Sakpe and near

Lemu, pure white sand is found, a much more fertile soil as far as I can judge, which makes the country in the eyes of the native 'more beautiful' —by which he really means 'more useful'. Lastly, the low broken hills of Nupe are ferruginous, and on their slopes iron ore is mined by the natives.

VEGETATION AND NATURAL RESOURCES

The geographical position of Nupe country makes it a typical area of transition from the southern forest belt to the arid savannahs of the north. Narrow strips or patches of thick rain-forest-like vegetation accompany river valleys and watercourses; but then, inland, we find a country of thin forest, shrub, and 'orchard-bush', alternating with beautiful open park-land, such as round Bida and Agaie, where intensive cultivation has cleared bush and shrub. The plant-life, again, reflects the geographical position of Nupe midway between north and south. Nupe is one of the northernmost countries in which the oil-palm is found, and yam and the southern variety of maize are cultivated; it is, at the same time, the southernmost habitat of the date-palm, the shea-nut tree, and millet crops. The trees and plants which are important for Nupe production and diet are these, in the order of importance. In the drier inland areas we find the locust-bean tree (*Parkia filikoidea*), in Nupe *lonci*; the shea-nut tree (*Bassia Parkii*), *koci*; the indigo tree or vine (*Lonchocarpus cyanescens*), *eci* and indigo grass (*Indigofera arrecta*), *tsentse*; baobab (*Andansonia digitata*), *kuci* or *kuka*; silk-cotton tree (*Malvaceae*), *lembubu*; date-palm, *dobina*; and finally the mango, *man-goro*, a European importation. On irrigated land and in the thick groves near watercourses grow the oil-palm and other, less important, varieties of palm-trees, kola-nut tree (*Sterculia acuminata*), *ebì*, and banana, *yaba*. Only the kola-nut tree, the mango, and partly the banana are cultivated, all other trees growing wild. Nupe cultivation comprises the following kinds of crops and edible plants and roots: three millet varieties, bulrush-millet (*Pennisetum*), *mayi*, 'late millet' (*Spicatum*), *kpayi*, and guinea-corn (*Sorghum vulgare*), *eyi*; yam, *eci*; cassava, *rogo*; maize, *kábà*; ground-nuts, *gužya*; rice, *jenkafa*; sugar-cane, *kpãsanako*; and onions, *lubasa*, in the river marshes; further sweet potatoes, *duku*; beans and ground-beans, *ezo* and *edzu*; red pepper, *yaká*, and various kinds of greens which are eaten as vegetable. Of plants utilized commercially and in native industry cotton, *lulu*; henna, *lali*; hemp, *rama* or *egba*, 'rope'; and gourds, *evo*, are the most important.

In this enumeration of crops and plants of Nupe we have left the field of physical environment in the narrow sense. This rich and varied system of cultivation reflects already a standard of civilization, technical achievement, and inventiveness of a people which has learned to master its environment. Some of the plants and crops mentioned have been adopted comparatively recently and introduced into Nupe from the north and south. As the Nupe names for hemp, henna, or cassava are borrowed from Hausa the plants themselves represent 'borrowed' cultural goods. The cultivation of onions was introduced into Nupe from

Hausa, and partly from Bornu, in historical times.[1] Nor is the cultivation of yam an original cultural possession of the Nupe, which is proved by two facts: first, that the Nupe north and east of the Niger are unfamiliar with certain important ways of preparing yam common in all 'real' yam countries, e.g. the drying of yam; and second, that yam, though to-day an important staple food, has still no place in their sacrifices, ritual meals, and first-crop ceremonies: only corn and millet may be used for these ritual offerings.[2] Cassava, finally, has only been introduced in the last thirty years; thirty years ago, I was told by a missionary, it was almost unknown in Nupe. Thus communication and culture contact have helped to mould the physical environment of to-day. This manifold agricultural system, however, could not have been evolved if the natural conditions of the country had not been favourable. The meeting of south and north in the vegetation of Nupe, the coexistence of marsh-land and savannah country, the natural irrigation and the strips and patches of thick forest, all this was as essential to the development of the productive system of the country as was the inventiveness and stage of civilization of its people. We cannot attempt to decide which factor, environment or civilization, has had the larger share in this development. The rigid distinction between environment and culture has long been abandoned as misleading and futile. For our investigation it is irrelevant. We can well regard the environment as it appears at present, the natural resources as they are utilized by the people to-day, as a unitary complex of factors the effect of which, upon the life and well-being of the people, we have to examine.

CLIMATE

Nupe, lower lying than any of the neighbouring districts, with its two big rivers, their dry, blazing sand-banks in the dry season, and their vast swamps in the rains, is one of the hottest and at the same time most humid districts of Nigeria. The river valleys especially, and the hollow in which Bida is situated, are damp, airless, and unhealthy. The following figures give the average temperature, humidity, and rainfall in Bida for 1933:[3]

TABLE I

	Jan.	Feb.	Mar.	Apr.	May	June	July	Aug.	Sept.	Oct.	Nov.	Dec.	Annual total
Minimum temp.	60	70	72	72	71	71	68	68	68	70	70	67	..
Maximum temp.	93	98	102	103	98	88	92	90	85	91	96	96	..
Humidity (per cent.)	60	50	66	71	78	92	92	92	85	76	75	62	..
Rainfall (in inches)	2·99	..	..	1·99	3·06	12·33	15·41	15·82	11·87	2·29	0·32	..	66·08

[1] It is still practised to-day by the Bornu settlers of Kutigi.

[2] There is one exception: Mokwa, in the north-west corner of Nupe, where yam is sacrificed at certain annual rites. But the exception proves the rule, for Mokwa is the gate for cultural influences from Yoruba.

[3] This table was copied from the readings taken regularly in Bida Middle School.

The highest temperature measured in Bida was 106 in the shade, only a few degrees lower than in the hottest (but driest) district of Nigeria, Bornu. The humidity of Bida, on the other hand, almost equals the humidity in the rain-forest belt. The combination of features from south and north which seems characteristic of Nupe country has its most unfavourable aspect in climatic conditions. The influence of the unfavourable climate upon the health of the natives is evident .in the large proportion of people suffering from lung trouble and rheumatic diseases. Climate and soil combine to even more deadly effects: full of malaria-carrying mosquitoes, the river forests infested with tsetse-fly, and all watercourses polluted with bilharzia, Nupe is indeed an ill-favoured country.

The tsetse-infected areas have played their part in Nupe history. The forest belt in the south, of which the strips of river forest in Nupe are the northernmost outposts, marks the southern boundary of cattle and horse in Nigeria. The parts of Nupe which are free from tsetse are also safe for horses and cattle (more precisely, the northern breed of cattle, which is not immune from trypanosomiasis). Nupe country, with the neighbouring Ilorin—the southernmost country in which horses can be kept and to which the nomadic Fulani herdsmen can take their cattle—became also the southern outpost of the Fulani Empire, the southern-most stronghold of that race of cattle-people and horsemen whose spectacular conquest of Nigeria was stemmed only by the natural bulwark of the forest belt.

HEALTH AND DISEASE

In the Census of 1931 Nupe appears among the districts with the highest proportion of blindness, leprosy, and insanity.[1] In the case of leprosy the Census estimate of over 5, and possibly over 10, per thousand is hardly exaggerated—even casual observation shows this, although the fear and secrecy that surround this disease among the Nupe make a more precise estimate impossible. Information which I obtained on the spot, from the Medical Officer in charge of Bida Native Administration Hospital, rather went to show that blindness is not more frequent in Nupe than elsewhere in Nigeria. As regards the proportion of insanity, I have seen too few cases to venture any definite opinion. A remark on the nature of the mental disorders, however, may not be without interest. Of the five cases which I have seen three showed clear symptoms of paranoid schizophrenia—strongly delusional thinking, to the extent of persecution mania, combined with violent aggressiveness which appeared and subsided with marked suddenness, and involving no general degeneration of normal intellectual functions. Two cases were simple forms of imbecility.[2]

[1] *Census of Nigeria*, 1931 (London, 1933). The Census figures refer partly to the tribe, i.e. to random samples of Nupe (ii, pp. 110–11), partly to the political district of Bida Emirate (ii, p. 391), and partly to Niger Province as a whole ('Nupe Province' in the old terminology), the population of which consists to two-thirds of Nupe (i, pp. 41–2, ii, p. 38).

[2] See p. 402.

SURROUNDINGS OF BIDA

THE KADUNA RIVER NEAR GBARA

Sleeping sickness is the great scourge of the country. A Sleeping Sickness Commission which visited Nupe in 1936 found 70 per cent. of the people infected—the highest figure in the whole of Nigeria. Bilharzia and other worm diseases are no less widespread. The prominence of venereal diseases is characteristic of Nupe as it is of the whole of Nigeria and indeed of the whole of semi-civilized Africa. Dysentery, malaria, and yaws complete the unhappy picture. It is worth noting, however, that typical deficiency diseases, including boils and ulcers, are comparatively rare. A statistical table, compiled from the attendance figures of the N.A. Hospital and Dispensaries in Bida Division, may illustrate the distribution of the more important diseases occurring in Nupe.

TABLE II

The figures for Bida Hospital refer to in-patients treated during April, July, October 1935 and January 1936. The figures for the Dispensary of Lemu give the attendance in January 1936. For another dispensary (Kutigi) only the order of frequency of the various diseases could be ascertained; it is indicated in the third line by roman numerals.

	Venereal diseases	Malaria	Ulcer, scabies, &c.	Bronchitis, pneumonia	Dysentery, enterics	Eye-diseases	Rheumatic diseases	Leprosy	Bilharzia, worm diseases	Various
Bida Hospital	35	14	15	13	9	3	5	2	80 per cent. of all cases	128
Lemu Dispensary	21	18	3	54	2	2	68	4	?	106
Kutigi Dispensary	II	IV	III	VI	?	V	I	10 cases	?	?

The description of health conditions has a more special bearing on the anthropology of the Nupe people. First, it is of a certain significance in connexion with certain cultural elaborations of the theme of disease among the Nupe;[1] second, it involves relevant questions of mortality and population movement—a subject to which we shall turn presently. Finally, with respect to mental disorders: psychology and sociology have long realized that certain tensions and maladjustments in the social system tend to manifest themselves in the sphere of psycho-pathology. We shall see that this correlation is true also of Nupe society.

POPULATION MOVEMENT

It is unnecessary to stress the importance of population studies for the understanding of a society and the nature and working of its institutions. But it may be necessary to justify the inclusion of a discussion on population movement in a chapter on environment. A first justification lies in the fact that, in a study of social organization, environment and popula-

[1] Most instances of this kind, however, I must leave for future publications. To one typical instance, the part which leprosy plays in the mythology and ritual of the *gunnu* cult, I have referred in the description of this cult in *Gunnu*, A Fertility Cult of the Nupe in Northern Nigeria', in *J.R.A.I.* lxvii, 1937, pp. 91-130.

tion movement are to some extent methodologically of the same order. Both represent in certain respects 'data', given facts—factors external to the field of social phenomena which we investigate. Moreover, population movement and environmental conditions are inseparable from one another. Population movement reflects the effects of a complex of heterogeneous factors of which physical environment is one of the most important. It bears on possibilities and means of production, on nutrition, health, and livelihood in general.

But we shall also encounter the effects of other factors upon population movement, namely, specific 'cultural' factors—social and economic conditions, 'standards of living', moral concepts—and certain historical events which have influenced the distribution of population in Nupe country.

Birth-rate and Fertility

The Nigerian Census places Nupe birth- and fertility-rate at the bottom of the scale.[1] The proportion of live children per mother among the Nupe is 1·8 (the Yoruba are the only other tribe with an equally low rate), as against an average for all tribes of 2·6, and a fertility-rate of 2·4 in the tribe with the next lowest figure. Fifty-eight per cent. of Nupe women in the age group 30–39 are sterile, as against the total average for Nigeria of 22·7, and the next highest sterility rate of 27·1 among the Yoruba. These figures contain certain inconsistencies, and leave certain relevant questions unanswered. Thus the rate of live children per mother is equal among Nupe and Yoruba, while the proportion of sterile women among the Nupe is exactly twice the corresponding figure among the Yoruba. This would imply that infant mortality among the Yoruba is twice as large as among the Nupe—which seems hardly probable. Moreover, the proportion of live children per mother does not indicate to what extent the low figure is due to still-birth, infant mortality, constitutional sterility or, possibly, birth restriction. Finally, the statistics ignore the sociologically most important distinction between rural and urban areas.

The last point can to some extent be answered indirectly. The following figures give the birth-rate of three Nupe towns and one district (Kontagora) which has a very large proportion of Nupe among its inhabitants. Though only approximate these figures are well worth quoting in this connexion as they refer to localities representing different degrees of urbanization: the purely urban area of Bida town side by side with the much less urbanized village-capitals of Agaie and Lapai Emirates.

TABLE III

	Birth-rate per 1,000
Bida town	12
Agaie town	36
Lapai town	27
Kontagora Division	26

[1] *Census of Nigeria*, i, p. 55.

In the course of our investigation my wife and I attempted to ascertain further statistical data which could throw light on these points. They were obtained by the method of house-to-house investigation in three selected localities, in the villages Kutigi and Jebba Island, and in one town ward of Bida. The scale of this statistical research, carried out single-handed, was of necessity very limited. Nevertheless, certain significant facts could be ascertained (Tables IV and V).

TABLE IV

	Mothers (age group 30–40)	Total children born	Children alive	Children dead	Births per mother	Live children per mother
Villages	101	206	108	98	2	1·06
Town	144	230	126	104	1·5	0·8

TABLE V

	Mothers	Children died at age of					Total
		Birth	1–2	3–5	6–8	9–15	
Villages	101	29	25	27	8	9	98
Town	41	21	15	27	7	4	74

Table V shows, first, the distribution of infant mortality over different age groups. Infant mortality in the villages seems, on the whole, considerably lower than in the town, remarkably so at, or shortly after, birth and in the first five years of the infant's life. This seems in the main due to the spread of venereal infection in the town, and also to the effects of abortion and artificial birth restriction which, as we shall see presently, is practised in Bida. The highest mortality, both in urban and rural districts, occurs at the age of 3–5. This peak of mortality seems due primarily to malaria, which is especially fatal at this age.[1]

Table IV (examining a larger group from the urban area) attempts to establish a comparative birth-rate for urban and rural areas. For the low fertility-rate of the Nupe women in general two physiological explanations suggest themselves: first, reduced fertility may be the result of certain endemic or widespread diseases, such as sleeping sickness and gonorrhoea; or second, it may be the result of prenatal deficiency of vitamin E (a vitamin contained, for example, in palm-oil). The effectiveness of these two physiological factors cannot be denied.[2] However, the striking difference in the birth-rate of town and villages demands a different interpretation. The distribution of venereal diseases, definitely higher in the town than in the rural area, would fit into the picture. But of sleeping sickness rather the opposite is true; and the vitamin deficiency

[1] For this information, as for the other medical information in this chapter, I am indebted to Dr. M. Ellis, of the Nigerian Medical Service, who at the time was in charge of Bida N.A. Hospital.

[2] A study of diet among the Nupe has shown that the women's share of the daily meals (i.e. the meals cooked with palm-oil) is only about one-fourth of the men's share.

should be less marked in the town, where rich food is the rule. Physio-logical factors are thus not sufficient to explain the low fertility-rate in Nupe. This is confirmed by the data of Table IV. For in the context of this table, which refers only to women who have had children and ex-cludes sterile women, the difference in birth-rate precludes to some extent the explanation on the ground of constitutional sterility and suggests instead the influence of another factor: the existence of· birth restriction in the town, in other words, the effects of *social* motives.

Nupe religion and morality, as we shall see later, emphasize very strongly the idea of progeny. Nevertheless, in the higher social strata, especially in Bida town, the women often prefer childlessness, or at least do not want more than one child. Childlessness opens to them certain economic opportunities of which women with children, or many children, cannot avail themselves as easily. The Bida women know how to bring about abortion, and even know the use of contraceptives—or rather of certain practices and drugs which are believed to work as contraceptives. Many of them are clearly mere superstitions and the expression of magical beliefs; whether certain drugs which one can buy (in the greatest secrecy) from medicine-men and barber-doctors are more effective, I am unable to say.[1] However this may be, sterility of the Bida women is, to speak with Durkheim, a typical 'social fact'. In our own terminology, it represents a typical case of that 'indirect' influence of environment which determines population movement, working through considerations of economic benefit and standard of living. And this influence becomes evident in our case not only as an abstract social trend, derived from statistical correlations, but still more in the form of conscious and tangible behaviour.

Sex Ratio

Statistical figures show a surprising fact: a marked preponderance of females among the adult population, but hardly any preponderance of females—indeed, in Bida town, the reverse relation—in the sex ratio of non-adults.

TABLE VI[2]

	Adults		Non-adults		Females per head of male population	
	Male	Female	Male	Female	Adult	Non-adult
Bida Emirate ·	57,759	66,546	22,949	24,204	1·15	1·1
Agaie-Lapai Emirate · ·	20,148	23,915	6,139	5,938	1·1	0·9
Bida town · ·	7,714	11,602	3,240	2,675	1·5	0·8
Bida Emirate excl. of Bida town ·	50,045	54,944	19,709	21,529	1·1	1·1

[1] The Nupe 'doctors' know two kinds of contraceptives: temporary contra-ceptives of a magical nature (e.g. a magical belt), and permanent contraceptives—powders which are taken internally. These drugs are considered 'evil', immoral medicines, but are made and sold all the same.

[2] *Census of Nigeria*, ii, pp. 176 et seq.

This discrepancy is partly explained by the fact that girls marry at an earlier age than boys, and also by the fact that polygamy, especially the large-scale polygamy in Bida town, implies marriage of young girls to much older men. Married girls being counted in this table as 'adults', these factors must upset the 'normal' sex ratio in the higher age groups of non-adults. But this explanation only underlines the general social problem emerging from these figures: how are we to interpret the divergence between the sex ratio among adults (implied in polygamous marriage), and the sex ratio among non-adults? In other words, how can the sex ratio in actual polygamous marriage be harmonized with the sex ratio on which such marriage potentially depends? There is, first, the heavier mortality among men, whose numbers, only a generation ago, were constantly reduced in the almost permanent wars in Nupe. But the comparison between the figures referring to Bida town and to the rural districts in the Emirate respectively reveals that there is also another influence at work. In Bida town the difference between the two sex ratios is 0·7, in the rural districts the figures are identical. That means that marriage in the villages—monogamous marriage, or polygamous marriage on a small scale—can rely on local women, whereas Bida must import its wives from outside. Formerly slave girls constituted a large contingent of this urban importation of wives-to-be; to-day, in smaller proportion, girls from the country drift into Bida. We shall see later that genealogies and marriage statistics fully endorse this explanation.

Population and Emigration

Translated into terms of general population movement, the strikingly low birth- and fertility-rate among the Nupe can mean only one thing: a decreasing, or at least a stationary, population. The general population statistics in the Census can, on the whole, be taken to confirm this conclusion. But the nature of the available statistics does not allow more than this indication of a general trend. The total population of the Nupe tribe was given as 349,008 in the Census of 1921;[1] ten years later the figure is 326,017. These figures, implying a fall of over 20,000 in ten years, cannot be accepted as anything but a very crude approach to the true situation.

The difficulties which stand in the way of exact population statistics in a West African territory need not be stressed specially. Yet the earlier Census figures were likely to have underrated rather than overrated the population; with the improved technique of registration (e.g. for taxation) in the last ten to fifteen years one would have expected an increase rather than a decrease in the numbers that appear in the Census, even if the population had remained stationary or had decreased slightly. Certain other sources of error, however, seem not to have been eliminated, above all, inconsistencies in tribal classification. The native and British officials who compile the Census lists are frequently insufficiently acquainted with tribal and sub-tribal names and distinctions.[2] Thus,

[1] See C. K. Meek, *The Northern Tribes of Nigeria*, Oxford, 1925, vol. ii.
[2] It may therefore well be that the 1921 Census which was compiled under the

for example, the Gana-Gana (Dibo) sub-tribe of the Nupe is classed
sometimes under 'Nupe' and sometimes as a separate group. In the
Census of 1921 their number is given as 19,700, in the Census of 1931 as
2,897;[1] into which tribal category the rest of them disappeared I have
been unable to discover. A last example: only in 1936 did the Administration of Ibadan Division discover that the people who were listed in
their statistics under the heading 'Tapa' (Takpa) were identical with the
'Nupe' of the Northern Provinces, Takpa being the Yoruba name for
Nupe.

The difficulties and sources of error which render tribal statistics so
uncertain do not affect in the same degree population statistics compiled for certain single Provinces, political Divisions, and especially
townships. Here the improvement in registration has had its full effect;
and I may add that in the preceding discussion I have used only these
more reliable statistics. Here are certain figures illustrating population
movement in Niger and Ilorin Provinces—the two Provinces in which
the bulk of the Nupe people are living.

TABLE VII

	General Census 1921	General Census 1931	Local Census 1934
Bida Emirate . . .	171,958	171,458	168,247
Bida town . . .	29,848	25,231	23,286
Nupe in Ilorin Province .	64,652	65,040	53,600
Nupe in Niger Province .	233,840	226,132	..

Again we find a marked decrease in population and a decrease which
cannot be dismissed as due to miscalculation. Evidently, a decrease
in population even considerably smaller than that shown in these
figures cannot be due merely to unfavourable birth- and death-rate.
Emigration seems the only alternative, and I have indeed found evidence
of this. A continuous emigration on a small scale and the existence of a
floating population of traders and craftsmen drifting to the prosperous
centres in the south could be established beyond doubt.[2] The study of
life-histories and genealogies among the Nupe shows further that
emigration of considerable importance occurred, roughly, in the last six
to ten years. The drift of the emigration was again mostly south, to
Ilorin, Lokoja, Ibadan, Oshogbo, and Lagos, that is, to the wealthier
and, above all, less heavily taxed districts of Southern Nigeria.[3] In-

direction of an anthropologist, Dr. C. K. Meek, is in many respects more correct
than the more comprehensive and elaborate recent Census.

    [1] *Census of Nigeria*, ii, p. 70; on p. 30, however, there are, again, 18,220
Gana-Gana.

    [2] A census of Nupe people living at present in Lokoja, for example, showed
the following distribution of professions among 60 family heads: 2 farmers, 4
mechanics, 5 barbers, 15 tailors and embroiderers, 4 black- and brass-smiths,
9 Koran teachers, 3 mat-makers, 2 carpenters, 5 canoemen, 5 N.A. messengers,
interpreters, and other small officials.

    [3] These are the comparative tax figures for 1934–5 per adult for Bida Emirate
and Ilorin and Ibadan respectively: Bida town, 9s.–10s. 6d.; Bida Emirate,

vestigations among the Nupe community of Ilorin and Ibadan have elicited the information that in 1934–5 a big wave of Nupe emigration had reached these towns.[1] These two years, my informants explained, had been bad years, with a severe food scarcity in the north, high prices, and shortage of money. The reason is indeed convincing: 1933–4 marked the nadir of the economic depression in Northern Nigeria, which almost paralysed trade and native industry. To the mobile professions of trader and craftsman emigration appeared in many cases as the natural solution.

Density of Population

The following table illustrates the density of population in different parts of Nupe country. The first three figures are taken from the Census of 1931, the other figures, referring to districts of Bida Division, are compiled from the local Census of 1934.

TABLE VIII

Locality	Density per sq. mile	Locality	Density per sq. mile
Bida Division	35·22	Mokwa district	12
Agaie-Lapai Division	21·70	Kutigi ,,	13
Lafiagi-Patigi Division	30·00	Districts west of Kaduna river ('Trans-Kaduna')	17·6
Badeggi district	22		
Gbangba ,,	50	Districts east of Kaduna river ('Cis-Kaduna')	55
Jima-Doko ,,	53		
Kacha ,,	60		

The striking difference in density of population east and west of the Kaduna river needs explanation. It lies in the historical fact of the Fulani conquest of Nupe and the immigration of the Fulani rulers and their huge army of warriors, slaves, courtiers, and other dependants into the area east of the Kaduna, where they settled, occupied the land, and built their capital and numerous villages. The history of the conquest and the political reorganization of the country which it entailed will be described later in more detail. But here already we realize the far-reaching influence which this difference in population density must have upon the social organization of the country, and upon the distribution of natural resources on which its economic life depends.

districts, 9s. 6d.–15s.; Ilorin town, 9s.; Ilorin Emirate, districts, 10s.–11s.; Ibadan town, 7s.

[1] During 1935 200 people from Bida Emirate migrated south. (Personal information received from the District Officer, Bida Division.)

CHAPTER II

CULTURE, TRIBE, SOCIETY

THE description of environment is concerned with a solid, easily defined, almost self-evident reality. A description of the general demographic and cultural constellation deals with the fluid entity of groups and systems of unity, the mere circumscription of which involves already theoretical definitions and classifications. These definitions and classifications must be based on facts which only the full analysis of the society can establish. This chapter will thus have to anticipate certain results of the general description which forms the main body of this book. It will not attempt to anticipate the descriptions themselves. Its aim is only to sketch in a background, to stake out a field of demographic and cultural facts by which is bounded that social reality with which this book is dealing.

PROBLEMS OF DEFINITION

Let me draw a tribal map of the part of Nigeria where Nupe country lies: in the north the neighbours of the Nupe are Kamberi, Kamuku, and Hausa; in north-east and east lies Gbari country; in the south, on the river, the country of the Kakanda; and west of the river, Yagba (a section of the Yoruba) and Ilorin Yoruba; and in the north-west, finally, the people of Borgu and Bussa. Colonies of Nupe, small sections, split off from the main body of the tribe, are scattered all over Nigeria, especially in villages and towns on the Niger. The largest of them, a group of about 15,000 people who call themselves Bassa, or Bassa Nge, lives near the confluence of Niger and Benue. They appear to have emigrated from the mother country about a hundred years ago, before the Fulani conquest; they settled first on the right bank of the Niger, on the hills of what is to-day Lokoja, and moved later, when the new town of Lokoja was founded by the Niger Company, to the left bank where they are living to-day.

The Nupe are known as *Nufawa* (sing. *Nufe*) among the Hausa, as *Abawa* (sing. *Bawa*) among the Gbari of Kuta, and as *Anupeyi* and *Anufawhei* among the Gbari of Paiko and Birnin Gwari; the Yoruba know them as *Takpa* and the Kakanda as *Anupecwayi*. The Nupe call themselves *Nupeci* or, in the plural, *Nupeciži*, their language *Nupe*, and their country *kin Nupe*, Land of Nupe. No special word for 'tribe' exists in Nupe; the Nupe speak of *za Nupe*, Nupe man, Nupe peoples.

This book is concerned with the culture of the people that calls itself Nupe. But what does 'people' mean here? What is the social reality to which the term Nupe people or Nupe tribe refers? The three meanings of *Nupe*, people, language, and country, do not coincide. Disregarding the split-off sections we may say that the Nupe tribe inhabits, roughly, the same territory. But it is not, and never was, 'one country' in the sense of a group united politically, or by facts of close contact and 'common life', thus marked off from other, similar areas or groups. Of such facts of common life which would link the whole tribe we find only one—a weak, potential link, determining individual action only, namely, the rule of hospitality which every Nupe must extend to his fellow tribesmen (but which he would not refuse to strangers).[1] Otherwise the common life that exists in Nupe takes its course in a very much more narrow compass, in scattered villages, towns, or groups of villages—small circles on the spacious tribal map.

Politically the Nupe people are scattered over several 'countries', seven Emirates and chieftainships to-day, and four or five in pre-European times. Even the ancient Nupe kingdom has not, as far as our evidence goes, included the whole group; sections of Nupe have always lived outside its boundaries, and other tribes or tribal sections beside the Nupe have formed the nationals of these countries of Nupe. To-day the largest of them is Bida Emirate with a population of 171,458, the core of the ancient kingdom of Nupe whose present rulers still take the title *Etsu Nupe*, King of Nupe. Some of the other, smaller Nupe states are ruled by independent kings (in modern terminology, Emirs): Patigi and Lafiagi, comprising an area of 3,023 square miles and a population of 90,702, and Agaie and Lapai, with an area of 2,587 square miles, and populations of 24,174 and 25,000, respectively. Other Nupe territories are but small chieftainships, political districts, under the rulership of Hausa, Yoruba, or Gbira kings: Zuguma (with a population of 5,000) under the Hausa Emir of Kontagora, Shonga and Shari (appr. 17,000) under the Fulani-Yoruba Emir of Ilorin, and Eggã and its hinterland (5,000) under the *Atta* of Gbira. In Bida, Patigi, Lafiagi, and Agaie the Nupe represent the vast majority of the population; in Kontagora, Lapai, Ilorin, and Gbira they are a small minority, living side by side with Hausa, Yoruba, Yagba, Gbari, Kakanda, and Gbira.

If the Nupe tribe is thus not a local group in the strict sense of the word, it is not a linguistic unit either. Nupe is spoken to-day by the bilingual Gbari of Paiko and Lapai and the Kakanda on the Niger. On the other hand, some of the split-off sections and colonies of Nupe, though still laying claim to tribal membership, have abandoned and forgotten their mother tongue. True, these facts reflect only comparatively recent historical changes. But language as such, in its very structure and organization, proves the same divergence between the two social realities, tribe and linguistic group. Nupe language belongs to the group of Sudanese languages, and within this category forms, together with Ibo, Edo, Ijo, Andoni, and Yoruba, the 'Kwa-group' cf West African languages.[2] Nupe is related more closely, in structure and vocabulary, to Gbari and Kakanda (I am speaking here only of languages which I have studied myself). But to speak of Nupe language pure and simple is incorrect. There exist to-day five markedly different dialects: a dialect which we will term Nupe proper, and the dialects of Ebe, Žitako, Bassa,

---

[1] There exists a fine distinction, though: fellow-tribesmen who claim hospitality are, where possible, given a sleeping hut to spend the night in, and are often invited to share a meal with their hosts; strangers sleep in the entrance hut of the compound.

[2] See D. Westermann, *Africa*, viii, p. 145, 1935.

and Kupa. Nupe proper differs from Ebe, or Bassa from Žitako, no less than Nupe differs from the languages of the other, related, tribes, Gbari and Kakanda. Dialects, language, language group, or linguistic class—these are all fluid categories, shading over into one another, and none of them capable of being identified with tribe or people.

Political group and language group thus imply the existence of the tribe, they do not explain it. The objective reality of political and linguistic organization leaves undefined the nature of that elusive human substratum, tribe or people. Nor can we count on any external symbols of tribal unity to help us with the definition. No tribal costume, or tribal emblems, exist, no tattoos or face-markings characteristic of all Nupe.[1] Yet to the Nupe man himself the Nupe tribe or the Nupe people is a clearly defined, unmistakable entity. He will rarely hesitate whether to describe the population of a district or village as Nupe or to put it down as alien, non-Nupe. This is, of course, an expression of traditional, historically accumulated, and transmitted knowledge. People and tribe themselves represent but the product of complex historical processes, contacts, and ramifications. These processes are no longer traceable to-day; but even if we could trace them they would tell us nothing about the nature of this social fact which we witness to-day, the classification of groups which do not speak the same language and do not live together in 'one country' unified by political organization, under the heading of 'one tribe'. The only definition of tribe that seems possible is the tautological statement that a tribe or people is a group unit the members of which claim to form a group unit. But perhaps there exists some other, objective, social reality which can help us to define this evasive concept?

We have not examined yet that paramount social reality, culture. But culture no less than language or living-together seems a fluid criterion of tribal unity. The only definition of tribe that we can give in terms of culture is to call the tribe a group possessing more or less the same culture—as it possesses more or less the same language or lives more or less in contiguity and 'togetherness'. In Nupe the unit of culture is in certain respects smaller than the unit of the tribe. The different 'countries' of Nupe represent different, and differently organized, cultural 'provinces'. Culture varies with environment and the productive organization which it entails; it expresses the changing dominant interests involved in social, political, and economic conditions. We can thus speak of a riverain Nupe culture, a hunters' or peasant culture, and distinguish town from rural culture, or the culture of the ruling group from the culture of the subjects and commoners. The cultural unit is also wider than the unit of the tribe. Nupe shares its political and social system with many tribes in West Africa, its traditional religion with neighbouring groups in the north, east, and south, its modern religion, Islam, with the whole Sudan. There is, in fact, good sense in speaking of a West African culture, or a culture of the inland groups of West Africa (as against the culture of the groups in the rain-forest and near the coast). Finally, culture appears also, as it were, crystallized in the form of

[1] See below, p. 22.

a tribal culture, and the area of cultural unity reveals itself in some respects as coextensive with the tribe.

This is not merely an enumeration of isolated 'traits' selected at random. Each cultural factor which we reviewed affects, and is interdependent with, a wide range of other cultural factors. Culture, as anthropologists are realizing, is not a sum total of discrete traits; it possesses a definite structure and identity; its traits or elements, interdependent and mutually determined, build up a 'pattern' that tends towards coherence and consistency. This consistency—a functional consistency—reveals its existence to the student of the society in those cultural characteristics which he learns to regard as 'typical' or 'non-typical' of a culture. Each of the three cultural units which we enumerated shows, in some measure, the features of this consistency and identity. We will not here probe deeper into the nature of this consistency which seems to crystallize in different degrees of intensity and comprehensiveness. But we must clarify our concept of culture. So far, we have used the word in a rather vague sense. It is not the same culture, the same category of culture, which we discovered in these three relations between cultural and tribal unit. Cultural unity is, speaking generally, unity and correspondence in forms of social behaviour. When speaking of culture units wider than the unit of the tribe, we referred to a correspondence of behaviour among disconnected groups which we as students of cultures and peoples discover, classify, and name; it is a correspondence upheld by the unconscious processes involved in tradition and the perpetuation of custom; it impresses upon the groups a certain external *uniformity*. When speaking of the smaller cultural units which reflect common environmental conditions and common interests, common spheres, that is, of organized social life, we refer to something that goes beyond an externally visible uniformity. We mean a *conformity* of behaviour, a conscious unity created by, and embodied in, a common group life and the mutual control and adjustment of behaviour among the people who form the group.[1] The identification of cultural group and tribe implies, in the observer's interpretation, something of both.

But were this all it would enable us only to define the tribe as a natural species is defined—unknown to the subject of the definition. It would amount to colouring a certain space on a cultural map and calling it 'Nupe tribal culture'. It would not explain the crucial point in our argument, that the people are themselves conscious of the reality of the tribe. But culture has also another, new, meaning: it represents the conception of the people themselves. To the Nupe the tribe possesses a certain culture, specific to it and only to it, irrespective of variations within or similarities with groups without the tribal boundaries. Their awareness of this unity is expressed in the form of almost axiomatic statements, 'the Nupe do this or that', 'this and that is a Nupe custom',

---

[1] The historian may attempt to link the two, and derive 'uniformity' from an original 'conformity', that is, explain the present cultural correspondence among disconnected groups by cultural diffusion from a centre in which culture was identical with organized common life. But considerations of this kind remain outside this discussion.

contrasting Nupe usages with customs and forms of behaviour characteristic of other tribes. You discuss, for example, the worship of human
figures and idols of the kind you see in every village and every house in
neighbouring Yoruba; or the face-like masks which the Yoruba and
many southern tribes wear in their ritual dances; or perhaps the ceremony of spirit possession which the Hausa who live in Bida town perform on Bida market. Your Nupe informant will tell you positively: no
—we have none of this; only Yoruba do it, or Hausa do it, as the case
may be. Or you ask a Nupe man what all Nupe have in common. He
will, as a rule, enumerate the same few traits. All Nupe, he will say,
have the *ena gbarúfuži* (age-grade associations), all Nupe have the same
system of *tici* (ranks), and all Nupe have the *gunnu* cult. Of the Nupe
community in Lagos, a group which has forgotten its traditions and
abandoned its language, I was told that they were still Nupe, because
they still practised the Nupe *kuti* (ritual) of the *ndakó gboyá* (a ritual
closely linked with the *gunnu*). Yet on closer examination this shib-
boleth of Nupedom proves only half true. Worship of idols and human
figures exists also among the Nupe, in the riverain area; mask dances
with face-masks are practised in a large section of the Nupe, in Mokwa
and the neighbouring villages. The age-grade associations are common
both to Nupe and Hausa. The rank system is common all over Northern
Nigeria, but the details in its organization (very significant details) vary
considerably among different groups of the Nupe. The *gunnu* cult exists
also among Gbari, Gara, Basa Kom, and, what is more important,
appears in Nupe itself in strikingly different forms in different parts of the
country.[1] Finally, as regards the Nupe colonies outside Nupe country:
I have visited the Nupe communities in Lagos and Ibadan. They are
descendants of Nupe slaves and serfs, completely Yoruba-ized to-day in
language, custom, and everyday habits. It is true they have the *ndakó
gboyá* (which they call by the Yoruba name *igunnu*). But the *ndakó
gboyá* is completely absent among the eastern section of Nupe, the Dibo,
and also, I believe, among most groups of the Ebe, the northern section
of the Nupe tribe.

Objectively, then, the rigid distinction of Nupe and non-Nupe on the
basis of cultural characteristics often proves incorrect, and must do so,
since culture is both wider and narrower than the tribe. True, there exist
certain traits, or 'patterns' of traits, which are typical of all the Nupe,
and possibly only of the Nupe—facts of material culture, social organization, religious beliefs. Like the Nupe who mean to uphold the identity
of their tribe, I shall speak of things 'the Nupe do' or 'do not do'. True
it is that the people admit the existence of certain cultural variants which
qualify the cultural unity of the tribe. But the essential fact to us here is
not the objective constellation of cultural traits. The identification of
Nupe tribe with a core of Nupe culture represents a concept, a spiritual
reality, rather than a critical interpretation of cultural facts. It reflects
not the quasi-scientific calculation of more essential against less essential
traits, or of a majority of common characteristics as against a minority of

[1] See *J.R.A.I.* lxvii, 1937, pp. 91–130.

dissimilarities, but a phenomenon of a different order, a theory and ideology which ignores divergences *ex definitione*. It represents, in one word, the theory of the Nupe tribe. Our tautological definition of tribe then reads thus: a tribe or people is a group the members of which claim unity on the grounds of their conception of a specific common culture.[1]

To define the unity as conceptual does not make it less real or less significant. The awareness of unity is the basic element in all social unity. Consciousness of commonness is the primary element in social commonness. 'Communities, for all their external marks, are not objective things, they are spiritual realities.'[2] The tribe is not a community in the strict sense of the word: it lacks, as we have seen, the element of 'common life' and co-activity. But communities exist in different degrees of intensity; they have a different compass of social inclusiveness; there is not *one* community, but a complex hierarchy of communities.[3] The consciousness of a uniform culture defines the widest, loosest unit in the hierarchy of communities—potential rather than actual 'common life'. One turns easily into the other. 'One of the great processes of society . . . is that thereby the common is built out of the like, common interests growing out of what were at first merely like interests.'[4] We add that the consciousness of uniformity is the first step towards conformity of culture.

At the same time this uniformity of conduct which is conscious of itself is more than merely a potential stage of social existence. It represents, in itself, a specific social reality. Let me define here a vital concept of social existence which will occur throughout this book: social integration. The essence of integration is co-activity—potential or actual; social integration is predictable co-adaptation of behaviour in a group. It reveals itself in the certainty with which, in the group, certain actions of individuals or group sections will call forth appropriate response actions of other individuals or group sections. Now uniformity of behaviour is, sociologically, meaningless. Conscious uniformity, however, is predictable uniformity; the knowledge that a certain familiar pattern of activity will be repeated endlessly throughout the group represents a first form, and a degree at the same time, of social integration.

These two types of integration, uniformity and conformity, do not exhaust the forms of unity of behaviour existing in society. We shall meet in this analysis also with a third interpretation of cultural commonness or likeness, namely, the co-adaptation of behaviour involved in all organized associations. We shall speak of it as *co-ordination* of behaviour, for it represents essentially a planned, controlled organization of behaviour in the group, regulated and enforced by specific social mechanisms. In

---

[1] This definition claims to hold true for all large tribal groups ('peoples') of a similarly complex structure. It does not apply to smaller and more homogeneous groups. The factor of size and numbers is of importance. Evidently, for a small group on a Pacific Island tribe equals local group; or among American Indian tribes the tribal unit may coincide with the political group (see A. L. Kroeber, *Anthropology*, 1923, p. 232).
[2] R. M. MacIver, *Society*, p. 66.   [3] Ibid., p. 10; *Community*, p. 23.
[4] R. M. MacIver, *Society*, p. 8.

this book we shall be dealing mainly with the political association, which seems characterized by two sets of factors: first, by its inclusiveness, being the relatively widest unit of co-ordination, and, underlining it, by the conception of a collective identity emphasized, above all, in inter-group dealings. And second, by the nature of its regulative mechanism (here the 'Government'), which rests, in the last resort, on the employment of force and coercion, and which controls both co-ordination for the purpose of internal stability ('law and order') and co-ordination for the purpose of external, inter-group, action ('offence and defence'). Cultural groups and communities have fluid boundaries; the association (in our case the political unit) is or is not rigid, but its boundaries—the boundaries of the group and sphere of conduct within which the co-ordination is to be valid—are by definition rigid. The consciousness of this validity defines the membership of the political association—in modern terminology, nationality. The political unit, unlike culture and community, is unequivocal: one either is or is not a citizen of a country; one either comes or does not come under its laws and restrictions. However, one remains at the same time a representative of a culture which may not simply coincide with the cultural uniformity upheld by the political system. One remains also a member of a community or of communities which may exist apart from the 'common life' embodied in political co-ordination. Planned co-ordination of behaviour cannot ignore these other forms of integration—cultural likeness and commonness. Whether it utilizes them, creates them anew, or simply accepts their existence, they are the cultural raw material out of which it must fashion its unity.

The three planes of integration, and the group units which they define, thus cut across each other, overlap, and possibly grow out of each other, It will not always be easy to separate them clearly in the concrete description. The preceding analysis has to some extent defined their theoretical boundaries. In what follows we can attempt to isolate, in our concrete material, these three social realities: the integration of (conscious) cultural uniformity or the tribe; the integration of cultural conformity or the community; and the cultural co-ordination typical of organized society, above all, the political system and its paradigm, the state.

THE TRIBE

The conception of a common tribal culture is kept alive, as part of Nupe tradition, by the transmission of traditional knowledge. It forms part of the general ideological background of all institutionalized behaviour. For many forms of customary behaviour membership of the tribe constitutes a convincing *raison d'être*. The tribe, lacking all unity of comprehensive co-operation, also lacks the unity of a common centre of cultural teaching. The consciousness of a common tribal culture is thus maintained by the scattered, disconnected mechanism to which the transmission of traditional knowledge is entrusted in Nupe. It is implied in the nature of this transmission that the same *raison d'être*—'we do this or that because we are Nupe'—is quoted in support of widely different and divergent cultural activities. In the riverain districts they tell you: 'The Nupe know only two funeral rites, the ceremony of the Eight Days and the ceremony of the Forty Days; but the Mohammedans have introduced a third ritual, the Hundred-and-twenty Days.' Go to the Nupe round Bida or in Trans-Kaduna, and you learn 'that all Nupe perform the Hundred-and-twenty Days'. In Bida they say that 'no Nupe eats eggs, for they make the women sterile'—but in other districts I have seen people eat eggs and think nothing of it. A contradiction?— only so far as concepts which are never checked against reality can imply contradiction.

I have said already that for certain cultural practices the people admit that no general rule can be formulated and that different sections of Nupe follow different practices. But this admission of differentiation is, with regard to actual facts, no less inaccurate than the comprehensive statement about customs that are 'typically Nupe'. The cultural theory which allows for variants in the tribal culture is no less a theory and no less an ideology. This qualified ideology of cultural unity becomes specially important in connexion with another fact, namely, that the Nupe theory of tribal or cultural unity does not imply a belief in common stock or origin of all members or sections of the tribe. On the contrary, the Nupe assume different origin, and subsequent processes of fusion and sometimes differentiation, to account for the existing tribal sections. The Nupe count eleven or twelve such tribal sections or, as I propose to call them, sub-tribes. Here are their names: Ebe, Gbedye or Gbedegi, Kusopa, Benu, Beni, Dibo or Žitako (also known as Gana-Gana among the Hausa), Kyedye or Kede, Ebagi, Bataci, Kupa, Cekpā, and perhaps also Gwagba—a section formed but recently, something between sub-tribe and political faction. One group in Trans-Kaduna, which is believed to represent the oldest section of Nupe, has no second sub-tribal name; the people refer to themselves only as Nupe, or Nupe zam, 'pure Nupe'. In this area no real conception of the sub-tribe exists; the different villages regard themselves as independent cultural units, of independent origin, united only by the one, widest link of triba membership.

The different sub-tribes are supposed to be not only of different origin but also of different age and to have evolved as sub-tribes at different periods. According to Nupe tradition there were five 'original' sub-tribes in existence at the time of the culture-hero of Nupe, Tsoede, of whom we shall hear more presently, namely the Ebe, Beni, Ebagi, Bataci, and Dibo. The origin of the Kyedye and Gbedegi is linked, in this tradition, with the coming of Tsoede. The riverain Kyedye are supposed to have come with him to Nupe country and to have been settled by him all along the river Niger and established as the Lords of the Water and as local rulers over the aboriginal inhabitants of the area, the marsh-dwelling Bataci. The Gbedegi are believed to have been of Yoruba origin, and to have been Nupe-ized by Tsoede and his men. Cekpā and Kupa, the sub-tribes on the southern bank of the Niger, are said to have lived first in the area north of the river, in Nupe proper, but to have crossed later to the other side where they settled and became, in the course of time, independent sub-tribal sections.[1] In the case of the Kupa the tradition is more concrete; it describes them as Ebe people who have crossed the Kontagora river (called in Nupe Eku, to cross the river is, in Nupe, *lá 'kú pà*, and this is supposed to be the origin of their tribal name) in the time of the big Nupe wars of conquest, about 1800. The Kusopa, the Forest Tenders, appear in Nupe tradition out of nothing. Somehow they grew into a separate sub-tribe the identity of which is based on their habitat in the thick inland forest west of the Kaduna and also on their special occupation, which is the cultivation of kola-nut trees. Gwagba is a deprecatory nickname given originally to a small section of 'Nupe *zam*' from Gbara, followers and henchmen of the Nupe kings who, in the wars for the Nupe throne, fled to Zuguma. *Gwagba* means, literally, Those who threw up their Hands, the Defeated, but it is applied to-day to the whole group of Nupe living in and around Zuguma town. The Benu, finally, represent another sub-tribe of recent origin, formed in historical times. They are people of Bornu origin (*Benu* being the Nupe corruption of *Bornu*), from Kukawa, the ancient capital of Bornu, who came to Nupe country towards the end of the eighteenth century, at the time of *Etsu* Ma'azū and settled, with his permission, in Trans-Kaduna. They came as wealthy traders, bringing with them certain new agricultural techniques—onion growing—horses and cattle (the latter soon disappeared in the tsetse-infested country). They soon became the dominant group, economically as well as politically, in the region where they settled, but they Nupe-ized themselves, intermarried with the Nupe, forgot their language, and abandoned most of their original cultural traits. Thus they are to-day a section of the Nupe, speaking the Nupe language, and conforming in their whole social structure to the standards of Nupe culture. Only their great annual festival, the *gani*, and the title of their chief, *Zonuwa*, are reminiscent of the ancient culture of Bornu.[2]

The name Nupe has also been extended to other originally alien groups living in Nupe country, which have become Nupe-ized and are hardly distinguishable to-day from the people among whom they live. In many villages and towns of Nupe we find groups known by the name of *Konú*, Prisoners of War,[3] or Eyagi-Nupe, Yoruba-Nupe, people of Yoruba origin, who are the descendants of slaves captured in the wars of the Fulani kings of Nupe against the Yoruba; they were later freed and, by order of the king, settled in various districts of the kingdom. In Bida town I met the makers of horse-trappings—a craft imported from Hausa—who assured me that they were Hausa no longer. 'Yes, our fathers were Hausa,' they admitted; 'but we are Nupe'—claiming Nupe-

[1] They speak, in fact, the same dialect—proof that the tradition is not without historical foundation.
[2] See Sir Richmond Palmer, *The Bornu Sahara and Sudan*, 1936, p. 148. I have given a more detailed description of this process of cultural fusion in *Man*, 1938, 85.
[3] *Konú* means 'war' in Fulfulde; the adoption of this term reflects cultural conditions in the early times of the Fulani régime, when the rulers still used their own language.

ization after barely one generation. The people in the north of Nupe country, near the boundary of Gbari, are known as *Gbari bautá*, Gbari slaves. They represent the original Gbari population of an area conquered by the Nupe and incorporated into the kingdom about 1800. In the north-east, too, Nupe culture is absorbing groups of Gbari, in a smooth and silent development which is still observable to-day. In Kataeregi, for example, in the north-east corner of Beni country, one or two old men still speak Gbari and remember their tribal origin; but the younger people speak only Nupe, regarding themselves, and being accepted, as Nupe and Beni full and proper. On the river, in the south, we have another group which has for some time been under Nupe political influence and has partly adopted Nupe language and culture: the Kakanda. They are not, however, regarded as part of the Nupe tribe —or not yet. Whether or not the consolidation of their cultural links will advance further and will eventually lead to an adoption into the tribe we cannot say for certain; perhaps the Kakanda will, with the completion of cultural assimilation, some day be regarded as another, thirteenth, Nupe sub-tribe.[1] In one or two cases, finally, people of one sub-tribe have emigrated into the district of another sub-tribe, living there as settlers in a 'foreign' land. Thus we find a group of Beni villages in Dibo country, emigrants from Beni during the Fulani wars, and also two small groups of Ebe in Trans-Kaduna, in the area of the section which calls itself 'pure Nupe'.

Thus one can 'become' a Nupe—*a že Nupe*, they have become Nupe, is what the Nupe say of their cultural proselytes. It is, of course, impossible to define precisely the point when cultural assimilation warrants, or might warrant, inclusion in the tribe. But it may seem as if this elastic application of the tribal name, which takes into account *de facto* cultural similarities, contradicted the 'theoretical' and 'conceptual' unit in which we saw the definition of the tribe. The unobtrusive assimilation of a small group on the fringes of some Nupe section and its eventual absorption in this section (as in the case of the Kataeregi Beni) can be easily understood. But the so-to-speak official inclusion of a new section, under a separate heading, seems to presuppose something like a cultural tribunal which grants tribal membership to new, 'naturalized' groups. This contradiction is due not to an obscurity in our definition but to an obscurity in the facts themselves—and an obscurity which cannot be eliminated. The substratum with which we are dealing has, as it were, changed under our hands. The concept of tribal culture has changed into the concept of a culture vested in a political unit and its deliberate, conscious expansion. The proselytes of the Nupe tribe or Nupe culture were in reality proselytes of the Nupe kingdom.[2] (It is,

---

[1] A few informants, in fact, already classified them as a sub-tribe of Nupe— but these were informants from sub-tribes adjacent to the Kakanda, that is, from groups which, so to speak, could directly watch the cultural changes. Groups farther away kept to the established, traditional definition of the Kakanda as a separate tribe.

[2] This is the conception of the people themselves. All informants spoke to me of the various sub-tribes as having 'become one through Tsoede' (the ancestor-

in fact, doubtful if a tribe not backed by any political organization could make proselytes on any larger scale.) Later we shall see more clearly how it happens that tribe and kingdom become, for the people, one and the same thing. But the mark of the 'theoretical' tribal distinction is not obscured completely. It is visible in the qualified adoption of these new 'naturalized' sections. They 'have become Nupe'; but they are still called 'Gbari slaves' or Yoruba-Nupe. And perhaps now, since the expanding Nupe kingdom no longer exists, there will be no thirteenth sub-tribe of Kakanda-Nupe, after all.

THE SUB-TRIBE

The fact of common origin which is excluded from the concept of the tribe becomes an essential element in the definition of the sub-tribe. The sub-tribe is thus not a 'tribe' on a smaller scale; it differs essentially from the wider unit of the tribe. If the Nupe tribe possesses no external symbols, costumes, or body markings, such emblems exist to some extent for the sub-tribe. The Nupe practise body and face markings, *etsa*, 'patterns', which are cut into the skin of newborn babies, male and female, and which differ in the different sub-tribes.[1] The sub-tribe, too, has its ideology in which the conception of unity and differentiation from other groups is expressed. The ideological criteria are two: one we have just discussed, the unity of origin and of historical continuity. The other is, again, the criterion of cultural unity. But the physical fact of the smallness of the group as compared with the tribe makes 'culture' here a more concrete, so to speak more concentrated reality. No Nupe term which corresponds to our 'sub-tribe' or 'section' exists. The Nupe refer to the various sub-tribes as to 'lands', they speak of *kin* Beni, land of the Beni, or *kin* Kusopa, land of the Kusopa, and even of *kin* Kyedye, land of the Kyedye, a 'land' which consists of a narrow strip of territory running across river banks and islets. The sub-tribe is thus, like the tribe, a territorial unit. But again the fact of physical size changes the meaning of the concept. The smaller locality is, in fact, more of one 'land'; it implies a more unified environment. This is partly expressed already in the names of the sub-tribes, some of which refer to the nature of the environment in which the group lives and to the nature of the occupation by which it earns its livelihood. The Bataci or Marsh Dwellers are a group of marsh-land farmers and fishermen whose hunting-grounds are the pools and backwaters of the Niger. The Kusopa or Forest Tenders work the famous kola-nut plantations of Labožˇi and

king of Nupe), or explained the development as due to the fact that '*one Etsu* established his rule (or law) over the whole country'.

[1] I must add, however, that even here these external symbols of group unity are not quite unequivocal. Fashion is changing the markings to-day—and there is no reason to assume that this has not always been so. I have seen fathers and sons whose faces bore different markings. The markings of the Bida people, like other fashions associated with the capital of the kingdom, have been adopted by the people of the districts. And the modern Bida and Beni markings are in turn said to have been adopted originally from the Yoruba, whose less conspicuous facial marks the Nupe found 'nicer' than their own crude slashes. (See Appendix II.)

Kudu and occupy the rich oil-palm district of Yeti. The name Kyedye, finally, is often used synonymously for all canoe-men and fishermen on the main river. Unity of environment, a uniform productive system, a uniform material culture, represent a first aspect of the cultural unity of the sub-tribe.

Then there is language, certain linguistic differences which throw into relief the cultural boundaries between sub-tribes. The Žitako, Ebe, and Kupa still speak dialects which differ considerably from each other and from the Nupe spoken in the rest of the country. To-day most people in these sub-tribes are bilingual and understand and speak both their own dialect and 'Nupe proper'. The Gbedegi, too, are said to have spoken a special dialect, only a generation or two ago. No trace is left of their language; I found only one old man in Jebba Island who could speak a little Gbedegi. In the area where Nupe proper is spoken only insignificant dialectal differences exist. This linguistic unification within Nupe is the counterpart of the expansion of Nupe language (Nupe proper) and culture beyond the tribal boundaries. Both reflect the same development. The linguistic unification proceeded from the political centre of Nupe kingdom, the area of the Beni, Kyedye, and Bataci sub-tribes. Their dialects, identified with the language of the Nupe state, gradually came to embrace all other tribal sections. The language map of Nupe reveals the phases of this process, the stages in the growth of a supreme, unified culture. We can see the resistance to assimilation increase as we move away from the centre of expansion: the dialects spoken on the borders of the kingdom are losing their identity more slowly and more reluctantly than the dialects of the groups in the centre. The last phase of this development is not yet completed. We are yet to see the full Nupe-ization of Žitako, Ebe, and Kupa.

But in the centre of this expansion the differentiation between cultural centre and periphery gains a new meaning. It is conceived of as a differentiation not of dialects representative of tribal sections, but of dialects, or forms of *patois*, representative of a cultural and social milieu and upbringing. To-day we have a Bida-Nupe, a 'higher', more refined Nupe (a Nupe which, for example, has replaced many Nupe words by words adopted from Hausa and Arabic); and we have, besides, the cruder, 'low', peasant Nupe—sometimes called 'pagan' Nupe—spoken in the districts. However, this new attitude towards cultural differences, this evaluation on the scale of a 'lower' and 'higher', a more or less refined culture, belongs to another chapter.

The cultural unity of the sub-tribe manifests itself also in the religious field. Certain cults and rituals are peculiar to single sub-tribes, and inter-tribal contact and assimilation have hardly obscured these cultural boundaries. Certain cults, bound up with conditions of environment, seem linked naturally to special areas: a sacrifice to the mythical ancestor of kola-nut planting among the Kusopa; cults which have to do with the water, with floods, with the dangers of the river, and success and safety in fishing, among the riverain groups. The *elo* ritual, and the *mamma* cult, masked ceremonies, are known only among the Gbedegi; the *žikinta* among the Ebe, the *gani* among the Benu, the 'white' *gunnu* among the tribes on the southern bank of the Niger, and (a negative evidence mentioned already) the *ndakó gboyá*, which is regarded as 'typical' Nupe by Hausa and Yoruba, is unknown among Dibo and Ebe. There are also other rituals and cults which cannot be assigned (at least not to-day) to a certain sub-tribe, and finally rituals and cults which represent the cultural possession of single village communities. In brief, the possession of a common cult means only an external uniformity of culture. None of these rituals implies co-operation and actual contact in the group at large. They are still but the expression of parallel, 'like', behaviour and not of concrete co-activity and 'togetherness'.

This is equally true of the other cultural features on which the cultural identity of the sub-tribe rests. The consciousness of a cultural uniformity is supported by the actual existing uniformity. But there is still no organized centre of co-activity behind this uniformity or behind the transmission of the consciousness of this uniformity. We can only say this: the sub-tribe, much more than the tribe, constitutes a potentiality of such co-activity and intensive 'togetherness'. The links of a common language, of similar economic pursuits, similar interests, parallel religious ideas, may grow easily into links of co-operation and 'togetherness'. Only in two cases, however, has this potentiality become reality— among the two sub-tribes Kyedye and Beni. In no other section are there contacts and forms of co-activity which make the sub-tribe 'one country', and its people 'one group'. How, then, does that cultural uniformity crystallize into the unified, conscious commonness of 'one country'?

I have described elsewhere the growth and organization of one of the two sub-tribes which have evolved such unified structure.[1] Let me repeat here the main facts. The growth of the Kyedye organization was the growth of a colonizing and conquering group. Expanding from one centre—Murègi, near the confluence of Niger and Kaduna—the Kyedye established themselves in the course of time all along the river banks. They built their settlements on the land of the aboriginal sections, Bataci and riverain Gbedegi, and claimed rulership over them. Twin villages arose, half Kyedye and half Bataci or Gbedegi, from which the Kyedye administered the district, assuming judicial authority and levying taxes. This colonization is still going on, and their rulership, rigidly centralized, is still alive and undisputed.[2] Close contact, intermarriage, and regular new emigration link the settlements, old and new, capital and colonies. Delegates from Muregi, relatives of the Kyedye chief, reside in the settlements, and these administrative 'posts' are correlated with the ranks which the delegates hold in the Kyedye hierarchy; promotion in rank involves promotion to a more important as well as more lucrative post. This closely knit ruling group precludes all permanent links between the cultural groups which this political development has thrown

[1] See 'The Kede: A Riverain State in Northern Nigeria', in *African Political Systems*, Oxford University Press, London, 1940, pp. 165–95.
[2] Only twenty or thirty years ago have the Kyedye established themselves on the river Kaduna, or on Jebba Island, a place which had only then become of economic importance.

together. There is no intermarriage, and almost no cultural give-and-take; to-day the Kyedye are Mohammedans (or semi-Mohammedans), but the Bataci and Gbedegi have remained pagans. Yet in one significant field cultural unity has evolved, over and above the differences of culture, tribal origin, and social status, and over and above also the co-operation embodied in the political structure. With the political ruler-ship the Kyedye have assumed spiritual authority as well; myths and sacred insignia confirm the position of the *Kuta*, the Kyedye chief, as the ruler over the whole riverain area and its people; and two most important sacrifices to the river Niger, which secure large catches and safety from floods, the *ketsá* and *ndáduma*, are linked with his person and office. Every new appointed *Kuta* will send one of his near relations to Jebba and Buka, the two places where these sacrifices are performed, with two white bulls to be sacrificed to the river spirits by the priests of these cults. By these sacrifices the chief secures 'greatness' for himself, and success and welfare for his subjects.

The Beni organization presents an entirely different picture. Unlike the Kyedye system it exists no longer; it was broken and destroyed by the Fulani conquest. It took the form of a confederacy formed by the twelve 'towns' of the Beni: Bida, Tafiẽ, Esã, Doko, Towagi, Egbe, Gaba, Nupeko, Eda, Panjuru, Ewu, Yesa. The political bonds were twofold: the twelve towns recognized the supremacy of one town, and paid a small tribute to its chief, or 'town-king'; further, in case of war, the twelve towns were bound to fight together and to support each other, again under the leadership of one town.[1] Mythology, and the existence of certain common sacred insignia of the twelve town-kings of Beni, supply the spiritual background for the political unity. Moreover, the *gunnu* cult, this most important religious cult of Nupe, appears among the Beni in a special form, namely, as a cult which utilizes comprehensive co-operation between the priests of the whole country, thus underlining, in the religious sphere, the unification of the sub-tribal section.[2]

One might ask why it was that just these two sub-tribes evolved a comprehensive political and cultural unit. The origin of the Beni con-federacy is hidden in the dim past of a Nupe of which we have no records. As regards the Kyedye we can, to some extent, answer the question. In the environment of the river valley, and in the pursuits of a riverain people, lies the germ of territorial and political expansion. Long fishing expeditions, an extensive river trade, on which the liveli-hood of this riverain group depends, demand extension of political in-fluence as security for the very wide area of their economic activities. Trading-posts become political outposts, and fishing colonies become strongholds of territorial expansion. The spirit of adventure and enter-prise, finally, which alone could have built up this efficient organization, is part of the life of this riverain people.

Of the enterprising spirit of Kyedye chiefs, born colonizers and

---

[1] This chief town of the Beni seems to have been Tafiẽ till the Fulani con-quest; after that the headship passed to Bida, till it disappeared finally with the absorption of the Beni confederacy in Nupe Emirate (see p. 82).

[2] See *J.R.A.I.* lxvii, 1937, p. 98.

pioneers, the history of the Royal Niger Company can give many instances. But let us read these examples correctly. They show, first, that political integration tends to widen its basis so as to embrace all spheres of cultural activity; political unification calls into being other forms of contact and co-activity, and thus cements its own unity with the help of a more comprehensive and more intimate 'togetherness'. But these examples show also that the creation of such co-activity and togetherness does not simply follow from the potentiality of cultural uniformity. In the case of the Beni confederacy cultural uniformity appears intensified into co-activity and togetherness; among the Kyedye the political fusion of different sub-tribes, different cultural areas, created the wider area of co-activity and common life. Obviously, the nature of this co-activity and common life is different in each case. The commonness that grows from uniform culture and the commonness that is superimposed upon a cultural diversity represent two different social realities. What we have said above of the links of cultural uniformity which 'grow easily into links of co-activity and togetherness' was not, therefore, quite correct. We have before us not a simple quasi-automatic process of 'growth', but two specific, alternative forms of social development.

CHAPTER III

INTRODUCTION TO NUPE KINSHIP

BEFORE attempting the analysis of the Nupe community we must examine certain essential aspects of the kinship system of the country. This description cannot claim to be more than a brief outline. It is concerned only with the main principles of kinship structure among the Nupe so far as they bear on the subject-matter of this book.

The basic structure of the Nupe kinship system is the *extended family*: all individuals who can trace their descent to a certain initial, nucleus family—a husband and his wives—regard themselves as related and as forming one kindred. The Nupe have only one word for kinship, *dengi*, which defines relationship in the widest as well as in a more restricted sense. The vagueness of the terminology reflects the inherent vagueness of this concept of relationship. The extended family is a fluid unit in two respects. First, as the women of the family marry outside, into other houses and families, their connexion with the family from which they come, although never admitted to have ceased entirely, becomes weaker and less effective generation after generation. Secondly, the constant growth and expansion of the kinship unit which this principle of reckoning descent entails leaves the boundaries and 'fringes' of the family unit only vaguely defined. People cannot, in fact, trace their descent back farther than two or three generations, and in every family there are a certain number of 'relatives' who are known to be *dengi*, related, without anyone being able to define the degree or nature of the relationship. Moreover, individuals and sections may split off from the main family group, move to other parts, and thus disappear from the view of the rest of the kinship group.

It is implied in these facts that the effective kinship unit is represented, not in the vaguely defined 'theoretical' extended family, but in that section of it which remains living close together—whose members keep, as it were, in each other's view—in the particular case, the kinship section inhabiting one house. This kinship section is, in fact, referred to as a 'house'—*emi* in Nupe. The Nupe reckon relationship in 'houses', saying, for example, that people belong or do not belong to the same 'house', that is, are or are not related. Technically, the 'house' is a compound of a number of houses (to be described later in more detail), enclosed by a common wall and sharing a common gateway or entrance hut, called *katamba*. The term *katamba* is frequently used synonymously with 'house': in enumerating the kinship groups of a village the Nupe will tell you that the village numbers so many *katamba*.

To some extent the house-group, too, is subject to the natural fluctuations of increasing or decreasing population. An overflowing population may necessitate the building of new houses and compounds, mostly placed close to the original home, but in some cases at some distance from it, in another part of the village, perhaps in another locality

altogether. Thus one 'house' (in the abstract sense) may be found distributed over a number of adjacent compounds, occupying a part or the
whole of the separate cluster of compounds which constitutes the subdivision of the Nupe village, and is called *efu*—a term best translated
with 'village ward'. Or we may find separate small hamlets, called *tunga*,
which are regarded as dependencies of the original house and village.

HOUSE OF A VILLAGE CHIEF

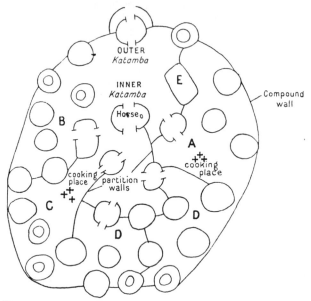

◯ *Sleeping huts* ◖◗*Katamba* **A**.. *partition of family head.* **B**...*partition
of unmarried sons.* **C**...*partition of unmarried daughters.* **D**...*partition
of married sons and younger brothers* **E**...*sleeping hut of family
head.* ◎ *Granaries.*

Both terms, *efu* and *tunga*, will play a considerable part in our discussions of the Nupe community. The fluid transition between 'house' and
'ward' is reflected in the often synonymous use of the two terms: thus
the quarter of the blacksmiths (*tswata*) in a certain village will be known
both as *emi* and *efu tswata*, or the part of the village in which the chief
(*Žitsu*) resides both as *emi* and *efu Žitsu*. Decrease in the size of the kinship group (owing to death or emigration), on the other hand, may cause
the break-up of the house-group and lead the people to abandon their
home altogether. Individuals who are left without a large family may
join friends or neighbours as adopted members of their house.

    In Bida the situation is altered by a number of circumstances peculiar
to the urban society. Space for local expansion being limited, families
are much more widely scattered than in the village, even beyond the

single *efu*, and the family section inhabiting one house is reduced to the smallest size. Moreover, independent economic position and independent, possibly even divergent, political interests and connexions cause adult family members to leave the paternal home and to set up households of their own. Even the wider local unit, the *efu*, is no longer based on kinship, but is largely replaced by a local unit the composition of which is determined by the factor of political allegiance and partisanship.

The size of the house-group varies widely: the largest group which I encountered numbered about sixty individuals, including men and women, adults and children. The smallest groups are found in Bida, and may comprise not more than six or eight people.

The effective kinship unit—the 'house' in the abstract sense of the word—expresses itself conspicuously in the recognition of a common family head, who is called, significantly, *emitsó*, Owner of the House. We shall learn later of the political, religious, and economic prerogatives vested in the person of the family head. Here I will only add that where a section of the house-group splits off from the main body and establishes itself in a new, separate, house it cannot claim to be at once recognized as a new unit, entitled to a separate *emitsó*, but continues to acknowledge the old family head. In the course of time the head of the new group may gain the position of an independent *emitsó*. The following diagram illustrates a case of this kind. The members of the family group placed to the right of the dotted line separated from the main family body in 1934 and moved to a newly built house in another part of the village (Kutigi). The reason given was that the old house had become 'too crowded'. The head of the new group expected to be recognized as *emitsó* after the death of the old family head (marked FH in the diagram).

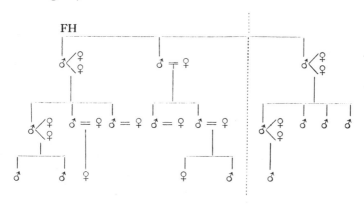

The 'house' is subdivided into a number of family sections, each of which inhabits a division of the compound. The single section represents an even more effective unit than the house-group and its members enter a more intensive co-operation: they keep house together, eat together, and also form a common productive or labour-unit. No special

name exists for this group *qua* group, only a name referring to its
organization as a labour-unit, or *efakó*. To-day these smaller sections
are often reduced to the small individual family consisting of a father,
his wives, and unmarried children; as often, however (and regularly,
under traditional conditions), they embrace larger units and represent
'sections' in the strict sense of the word, cut from the house-group, and
repeating its composition on a smaller scale. Such a section embraces,
for example, a number of brothers, their wives, children, and grandchildren. The attached genealogy may illustrate the relation between
the 'house' and the smaller kinship unit.

This genealogy shows another household in Kutigi whose family head
is a certain Kolo, a man of about 50 or 55. Brackets indicate deceased
family members. A dotted connecting line means that the nature of the
relationship cannot be ascertained concretely but is only referred to
vaguely as implying relationship of 'younger brothers'. Family members
working together in the same *efakó* group are marked with the same letters
(e.g. all individuals marked *a* form one *efakó* group, all individuals marked
b another, &c.). The family members marked SH have left the original
family home and have built themselves a separate house. Women and
small children are ignored in the chart.

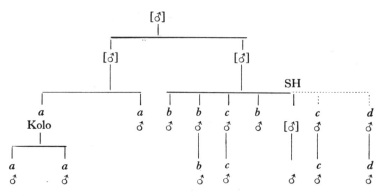

Each of the sections of the house may one day contribute the family
head for the group at large. The position of the family head falls to the
senior male member of the house-group, who is succeeded by his
younger brother in the classificatory sense, i.e. the man next in seniority
of the same generation, and, when the generation is exhausted, by the
oldest man of the next generation, i.e. the eldest son of the eldest
brother. This rule, however, is not applied rigidly and allows of some
latitude so that personal qualifications can also be taken into account.
Especially is this so where succession to family headship entails the
assumption of a certain important position in the community (e.g.
priesthood, or position of an elder). This brings us to the question of
the transmission of rights and duties vested in family membership and
to the method of reckoning descent.

The family has been regarded by many anthropologists as a typical *bilateral* unit—a group in which the transmission of rights and duties follows both the paternal and maternal line. We know now that such family structures are extremely rare, and that in most societies succession in paternal and maternal line supplement each other and are assigned different spheres of validity, certain rights and duties being transmitted in the paternal and others in the maternal line. For the Nupe family we

HOUSE OF A BIDA NOBLEMAN OF LOW RANK

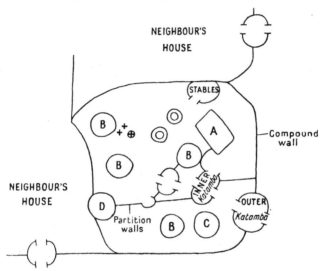

○ *Sleeping huts* ⊂⊃ *Katamba.* **A**.. *Sleeping hut of family head.*
B.. *Sleeping huts of his wives.* **C**... *Sleeping hut of unmarried son.*
D... *Sleeping hut of unmarried daughter.* ⊕ *Well.* ◎ *Granaries.*

can say that rights and duties which are transmitted through the father greatly outweigh in scope and importance those transmitted through the mother. Kinship membership itself and the access to the political and religious rights vested in it are determined by paternal descent. As women in Nupe neither own nor work land, this most important property is inherited through the father. The rights to certain forms of financial support (e.g. for the payment of bride-price or support in old age) are equally derived from descent in the father's line. As Radcliffe-Brown has shown, the division into paternal and maternal succession depends also on the nature of the benefits and duties that are transmitted from individual to individual, some being transmitted more satisfactorily through men (i.e. the father) and others through women (i.e. the mother).[1] Thus the personal property of the Nupe women is inherited by their daughters—as the personal property

[1] R. A. Radcliffe-Brown, 'Patrilineal and Matrilineal Succession', *Iowa Law Review*, xx, 1935.

of the men is inherited by their sons. As in the Nupe economic system the women frequently enjoy a financially more advantageous position than the men we find also that, in the event of economic stress, a mother may take over some of the financial duties normally discharged by the father.

Generally speaking, matrilineal descent in Nupe, including here both descent from the mother as an individual and from her family, has essentially the significance of an ultimate safeguard in case the patrilineal arrangement proves insufficient. In Bida society, with its great inequality of wealth and status, rich or powerful maternal relations may be as valuable as paternal relations; political connexions, especially, through the mother's family will often be utilized profitably. We realize that these 'matrilineal' rights do not follow rigid rules of descent and succession; rather they represent a 'second line of defence' on which individuals can fall back in case the 'first line of defence'—claims derived through the father—has failed. If we speak of the Nupe extended family as 'patrilineal' it will be understood that we refer only to the preponderance and the more rigid formulation of rights and duties transmitted in the father's line. The kinship organization as such, in which the alternative methods of reckoning descent stand in that relation of 'first' and 'second line of defence', can be most aptly described by a term which was suggested by R. W. Firth as 'ambilateral'.

The rule of succession to the rights and duties derived in the paternal line, which, as we have seen, imply a succession running through one whole generation before descending to the next, is expressed very clearly in the Nupe kinship terminology, about which I will only say a few words. It is of the classificatory type and corresponds to the generation pattern: it subsumes all members of the kinship group who are of the same generation under a common term. Thus members of the same generation are all 'brothers' to each other, 'sons' to the generation above them, 'fathers' to the generation below, 'grandsons' to the second generation above, and so forth. Within the generation seniority is specially defined: elder brothers are distinguished from younger brothers, and also the father's elder brothers from the father's younger brothers. The former, who represent the potential family heads senior to one's own (real) father, are called 'father', the latter, who may be placed as junior relations under one's father, 'little father'.

Let me summarize the main kinship concepts with which we shall be concerned in the course of this book. We shall largely disregard the fluid and vaguely defined large kinship unit formed by all individuals who are regarded as being *dengi*. When speaking of kinship group, or large family group, we shall always mean the 'house-group'. To the smallest unit, finally, we shall refer either as the family section, or as the household or labour unit, according to the aspect under which we are considering it. I must add, however, that the Nupe also recognize a much wider unit derived—in a very vague sense—from kinship factors. Thus a whole village is sometimes spoken of as representing one *dengi*, and as having 'one ancestor'. This interpretation does not refer to concrete common descent from an original family, but rather reinterprets the existing political structure of the community in a kinship sense. The ancestors of the chief who are regarded as founders of the village are also thought of vaguely as ancestors of the whole community. These essentially mythical kinship links exercise no influence upon concrete kinship claims and obligations.

Political factors are also responsible for the development of the large units which characterize kinship among the ruling family. We shall see that the ruling house of Nupe crystallized in three dynasties, which trace their descent from different sons of the founder of the ruling house, and divide between them the rights and duties vested in the ruling house. The ancestors of the three dynasties lived only two or three generations back; but already certain religious observances (prayers on their grave) mark them off from all subsequent royal ancestors. In this rigidly defined system of reckoning descent in the father's line back to these almost sanctified 'first ancestors', and in the relationship with one another which is in the nature of mutual obligations for the sake of the larger unit, the royal house itself, the three dynasties correspond from kinship point of view to incipient *clans*—the only analogy to clan structure which we find in Nupe.

Let me say in conclusion that kinship structure in Nupe is not that dominant, all-enveloping structure which we know from many primitive societies. Although it bears upon religious life, education, and the organization of production, it is greatly overshadowed as a determinant of social behaviour by the factors of political organization and, in economic life, by economic interests proper. Indeed only because of its lesser significance in social life could we omit the detailed description of Nupe kinship from the sociological analysis with which this book is concerned.

CHAPTER IV

THE COMMUNITY: VILLAGE AND TOWN

THE description of 'areas of common life' must start with the description of the external arrangement, that is, forms of settlement. The Nupe live in large villages or towns. They have only one word for both, *eži*, thus defining the essentially identical nature of the two forms of settlement. There exists another Nupe word, *tunga* or *kangi*, which is applied to very small settlements. But this name refers not so much to the size as to the different sociological nature of the settlement; for the *tunga*, unlike the *eži*, does not represent an independent local unit but a 'daughter-settlement', a 'colony' of a village or town.

The size of the *eži* varies considerably. Nupe Emirate counts three villages with a population of over or near a thousand: Doko with 800 inhabitants; Mokwa with 2,000; and Kutigi with 3,000. But there exist also smaller 'towns', villages the population of which had been reduced by emigration and which may be, in size, hardly bigger than a large *tunga*. The local arrangement of the Nupe village, large or small, is nearly always the same: clusters of compounds scattered comfortably over an area, each 'cluster' consisting of a number of walled compounds, 'houses' in native terminology, and forming what the Nupe call an *efu*, or ward. These village wards are separated by stretches of open land, spacious cultivated fields, studded with clumps of trees. More rarely the *efu* stand close together and are separated only by narrow thoroughfares between the walls of neighbouring compounds. This latter arrangement is typical of many riverside villages where, in narrow space, house presses upon house and compound upon compound. Each *efu* has its own name, derived either from a topographical peculiarity, e.g. Takogi, meaning 'the one below', or Kpacinefu, 'the river bank *efu*', or from a sociological feature, namely, the rank or profession of the people living in the *efu*, e.g. *efu* Žitsu, '*efu* of the chief', or *efu* Tswata, '*efu* of the blacksmiths', and so forth; or, finally, the name of the *efu* may refer to the origin of its inhabitants, betraying them as immigrants from another village or tribe, e.g. Yafu (abbr. for Eyagi-fu), 'Yoruba *efu*', or *efu* Daži, '*efu* of (the people of) Daži'.

The Nupe *eži* with its scattered *efu* clusters is encircled by a large town wall, or more correctly, used to be encircled by a town wall. It exists no longer, but its ruins can still be seen in many places, and all the people insist that formerly all 'towns' were protected by such walls. These crumbled ruins of the old town wall provide us with a piece of important historical evidence, which tells us, I think, why the Nupe have chosen just this type of settlement, in large populous 'towns', and not, for example, settlement in loosely linked, scattered homesteads; it allows us to grasp at least one of the motives behind this social development: the dangers of war.[1] Large villages represent in a country of

---

[1] The other motive is economic and is entailed in the organization of the Nupe system of production and exchange. (See p. 366.)

constant warfare the only safe method of settling. The small outlying settlements could quickly seek the protection of the walled town; a large concentrated population meant comparative security from raids, comparative safety in unsafe times. We have more historical data to support

SKETCH MAP OF DOKO

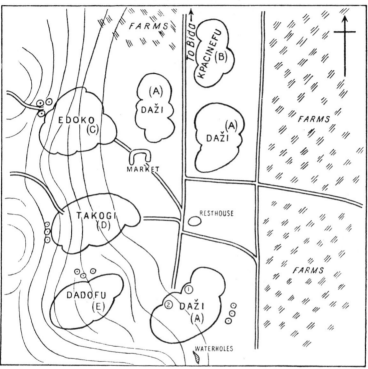

A–E are the five *efu* or wards, of the village.   ⊙....roast ovens.
①...house of chief *(Etsu Daži)*.   ②....house of village priest *(Žigi)*.

this interpretation. One or two Nupe villages have sprung from the amalgamation of small groups, and in one significant case this fusion of component groups into a single large 'town' can definitely be traced to the time of the Fulani wars. What is to-day the village of Doko originated then out of the fusion of a small hill-side village, called Edokó, with a village situated originally about two miles away, in the plain, by the name of Daži. To escape from the Fulani raiders the people of Daži moved to Edokó, into the protection of the hill-side. The new twin-town was called Doko, with Edokó and Daži as two of the five *efu* which form the village to-day; and the chief, who comes from the stock of the Daži people, still takes the title *Etsu* Daži, king of Daži.[1] We possess also

[1] How far a development such as this, with a large village growing out of the fusion of two or more component groups, is typical of Nupe settlement in general

negative evidence to show that with the pacification of the country the reverse process has set in: Jima, once a capital of Nupe kingdom, a huge town to judge from the ruins of its town walls, is reduced to-day to a tiny village; most of its people have moved outside, and the eight former town-wards, still known by their old typical *efu*-names, are to-day scattered outposts, village 'colonies'—*tunga*.

The origin of the *tunga* settlements of Jima represents an unusual development. Normally the *tunga* reflects the expansion rather than the breaking up of the 'mother-town'. But the term *tunga* is not unequivocal. It refers to three different types of settlement. The first, the release of small groups for the foundation of 'daughter-settlements', is a direct consequence of the concentration of a large population in a single town. A growing population in the village, the need of new land, may lead to small groups moving into the uninhabited bush, to occupy virgin land and to found new settlements. A small section of one family at first, a few young men with their wives and children, the *tunga* may grow to a small hamlet embracing two or three large family groups. Or immigrants from another part of the country may choose to settle on the land which belongs to a certain village, and under its political protection: this settlement, too, will then be called *tunga*. Finally, the big landlords of Bida have settled their slaves and dependants on the land all round the capital, in small hamlets, called again *tunga*. But these settlements are in a different category, they represent not colonies of villages or towns but private property, farm settlements of individual landlords. A *tunga* is thus easily identified, for it is always referred to as a *tunga*, a 'colony', *of* a certain village or, in the case of private settlements, *of* a certain landlord. *Tunga* settlements seldom grow beyond three family groups. Should the population expand further, the *tunga* would again release some of its members who would leave the old settlement and found a new colony near-by. But it seems to have happened very rarely that a *tunga* grew into a 'town' proper—Gbangba, a prosperous village north of Bida and to-day the seat of a District Head, is the only example I can quote. Gbangba, however, was not a village colony but a *tunga* founded by people from Bida. On the other hand, I have seen several cases of *tunga* settlements which have grown out of each other, dependencies of dependencies. The *tunga* is itself a much more mobile settlement than the village proper. A *tunga* is often abandoned, and the people move to a new place, if there have been two or three bad harvests, or repeated cases of illness.

We understand the mobility of the *tunga* when we realize that these small farm settlements, founded by younger branches of families, can have none of the spiritual bonds—religious and ancestral—that would tie the 'real' village more permanently to the locality.[1] The same factor

I will not examine here. I may say that I have found two other typical instances; one I have described in *Man*, 1938, 85. There may be many more, of which the traces have become much more obliterated.

[1] An exception is provided by certain cults which are linked with individual families and not with the village as such; a sacred shrine of this kind may thus be carried to a *tunga*. The *tunga* Shebe Woro, for example, harbours the sacred chain and the shrine of Tsoede—two paraphernalia of the *ndakó gbǫyá* cult.

COMPOUNDS IN KUTIGI

JEBBA ISLAND

also explains why *tunga* settlements rarely (if ever) develop into real 'towns'. The factor of size and numbers, too, plays its part. In order to provide that self-contained social and political life that is typical of the Nupe 'town', and in order to afford its inhabitants the political security which is part of the *raison d'être* of that form of settlement, a much larger concentration of people is necessary than the village *tunga* is likely ever to achieve in a sparsely populated country with so low a birth-rate. But the attitude of the people is as important: they cannot conceive of a *tunga* becoming an *eži*—a rival settlement to their mother-town. The village *tunga* has no social life of its own: it possesses no market, no independent political organization, often no age-grades of its own, and celebrates its feasts and ceremonies with the 'mother-town'. 'Towns', on the other hand, are independent, self-contained units, which have little in common with each other, and often know nothing of their next-door neighbours. To become a 'town' would thus mean for the *tunga* to deny the very essence of its social identity.

Every village then counts, 'owns' as the Nupe say, a certain number of colonies, which surround it in a radius of six to seven miles, right up to the point where the area of the next village begins. Kutigi, for example, possesses six *tunga* settlements founded between 1860 and 1910. Five were founded by people from the two largest *efu* of Kutigi, one by people from Etsú, a neighbouring 'town', who preferred to settle on the more open and fertile land of Kutigi. Doko, a much smaller village but situated in a more densely populated area, owns nine large *tunga* settlements and a number of smaller, secondary, dependencies. Two of the large *tunga* settlements were founded by people of the Cekpã sub-tribe who fled from their homes during the Yoruba wars and settled in more peaceful Beni country. The other seven are village colonies proper. Interspersed between these colonies of Doko are four 'private' *tunga* settlements, founded by slaves and other dependants of Bida landlords.

The following examples may illustrate the organization of two comparatively recently founded *tunga* settlements:

Zaboru, a *tunga* near Sakpe, consisting of two compounds, was founded by the man Zaboru, together with his elder brother, the present Village Head of Sakpe, about thirty years ago. The two men went out together to find a place with new farm-land, and built first temporary, later permanent huts. The elder brother returned to Sakpe after the death of their father to assume his position as the new head of the family. In his place a third, youngest, brother, who had just married, went out to the *tunga*, about ten years ago, where he is still living.

Shebe Woro, belonging to the 'town' Shebe and consisting of two compounds, was founded in 1933, when a certain Kolo left Shebe 'because the place was too full'. Together with some relations and two friends he occupied a new place, about three miles away, deeper in the bush, and founded there the settlement now called Shebe Woro, which means, New Shebe.

Let us now go inside a Nupe village. I have described already its typical lay-out—the scattered *efu* and the walled compounds or 'houses' which make up the *efu*. The Nupe house consists of a number of huts, mostly round, built of clay and thatched with grass, which are surrounded by a high mud wall. The wall opens upon the path or open space in front of the house in the *katamba*, a hut more spacious than the rest, with big doors which make the *katamba* a gateway or entrance-hall of the compound. Inside the house are smaller partitions and a number of smaller *katamba*, all invisible from outside. You only see the tops of the grass roofs protruding from behind the compound wall. Sometimes the house of a chief is built in a different, more imposing style with a large square or semicircular *katamba* which has a high gabled roof and windows let into the walls. Often huts or entrance-halls are decorated with ornaments worked in relief into the clay. Some houses are more beautifully decorated than others—a sign both of difference in prosperity and in ambition or aesthetic leanings. There are the signs of occupational specialization: one or two blacksmiths' furnaces; a house decorated with crude plastics in relief of animals, or with a pair of horns surmounting the roof—a hunter's place; a platform of dyeing pits in one corner of the village, and perhaps the half-open sheds of the weavers. To-day one small mosque at least is found in every village of Nupe. Pagan sacred shrines or sacrifice places are mostly hidden inside the houses; only in the riverain villages did I find a sacred shrine placed in the open, in the middle of the village. The sacred groves where the annual sacrifices are performed are always some distance away from the village, hidden in the thin bush and brushwood which surround the village. Most villages are situated near a watercourse, be it only a little stream or brook. From here the women fetch the water, and here you may see them at all hours of the day washing dishes and calabashes or laundering their clothes. There are also wells in most of the villages, well-dug deep wells—the Nupe are excellent well-builders—with a strong timber framework and a solid, clean platform round the mouth of the shaft; standing on the platform, the women draw water in buckets or earthenware pots tied to long ropes of native hemp. The big, round roasting-ovens of clay which look like huge red eggs scattered on the outside of the village, and in the bigger places the square of open booths which forms the market, complete the picture of the Nupe village. Once or twice a week this square is overflowing with people, men and women of all ages: they buy and sell, they listen or dance to the music of drummers and flute-players, they have their heads shaved, they talk, chat, cry out their wares. They are a mixed crowd, and the nearer the village is to the main roads of the country, the more mixed it is: people from the village, peasants from the *tunga* near-by, traders from Bida, travellers and occasional visitors from places and countries far away.

The market gathering is not the village community. Yet the boundary of what we have called the area of common life is, of necessity, fluid. It is redrafted and reset with every new bond of contact and every new channel of communication. But we may say this: the village and its dependencies form the core of this area of common life. Between them takes place the intensive life of the community, of regular and habitual co-operation in all spheres of life. Within this area marriages are arranged, pacts of friendship made, visits, feasts, and meetings organized regularly. Contacts and forms of intercourse may stretch beyond this area—they regularly do in trade connexions or in the contacts involved in the political system of the country. Moreover, modern communications have greatly extended their scope. Yet these contacts and single lines of intercourse hardly affect the self-containedness of the community. A sign of the tendency to seek regular contacts with places and groups without is travelling. And here we see that the villagers evince little interest in travelling and in visits to other towns and countries.[1] In the small Beni village Pichi, about five miles from Bida, only three men out of fifty have been across the Kaduna river or outside the area of their sub-tribe. Most peasants, at least the older men, with whom I have discussed travelling, said in so many words that travelling had no interest for them.

Again, the self-limitation of community life expresses itself in the parochial outlook of the villagers. There is a striking lack of interest in the life and customs of the peoples 'outside'; or the interest is of that lofty and self-centred kind that will credit anything unusual reported of 'foreigners'. When discussing with villagers the customs, for example, or the religious rites, of neighbouring communities you will be told: 'We don't know; we do this and that, but they may have different customs', or you will be given unreliable, second-hand information, often biased and sensationally made up. Certain of these opinions have become quite firmly rooted—commonly accepted popular theories about other communities. The people of Jebba Island professed to know nothing about the religious practices of Gbajibo, a village some twenty miles up the river—'they have quite different customs there' is what they told me. A visit to Gbajibo revealed that the religious practices of the two places were almost identical. In Bida and Doko I was told that the people of Etsú were blacksmiths by origin and possessed special blacksmith magic. The people of Etsú themselves had a quite different tradition of origin and their magical rites had nothing to do with blacksmith work. In several Nupe villages the people told me that while they themselves performed the *gunnu* ritual in the open, other villages possessed special sacred *gunnu* huts. I examined every case, but found no trace of this reported difference. This tendency to assume non-existent and exaggerate insignificant cultural differences between one's own village and other communities represents, on the ideological plane, the assertion of the cultural identity of the community. As in the case of the tribe, we find the social group sustained by an ideology which ignores and overrides empirical facts.

We must, however, qualify these statements about the self-contained nature of the village community. There exists one kind of interest and knowledge—and this time keen interest and on the whole well-informed knowledge—which embraces groups outside of the village community, namely, interest and knowledge bearing on the kingdom, its countries

[1] I am speaking here of the inland villages and not, of course, of the riverain Nupe, whose very existence depends on travelling. Nor do I refer here to migrations and similar permanent changes of residence.

and peoples, its organization and its personalities, and above all its centre, the town of Bida. It seems characteristic that of the people of Sakpe, a backwood village in the centre of Bida Emirate, a large number have been to Bida, thirty miles away, but no one to Labôži, which is only ten miles away but lies in the opposite direction to Bida. There is only an apparent contradiction between this parochial outlook with respect to the community next door and this interest for the kingdom and its capital. It reflects the centripetal structure of the system of cultural 'co-ordination' which we identified with the Nupe state. But let us examine first, under the aspect of community and common life, its capital, Bida.

Bida as it exists to-day is a comparatively young town. It was founded by the first Fulani Emir of Nupe about 1860. The old Beni village of Bida which stood on its site, a small village of four *efu*, forms to-day the 'old city' of Bida, its innermost part, known as *ba nîn*, the Inside. At the time of the British occupation Bida is reported to have had a population of 60,000. Later it dropped rapidly: the enormous households of the feudal lords dissolved, slaves and private armies disappeared, and absentee landlords moved out into the country to live on their land. The old trade-route to the south which ran through Bida was diverted by the British, who suggested the shorter route from Zaria to Lokoja.[1] Trade began to avoid the defeated, impoverished capital. Some ten years ago Bida counted over 30,000 inhabitants; the last figure, for 1934, is 23,286. But the cosmopolitan character of the population still betrays its character of a metropolis: all tribal sections of Nupe are represented, and besides almost every tribe of Nigeria: Hausa, Yoruba, Yagba, Bunu, Kukuruku, Dakakari, Kamberi, Koro, Asaba, Gara, Tiv, and many more. The Nupe of Bida total over 20,000; of the strangers, Yoruba with nearly 600 and Hausa with 400–500 constitute the largest contingent in this medley of tribes and races.

And now the town itself. From a broken-off plateau that forms its northern edge, from the foot of two flat-topped hills, the town sweeps down into the plain. The town wall embracing the wide expanse of Bida runs over the edge of the plateau, climbs down into the plain, crosses two rivers and opens its gates upon four roads. This wall was estimated to measure twelve miles in circumference. To-day it has lost its former importance. It has broken down in many places and has been left un-repaired. A go-ahead Administrative Officer some two years ago had ordered all town gates to be pulled down—to make room for the in-creased motor traffic (which never came). Also, the town no longer fills the space within the wall, and many ruins and deserted places inside the wall betray the changes that have overtaken Bida and its people.

Four big roads lead through Bida, roughly in the shape of a cross, from east to west and north to south. The road from the Kaduna river enters Bida in the west, by the 'Wuya gate', so named after the village on the banks of the Kaduna. Just outside the west gate is 'New Bida'—a nucleus of New Bida—consisting to-day only of a few official buildings, among them the Emir of Bida's newly built residence. We leave New Bida behind, with its brick buildings, its tin roofs, and glass windows, and

[1] Dr. W. B. Baikie, R.N., *J. R. Geogr. Soc.*, 1867, p. 362.

A VILLAGE *KATAMBA*

A *KATAMBA* IN BIDA

enter the native town. In the town as it presents itself to the eyes of the visitor there are but few traces of modern influence. There are the modern roads, metalled, with stone parapets and bridges of concrete. But the houses which line the streets are still the same century-old Nupe houses: the big, naked wall enclosing the compound and, hidden behind it, the array of small thatched huts. As in the village, the compound wall opens upon the street in the *katamba*, the gateway or entrance-hall of the Nupe house. Its style and lay-out and the state it is in indicate better than anything else the status and position of the people who live there. There are the round gateways of the wealthy, some painted black, some in gay colours, with ornaments worked in relief into the clay, and the roomy gateways of the royal princes, with window recesses, and pillars and buttresses to support the high-gabled roof. Some *katamba* have raised platforms in front of the door, carefully levelled, and stained with the juice of the locust-bean which gives them the appearance of smooth asphalt. Others have coloured earthenware plates inlaid in the clay of the wall; others show, worked in relief, figures and emblems which took the builder's fancy or which are to indicate the owner's profession, such as the likeness of the wooden writing slate—the 'trade-sign' of the learned Koran-teacher. And then there are the naked, sober *katamba* of the simple craftsman or farmer, and the dilapidated, neglected, and roof-less entrance huts of the poor. *Katamba* follows *katamba*, house follows house, as we walk along the road. Side-streets branch off, winding between the compounds, a maze of small streets and paths, which are often just wide enough for a man on horseback to pass through. Here and there the walls recede and give room to an open square with a few trees, a little grass or a patch of cultivated ground, where goats and sheep graze, children play, and a few men, sitting in the shade, enjoy the hours of leisure.

We pass a blacksmiths' quarter, easily known by the open forges with their many doors and small triangular windows all round the walls. A little off the road live weavers and bead-makers. The road opens into a large square. To the right is a market, one of the three big day-markets of Bida, noisy and crowded with people who are buying and selling: foodstuffs, firewood, cloth, small pots. To the left, occupying one whole front of the square, is the residence of the Masaba dynasty. Two small bronze cannons formerly flanked the entrance-hall as symbol of the royal might. In the centre of the square stands a small throne hall; it used to be a pretty building, with painted and decorated pillars all round. But to-day, only a year since the death of the last *Etsu* from this house, it is already in a state of disrepair and neglect which symbolizes, more convincingly even than the disappearance of the bronze cannons, the passing of royal power. Houses of nobility and high office-holders occupy the other sides of the square. Walking on, past the long wall of the royal residence, we come to the street of the brass- and silversmiths. At all hours of the day their forges are busy, but not too busy to greet you with a little flourish of hammering on their anvils. Their women-folk are sitting outside the huts with baskets full of brass- and silverware in front of them, offering the products of the street to those who pass by.

It is a little over a mile from the west gate to the centre of Bida where the four main roads meet. Here stands another royal residence, the house of *Etsu* Usman Zaki—to-day almost in ruins. But the ruins, the enormous lay-out, the faded paintings and decorations, still speak of the ancient greatness. It is only ten years since the last ruler from this house, *Etsu* Bello, died. But ten years in this country, ten years with no royal household, no army of servants and slaves to take care of upkeep and repair, have sufficed to turn the king's palace into a desolate, half-deserted ruin in a corner of which the king's last descendants find ample room. Behind the house of Usman Zaki is the big town mosque where the Friday services are held, a building of red clay, with a tin roof perched on top, bare and singularly unattractive. In front, and all along the north wall of the royal residence, filling the wide open square, stretches the big 'night-market'—the centre of Bida's pulsating life. It starts in the late afternoon, when peasants return from the farms, craftsmen stop work, and the women leave the houses, dressed for the occasion. Soon the large square is packed with people: men, women, children; townspeople and villagers, buyers and sellers, and those who come to the evening market to watch the crowds, meet friends, or to enjoy the excitement that goes with such public gatherings. The market is easy to survey. Every important commodity has its proper place. Horses and live stock, saddlery and fine coloured grass mats are sold behind the mosque; leather work, caps and straw hats, timber for roofing and coarse mats, in front of *Etsu* Usman's house. The butchers have a hut of their own, and so have the barbers, while traders and brokers who deal in cloth, gowns, ornaments, and swords occupy the long rows of booths which form the one rigid structure in this moving, seething multitude. Women are sitting in long rows all along the street, so close to each other that you can hardly move, selling food, native soap, kola-nuts, ornaments, silver bangles and glassware, beads and European cloth—anything that can be bought and sold in West Africa. Sometimes there are drummers, or a group of girls will sing and dance somewhere in the crowd; the 'young men about town' walk up and down the street, shouting greetings to friends, and joking with girls. When it becomes dark the big trade ends; only the women continue their trade in the light of little clay lamps which they place in front of them—a truly enchanting illumination.

But then, in the dark of the night, the market changes its face: the respectable meeting-place of buyers and sellers becomes a market of Venus Pandemos. The women who remain so late are not dressed for work or trade: they wear their most beautiful dresses, light-coloured and embroidered cloth; they have bangles on their wrists and rings on their fingers; their eyes are painted with antimony, and their fingers and hands stained with henna. They never carry loads themselves—they always have a small girl with them to carry their baskets and bundles. They all sell kola-nuts—a man's article. They are always surrounded by men with whom they gossip and joke, and then, a whispered appointment, one of the men leaves, followed after a while by his companion for the night. One light after the other is extinguished. The market grows

THE PALACE OF THE ROYAL HOUSE OF MASABA

THE PALACE OF THE ROYAL HOUSE OF USMAN

dark and quiet. After 9 o'clock the market-place and the streets are almost deserted.

But let us return to our daylight inspection of the town: we were standing at the crossing of the four main streets of Bida. Turn to the north, and you come to *lálemi*, the strangers' quarter of Bida, where Hausa and Yoruba are living in houses and huts built in their own tribal style and fashion. They are traders by profession, and shops and stalls line the long road to the north gate—shops in which you can buy every-thing at every hour of the day, from native food to a European wrist-watch, from the powders and amulets of the Hausa medicine-man to brass buttons or bicycle spare parts offered for sale in a Yoruba man's shop. The road to the east bridges a stream and a stretch of marsh-land that runs across the town, with its fields of rice and sugar-cane; it runs past another quarter of brass-smiths, skirts the quarter of the *masagá*, the Bida glass-makers, and leaves the town by the Badeggi gate, so called after a village thirteen miles from Bida on the small rickety railway line (the oldest railway line in Nigeria) which links Baro on the Niger with Minna on the main line of the Nigerian Railway. The south road crosses another stream, with yellowish, dirty water in which children are bath-ing, grooms watering horses, and women washing their clothes and cleaning pots and pans. It runs on through a thickly populated part of the town, past a beautiful old mosque perched precariously on the edge of a deep trench; another day-market, and another royal residence. Another weavers' quarter, and another group of blacksmiths. Old Bida and New Bida mix for a while: still inside the town walls are Prison and Hospital; on the other side the Native Administration Workshops and the Middle School. And beyond this, the European Reservation, the Government Offices, and then open fields and farms.

This, then, is Bida. Like all large towns it is both more and less than one community. More, in that contacts, communications, and forms of intercourse stretch far beyond the town boundaries; and less, in that within the town walls of Bida there exists a vast number of different, almost independent, strata and 'areas of common life'. Some, perhaps the weakest and least tenacious, are defined by tribal origin. The social differentiation of rich and poor, of social status and political rank, create others—strata in which life is lived in different fashion, in which different values are valid and different patterns of behaviour accepted as normal. But we have also observed the division of the town into three large districts, almost exact copies of each other, each with its day-market, its quarter of craftsmen, and its royal residence. The three districts are separated, geographically, by the two streams which run through Bida, and they are spoken of as three *ekpã*, 'banks', and given the name of the royal house that stands on their ground. Here we deal with units of a different order: they represent political factions, organiza-tions of partisanship and patronage, which cut across the other social, cultural, and tribal strata. They reflect specific political and economic interests, they are vested, ultimately, in that paramount political organ-ization, the state. But that we shall understand more clearly as this description proceeds.

CHAPTER V
THE POLITICAL ORGANIZATION OF THE VILLAGE

THE political organization of the Nupe village differs in certain respects in different parts of Nupe-land, but the general outline of the system remains, with one or two exceptions, the same. Every Nupe village, as it constitutes a separate community, also constitutes a separate political system. The area over which its sovereignty extends is formed by the village and its *tunga*, the 'town' and its 'dependencies'. At its head stands the 'town-king', *Žitsu*, who, to use the language of the people, 'owns' the village—*u wũ ži*—and the land on which it stands. By this right of 'possession' he controls the lives of his community and the main resource from which it derives its livelihood, land. The close identification of chief and locality is often expressed in the title which the chief assumes and which is identical with the name of the village: the chief of Jebba (the correct name of which is Gebba) is known as *Gebba*, of Bele as *Belé*, and the old Beni 'town-king' of Bida styled himself *Bida*. In the chief, then, the collective existence of the village community is represented as in a symbol.

This political configuration is to some extent thought of as having evolved gradually in the course of time. But the Nupe village (unlike the kingdom) possesses no elaborate mythology which tells of the origin and the growth of the present polity. We have spoken of the vague interpretation in a kinship sense of the past of the village, according to which the people of the village have all descended from some common ancestor. As regards the specific political features, we find equally vague traditions of half-forgotten ancestors who were the founders of a village and the first settlers in the locality (we can disregard here the recent memories of fusion and separation of villages). The following tradition, referring to the village Doko, is a typical instance:

Two brothers came from beyond the river, from a place called Gaze (a village on the river Kaduna). They came to a place now called Kopa [Kopa is about five miles from Doko, on the other side of the hill on the slope of which Doko is situated]. There was nothing in this place then save bush. They settled there, first as hunters, later they began to work the land. After two years the younger brother left Kopa and came down the hill to the place where Doko is to-day. He settled there and called himself chief. He became the first *Žitsu* of Doko, *Žitsu* Lefiya.

These traditions of origin become more articulate only where the tradition of the village can be linked with the semi-mythical history of Nupe kingdom and its ancestor-hero Tsoede. In a number of Nupe villages the people trace their line of chiefs back to one who was confirmed in his office by Tsoede, and invested by him with certain insignia and magical emblems. Of both Tsoede and these insignia we shall hear more at a later stage. Here it may be said that the ancestral chief thus marked off by tradition is not, as a rule, identified with the first chief and founder of the village. It is mostly the second in the line of chiefs whom tradition associates with the ancestor-king of Nupe. Thus Lefiya, the first chief of Doko, is said to have been succeeded by a certain Dibo Saba upon whom Tsoede conferred insignia and chiefly magic. Or in Pichi tradition has it that a certain Dikwa founded the village and assumed chieftainship first, and that it was his successor, Goga, who was invested by Tsoede with the emblems of rulership. This mythological feature is of great significance, for it proclaims, projected in the manner of myths into the dim past, two facts in which we shall discover the very essence of village society: the fact that the village is conceived of as possessing a social identity of its own, and at the same time the fact that it depends for its continuous existence on the sanction of king and kingdom of Nupe.

We notice also another interesting fact, namely, that while normally Nupe families cannot trace their ancestry back more than three or four generations, these chieftain families proudly record a long list of ancestors, embracing ten or more generations. The explanation lies, again, in the political significance of this link with the past which, like the mythology that surrounds it, endorses the existing political constellation. In the case of ordinary kinship groups the genealogy has no significance beyond that of establishing, rather vaguely, present relationships; in the case of (hereditary) chieftainship it is to establish a convincing—and unique—pedigree for political claims.

THE COUNCIL OF ELDERS

The chief rules over his community assisted by the village elders, the *nŭsaži* or Old Ones, or, as they are also called, the *ticiži*, the Titled Ones. They are the heads of families or of groups of families which live together in one compound or one *efu*. Their appointment to the position of an elder is expressed in the titles which the chief confers upon these members of his council. The office of the elders is only very loosely specialized. Certain titles reflect the special occupations which *nŭsaži* and their families follow—titles of hunters, drummers, blacksmiths. When the community is in need of the services of these professions—for the purpose of organizing a large-scale hunt or of preparing a ceremony at which the village drummers are to perform—it will secure them through the elders who represent the profession on the village council. Sometimes a religious office is combined with a political rank. But more frequently the important priestly offices, for example the priesthood of the *gunnu*, the main cult of Nupe, although bestowed on family heads, are not connected with a political position. The holder of this religious office has no seat or voice in the village council except when questions of ritual—his ritual—are discussed. Apart from these more specialized offices the rank of the *nŭsa* is exactly what the name implies: the rank of a man whose age and experience and the headship over a large family entitle him to assume an active part in guiding the fate of his community.

Titles and composition of the council of elders vary, but the same rule is valid in every Nupe village: so many 'houses' or family groups, so many elders. No 'house' may be excluded from the share-out of village offices, nor may one 'house' 'own' more than one title—at least not in theory. The senior members of the house sometimes accompany their family head to the meetings of the council in the chief's house. Or if an elder is himself too old, or an invalid, a younger relative may do his work for him; but there would not as a rule be two holders of a *nŭsa* rank in the same house.[1] These rules, however, are not, in fact cannot be, rigid. A powerful chief may appoint a friend or favourite to a rank to which he would not normally be entitled, or refuse a rank to the legitimate claimant for reasons of private enmity or jealousy; an immigrant group may demand that a rank be conferred on its head as a confirmation of established citizenship; or an expanding family may claim additional titles for its members. New ranks may thus be created, new titles introduced, which do not correspond to the traditional system of village ranks.[2] On the other hand, titles may disappear with the family in which they were vested or with the special profession to which they referred. The title *Ndace*, Father of Hunting, originally a title common everywhere in Nupe, is missing to-day in many villages; the titles *Etsu Dzā*, Head of the Drummers, and *Majī Tswata*, Master of the Blacksmiths, have disappeared here and there where strangers (Hausa) have taken over the work of drumming and smithing and have disorganized this originally family-owned profession.

The equation: so many houses, so many titles, may also be upset (at least temporarily) by the opposite trend: in an expanding family group sections may split off from the main body, and build themselves a new house, without being awarded a separate rank. The *tunga* very rarely 'owns' a *nŭsa* rank. Founded by young people, it usually keeps its status of a 'junior branch' even in subsequent generations. However, a son or younger brother may be called to succeed the family head in the village and leave the *tunga* to assume his inheritance and position in the 'town'.[3]

Thus the institution of ranks of elders has two aspects: one is the official recognition, by the community at large, of the headship of certain individuals over the component groups of the community—kinship groups and 'houses'—a headship which implies both a certain moral control and control of the economic resources of the group; and the other the division of the political executive of the village between a number of selected individuals. The closer examination of the first aspect belongs to the chapters on kinship, land-tenure, and economics. We are concerned here more especially with the second aspect. But we shall see that the two are closely intertwined. The acceptance of a family head into the village executive enhances the position of authority which he normally occupies in his kinship group; but it signifies at the same time that he may be called upon to use this moral authority in the service of the village at large. Appointment to a village rank also strengthens the measure of

---

[1] Thus an old, blind *nŭsa* in Jebba no longer took part in the meetings of the village elders. But no successor was appointed until his death.

[2] In Mokwa, for example, the new title *Majī Koshagba* (lit. Master of Grave Digging) was conferred on the head of a Hausa family which had settled there during the Fulani wars.

[3] See p. 37.

TWO VILLAGE CHIEFS

THE POLITICAL ORGANIZATION OF THE VILLAGE 47

economic control which he exercises, by granting him access to special economic resources (above all, fruit-bearing trees) unattainable to the other members of his group. Thus supported, the titled family head is qualified to assume his double role, as official agent of the community at large and as representative of his group *vis-à-vis* the village community.

The relation between the two roles and their relative preponderance varies with the rank which an elder may attain. For the *nusa* ranks are not of equal order. They are defined by strict order of precedence, and there is never any doubt which title ranks higher or lower. The measure of political responsibility closely corresponds to the place in the scale of village ranks. In some villages we even find a formal distinction between the 'great' and 'small' ranks, the former three or (more often) four in number, forming as it were the 'inner council'. Where the village is arranged in a number of separate large clusters of compounds (as in Doko, Kutigi, or Sakpe), the distinction between 'great' and 'small' ranks also implies a distinction between headship over the whole cluster of compounds, the *efu*, and headship over single compounds or 'houses' only.[1] The professional ranks of blacksmiths and drummers are always at the bottom of the list of village ranks. The political importance of the rank of the Head of the Hunters and of the ranks which are combined with priestly offices differs in different communities.

It would be wrong to think of the village council of elders as of an elaborate, rigidly formalized, instrument of government. The full council is rarely summoned except on important occasions, such as the election of a chief, or the visit of the *Etsu* and his delegates or the District Officer. The normal routine work of village government is carried on by the chief and his 'inner council' of two or three elders of highest rank. And here again we have no formal appointed assembly, but rather casual meetings in the houses of the chief or of one of the elders, at which current questions are discussed and the necessary decisions taken. If more elders have to be consulted or instructed, a messenger will be sent to their houses, or they will call individually at the house of the chief or the head *nūsa*. If in the case of the *nūsaži* of high rank their position of authority transcends the component groups to the headship of which they have risen in virtue of their kinship position, this latter aspect preponderates in the case of the *nūsaži* of lesser rank who are excluded from the 'inner council'. They are executive organs of the village in the indirect sense of intermediaries through whom decisions of the chief and the leading elders reach the various kinship and local groups, and through whom, in turn, these groups can voice claims and interests so far as they call for action on the part of the community.

The graded scale of village ranks does not command an unequivocal corresponding system of appointment and succession. Succession to the lowest, professional, ranks is invariably hereditary. So is succession to the priestly ranks or the ranks linked with a priestly office: the secret

[1] In eastern Nupe, especially among Dibo and Beni, the number four plays an important part in the arrangement of *efu* as well as in the order of ranks. We find four *efu* and four ranks, or four head ranks and four secondary ranks, or four ranks plus the chief's rank.

of the ritual office remains vested in one family group. But succession to the other ranks involves a certain ambiguous situation. Only a few communities have worked out the principle of precedence consistently, evolving a system of promotion from lower to higher rank—Jebba Island and Mokwa are examples. In these communities every vacancy is made an occasion for a reshuffle of the ranks. A *nũsa* whose seniority and standing qualify him for the rank that has fallen vacant is appointed, his own rank going to another *nũsa* deserving promotion, and so forth, till finally one of the lowest ranks becomes vacant, which is then duly bestowed on a fitting, as yet untitled, candidate. But in other communities all promotion from one rank to another is excluded, the titles in almost caste-like rigidity remain linked with 'houses', and a man can claim only this one title whether or not it is one for which his age, experience, and personality would qualify him.[1] The people are themselves well aware of this ambiguity. It is overcome, in practice, in various ways. First, the appointment to the rank which has fallen vacant may be postponed till the candidate has reached the age and gained the status appropriate to the rank; a 'young man' of Kutigi (he was about 45) had been waiting for ten years for the title which his father's brother had held before and which had been 'reserved' for him; every time I saw him and asked how his affair stood, he replied with the same words: *n'wa ke degi*, 'just a little longer'. Or one may introduce new titles, intermediary ranks, by which device the rigid order of traditional ranks is circumvented. Finally, hereditary succession in Nupe is never understood in the narrow sense of a quasi-automatic appointment. Often it is a selection from a number of candidates of suitable seniority—younger brothers or eldest sons (in the classificatory sense) of the deceased. Though seniority counts above all, old age and debility will disable a prospective successor to family headship. Apart from seniority, other attributes are also essential: good reputation, skill and experience as farmer, a friendly temper, and good health; a leper or a man suffering from elephantiasis or blindness is ineligible; so is a complete invalid. But so long as his impediment (e.g. a short leg, a crooked arm) does not interfere with his work on the land and his ability to move about, it does not matter. The main attribute is *ánkali*—intelligence. In Kutigi a serious quarrel had broken out between the chief and some of his elders who refused to give their consent to the appointment to a high rank of a man whom they considered 'to have no brains'.

The following genealogy illustrates the succession to the position of a certain titled family head, the *Ndagoro* of Mokwa. We

---

[1] An interesting transition from hereditary ranks to ranks of the promotion type has evolved in Faže, a village in Ebe country. Only recently the former system of hereditary ranks was replaced in this village by a promotion system, the depopulation of the village in the Fulani wars having made this step necessary; for some of the families in which the most important ranks had been vested had died out, and only promotion from lower to higher ranks could prevent this untoward vacancy. This local development cannot, for various reasons, be taken as affording the explanation of the origin of the promotion system of *nũsa* ranks in Nupe. But it clearly shows that the people are aware of the inherent conflict between the rank system based on precedence and the strict rule of hereditary succession.

observe the general scheme of Nupe inheritance, one generation being run through before the next generation is admitted to the succession; but we notice also that the progress of succession left out two men of the older generation.

Genealogy of the *Ndagoro* of Mokwa

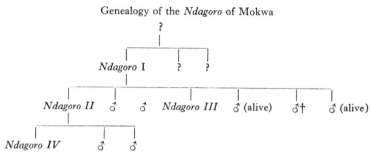

The same qualifications would also make a stranger who has settled for some time in a Nupe village eligible for a higher or lower *nŭsa* rank. But 'good reputation' would be understood according to local standards, which may not be the standards of the applicant. A lute-player in Doko, who had been living there for some twenty years, a fairly prosperous and well-liked man, still went without title. Lute-playing, though appreciated in Bida, was not in the eyes of the villagers a respectable profession. Had he been a farmer, or even a drummer, he would have been awarded a title long before.

If a 'new man' desires to be granted a title he broaches the subject first with one of the titled *nŭsa* with whom he is intimate; the latter will bring it before chief and council of elders, who will then discuss the question at their leisure. If, on the other hand, a rank falls vacant, especially one of the higher ranks, the official discussions will start at once, and all the men of the village will be talking about it and surmising likely successors. In the lowest ranks succession is a simple matter. In hereditary ranks, particularly in small families, the decision may also take but little time. When the *Ǹjukó* of Jebba Island—the hereditary Keeper of the Chain of Tsoede—died, his successor was known a week after his death, and the title was conferred upon him within a month. But sometimes the appointment of a successor is a serious and long-drawn-out business, and often enough, as we have seen, feuds may break out over the appointment of the most suitable candidate. Discussion follows discussion, often for weeks and months, especially if it happens to be the rainy season when everybody is busy and can spare only an evening or two in the week. The elders meet first, in small groups, in their own houses; later when the discussion has reached a more advanced stage they meet in the house of the *nŭsa* of highest rank and finally in the house of the chief. As always in meetings of this kind the assembly gathers in the entrance hut of the house; the younger men sit near the outer door, the elder men on the inner side of the hut. They are rarely given anything to eat or drink except perhaps a few kola-nuts in the house of the chief.

The meetings (which I have had many opportunities of attending) are quiet and dignified, the discussion flows slowly, no loud word is spoken; the young men are mostly silent, only the elder ones take part. If controversies or disagreements occur, they are never apparent in the discussion itself. Rather they reveal themselves in the disconcerting practice that what had seemed to be happily settled in one discussion will be questioned again in the next; and men whose agreement seemed to be successfully secured to-day will call another meeting of their own to-morrow or the next day and start the discussion all over again.

The appointment to a new rank is a matter of little ceremony. It is identical with the modest ceremonial that accompanies succession to the position of a family head (to be described in a later chapter) with which, in fact, it frequently coincides. Appointments to high *nūsa* ranks usually fall in the long period of mourning for the late holder of the rank, and so exclude any festivity or general celebration. Appointment to a new rank, which would mostly fall to a comparatively young man, is sometimes made the occasion of a little feasting: beer or palm-wine for the guests and a dance in the afternoon and evening to which neighbours, friends, and above all the comrades from the age-grade association are invited. But more often there is nothing; the selected candidate would be summoned to the chief's house before the assembled council of elders, and would be informed that *nw'a gi Tsowa*, 'he had been appointed (lit. had eaten) *Tsowa*', or some other such rank, and that is all. Only by the self-importance with which the new *nūsa* carries himself in the next few days or weeks will you be able to say that this had indeed been an important occasion. If by mistake you address him by his old title, he—or others who know—will put you right at once.

Perhaps I should mention that I have myself gone through this experience when the people of Jebba Island decided to bestow a rank on me, who had become in their eyes a 'full Nupe', and who at any rate was insisting on being treated as one when it came to religious meetings or confidential discussions of village matters. I had to make a few small presents (from which even a 'real' *nūsa*-candidate might not be exempted) to chief and elders; they were 'sitting' for three days, discussing the most suitable title, till eventually the senior *nūsa* informed me that I had been given the title *Shaba* (a very high rank but, needless to say, introduced *ad hoc*, and copied from the rank-list of other villages). A day or two after my appointment I walked through the village and met some people who used the customary greeting for Europeans, *zaki*; but my companions called the people sharply to order, informing them that I was *Shaba* of Jebba now, which information at once elicited the greeting corresponding to the *Shaba* rank, *gbako nyenkpa* (body of iron). In a week or two there was nobody within ten miles of the place who did not know of my new rank.

CHIEFTAINSHIP

Chieftainship in Nupe is, like the system of *nūsa* ranks, characterized by the coexistence of two systems of succession: promotion and hereditary succession. In Jebba and Mokwa the chief's rank is merely the highest in the order of village ranks, and one of the senior elders of the village is promoted to the position of the chief. In all other areas chieftainship is hereditary and bound up with one 'house'. Chieftainship of the promotion type goes invariably hand in hand with a rank system of promotion type. But hereditary chieftainship does not invariably imply hereditary *nūsa* ranks. In Dibo country, for example, chieftainship is hereditary, but the *nūsa* ranks in some villages follow promotion. The elected chief is by no means regarded as less closely identified with the village which he 'owns' than the hereditary chief. The rule that he assumes the name of 'his' village as title holds good both for elected and hereditary chiefs: the *Gebba* of Jebba (Gebba) is, as we have just seen, an elected chief.

Neither chieftainship by election nor hereditary chieftainship implies an automatic, rigidly fixed, succession. Under the former, any elder who has reached an important rank is eligible for the final promotion. The latitude which this arrangement allows is illustrated in the succession to the chieftainship in Mokwa, where, in the case of the last five chiefs, the following rank-holders were elected as chiefs: *Sámaza*, the fourth on the village rank-list, *Sojekó*, the second on the village rank-list, *Majī Bagidi*, the eighth, and *Sarkin Zongu*; this last rank, borrowed from Hausa, has been abandoned during the régime of the present chief. It was attached to the position of a caretaker in the camp prepared for the trading caravans stopping at Mokwa—a responsible and lucrative, though from traditional point of view inferior, post. (See chart I, p. 54.)

Hereditary succession to chieftainship follows the same elastic rule which governs succession to hereditary *nūsa* ranks.[1] A few communities have adopted the practice of appointing beforehand the successor to chieftainship, an 'heir presumptive', mostly known by the title *Shaba*. But it can be shown that this practice is of comparatively recent origin, in fact, a copy of the system of succession characteristic of Nupe kingship. The larger the family group or 'house' of the hereditary chief, the more scope there is for the selection of a fitting successor. Expansion of the chieftain family may lead to a splitting-up of the 'house' as a result of which the chief's office, vested in two or more related houses, is taken in rotation by these families. In at least one case hereditary succession itself was abandoned, and replaced by free election: in Doko the line of hereditary succession was interrupted two generations ago, and a 'new man', a man of outstanding ability, was appointed as successor by the old chief and accordingly 'elected' later by the elders of the village. The genealogy of the Doko chiefs (p. 52) up to the appointment of this 'new man' may illustrate the latitude allowed even in strictly hereditary chieftainship. We see that sons, grandsons, younger brothers, and brothers' sons are all equally admitted to the succession of village chieftainship.

The appointment or election of the new chief is a matter for the council of elders. It is presided over by a certain *nūsa* of high rank who is in many places called *Ndeji* (a corrupted form of *Ndeži*, viz. *nda eži*),

[1] In one village, Etsú, I found matrilineal succession to hereditary chieftainship, through the mother's brother's son, although in all other respects the rules of inheritance were the same as everywhere else in Nupe. I am unable to explain this isolated instance, unless perhaps historically.

Genealogy of Doko Chiefs

```
                    1. Lefiya
            ┌───────────┴───────┐
    2. Dibo Saba            3. Kolo
                                │
                            4. Yisa
                                │
                                ♂
                                │
                            5. Tsado
                    ┌───────────┴───────┐
            6. Jiya                7. Yisa
                                        │
                                   8. Gana
                            ┌───────────┴───────┐
            9. Tsado                        10. Yansako
```

Father of the Town, and who stands somewhat apart from the other village ranks. He plays the part of the chief 'elector' or 'king-maker'; he is never himself a candidate for chieftainship, but is entrusted with the rule of the village during the interregnum. We shall hear more of him presently. The Nupe dislike a long interregnum: as a rule only a few weeks, filled out with discussions and the consultation of diviners, elapse before the appointment of a new chief.[1] This appointment will eventually need the confirmation of the *Etsu* Nupe and, to-day, of the Administrative Officer. This last rule, however, applies only to those chiefs who are recognized as official Village Heads under the modern Native Administration. In the reorganization of the Emirate under British rule only the larger villages have been created seats of official Village Heads. Their number does not comprise all the places which are 'villages' or 'towns' in traditional native conception.[2] A significant terminological dualism has been the result: the people speak of *Žitsu*, 'town-king', when referring to their traditional, officially unrecognized, chief, and call the officially appointed Village Head *Etsu Nyenkpa*, 'Money Chief' (i.e. tax chief).

I can offer no explanation for the coexistence of these two different systems of chieftainship, of hereditary and promotion type. There is no evidence of either having developed from the other. Nor can local conditions, economic factors, or the factors of size and population be made responsible. But I could discover the sociologically interesting correlation between the system of succession and the religious elements which surround Nupe chieftainship. In the villages where chieftainship is hereditary we find that vague mythology of origin which tells of the first occupation of the land, and of the foundation of the village by the

---

[1] I have been told that formerly unanimity between the various diviners of the village was considered necessary. In Mokwa my informants stated that the normal duration of the 'interregnum' is ten days.

[2] In connexion with a scheme to raise the salary of Village Heads the number of Village Headships in Bida Emirate has recently been further reduced.

ancestor of the present chief. A certain special magic and sacred insignia are linked with the house in which chieftainship is vested. Thus the chiefs of various Beni villages and of Sakpe possess the brass bangles of Tsoede; chiefs in Dibo country an iron staff; chiefs in the riverain area the sacred chain of Tsoede. The magic ritual which is associated with chieftainship varies as widely: in Doko it is a harvest rite, the 'eating of the bulrush-millet'; in other villages it appears as magic against barrenness, as a rain sacrifice, an ordeal, or as a general rite to secure health and prosperity of the community. But invariably the chief's ritual, whatever its more specific aim, will be performed as funeral rite and ceremony of installation of chiefs, and also whenever certain great calamities befall the community—a drought, famine, or epidemic. The chief is not himself the priest of this magic, and often has not the insignia in his own possession. Insignia and magic are entrusted to another member of the chief's family. The office of the *Zigi*, the village priest, is kept in the junior branch of the chieftain house, and *Zitsu* and *Zigi*, Town-king and Town-priest, appear in the genealogies as elder and younger brother (in the classificatory sense).[1]

In the communities, on the other hand, where the chief is elected from the senior rank-holders, his house 'owns' no special magic or insignia, and there is no mythology of a founder of the village, but tradition speaks of the village as having 'always been there'. The religious duties fall, instead, to the *nŭsa* who acts as chief 'elector' and who is entrusted with the rule of the village during an interregnum. This man's office will be hereditary and sacred, he will own insignia or a special powerful magic, which is, again, invoked at the death and the appointment of chiefs or in the case of great calamities. A supernatural agency, a mystic safeguard, is thus always assumed behind the chief's authority. But Nupe village organization has evolved two different solutions, in accordance with the two different systems of chieftain succession: one makes the chief or his family the agents of the supernatural power which supports the claim to chieftainship; the other separates the political rule from the mystic safeguard and, instead of a hereditary king, brings into being a hereditary 'king-maker'. (See chart II, p. 55).

This division of religious and secular office seems to eliminate effectively conflicts between chief and priest. The priests of the village cults, experts in religious matters only, have no influence in political affairs; they are, as we saw, not even granted the general prerogative of their age: a seat on the council of elders. The priest of the chief's cult, if of the chief's family, is classed as a 'younger brother' and thus equally barred from the position of an influential elder. Only the priest-king-maker (where he exists) could gain the position of a rival power and interfere with secular affairs. However, by his office the main 'elector' of the chief, he should be a supporter and ally of the chief, whose office reflects to some extent his own authority, rather than his adversary or rival. He may prefer a puppet at the head of the village—I saw an instance

---

[1] See the genealogy given in chart II, p. 55.

I

Rank System from Mokwa (Promotion Type)

Rank order	Title,	Office.	Locality ('efu' or 'emi')	Succession	Insignia, magic, &c.	Remarks
1	Lile	Chief	Efugbo or efu Lile	Promotion	..	Present chief was promoted to chieftainship from rank Sarkin Zongu
2	Shaba Lile	..	Gunnuba (so called because gunnu priest lives here)	,,	..	Title introduced under Fulani influence; replaced original title Sojekó.
3	Ndeshi (Sheshi)	'Kingmaker'	Ilancita	Hereditary	Sacred chain, priesthood of Tsoede	Title Ndeshi corresponds to Ndeži, 'Father of theTown'.
3a	Guye	Successor to 3	Etisheshi and Korofugi	Hereditary in family of Ndeshi[1]	..	..
3b	Tswashe	Successor to 3a	Ntaci	As 3a	..	..
4	Sámaza	..	Gbaye and Yafu	Promotion	..	Was promoted to present rank from Tsonkwa.
5	Ndagoro	..	Goro	,,	..	
6	Maji Koshegbe	..	Kpege	,,	..	Newly introduced rank.
7	Tsonkwa (Tsowa)	..	emi Ndakogi	,,	..	..
8	Maji Bagidi	..	Ilancita	,,	..	..
9	Maji Dende	..	Goro"	,,	..	..
10	Maji nya Kota	..		,,	..	..
11	Maji Guye	..	Kpege	,,	..	..
12	Maji Tswaci	Head of Blacksmiths	Tswata	Hereditary	..	..
13	Etsu Dzã	Head of Drummers	emi Dzezi	,,	..	..
13a	Shaba Dzã	Successor to 13	emi Dzezi	Hereditary in house of Etsu Dzã[2]	..	..
*	Wangwa	..	efu Wangwa	..	..	This rank no longer exists. The position of the head of the efu has fallen, quasi-unofficially, to the Liman, the Mohammedan priest, who is not yet, however, officially admitted into the village council.

[1] These secondary ranks defining succession to the hereditary rank of 'king-maker' I have found only in Mokwa. The Sheshi, Guye, and Tswashe regard each other as elder and younger brothers respectively. I was told that originally the office of Sheshi was inherited matrilineally, and that this is the explanation why it has become divided between three kinship sections living in different efu. Though this explanation is, logically, incorrect, and although these three offices have actually been inherited in paternal line since the people can remember, the fact remains that the three groups which succeed each other in rotation are vaguely thought of as of matrilineal origin. The aloofness from the other village ranks which characterizes the office of the 'king-maker' is thus further enhanced by the different conception of succession.

* Secondary professional ranks of this kind are found also in other craftsmen groups, e.g. blacksmiths. Sometimes there exists also a third rank of this order, with the title Kpotũ. This organization of craftsmen ranks will be discussed in Chapter XIV.

II

Rank System from Doko (Hereditary Type)

Rank order	Title	Office	Locality ('efu')	Succession	Insignia, magic, &c.	Remarks
1	Etsu Daži	Chief	Daži	Hereditary	Sacred bangles, chief's ritual	Žigi (priest) is of chief's family.[1]
2	Shaba	..	In tunga	A relation of chief, promoted to present rank from Lile at death of late Shaba, 1935	..	Newly introduced title, copied from Bida ranks.
3	Lile	Formerly 'Heir Presumptive'	Daži	Present holder chief's younger brother	..	..
4	Kpotū	..	,,	Present holder chief's elder brother (died 1936)	..	Newly introduced title, copied from Bida.
5	Makū	..	,,	Tentatively introduced (see p. 56)	..	As 2 and 4
6	Ndefie	..	Edokó	Hereditary in one 'house'	..	..
7	Dzoko	..	Takogi	,,	..	..
8	Boke	..	Kpacinefu	,,	..	..
9	Shabaeži	..	Ndadofu	,,	..	..
10	Bodo	..	Daži	,,	..	..
11	Žitsu Bebi	..	Edokó	,,	..	..
12	Maji	..	,,	,,	..	..
13	Maji Egbe (or Ndace)	Head of Hunters	,,	,,	..	..

[1] The typical relationship between Žitsu and Žigi, chief and priest of the chief's ritual, as described above exists no longer, as the present chief comes from a new family. The relationship between chief and priest as it existed in the original chief's dynasty is shown in the attached genealogy.

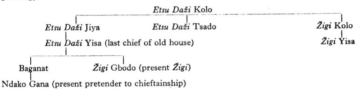

Etsu Daži Kolo

Etsu Daži Jiya — Etsu Daži Tsado — Žigi Kolo

Etsu Daži Yisa (last chief of old house) — Žigi Yisa

Baganat — Žigi Gbodo (present Žigi)

Ndako Gana (present pretender to chieftainship)

of this: a young man, son of the late chief, but inexperienced, timid and unintelligent, had been put forward as candidate by the 'king-maker', himself a shrewd and keen man, when the Administration looked for a successor to the vacant chieftainship of Sakpe. (The young chief, whose rule not unnaturally proved a failure, was deposed after two years.) But such cases are rare. As a rule the division of secular and priestly office works out harmoniously. Only once did I find an open conflict; but it revealed, not a failure of the established system, but rather a departure from it, brought about by extraneous influences.

It was the case of the chiefs of Doko, to which I have already referred. Here the kinship bond between chief and priest, Žitsu and Žigi, had been dissolved when the new family succeeded to the chieftainship. The priest of the chief's ritual became, from the priestly partner in the two-fold office of chieftainship, an independent, and thus dangerous, agent. The descendant of the original chief's family, a young man, Ndakó Gana by name, used the spiritual power vested in his house as a weapon against the ruling chief whom he regarded as an usurper. He refused the chief the use of the sacred insignia—the bangles of Tsoede—without which the annual chief's ritual cannot be performed. Finally, in 1934, he asked me to intervene for him so that he should be given official authority to keep in his possession the invaluable insignia, which the chief was demanding back not so much for religious reasons (for some of his brothers and sons were already posing as Mohammedans); as in order to deprive the rival family of this convincing evidence of their claim to the rule of Doko. The case remained undecided, and the rivalry between the two men unrelieved, till in 1936 the chief offered the 'pretender' official recognition of a sort, namely, the title *Makŭ*. The highest rank next to the chief's, *Shaba*, had just fallen vacant, and a reshuffle of titles had taken place. Ndakó Gana, however, rejected the title *Makŭ*—a new title, introduced *ad hoc* (copied from the dynastic ranks in Bida)—as a meaningless, makeshift sort of rank and demanded instead the rank of *Shaba* itself. The deadlock was finally overcome by an appeal of both parties to the *Etsu*; he managed to persuade the young man to accept the offered rank, at least as an earnest, and as more fitting to his age.

VILLAGE GOVERNMENT

The tasks of government which fall to the village chief are these:

1. He appoints the village elders from the ranks of the family heads and is thus bound, as by a constitution in the modern sense, to accept their co-operation and advice in all matters of village government.
2. He controls the land resources of the community and in this capacity apportions farm-land, trees, fishing rights, and levies certain tributes and land dues from the families holding village land. With this aspect of village government we shall deal later on in detail, in the chapter on land-tenure.
3. He is not, as we have seen, the religious head of the community. But he organizes, directly or indirectly, and partly finances, certain religious rites linked with chieftainship.
4. He arbitrates in litigation and wields (though now only on a limited scale) a certain informal judicial power.
5. He organizes all large-scale co-operation and concerted action of the village community.

We have already spoken of the composition of the village council and the co-operation between chief and elders. Let me add some concrete data to illustrate the working of the village 'constitution'.

A Doko farmer had quarrelled with a neighbour over some trees; people from a village near Mokwa came into Mokwa to borrow masks for the *elo* ritual which they were going to perform, having lost their own masks; a family head in Sakpe accused his sister's son who lived in his house of having stolen rice from his farm; a girl in Laboži denounced two strangers who had been given hospitality by a neighbour and whom she saw stealing their host's clothes; a young man in Jebba accused his wife of adultery; another man in Jebba complained that a certain hunter who was reputed to possess strong and deadly magic had threatened his life; a family head in Kutigi that his family was too highly taxed; a man in Pichi that a neighbour had beaten his goat (which the other man had found eating his grain): these are some of the cases which a village chief and his elders may daily be called upon to decide.

The procedure is nearly always the same. The various news, requests, or complaints are communicated at once to the chief, directly, if the supplicant or bearer of the news has the chief's ear, that is, is himself a titled elder, and indirectly, through the family head or the *efutsó* (head) of the *efu* in which he lives, if the bearer of the news is an ordinary peasant. Upon receiving the news the chief will summon the head *nūsa* (the *Sheshi* in Mokwa, the *Lile* in Doko, the *Ndeji* in other villages), and he in turn will call together the other members of the council whose co-operation is required: two or three of the senior elders—the members of the 'inner council'—and always the *nūsa* to whose kinship group or *efu* the litigant or supplicant belongs. Not only does this *nūsa* act, as we have seen, as the official informant of the chief on all matters concerning his group and locality, but his intimacy with the people whose case is to be heard, and his moral influence, make him an important witness and, when a decision has been reached, a guarantor of its execution. Before this tribunal, then, supplicants and litigants in the village appear. The discussion that ensues is informal, and devoid of the stiff procedure that characterizes, for example, the Native Court. Supplicant or plaintiff state their case in a few sentences—the Nupe are not fond of long speeches and elaborate expositions. Obscurities in the statement are unravelled in patient cross-examination, in which everyone present can take part. Then, at one point, the chief or a *nūsa* may suggest a solution, which may be agreed to by the others with the stereotyped expression *u ge*, 'it is well', or revised in renewed discussion. Very rarely do tempers flare up and the discussions become heated. The final decision of the chief and his council is pressed home in the form of advice, persuasion, warning. A discussion of this kind rarely lasts longer than two or three hours, after which time it will be interrupted to be resumed on a following day. Mostly one or two sessions suffice to arrive at the final decision.

But then, in more difficult cases, in which many witnesses have to be called and thorny problems of arbitration settled, the decision is taken out of the hands of the village executive. For the chief is not entitled to dispense formal justice and to enforce arbitration. He must send all legal cases to the professional Mohammedan judge (*Alkali*) of the district; moreover, litigants who are dissatisfied with the chief s decision may themselves bring their case before the professional judge or the District Head (a point to which we shall return later). This limitation of village jurisdiction makes it impossible to pronounce in more detail on the efficiency of the village council and the way in which it handles, or could handle, more severe conflicts. The gamut of advice, persuasion, and warning is the only one which it can use: the more strident notes of authoritative orders and severe reprimands are outside its scale.

That they, too, have a rightful existence in the administration of village affairs is shown in the organization, by chief and elders, of all concerted

activity that exists in the village: common labour and communal ceremonies and sacrifices, fights and wars in pre-European times, and tax-
collection for the modern Native Administration. Tax-collection in the
village has become a little ritual of its own, interesting enough to be
described here. Some time before the N.A. lorry is expected from Bida
on its periodical tax-collecting visits you will find the chief sitting in his
house, or in a booth in the market, surrounded by the people who have
come to pay their tax. The two or three head *nŭsaži* will sit with him.
The 'tax Mallam', who is attached to the Village Head as scribe and
'accountant', makes entries in his little book and is busy writing out tax
receipts. Little heaps of coins pile up before them. On this day the
normal routine of village life is interrupted: the men do not go to their
farms and often forgo their midday meal at home, and even a ceremony
that might fall in that time will be postponed until the 'tax ritual' has been
concluded.

A large proportion of co-operative village work is done to-day by the
order of the N.A.: the repair of a rest-house, the clearing of a motor-
road, &c. But the concerted action of the village community is still as
efficient in spontaneous, unsolicited work. I have seen the men of a
village repairing a bush bridge leading to their farms a day or two after
the news that it had been swept away by floods was reported to the chief.
And although there exists to-day an efficient body of N.A. police, in an
emergency it falls frequently enough to the people of a village to organize
the pursuit of a criminal and to escort him to the District Head—a task
which the young men at least undertake with efficiency and relish.

BALANCE OF POWER

To repeat: the village elders are the mouthpiece and the agents of the
chief, through whom his orders reach the community; and they are also,
in turn, the informants on whom the chief depends, and the mouthpiece
of the people whom they represent both in their official capacity and as
heads of kinship and local groups. Again we may call the chief a symbol
of the collective identity of the village community, in the sense that,
through his orders, he expresses its collective will and interests. Yet the
degree of perfection which this political system, with its well-planned
harmonious co-operation between chief and elders, attains in practice
varies considerably. Autocratically inclined chiefs find means to evade
the check on their power which an efficient council of elders implies.
We have spoken of certain chiefs who appointed their friends and
favourites to the position of titled elders in disregard of more legitimate
claims, thus creating for themselves a personal following in the village
council. I was told of chiefs who in the past have overridden the authority
of the elders, levying tribute and refusing legitimate grants of land, until
the elders appealed to the overlord of the country, the *Etsu* Nupe,
against their overbearing ruler. If they failed to obtain the support of
the king, my informants added, they would carry on as if there were no
chief—go on strike, as it were. I have myself witnessed all variations
possible in this fight for balance of power: an autocratic chief who

seemed to have managed perfectly to turn his elders into mere puppets; a chief (the chief of Doko) whose overbearing behaviour caused a *tunga* group to refuse him the customary 'tithe' of fish caught in a pond on their territory; and also a chief who had tried, in the appointment of a rank-holder, to go against the majority of his council, but was brought to heel by the organized 'strike' of the elders: this happened in Kutigi, where, during the great Mohammedan festivals, the elders declined to attend the traditional ceremonial gathering in the chief's house until he gave in rather than prolong this assault on his prestige. That this religious 'strike' concerns a Mohammedan ceremony is incidental. Refusal to co-operate in established ceremonial activities may well check a chief's high-handedness (though I have not seen another case of this kind): the congregation is as indispensable as the 'owner' of a special magic and the chief organizer and 'financier' of communal rites.

Into the problem of political balance enters yet another factor—the economic aspect of chieftainship. The ability of the chief to free himself from all checks on his authority may depend ultimately on the economic resources of which he can avail himself—of the economic resources, that is, allowed him by the village constitution. (We may leave out of account for a moment the existence of the supreme control of village chieftainship by the overlord of the country.) Having to appoint the heads of family groups to the position of village elders, the chief cannot eliminate completely these agents of 'public opinion'. But decisive economic superiority may spell political power uncontrolled— the ability to win over, bribe, or force opponents into submission.

The political power of the chief is sustained by a number of important economic privileges. First, the chief receives (or rather used to receive) a land-tax in kind, known by the Arabic-Hausa name *dzanká*, 'tithe', from every family head. He also receives a certain gift in kind, or sometimes money, when allotting land to new tenants. The nature of this payment as a gift and not as a regular tax is expressed in the rule that on its receipt the chief has to make the usual small return gift with which the Nupe always dismiss a bearer of presents. A special right to fruit-bearing trees assigns to the chief a source of income not available to other members of the community. The communal farm-work, *egbe*, which the Nupe farmers carry out for one another is always performed first, and on the largest scale, on the chief's farms, so that he can count regularly on a larger and more docile team of workers than any other citizen of the village. Finally, the chief has special rights to the fish caught in the ponds or backwaters in his territory, and to certain game killed by the hunters of his village. As regards the former, he again claims *dzanká*, tithe, of every catch; hunters have to surrender to him the skins of leopards or lions, or meat of leopard and lion, or one leg of a buffalo—here the rules vary locally.

Some of these prerogatives have disappeared to-day. The general money tax of the Emirate has replaced the former land fees and tithes. Besides, the chiefs of larger places, official Village Heads under the N.A., receive a fixed salary. Only in a few small villages the annual gift in kind has survived, though reduced in amount and only in the nature of a voluntary present. It is, I was told, only the 'old men who are still doing it'. The value of the right to communal farm-work has also lost its former importance. A number of salaried Village Heads have abandoned almost completely their former agricultural work, being too busy with their official duties. One village chief, who is District Head at the same time (in Kacha), has found it impossible to spare even his sons and brothers for farm-work, needing them as messengers and the like. Instead, he has adopted the most recent innovation in Nupe economics, and engages wage-labour to work his land. The chiefs of small villages, however, who draw no wages, and have been given no official position under the N.A., have lost the most important of the old economic prerogatives—unless their people voluntarily continue the old practice—without benefiting from the new. Only the right to special fruit-bearing trees, game, and fishing has survived everywhere without change. It is not surprising, therefore, that the old term *Žitsu* is more and more losing its splendour, overshadowed by the matter-of-fact term *Etsu Nyenkpa*, Money or Tax Chief. And often the small chiefs, who have been passed over in the political reorganization of the Emirate,[1] tell you that to-day there is little difference between chief and commoners.

How far did the former economic prerogatives in reality establish a definite, unassailable economic superiority of the chief? The approach to this question must be through the comparison between traditional income and expenditure of chief and elders respectively. Here we see that some of the economic prerogatives of the chief are shared (though in lesser degree) by the other family heads and titled elders. The *nùsaži*, like the chief, have a right to the possession of fruit-bearing trees; they too can avail themselves of communal farm-work—though only after the chief. And if they have a large family, many sons and younger brothers helping in the farm-work, their normal income may not be very much lower than the chief's. Of the economic prerogatives of the chief only the land-tithe (or its modern counterpart, the chief's salary) and the game and fishing rights are exclusive to his official position. The game rights contribute mainly to the symbols of chieftain status—the possession of a leopard or lion skin, allowed only to the chief. The additional capital resources vested in chieftainship—additional in the sense that they are unavailable to ordinary family heads—were thus derived in the main from the tithe.[2] I have calculated that the annual land-tithe of a village the size of Doko would amount to about seventy bundles of corn —twice the annual yield upon which an average peasant household could reckon.[3] Now, on this evidence we are justified in saying that the

---

[1] See p. 52.

[2] Certain other irregular forms of income it is impossible to estimate to-day: occasional land fees from new tenants, fines or gifts from parties between whom the chief was arbitrating. Moreover, certain chiefs received a small share of the tax money they levied for the *Etsu* Nupe (see p. 116); but this last income, derived from the kingdom, no longer reflects the village system as such.

[3] There is a certain margin of error in this calculation. The constant extension and subdivision of Nupe family groups and households make it impossible to define with any precision the size of the households originally responsible for the payment of the tithe. I have taken an average of the larger groups, such as are

chief's special income did not, normally, constitute an insurmountable economic barrier between himself and his subjects. This is further shown by the fact that the characteristic possessions of a chief—possession of things generally valued in the society—were not unattainable by others.

His surplus income the chief uses as follows: some of it he must devote to special expenditure attached to his office, the purchase of a goat or fowl for the annual sacrifices, or some other large contribution (larger than that of the other family heads) towards the cost of the village ceremonies. Occasional liberal presents to the elders, food, kola-nuts, beer, gowns are also indicated; a niggardly chief is much disliked. The larger part of his income the chief spends on himself, his family, and generally on things the possession of which are demanded by his status and prestige. Some chiefs, with a view to profit as well as prestige, have bought slaves or taken pawns. Every bigger chief possesses at least one horse. His dress is always of the more expensive kind—embroidered trousers, a turban, and an indigo-dyed gown, possibly an embroidered Bida robe. Many chiefs possess the beautifully carved staffs which are made by the craftsmen in the river valley and sold for sums up to two pounds. One or another chief owns an old flintlock gun, and some chiefs pride themselves on building bigger and more ornate houses than the majority of the people possess. Finally, as the most conspicuous symbol of economic advantage in this country of extremely high bride-price, two at least of the bigger chiefs I met had what among the Nupe peasants is considered a very large number of wives (5 or 6 as against the usual 1 or 2), and so had some of their sons and younger brothers.

Set against this the economic position of a well-to-do family head and rank-holder. He too used to own slaves or pawns. The higher rank-holders often possess large, imposing houses. They carry carved staffs, own a horse, turban and state gown, and a gun. Some of them may have three or four wives. With regard to the accoutrements of his office—the religious elements linked with chieftainship, its insignia and symbols of rank—the chief stands on a plane by himself; as regards things 'that money can buy', or liquid capital, he is placed only one step higher than his citizens of rank. The surplus capital which he derives from his office is not, as we can see, large enough to be turned into an effective instrument of political ambition.

Involved in this is the question how far the temporary economic benefits linked with the chief's office can be used so as to be turned into a lasting economic advantage, enjoyed by the descendants and the whole family of the chief. For the communities in which succession to chieftainship follows promotion or rotation the question answers itself: the surplus income vested in the chief's office is not sufficient, once acquired, to endow his whole 'house' permanently with economic superiority.[1] In

presided over by the *nusa* ranks, and the smaller family groups (approximately 100 in number) with which we should have to reckon to-day.

[1] Here is a significant illustration: in Mokwa and Jebba, two villages of 'promotion type', the imposing houses of the late chiefs have fallen into disrepair; the descendants are no longer able to command the communal labour without which the upkeep of the large house is impossible.

hereditary chieftainship, the accumulation of surplus renders such development more likely. But even here the existence of the special chief's cult, which imposes additional expenses on the chief (higher than in the case of cults to which he need only contribute his share), should tend to adjust more equitably the economic balance between chief and elders.[1]

However, we have other evidence to show that the chief's position, economically privileged though it may be, is not *meant* to lead to the formation of an essentially different, sharply separated, permanently privileged ruling class; evidence, in other words, to show that the political organization of the village is meant to preserve the social homogeneity of its community. This evidence lies in the rules of etiquette defining the behaviour of the people towards their chief. People everywhere show reverence to their chief: they kneel down by the door when entering his presence. Often there are raised platforms in the chief's entrance hut, near the door leading to the inner part of the house, on which he would sit, while the others are squatting on the ground in front of him. Or the chief would sit on a leopard skin or at least a cow-hide, while the others are assigned seats on grass-mats. The chief, finally, is addressed by special formulae of greeting reserved for his title. Yet again, this attitude of reverence represents only the highest grade of respect as it is shown similarly to all *nũsaži*, graded in accordance with age and rank. In every house young men or visitors of lower status and seniority would squat near the door while the head of the house, or honoured guests, occupy places on the inner side—the more honoured side. Special greetings of the same symbolic nature as the salute reserved for the chief are typical of the various ranks. Here as in the case of economic privileges etiquette marks off the chief not as standing on 'a plane by himself' but merely as the most prominent in a graded order of prominence. If on state occasions, wearing his state robe and turban, the chief is conspicuously marked off from the rest of the people, when going out to his farms there is nothing to distinguish him from an ordinary farmer; like him he carries his hoe across the shoulder, a straw hat on his head, and wears only the cheap blue cloth slung loosely round the body. There is thus ample 'neutral ground' in the matter of etiquette and distinction of status between chief, elders, and the rest of the people.

But above all, the attitude of reverence and the special chief's salute are reserved for the chief's person; they are not enjoyed equally by his relations merely in virtue of their being his relations. The exalted social position of the chief does not extend to his family—there exist, even in hereditary chieftainship, no symbols of a hereditary class differentiation. Later, in the discussion of social classes in the kingdom, we shall understand fully the significance of this 'democratic' element in Nupe village chieftainship.

---

[1] In 1936 the chief of Doko bought five sheep for sacrifices connected with the 'chief's cult', contributed beer to other ceremonies, and presented two gowns to men with whom he was anxious to keep on good terms—not counting occasional small gifts and contributions, e.g. to family feasts, &c. Altogether an expenditure of approximately £2–3, or 30 to 40 bundles of corn, that is, roughly half of his income from tithe.

There is one exception—which proves the rule. In Kutigi all the members of the chief's family are addressed as *wacī*, 'Great Ones', and though not shown special reverence are regarded somewhat as a class apart. The explanation is this: the rulers of Kutigi come from an alien group, those Bornu immigrants to whom I have referred already. Owing to their economic and educational advantages (they were Mohammedans in a pagan and rather primitive country) they had established themselves as the dominant group, and the leaders of the immigrants became the political rulers of the original inhabitants. In this position they were confirmed by the *Etsu* Nupe. In the Fulani dynasty of Nupe the Benu had an example close at hand how an alien group could arrogate to itself the position of a hereditary ruling caste. They followed it in every detail: from the Fulani kings they adopted the salutation *wacī*; and like them they managed that the recognition of social superiority was extended not only to the actually ruling chief but to his whole kinship group—a whole hereditary ruling class.

BINDING FORCES

Let us try, in conclusion, to define the specific nature of the political unity achieved in the Nupe village. It must be emphasized, first of all, that it *is* a specific unity, and that it is achieved by mechanisms peculiar to itself. In other words, political organization is not—as is the case in many primitive societies—simply absorbed by religion, magic, or kinship, and the mechanisms of control which these domains of culture entail. Nor is it, on the other hand, possessed of any of the conspicuous instruments of political control which characterize other societies: a police or military executive, a disproportionate chieftain power, or an elaborate apparatus of coercion. Moreover, the connexion between political control and religious and kinship agencies is very close. Political organization delegates to the kinship system the important task of providing the executive organs for the community in the persons of the *nūsaži*, who, as we have seen, are village elders and family heads in one. And religious beliefs and practices supply the spiritual sanction of chieftainship and authority in general. But as important as these specific contributions of religion and kinship are certain less specific influences, by means of which both religion and kinship help to sustain the system of political control. Thus encouragement of intermarriage within the village community adds the strength of interlocked kinship relations to political ties; and the communal religious rites exercise, and underline in their own impressive fashion, the unit of the village group.[1] They do it consciously and openly: their dedication to the support of the village community expresses itself in the prayer formula which occurs in every religious ritual whatever its avowed purpose or the occasion of its performance: *eži u de lafiya*, 'may the village prosper'. Political control, kinship, and religion thus define coextensive social units. Only because

[1] This interdependence of political unit and religious congregation is analysed more explicitly in the case of the *gunnu* cult. (J.R.A.I., lxvii, 1937, pp. 91–130.)

of this coextensiveness of the spheres of religious and political control
could the village elders of Kutigi to whose 'strike' we referred above
effect that political adjustment by religious pressure. And again only because of this coextensiveness of the spheres of political and kinship control
could, in another instance, a family head be excluded from the ranks of
the titled elders on the grounds that one of his sons had twice been caught
thieving. The family head was identified with the moral standards
obtaining in the kinship group the headship of which would have
entitled him, in the normal case, to a position in the political executive.
'How can a man who cannot keep order in his own house,' said my informant, 'keep order in the village?' But these three agencies of control
are only three in a multiplicity of coextensive forms of social organization: economic pursuits, the contacts of everyday life, recreation, education. The political activities take place within this one area of common
life. Expressed in one formula: the political system and the closely
knit social life of a single community organize an identical human
substratum.

Here we may, in parenthesis, touch upon the theoretically interesting
question whether this system of 'multiple control' which the political
organization is capable of utilizing can be taken to explain the absence,
in the Nupe village, of the more conspicuous, specifically political
instruments of control. However, this question cannot be solved on
the basis of Nupe material alone. For here the issue is confused by
the fact that the state organization, superimposed upon the village
system, obviates the necessity of the more essential of these instruments,
especially with respect to legal and military executive. Indeed, the fact
that the state removes graver legal cases from village jurisdiction re-
leases the social system of the village from certain social pressure
which must otherwise have necessitated a more strongly marked political
authority.

This brings us to the question of the resistance of this delicately
balanced system of multiple control to outside influences and, generally,
the influence of change. Its efficiency is clearly a function of the uniformity of social interests obtaining in the community. It will fail as
soon as the closeness of community life is broken by a strong divergence
of interest. Extraneous changes creating new aims which are apt to dissociate the political executive from the rest of the people may disturb its
equilibrium, which could then be readjusted only by a corresponding
strengthening, at the cost of the other agencies in the multiple machinery
of control, of political power as such. The most radical adjustment of
this kind is that brought about by the modern political changes which, in
accordance with the system of Indirect Rule, have turned the village
chief into an official agent of the Administration. In this capacity he
may have to give orders, enforce laws, and exact actions unpopular with
his people. He is bound to stand for aims and interests which may
threaten to estrange him from the community. An inconsiderate Administrative Officer may still more widen the rift. Twice I have come
across chiefs who, in their official capacity and by the order of a District
Officer, had to forbid all dances and festivities in a district which was

behindhand with the tax, at a time when he should have organized, as chief, the village rituals that precede the harvest.

As long as a chief in his capacity as a paid official of the N.A. organizes common labour for road-work—the value of which the Nigerian peasant is soon coming to realize—the capture of a criminal, or certain obvious hygienic practices, he will be backed by public opinion. But when enforcing an unpopular tax, pressing children for the Government schools (which was frequently enough the case a few years ago), or—a case I witnessed myself—sentencing to a fine in accordance with some ambitious by-law a man who had been defecating on the public road, his authority no longer serves the accepted common interests and can no longer reckon with common approval.[1] Here the backing by the Administration must provide the extra power which is to weigh the scales in favour of the chief and to reset the political balance between chief and community. Here and there the Administration even felt compelled to replace a traditional chief, who proved incapable of carrying out the tasks which his position under the N.A. assigned to him, by a more willing or more enlightened man, possibly one who had had the advantage of education and could thus better see the 'white man's' viewpoint.[2] But this solution was not an unqualified success: Government backing was not capable of making up for the loss of the moral unity which supports the traditional chief in the execution of his traditional duties.

The case of the present chief of Jebba Island is an illuminating instance—although here the Administration is only indirectly responsible for the departure from the traditional rules of chieftainship. After the death of the last *Gebba*, who was said to have been a rather inefficient Village Head, a complete outsider was appointed as chief, a stranger who had been living for some time in the late *Gebba*'s house and had been acting for him as semi-official messenger in his dealings with the District Head at Mokwa. It was on the advice of the District Head that he was made the new Village Head. The District Head, himself a stranger who did not know the local situation, preferred to have a man he knew for his subordinate, and a man who had been to the Government School and who was, incidentally, a Mohammedan like himself. Elders and 'kingmaker' were not consulted. The village elder who would have been appointed chief if the latter had had their way held at the time the title *Wangwa*. He set up something like an independent rule of his own. Except for official business—tax-collection in particular—the people ignored the other, shadow chief, completely. An unhealthy situation arose and was left to exist for two years, during which time there was no real authority in the village, and legal offences and unruly conduct in general were increasing rapidly. In 1935 I had the opportunity of drawing the attention of the Administration to this fact.' The man *Wangwa* was recognized officially as a 'second-in-command' and prospective

[1] This case happened in a community half Yoruba and half Nupe. The progressive chief was a Yoruba, the victim (who came to me to complain) a Nupe. I could, in fact, hardly imagine a Nupe chief to be sufficiently appreciative of hygienic principles to take such a step.

[2] This happened twice, in Jebba Island and Sakpe.

successor to the chieftainship (it being thought inadvisable to depose the once appointed chief). At the same time the elders promoted him to the highest village rank next to the chief's, *Tsadú*. Having been granted this responsible position in the village government, the ex-rival of the chief seems prepared to use his influence and moral power in support of the official Village Head whom he may succeed some day.

This book cannot venture to answer the question how far the authority of the traditional chief can be strained without alienating him from the people and the elders, or without forcing the latter to abandon their role as free spokesmen of the community and become mere pawns of the chief.[1] But it must be said that in many respects the adoption of new governmental duties by the traditional chiefs is proceeding smoothly and efficiently. This readjustment seems due less to political measures as such than to the comprehensive effectiveness of culture change, which gradually diminishes certain divergences in the views to which the political executive is committed and those of the people themselves. Already many Nupe villagers appreciate medical help and education, and are sending their children to school without pressure from the chief.

For completeness' sake we must add that the balance of 'multiple control' may be endangered also by the opposite development, namely a separation between political executive and community in which the latter represents the new extraneous influences. For individuals or sections of the community may dissociate themselves from the unity of common life, alienated by modern education, new economic enterprise, or conversion to Christianity, and may thus no longer be amenable to the traditional authorities. However, this danger has not yet arisen in the Nupe village, chiefly because the 'progressive' elements flock to the town rather than stay in the village, and also because Christian influence is inconsiderable.

Yet it would be a mistake to assume that the factors that weaken the homogeneous village community are all of recent date and the results of modern colonial development. Disturbances of the 'balance' very similar to those just described, and like them entailing a strengthening from outside, as it were, of the chief's authority, were also at work in the pre-British Nupe kingdom. They are embodied in the very existence of the kingdom as a political and social superstructure which is the carrier of new values and new, manifold, cultural influences.

First the purely political factors. We have heard of the insignia and emblems of chiefly power which, according to tradition, were bestowed on village chiefs by the ancestor-king of Nupe; the most ancient form of

---

[1] It is possible that in communities in which the 'multiple' system of control is less delicately adjusted, and the political authority of the chief more independent of the other principles governing community life, the political power of chief and elders can be used more freely for new tasks. This adds, I think, a new meaning to the following statement by Sir Donald Cameron: 'The Native Authorities Ordinance also makes provision for the limitation in particular instances of the powers which may be exercised by a Native Authority, for some of these are well organized and experienced while others are of . . . weaker mould.' ('Native Administration in Nigeria and Tanganyika', *Journal of the Royal African Society*, xxxvi, Supplement, p. 13.)

village chieftainship is thus thought of as an office held 'by the grace of the king'. I have also mentioned that the appointment of the village chief is subject, to-day as of old, to confirmation by the *Etsu* Nupe. The chief thus becomes the official representative of the king, responsible to him for law and order and the collection of tax, but also able to rely on his sovereign's spiritual or political support. The people of the village can appeal to the *Etsu* if they are dissatisfied with their chief, and in the case of rival claims to chieftainship the king would be called upon to decide between the claimants—a role which he did not always undertake impartially; bribes offered by a chief threatened with the loss of his position or a new claimant would easily influence his decision.[1] The control of the king over his chiefs is expressed already in the ceremonial of the appointment. The chief-elect, accompanied by the head elders, would be summoned to the capital to receive his appointment and to be vested with a gown, turban, and sandals as insignia of his office, in a ceremony which closely resembles the investiture of officers of state or members of the royal nobility. The *Etsu* Nupe may also be called in to arbitrate in internal disputes, e.g. over the succession to local ranks —we remember the example from Doko. Lastly, legal cases come under the jurisdiction of the *Etsu* and his appointed agents, thus removing from the orbit of the community the right to see offences punished and retaliation achieved.

Another source of 'disturbance' lies in the impact of Islam. It led in many cases to a spiritual separation of chief and community, for many chiefs embraced Islam (at least nominally) long before the rest of the people. Thus these chiefs can no longer organize, and rarely even show interest in, the traditional religious ceremonies which weld the community into a single congregation. Nor can they base their authority, hereditary or not, on that spiritual commonness of which it was once an expression. They rely instead more or less openly on the closer association with the Mohammedan rulers of the country with whom they now share the creed—at least one feature of their exalted position. In its ever-increasing scope of proselytizing, Islam drives the wedge of another class distinction into the structure of village society. The distinction between Mohammedans and pagans in a village often has this effect, that the two sections differ not only in religious observances, but also in general mode of life, dress, important food habits (Mohammedans do not drink sorghum-beer, the traditional ceremonial drink of the Nupe peasants), their—often imaginary—educational qualification and, again, in the degree of the affinity they could claim to the highest social stratum in the country.

In other spheres of life—economic, educational—similar influences are at work, striking at the very roots of social homogeneity. But we may cut short our description; we shall meet with these influences again later. Our present discussion has established the main facts. For at least a century and a half the Nupe village did not exist in that self-centred, secure isolation in which the balance of its social system could fulfil

[1] Bribes to the *Etsu* are said to have played an important part in gaining the assent of the king when the new chiefs of Doko usurped the chieftainship.

itself ideally. Through the person of its head, first of all, the village organization is bound to duties towards, and linked with the fate of, the wider political organization—the kingdom. Through religious, economic, and educational factors which follow in the wake of political absorption the one-ness of community and political organization which proved the essence of the village society is finally broken. The communities themselves, their areas of integrated social life, are broken open and forced partly into a system of integration, under the dictate of a concept of social unity which is that of the centralized political system of the state. I say 'partly', for the latter has to some extent left intact the social identity of the village. This is not meant only historically, but refers to the relation and actual inter-penetration of two essentially different social systems. Nor does it refer merely to a distinction between political autonomy of the village, or certain villages, as against political domination by the kingdom. One may perhaps speak of a partial autonomy of the villages under or within the kingdom, but the essential point is the different solution of the problem of political integration in one and in the other case. We have met with the analogous difference when we discussed the two different systems of political unification evolved by the two sub-tribes Kyedye and Beni. Let me formulate it again: it is the difference between an organization growing out of and utilizing the potentialities of uniform culture and common life, and an organization relying on the extraneous machinery of political control; between a political integration which remains true to the concept of Community, and an organization which forces unity upon diversity of culture and common life—the State.

CHAPTER VI
POLITICAL HISTORY OF NUPE KINGDOM
THE STATE

IT will have become clear that we regard the state as a specific form of political organization. Not every political system represents thus a state. This book can do no more than suggest a descriptive working definition of that difficult and much discussed concept. If we accept the definition of a political system suggested above, on the basis of its inclusiveness and the nature of its ultimate sanctions, we may regard the state as a social system in which these two characteristics crystallize in specific forms. Thus we arrive at the following threefold definition: (1) The state is a political unit based on territorial sovereignty. Membership of the state, i.e. citizenship or nationality, is determined by residence or birth-right in a territory. The state is thus inter-tribal or inter-racial, and distinguishes nationality from tribal or racial extraction.[1] (2) A centralized machinery of government assumes the maintenance of law and order, to the exclusion of all independent action.[2] (3) The state involves the existence of a specialized privileged ruling group or class separated in training, status, and organization from the main body of the population. This group monopolizes, corporately, the machinery of political control. It is regarded as a 'representative' group, and its actions and decisions are accepted by the people as actions and decisions on behalf of the country at large. These three factors must appear combined to justify our terming a political system a state.[3] The three factors of state structure represent interdependent social necessities which follow from one another and can be reduced to the basic principle of territorial sovereignty maintained over groups of different cultural and ethnic extraction. Such sovereignty must involve a certain measure of centralization, powerful enough to counteract separatist tendencies (Lowie), and also the creation—or continued existence—of a group of rulers and administrators who, by special training and tradition, are raised above the complexity of cultural and ethnic groups. Historically, an inter-tribal sovereignty of this nature can only have arisen from the ascendancy of one ethnic group over others. Certain students of society have interpreted this fact as implying the essential identity of state

---

[1] Cf. Sir Henry Maine's statement that the 'most nearly universal fact concerning the origin of known states' is that they 'were formed by the coalescence of groups' (*Lectures on the Early History of Institutions*, p. 386).

[2] Political order in the state is 'distinguished most of all by this trait, that it is a peaceful order which allows of no individual violence and only permits itself to enforce justice' (N. M. Korkunov, *General Theory of Law*, New York, 1922, p. 341).

[3] Obviously, there exist transitory forms in which only one or two of these political principles are manifest. The Beni confederacy represents such an incipient state organization. Yet if Lowie says: 'Some sort of state is a universal feature of human culture' (*The Origin of the State*, 1927, p. 44), we feel inclined to alter this to 'some sort of political organization'.

origin and conquest, state organization and alien domination.[1] I will not go too deeply into this controversial question. But we cannot pass without comment the fact that the structure of the Nupe state as it exists to-day, with its ruling class of Fulani conquerors, and also its growth so far as we can with any claim to accuracy trace it back in history, indeed support this theory of the origin of the state.

Our discussion of the principles of state organization has thus led to an historical interpretation. Indeed the description of Nupe kingdom would be incomplete without the description of its growth and development. Its inter-tribal and inter-cultural nature cannot be fully understood without the inclusion of the historical viewpoint. Our three-fold conceptual system of cultural unit, community, and state must itself be envisaged under the aspect of a dynamic process rather than of a static differentiation. For the deliberate political co-ordination of forms of conduct must tend to influence other spheres of cultural activity as well. In Nupe as everywhere, social patterns, common ideal types, spring up by themselves as 'natural products of long association'.[2] Political unification goes hand in hand with dissemination of culture and with an extension and reinterpretation of racial and community boundaries. The 'inter-cultural' and 'inter-tribal' state gives way to a new 'state culture' and a new paramount group-unit, the nation.

It will be for a later chapter to examine how and how far this unification has been achieved in the Nupe state. But we must point out at once that this absorption of heterogeneous elements could only achieve a relative unity. The antagonism between the original heterogeneity and the subsequent unification is never allowed to disappear completely. It survives in certain forms of cultural and racial discrimination. The culture of Nupe, more correctly the culture typical of that section which formed the core in the historical growth of the kingdom, became the representative culture of the whole country, set up as a standard and 'ideal type' for the heterogeneous population. The sections of the Nupe tribe which were the carriers of this culture became the representative group of 'real' Nupe, sharply distinguished from the groups which have become Nupe-ized and absorbed in the state in the process of political expansion. A tribal and territorial section thus gained the position of a cultural *élite*, considerations of political status came to determine the evaluation of cultural features, and facts of cultural and tribal extraction were re-interpreted in the sense of political class distinctions. Here we understand the anomalies in the application of the name Nupe which we discovered in our discussion of Tribe and Culture: why the people in the capital regard the Nupe spoken in the districts and on the borders of the country as an inferior brand; or why the Nupe still speak of 'Gbari slaves' although culturally this tribal section has become indistinguishable from the Nupe proper. The 'real' Nupe call themselves *kintsoẑi*, Owners of the Land, as against all who have come later into the country —settlers, aliens, citizens of Greater Nupe. For all the groups outside of

[1] F. Oppenheimer, *The State*, 1923.
[2] A. E. Ross, *Social Control*, p. 222.

the 'core' of the kingdom, whether they are Nupe, aliens, or Nupe-ized aliens, the Nupe have a common name: *zaži kati*, 'Outside Peoples', and the cultural evaluation implied in this term is felt acutely by these groups. It was extremely interesting to see how strongly the people of Lemu, Nupe-ized since three generations only, resented being called *zaži kati*, although they frankly admitted their Gbari origin. 'This name', they said, 'does not apply to us; we have been Nupe and Beni for a long time. The Gbari in the north and east, in Wushishi and beyond Kataeregi, they are Outside Peoples.'

The Fulani conquest added a new chapter to this ambiguous history of cultural and political unification. But here 'representative' and 'absorbed' groups have exchanged places. The Fulani conquerors of Nupe, numerically an insignificant minority, were absorbed completely by the culture of the people whom they subjugated. Some of the Fulani came from nomadic herdsmen stock; the majority belonged most probably to the 'town Fulani' (as they call themselves), who had long been settled in the northern Hausa states and whose culture had become identical with that of Hausa. The former surrendered their identity completely; the latter had little, if anything, of their own to give. The Hausa traits visible in Nupe culture to-day did not reach the country through the Fulani; and Mohammedanism, the religion of the Fulani conquerors, was firmly established already at the time of the early Fulani infiltration. In Nupe the Fulani lost their language[1] and the last characteristics of their race and original culture. Racially, after generations of intermarriage, they are indistinguishable from their subjects; culturally, they are as much Nupe as the Nupe themselves. Many are even eager to step into the cultural heritage of the country over which they rule. They read and quote the history of ancient Nupe with the same enthusiasm and pride with which they learn or talk about their own historical heroes, the first Fulani emissaries.[2] Yet they remain a separate social group, conscious of its alien origin, and still distinguished by a special tribal name: they call themselves, and are called by their subjects, *goiži* (a name which distinguishes these settled, 'town Fulani' from the nomadic cattle people, who are known as *bororóži*), never Nupe. They are a 'representative' group in a different sense—the small *élite* of conquerors and rulers. The historical memory of their alien origin—for it is only this to-day—buttresses their detached social position. Racial antagonism which might have disappeared in a homogeneous community here, in the framework of the state, blending with the antagonism of class, remains alive, and even strengthens with its sentiments the inner tension of the society. It flares up with every open friction between rulers and ruled. We have again a political and social cleavage in the guise of 'racial' discrimination.[3]

[1] *Etsu* Mohamadu (1897–1915) was given the nickname '*Etsu* with two tongues', being the last Fulani ruler who—already a striking exception—could still speak Fulfulde.

[2] For some time I carried on a correspondence (in Hausa) with two of the most prominent members of the Nupe-Fulani community who had asked me to let them have all information I could obtain on the ancient history of Nupe.

[3] The following is a significant anecdote: the *Etsu* Nupe once confided to me

Visualize this intricate racial and cultural pattern: two *élites* of different order—*kintsoži* and Fulani—and surrounding them, almost in concentric circles, ethnic groups of varying cultural dissimilitude, each cultural grade also a grade on the scale of political evaluation. This is indeed the exact picture of the historical growth of Nupe kingdom. Through conquests and expansion, with fluid, ever-changing boundaries, Nupe kingdom maintained its conspicuous centre, the core of its political and cultural growth. Like a tree, it grew from the centre, and you can still trace the rings which mark its growth.

FOUNDATION OF THE KINGDOM

Before embarking on the historical account we must clarify the concept of 'history' as we propose to use it. For there is a certain ambiguity in the term 'history' as it is used by anthropologists. History can mean two things: first, what we may call 'objective' history, that is, the series of events which we, the investigators, describe and establish in accordance with certain 'objective', universal criteria of connexion and sequence. Second, the 'ideological' history, which exists in the society which we study, and which describes and arranges events in accordance with accepted traditions about past happenings and developments. The two may coincide (as they do in modern history); or the second may at least supply some source of information for the first. But also it may have significance only as a sociological datum *per se*, i.e. as a system of accepted beliefs and traditions influencing social behaviour in the group. As such, it is often indistinguishable from mythology and from what Malinowski has called significantly the 'mythical charter' of customs and existing cultural usages.[1] Different societies may stress in a different measure either the mythical, supernatural or the rational, pseudo-scientific nature of what they accept as an account of their past. The Nupe are what we may call an historically-minded people. The highest, constantly invoked authority for things existing is, to the Nupe, the account of things past—but an account which is clothed in terms of a sober, pseudo-scientific 'history'. Such is also the nature of the Nupe tradition of the origin of their kingdom. Only for the more recent periods do we possess 'objective' sources; the earliest period of Nupe kingdom is described only in their own 'ideological history'.

The earliest history of Nupe centres round the figure of Tsoede or Edegi,[5] the culture hero and mythical founder of Nupe kingdom. The genealogies of Nupe kings which are preserved in many places in Nupe country, and which have also found their way into the earliest written records of Nupe history which were compiled by Mohammedan scholars

his grievance against a certain rather unruly relative of his whom he believed to have intrigued against him. He added: 'All Nupe are bad people, you know.' The said relative, himself, of course, as much Fulani as the *Etsu*, retaliated by informing me that 'all Fulani were liars'.

[1] B. Malinowski, in *Encycl. Soc. Sc.*, London, 1931, vol. iv, p. 640.

[2] Tsoede is, linguistically, a contraction of *Etsu*, or *'tsu Ede;* the Nupe more often use the name Tsoede, the Hausa the name Edegi.

THE CHAIN OF TSOEDE

THE SACRED BRONZE FIGURES ON JEBBA
ISLAND

and court historians, place his birth in the middle of the fifteenth century.[1] At this time, the tradition runs, there was no kingdom of Nupe, only small chieftainships which, among the Beni, were united in a confederacy under the chief of Nku, a village near the confluence of Niger and Kaduna. At that time the Nupe people were tributary to the *Atta* (king) of the Gara, at Eda (Idah), far down the Niger. The tribute was paid in slaves, and every family head had annually to contribute one male member of his house. These slaves, as tradition has it, were always sister's sons. It so happened that the son of the *Atta* Gara came hunting to Nku in Nupe country. Here he met the daughter of the chief of Nku, a young widow, fell in love with her and lived with her for some time. When the death of his father recalled him to his country, to succeed to the throne of the Gara, this woman was pregnant. He left her a charm and a ring to give to their child when it was born. This child was Tsoede. Then the old chief of Nku died, his son became chief, and when Tsoede was 30 years of age the new chief sent him, as his sister's son, as slave to Eda. The *Atta* Gara recognized his son in the new slave by the charm and ring which he was wearing, and kept him near his person, treating him almost like his legitimate sons. Tsoede stayed for thirty years at his father's court. Once the king fell victim to a mysterious illness which nobody could cure. The court diviner prophesied that only a fruit from a very high oil-palm outside the town, plucked by one man, would cure the king. All his legitimate sons tried, in vain, to obtain the precious fruit. Finally Tsoede made the attempt, and succeeded. But in this attempt he cut his lip so badly that he looked almost like a man born with a split lip. From this time—and this still holds true to-day—all hare-lipped boys born in Nupe are named Edegi. Tsoede's achievement, which made him still more beloved by his father and honoured by the court, evoked the jealousy of his half-brothers. Thus, when the *Atta* felt his death coming he advised his son to flee, and to return to his own country the rule of which he bestowed on him as a parting gift. He assisted him in his flight, he gave him riches of all kinds and bestowed on him various insignia of kingship: a bronze canoe 'as only kings have', manned with twelve Nupe slaves; the bronze *kakati*, the long trumpets which are still the insignia of kings in the whole of Northern Nigeria; state drums hung with brass bells; and the heavy iron chains and fetters which, endowed with strong magic, have become the emblems of the king's judicial power, and are known to-day as *egbã Tsoede*, Chain of Tsoede.[2]

Now comes the story of Tsoede's adventurous flight from Eda, travel-

---

[1] See Appendix III. There exist several versions of the myth. I am giving here the version which I learned from the *Etsu* of Patigi, the last living descendant of the Tsoede dynasty.

[2] The villages where these chains are found (all lying in the Niger valley) were entrusted with the special mission of acting as the 'King's Hangmen'. I have described this organization in *Man*, 1935, 143. Two places on the Niger, Tada and Jebba Island, possess sacred bronze figures which, like the chains, are linked with the tradition and worship of Tsoede. According to some versions of the Tsoede myth they too were a gift from the *Atta* to the departing Tsoede; the *Etsu* of Patigi, my informant for the version given here, denied this.

ling up-river, hotly pursued by his half-brothers and their men. On the way he is helped by two men, whom he later rewards by making them chief and second-in-command of the Kyedye tribe. When he reaches the Kaduna river he turns into a creek called Ega, and lies here in hiding till his pursuers, tired of their fruitless search, return to Eda. Tsoede and his men leave the canoe and sink it in the river; the people of Ega still perform an annual sacrifice on the spot, where, as the tradition has it, Tsoede's canoe was sunk, and at these ceremonies they are able, you are told, to see the bright bronze of the canoe glitter in the water. Tsoede then went to Nupeko, a village near-by, killed the chief, and made himself chief of the place. He conquered Nku, the town of his maternal uncle, made himself the ruler of all Beni (or Nupe—all informants are vague on this point), and assumed the title *Etsu*, king. He made the twelve men who had accompanied him from Eda the chiefs of the twelve towns of Beni and bestowed on them the sacred insignia of chieftainship, brass bangles and magic chains. The present chiefs of Beni (as far as their 'towns' still survive) claim descent from these twelve men, and still treasure bangles or chains as insignia of chieftainship. Tsoede carried out big and victorious wars against many tribes and kingdoms, conquering in the south the countries of Yagba, Bunu (two sections of the Yoruba), Kakanda, as far as Akoko, and in the north the countries of Ebe, Kamberi, and Kamuku. He resided first in Nupeko, which name means 'Great Nupe', for eight years, and when Nupeko grew too small, he built the new capital of Gbara, on the Kaduna, which was to remain the *eži 'tsu*, the King's Town, till the Fulani conquest. At that time his residence is said to have counted 5,555 horses, so many in fact, that there was no room for them in Gbara, and one of Tsoede's sons, Abdu, who was in charge of the horses, crossed the Kaduna and founded on the opposite bank a place which is still known by the name of Dokomba, 'Horse Place'.

Apart from the royal insignia and emblems of magic Tsoede is said to have brought to Nupe from Eda certain crafts and techniques hitherto unknown in the country. He brought with him blacksmiths and brass-smiths who taught the crude blacksmiths of Nupe their more advanced technique; the canoe-men who came with him imported into Nupe the craft of building large canoes of which the Nupe are said to have been ignorant at that time. Tsoede is also believed by some to have introduced human sacrifices—there is a gruesome story of the first sacrifice, the victim of which was Tsoede's mother's brother—and to have established first the custom of bride-price.

We can to some extent ascertain what there is of historical truth in this tradition. Certain indirect evidence tends to confirm the main facts of the Tsoede tradition. The alien, southern provenance of some of the cultural goods, which in the tradition are linked with Idah and the coming of Tsoede, seems fairly certain. Some at least of the sacred bronze figures in Tada and Jebba, cast in *cire perdue*, a technique unknown in Nupe and the north, bear the stamp of the culture which we are wont to associate with Benin—and Benin, as we know, has for a long period been the political overlord of Idah; the same is true of the beautifully cast brass bells—among them the square-shaped bells typical of Benin work—on the state drums found all along the Niger. The heavy iron chains and fetters, on the other hand, are most probably of Portuguese origin; they may have been brought in by slave-traders from the coast and have found their way up the river into the hinterland—the home of these precious trading goods.[1] Even the approximate date of the immigration of Tsoede and his band can be fixed with some accuracy. For on this point all the various genealogies of Nupe kings, obtained from quite different sources, tally. Giving the years of reign of every Nupe king, back to Tsoede, they all place the life of Tsoede in the same period, the early fifteenth century. It is interesting to note that the royal genealogies in two great neighbouring kingdoms, Yoruba and Ewe (in Togoland), also trace back the history of their royal ancestors to the same period, about 1400.[2] We may not be mistaken therefore in assuming that the beginning of the fifteenth century marks the end of a big wave of immigration which eventually led to the firm establishment of a number of new West African societies—kingdoms, in our three instances. For Nupe we can go farther than this. The same period saw the first contact of the Guinea Coast with Europe. In 1498 the Portuguese established themselves in Benin. But at that time they found a Benin already on the verge of collapse, the once powerful kingdom weakened and in obvious disintegration. Idah, once tributary to Benin, and master over Nupe as of many other dependencies, must have weakened with it. The myth of Tsoede's delivery of Nupe from the yoke of Idah may well contain a kernel of historical truth (whatever form the events may have taken in reality); the foundation of an independent Nupe kingdom may have been one of the historical results of the disintegration of Benin and its vassal states. The ancient contact of Idah and Nupe as well as the former sovereignty of Idah, are undoubtedly historical. The tradition of Tsoede is as well known in Idah as in Nupe. And when some years ago the *Atta* of Idah came to Bida—he was keen to visit that country of which the tradition of his tribe had so much to tell—a significant political imbroglio threatened the meeting of the Nigerian potentates. It arose from a question of precedence; the Idah man insisted on being given a higher seat than the *Etsu* Nupe, basing his claim on the unforgotten historical fact of Nupe's ancient vassalship to Idah.

This bare framework of facts—if facts they are—has absorbed many other features, legends, traditions, embellishments; which of them contain any historical truth it is impossible to say. But we are not concerned here to determine what is and what is not historical truth in the rich cycle of traditions round the figure of Tsoede. The myth as it stands, and as it is treasured by the people of Nupe, is to us a sufficiently significant social reality. It represents the typical 'mythical charter' of

[1] Exactly the same chains and irons have been found on the Gold Coast; small models of these fetters, of brass, iron, or gold, are sold as charms all down the river and the creeks of Southern Nigeria. A common origin suggests itself forcibly.

[2] See Bishop Johnson, *History of the Yoruba*, and D. Westermann (personal information).

the kingdom, and its common knowledge constitutes the first and foremost of these common beliefs and forms of cultural 'commonness'
which supply the background of political unity. I have found the consciousness of this tradition developed most strongly in the river area and
among the Beni, that is, in the area that marks what I have called the
'core' of the expanding kingdom. It is totally absent to-day, and most
probably has always been absent, among the Dibo, who have never
formed part of the old kingdom, and among some of the Nupe-ized
groups (such as the 'Gbari slaves') which, absorbed into Nupe in more
recent times, have remained culturally 'Outside Peoples'. The distribution of the 'mythical charter' of Nupe kingdom and the boundaries of
the kingdom itself coincide.

To go on with the tradition of Tsoede. For sixty years he reigned in
Gbara; he died, 120 years old, on one of his military expeditions to the
north, near Gbagede. Some of his belongings, two stirrups and his
sword, are still kept as almost sacred treasure by the people of Gbagede
(who are Kamberi, not Nupe). At the time of Tsoede's death the kingdom of Nupe was expanding towards the north, and his four sons who
succeeded him as kings of Nupe, one after the other, are said to have
founded Mokwa, in the north-west corner of Nupe, as their temporary
capital. Another of his descendants, Abdu Waliyi, founded the capital
Jima, on the Kaduna opposite Gbara.[1] The fifteenth king after Tsoede,
Jibiri, who reigned according to Nupe genealogies about 1770, was the
first Nupe king to become Mohammedan. He was deposed by his son
and died in exile, in Kutigi, where his grave can still be seen. Under
Etsu Ma'azŭ, the nineteenth king of Nupe, Nupe kingdom reached its
greatest power. During his reign, about 1810, Mallam Dendo, also
called Manko, 'Great Mallam', a Fulani from Kebbi who was destined
to change the whole fate of Nupe kingdom, is said to have first appeared
in Nupe country as an itinerant preacher, diviner, and seller of charms.
With *Etsu* Ma'azŭ we also reach, for the first time, in this account, the
plane of 'objective history'; his death is recorded by one of the first
European visitors to Nupe as having occurred in 1818.[2]

THE FULANI CONQUEST

We enter now a period of Nupe history which is illuminated by the
light of 'real' history. It is described with many details in the written
records of Nupe court historians, the earliest of whom was a certain
Abduramani, a Mohammedan scholar who seems to have lived in Rabá
in the early days of Fulani rule. It was during this period, too, that
European travellers first penetrated into Nupe.[3]

[1] In addition to the historical capitals of the kingdom, Gbara, Mokwa, Jima,
and finally Rabá (see below), the Nupe records also mention certain other places
at which the Nupe kings are said to have resided temporarily at various times,
viz. Etsú, Jengi, and Yeti.

[2] Journal of Rev. J. F. Schoen and Samuel Crowther, *Expedition up the Niger*,
1842, p. 191.

[3] I owe to the kindness of the Administration the opportunity of having been
able to consult unpublished Government records, compiled by the first officers
who were serving in this area; I must acknowledge specially the very complete
'Notes on Nupe History', by Major Burdon (1902).

From that time Nupe history is linked indissolubly with the fate of the Fulani conquerors of Nigeria who had made themselves rulers of the main Hausa states in the beginning of the nineteenth century. The history of the Fulani *Jihad* has often been described,[1] so I need say only a few words. The Fulani established their suzerainty over Northern Nigeria in a loosely organized, decentralized dual empire, the western part under the supremacy of the Sarkin Musulmi of Sokoto, and the eastern under the Emir of Gwandu. Nupe kingdom fell to Gwandu's share. The Fulani conquest was achieved in two phases and by two methods: a gradual infiltration of the foreign country by Mohammedan Fulani, and then, ultimately, a military conquest. The same policy was adopted in Nupe. Mallam Dendo was one of those Mohammedan preachers and emissaries to 'heathen countries' who was to collect an ever-increasing group of followers as the nucleus of future conquest. His followers seem to have included men of all stations: cattle Fulani to whom in their semi-nomadic life Nupe had become a second home; Fulani and Hausa mercenary soldiers who took service in the Nupe armies; merchants from northern towns; and Mohammedan priests and missionaries; I estimated their number at the time of the conquest at not more than 1,000 or 1,500. When Mallam Dendo became strong enough to venture the decisive blow, he applied to the Emir of Gwandu, his overlord, for military help and for a *tuta*, flag, which signified his official recognition as a leader and accepted feudal chief of the Fulani Empire.

The opportunity for the Fulani to make themselves masters of the country soon came. Almost immediately after *Etsu* Ma'azū's death internal trouble broke out. The claim of Maazu's son Jimada, the legitimate heir to the throne, was disputed by his father's brother's son, Majiya II. The details of this feud are not clear. According to some accounts Jimada was Majiya's father's sister's son, who had been appointed regent for the boy-king Majiya; later, when Majiya grew up and demanded his kingdom, Jimada refused. Other accounts make the two claimants sons of elder and younger brother respectively, namely, of *Etsu* Ma'azū (the nineteenth king of Nupe) and *Etsu* Mama (the twenty-first king of Nupe). Majiya claimed the throne by the right of general Nupe succession, being the elder brother's eldest son; Jimada, however, was regarded as the legitimate heir according to the ancient Nupe rules of royal inheritance which decreed that the son 'born in the purple' should become king.[2] Whatever the origin of this dynastic feud, it led to a temporary division of Nupe kingdom into a western and eastern half: Jimada reigned in Gbara, the ancient capital of Nupe, and Majiya built himself a capital in Rabá, on the Niger. Majiya gained the friendship of Mallam Dendo and the Fulani group in Nupe, and with them on his side he became by far the more powerful, and soon snatched the other half of

[1] See A. C. Burns, *History of Nigeria*, Oxford, 1929; A. W. Bovill, *Caravans of the Old Sahara*, Oxford, 1933; C. K. Meek, *The Northern Tribes of Nigeria*, Oxford, 1925, i, pp. 98–102.

[2] In Africa this rule of inheritance is unique, and cannot, according to Nupe tradition, have applied to Tsoede himself and his four sons who succeeded him. All informants insisted that it became, at some unspecified period, the rule of succession in the Nupe dynasty.

Nupe kingdom from his rival. He defeated Jimada in the war, killed him at Ragada, near Jengi, and thus made himself the undisputed king of Nupe, about 1820. Idirisu, Jimada's son, fled with the rest of his followers to Labǒži, and later across the river, to Eggã, where he stayed, an exile and fugitive, powerless against Majiya's army. Nupe was not to remain at peace for long. Majiya's gratitude to the Fulani who had helped him to defeat his rival soon changed to jealousy and fear. He turned against them, only to be himself defeated, and to lose his throne to his sometime friends and allies.

This is the story that is told in Nupe of the rise of the Fulani and of the final struggle for the Nupe throne. Majiya, as king of Nupe, had learned of the fame of Manko as a preacher and Mohammedan scholar and diviner. He invited him to his court and installed him there in the influential position of his private counsellor and diviner. He trusted his prophecies and his advice and was convinced that his victories in the field were due to Mallam Dendo's *asiri* (lit. 'secret', that is supernatural powers); he rewarded him magnificently, gave him money, slaves, horses. He took Mallam Dendo's youngest son Masaba into his house as his foster-son, as the Nupe do with sons of friends. More and more of Mallam Dendo's kin and fellow countrymen came to Rabá to take service under him or under the king, till at last Manko's power and influence were more than equal to that of the king himself. Majiya now thought it high time to rid himself of the dangerous rival. He drove Mallam Dendo and all his followers from Rabá, and chased them from his territory, across the Niger, into Ilorin country.

Here another Fulani emissary, Mallam Alimi, had already been established for some time as king over the Yoruba of Ilorin. He now gave protection to the Fulani refugees from Nupe. But *Etsu* Majiya, desirous of uprooting for ever the power of his dangerous vassals, decided to attack Ilorin and to conquer this southern stronghold of the Fulani invaders. He attacked Ilorin with 4,000 horsemen and 10,000 foot-soldiers. He marched for two days from Rabá to Ilorin, and halted his army at the gates of the town. The victory seemed his. This war of Majiya against the Fulani of Ilorin, as it is told in Nupe, is a magnificent epic. There were five Fulani emissaries in Ilorin at that time: Mallam Baba, who had fled with Dendo from Rabá and later became the first Emir of Agaie; Mallam Dendo himself; Mallam Musa, another fugitive from Rabá; Mallam Maliki, who had resided in another Nupe town, Lafiagi, and had been driven from there by Majiya; and Mallam Alimi, the Emir of Ilorin. Dendo was the youngest of the five, but his keen intelligence made him at once their leader. He first sent word to Idirisu, Jimada's exiled son, asking for his support in this fight against Majiya, the murderer of his father. Then Dendo prepared his most powerful *asiri*. Two brave men were sent out at night to steal into the enemy's camp and to bring back some earth. Dendo dug a large pit close to the town wall. He put the earth into this pit, and covered its mouth with grass. On a Friday morning he entered the pit, taking with him fourteen dates. He stayed there till the hour of evening prayer, but what he did in the pit, what secret magic he performed, no one knows.

When he reappeared, he called again the two men who had brought the earth the previous night, and ordered them to scatter it by night all round the town walls. Next morning Majiya attacked. A thick mist had fallen over the country. Majiya's troops were unable to move in the mist. Then a sand-storm sprang up, blinding men and horses. The horses bolted, and Majiya's cavalry, placed (in accordance with Nupe military principles) behind the infantry, trampled down their own men. When the small army of Ilorin sallied forth from the gates of the town, it met an enemy already half defeated. Majiya was beaten, he fled across the Niger, back to the protected Rabá, with only 1,000 horses and 1,070 men left of his huge army. This was not the end. Idirisu and his followers joined forces with Mallam Dendo. Together they pursued Majiya's troops, marching their men up the Niger as far as Gbajibo, fifty miles north of Rabá, where they were able to cross the river unmolested. Here Mallam Dendo is said to have used a clever ruse: for a week he collected horse-dung, and then threw it into the water; drifting down the river it reached Rabá; and the Nupe, who had hardly recovered from their defeat at Ilorin, thought that an enormous army of horsemen was approaching Rabá and had already crossed the river. Majiya fled into the interior, to Zuguma, leaving Rabá unprotected, an easy prey to the Fulani army.

Mallam Dendo repaid Idirisu's help badly. He let him remain a puppet king of Nupe exiled to Eggã,[1] while he installed himself in the capital Rabá as the real ruler. Dendo and his people collected taxes and tribute; they had the command of the larger part of the army; they began to dispense justice, and generally to direct the affairs of the kingdom. A revolt of Idirisu ended in his being killed by Mallam Dendo's troops, whereupon Dendo, 'true Fulani' (say Nupe informants), turned back to Majiya, previously his enemy, offering him friendship and recognition as king of Nupe—another puppet king, in far-away little Zuguma. Two years after this unification of Nupe, in 1833, the year when Oldfield and Lander visited Rabá, Mallam Dendo died.[2] He left four sons (two having died before their father) and two daughters, the sons being Abdu Gboya, Usman Zaki, Mamudu Gwogi, and Masaba (Mama Saba), the daughters Gogo Sabaci and Gogo Wodiko.

During Mallam Dendo's lifetime Mallam Baba, one of his companions on the flight to Ilorin, set out to conquer a kingdom for himself. Following Dendo's advice, he took twelve men, crossed three rivers, travelling by night and hiding by day from the Nupe troops who might intercept his party. The small troop raided the country, and growing as it marched, finally reached Agaie, which Mallam Baba made the capital of another (much smaller) Fulani Emirate in Nupe country. Revolts of the Nupe of that part, and attacks of Majiya, whose sovereignty had extended over Agaie, were in the end defeated, and soon Mallam Baba could enlarge his small kingdom by new victories: over part of the Bataci tribe on the river; over Kacha, which subsequently fell to Bida;

[1] In 1833 Oldfield, whose ship, the *Quorra*, was anchoring off Eggã, met there the exiled Idirisu (Laird and Oldfield, op. cit. ii, pp. 38-9).
[2] Laird and Oldfield, op. cit. ii, p. 76.

and over the Gbari of Payi, which became later the independent Emirate (again under a Fulani) of Lapai.

Mallam Dendo is said to have advised his sons not to seek, after his death, official secular power, but to remain what he had been: the un-crowned king, nominally only an emissary of Islam and the spiritual head of the country. But the division into real and nominal, spiritual and secular rulership did not work. Two years after Majiya's death (1835?) Tsado, his son, like him puppet king of Nupe in Zuguma, revolted again against the hated Fulani. He was defeated and killed by one of the Fulani generals near Egbako. His son, Dzurugi (The Red One), re-turned to Zuguma. But now Usman Zaki, the second son of Dendo, himself adopted the title *Etsu* Nupe, demanding the ancient regalia from the exiled shadow king in Zuguma and making Rabá again the official capital of the kingdom. From this time the legitimate dynasty of Nupe abandoned all legal claim to the rulership over the country, and the new Fulani dynasty assumed full powers. Of the other descendants of Mallam Dendo, Abdu Gboya, Usman Zaki's elder brother, whose leanings were more scholarly than warlike, became *Alkali* (judge) of the kingdom, and Mamudu Gwogi, Usman's younger brother, *Shaba*, or Heir Presumptive.

From this time the history of Nupe kingdom is the history of constant intrigues, fights, wars, and rebellions. Fights between the sons of Mallam Dendo, wars against other tribes and against factions in Nupe, and rebellions of the descendants of the old Nupe dynasty, who did not give up hope of recovering the throne from the Fulani, or rebellions of powerful generals of mercenary troops who claimed the rulership for themselves, and often rebellions of both, one using the other as a pawn in this game for the throne of Nupe. Masaba, the ambitious and most popular youngest son of Mallam Dendo, born of a Nupe mother and educated at the court of the Nupe *Etsu* Majiya, claimed the throne on the grounds that he was a real Nupe and not, like Usman Zaki, a Fulani by descent. He won the support of Tsado in Zuguma and Idirisu in Eggā, the two shadow kings of Nupe, and finally even the support of the Emir of Gwandu, the spiritual head of the Eastern Fulani Empire. Masaba led two revolts against Usman Zaki, the first from Rabá, shortly after the latter had assumed power, and the second, from exile in Lade, south of the Niger, in 1841.[1] It was successful and forced Usman Zaki to leave Nupe kingdom together with Umaru, the son of his eldest brother Majigi, and to return to the home of his ancestors, Gwandu. Masaba became king of Nupe.

Let me enumerate the main facts in the involved history of Fulani-Nupe, with its revolts, its constant bloodshed, and its fratricidal wars. During Masaba's reign Nupe kingdom grew extensively. Masaba, re-siding first in Lade and later in Rabá, conquered the Kamuku in the north, the Gbari in the east, and the Kakanda in the south; he entrenched himself firmly on the Yoruba side of the Niger, snatching the country from other Fulani chiefs who had gained a foothold there. A revolt of one of his mercenary generals, the Bornu general Umar Bahaushe, drove

[1] Schoen-Crowther, op. cit., p. 161.

Masaba from Rabá, and the king had to seek refuge in Ilorin. Umar Bahaushe, for some time undisputed master of Nupe, attempted to make himself *Etsu* Nupe. All Fulani rallied against him, Usman Zaki and

SKETCH MAP SHOWING THE DIVISION OF ROYAL LAND

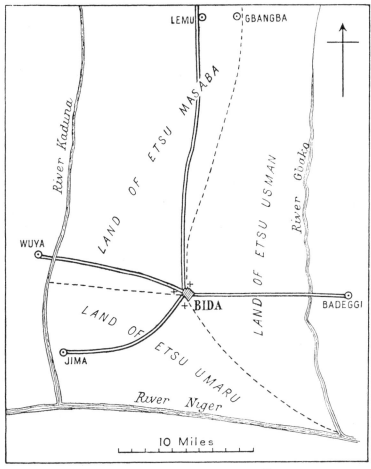

+ ...... Royal Estates *(esoži)*

Umaru Majigi returned from Gwandu, their self-chosen place of exile, and joined forces with Masaba against the usurper. For three years the Bornu general drove the Fulani armies before him and beat them in battle after battle. At last the luck turned. The Fulani army under Umaru, son of Majigi, fleeing from the usurper's army across the Kaduna river, found protection in the walled town of Bida. With the arrival of Masaba's troops from the south, and with the assistance of the town-king of Bida and the twelve Beni towns whose confederacy is brought into play for the last time in Nupe history, Umar Bahaushe's army was defeated after a three months' siege of Bida. The rebel general was killed, and when the *Dayspring* reached Rabá, in 1857, Dr. Baikie saw the head of the unfortunate Umar Bahaushe impaled at the landing-place.[1]

Then came a time of comparative peace. Bida became the centre of the new kingdom. Usman Zaki, now reinstated, was the first *Etsu* Nupe to reside there. He died in 1859 or 1860, and was succeeded by Masaba, whose second reign lasted till 1873. Under his rule Bida was transformed from a huge war-camp into a capital worthy of the most powerful kingdom of Central Nigeria. Many great buildings in Bida date from this time: the three royal palaces, the great mosque, and the lay-out of the night market. Masaba, suppressing revolts of the Gbedegi in Mokwa, of the riverain Kyedye, fighting wars against the Kukuruku, Kakanda and Bassa Nge in the south, and Gbari and Agaie Fulani in the east, consolidated the country internally and expanded its boundaries farther and farther afield. Of the two descendants of the original Nupe dynasty, one, Yisa, of Jimada stock, had fought on the side of the Fulani against the usurper Umar Bahaushe, and had then settled, half guest, half hostage, in Bida. The other, the descendant of Majiya, after having revolted, in vain, several times, fled again to the refuge of his father, Zuguma, in Kontagora. In *Etsu* Masaba's time, Nupe kingdom is said to have stretched from Mulye and Awawu, in Ebe country, in the north, to Akpara in Bunu in the south, and from half Yoruba Tsaragi (Shari) in the west, to Payi, in Gbari, in the east.[2] After Masaba's death Umaru, the son of Majigi, became *Etsu*. He reigned from 1873 till 1884. He is said to have been a fanatic Mohammedan, and he, too, helped to extend the boundaries of Nupe kingdom. He fought against Bunu and Gbira—and in this fight used for the first time gunpowder bought from the first Niger Company trading-post which had newly been established in Eggã, on the Niger. He quelled a revolt of the Kusopa under a chief from Yeti who joined forces with the exiled Nupe king of Zuguma, and another rising of the Kyedye. In this fight he had the help of the Kakanda, now tributary to the Nupe, and of the Niger Company troops which then for the first time played an active part in Nupe politics.

Etsu Maliki, who succeeded Umaru Majigi, reigned from 1884 to 1895. He is said to have been the wealthiest *Etsu* of Nupe, but (which means, perhaps, the same) avaricious and cruel. Under his reign taxes reached an almost insufferable height. His reign was on the whole peaceful except for the usual border raids and punitive expeditions against recalcitrant vassal tribes. Abubakari, 1895–7, followed. It was under his reign that the Niger Company troops were fighting against the

[1] A. C. G. Hastings, *The Voyage of the 'Dayspring'*. London, 1926, p. 90.
[2] About that time Dr. Barth, travelling in Hausa, was told of the great warlike kingdom of Nupe, whose boundaries he records; they are almost exactly the boundaries given above: Faže (in Ebe) in the north, Bunu country in the south, Tsaragi in the west, and Liffe (?) in Oban, in the east. (Henry Barth, *Travels and Discoveries in North and Central Africa*, London, 1857, vol. iv, Appendix V, p. 545.)

Nupe, finally taking Bida, in 1897, deposing *Etsu* Abubakari and appointing Mohamadu in his place.

The story of the Niger Company campaign has been often written. Between 1870 and 1890 the Royal Niger Company had established trading-posts all along the river, its northernmost posts being situated on Nupe territory. Shortly after the accession of Abubakari trouble broke out in the south of Nupe kingdom, in what is to-day Kabba Province, where the Yagba and Gbira had revolted against Nupe suppression. The Niger Company, which had many important trading-posts in this part of the country, promised them protection from Bida. *Etsu* Abubakari, no friend of the white man, decided to kill two birds with one stone, to 'pacify' Kabba country and to oust the hated Europeans. He moved his army south, under the command of *Maku* Mohamadu. But the latter, who nursed a grievance against the *Etsu* for having refused his claim to the title of Heir Presumptive, made a pact with the British; in exchange for the promise of Sir William Wallace, who commanded the Niger Company troops, to make him *Etsu* of Nupe, he agreed to keep his army out of the fight. The Kyedye, always ready to revolt against the central government, manned their canoes, placed them at the disposal of the Niger Company and, under the command of a gunboat, undertook to guard the river so that no reinforcements should reach the beleaguered capital. The Niger Company troops marched on a city depleted of soldiers and arms. After twelve days' fighting the stubborn resistance of Bida was broken. Abubakari was deposed, and Mohamadu, Sir William Wallace's ally, appointed *Etsu*. The chief of the Kyedye was rewarded with the grant of the semi-independent status which his country had lost under the Fulani, and was placed directly under the authority of the Niger Company (a prerogative which was later withdrawn). Moreover, acceding to the request of the Kyedye chief, Patigi, the territory on the southern bank of the Niger opposite the Kyedye capital Muregi, was detached from Bida and given, as a separate Emirate, to Idirisu, the exiled Nupe king of the Jimada branch, who had been living in Bida as the 'guest' (hostage, in reality) of the Fulani kings.

The Niger Company and later its successor, the Government of Northern Nigeria, continued for some time this policy of breaking up the too dangerous big Nupe kingdom. Kolo Yisa, a grandson of the exiled Majiya, had thought of using the defeat of Bida for his own ends. He hurried to Zuguma, where his ancestors had lived as puppet kings of Bida, made himself king over the territory, and was later confirmed in this position by the Government. Yagba, Bunu, Bassa, and Kakanda had become independent districts and provinces immediately after the conquest of Bida. Now also the Nupe possessions on the southern and western bank of the Niger were taken away from Bida and placed in a different province, Ilorin, where they were divided up between the Emirs of Ilorin, Shonga, and Lafiagi (1900–5). Of the Nupe Empire that had reached from the Benue in the south to Gbagede in the north, only Bida Division remained, bordered on all sides by countries populated by Nupe, but ruled by different sovereigns.

Etsu Abubakari, who had been banished to Lokoja after the conquest of Bida, made one attempt to return to his country and to recover throne and independence. He succeeded in collecting a following large enough to threaten Bida. He defeated *Etsu* Mohamadu and drove him from Bida (1906). But the British, by this time firmly established, helped Mohamadu, brought him back to Bida, and sent Abubakari back to Lokoja, where shortly afterwards he died in exile. Mohamadu died in 1915, succeeded by *Etsu* Bello, 1915–26, *Etsu* Mallam Saidu, 1926–34, and finally the present *Etsu*, Mallam Mohamadu Ndayako.

Viewing the historical growth of the Nupe Empire as a whole we discover the familiar two trends which, closely intertwined, force political systems into an endless twofold development: from expansion to military and political consolidation, in the course of which the necessity of further expansion seems invariably entailed. The roots of this development are no less evident in Nupe history than in the political developments of our own history. First, newly conquered territory demanded in due course conquest beyond its boundaries in order to ensure the pacification of the conquered areas and to prevent interference from tribes or states without. And second, the expanding territory absorbing more and more alien groups, all to be controlled and governed from a small nucleus-country, by a population less than one-fifth the size of the population that was brought under political control, necessitated continuous 're-conquests' and wars of consolidation. In the field of social organization this development becomes manifest in the rise of the feudal system; in the military sphere, in the ever-increasing employment of mercenary troops.

Not every step in the expansion of Nupe kingdom was carried out by war. There is evidence of peaceful expansion as well. Certain communities and tribal groups are said to have 'submitted' (*gba*) voluntarily to the Nupe state, accepting the position of tributary groups and claiming at the same time the political protection which the Nupe overlords extended to their subject groups. But accepting this 'protection' meant largely avoiding the more disastrous subjection. Though not the direct result of war and conquest, it was yet a submission to the threat of war and conquest which the momentum of a steadily expanding Nupe must have seemed to entail to her weaker neighbours.

To discover with equal certainty the first stimulus of the whole development, the force which, as it were, set the stone rolling, is impossible. The origin of Nupe rule and expansion is buried in the mythical past. Whether it was the immigration of a large tribal group (condensed in the myth to the small band of men round Tsoede) or a small *élite* of the kind Pareto likes to discover in every political achievement, we have no means of deciding. We do not even know what the original social structure and economic system of this immigrant group was, or whether it contained any stimulus to territorial expansion or conquest. Only in the Fulani conquest does this first 'stimulus' lie open to historical examination. We have described to some extent the gradual infiltration of Nupe by the Fulani, who came as herdsmen, mercenary soldiers, and Mohammedan preachers. Here a distinct tribal section, a semi-nomadic group on its wanderings from west to east and south-east, was the carrier of conquest. It was separated from the groups which it subjugated by ethnic descent and social structure, consisting apparently of a loose aggregate of kinship groups and self-constituted warlike bands, and only partly by its system of livelihood; for the predecessors of the Fulani, the Nupe rulers, had already been soldiers and had themselves evolved an urbanized civilization in which Mohammedan culture played its part. But the analysis of Fulani political history goes beyond the scope of this book.

We can study some of the stimuli which, though perhaps it did not initiate, yet certainly influenced and directed the political growth of Nupe. Limiting ourselves to the periods that come under the heading of 'real' history, we can point out the essential difference in the policy of expansion before and after the Fulani conquest. The expansion of the pre-Fulani kingdom appears to have been most marked in the north, and of the Fulani era, in the south. Tsoede's grave, symbolic to all Nupe kings of what we might call his 'political testament', lies in Gbagede, 100 miles north of their northernmost capital, Rabá. The Fulani Emirs, on the other hand, drove their armies farther and farther south; only in recent times, less than two generations ago, did they begin to 'consolidate' the Gbari provinces, thirty or forty miles north of Bida. The conquest of the northern territories, inhabited by primitive pagans who possessed no handicrafts or remarkable wealth, had evidently two main aims (apart from the necessity of pacifying the border countries): first, to tap the rich, easily accessible reservoir of slaves which the Nupe found among these primitive and poorly protected groups; and second, to protect and attract the trade from the wealthy centres of civilization in the Hausa states. Of this latter aim we have concrete proof. The main trade-routes from Hausa passed through, and partly ended in, Nupe, crossing on their way the territories of unruly hostile tribes. Rabá was the goal of the huge caravans that carried regularly *kanwa* (potash) from Lake Chad over Kano to the countries of the south.[1] When the first European explorers, in the times of the last indigenous Nupe kings, reached Nupe country and Rabá, they found it a town rich in cattle (the humped, northern, breed), horses, camels, and ostriches—which must all have come from the north—and the markets full of precious goods from Hausa, Bornu, and North Africa.[2]

The turning to the south represents a new political interest, bound up with a later phase in the history of West Africa. Fulani-Nupe, as the southern outpost of the Fulani Empire, carried its wars of expansion into the pagan south and no longer into the northern countries which had come under the sovereignty of various Fulani potentates to whom Nupe was tied by common allegiance. The south offered, over and above new densely populated areas for slave raiding, the command of the main route for the slave-trade, down the river to the coast whence ships took the slaves to foreign ports. Not until the Fulani subjugated the Kakanda

[1] See Barth, op. cit. ii, p. 115.
[2] See J. and R. Lander: Rabá had large herds of 'horned cattle remarkable for size and beauty' and a 'prodigious number of excellent horses' (op. cit. ii, pp. 312–13).

tribe could Nupe canoes, with slaves and various goods, travel unmolested between Nupe and Lokoja and Onitsa, having had, before then, to stop at Eggä and to tranship their loads to Kakanda boats.[1] The highly developed trades and crafts of the south, capable of supplementing the northern trade, proved another attraction to a kingdom that had grown rich and fastidious. We have heard of the Yoruba slaves imported by the Fulani *Etsu* Masaba because of their skill in weaving and dyeing. Finally, the south became of paramount importance as the main door to European imports. This importance reached its climax when *Etsu* Umaru bought gunpowder for his long-barrelled flintlock guns of Arab pattern from the store of the Niger Company on his territory—north and south matched again in most profitable manner.

Our sketch of the growth of this West African kingdom has shown political expansion dominated by economic interests. If other motives— a collective desire for military adventures and glory—were decisive in shaping it, they are now invisible in the historical perspective. The impetus of religious zeal, which drove the Fulani armies across Northern Nigeria, was spent when, as rulers of Nupe, the Fulani turned their faces southward. I will not pursue farther this question of political philosophy, of the ultimate stimulus behind political expansion. But we shall see that economic considerations were involved in the building and maintenance of the kingdom in many other, more subtle, ways. The incentive of gain will appear not only as an abstract, impersonal, historical stimulus, but as a concrete element, directly affecting individual action and directly shaping the motives and interests by which the individual agents of the political system are animated.

[1] See *African Political Systems*, Oxford University Press, 1940, p. 170, n. i.

CHAPTER VII
POLITICAL HISTORY OF NUPE KINGDOM
(continued)

KINGSHIP

IN the tradition of Tsoede, that 'mythical charter' of Nupe kingdom, the essence of the Nupe state is already clearly expressed, sanctioned, almost sanctified, by that paramount authority that attaches to pre-historic events: it outlines a system of political domination, growing by conquest and expansion, and governed by a group detached in origin and status from the rest of the population, and claiming its supreme position by the right of might. The small river kingdom which figures, in the Tsoede tradition, as the nucleus of the great Nupe of later times, and the vast empire under the Fulani Emirs, are essentially of the same nature. The twofold process of expansion over alien groups and cultures, combined with cultural assimilation and absorption, is reflected in both, in the ideological history of the Tsoede myth as well as in the 'real' history of the Fulani kingdom. In one there is Tsoede, who conquers Nupe with the help of alien magic, who brings into Nupe the insignia of alien rulership and culture, but who, himself half Nupe by descent, creates a new, independent, and united Nupe. In the other there is this remarkable piece of empire-policy when Masaba claims succession to the Nupe throne on the grounds of his being half Nupe by birth and full Nupe by education. If the mythology of Tsoede establishes the essence and growth of kingship, later history shows its vicissitudes involved in such system of domination which forces unity upon heterogeneous groups and cultures, revolts and feuds, kings deposed and exiled, usurpers and shadow kings.

We know little about the system of kingship in pre-Fulani times. I have mentioned one piece of information already which I obtained from various sources, namely, the ancient rule of succession which made the eldest son 'born in the purple', that is, the son first born during the father's reign, the heir to the throne of Nupe. A few other facts concerning the person of the king I was able to ascertain from the *Etsu* of Patigi. Certain ritual rules obtained at the king's court—and some of these rules are still observed in Patigi. Thus the *Etsu* may only wear white; he can travel and go out whenever he likes, but may not eat any food save that prepared by his wives; nor may any stranger watch him eat. Finally, no one may be killed in the presence of the king or in the town in which he is residing.[1]

---

[1] This helps us to understand the organization of the 'King's Hangmen', the crucial fact of which was that the royal executioners killed their victims in places far away from the king's capital. Another effect of this observance, which is still visible, is the rule which forbids the performance of the *ndakó gboyá*, a cult believed to lead to the death of witches, in Patigi, the present 'king's town', or anywhere within a distance from which 'the shrieking of the spirit could be heard in Patigi'. (See *Man*, 1935, 173.)

Although the present-day political system of Nupe appears to represent in many respects only a copy and continuation of the pre-Fulani system, the characteristic features of ancient Nupe kingship—the former rule of inheritance, the ritual taboos, and the sacred emblems and form of magic linked with kingship—have disappeared under the Mohammedan Fulani Emirs. But already a new background of religion and myth is forming behind the modern kingship. The memory of the ancestor of the Fulani rulers of Nupe, Mallam Dendo, has become sanctified. The stories of his life and exploits, emphasizing his supernatural faculties, have the flavour of myths. And his tomb at Rabá, over which a mosque has been built, became a place of worship and pilgrimage. At the time of the election of the present Emir, when a number of important political posts were due to change hands, the *Rani*, a Fulani prince anxious to obtain one of these posts, went to Rabá, fasted for seven days, sacrificed in the grave-mosque, and prayed to his ancestor for help.

The disappearance of ancient Nupe kingship reflects the far-reaching historical changes which Nupe kingdom had undergone in the Fulani conquest. In pre-Fulani Nupe the link with magic and myth, ritual rules and taboos, and possibly even the law of succession, separated the king from the rest of the people, even from the members of his own house. Fulani rule, only recently established by undisguised conquest, and dependent upon the co-operation of a band of war-chiefs and faction-leaders, turned semi-sacred kingship into rulership of the strongest. The king becomes a *primus inter pares*, the highest rank-holder in a royal nobility ruled by precedence and promotion. The exclusiveness of primogeniture gave way to a system of succession that allowed for balance of power and could satisfy rival claims. This final balance was not achieved at once. Of the seven sons of Mallam Dendo three only were destined to found royal houses, two directly, Usman Zaki and Masaba, and one in the second generation, Majigi, through his son Umaru. Having once concentrated military and political power in their own hands, these three families eliminated the other sons and grandsons from the succession, paying them off with political offices the importance of which decreased from generation to generation. This resulted in three dynasties which succeed to the throne in strict rotation. In the genealogy given in Appendix II this development is clearly visible. This historical explanation of the present system of kingship is borne out by the views of the people themselves. One of my most enlightened informants, a very learned man and himself a member of the royal nobility, defended the present form of succession against the old primogeniture on these grounds: the old system could work in ancient Nupe, when there was a powerful *kuti* (magic) behind the *Etsu*'s authority. For the Fulani dynasty, which came to power as a large group, composed of jealous relatives and partisans, a divided succession was the only solution. The country too, he added, could only benefit from such balance of power.

We may mention here another change from pre-Fulani to Fulani kingship which concerns the political status of the Nupe state. While the Nupe kings were absolute masters in their own country, the Fulani

Emirs were, in a loose sense, vassals of a larger state, the Fulani Empire of Gwandu. Beyond an annual tribute by Bida to Gwandu (reduced to-day to a nominal gift) and the merely symbolic confirmation by the Emir of Gwandu of every newly appointed king of Nupe, expressed in the traditional bestowal of a flag, the vassalship involved little interference with the internal government of Nupe. The Emir of Gwandu acted mainly as the guarantor of the various political systems under his suzerainty. In this capacity he was sometimes appealed to in boundary disputes and suchlike, and he would support his arbitration if need be by military action, as happened in the dispute over rights to raid between Bida and Agaie (see p. 115). In turn Bida, like all other Fulani vassal states, could be called upon to send military help to her suzerain. The overlordship of Gwandu was also appealed to in the early dynastic disputes between the descendants of Mallam Dendo. It was due to the advice of Gwandu that Usman Zaki ceded the throne to Masaba; Gwandu helped the Fulani against their rebellious general Umar Bahaushe; and Gwandu supported later the reinstatement of Usman Zaki. The influence of Gwandu upon dynastic affairs disappeared, characteristically, with the gradual establishment of a fixed system of succession which could itself safeguard balance of power and the conciliation of rival claims.

The rival character of the threefold dynastic structure is abundantly manifest in present-day Nupe. Every possession or privilege linked with Nupe kingship reflects the tripartite arrangement. The three highest ranks in the hierarchy of the kingdom are vested in the three royal 'clans': the ruling king, head of one royal house, takes the title *Etsu*; the head of the royal house next in succession, the title *Shaba*, 'Heir Presumptive'; and the head of the third house, the title *Kpotū*. The land of the Beni round Bida where the Fulani settled after their decisive victory, appropriating all vacant land, is divided into three parts: the family of Usman Zaki owns the country east of Bida, the family of Umaru Majigi the country in the south, and the family of Masaba the country in the west.[1] Bida town is divided, as we have seen, into three *ekpã*, each with its royal palace, and each bearing the name of one of the three royal families. Every king adding more land and power to his kingdom is adding at the same time more land and power to his own family, and distributes land and wealth among his own followers and favourites. Every *Etsu* Nupe uses the period of his reign to increase to the utmost the wealth and power of his house. The only balance of power lies in the rigid system of succession. For favouritism and extortions from the ruling *Etsu* may win for the house of his successor the favour of the masses; oppression from one may mean help from the other; the increase of power in one royal house will eventually be balanced by the growth of the house that succeeds it to the throne. It is a precarious balance, and its history, which is the history of Bida to-day, is written in rivalries, feuds, intrigues, and revolts, which threaten constantly the peace of the country and tear the people of Bida into rival factions.

The struggle for dynastic power is as apparent in the economic field.

[1] See sketch map, p. 81.

The control over the wealth and the potential resources of the country, though not exclusively the king's, is yet sufficiently his to render his economic position unassailable. The king of Nupe derived his income firstly from the taxes and tributes which his officers collected, and of which he received the largest share, and secondly, from the wars and raids which the king's armies carried into foreign lands. The king's private estates constituted a third important source of income. These estates were worked by slaves who lived in small hamlets on the royal lands called *esoži*. We shall discuss the organization—past and present—of these royal estates later, in the chapter on land tenure. Here we need only say that not all the Emirs of Nupe were equally keen farmers; some, *Etsu* Mohamadu for example, let things drift; they took little interest in their estates, neglected their *esoži*, and cared only about the regular payments of their share in the yield of the farms.

Other sources of income are less clearly defined—profits made from commerce (above all, from slave-trade), in which an *Etsu* Nupe, like every Nupe nobleman, might sometimes engage; or proceeds from bribes, extortion, and the confiscation of estates belonging to rebels and other 'enemies of the country'. One interesting variety of this latter kind is the exploitation of a religious institution, a 'king's cult' of comparatively recent origin, the anti-witchcraft society which is known in Nupe as the *ndakó gboyá*. The Fulani Emirs had ingeniously grasped the control over this powerful and lucrative secret society and shared the proceeds with its members; the share of *Etsu* Bello in one year is said to have amounted to over £100.[1]

Another source of income, which will gain the economist's special appreciation, lay in the royal monopoly of the kola-nut trade. You will find to-day two kinds of kola-nuts on the markets of Nupe (or for that matter Nigeria): the small cheap kind, which is imported from the Gold Coast and Southern Nigeria, and the large, most expensive kola-nut which is grown in Nupe country, on the farms of the kola-nut planters of Laboži. Till the days of British rule this latter kind, famous all over Nigeria, could be procured only by the members of the nobility; no commoner or peasant had any opportunity of obtaining Laboži nuts. The trade in these nuts was a strict monopoly of the *Etsu* Nupe, the kola-nut growers being forbidden to sell their crop to anyone except his own agents.[2] Stories are current of traders smuggling the precious fruits out of Laboži by night, lest they should be seen and caught by the men of the king. In the kola-nut monopoly an instrument of sharp class-prerogative was cleverly combined with an efficient economic measure.[3] But to what extent the *Etsu* Nupe disposed of the kola-nuts as gifts to his courtiers and favourites, and to what extent he made money by selling them to the nobility of the country, I am unable to say.

[1] See p. 142 and *Africa*, 4, 1935.
[2] The *Etsu* Nupe in turn supplied the kola-nut planters with slaves to help them in their work. In pre-Fulani days the kings of Nupe are reported also to have presented one slave every year to Laboži to be sacrificed in the annual ritual with which the Laboži planters secured the thriving of their crop.
[3] See p. 129.

Out of this large and varied income the king gave directly very little to the common weal: he 'financed' certain public works, the repair or the building of the city mosque, his own palace, and the town walls and gates. The work itself was organized by the members of the lower nobility and carried out by their slaves and serfs; the king contributed only food and drink for the labourers, and small presents for the men in charge of the work. From his income, but assisted by gifts from other members of the royal house, the *Etsu* also paid the annual tribute to the Emir of Gwandu, by which the kings of Bida recognized the sovereignty of that ancient centre of the Fulani Empire.[1] Finally, the king, equipped his army with horses and arms, and formed of his personal slaves the police force which had to keep order in markets and streets. But indirectly the king contributed very considerably to the economic life of the country. The court was the centre round which the economic and cultural life of the capital revolved. The splendour of the court life of Nupe, famous in Nigeria, meant work and income for thousands, incessant production in the workshops of the craftsmen, and rich business for the merchants. Beautifully built houses to live in; gorgeous gowns, horses, saddles, arms, to be given as presents to courtiers and members of the household; food and drink, music and dances, for the great feasts celebrated at court, these were (and still are) the daily needs of the royal household. Presents play an important part in the etiquette of Nupe kingdom: from a small bowl of kola-nuts to a silk gown or a horse range these expressions of the king's favour. And at the great Mohammedan festival of the year, the *Sallah* as it is called in Nigeria, every one of the hundreds of people who by the right of birth or status are entitled to the king's attention are honoured with a smaller or larger gift. To be left out means disgrace; and the sending of a present to a man with whom the *Etsu* was known to be on bad terms expresses conspicuously reconciliation and new favour.

Of the former sources of royal income only two have survived under modern conditions: profits from occasional trade, and the proceeds of the royal estates (materially reduced by the transformation of slave labour into labour on the métayer system, or even wage-labour; see p. 200). To this we have to add to-day the Emir's considerable salary. On the other hand, his expenses, too, have been greatly reduced: public works, the upkeep of a police force, even the building of the royal residence, now form items on the list of Native Administration expenditure. But all the current expenses, all those demanded by status and prestige, by the etiquette of the kingdom, and by the necessity of winning supporters for himself and his house, are still as much part of the unwritten obligations of an *Etsu* Nupe as they ever were.

A DAY OF COURT ROUTINE

Every morning the *Etsu* mounts his horse and, accompanied by members of his household and some of his officers of state, rides round

[1] In the first period of British rule this tribute consisted of 100 gowns worth £300, 200 gowns worth £125, and one silver sword worth £10.

the walls of his house. This morning ride is still part of the daily routine of the *Etsu* Nupe, even up at his modern brick residence which stands by itself on the hill outside the town. He may extend his ride to visit his *esoži*, a short distance away, and inspect his farms, or possibly to inquire after his guests—for visitors of standing who have come from far away are assigned quarters in the *esoži*. Once when I accompanied the *Etsu* on this ceremonial morning ride he went to see a Nupe Mallam who had returned from the pilgrimage to Mecca and stopped in Bida as the king's guest on his way home. Another time two noblemen from Sokoto, relatives of the Sultan, had come on a visit to Bida and were invited to stay in the *esoži*. Later in the morning, back in his house, the *Etsu* receives the first official visitors of the day: the *Etsu Dogari* and the *Sarkin Yandoka*, the chiefs of the two police forces of the Emirate, who come to bring him the 'news of the town'—arrests made on the market the night before, a case of small-pox in one of the town quarters, and so forth. The *Alkali* and his Chief Assistant drop in to pay their respects, possibly to report on an important law-case, before they go down to the Court House in the centre of the town. The guild-head of the traders may present himself in order to inform the *Etsu* of the arrival in Bida of traders or a trading caravan with new attractive goods which the *Etsu* might care to inspect. Messengers come and go—from the Native Administration Treasury, or the Divisional Office, the Bida Town Council, or from a District Head. In the meantime the highest officers of state, the members of the Emir's Council, have arrived in his house for the daily *nkó*, the Council of State. At the *nkó* all matters of importance are discussed; or there may be legal cases on the day's agenda. For the *nkó* has also judicial functions and tries cases referred to it from a lower court. The session of the *Etsu*'s Council concludes the official duties of the day. In the afternoon the *Etsu* might see friends or visitors in his house, or drive through the town in his splendid motor-car—one of the modern symbols of royal prestige.

The climax of Bida Court life is the celebration of the Friday. On Thursday night and again on Friday afternoon the *Etsu* rides in great state to the mosque in the town, and on Friday at his return he holds a reception in his house which is attended by every man of rank and standing. Envisage this Friday procession: king and courtiers on horseback, in their sumptuous gowns, the king under the great silken state umbrella, the horses with trappings of silver and beautiful cloth; a bodyguard carrying swords, and police with their staffs, are running ahead, shouting the *Etsu*'s name or blessing formulae or little proverb-like sentences which illustrate the king's greatness; drummers are beating their drums, three mounted trumpeters blow the huge bronze *kakati* in an incessant deafening chorus; with it blend the shrill notes of the *algeita*, the Hausa oboe, while another musician is beating an iron double bell with a wooden stick, shouting and singing at the same time. All streets are lined with people, adults and children, who watch, fascinated, this procession, bearing witness to the impressiveness of this display of royal power. And then, back again in the royal palace: the wide place in front of the house and the courtyard are crowded with people; the *talakaži*—

the commoners, men without name and rank—sit and stand outside, chatting and watching what there is to watch; the members of the privileged classes, titled nobility, and Mohammedan priests, are sitting in the inner courtyard and in *katamba* (entrance-halls), each *katamba* reserved for a special group. Only royal princes and the highest officers of state are admitted to the presence of the *Etsu*; they sit in the inner part of the house together with personal friends and favourites of the king.[1] All these people come to pay their respect to their sovereign, to see and to be seen, to exercise prerogatives, or to proclaim their connexion with the privileged and mighty. This external arrangement of the Friday ceremonial is indeed a symbol of the whole social structure of Nupe kingdom with its rigid system of etiquette and precedence, its differentiation of status, rank, and prerogatives, and its display of wealth and power. This structure we must now analyse in detail.

THE ROYAL NOBILITY

The descendants of the house of Mallam Dendo, under their three heads *Etsu*, *Shaba*, and *Kpotū*, form the royal nobility of Nupe, the *ena gitsúži*, the Group of Those who will become King. They are *gitsúži* in the sense that from their ranks the new king is elected. The titles of nobility which they hold by the privilege of birth may lead every one of them, by slower or more rapid promotion, eventually to the highest rank, kingship. In most cases the royal prince who succeeds to the throne has reached first the rank of *Shaba*; the change from old to new king is thus made almost automatic, a dangerous interregnum is avoided, and the fight between the rival factions is confined to the less dangerous sphere of competition for the ranks next to the king. Only twice was a man who had not reached the title of *Shaba* (or, if the *Shaba* had died, the title of *Kpotū*) made *Etsu*.[2] In 1936 there existed, or more precisely, were actually held, 41 royal ranks, of which 10 fell to the house of Usman Zaki, 17 to the house of Masabá (the house which had supplied the last

---

[1] The arrangement at these receptions, the way in which the people who are admitted to the presence of the *Etsu* group themselves, is invariably the same. It is shown in this diagram:

Two bodyguards with ostrich fans
Etsu (on state bed)

Gitsúži   *Ndeji*   *Sarakiži*
                    Mayaki
          Liman-Alkali
              Mallams

[2] These exceptions were *Etsu* Mohamadu who, only *Makū*, was appointed *Etsu* by the Niger Company, and the present *Etsu* who had been *Nágenu*, but had held the important office of a District Head of Jima. It is the present tendency of the Administration to abolish the office of *Shaba* and to make the appointment to kingship a free election from the royal ranks. After the death of the late *Shaba* in 1935 no new *Shaba* has been appointed. It is not yet clear what effect, if any, this innovation will have upon the internal dynastic organization. The threefold system is so deeply rooted that I believe the effect will be only to abolish a name, and that the rank next in order in the dynastic section will assume the main function of the abolished rank, that is, headship of the dynastic clan.

Etsu), and 14 to the house of Umaru, the present ruling house. The death of a high rank-holder and the subsequent appointment of a successor is frequently made an occasion for a far-reaching reshuffle of ranks, called in Nupe *wúruwúru*. It goes hand in hand with a large-scale exchange of houses, younger brothers or sons moving into the vacated house of their older brothers or fathers (vacated by death or promotion), for the state residence of the highest *gitsú* ranks goes with the title. Rarely would a new house be built in Bida to-day for a *wací*, a Great One, as the members of the royal nobility are also called; 'only *talakaži*, Poor Ones', said an informant, 'must build themselves new homes.' Appointment to a first rank and promotion to a higher rank is granted by the king in council with royal princes and the other officers of state. Any able-bodied man in the Fulani families who has reached senior age and who has proved his ability and loyalty can claim to be admitted to the ranks of the titled *gitsúži*.[1] But there is no rule. Favouritism, intrigues, bribes play their part in appointment and promotion. The ranks which a family can accumulate reflects its influence at the court and its favour with the ruling king. It is no accident that the royal house of the last *Etsu* (who had only just died) counts more ranks than either of the other two dynasties. Unlike the system of ranks which we found in the village these royal ranks do not leave an old man or an invalid who can no longer fulfil his duties in the possession of his office. In such a case a younger man is appointed to the rank, and the old holder is known as the 'Old *Kpotú*', or whatever the rank may be. A similar difference between the rank systems of village and state lies in that perfect health is an indispensable condition of appointments to any state rank. Deformity, even of the slightest kind, is ruled out. The younger brother of one of the Emirs of Bida, who had a withered arm, was unable to obtain any title at all. In the state system of ranks, which was based on service in the war and on offices vital to the safety of the state, respect for old age or consideration for even minor disablements has no place.

The investiture—it is the same for royal princes and for officers of state—is an interesting ceremony, an impressive proclamation of the main facts on which the feudal kingdom is built: social promotion, the oath of fealty and loyalty and responsibility towards king and country. A propitious day for the investiture is first fixed by Mallams or diviners. Then follows the invitation to the ceremony—gifts of kola-nuts sent by the candidate to all men of rank and standing. Drummers in the house of the *Etsu* announce the beginning of the ceremony; all rank-holders are assembled in the *Etsu*'s house. He addresses the candidate ceremonially, proclaiming three times his appointment. The *Alkali* (or *Liman*), as representative of the clergy of the kingdom, clothes the candidate in an embroidered gown and rich cloak—gifts of the *Etsu*—and places a turban on his head. Then he leads the prayer, and the *Etsu* addresses a final exhortation to the new officer of state: 'Practice for-

---

[1] The Nupe of Patigi have preserved a linguistic distinction which has disappeared in Bida, namely, between royal princes who have received titles and those who have not. The former are called *b'rama* (their traditional salute is *lerama*, i.e. behold the *rama*), and the latter *gitsúži*.

bearance; do not set the hearts of your men against each other; beware of conceit, and do not fail the people.' All present repeat, like a formula of confirmation: *Hakíka, hakíka*, 'verily, verily'. Drummers and musicians intone the songs and drum rhythms which are associated with the family and rank of the newly knighted; he mounts his horse and rides, accompanied by all rank-holders, through the town, dismounting at each house of a prince or *saraki*, making his greetings to the head of the house. If the newly appointed (or promoted) nobleman is a member of the royal dynasty he stops at each of the three royal houses and says a prayer at the grave of his ancestors. A great festivity in his house, lasting for several days, to which everybody in the town is invited, noblemen and commoners alike, concludes the ceremony.

Descendants of the men who conquered the country and appropriated all vacant land, the *gitsúži* may become, through ordinary inheritance, owners of land and considerable wealth. But the appointment to a royal rank meant more than this chance of inheritance: it meant status, influence, and access to increasing power and wealth. The princes of rank were admitted to the *nkó*, the Council of State, but had little influence, it seems, upon the actual government—this was entrusted to the council of the more competent, appointed, officers of state. The power of the *gitsúži* rested in the main on two things: the part they played in the wars, and their position as *egba*, royal fief-holders and delegates placed in charge of the districts of the kingdom. We shall speak presently in more detail of these services which the royal nobility rendered to king and state. I will give here a list of all the ranks held at present among the *gitsúži* of Bida. To illustrate the system of promotion I have indicated certain changes in the distribution of ranks which had been anticipated by the *Etsu* and his council after the death of the *Shaba* in 1935; as already said, the Administration was not prepared to endorse this reshuffle, which would imply the reoccupation of the post of *Shaba* (see p. 93, n. 2). The list also shows some of the fiefs which were connected with the ranks in pre-European times, and finally the offices under the present-day Native Administration which are linked with certain *gitsú* ranks.

DYNASTIC RANKS IN BIDA 1936

1. *Ranks held by Members of the emi 'tsu Maru (House of Umaru Majigi)*

Etsu, appointed 1935, former title *Nágenu*.
Shaba, died December 1935; till 1934 District Head of Sakpe. Fief in pre-European times: Mokwa.
'Old' *Makū*, till 1934 District Head of Kacha, then retired; previous title *Lukpā*. Fief in pre-European times: Kacha.
Makū, younger brother of 'Old' *Makū*; no official position.
Ginya, present District Head of Badeggi.
Cekpa
Gara
Lafyene (Lakpene)
Uban Dóma
Tswáyi

Táka, held by eldest son of *Shaba*.
Sontwáraki
Wacĩ Taba, held by younger brother of *Shaba*.
Nda Iya
Nágenu, held by younger brother of *Etsu*, appointed 1935; no previous title; District Head of Jima.
'Old' *Natsu*, retired from office 1934.
Natsu, son of a former *Kpotũ*, younger brother of *Ginya*; on the Bida Town Council.
Shabarabá, a new *ad hoc* introduced rank, bestowed in May 1936 on the eldest son of the late *Shaba*, as no higher rank was vacant.

2. *Ranks held by Members of the emi 'tsu Usman* (*House of Usman Zaki*)

'Old' *Kpotũ*, died in 1936; for some time District Head of Sakpe. Fief in pre-European times: *Edupkã* (countries beyond the Niger).
Kpotũ, son and nephew of former *Kpotũ*; District Head of Kutigi. He will shortly be asked to resign, that is, to become an 'old' *Kpotũ*, on the grounds that his health is not very good. The *Etsu* does not contemplate promoting him to the vacant post of *Shaba* in accordance with the general rules of succession.*
Nágya, till 1935 District Head of Mokwa, now member of the King's Council. He is chosen to succeed to the rank of *Shaba*. Fief in pre-European times: *Edukpã*.
Rani, since 1935 District Head of Mokwa.
Kusódu, younger brother of the late *Etsu* Bello, living in his Bida house. Fief in pre-European times: Kamberi country.
Wacĩ Tswa
Shaba Gíni
Fogũ
Lafarma
Kafa
Cata

* The ground of ill health is a pretext rather than the true reason—and this is very significant. The *Kpotũ* does not belong to the house of Usman Zaki, although he is generally regarded as belonging to this dynasty. He is a descendant of Abdu Gboya, one of the sons of Mallam Dendo whose offspring had failed to secure succession to the throne of Nupe. He is, in fact, the only member of these 'second-rank' royal families who had obtained, still in the fourth generation, one of the three highest dynastic positions. His premature resignation is a striking evidence of this dynastic policy to restrict succession to the throne to the three 'houses'.

3. *Ranks held by Members of the emi 'tsu Saba* (*House of Etsu Masaba*)

(Late *Etsu* Saidu, died 1935.)
Wacímbe
Nákorji, District Head of Gbangba. Chosen to succeed to office of *Kpotũ*. Fief in pre-European times: Yeti.
Lukpã
Tsaduya
Tsaci
Tswasha Giraba†
Tsuroma†

Benú, Fief in pre-European times: Kin Agbadya (Lokoja).

Tswanku
Tsoyida
Tswankúku
Rofiẽ
Cecekó
Nkoci
Tswashakó
Yitsa
Ndáma

† Two established *gitsú* titles, *Fokpo* and *Gbaruku* (a Dibo word, meaning Old One), are not represented in this list, i.e. are not held at present. On the other hand, new titles are constantly introduced to cope with an increased demand; e.g. *Tsuroma* is a Bornu title (*Ciroma*). The rank *Tswasha Giraba*, lit. '*Tswasha* bestowed in Rabá', seems to have been a newly introduced, additional, rank at one time, in Rabá, as the meaning of the title indicates. The *Etsu* bestowed a new title of this kind shortly before I left Bida on the younger son of the late *Shaba*, making him *Shabami* (lit. '*Shaba* of the House').

OFFICERS OF STATE

Placed under the royal nobility in rank but its equal in political influence is the titled office nobility of the kingdom. Its members are known as *ticiži*, the Titled Ones, or *rowni*, the 'Turbans', so called because the gift of a turban by the king is the symbol of the bestowal of rank and office. There are three groups of officers of state, each of which is thought of as a sharply defined social order or estate—*ena* in Nupe, which means 'group', 'society', 'order': first, the *sarakiži*, a twofold group of civil and military nobility, consisting of the *ena Ndeji*, the Order of Town Elders, and the *ena 'kū*, the Order of War. Second, the *ena manži*, the Order of Mallams, comprising the judiciary and the clergy of the kingdom, the *Alkali*, judge, and *Liman*, religious head of the Nupe Mohammedans, with their scribes and assistants. The third class of state officials, lowest in rank but still possessed of great influence, is the *ena wuži*, the Order of (Court) Slaves; we shall deal with this group later, in the chapter on slavery.

We shall see that many of the titles of the *saraki* nobility are identical with the ranks bestowed on the village elders. Of some ranks we know that they have been copied comparatively recently by the villagers. Whether this adoption of state ranks by the village communities explains all the existing correspondences, or whether they are due, historically, to the evolution of the kingdom from a village community, we have no means of deciding. To-day, it is a correspondence in name only. The identical symbols of status in the kingdom and in the village refer to very different social contexts. The differences in the official duties and in the rules of appointment will become clear presently. Here I will only mention the difference in the social conceptions upon which the two rank systems rest. Both must be interpreted as systems of selection by means of which the society obtains its leaders. But selection in the village means offering 13 ranks to, say, 200 adult men or—expressed more correctly—13 families; in the kingdom, it means admitting to leadership 30 men out of a population of hundreds of thousands. In the village, the position of importance and responsibility already attained by the individual who qualifies for the rank (through seniority, experience, and headship of a kinship group) is at least equal to the new benefits entailed in the appointment; in the state ranks these benefits far out-weigh any position one could have made for oneself previous to the appointment—often the latter is negligible. At the same time many of the state ranks, subject to changing political fortunes, are held more in-securely. In the village, then, rank is essentially a form of assured public recognition: in the state it represents a hotly contested and often capricious elevation to the privileged *élite*.

I have called the *saraki* nobility an office nobility to contrast it with the hereditary nobility of the *gitsúži*. The *saraki* ranks are, at least in theory, always open to new blood. Only one or two of the higher ranks are to-day hereditary in practice, having become the prerogative of certain families which, once established in their influential position, secured these offices for their descendants and relatives. Civil and military nobility are mutually exclusive, and are ruled by rigid pre-cedence and promotion. Promotions and first appointments are granted by the king in council with his princes and other officers of state. These ranks, unlike the *gitsú* ranks, cannot be accumulated in the same family; they are bestowed exclusively on one member of the family group, and no other close relative can claim a title or office in addition to the one already bestowed on his 'house'. Only the less rigidly defined benefits of status and economic privileges that go with the elevation to the nobility extend, to a lesser or greater extent, also to the other members of the family group. Outsiders, even commoners, who have won the favour of the king may be admitted to the nobility of the *sarakiži*. Success in war and outstanding military achievement constituted formerly the main claim to *saraki* rank. Wealth and financial influence, which, under the old system were bound up with big land ownership and the slave-trade—prerogatives of princes and noblemen—have come into their own in modern times and are demanding recognition. The granting of titles to rich traders in return for huge presents has, in fact, become a new feature in the Nupe nobility.[1] The result is that the *saraki* group em-braces people of very different origin: descendants of the old office nobility of pre-Fulani Nupe as well as families of Nupe commoners who had become partisans of the Fulani conquerors, and also strangers, Hausa, Yoruba, Fulani mercenary soldiers, or rich traders who have earned the gratitude of this or that *Etsu* Nupe. The titles themselves equally reflect the situation, new titles being frequently invented or borrowed from Hausa or Bornu.[2]

---

[1] *Etsu* Bello and *Etsu* Saidu are said to have 'sold' certain titles for prices varying from £5 to £20 to ambitious, wealthy traders; they are even reported to have conferred important state offices, offices to which the candidate was entitled by birth and standing, such as the office of the *Alkali*, on the payment of a 'fee'.

[2] In present-day Nupe Hausa names have replaced to a large extent the original Nupe titles. The traditional Nupe name, for example, for *sarakiži* (which is a corruption of the Hausa *sarakuna*) is *agabi*, but this name is only pre-

Civil and military officers received no salary. The payment for their services took the form of a share in the booty of slaves, horses, or other property, made in the war by their household troops; of landed property and fiefs bestowed by the king upon his loyal servants; and, finally, of status and exalted social position linked with title and office. Every promotion to a higher rank, as it involved a larger measure of political influence, involved also claims to larger and more lucrative fiefs.

The *Ndeji*,' Father of the Town', is the head of the civil nobility. He is in charge of the affairs of Bida, and all reports or complaints are brought to him first. He is closest to the king, always about his person, the most powerful of all the officers of state because he 'has the king's ear'. He and the other civil rank-holders are the *shawraciži nya minîn*, the Councillors of the Inner House, so called because they hold their daily *nkó* (council) with the king himself.

The *ena 'kü*, a creation of the kingdom, has no parallel in the village organization. Service in the war, open to every man in Nupe, nobleman or commoner, is compulsory for this class of professional soldiers. The 'war-ranks' imply tasks for experts, and special responsibility for the execution of these tasks to king and commander of the army. Thus the different titles have specialized meanings: the *Maiyaki* is the General-in-Chief, the *Uban Dawaki* and *Dokoyiringi* are in command of the main body of horsemen, the *Sokyara* is in charge of the mounted vanguard, the *Ejukó* of the archers, the *Sónkali* of the foot-troops, &c. The *ena Maiyaki*, too, holds its daily *nkó*, but not in the presence of the king. They, too, receive reports about the affairs of the town, and also of the country at large; but their main work is the discussion and preparation of military expeditions.

Only for the four or five highest ranks of the civil and military nobility is the order of precedence really rigid and generally valid. The significance of the remaining ranks changes frequently; bestowed as they are by the king on individuals to whom he owes gratitude or recognition for their services, they may lose their importance under another king, who has other, new men to reward and to distinguish. On pp. 100–1 is a list of the *saraki* ranks which exist in Bida to-day. Where possible I have indicated previous ranks and promotions, and also the first appointment under one or other *Etsu*.

The *ena manži* derives its name from the fact that the judicial and religious offices which it comprises are bestowed on Mallams, men of learning and scholarship. Profound knowledge of the Mohammedan literature, which is religious and juridical in one, is the only way to these ranks which are, like all other ranks in the kingdom, bestowed by the king. But the specialized training, the very necessity of finding a man of so special an education, limits the number of possible candidates. With knowledge and scholarship the office is handed on from father to son, political influence and power of certain families do the rest, and the result is that the offices of the *Alkali*, Judge, and *Liman*, Head of the Mohammedan clergy, become hereditary almost more rigidly than

served in Patigi. Or again, the highest military rank to-day is called by the Hausa name *Maiyaki*, instead of *Somasü*, which is the old Nupe title.

the *saraki* ranks and offices. Thus the present Chief *Alkali* of Bida as well as his assistant is himself the son of an *Alkali*. The same few families supply to-day the judges for the district courts in Nupe and indeed for many courts outside Nupe country, where the reputation of Bida scholarship has found recognition. And, as a final result of this tendency to make these offices the prerogative of a small group, we find since the time of *Etsu* Mohamadu the two offices of *Liman* and *Alkali* combined in one person.[1]

The office of the *Alkali* in Bida, the highest Mohammedan judge of the kingdom, dates back to the first period of Fulani rule. Its importance and distinction is expressed in the fact that Mallam Dendo's eldest son chose for himself the office not of a temporal ruler but of judge of Nupe. Many of the men who held these offices were of great learning and outstanding ability. Some have left behind records of the history of

1. *Ranks of the Ena Ndeji*

Title	Tribal origin	Previous ranks	Biographical remarks
Ndeji	Nupe from Dibo	*Magajin Gari*	Grandfather was *Ndeji*, appointed by *Etsu* Masaba; the father had no title. To-day highest official of the N.A.; head of the Emir's council.
Nyáfyenye	Fulani	*Magajin Gari*	Father and grandfather both *Ndeji*; first appointment under Usman Zaki.
Magajin Gari	Nupe	..	Father was *Nyáfyenye* and later *Ndeji*.
Sonfadakó	,,	*Gadza*	Father had no title; his first appointment was under *Etsu* Maliki, his second under *Etsu* Mamadu.
Gadza	No holder at present, but formerly a very important title.		
Sakiwa	Fulani	..	Father was *Ndeji*, titled under Umaru Majigi.
Mamasŭ	,,	..	Father held a lower title; he himself was titled under *Etsu* Maliki.
Etsu Basa	Benu-Nupe	..	A hereditary title held in one family.
Etsu Gbari	Nupe	..	Father was *Uban Dawaki*.
Tsadza	Fulani	*Galadiman Gari*	Father and elder brother have held same title.
Ndasŭ	Hausa	..	Newly introduced title.
Galadiman Gari	Fulani	..	Father was *Gadza*; he himself was appointed under *Etsu* Bello. He became later a 'ward-head' of the modern town-administration.
Kotonkomu	Nupe	..	Father held same title.

[1] There exist two different kinds of *Liman* offices: the *Liman Ratibi*, the minister of the weekday service held in the various mosques of the town, and the *Liman Jemaa*, the minister of the Friday service, which is held in the big city mosque, in the presence of the king. In every part of the town there is a *Liman* of the first kind; but there is only one *Liman Jemaa*. And it is to this highest priestly office that we referred above.

2. Ranks of the Ena Maiyaki

Title	Tribal origin	Previous ranks	Biographical remarks
Maiyaki	Hausa	Dokoyiringi, Uban Dawaki	Father received title of *Maiyaki* in the war. To-day official of the N.A.; on the Emir's council.
Uban Dawaki	Nupe	Sokyara	Father *Maiyaki* and *Uban Dawaki*. To-day on the Bida town council.
Sokyara	,,	Wambayi	Father was *Sokyara, Uban Dawaki*, and finally *Maiyaki*. He himself was formerly on the Bida town council.
Dokoyiringi	,,	Wambayi	Father was *Uban Dawaki* and *Maiyaki*.
Ejukó	,,	Tswakoko	Father already *Ejukó*.
Sondzamitsu	,,	..	Father had no title; son got his under the late *Etsu* bȩcause of his wealth.
Sonlawu	,,	Sarkin Barayi	Father had no title; son received his in the war.
Sarkin Barayi	Hausa	..	Father was *Maiyaki*.
Tswakoko	Nupe	..	Father was *Nagun*.
Nagun	,,	..	Father was made *Nagun* in the war.
Saganuwa	Hausa	..	This title is hereditary in one family, followers of the Hausa general and relative (by marriage) of Manko, Handi Boshi.
Wambayi	,,	..	Father was a serf (*bara*) of *Etsu* Abubakari.
Sanaji	Nupe	..	..
Galadiman Masŭ	Komú-Yo-ruba	..	Held in Bida now instead of the old Nupe title *Somasŭ* (the Nupe equivalent of *Maiyaki*), but is to-day a very small and unimportant title.
Luci	Nupe	..	Formerly a powerful man; lives to-day on a farm in Trans-Kaduna.
Rwafi	Hausa	..	An hereditary title, held by relatives of the Hausa general of Manko, Handi Boshi.
Sonfadákwa	Nupe	..	..
Barixe	,,	..	Father was *Sojetsu*.
Sojetsu	,,	..	Received title from *Etsu* Bello; rich landowner.
Magayaki	,,	..	Received title in the war, under *Etsu* Maliki.
Songubi	,,	..	..
Sónkali	,,	..	..
Manlawo	,,	..	..
Mamasŭ	,,	..	Father was *Sonlawu*, a title which he received in the war.

Nupe. The judicial organization of the kingdom left them free hand to interpret and apply, even to alter and create laws. The names of past *Alkalai* are known to everybody, and are associated with certain new laws or special judicial practices. Of this aspect of their activity we shall hear more at a later stage. But one point (already mentioned) must be stressed here. The office of *Liman* and *Alkali* could become hereditary; many judges and Mohammedan scholars are of Fulani stock; but this reflects only the political influence and partly also the tradition of learning in these families. As representatives of Mohammedan scholarship *Liman* and *Alkali* are only the most exalted exponents of a professional class which comprises men of every status and birth—the Mallams, 'learned men', who are held in high esteem by everyone. Even without rank or title, when of little and insignificant learning, they are placed above the ordinary commoner. They may marry the daughters and sisters of the high-born. The *Etsu* himself, descendant of a Mallam, puts a 'Mallam' before his name. Like his ancestors he honours and receives at his court all Mallams of reputation. They are a class between the classes, a mobile, privileged intelligentsia.

The description of the hierarchy of Nupe kingdom is incomplete without the mention of a last group of minor rank-holders, composed of the heads of the Bida craft-guilds. The guilds are closed occupational groups, the members of which live together in one locality and practise certain hereditary crafts such as glass-making, brasswork, weaving, &c.[1] The guild-heads receive their titles, together with the usual gift of a turban, from the *Etsu*. Though low down in the scale of ranks, they have yet an official standing, and are raised above the ordinary commoner and peasant. Their headship implies authority over all the members of their craft in town and village. Formerly the guild-heads received a small annual tribute of products of their craft from their fellow craftsmen. Like the members of the nobility, the titled guild-heads are summoned to the *Etsu*'s Council at the *Sallah*, the great Mohammedan festival; and, like the privileged nobility, they are exempted from taxation. Their only tribute takes the form of an annual gift—an *emisa*, or 'salute'— again of products of their craft, the cost of which is borne jointly by the whole guild, and which is presented to the *Etsu* at the *Sallah*.

Certain craft-guilds are linked with the dynastic division of the capital and are divided into three sections each of which resides in a different *ekpã*. The groups of craftsmen also bear more special allegiance to the royal house in whose *ekpã* they live and with the ancestor of which they associate their coming to Bida and the foundation of their guild. But over and above this party allegiance guilds and guild-sections are closely linked with the ruling king·of Nupe. For the king and the court represent the most important customers of the Bida craftsmen. All orders which the court intends to place are given through the guild-head, who guarantees their execution and acts as an official 'controller' of his group of craftsmen.

A position similar to that held by the guild-heads is also assigned to the head of the Bida brokers, the *Etsu Dilali*, who again plays the part of an agent of the king in all matters concerning commerce and trade in the capital.

[1] The organization of the Bida craft-guilds will be described in more detail in Chapter xiv.

We shall see later that the explanation of this incorporation of artisans and brokers in the rigid bureaucracy of the kingdom lies in the control which the state exercises over crafts and merchandise; only by means of a control of this kind could the head of this warlike state secure an unimpeded supply of the commodities that were vital to the court and the state: arms, clothes, and saddles for the soldiers, food for the huge capital, and the luxuries that were needed for the display of royal power and wealth. We find convincing evidence for this interpretation in the fact that the different crafts are not of equal standing. Some rank higher than others, and this grading is not correlated with economic success: the very prosperous butchers are last on this list, blacksmiths and brasssmiths, on the other hand, head the list, 'for they are makers of arms'. Only the glass-makers, a strongly independent and important craft, stand aloof from this order of craft-guilds. This is a list of the craft-guilds in Bida, with the titles of the guild-heads, arranged in order of precedence.

The figure in brackets shows the number of *ekpā* in which they live. The titles of the guild-heads are given in italics.

Brassworkers (2): *Muku.*
Blacksmiths (3): *Dokodza.*
Carpenters and Builders (1): *Egbaba.*
Barber-Doctors (3): *Sokyara.*
Beadworkers (2): *Majĩ Lantana.*
Leatherworkers (scattered in the town): formerly *Majĩ Kimpa.*
Weavers (3): *Leshe, Majĩ, Ndakó.*
Butchers (3): *Sonfawa.*
Glass-makers (1): *Masagá.*

SLAVERY

The lowest in the complex order of social classes in Nupe are the slaves (*wuži*, as against *egi*, freeman, lit. child). But in this one class there are shades and distinctions of social status. Some slaves have risen to positions of wealth and influence. Others have remained menial workers in the households and on the farms of their masters. Pre-British Nupe numbered its slaves by the thousands. Twenty to thirty slaves was a moderate average for the household of a man of consequence. The prosperous craftsmen of Bida town, blacksmiths and weavers, always had slaves to work for them; even in villages one found households with one or two slaves.

The people of Nupe obtained their slaves by two methods: first, there were the slaves captured in the war, who became the property of the man to whose share in the booty they had fallen; and second, there were slaves bought in the markets of Bida.[1] The majority of the latter, it seems, were slaves sold by their captors—noblemen who had taken more slaves than they needed for their household. Slaves were also sold abroad, mostly to the south. Many Nupe men of rank were engaged in

[1] Lander reports that 200 slaves were on sale in the market of Rabá, the then capital of Nupe (op. cit. iii, p. 313).

professional slave-trading; they acted as middlemen between the slave markets of the north, Kano, Katsina, and others, and the buyers in the south, on the river and coast.[1]

At the time of the Fulani conquest the price paid locally for an able-bodied male slave was 40,000 cowries, i.e. £1, and for a female slave 50,000 cowries, i.e. £1. 5s.[2] The price of slaves rose very high in later times. Shortly before the British occupation it had reached the sum of £7 for male, and £7. 10s. for female slaves. As my inquiries from various informants showed, this price had become almost standardized in the last decade before the British occupation and was valid throughout the country. It is interesting to note that this rise in price took place at a time when the largest market for slaves from Nupe was disappearing, shipments of slaves to countries overseas, especially to the Americas, having come to an end. We cannot say how this rise in price started, nor what might have been its cause. I can only suggest that it was due to increased difficulties of supply. Half a century of wars and raids had denuded the country of people who could with no great difficulty be made slaves. Slave-raiders were forced to obtain their human chattels in more distant areas and by more serious warfare—in the language of the economist, under conditions of higher 'cost'. Whatever the cause, this rise in price meant that the commoners and peasants of Nupe could derive from the wars and raids by which their rulers gained their fortunes not even the benefit of cheaper slave labour. Commoners and peasants would suffer when their country was defeated and their villages invaded by the enemy, or when, in civil wars, rival troops fought on their land. But the fruits of victory—rich booty in slaves—they could share only at a price: the same price which foreigners had to pay when buying slaves from Nupe in the open market.

Slaves were, in the strict sense of the word, the property of their masters. If anyone killed a slave belonging to somebody else this was not regarded as a case of murder or manslaughter, but only as an offence demanding restitution of the 'destroyed' property, i.e. the full purchase price had to be paid over to the owner. But the slaves who were kept in the houses of the Nupe nobility were on the whole well treated. The master of a slave was quite within his rights if he chose to maltreat him, sell him again, or even kill him. But there is no doubt that this happened rarely—if ever. Many slaves, in fact, preferred to stay on in the houses of their ex-masters when slavery was abolished, in the position of an unpaid servant or retainer, rather than to start life on their own, especially if they were of advanced age. Custom even guaranteed the

[1] Barth states that most of the slaves from Kano were carried by small caravans to Bornu and Nupe; 'the best of slaves now go to Niffee (Nupe) to be there shipped for America. . . . Slaves are sent from Zinder to Niffee. Indeed it now appears that all this part of Africa is put under contribution to supply the South American market with slaves' (Dr. Barth, op. cit. ii, pp. 132 and 135). Lander mentions that the slaves brought to Rabá were purchased by southern peoples, traded down the Niger, and from there 'delivered from hand to hand till they at length reached the sea' (op. cit. ii, p. 298).
[2] See Schoen-Crowther, *Journals*, p. 194, and J. and R. Lander, op. cit. ii, p. 298.

slaves a not inconsiderable measure of economic and social independence. An adult male slave would work for his master in the same way as sons and junior relations work for the head of the household. If he was put to farm-work, he would be given a small plot of his own to cultivate in his spare time. Or if he helped his master in a craft or in trade he would be able to count on a regular commission. Other slaves, who made good soldiers, were put into their master's private army, in which they would serve as foot-soldiers, armed and equipped at their master's expense. In the wars they would have their share of the booty. Slaves could thus acquire property, and the more fortunate owned horses, sheep, cattle, money—even slaves of their own. But when they died their property fell not to their wives and children but to their master.[1] Female slaves became personal servants of their mistresses or possibly concubines of their master. Unlike the male slaves they had no income of their own; what they might earn—by handicrafts or trade—would be their master's property.

Frequently the master would have to find wives for his male slaves; he would buy either a slave girl from the market, or possibly a girl belonging to another master—a slave girl to whom his own slave may have lost his heart. In the latter case a very reduced price would be paid, but the children would belong to the owner of the girl. But a slave might make money enough during his service to pay the bride-price for a free woman —mostly a widow, for whom a low bride-price is paid. In such marriages the free wife would in no way share the conditions of slavery, she would have her own house and work (a farm or trade) and might in due course be able to ransom her husband. Or a slave who had done well might be able to buy his own and his children's liberty. In this case he had to pay the full purchase price, except in the case of very old slaves who were no longer good for work—they would be released for half the amount. But if the offer to ransom a slave came from the slave's (free) relations, the owner would ask an exorbitant price, up to £20 or £30. Very rarely would a master let a slave free without the payment of the ransom, for example, as reward for faithful service. In all these cases the slave would bring two men as witnesses of the act of manumission.

A slave girl often became the wife of a free man—her own master or another man who bought her from her master, the purchase price replacing in this case the usual bride-price. This was not, however, real marriage; the slave girls became only concubines, not wives, and no religious or legal ceremony accompanied the marriage. Once they had borne their 'husband' a child, both mother and child became automatically free (though the status of a concubine remained unchanged). The families of the Fulani nobility count an innumerable offspring from this type of concubinage.

Children born of a free father and a slave mother were thus free

---

[1] To-day, more than thirty years after the abolition of slavery, this rule still holds in a modified form, with respect to ex-slaves who die without issue. In a court case heard before the Chief *Alkali* in Bida in 1936 the considerable property (cattle) of an ex-slave who had died without heirs was thus awarded to the son of his ex-master.

themselves; so were children born of a slave father who married a free woman, and also of a slave father who bought a girl slave for himself and married her. If, however, slave married slave, the marriage being arranged—i.e. the purchase price for the girl paid—by the slave's master, the children remained slaves. But these slaves in the second generation were slaves of a different kind. They were no longer called *wuži*, but *mangi*, 'born as child' (i.e. as freeman). Though not really free they were exempted from many of the disabilities of slavery. The children of a *mangi* who married another *mangi* were themselves *mangi* slaves again. But a *mangi* could not be sold by his master, nor could he be maltreated or killed—in the latter case his parents could obtain legal redress and would be paid the usual purchase price as 'blood-money' At the death of a *mangi* only half of his property could be claimed by the master, the other half was inherited by his own family. The *mangi* also had family farms of their own, and were generally treated like full members of the household in everything except that they were not entitled to any share in the inheritance of their master's property. A *mangi* was brought up together with the children of the house, was given the same education, and, like the sons of the house, served in the mounted household troops. Many *mangi* would free themselves, or at least marry free women. But the names of these house-born slaves invariably betrayed their origin; for they were named by their masters, and given not the usual Nupe names but names made up of some well-known blessing formula, of the first words of a proverb, and such like, for example: Adetsua, from *a de 'tsu à sei Sokó*, 'there is no Lord but God'; Barsu, from *bar su ga Allah* (Hausa), 'leave them to God'.

It would be wrong, however, to assume that slavery in Nupe carried with it a stigma. True, the people of Bida still speak with contempt of the 'pagans' and 'slaves' (the two terms are almost synonymous) into whose countries their fathers had carried their profitable raids. But, characteristically for Nupe, the stigma attaches to the humble status rather than to the misfortune of having been made a slave. It disappeared with the signs of success and prosperity, open to slaves as to anyone. The wretched slave who could never rise above a menial labourer had to bear the ignominy of his position. But in the case of the trusted slave in a noble household, and above all the successful, freed slave, the taint of slavery meant little more than, in their own words, 'luck of war'. Slaves who served in the houses of the high nobility did indeed share some of the splendour that surrounded the position of their masters. Able and faithful slaves were rewarded with the position of head slaves, overseers, bailiffs; their masters bestowed upon them rich presents and gifts of land—more land than they cared to work with their own hands, having become men of wealth and importance. Their masters bestowed upon them, above all, special titles, household ranks— the ubiquitous symbol of social rise in Nupe, which in this case obliterated even the last external symbol of slave status, the typical slave-names.

The royal houses of Nupe, like every nobleman's house, had their host of slaves: slaves for menial work—in the house and on the land—as well as the titled slaves of respected position. At the court this latter group of slaves formed the *ena wuži*, the Order of Court Slaves, a distinguished slave *élite* into which only few selected slaves could ever hope to be admitted. From the slaves captured in war those of high birth and status, chiefs or distinguished warriors, were selected for the court. These, too, were given ranks and titles, and could rise high in the service of the king. Theirs was the specialized service of officials and trusted royal agents. There were those who looked after the king's vast household; those who were in charge of the *Etsu* Nupe's no less imposing harem—both offices formerly entrusted to eunuchs.[1] Other slaves formed the king's bodyguard and police force; they were provincial delegates, tax collectors, trusted messengers, 'liaison officers' between the king's palace and the houses of his noblemen, and between the king and the army in the field. These slaves, like the other rank-holders, owned land and held fiefs. The Nupe kings in Rabá are said to have had only four titled court slaves; the slave ranks that existed at the court of Bida some thirty years ago (and the ranks still exist, although their holders are no longer slaves) were more than three times that number. Under *Etsu* Maliki, one of the last independent kings of Nupe, the most responsible state offices were taken from royal princes and *sarakiži* and entrusted to slaves. The position of the slaves as officers of state thus seems to have overshadowed more and more all other state ranks. Slave ranks were ranks bestowed *ad personam*, and ranks bestowed by the king personally, independent of the council of princes and ministers; and this gives us the explanation for their rise in importance. The offices linked with civil and military rank also depended to some extent on the personal favour of the king. But once appointed, these men stayed on, servants of the kingdom rather than of the king. They had behind them the claims of powerful families, they were exponents of political factions, and could play on that 'balance of power' between the dynasties. The slaves were personal servants in the full sense of the word. They were brought into office, not by family claims or promotion or a rigid rule of succession, but by personal appointment, selection, and trial. They were bound to the king's service generation after generation, by the strongest bond: their position of unfree men. It frequently happened that a new *Etsu* took over the slaves who had served his predecessor and left them their ranks and possessions. The rise of the slave officials at the Fulani court is the counterpart of the rise of a powerful, dangerously independent feudal nobility.

The following is a list of slave ranks held to-day, not by slaves, but by former slaves or descendants of slaves at the court of the *Etsu* Nupe. I have again tried to indicate in what manner they received their title, and also in certain cases the office which some of them are holding to-day in the Bida Town Administration. That so many of these former slaves

---

[1] In the pre-Fulani kingdom the court is said to have employed only a few slaves—all eunuchs. All slave ranks which have a *nda* in their title, meaning 'father' (ranks that are still in use—see attached chart), were originally ranks reserved for eunuchs.

had been placed in responsible positions proves what I have said about the selection and rise of slave officials at the court of Bida.

Slave Ranks

Title	Tribal origin	Present office	Biographical remarks
Gabi Seidi	Kupa	'Officer of Liaison' between Etsu and District Officer	A rich slave who under Etsu Bello bought his title for £16.
Ndatwakí	Yagba	On the Bida Town Council	Father was Ndatwakí under Etsu Maliki; he himself received the same title under Etsu Bello.
Dzwoáfu	,,	,, ,,	An hereditary slave title, first granted under Etsu Usman.
Ndamáraki	Bunu	,, ,,	Father was Ndamáraki under Etsu Masaba.
Sántali	Benu-Nupe	..	Grandfather was a slave of Usman Zaki; they remained slaves of this house.
Masántali	Yagba	..	Grandfather was a slave of Etsu Umaru Majigi; they remained slaves of this house.
Swajiyá' tsu	,,	..	Father held same slave rank.
Ndatódo	,,	..	Father held the same title and also title of Ndamáraki.
Manfáda	,,	..	Another slave title which has become hereditary in one house.
Sonmáži	Kusopa-Nupe	..	Id.
Ndádari	Nupe	..	Id.
Shangbo	Nupe from Rabá	..	Father was a saraki (Somasū) of Etsu Majiya. He was made prisoner in the war and became a slave of Etsu Masaba.
(Sarkin Dogari	Hausa	Head of police force	To-day not regarded as slave title. Formerly bestowed on a personal slave of the ruling king.)

WAR

It will be understood that this description is based entirely on information and the historical recollections of informants. However, the wars that were fought in Nupe and by the Nupe are not so far distant that there are no longer eyewitnesses left, or people who have themselves borne arms in these wars. Thus information could be checked and cross-checked. For certain details I could, moreover, count on most authoritative informants, who had played a leading part in the last wars of the kingdom; the description of the military organization, for example, is based on information obtained from the late commander of the *élite* troops of Nupe, the king's bodyguard.

War was essentially a concern of the Nupe state. No warfare or organized fights occurred between the villages or tribal sections of the country.[1] But villages and tribal sections were frequently involved in the wars of the kingdom, either themselves causing wars by rebelling against the central government, or being forced to take sides in the wars which the kingdom waged against other groups. Thus the Beni and Gbedegi sided with Bida against the rebellious Kusopa, and again in the Kyedye war, while other tribal sections, such as the riverain Bataci, Kupa, and Ebagi, came to the aid of the Kyedye. In the later times of the kingdom, to which my records chiefly refer, the wars were indeed largely caused by internal disturbances and were directed against rebellious provinces or feudal lords—being reconquests rather than conquests. Historical records mention ten major wars in the thirty years that preceded the British conquest, between 1864 and 1895. Most of these wars are still vividly remembered, and old men would even recall characteristic incidents in the various campaigns. My informants, not unnaturally, greatly extolled the soldierly virtues of the Nupe people. But there is also Barth's testimony that the Nupe army, especially the cavalry, was well known in the Hausa states.[2] Twice, in fact, (in 1880) the Nupe were called to Hausa to help their allies, the Emirs of Kontagora and Gwandu, to put down rebellions in their countries.

The Nupe army was comparatively loosely organized. It possessed only a small nucleus of regular troops, represented in the king's bodyguard; the rest of the army consisted of levies of slaves, volunteers, and mercenary soldiers, raised by the houses of the feudal nobility. But these household troops, too, were largely composed of trained and experienced soldiers.

The king's bodyguard comprised both infantry and cavalry. The foot-soldiers, called *dogari nya dakári* (i.e. 'guards on foot'), were equipped with guns or bows and arrows, and were under the command of the *Etsu Dogari*. The troops who carried guns were mostly slaves, the sons of slaves from the king's household, the others were free men, mercenary soldiers—among them many foreigners, from Hausa, Bornu, and Yoruba—who had taken service under the *Etsu* Nupe. Under *Etsu* Maliki this royal bodyguard numbered 80 men. The royal horse troops, a slightly larger group, were called *lefidi*, after the cotton-wool armour which they wore. Their weapons were swords, spears, and big leather shields. They were commanded by the *Etsu Lefidi* (who was also called *Zarmi*). One of my informants for the present description was the *Etsu Lefidi* of the royal house of Usman Zaki. He was of Hausa origin, a freed slave and the son of an *Etsu Lefidi* who had served under Usman Zaki himself. The horse troops were composed again of slaves and mercenary soldiers. The slaves who served in the royal cavalry were the sons of titled slaves, every court slave of rank having to send one of his sons into the *Etsu*'s bodyguard, and the volunteers were all foreigners. In the reign of *Etsu* Maliki the *lefidi* numbered 100 men.

The troops which were contributed by the various houses of the

---

[1] The only exception was the warlike Kyedye sub-tribe.
[2] Barth, op. cit. iv, p. 545. Lander reports that Mallam Dendo could 'command 1,000 horsemen, well equipped, and an uncountable number of foot-soldiers' (op. cit. ii, p. 296).

nobility were of three categories: ordinary foot-soldiers, called *dakári*, foot-troops carrying guns, or *bindigacizí*, and horsemen, or *dokocizí*. The *dakári* were composed entirely of volunteers, i.e. men who had entered the service of a feudal lord as soldier-*bara* or 'clients'.[1] They were all young men, and their ranks comprised peasants and townsmen, Nupe as well as foreigners. Every noble household had its own *Etsu Dakári*, Chief of the Foot-Troops, a *bara* of higher rank, who was in charge of these volunteers and responsible for their training. The *dakári* wore a sort of leather apron, called *walké*, and caps, and were equipped with shields and bows and arrows or spears. The troops which carried guns were, like the king's bodyguard, slaves. The cavalry represented the *élite* of the Nupe army. It was composed of senior *bara*—men whose sons might be fighting in the foot-troops—and younger relations, sons and brothers, of the feudal lord himself. The horsemen wore short shirts of strong coarse material, called *ewogí*, i.e. small gown, into which leather amulets were sewn, caps or turbans, and, over the *ewogí*, a *sulke*, a chain mail. They carried shields, swords, and spears. In the Kyedye war certain feudal lords could muster the following troops: the *Kusódu* 100 foot-soldiers, 200 guns, and 200 horses; the *Kpotu* 100 foot-soldiers, 100 guns, and 20 horses; the *Ndeji* 100 foot-soldiers, 200 guns, and 10 horses; the *Benú* 50 foot-soldiers, 50 guns, and 20 horses; the *Waziri* 50 foot-soldiers and 5 horses. Many of the feudal lords—princes and civil nobility—would themselves join the army at the head of their household troops; but they would have to place themselves under the command of the 'professional soldiers'—the military nobility—who would join the troops in a body.

Warfare in Nupe possessed its etiquette, its conventions, and rules, which show how highly developed and specialized a technique it had become. Two kinds of war are distinguished: the great wars planned and organized by the central government, and smaller raids and military expeditions carried out by individual feudal lords. In the latter case, the feudal lord would request the permission of the *Etsu* for undertaking a campaign against this or that village or tribe. Without the sanction of the king his military expedition would amount to *cin amana*, a breach of the peace (lit.: devouring friendship), and might itself become the cause of a punitive expedition sent out by the central government. In the 'real' war, before hostilities are opened, a messenger of the king, called *kuru*, is sent to the enemy's camp to deliver the 'ultimatum', that is, to inform the enemy of certain demands of the kingdom the rejection of which would be followed by war. A titled royal slave of high rank acts as messenger. His person is inviolable—in theory; but during the Kusopa revolt three royal messengers were killed, one after the other, by the rebellious tribesmen. The next step is the appointment of a commander-in-chief of the armies, in the person of a royal prince who will then be known as *Nna 'Kũ*, Mother of War.[2] Sometimes soothsayers and Mallams are

---

[1] For the definition of *bara* and 'client' see p. 123.

[2] Owing to erroneous information I have mentioned this title as *Nda 'Kũ*, Father of War, in a previous publication (*Africa*, 1935). I must add that I was unable to obtain any explanation of this rather surprising matrimonial touch.

asked to divine a victorious general. Invariably his rank would correspond to the importance and scope of the war that is planned. At the same time his office is only nominal. Although he would take the field at the head of the army, and although he would bear the responsibility for success or failure, the actual organization of the campaign is left to the professional soldiers: in an important war the *Maiyaki* himself would take command, in a minor war his next in rank, the *Dokoyiringi*.

Now the council of war meets in the house of the *Maiyaki* to discuss the question of raising the levies. The various feudal lords are informed that they are expected to produce so many guns and horses. Preparations take one or two months—the troops must be raised, recruits trained and equipped, and food supplies provided for the campaign. Finally diviners and Mallams are summoned again by the commander of the army to decide on a propitious day. On the appointed day, drummers and trumpeters sound the assembly, and the troops leave Bida on their march into enemy country.

The Nupe never fought by night. Their method was to move up as close as possible to the enemy, hiding in bush and scrub, camp for the night, and attack in the early hours of the morning. In open battle the attacking troops would be arrayed in a long straight line facing the enemy. But often the war would turn into the long siege of a walled village or town, close to which the army would put up its war camp, the troops surrounding the town and cutting the population off from their farms, supplies, and reinforcements.

This was the typical formation of the Nupe army in open battle: first came the foot-soldiers, the various household troops each under their *Etsu Dakári*, commanded by an officer of the king, the *Sónkali*. Behind them, at a distance of a quarter of a mile, a first troop of horsemen halted, under the *Sokyara*, and with it the lesser military and civil nobility. Behind this group again another, larger, detachment of cavalry was posted, under the highest generals of the army, the *Uban Dawaki* and *Dokoyiringi*. With these troops were the higher civil and military nobility and certain princes of lesser rank. The infantry would move first, sent into the battle by the shouts of the *Sokyara*: 'Kay Dakári', 'Forward! foot-soldiers'. When they had engaged the enemy, the cavalry of the *Sokyara* would charge after them, the *Dokoyiringi* giving the signal with shouts of 'Kay Sokyara'. The *Dokoyiringi*'s own troops would charge last, to the signals of the long bronze trumpets which only the troops of the highest military ranks may carry. There would also be drums and flutes, and the soldiers would shout the *kirari* of their leaders and sing their war songs.

In the rear of the troops the reserve was placed, which would come into the fight only if the other troops were unable to master the situation. It was commanded by the *Maiyaki*, with whom were also the princes of highest rank, including the commander-in-chief. In the last big war, against the Yagba (the same war which ended in the conquest of Bida by the British), the infantry is said to have numbered 6,000, the cavalry of the *Sokyara* 400, those of the *Dokoyiringi* 1,000, and the reserve 2,000 men.

An unsuccessful army would never retreat, or return to Bida with the goal unachieved. One would call for reinforcements from the capital, which would be sent out together with a new *Nna 'Kŭ* to replace the unsuccessful commander-in-chief. If these troops too were unable to bring the war to an end, the *Etsu* would take command personally, at the head of a third army composed largely of his own bodyguard and of the household troops of noblemen who had not joined the troops previously. During the king's absence from the capital a regency council, headed by the *Ndeji*, would be appointed to look after things at home. In the Yagba war the *Etsu* did not join the army but stayed behind, with his body-guard of 200 men, which, together with the household troops of four noblemen who had remained in Bida, were the only trained soldiers to oppose the British attack. The king and the noblemen of high rank took the field accompanied by their whole household staff of slaves and servants, and often by their wives as well. They stayed in the Great Camp—consisting of huts of grass and matting—which was put up behind the fighting line or established in a hamlet near-by. A number of Nupe villages betray by their names that at one time the Great War Camp, *edokó*, had stood on their site.

The Nupe war was carried on till the capital of the enemy, that is, the village or walled town in which the chief resided, was captured. If the chief and the other leaders fled, they would be pursued until they were captured or until further pursuit became impossible. Often a fugitive chief sought refuge with the king of a neighbouring country whose territory the Nupe troops would have to respect. All captured places were looted and burnt, and the whole enemy country devastated. But slaughter was avoided as far as possible—the defeated enemies were more valuable alive, to be sold later as slaves. Only when rebellions had to be put down by force of war the enemies, above all chiefs and leaders, would be killed mercilessly, either in the battle, or later in Bida, whither they were taken to be executed.

No less well defined than the etiquette of warfare were the rules and conventions governing the economic aspect of the Nupe wars—the division of loot and booty. All booty taken before the decisive battle—the capture of the enemy's capital—belonged to the king and was dis-patched to him immediately. Upon the capture of the town *wasóso* was declared, free looting, in which everyone who fought in the battle could join. The shares in the spoils of war varied according to rank and position. The slave soldiers had to deliver everything to their masters but were rewarded with a small share in the booty they had taken. The *bara* soldiers could keep all booty in kind—(called *dukiya*, wealth)—but were expected to present some of it to their overlords as 'gift of thanks'; of the slaves whom they captured they had to surrender half the number to their overlords. The independent fighters, i.e. the sons of noble houses, kept whatever they captured, both 'wealth' and slaves, except for a voluntary gift to the head of the house. If I have at various occasions in this book called war in Nupe a profession and a source of income, these facts substantiate that view.

Let me conclude this description with the report of an eyewitness of standing—the youngest son of *Etsu* Masaba—who had fought in one of the last great wars of old Nupe, against the Kyedye. I have referred before to the origin of this war. It was the answer of the central government to the capture by the rebellious Kyedye of the town Kacha, which, having submitted to Fulani rule, appealed to Bida for protection against their unruly fellow tribesmen. It was, incidentally, also the last war in which the Niger Company assisted the Bida government. In the next war Niger Company troops were to turn against the Fulani, and (helped by the same Kyedye) to defeat the armies of the kingdom.

Since the time of Manko, *goy* and Kyedye were always at war. It happened like this. The Kyedye refused to recognize the Fulani kings. They contended. that they were independent 'kings of the water'. So Manko sent his son Ibrahima from Raba to the *Kuta*, to come to an arrangement and to stop hostilities. But the Kyedye killed the messenger, cut his body to pieces, and threw it to the fish. Thereupon Manko went to fight them, but could not do much. So the wars between the two went on and on.

Later, at the time of *Etsu* Umaru, the Kyedye attacked Kacha under their *Kuta* Usman, because Kacha had submitted to the Fulani and accepted their *egba* (delegate). The Kacha people fled to Bida and asked for help. *Etsu* Umaru sent out a big army led by *Shaba* Mamudu. Most of the *gitsúži* went with him, and I was among them, also many *sarakiži* both from the *ena Maiyaki* and *ena Ndeji*. We were three days on the way, stopping twice for the night (Kacha is about 40 miles from Bida). We made camps of grass huts; some of us lived in a *tunga* near-by. For the great men we built huts with grass fences round. The army had guns and men and horses—you could not count them. In Kacha the water was covered with Kyedye canoes. We attacked at once, shooting from the banks down upon the canoes in the water. The boats of the Niger Company were helping the Fulani then. They closed the Kacha river in the back of the Kyedye. The Kyedye fled, and we crossed the river in canoes which they had left behind. The *Dokoyiringi* led the pursuit, accompanied by *Shaba* Mamudu. The rest of the troops followed later. We pursued the Kyedye on the other bank, both on land and water, for three days, as far as Lafiagi and Shonga. This was a war not only against the Kyedye, but also against Kupa and Ebagi, who were helping the Kyedye. All villages and hamlets were burnt down, numberless men and women captured. We made more than 2,000 slaves. Later they were all sold (although the Niger Company had asked for the release of the prisoners of war). At Shonga the war ended. Many Kyedye had been run down and captured or killed, but some hid in the creeks and the river forest. The chief and the seven elders of the Kyedye fled with their wives and children to Ilorin. It did not help them. Emir Aliyu (the Fulani Emir of Ilorin) sent them back as prisoners co Bida. Here they were held as hostages till *Etsu* Umaru's death. But shortly after his death *Etsu* Maliki condemned them to death, and they were strangled secretly at night in the houses where they lived.

In war, which is political action *par excellence*, the essence of state structure must reveal itself most clearly. We observe what we have recognized as an element of state organization: the monopoly position of the ruling group with regard to the employment of the political machinery, in this case military action. We see, too, that this monopoly of control is vested in the ruling group *corporately*: its individual members, though they control severally the executive side of the political machinery, can only use it subject to the agreement of the administration as a whole (of which they form part), else the military machinery is directed against them as breakers of the 'king's peace'. Finally, wars are planned and the military machinery is set in motion by the ruling group as a *representative* group, that is, on behalf of the country at large. In wars against outside enemies the interests of the country and the people are perforce identified with the interests of the ruling group—expansion, conquest, or the destruction of a rival power. But in wars waged against internal enemies—rebellious sections or dangerously independent members of the government—the military action is taken as much in the interest of the ruling group (safeguarding, above all, the revenue) as in the interest of the state and the people in that it re-establishes order and public security. Thus in the Kacha war, referred to above, the ruling group, as the representative group of the state, protected one subject group against abuses by another. The government can take sides and place the political machinery at the support of one section against another only because it is vested in a group (as I put it in a previous section) raised above the heterogeneous component sections of the state. The monopoly control over the machinery of force thus reveals its twofold significance: as a privilege or prerogative, in the sense that it can be used (in war proper) for conquests and expansion, thus serving the specific interests of the ruling group; and as a constitutional duty, in the sense of being used internally, for the purpose of maintaining the 'king's peace'.

These two functions are not, however, securely balanced, and we shall discover the effects of this unstable equilibrium in the internal administration of the country, to the description of which we must now turn.

CHAPTER VIII
POLITICAL HISTORY OF NUPE KINGDOM
(continued)

THE FEUDAL STATE

WE have seen how in the history of the kingdom a certain territorial nucleus evolved, an area of 'Nupe proper'. This concept of a territorial 'nucleus' also forms the basis of the division of the country for the purpose of government. For the purposes of political, judicial, and tax administration the kingdom was divided into four zones. First, the area of the conquered tributary countries outside the boundaries of the 'kingdom proper', in Nupe terminology, the countries of the *zaži kati*, the 'Outside Peoples'. Second, within these boundaries, an innermost core, the countries of Beni and Kyedye; having formed the nucleus of the rising kingdom they are now assigned the privileged position of royal domains. The third zone comprised the wider 'ring' of remaining towns and districts of the kingdom, most of which lie in Trans-Kaduna. Bida town, the seat of the central government, formed an administrative district of its own.

Under the name of Outside Peoples were comprised the conquered territories of Gbari, Gbira, Kamberi, Kakanda, Yagba, Bunu, and certain sections of Nupe (Dibo and Ebe mostly). These districts were not administered fully by the central government. Their political dependence entailed two things: an annual tribute to Bida, and the recognition by other Emirates and chieftainships of the political status of these territories as 'under the protection' of Bida. It was a one-sided 'protection': Bida itself was free to raid her own outside peoples, but no other country could do this or levy taxes in these territories with impunity. The guarantor of these 'treaties' was, in the last instance, the Emir of Gwandu, the highest feudal overlord of all Fulani Emirs in this part of the world.[1] The central government in Bida did not assume jurisdiction over these countries, nor did it interfere in their own political administration. The tribute was paid in slaves and was collected annually by royal messengers, *tuci*, or as they were also called *ajele* (from the Arabic *ajala*, to dispatch), who visited these countries at the head of small armies, ready to quell any disturbance or to bring recalcitrant tax-payers to heel. Of the tribute levied a little more than half went to the king, the rest to the royal messenger. The office of tax-collector in the outside areas of the kingdom was entrusted mostly to the royal nobility, and the districts over which they were put in charge were linked with

---

[1] Such an 'international' agreement existed, for example, between the *Etsu* Nupe, the *Sarkin Sudan* (the Emir of Kontagora), and the Emir of Zaria with respect to Gbari country. These treaties were not always kept by the parties concerned. Thus the *Etsu* of Agaie used to raid the territories of his brother Emir, the *Etsu* Nupe, and had eventually to be stopped by a big war which was led by the Emir of Gwandu himself.

certain ranks. Thus *Edukpã*, the Countries beyond the Niger, were always the province of the *Nágya*, the country of the Kamberi of the *Kusódu*, of the Gbari of the *Etsu Gbari*, of the Yagba of the *Makũ*, and so on. Political influence, however, could alter the rule, and a rich district would sometimes go to the more powerful royal prince irrespective of his rank. Thus *Etsu* Maliki, to win over the powerful *Kpotũ* Abubakari (who became *Etsu* after Maliki's death) transferred the rich fief of *Edukpã* from the *Nágya* to him. Power and the possession of a strong private army was essential for the post of an *ajele*. An *ajele* who failed in his task was dismissed from rank and office and replaced by a 'stronger' man.

It is no accident that the two royal domains of Nupe kingdom were the two political organizations which embraced the whole tribe, the two small 'states within the State', Beni and Kyedye. The political unification which they had evolved was recognized and utilized by the political administration of the kingdom. These areas were placed directly under the king. The chiefs of Beni and Kyedye acted somewhat as royal agents. Their appointment and succession was subject to the confirmation of the king, and a gift of sandals, a gown, and a turban which he presented to the new *Žitsu* symbolized, as we have seen, the fact that the local chief held his office 'by the grace of the king'. The town-kings of Beni and the *Kuta* of the Kyedye administered law in all cases which came under the category of *gyara*, 'reparation', and were required to refer graver cases, cases involving *sheri'a*, 'judgement', to the central authority—a point to which we shall return later. The town-kings also collected the tax in their areas on behalf of the king. This tax, *edu*, levied in these areas as in the whole kingdom, was in money, thus differing from the *dzanká*, the local tithe in kind. The tax was collected first by the head chief of the district, i.e. the *Kuta* among the Kyedye, and the town-king of Tafiẽ and (in Fulani times) Bida among the Beni, who placed the money into the hands of the royal tax-collectors appointed for these two royal domains. Of the tax levied in the domains the *Etsu* received two-thirds, the royal tax-collectors and the head chiefs of the two districts sharing between them the remaining third. In the time of *Etsu* Masaba, however, the *Etsu* took all and the town-king of Bida, in order to obtain his share, levied an additional tax of his own. The total tax paid by a Beni village in Fulani times is said to have amounted to £2 under *Etsu* Masaba and £3 under Umaru Majigi; later, under the greedy Maliki, it rose higher and higher till *u de iyaka à*, 'there was no limit'.[1]

The rest of Nupe kingdom was divided up into smaller and larger

---

[1] The Bororó Fulani who came regularly to Nupe with their cattle formed another such royal domain with respect to taxation. The organization of this nomadic group evidently lent itself to no other method of administration. Their tax was collected by their own group head, the *Diko*, and then handed over to the royal tax-collector, who was known as *egba Bororó* (Delegate to the Bororó). He was himself a Fulani, who lived—and is still living—in Bida. When the *Etsu* Nupe recently wanted to buy cattle for his new experimental farms he arranged the deal through the man who used to be *egba Bororó*, making use of the old connexion for the new purpose.

'countries' comprising each a town with its dependent villages and *tunga* which were administered as fiefs through feudal lords or *egba*. The *egba*—a member of the royal house or of the office nobility, or a court slave—received the fief from the king together with his rank with which the fief remained permanently linked. Mokwa was known as the town of the *Shaba*, Eggā as the town of the *Ndeji*, Kutigi and Enagi belonged to the *Ndatwaki*, and so on. Promotion to a higher rank brought with it appointment to another, more lucrative, fief. The feudal lord himself lived in the capital and rarely visited his possession. The local affairs, the collection of tax, were in charge of his representative, one of his slaves or serfs who was residing on his lands as *egbagi*, Small Delegate. Of the tax collected in these fiefs, again a money tax, a quarter went to the king and three-quarters were retained by the *egba*, who returned a small share to his *egbagi*, salary and commission in one. Sometimes the towns or districts also paid an additional tribute in kind both to *Etsu* and *egba*. I have been able to collect some data about the tax levied in these areas. The uniform information which I obtained from different sources leads me to believe that the facts are substantially correct. The town Kutigi, according to my informants, paid under *Etsu* Umaru a money tax of 20,000 cowries (about 10s.) to the *Etsu* through the *egba*; to the *egba* himself 10,000 cowries (5s.) and to the *egbagi* 5,000 cowries (2s. 6d.). In addition to this, the people of Kutigi sent the *Etsu* 20 mats of the kind which has made Kutigi the centre of a famous mat industry, worth over £1, 4 bundles of corn worth about 7s. 'for the king's horses', and 10 mats and 1 bundle of corn to the *egba*. In modern money, the total tax of the town which at that time had eight *efu* and a population of perhaps 500, amounted to between £2 and £3.[1]

The feudal lord in Bida was responsible to the king for law and order in his district. The appointment of the village chief was, again, subject to royal confirmation. The overlordship of the king also implied the right of appeal of the villagers to the king against oppression or injustice from their feudal lord.[2] Lastly, the *egbagi*, together with the village chief, administered justice in the smaller cases and sent all bigger cases to Bida, where the *egba* himself would plead the case of his tenants before the court of *Etsu* and *Alkali*.

A variety of the fiefs just discussed were bestowed on individuals, relatives, courtiers, or favourites of the king, as personal fiefs, independent of rank and office. Even women could hold fiefs of this kind. These fiefs were sometimes hereditary and sometimes reclaimed by the king after the death of the holder. They were very small, single towns or villages, but one person could hold two or more such fiefs—which, however, were never adjacent lest the power in the hands of one person

---

[1] Oldfield reports that in 1832–4 (i.e. under *Etsu* Usman) Eggā, one of the largest towns of Nupe at that time, paid an annual tax of 120,000 cowries, that is, about £3 (Laird and Oldfield, op. cit., ii, p. 39). This fits in very well with the data I obtained.

[2] The people of Mokwa once availed themselves of this right to lodge a complaint against their feudal lord. When I asked my informants what the result had been, they shrugged their shoulders and said: 'The *Etsu* promised to help us; but does one Fulani go against another Fulani?'

became too great. The towns or villages which were granted as such personal fiefs could lie anywhere within the boundary of the kingdom, on the royal domains as well as in the areas held as office fiefs by *egba*. The personal fiefs involved no legal or administrative authority, only the authority of levying an additional tax called *edugi* (small tax) over and above the royal tax, *edukó* (big tax), after the latter had been collected. There was no limitation to this additional tax, which must often have exploited the peasants ruthlessly. Yet I have also seen close personal attachment between villages and their lord still existing to-day, bearing witness to the existence of more friendly ties between feudal lord and tenants.

It is clearly impossible to state in more detail how this administrative system worked, and especially how far the administrative and judicial authority of the feudal delegate worked in harmony with the existing traditional authority vested in village chief and elders. Later on, I shall give more data about the working of this legal machinery. But it is easy to understand that the powerful feudal lord and his delegate could uphold political and legal authority by the very fact of their power and influence. They could, for example, secure redress or punishment where the village chief's limited power might be too weak to enforce judgement or arbitration. But this intervention might easily distort justice rather than further it. As aliens, never linked permanently with the people over whom they rule, the fief-holders were bad guardians of tribal law and traditional justice. This, in fact, reflects the fundamental conflict involved in the system of feudal administration. The feudal lords were officially responsible for the well-being of their subjects; they were agents of a central authority which was vitally interested in the maintenance of peace and order; they themselves, like their royal master, depended on the people of the fief for tax, supply of food, and supply of men for their armies and wars. But the connexion of fief with rank, involving as it did a change of the fief with every promotion, did not allow the mutual attachment between the feudal lord and his subjects to grow really strong and permanent—too strong and permanent for the safety of the king and the unity of the state. To balance the danger that might arise from a too firmly entrenched feudal lord, the kingdom had to risk the other danger of maladministration and discontent among the people on the fiefs.

This policy of preserving the balance of power between dynastic and feudal interests which had to be re-established and readjusted with every change of régime is reflected in the many changes which the administration of the kingdom has undergone in the hundred years of Fulani rule. *Etsu* Masaba, intent on building up an enormous dynastic power, divided the whole of Beni and Kusopa country, town for town, among his sons and daughters and other followers as personal fiefs. There was no place in the kingdom, the Nupe say, which had not its private 'owner'. The Nupe nicknamed this generous king *ndă na ma gă na*, Father of Distributing. *Etsu* Umaru, who succeeded him, adopted the opposite policy in order to win the support of the native tribes against the feudal lords who had supported his predecessor. He abolished all private fiefs in

Beni and re-established the integrity of the Beni confederacy in the form
of a royal domain. *Etsu* Maliki, levying tax upon tax on a country
depleted by civil war, and having to defend a weakened kingdom both
against powerful feudal lords and a restive population, invented a new
system of government: he now applied the *ajele* system which was
formerly restricted to the Outside Peoples to the kingdom itself. He divided the country into six large districts placed in charge of his delegates—
trusted slaves, who, accompanying the fief-holders on their tax-collecting
expeditions from fief to fief, collected the royal tax at the head of an armed
force strong enough to cow into submission rebellious subjects as well
as any too independent feudal lords.[1] When *Etsu* Abubakari came to the
throne, he found all the wells of supply dried up. The taxing system of
his predecessors had left nothing in the country that could be made into
money—nothing except human beings. He started raiding his own
provinces to find slaves for the market, breaking down the most fundamental distinction of political status, that between the citizens of the
kingdom proper and the conquered *zaži kati*. But, my informant
added philosophically when he finished his sad story: 'A gown is dirty
—you wash it; behold, the water is dirty—with what are you going to
wash the water?'

In this ever-changing pattern of feudal administration the capital
stands somewhat apart, being administered directly by the king and his
officers of state. The threefold territorial and tribal division of the kingdom into an innermost core, a kingdom 'proper', and an outside area
reappears on a smaller scale in the division of Bida and its population:
here we have *ba nîn*, the Inner City, where the Beni of pre-Fulani Bida
live; the Greater Bida, and finally the Strangers' Quarter, *lálemi*. But
the order of status and prerogatives is not the same. Greater Bida included all the people who had come to Bida when it became the capital
of the kingdom—the members of the ruling class, Fulani and Nupe
nobility, with all their followers, hangers-on, with traders, Mallams,
warriors, drummers. A privileged class here again, this group was free
from all taxation, and this privilege also extended to all settlements
which they founded, the *tunga* in the country, which were worked by
their dependants, slaves, and serfs. The Nupe craft-guilds which had
come with the Fulani rulers from the former capital of the kingdom,
Rabá, were equally exempted from tax save for an annual 'salute' to the
Etsu. To the people of *ba nîn* the people of Greater Bida, Fulani and Nupe
alike, are 'strangers'. But in the kingdom they themselves, *kintsoži*,
Owners of the Land, were a group deprived of all privileges. They were
taxed exactly as the other peasants in the country; and so also, by gate-
tolls and market dues, which were collected by the king's police force,
were all Nupe from the country who came to sell their goods in Bida
market.

Finally, there are the strangers—'real' strangers—of whom this cosmopolitan capital was (and is) always full: people from Hausa and
Bornu, Arabs from the Sudan and Tripoli, Yoruba from the south.

[1] These districts were: Cekpã (the country of Patigi), Gbakokpã (Badeggi and
Kacha), Eggã, Beni, Kyedye, and Kusopa.

They come to Bida as traders or itinerant artisans, some for a short period only, others to stay. The trading caravans from the north stop outside the town gate in the *zongu*, camp, reserved for them. There are three such *zongu* in Bida, each situated on the territory of one of the royal houses; the caravans must stop in the camp that belongs to the ruling house—another expression of that comprehensive dynastic division into three. The traders from the south, individual traders and the strangers who settle down in Bida for longer periods, perhaps permanently, live in *lálemi* under their own headmen, the *Sarkin Hausawa* (or *Madúgu*, as he was originally called) and the *Sarkin Yorubawa* (or *Asari*), the Chief of the Hausa and the Chief of the Yoruba. These two men are the recognized ward-heads of the aliens' quarter, and latterly have held an official position on the Bida Town Council. Strangers from the rich countries of north and south were always welcome in Nupe. They were treated with special consideration by the rulers of Bida, they paid no regular taxes, only comparatively small market dues, and they were looked after by their own headmen, who were appointed to watch the interests of their fellow countrymen, as, for instance, in all matters concerning financial transactions. This treatment of strangers contrasts curiously with the ruthless treatment of the native peasants. It reflects the vital part that trade played in this country, in the households of this society which depended for its existence on foreign markets where imported arms, horses, and all the paraphernalia of court life might be bought, and where the valuable commodities of the kingdom, embroidered gowns, beads, brass- and silverware, and slaves might be sold.

Cutting across this threefold division of Bida there exists another division, still more important for the life of the town: the division into small local units, factions rather than organized town wards, which form themselves more or less spontaneously round the houses of the powerful nobility. This is, in fact, how the Bida people refer to the different parts of the town; they call them by the title of the most prominent member of the nobility who has his house in that locality, *efu Ndeji*, or *efu Dzwoáfu*, *efu Sokyara*, and so forth. This link of locality is explained partly by the fact that powerful men tended to settle their henchmen, slaves, and serfs in their neighbourhood, and partly by the fact that the people of the locality were ready to acknowledge as their patron the member of the titled nobility, living in their midst, who at the time had the greatest influence, the man whose rank and power promised protection and support to those who rallied round him. But it is not the strong, permanent link of the kind we found in the Nupe village. Nor is there real continuity in this voluntary allegiance of a group of commoners to a noble patron. As the ranks change hands so the allegiance will change; every change on the political horizon may dissolve the local faction and reset the face of the town.

Just as these rank-holders are themselves dependent upon the favour of the king and the royal house, and as they group themselves in accordance with that tripartite dynastic division, so these small local factions are subordinated to the threefold arrangement. We remember the three *ekpã*, the three 'banks', on which Bida is built: the large number of *efu*, linked with a title or name, encased in these *ekpā* which bear the name of a royal house, the group of commoners rallying round a noble patron, and the nobility rallying round a dynastic head—this is one of the most conspicuous symbols of the political relationships which rule the capital.

The political administration of Nupe kingdom (like every political administration) can be regarded as an organization guaranteeing order and security to the subjects of the state—individuals and groups—in return for specific forms of submission: submission of individuals to the established rules of conduct; surrender, by groups, of all independent political action; and surrender, by individuals and groups, of portions of their property in the form of taxes and tributes. The law-abiding, tax-paying citizens are thus promised protection against enemies at home and abroad, and general security for carrying on their daily work, holding markets, using the roads, and enjoying the fruits of their labour. With regard to individuals, a legal machinery safeguards their civic rights, that is, their claims to this protection. With regard to subject groups, we may speak of constitutional rights in which this safeguard of security is embodied. The element of reciprocity implied in these constitutional rights, namely, the promise of security in return for a surrender of autonomy, is clearly understood by the people. This is shown in the current interpretation of such political measures as the suppression of the Kyedye attack on the town of Kacha described above. The intervention of the central government on behalf of Kacha is positively linked with the previous surrender of autonomy (*a gba ya Bida*, 'they submitted to Bida').

A striking feature of the internal organization of Nupe are the considerable regional differences in the completeness and directness of administration and the frequent changes which it has undergone in the fifty years of Fulani rule. These variations and changes have a threefold explanation: (1) They interpret, in terms of political status, the cultural and ethnical provenance to which we referred in the preceding chapter. (2) They are a compromise between the superstructure of the state and certain claims to autonomy, admitted mainly because of the difficulty of establishing a more complete control—for example, over the strongly organized river-state of the Kyedye, or over the newly absorbed 'outside' groups on the periphery of the kingdom. (3) They are a compromise also between centralization and delegation of power. The delegation of power represents an essential structural characteristic of the Nupe political system. The ever-expanding kingdom, increasingly dependent on the military help of the nobility, had to secure their services more and more by granting them landed property in the form of fiefs, and thus investing them with a portion of territorial sovereignty. But then, only through this indirect—feudal—administration could the expanding state hope to reach and to control its entire population, above all those scattered village units which never evolved a larger political system than could be fitted easily (like the Beni confederacy or the Kyedye political organization) into the large-scale framework of the Nupe state.[1]

[1] Compare the similar situation in Imperial Rome: 'The state had to appeal to private persons of wealth and influence because it was not able to transmit its

But to 'reach' and to 'control' means often wholesale exploitation rather than protection and security. Here the fundamental weakness of a sovereignty vested corporately in a ruling group, the members of which are entrusted severally with executive power, is clearly revealed. In other words, in the employment of the political machinery the aspect of duty towards the state is not invariably harmonized with the aspect of class privilege. Thus the peace of the country was often disturbed by the rulers themselves: one feudal lord breaking into the térritory of another, levying illegal taxes; a royal messenger misappropriating tributes which he was to collect for his royal master; or a royal prince raiding on his own the countries which had paid their tribute and thus bought their claim to the 'king's peace'. King and notables alike would rally against the man who thus betrayed his loyalty to the kingdom. Punitive expeditions, loss of office, and heavy punishment were the reward of those who broke the 'king's peace' and committed what the Nupe call *cin amana* (see p. 110).

Revolts were quelled, raids answered with raids, war fought with war, and the 'king's peace' eventually re-established. But under conditions like this, protection and public security could be, at the best, only very unequal and unstable. The stress and tension of the system revealed itself in the various attempts on the part of the peoples of Nupe to secure better safeguards for their civic rights. Direct rebellion was the crudest, and, in fact, least efficient, weapon. Siding with one feudal lord against another, with pretenders against the ruling king, and princes against their royal overlord, meant obtaining, if not permanent security, the promise of protection and favours. Villages and districts could not choose their overlords or feudal delegates: but there are one or two indications that they could change their political status. Thus the villages of Sakpe and Kutigi claim that they obtained under *Etsu* Masaba, in return for heavier taxation, the legal franchise normally granted only to royal domains. I have mentioned the frequent efforts of the Kyedye to secure a semi-autonomous position. The Kusopa of Laboži, taking advantage of their exceptional economic position as the kola-nut planters of the kingdom, were also able to secure from *Etsu* Masaba the status of a royal domain equal to that of Beni and Kyedye.

PATRONAGE AND CLIENTSHIP

The privileges granted by one *Etsu* could be abolished by another. Security granted by charter could be infringed by powerful feudal lords. Where the group as such, village, or district, failed to obtain permanent security, individuals could seek protection of a different order: the declaration of voluntary allegiance to a feudal lord or an influential man in the capital bought his and his family's friendship and personal protection. This allegiance, which often went hand in hand with the voluntary adoption of Mohammedanism, would be initiated as a rule by

commands to the inert masses of the population in any other way' (P. Vinogradoff, in *Cambridge Medieval History*, i, p. 653).

presents which the applicant brought his patron-to-be. A short trial period established the readiness of the 'client' to fulfil his obligations, and the ceremonial gift of a sword and turban by the patron to his new henchman sealed the pact. Such a pact involved on the part of the client gifts, services, and a regular tithe paid from the produce of his farm; on the part of the protector, help against claims, just or unjust, of other people, against the abuse of power by other feudal lords, sometimes grants of land, and invariably assistance in all matters that had to do with the central authority. In legal affairs, e.g. court cases brought before the central authority in Bida, the protector, residing in the capital, with his knowledge of state affairs and his private influence, would give invaluable help to the powerless ignorant peasant. Even to-day, peasants from the country, when summoned before the court in Bida, invariably go first to see their protector in town, ask for his help or advice, and then appear in court accompanied by one of his men—an outward sign of their close connexion with the powers that be. This system of patronage is involved in the very structure of this rigid class society; it grows to an institution which impresses its stamp on the whole social life of Nupe and indeed all the Emirates of Northern Nigeria. We may call it by the native name, *bara*-ship, from the Hausa and Nupe word *bara*, servant or serf, or by the name by which the same institution was known in Imperial Rome and in the feudal system of medieval Europe: the *patrocinium*, or clientage.[1]

Clientage, this sacrifice of freedom for the sake of political protection, is common to country and capital. But in the capital it has a variety of meanings. First, there are the men who, anxious to obtain political protection, attach themselves loosely to an important personage as his loyal followers without surrendering their independence. These men, who do not work for their patron nor bring him gifts or tributes, are called *egi kata*, 'sons of the house'—the Nupe word for adopted children. Then there are men who become *bara*—real *bara*—because they are poor, and sometimes also because they shirk hard work on the land. Impecunious craftsmen thus hope to obtain a prosperous customer; Mallams a wealthy patron who can use their services; and ex-peasants become servants in the house of their master, are given food and clothes, money for tax, and have their children educated by their patron. Here 'protection' comes to mean freedom from all more serious responsibilities. And lastly, over and above securing material assistance, attachment to a man of rank and influence is a way to secure social promotion, the chance of becoming 'somebody', of being lifted from the ignominy of a commoner's life into the sphere of rank and importance.[2] The man in town who has no land to offer, offers himself and his services. The *bara* attaches himself to the household of his patron; he is servant, messenger, major-domo, soldier in his master's private army. He may rise to the position of a trusted friend and intermarry into his

[1] See P. Vinogradoff, op. cit. i, p. 563, and v, pp. 460–2.
[2] One of my Bida informants, himself a man with numerous *bara*, divided the *bara* into three categories: those who 'are afraid' and seek protection; those who shirk hard work and responsibility; and those who are out for 'greatness'.

patron's family. If he has been accepted as *bara* by an influential feudal lord, he may hope to be rewarded with the grant of land or a sub-fief. A title, finally, bestowed by patron on client proclaims publicly the *bara's* position as a henchman of a man of rank. These are the titles which are usually bestowed on *bara: Sonfada, Mižindadi, Tsowa, Tswanya, Tsadú.*[1]

In all these cases the benefit is mutual. The *bara* receives material support and possibly a rank; the patron gains servants, soldiers for the contingent which he is to muster for the king's army, and followers and henchmen to add to his prestige. The patron will choose his clients and will not accept everyone. A young man of about 25, who had become a labourer, told me that he intended eventually to attach himself as *bara* to a certain nobleman, but he was as yet too young and no one wanted him. To have gathered around oneself a large number of *bara* and *egi kata* is the final, most undeniable, mark of success. Whenever you visit the house of a nobleman, at any time of the day, you will find him surrounded by some of his *bara* or *egi kata*: possibly they have just returned from an errand or have come to discuss important questions with him, or simply to pay their respects and share, as they regularly do, his meal.

Often the loyalty of clients to their patrons extends to the whole family of the *bara* and is transmitted from generation to generation. But loyalty and ambition may come into conflict. Sons may choose a new patron for themselves, hoping for increased benefits from the new association; or the *bara* himself may leave his own protector when the influence of the latter decreases and look for another more influential patron.

The *élite* of clients are the *bara* of the royal princes. Not only are they servants of masters who have ample land and sub-fiefs to bestow, but they may also rise, with their masters, to the highest positions and become, some day, *bara* of a ruling king. These royal *bara* are almost equal in rank to the nobility of the officers of state. The *Etsu* Nupe has only two *bara*, the *Mižindadi* (lit. equal to major-domo) and *Sonfada* (lit. companion on travels—the present holder of this rank sits beside the chauffeur in the *Etsu's* car), not counting the freed slaves who play to-day more or less the role of *bara*. But the lowest *saraki* titles which the *Etsu* may bestow on his favourites are nearer clientship than nobility proper. Social climbers, rich and ambitious men, could buy themselves a clientship in the house of a royal prince or the king: *Etsu* Saidu, the late Emir, sold the title of *Mižindadi* three times over. Wealth buying a serf's title—this is indeed a paradoxical result of a social system which, intent on promotion and social rise, turns even the humiliation of clientship into a vehicle for a social career.

The complex pattern of clientship and the various motives which make free men seek patronage are illustrated in the following list of *bara* who were in the service of the late *Shaba*.

---

[1] Political ranks are frequently distinguished from *bara* ranks using the same title by adding the suffix *-kó*, meaning great, or the word *tsu*, meaning 'of the king', e.g. *Sonfada* and *Sonfadakó*, *Soje* and *Sojetsu*.

List of Bara in the Household of the late Shaba Usman

(*Bara* titles are printed in italics)

1. Ibrahima *Madawaki*—in Bida. Formerly warrior by profession, now matmaker. Made submission to *Shaba*; his father and the rest of the family are not *bara* of the *Shaba*.
2. Etsu Ndakó—in Bida. Wealthy trader. He is the type of *bara* who is out for social promotion—a '*bara* for greatness'. He began as *egi kata* of the *Shaba*, who had no rank at that time. When Usman became *Shaba*, Etsu Ndakó made full submission, in the hope of profiting by this allegiance to the 'heir apparent' who might become *Etsu* one day and then bestow a *saraki* rank upon his client.
3. *Sonmáži*—in Bida. Mat and straw-hat maker. His father was a *bara* of *Etsu* Umaru (of the same dynasty). The son followed in his footsteps, and served two *Shaba* in succession. He married a widowed daughter of his present master.
4. Yisa Gbodu—in Bida. Made submission to *Shaba*. Poor, a small trader by profession. Plays the role of a handy-man in the *Shaba* household.
5. Jiya Fugi—in Bida. Was formerly a *bara* of *Etsu* Mohamadu, the *Shaba's* father.
6. Yisa Sharu—in Bida. He is a Mallam by profession, and became *bara* of the *Shaba* before the latter obtained his rank.
7. Mamudu Yakagi—in Bida. As No. 1.
8. Umaru Zainu—in Bida. Was formerly a *bara* of *Etsu* Maliki (of a different dynasty). He is a tailor by profession. His patron is at the same time his most profitable customer, having all dresses needed by the family made by him.
9. *Babban Ndeji*—in Bida. His father held *Ndeji* rank. When he died, his widow married the *Shaba* and took her son with her, who then became a *bara* of his stepfather.
10. Etsu Saba *Manzo*—in Bida. As No. 1. Acts as personal messenger of the *Shaba*. The title *Manzo* means messenger (in Hausa).
11. Suleiman *Gadza*—in Bida. His father was a titled slave of the *Etsu*. He gave his son as *egi kata* to *Shaba*. When the father died Suleiman's elder brother inherited the title, and the younger brother, having no prospect of obtaining a *saraki* rank, remained with *Shaba* as his *bara* and received from him the *bara* rank *Gadza*.
12. Idirisu *Madawaki*—in Bida. A very wealthy trader who became *bara* in order to obtain a title. (Cf. No. 2.)
13. Mallam Yusufu—in Bida. His father was *Alkali* of Bida, he himself formerly *Alkali* of Mokwa. Later he lost his position and became *bara* of the *Shaba*, for whom he now acts as a private 'chaplain'.
14. Mallam Mamudu—in Bida. Also a private chaplain of the *Shaba* household.
15. Jiya Man—in Bida. Another Mallam. His father was already *bara* of the *Shaba*.
16. Ndakó Tétengi—which means 'little Ndakó', to distinguish him from his father, who was called Ndakó and was also a *bara* of the *Shaba*. At that time they lived in Bida. Later they built themselves a farm settlement (*tunga*) on land given them by their patron. They live there now, paying an annual *dzanká* to the *Shaba*.

K

17. Alhassan—younger brother of Ndakó Tétengi. Lives with him on the farm.
18. Suleiman Maidunki—in Bida. His father was a *bara* of *Etsu* Umaru. He is a tailor by profession—*Maidunki* means tailor (in Hausa). Cf. No. 8.
19. Kolo Langbogu—on a farm near Wuya. He obtained his land through his patron.

The social significance of clientship reveals itself, finally, in the formation of political factions. Every man of rank and standing collects round him a smaller or larger group of followers, henchmen, and clients, their families, their sons, brothers, and friends, who come to look upon this man as their protector and patron. The people of rank themselves are organized similarly, on a higher plane: we have seen how they attach themselves to a royal prince from whom they expect favours, support, and, some of them, promotion to an important office or rich fief. Let me try to reduce to figures this manifold system of integration that is the result of patronage and clientship. The old *Shaba* of Bida (as our list shows) had still in the days of his waning influence nineteen *bara*. Then there were his sons and younger brothers with their *bara*—some forty men altogether (not counting women and children). Of the other nobility, members of the royal house of Umaru Majigi to which he himself belonged, and members of the *saraki* nobility bearing allegiance to this house, some eight or ten were attached to the old man in personal allegiance, each of them with his own *bara*, bringing the total to over a hundred. The number of peasants, commoners, small traders, and Mallams who, living in his neighbourhood or on one of his *tunga*, regarded themselves as his clients in a looser sense, I can only guess. In Bida itself their group included all the streets round his house, twenty to thirty houses, and the people from this group would come to the *Shaba* or any important member of his faction, whenever they were in need of advice or protection. The following of the *Shaba* must thus have amounted to over 400 men, a thousand if we count their whole families, in a town of 30,000.

What was said earlier in this chapter about the division of Bida into local factions or 'wards' is now fully explained. You can map out the whole of Bida in such areas of personal influence and patronage. Rivalry and feuds between the leaders of the local factions may throw the whole town, indeed the whole country, into a civil war. This is what happened not long ago. In 1931 the trial of a witch in Bida had deeply stirred the passions of the people. A certain woman in the *efu* of the *Sokyara*, a powerful nobleman, though not at the time in favour at the court, was believed to be a witch and was accused by the people of the *efu* of having caused several deaths and cases of mysterious illness. The people feeling themselves menaced by her presence appealed for help to their patron, the *Sokyara*, who decided to expel the woman from his *efu*. She appealed to the *Etsu* and the *Alkali*; summoned before the court, she swore on the Koran that she was innocent, whereupon the *Alkali* let her go and dismissed the case. This to the enraged people appeared as a farce. The anti-witchcraft society to which the people of Nupe formerly used to entrust the discovery and punishment of witches had been forbidden some ten years previously. The modern method of obtaining protection against a witch, through the medium of the law courts, had evidently failed. Moreover, the people were aware of the enmity that existed between their patron and a powerful faction at the king's court, especially between the *Sokyara* and a certain favourite of the ruling *Etsu*, the *Uban Dawaki*, who had recently obtained his rank by what had seemed to many gross favouritism. The action of the *Alkali*, who was known to belong to the same faction, was supposed to be prompted by the wish to please the *Etsu*'s favourite and to discredit his rival. Enraged, and despairing of any other way out, the people took the law into their own hands and stoned the alleged witch and her daughters on their way home from the courthouse. Then the fight between the two factions flared up openly. Although certain members of the king's household had, as it was revealed later during the official investigation, taken part in the stoning of the witches, the *Etsu* accused the *Sokyara* and had him and his whole family arrested. The *Sokyara* and his brother managed to escape, and hid in their house. When this became known in the town the people of the *Uban Dawaki* faction thought this a good opportunity to deal the rival faction their death-blow. They set fire to the house of the *Sokyara*, who sought safety in flight while his brother died in the flames. Later the *Uban Dawaki* party tried to throw the blame on the *Sokyara* and accused him of having himself started the fire. Bida was in upheaval, the *Etsu* powerless, or pretending to be powerless, and only after the sternest measures could the government establish peace.

But we need not go to this extreme case to demonstrate the reality of this system of political factions.[1] Extend the 'circles within circles' of patronage and clientship wider and wider till they are bounded by the widest circumference—the three dynastic *ekpã*—and you understand their full import. Patronage and clientship are only small meshes in a texture which envelops the whole social life of the kingdom.

SOCIAL CLASS IN NUPE

The foregoing description has revealed a system of social gradation of remarkable thoroughness and indeed conspicuousness. We can speak of Nupe as a typical class society. But hitherto we have touched upon only one aspect of social stratification, namely, social differentiation so far as it results from differentiation in political rights and duties. We have studied social barriers—the barriers of rank and grade—where they are pivoted in the political structure. We have yet to learn the full extent of their influence upon the life of society at large and their relation to other trends of social stratification.

Social class is a complex phenomenon, the resultant of many factors,

[1] There is another hardly less drastic illustration: in April 1936 the same *Uban Dawaki* fell ill. At once rumour had it that he had been poisoned by the *Maiyaki*, an old enemy of his who was said to be jealous of the large following which the *Uban Dawaki*, though his junior in rank, could boast. That the medical officer diagnosed lung trouble did little to abate the rumour.

chiefly political, economic, occupational, and educational.[1] But so is the widest constellation defined on the basis of similarity or diversity of conduct—culture. The essence of social class lies in the specific fashion in which these various factors appear combined. To understand it fully we must view social class under two aspects. The first is that of firmly established and comparatively permanent differences in actual conduct—differences in standards of living, in habitual behaviour, occupation, and moral values.[2] The second aspect is that of the social agency which attaches to these differences of conduct the index 'inferior' or 'superior', and makes them reflect different grades on a common scale of values. Were we dealing only with differences of the first order we should be describing merely different cultural groups in which life is lived in different fashion, in which different customs are observed and different values valid. What turns mere cultural differences into differences of conduct typical of social class is the loss or absence of their self-contained and largely unconscious nature. Their permanence is no longer, as it were, self-chosen. The 'cultural' differences are now conceived of as results of unequal advantage and opportunity, and they are never allowed to lose their significance as different grades in the 'common scale'. It lies in the nature of things that this common scale, which depends essentially on the demonstrability of unequal opportunities, should rest above all on political and economic factors. The essence of class (as of any group) lies in the consciousness of group membership; the consciousness of class is the consciousness of this 'common scale of values'.

Let us examine first the social mechanism which maintains and propagates the consciousness of the common scale. It is essentially an educational mechanism (in the widest sense of the word). While perpetuating the various cultural traits characteristic of social class it perpetuates at the same time the common perspective from which these traits are set off as traits valued more or less highly by the society. One of the most efficient instruments of this mechanism is the convention of class symbolism and class etiquette, which not only regulates the intercourse between the classes, but also serves to demonstrate the reality of class barriers.

Nupe society is plentiful in such symbols of class distinction. The collective name for nobility, *rowni*, 'turban', marks already one of these outward signs of class: it refers to the turban of glazed blue cloth which only members of the nobility may wear. Another prerogative of rank is the right to carry a sword, or rather, have it carried by one's sword-bearer, the *zagi* (lit. 'little person', i.e. 'page'), and to appear on horseback on all official occasions. With regard to these emblems of rank the Nupe have kept abreast of the times: a novel symbol of status is an alarum clock, put in a little wooden case, which body-servants of men of rank carry after their masters.

[1] M. Ginsberg, *Sociology*, 1934, p. 162.
[2] Cf. M. Ginsberg, op. cit., p. 159: 'To the outward observer class is primarily a matter of behaviour, speech, dress, education, and especially habits of social intercourse.'

Or, in the sphere of etiquette: men of equal rank greet each other by cowering low (women go down on one knee) for half a minute or longer while exchanging the formulae of greeting and, if they are well acquainted, stretching out their hands several times in succession and lightly touching each other's fingers. A man of lower rank when meeting his social superior will bow very low or kneel down, and only if the difference of rank is slight or obviated by personal intimacy (as between a *bara* and his patron), will he venture to offer his hand. If he is on horseback, he will dismount; if he is wearing sandals, he will take them off, though it may be on the road, and put them beside him; if he enters the house of his social superior, he will keep close to the door, squatting there till he is summoned to come near. The man of higher rank will stand or sit still, or make a short perfunctory gesture of bowing, and hardly move his arm to meet the other man's hand. When sitting together in a group, the man of low rank always sits slightly behind the man of higher rank. In the presence of the *Etsu*, *Alkali*, the highest ranks, or royal princes, you may not rest your arms on the floor—this would be disrespectful: the proper posture is to squat cross-legged, the arms folded in your lap, and to bend forward a little so that it should not seem as if you were looking straight at your superior. The *Ndeji* and *Maiyaki* were the only men whom I have seen behave really freely in the presence of the king; all others, even the *Alkali* and the royal princes, acted in a conspicuously submissive and slightly constrained manner.

That one addresses one's superior always through a third person is a common feature of African etiquette. So is, I believe, the custom of pulling the sleeve or a cloth over one's hand when offering a gift to a person of superior rank. Of gifts as a symbol of Nupe class etiquette there is more to say. In Nupe (as in the whole of Northern Nigeria) kola-nuts are the commodity most universally used for gifts and presents. To announce your visit or to invite somebody's visit, to win the favour of another man or to express your appreciation of another man's services, you send a present of kola-nuts. Their quality and amount reflect precisely the social status of donor and receiver.

I have already mentioned the existence in Nupe of two kinds of kola-nuts, the cheap southern variety, and the expensive kola-nut from Laboži; the latter, as we have seen, could be obtained only by, or through, the *Etsu* himself—presents of Laboži kola-nuts were thus symbols of royal favour, and unobtainable by anyone who was not in one way or another connected with the court. When I attended the *Sallah* at the *Etsu*'s court in 1936, he had two bowls (teapots, as a matter of fact) full of kola-nuts in front of him, one filled with Laboži nuts and the other with the small cheaper kind. To watch him distribute the kola-nuts— the kind and amount as well as the gestures which accompanied the gifts—was to watch the rank system of Nupe come alive. He presented ten Laboži nuts through a servant to all the higher rank-holders, and five in the same manner to the less exalted officers of state. He then gave one especially big one with his own hands to the men of highest position— the *Ndeji*, *Maiyaki*, *Alkali* (and myself)—and threw one into the lap of favourites and friends whose rank called less for formality. Finally, small kola-nuts, in fives or tens, were handed out to messengers, dancers, guild-heads, and other people of lower rank.

Even language and music are used as symbols of class. There exist in Nupe special drum-rhythms, *take*, greeting formulae, *kirari* (Hausa, lit. 'calls'), and songs which are linked with certain noble families and important ranks. As soon as a family comes to power or a man receives rank and title, the drummers of Bida will compose such *take* and *kirari* in their honour. You can, in fact, have them made to order, at various prices; but an influential person will not need to order them, for the drummers, counting on his patronage, will supply him at once with this musical salute. Some of the *take* and *kirari* which one can hear to-day date back to pre-Fulani times; others were composed recently. Whenever a member of these noble families attends a festivity, the drummers would announce his arrival by playing 'his' *take* and singing 'his' *kirari*, and the 'master of ceremonies', who is always present at such gatherings, would recite a long list of illustrious ancestors to whom the nobleman can lay claim, the ranks which he had held, and the deeds which he achieved. Lastly, the Nupe address each other by titles only, and never by name, if the person addressed bears a title. Special formulae of greeting are linked with every rank, and thus mark position on the social scale by the most obvious system of signs—everyday speech.

Class symbols and class etiquette shade over into the more substantial differences of class. Behaviour which is pressed into the service of class manifestation becomes indistinguishable from behaviour which results from differences in social and economic advantage. The right to carry a sword or appear everywhere on horseback presupposes the economic ability to acquire these 'emblems of rank'. Submissive behaviour of a client towards his patron, or a member of the lower class towards a man of rank, is determined as much by the convention of class etiquette as by the special interest of gaining favour in the eyes of a person of consequence. Here we are dealing with the other aspect of class differentiation, those 'cultural' differences which are, or become, typical of different classes. They revolve round the two pivots: political and economic structure.[1] They involve the existence of political prerogatives and the varying measures of individual liberty and mastery over one's own destiny, enjoyed by the different classes. Here we can outline the existing classes of Nupe society. We have met their protagonists already: the ruling class of the kingdom, rich absentee landlords, men whose occupation was war and slave-raiding, and, low down on the social scale, commoners and peasants, heavily taxed, and gaining a scanty livelihood rendered insecure by the very facts that add power and prestige to the ruling class. We have also met the craftsmen in the town, who share some of the privileges of the nobility, and the Mohammedan intelligentsia who can attach themselves to the highest stratum irrespective of

---

[1] The two structures do not define identical strata, nor is the economic differentiation invariably reducible to political prerogatives. However, we will leave the examination of the exact relation between the two 'pivots' of social stratification for a later chapter.

POLITICAL HISTORY OF NUPE KINGDOM

their class origin. There is no sphere of life, not even an ordinary social gathering, in which the representatives of the various classes can meet, as it were, on 'neutral ground'.

The social stratification stretches beyond the formalized rank system embodied in the political structure. It embraces the whole country and absorbs and reinterprets in its own sense the cultural configuration of Nupe at large. On this wider scale the commoners of the town, the people of no name and title, rank higher than the people and tribes outside the capital, with their petty village titles and offices. The citizens of Bida look down upon the *gberizi*, the 'heathen' in the villages, ridiculing their habits and character, their fashions and the way they talk, their lack of education and 'urbanity'.

These differences of customs and habits are real enough. But they are underlined on the part of the Bida people by that credulity and fondness of exaggeration which we encountered already in the discussion of the village community and which, here even more strongly, expresses the biased self-centred interest of a group strongly conscious of its cultural identity. I have recorded many sensational accounts of the religious customs of the *gberizi* in which the Bida people firmly believe, unaware, or unwilling to admit, that they are quite untrue. Bida informants told me that among the peasants and pagans women practise the craft of medicine and not men as in Bida—another statement which I could easily disprove. Or I was warned not to believe anything that villagers say—'they are all liars'. Even if it were possible to test quantitatively this collective libel, it would, I am afraid, hardly reveal any real difference between town and country. What I have called, in the discussion of the village community, an ideology sustaining the assertion of group identity subserves here the assertion of (in a loose sense) class distinctions.

To return to the real, concrete, cultural differences linked with class. The framework of status which we have outlined is filled out with a multitude of minor traits, differences of conduct, extending even to walks of life which may appear only remotely connected with the central political and economic structure. We shall meet with these differences in every stage of our investigation; let me anticipate here a few typical instances as they would strike the observer of Nupe everyday life. He would note class differences even in one of the most elementary wants—nutrition: rich and poor have different food habits. The poor eat little meat, chicken very rarely (unless for religious reasons); but meat cooked in palm-oil is eaten every day by the wealthy, and chicken-and-rice, the most delicious food the Nupe know, comes on the table at least once a week. In Bida the sorghum or millet grain is always milled to fine flour; in some peasant districts it is boiled unmilled—a preparation of food which the more refined despise, although it is undoubtedly of higher nutritive value. The people of Bida drink palm-wine. the peasants in the districts feast on sorghum-beer.

Again, in the matter of recreation: among the peasants the men dance to the music of flutes and drums, or the women sing to the clapping of hands or the beating of upturned calabashes. Among the sophisticated people of Bida professional women singers, accompanied by their own drummers, perform for an audience which pays for its pleasures. The uneducated pagans like to sit together on afternoons and evenings in front of their houses, chat or weave mats, or just enjoy the peace of these hours of leisure. The educated Mohammedans meet in the house of a Mallam and read with him the holy books of Islam, using even their leisure hours for furthering their education.

As regards dress: a man of standing would always, even in the privacy of his home, wear trousers and the flowing white robe, and would never appear before guests and strangers without turban. Peasants and commoners normally wear a loin-cloth and a blue cloth thrown over the shoulder, and the blue Phrygian cap which is said to be the traditional head-gear of Nupe. Only on state occasions would they don robe and turban.

People of rank have adopted, with Mohammedanism, many features of Hausa culture. In their families the Hausa custom of removing the uvula of small children is practised—a custom absent among the lower classes and unknown among the peasants. They are fond of using Hausa words and phrases; for expressions concerning the delicate topic of sex they invariably use Hausa or Arabic circumlocutions. They despise the peasants and uneducated people of the lower classes who use the crude literal expression, and who cannot embellish their speech with the more elegant phrases borrowed from Hausa.

The various features enumerated above are clearly not of the same order. Characteristic though they are of the standards valid in the different strata of Nupe society they are not equally reducible to the central facts of class structure—political and economic conditions. The evaluation of certain habits as inferior or superior is as much a matter of convention as a result of social or economic inequality. That the poor man cannot afford meat or chicken-and-rice is due to his poverty; but the preference for milled or unmilled grain or for palm-wine or sorghum-beer respectively, is a matter of taste and habit, i.e. a 'cultural' trait pure and proper. Yet rendered permanent by education, linked with habitual group-behaviour which in other, more vital, spheres of life positively reflects economic or social prerogatives, these smaller traits, too, gain the significance of class-determined behaviour. Here we grasp another aspect of class differentiation. I have said that where the attribute of inferiority or superiority is disregarded, differences of habit and living conditions in general are reduced to cultural differences in the narrow sense. This gains special significance in a society like Nupe, which has grown out of a conglomerate of various tribal groups, each with its own more or less specific culture. Some of the food habits of the 'poor' peasants are indeed the original food habits of cultural groups which have been incorporated into the kingdom. I have mentioned that the Phrygian cap, worn by peasants and commoners, is regarded as the traditional head-dress of the country. Their 'uncouth' manners, their 'primitive' customs, are part of the pagan peasant culture of the country. Similarly turban and flowing robes, or the appreciation of professional musicians and Mohammedan learning, reflect the preferences of a specific cultural group, the 'town culture' typical of Northern Nigeria. These habits and customs exist, as it were, in their own right, quite apart from questions of economic or political opportunity. But as in the growth of the kingdom certain customs and habits have become representative of the *élite*, they have set the standard of cultural desirability and superiority in general. They have imparted to habits and customs which differ from the standard the stigma of lower, less 'respectable' ways of life. In this sense, then, class differentiation as we find it in present-day Nupe can be said to represent a direct result of the growth of the state.

The intensity of class cohesion and the vividness of class conscious- ness are determined by 'the amount and ease of social mobility', that is, inter-class movement.[1] We have denied to the economic and social stratification that obtains in the Nupe village the character of a social class, on the grounds that the higher and highest social orders were poten- tially attainable to all—universal mobility contradicts the conception of social class. Exclusion of all social mobility, on the other hand, would turn social class into hereditary caste. The Nupe state, a true class society, steers a middle course.

The social classes in Nupe represent to a large extent self-recruited, closed groups. A man born of commoners as a rule remains a com- moner, a craftsman a craftsman, and the ranks of nobility are filled with men of noble birth. But there exists promotion from grade to grade within the class, and a certain amount of inter-class mobility. Inter-class mobility in the fullest sense, that is, formal adoption into the higher orders, is attained, as we have seen, through service in war and, to less extent, through wealth and clientship. Its scope is narrow and closely controlled: there exist only thirty to forty ranks to which an 'outsider' may aspire, and only seven out of the thirty-seven civil and military ranks enumerated in our lists were granted to men whose families had held no rank previously. Moreover, adoption into the titled classes means only gaining a first foothold on the long social ladder. All social rise possible in Nupe is rigidly canalized by the hierarchy of ranks and grades. Here, viewed from the angle of social mobility, the Nupe rank system reveals its full significance: it controls and restricts as much as it aids social advancement. In the interest of governing the extensive king- dom, carrying on its wars, and administering its subject groups, political power had to be distributed and delegated. Individuals whose services were of value had to be attracted by the promise of admission to privileged positions. But by making social rise subject to the formal in- vestiture and, above all, by admitting individuals only gradually, through a step-by-step promotion, to increased power, the ruling class could regulate the infiltration of new blood as well as the accumulation of power by its members. We have seen that ranks and promotion are subject to changing political fortune; even the meaning of ranks and offices may change under different sovereigns. Recognition can be with- held or withdrawn from men who might prove dangerous or from families already too powerful. The hierarchy of ranks thus helps to pre-

[1] M. Ginsberg, op. cit., p. 163.

serve the precarious balance of power in the feudal state. It becomes, in the hands of the established ruling group, an efficient weapon to safeguard their class privileges.

Social mobility of a more fluid, indirect kind, which admits individuals to a close association with the privileged classes and indirectly to a certain share in their privileges, reaches a much larger proportion of the population. It is upheld by the institution of clientship and by the existence of the Mallam intelligentsia 'between the classes'. The possibilities of social mobility, above all, the extensive possibilities of this indirect mobility, account for the lack of cohesion among the lower classes of Nupe, or at least of Bida. The conspicuous symbolism of rank and the rigid definition of the social estates cannot but stimulate class-consciousness: commoners will always describe themselves as *tálaka*, and men of rank will leave you in no doubt about their consequential position. But this class-consciousness is blurred by thoughts and prospects of a social career that might raise anyone to a higher estate. Concern about betterment rather than sentiments of group solidarity define the nature of class-consciousness in Nupe. This can be seen most clearly in the attitude of the younger generation, who are just planning their future career. Only in two social groups do we find a more strongly pronounced and self-contained consciousness of common fate and common, class-bound interests; they are characteristically groups in which mobility, direct or indirect, plays hardly any part—the closed group of guild-organized artisans and (in the framework of their scattered communities) the peasantry.

How far social mobility took the form of local mobility, that is, of a movement to the town in the attempt to bridge over the cultural and social gulf between townspeople and peasantry, we cannot say. If it existed, it could only have been of very limited scope. For there were strong natural limits to such a development, above all, the scarcity of land near the capital.

Now to be complete and convincing, social rise must go hand in hand with assimilation to the habits and modes of life typical of the higher classes. This, in Nupe, proves no stumbling-block. The familiar instances of 'parvenus' who, though adopted into the higher social order, do not fit into the picture of its social life are unknown. The explanation is that cultural assimilation of this kind is much more widespread than actual mobility. The mechanisms of social mobility which we have enumerated all accord their benefits to individuals, not to groups; on the contrary, individuals may succeed where groups (local communities, tribal sections) would fail to achieve that improvement of social conditions and that increased security bound up with classes. But the assimilation of which we have just spoken must be regarded as a qualified form of social mobility which includes groups and whole sections of the population. Whole groups are free at least to imitate the external characteristics of the higher social orders. Where economic conditions allow it commoners and peasants adopt habits and modes of life of their betters—fashions in dress and housing, their way of talk, their food habits, and the forms of entertainment which they patronize. They also adopt, even more eagerly, the religious practice of the higher and highest classes, Mohammedanism. This is not 'real' social mobility; it serves only to blur the border-line between the strata. It involves attachment to a higher stratum only in the sense of external closeness and assimilation.

The assimilation achieved is irregular and of very unequal significance. Yet it is prompted by a definite motive running through the whole society—self-enhancement. The readiness of groups to identify themselves culturally with the representative stratum reveals an incentive to overcome that heterogeneity of cultures and groups in which we have grasped the essence of state structure. Potentially, this incentive may carry forms of cultural reorientation capable of wielding more intensive, more real, commonness. To examine how and how far this potentiality is utilized by the political system is to examine the crucial problem of this discussion: the dynamic relation between political integration and the heterogeneous raw material out of which it must fashion its unity.

BINDING FORCES

What then is the specific apparatus of control by means of which this heterogeneous society, severely divided by gulfs of culture, ethnic extraction, community, and class, maintains itself as a unit? And to what extent does it draw into its orbit and use for its own support these other non-political configurations and spheres of social life? When examining the political organization of the Nupe village from this viewpoint we discovered that there the basis of political control is extended to its widest possible limit: political organization utilizes the integrative forces of community life at large; it organizes into a unit what is integrated into the same unit by every existing institution. It might very well seem from our foregoing analysis of the Nupe state that here we have the exact opposite. A state machinery which concentrates political power in the hands of a small *élite* and ignores—save in order to transform into class barriers—tribal and cultural identity, seems committed to the narrowest system of political control: by coercion and physical force.

However, this section will show that such conclusions would be incorrect. One might, on general principles, reason that no state could afford to rely solely on coercive measures; and that it would rather utilize coercion only as a 'short cut' to bring about sentiments which, 'once established and sanctified, . . . may well flourish without compulsion, glorified as loyalty to a sovereign king or a national flag'.[1] A state that would disdain to call to assistance these bonds of inner unity seems to jeopardize continuously its safety, and to risk being shattered and broken up by unrest and revolts, possibly beyond repair. Such tension and unrest seems indeed characteristic of the political history of Nupe. But the historian would have to point out also that with all these grave disturbances Nupe kingdom yet maintained itself as a unit. Even when the Fulani took over the rule, testing most severely an already strained

[1] R. Lowie, *The Origin of the State*, 1927, p. 117.

political structure with the additional weight of alien rulership, the state did not break down but on the contrary appeared to have taken out a new lease of life.

Now we shall be able to prove the existence of strong trends of integration which form within the political unit, incidental to it or fostered by it, and which, bridging over cultural diversity and the rift of social and economic inequality, endorse in their fashion the unit wrought by political control. However, in our search for these 'binding forces' of more subtle and conciliatory type we shall discover that they do not all point the same way. They are indeed 'binding' forces—but what they tend to bind and draw together is not invariably the same group substratum.

We must examine first a significant negative instance—kinship. Kinship has no part in this integrative scheme, either ideologically or factually. No attempt is made to invest the conception of the state with that fiction of genealogical or kinship unity which is linked with the concepts of the sub-tribe and the village community. With the increased freedom of movement which is one of the results of political unification, kinship relations become more widely scattered: marriage between distant localities is increasing and is regarded more and more as normal. But these new kinship relations draw only a patchy, irregular pattern that can have little influence upon the integration of the people at large. Moreover, kinship relations are often subordinated to political interests; patronage and the adherence to political factions may even break up family units. The widest gulf, between rulers and subjects, and between the *élite* culture of Bida and the peasant sections, is bridged only by the sociologically less significant form of intermarriage between men of the upper and women of the lower classes. We shall see later that full intermarriage is rigidly restricted and rendered specially difficult, unless it follows already existing political ties of patronage. We shall, in fact, have to speak of a definite class endogamy among the ruling classes. Marriage and kinship ties thus cement the solidarity of the component groups of the state, not of the state itself.

We continue our search in the economic field. Political unification carries in its wake expansion of economic co-operation and interdependence. Economic areas were re-designed in accordance with the new, wider political unit and its centre of gravity, the populous capital, which depends for food and supplies on the agricultural districts. But the contribution of this widened economic co-operation to national solidarity is negligible if not wholly negative. In this reorientation of economic links the boundaries of the state have frequently been crossed and disregarded: trade became 'international'; craftsmen, traders, and even peasants are always ready to seek profitable new markets outside Nupe, and even to emigrate for the sake of better business prospects. Economic interdependence and co-operation even introduce new conflicts and forms of antagonism which set group sections against each other. We shall speak of the village artisans who openly admit (and partly resent) the competition of the superior Bida crafts. In times of crisis conflicts of this kind tend to become more strongly marked. During the depression of 1934–5 I could notice distinct resentment on the part of the peasants against the people of Bida, on whom they were dependent for the marketing of their produce, and whom they now held responsible for the disastrous fall in prices.

Legal unification goes a step farther. Dependence upon a common forum of morality evokes a certain group cohesion, a common orientation of mind at least in that all the component groups will share common hopes—and fears—and a common interest in whatever affects the judicial organization. If we can test the strength of economic co-operation by the facts of volume of trade and traffic and the relation between productive and consuming areas, we can test this moral reorientation by examining the measure of interest which the various groups evince in legal change. I shall show later how keenly the people everywhere in Nupe follow changes in the law. But I shall also show that this interest, all the more intense because such vital issues are involved, does not invariably foster the dissemination of true, or reassuring, knowledge: often it spells suspicion and fear of a biased jurisdiction and legislation. Whole sections feel themselves tricked and threatened by this dangerous law and reject co-operation with its agents and the groups which it seems to favour.

Dynastic and political changes engage the attention of the people no less strongly. When the late Emir died and a new Emir was appointed, and when the appointment of the highest royal ranks was to take place in Bida, the events elicited comments from many groups from which one would not have expected such interest in 'higher politics'. One day I was standing in a Bida street, talking to a brass-smith, when the *Kpotŭ*, one of the disappointed claimants to the throne, rode past. The brass-smith looked after him, shook his head, and said to me: 'It must have been a great shock to him when someone else was appointed *Etsu*.' In Kutigi, the district of the *Kpotŭ*, the older men knew all about the rumour of the *Kpotŭ*'s illness, which had been given out in Bida as an explanation or excuse for his not having been promoted to a higher rank. And in Mokwa, the district of the *Rani*, the elders told me with amusement of the abortive attempt of their District Head to obtain promotion by supernatural intervention: how he had gone to Rabá and prayed at the tomb of Mallam Dendo for the success of his political aspirations.

'Unity of interest' in this sense obtains also with respect to all things that affect the people, and the news of such events would travel fast from place to place. In March 1936, at a Bida wedding feast, I happened to hear girls sing a song the words of which sounded unfamiliar to me. I found it to be a new topical 'stanza' which referred to the activities of the Sleeping Sickness Commission which even then was working in eastern Nupe, i.e. Agaie or Dibo country. The song gave voice to the suspicions and fears of the people and their anxiety to escape, by whatever means, the unpopular treatment. The song runs as follows:

> The needle is coming,
> The Mallam of the needle,
> The father of threading.
> O let me go,
> And not only for my money [i.e. also for pity's sake].

The needle killed the men of Dibo,
And also the men of Baro [a town in that district].
O father, save me and let me go.
If you must use your needle,
Do not let it bite me.

The 'needle' is the injection needle, and the 'Mallam of the needle' the native medical assistant who was performing the injection and who, according to the testimony of the song, could be bribed to spare the patient the (very painful) injection. The testimony, incidentally, was true; some time later I learned that one of the native medical assistants had actually taken bribes from the people, and had been apprehended not long after I had heard the song.

To summarize: political co-ordination calls into being a co-ordination of interest—actual interest units—which in certain respects overcomes the heterogeneity of tribe, culture, and even class, and includes the whole people. Yet as economic co-operation goes its own ways, often disregarding political frontiers, so the other forms of 'reorientation' may tend to further the formation of new, even antagonistic, groups rather than to cement the political unit. The 'interest units' are, paradoxically, units that spell disunity. The paradox is easily solved: the common interests round which these units are focused are such that they show a different aspect and portend different things to rulers and ruled, or to adherents of different political factions. The units which they create may efface tribal and cultural divisions, and temporarily even the barriers of class: but in critical moments they will only put forth more forcibly the existing disparities and forms of antagonism.

We turn, then, to another group of integrative factors which seem to succeed where the interest units fail. They wield integration which endorses unconditionally the political unit. The secret of their success lies in that they attempt unity and integration in spheres in which the political interests suffer such integration to exist, and in which the divergent political interests are overcome by some stronger incentive to unity.

The study of the unity which the Nupe state has achieved, or is achieving, reveals the effectiveness of two main groups of such incentives. To formulate them tentatively: one is self-enhancement—especially a self-enhancement that (in the language of psycho-analysis) 'sublimates' the humiliating experience of political dependence and inferiority; the other, the appeal of the mystic and supernatural. The first incentive reveals itself in the progressive identification of the people with the cultural values typical of the social *élite*; the second, in their readiness to adopt new myths and embrace religious beliefs and practices, which are vessels of political 'propaganda' at the same time. The two incentives may join forces, self-enhancement being offered in the realm of religion —as in the spreading of Islam, the religion of the rulers and conquerors, among the subject groups of the kingdom. We can also discern the agency of a third incentive, more unspecific and subsidiary in nature, which, as it were, canalizes the influence of the other two, namely, the appeal to an historical (or quasi-historical) turn of mind. I have already called the Nupe an historically-minded people: here is more evidence for this bent. We shall see presently how under its influence ritual emblems become relics, and self-enhancement takes the form of exultation in past glories.[1]

Self-enhancement, then. These are the historical facts: the Nupe state has bound its many groups and peoples to its own fate, made them share its adventures, its conquests, the fruits of its victories and defeats. But the element of compulsion behind this commonness of fate disappears in its mental reflection. The commonness of fate is lifted up into the sphere of things eminently glorious and desirable. The people are eager to identify themselves with the kingdom and its fortunes, and share in a collective pride that ignores the social and cultural distance between rulers and ruled. Even the wars which deprived the Nupe of their own rights, chiefs of their independence, peasants of their wealth and land, become a cherished heroic memory. I was discussing the role of strangers in Bida with old Ndakotsu, one of my great friends, and I asked him whether there had been any Kamberi, Kamuku, or Gbari among the strangers who visited Bida regularly. Ndakotsu, last descendant of the Beni town-kings of Bida, who never became quite used to the idea that the *goiši* (Fulani) had robbed him of 'his' town, said ironically: 'Kamuku and Kamberi? Yes, but only as our slaves'—the 'our' evidently meaning a Nupe which credited to itself the successes of its Fulani rulers. When I first came to Mokwa my informants first of all showed me proudly the historical places near Mokwa where some of the battles in the wars of the Fulani against the usurper Umar Bahaushe had been fought, and insisted on describing them all in detail, as if this were the most important thing I had to learn. This did not prevent them later on from complaining bitterly about the tyranny of the Fulani and their indifference to the fate of the people.

This new, proud consciousness of a unity which embraces the whole kingdom is kept alive by every song telling of old times and every story relating the adventures and feats of the kings of Nupe. With fashions and cultural practices, songs and stories spread from the capital throughout the country. The songs composed in honour of the king or one of his noblemen by the drummers of Bida find their way into all the bigger villages of the country. In Mokwa I heard a song which had been composed in Bida in 1918 in honour of *Etsu* Bello's first motor-car, the first motor-car in the country. I put this song in here as an example not of the force of poetic expression which it possesses (in spite of the uncongenial topic), but as an example of its efficient 'propaganda for the kingdom'.

[1] There exist also certain other subsidiary stimuli, such as aesthetic appeal, which we may disregard here. One may put the question whether these various stimuli are to be regarded as universal or as peculiar to the culture which we are studying. More comparative material is needed to answer this question finally. However, one can fairly safely say already that the appeal of the supernatural is a universal trait of the human mind, while the appeal to self-enhancement, and still more so the appeal to historical appreciation, differs in effectiveness in different cultures; it is eminently typical of Nupe culture.

Song of Etsu Bello

The name of Allah is the beginning of all learning.
Let us speak of the day when *Etsu* Bello bought a motor-car.
On the day when *Etsu* Bello bought a motor-car,
The whole of Bida went out to build a road.
Younger brother and elder brother, they went out to build the road.
All the people on the farms went out to build the road.
The young bride, she went to build the road.
The bridegroom, he went to build the road.
But why did they all go out to build the road?
It was because *Etsu* Bello had bought a motor-car.
Because of that all people went out to build a road.
They said: Let us build a road on which the car can travel.
Then the man who wants to go to Baddeggi, in this car he will go.
And Zungeru, the man who wants to go to Zungeru, in this car he will go.
And Wuya, who will travel to Wuya, in this car he will go.
The man who will go to Jima, in this car he will go.
The man who will go to Kacha, in this car he will go.
The man who will travel beyond the river, in this car he will go.
Thus he will go, they said, and therefore let us make the road.
Etsu Bello has the money to buy the car,
But the car will benefit all the people of Bida, from the farms and from the
    city,
The great man and the servant.
They thank *Etsu* Bello because he bought the car.
Etsu Bello, who has horses, and who now has a car,
Etsu Bello can say: Though the horse may break his legs,
We shall go all the same.
On the day when *Etsu* Bello bought the motor-car,
The bottles of the glass-makers turned into red beads.
And the kernels of the gombara grass became necklaces.[1]
In that year when *Etsu* Bello bought the motor-car,
The men were beating the ground,
And the woman, she was sitting at home.
How did it happen that the woman was sitting at home?
Of old it was the woman who was beating the ground,
And the man he just stood and watched.
But because of this motor-car of *Etsu* Bello,
All the men were beating the ground, and that is that.[2]
And all the people, the whole of Bida,
They were saying their thanks to *mace da ciki*.[3]
And all Bida was giving thanks to *karan giya*,[4]
Who has sold the car to *Etsu* Bello.

[1] i.e. all the people who went out to see the motor-car were dressed in their
most beautiful dress, and the glass-makers of Bida were busy manufacturing
ornaments for the occasion.

[2] By 'beating the ground' is meant the levelling of the ground in the road
building. The same term is also used for the levelling of the floor in the Nupe
huts, a work which is reserved for the women. Therefore this comment on the
change of times.

[3] *Mace da ciki* (Hausa, pregnant woman), the rather irreverent nickname the
Bida people had for the District Officer at that time.

[4] *Karan giya* (Hausa, a grass with prickles—*Pennisetum*), another nickname
for the District Officer at that time.

And all the people were giving thanks to *Etsu* Bello,
Because he gave his money to buy a motor-car,
That motor-car that will become a thing of benefit
To all the human beings.

In myth and religion the 'binding forces' of the kingdom gather themselves to fullest strength. The *Etsu* Nupe is not, as we have seen, the religious as well as the political leader of his people; unlike the village chief, he cannot even claim kinship links with the priests of his country. But Nupe kingship is linked in so many ways with religious usages and forms of ritual symbolism that they inevitably become instruments of political solidarity. Rites and beliefs are focused upon the person of the king. Appeals for the help of supernatural agencies become appeals to agencies more or less clearly symbolic of the political system. The welfare and continuity of the community, unthinkable without these supernatural safeguards, become unthinkable without the state.

Out of the weak and irregular uniformity of beliefs and rituals and out of disconnected local cults and traditions the kingdom thus creates a new religious community. One of the centres of this religious unification is that 'mythical charter' which made the dynasty of Nupe kings descendants of the mythical culture-hero, Tsoede. Relics of Tsoede, regalia, instruments of ordeal, magical emblems, which exist in every town of the Emirate, are the symbols of this ancient sacred pact. The name and tradition of Tsoede is also associated with cults which secure childbirth, fertility, and well-being, with certain rituals which prevent floods of the Niger, drive away disease, or bring punishment upon a criminal.[1] To take one example only. In Mokwa exists a certain ritual called *Tsoede* or *sara* (Hausa, lit. malicious accusation, and also snake bite; refers here to the use of the ritual as ordeal), which is practised as ordeal, or whenever trouble befalls the community. It is performed by the *Sheshi*, that 'kingmaker' of whom we have heard before; he places the short 'chain of Tsoede', the insignia of his office, on the ground in the sacred grove, makes a sacrifice of beer and fowl, and speaks thus:

> God, we have come.
> God, everybody has come.
> This ancient thing of Tsoede
> Which is lying on the ground,
> It says we should bring beer.
> Because of the old saying which we have heard,
> Because of that we bring beer and fowl.
> Tsoede, make the whole town prosper [or whatever is
>   the special aim of the invocation].

A powerful secret society, organized to combat witchcraft, the order of the *ndakó gboyá*, became a *kuti 'tsu*, a King's Cult, only half a century ago. There is no doubt that the *ndakó gboyá* cult itself existed long before that. But under *Etsu* Masaba the head of this order, the grandfather of

---

[1] This latter cult I have described in *Man*, 1935, 143. The association of Tsoede with the main fertility cult of Nupe, the *gunnu*, is discussed in *J.R.A.I.*, 1937, p. 118.

the present head of the *ndakó gboyá* society, was invested with the pompous title of *Majï Dodo*, Master of the Monster, and with this royal recognition the organization of the society was made subservient to Nupe kingship. One after the other the heads of the society received their titles from the *Etsu* Nupe. Villages and districts which sought the help of the *ndakó gboyá* against witches had to apply first to the king. This new royal prerogative also entailed a considerable economic benefit: for the king shared in the income of the order which was derived from the gifts collected in the villages which had called in the *ndakó gboyá*.[1] But besides tapping a new source of income the co-operation between *Etsu* and anti-witchcraft society meant adding to the centralized temporal jurisdiction the power of spiritual, mystic jurisdiction over the supernatural enemies of society. This powerful prerogative of the king was, in fact, maintained by the Mohammedan Fulani Emirs till very recently.[2]

Every performance of these various rituals and cults in the villages and towns of Nupe—and many are still performed every year, long after the disappearance of the Tsoede dynasty—revived and perpetuated the consciousness of this unity which has grown into far more than an external bond of political unification. With the Islamization of the country many of these factors lost their power. The Fulani rulers could use the secret organization of the *ndakó gboyá*; they could seize by force, as they actually did, the royal insignia from the last Nupe king. They could not transfer the authority of the former 'mythical charter' to their own alien rulership. But they could introduce another, younger, and perhaps more powerful uniting force, Islam—Islam as creed and Islam as education. Mosques, a *Liman* and Mallams in every village, these are the instruments of propaganda.[3] And in every religious service, in every babbling little Mallam school this propaganda is enacted. Teaching Islam means teaching the holy cause which sent the conquerors down to this country. Praying to Allah means praying to the God of the powerful and sharing with them, if not their power, their beliefs. But Mohammedanism even becomes a real means of social approach between rulers and ruled. In a country still to a large extent pagan the adoption of Mohammedanism creates something like an intermediary social stratum, placed nearer to the rulers than the rest of the population. Formerly it involved—at least in theory—certain concrete benefits: an increased measure of security, above all, immunity from slave-raids (as the Koran forbids the enslaving of Mohammedans). This rule, however, was never strictly obeyed—unless the religious qualification was supported by the

---

[1] The *ndakó gboyá* society soon became a means of ruthless exploitation. The king and the members of the society were extorting money from the peasants all over the country on the grounds of ridding their villages of witches. This became so intolerable that eventually the Administration of Bida Emirate had to forbid all performances of the *ndakó gboyá*. (For a fuller description see *Africa*, 1935, 4.)

[2] It is interesting to note that when the independent Emirate of Patigi was created by the Government this new Nupe ruler appointed a second *Majï Dodo* for his country.

[3] Mokwa, a village of 2,000 inhabitants, possesses eight mosques, one of them built in 1934 during my stay in the village.

more solid one of political protection. Attachment to the ruling group thus fused with conversion to its religion. In the early days of Fulani rule hundreds of pagans are said to have flocked into the capital to seek out an important person as their patron and to declare to him —and not to the religious officers of Islam—their readiness to embrace Mohammedanism. They received their turban and sword, insignia of clientship and new creed in one. Of such men the Nupe say not 'they become Mohammedans' but '*a ze goiži*'—'they become Fulani'.

Whatever the true essence of Mohammedan faith may be in Nupe, and however sparsely Mohammedanism has so far spread, Fulani rulership did create, and is creating, another 'mythical charter' of the kingdom. It tries again, with its new means, to mould the religious elements into the intensive unit almost of a State Church.[1] The effect of Islam as a 'binding force' of the precarious political system that the Fulani had erected cannot be doubted. A striking example is that under *Etsu* Umaru the whole Trans-Kaduna revolted, refused to pay the tribute, and finally made war on Bida. The rebellious peasants crossed the Kaduna river, marched against Bida and almost reached it, being defeated at a place called Bidakoko, a few miles outside.[2] The whole Trans-Kaduna, that is, with the exception of one town—the strongly Mohammedanized Dabbã, the same town where Mallam Dendo started his proselytizing work in Nupe, and which now refused to join in the war against the rulers with whom they shared their creed.

The identification of State and Church is demonstrated in the annual Mohammedan festival, the *Sallah*, which is as much a pageant of the might and splendour of the kingdom as a religious feast. There are two *Sallah* feasts, the Small *Sallah* and the Great *Sallah*, separated by a two months' interval.[3] Their celebration may be called the climax of the whole year's cycle: the two feasts give the months in which they fall their names—*etswa salagi* and *etswa salakó*, 'month of the Small *Sallah*' and 'month of the Great *Sallah*'; and to these the people look forward and look back, in the long-drawn preparations and anticipation, and in recollections and memories. The *Sallah* feast is like a Friday celebration on an immensely enlarged scale. On the first day the king on horseback under the state umbrella and surrounded by his noblemen and state officials, leads the vast procession to the praying-ground outside the town, where the *Liman* holds the service. After the service the procession returns to the royal residence. Here a great display of horsemanship takes place, at which the bodyguard of the king, his police, and officers of state parade before him and his guests of honour—the foremost among whom are the District Officer and all the Europeans living

[1] See C. K. Meek, *The Northern Tribes of Nigeria*, 1925: 'Islam . . . has converted isolated pagan groups into nations; . . . it is largely due to Islam that numbers of tribes are now, before our eyes, forming themselves into nations' (ii, pp. 4, 10).
[2] It is said that this name Bidakoko was later given to the place of the battle, because *koko a tũ Bida o*, 'almost they (the rebellious army) had reached Bida'.
[3] The Nigerian *Sallah* is the *Beiram* or *Id* of other Mohammedan countries, which feasts are also celebrated twice, as 'Little *Beiram*' and 'Great *Beiram*'.

in Bida Emirate. On the second day of the *Sallah* the *Etsu* holds the great *nkó* of the year, a reception at which everyone who holds rank and title and every person of consequence comes to salute his sovereign, to offer gifts of loyalty and to receive counter-gifts expressing the king's favour. For two days tens of thousands of people crowd the streets of Bida and assemble in front of the royal residence—Bida people as well as peasants from the villages who flock to the capital to see the *Sallah*. There they watch their rulers ride past in all their splendour, equipped with their paraphernalia of rank; they listen to music, drum signals, and songs of praise; they join in the general rejoicing, made more joyful by the largesse and gifts of food and kola-nuts which a gracious sovereign causes to be distributed among his loyal subjects. Here, then, it falls to the elements of worship and secular display, inextricably fused, and supported by the stimulus of mass experience, to mobilize periodically sentiments of loyalty and the consciousness of unity.

From these manifold sources springs that common mental and moral orientation which we call national solidarity and loyalty to throne and country. Here are born the sentiments of unity which, in the words of Lowie, 'flourish without compulsion'. They crystallize largely round the figure of the king, thus giving substance to the self-description of the people of Nupe kingdom as 'king's men'. Yet the king is not simply the state—the factors checking his authority, his varying powers, show clearly that he is only an organ of the state. Nor is he a symbol of the power and unity of the state in the same concrete and personal sense in which the village chief can be regarded as a symbol of his community. Kings have been deposed and exiled; they have to fight and intrigue for their position; they are subject to the openly working balance of power. All this is well known—too well known for the identification of the person of the king with the unity of the society. Loyalty to a personal king of Nupe is factional; solidarity and loyalty on a national scale rallies round the throne and round the abstract principle of kingship rather than round the actual king.[1]

But the 'binding forces' are not wholly pivoted on kingship. They yield also a commonness referring to the country as such, the people as such, to a largely abstract and timeless collective identity which no longer needs the sustaining symbol of kingship. These 'binding forces' implant in the minds of the people of the state the realization that, over and above tribal sections, cultural and class divisions, they form a single human material, living an identical life. They teach a new meaning of the word Nupe, which is the meaning of *nation*. Collective pride, otherwise vested in the tribe or the local community, and its counterpart, the aloof or critical attitude towards other groups and their culture, fuses with and is supplanted by the sentiments of national pride—patriotism. Co-ordination of behaviour loses its aspect of a dictated order sanctioned by force, and becomes indis-

---

[1] It is possible that this was less so in the pre-Fulani kingdom, with its undivided rulership, invested with ritual functions and based on a unique, automatic, system of succession. Here kingship may well have been accepted in a much more concrete and personal sense as the symbol and pivot of political unity.

ETSU WITH BODYGUARD IN *SALLAH* PROCESSION

DISPLAY OF HORSEMANSHIP DURING *SALLAH*

tinguishable from the self-willed conformity born of a closely knit community life. The state itself becomes that twin-creation as which MacIver conceives it, and, with one side of its being, a community.

The process is not yet complete. Existing social divisions and divergent 'interest units' are not wholly submerged in the new consciousness of unity. Sociologically, the incompleteness of the development is visible in the reluctance with which certain sections, especially among the peasantry, respond to the cultural reorientation. Psychologically, it manifests itself in the ambiguous attitude of many individuals in the lower classes, vacillating between bitter resentment against the ruling class and readiness to identify themselves with its glory, of which we have seen examples. It is an attitude familiar in many societies similarly split by sharp distinctions of political and social inequality.[1] One might doubt whether this process of intensive unification will ever be completed now, with new influences coming in, new cultural and class divisions being formed which disturb the steady growth and blur the old border-lines. I do not myself think that this will be so. But in a wider sense the growth of the Nupe nation, even if it were to continue undisturbed, would never be complete: for the nation is a dynamic, not a static, unit, a unit which must constantly readjust itself and constantly absorb new 'raw material'—new generations, newly-formed classes, strata, groups.

The achieved integration of the state is then in some measure, like that of the village community, the integration of a 'multiple system of control'. Yet the state and the village community differ not only in the intensity and completeness but also in the quality of the integration which they achieve. We noticed that the 'binding forces' of the state appear in varying degrees of concreteness, from actual co-operation to moral orientation, and that those of most abstract appeal were the really effective ones. In this, I believe, lies the essential difference between the integrative mechanism operating in the village community and this new mechanism of creating nation-wide unity. Evidently, the very difference in size and numbers must play a decisive part. In the village all integrative agencies can address themselves to an identical group substratum, and can envelop it in the network of actual collaboration. The state, with its huge human substratum, its subdivisions and sections, precludes the full effectiveness of such direct and concrete integration. Direct contact and direct co-adaptation of behaviour are subordinated to indirect methods of bringing about conformity, through ideological persuasion. Actual concerted action gives way to efforts at securing parallel action, and 'common' interests in the strict sense are replaced by 'identical' interests. Instead of communal rites at which groups that in other contexts act as political units are welded together by the influence of religious experience, we have the spreading of common beliefs and practices designed to call forth identity of outlook and to foster, though not an identical group, a group conscious of identity.

Ultimately and rather surprisingly, then, the binding forces of the

[1] M. T. Herskovits has called it, by a suggestive term, 'socialized ambivalence' (*Life in a Haitian Valley*, p. 295).

state can be reduced to the fact of cultural assimilation. Yet it is not that random assimilation which is incidental to the expanding state, and which only superficially obscures social division, achieving but an insecure, external, likeness. This assimilation is designed to carry the foci of cohesion and solidarity—ideologies, and the institutions by which they are sustained. I said 'designed'. But how far are we justified in regarding this assimilation and the incentives behind it as deliberately conceived and employed by the political system and its agents? Certain practices such as the encouragement given to Mallams proselytizing among the pagans, the reward of increased security held out to converts, or the engagement of musicians and poets to sing the praises of the king and the kingdom, represent actual 'propaganda', still carried out under our eyes. Others, such as the supplanting of a local cult by a 'king's ritual', must have amounted to the same in former times (in the case of the royal interest in the *ndakó gboyá* society it can be proved to have been so only two generations ago). Other forms of persuasion, again, may have worked through the unconscious mechanism of habits and views formed imperceptibly. Often their agents are men who have been in the Fulani wars or who have in some other way been associated with the ruling group and then returned to their villages, where their stories and memories aid the other, institutionalized, 'propaganda' of the kingdom. In a wider sense, however, they all are deliberately conceived and employed: they are agencies of an assimilation conscious of itself and of the message which it carries.

CHAPTER IX

THE POSITION OF THE WOMEN
RANKS AND OFFICES

IT speaks for the consistency of the political system of Nupe that the position of the women, too, should be drawn into its orbit and even into the framework of official grades and ranks. Among the women of royal blood in pre-Fulani Nupe three women's ranks existed: *Nimwoye*, *Sagi*, and *Wogbo*. Precedence and succession in these three ranks corresponded to the succession in the three highest *gitsú* titles. At the court of ancient Nupe the titles were bestowed by the king on his mother or father's sister, elder sister, or daughter. The holder of the title had to be a *nyizagi gbakó*, a 'strong woman', that is, a woman of about 40–50 years. She had to be unmarried, or else her marriage would be formally dissolved on her appointment to the rank, and she would forthwith be regarded as unmarried. She lived, not in the house of her husband or father but in the *Etsu*'s own house. The Fulani adopted the first two ranks, abandoning, however, the condition of celibacy or nominal celibacy, and made the two daughters of Manko the first *Sagi* and *Nimwoye*. The two ranks have remained in the royal house of Nupe since then. After the split of the dynasty into three branches the women's ranks followed the new dynastic division, the title *Nimwoye* being assigned to the women of the royal house of Masaba, and the title *Sagi* being taken, in rotation, by the women of the royal houses of Umaru and Usman. This rule still holds good: the present *Sagi*, for example, is a sister of the late *Etsu* Bello of the house of Usman, and the *Sagi* before her was an elder sister of the *Shaba*, of the house of Umaru.

The women rank-holders occupied an extremely influential position at the court. They took part in the king's council, they could join in the war with their own troops of slaves and serfs, they held fiefs and owned land. Theirs was the position of 'kings over the women of Nupe'. Although these political prerogatives have disappeared, the position of authority vested in these women's ranks is unimpaired. All quarrels between women, especially women of the noble families, are brought before them; the women of Bida and the villages send them presents and receive counter-presents from them, much as is the custom between the noblemen of Nupe and their king. *Sagi* and *Nimwoye* are often the official representatives of the court at the family feasts of the Bida nobility. At the name-giving ceremony which was celebrated in the house of the *Shaba* in 1936 the *Sagi* came to bring presents and congratulations from the *Etsu*—an honour which was duly appreciated by all who were present.

Among the Bida women of low birth, the wives and daughters of commoners, we find another women's rank, *Sonya*.[1] She is, as the Nupe

---

[1] The Nupe word *Sonya* corresponds to the Hausa word (and the equivalent women's rank) *saraunyia*, lit. queen. *Só* or *So* is a Nupe root meaning head or chief.

put it, the 'Sagi of the poor'; what the royal princesses do for the women of the nobility the Sonya does for the women of her own class: she advises them and arbitrates in their quarrels, taking, however, the more serious cases to the Sagi. The Sonya might almost be called a female officer of state. All large-scale women's work that is done in Bida by order of the king is organized and supervised by her—for example, the beating of the floors in the houses of the king and the royal nobility: The Sonya is, above all, entrusted with the supervision of the market. She is elected by the Bida women who are regular traders on the market, and her rank is confirmed by the Etsu. The respect and deference with which all Bida women greet their Sonya illustrates the importance of her position. Formerly she was a royal fief-holder on a small scale, holding land of her own; she was also allowed to levy a small due on all business transacted on the market. Of this levy the Sonya returned one-third to the Sagi or Nimwoye as a symbol of her submission to the highest authority of these royal princesses over the women of Bida. To-day, the Sonya is still supervising the market and the work of the women. She has kept her status and her official position as well: for she has been made an official of the Native Administration and granted a small salary.

In every Nupe village, finally, we find a titled 'head of the women', called Sagi, like the royal princess in Bida. She is usually a woman about or over 50. She is elected by the married women of the village and her appointment is confirmed by the chief. In larger villages there may be a Shaba Sagi as well, an appointed successor to the headship of the women. The title Sagi itself seems to be of comparatively recent origin and was probably, like many other village titles, copied from the Bida rank system. The original title which it replaced was Lelu. This title, though no longer used, was explained to me in most villages to be the exact equivalent of the modern title Sagi. Yet this is not quite true: with the change in the title a subtle change in the significance of the rank has taken place. As I have described elsewhere, the Nupe chiefs used to bestow the rank Lelu on the woman who was believed to be the most powerful witch in the village. Her secret knowledge could thus be made to benefit the interests of the community. Turned into an organ of village administration, this woman could be used, in the opinion of the people, to check and control the subversive activities of the other witches.[1] With regard to witchcraft, then, the Nupe have adopted the proverbial policy of making a (reformed) criminal chief of police, or rather an imaginary criminal controller of an imaginary crime. Their belief in the efficiency of this measure has not changed. Yet the curtailed power of the present-day village chief, who is no longer free to act upon the advice of his female 'controller of witchcraft'; the general fear in the country, born of the experiences in the witchcraft trial in 1932, even so much as to mention the word witch or witchcraft; and in certain places also the growing importance of other more prosaic business for the head of the women, have all contributed to suppress the magical aspect

[1] See Africa, 1935, 4.

of the office of the village *Sagi* and to emphasize its harmless business side instead.

Thus we find that in many Nupe villages an efficient business-like head of the women has succeeded the *Lelu* or *Sagi* of the old type. In other places, again, the people would not admit the magic significance of the woman's rank. Yet the strength of the belief, concealed though it may be, was shown in a witchcraft case which I happened to witness in Gbajibo, a small village on the Niger above Jebba. Here the *Sagi*, the very business-like head of the local women, was yet behind the public outcry against an alleged witch. The women much more than the men were leading in this persecution; they had been the first to ostracize the victim; and when I questioned them about their motives, they all referred me to the *Sagi*. Her own motive appeared to be jealousy of the other woman, the alleged witch, in whom she saw a dangerous rival, possibly even for the position of a *Sagi*.

The office of the *Sagi*, modern or traditional, is invariably a much-coveted one. Her moral hold over the women, as our example has shown, is complete. It is equally strong in the less sinister spheres of communal life: like the *Sonya* in Bida, the village *Sagi* advises the women, organizes women's work, arbitrates between them, and receives small presents from every business transaction which they carry through.

MARRIAGE AND STATUS

The ranks and offices already discussed all belong to married women. But we have seen that they represent forms of status which the women acquire in their own right, on the grounds of descent, or personal ability, or both, independent of their status as wives of men who occupy this or that social position. We shall see later that the same principle applies also to the status won by wealth. In particular the status by descent of the Nupe women is affected but little by marriage, i.e. by the social status of their husbands; in so far as it is so affected, this change is in the direction of social advancement. Women of low birth who marry above their status into the aristocracy can claim the status of their husbands; and women who marry beneath their station do not lose their status but raise their husbands to their own social level. The men will be allowed to share most of the social and political privileges of the class into which they marry. Two cases were reported to me in which the men could even acquire *saraki* ranks after marrying a woman of the *saraki* nobility. But even if the men are not admitted fully into the titled class, their children would always acquire the status of their mother. Daughters may thus inherit the status of their fathers, and both sons and daughters that of their mothers; husbands may be adopted into the social sphere of their wives and parents-in-law. This social regulation may seem surprising in an otherwise strongly patrilineal society. But this one-sided interpretation of the change of status that goes with marriage is not an expression of matrilineal kinship tendencies, nor of 'feminist' leanings in Nupe society (though we shall find ample evidence of these, too); rather it expresses political interests, deep-seated class sentiments, which cannot admit of a lowering of status in any one high-born. Yet if, owing to the rigid class system, marriage between the classes is thus turned into a potential instrument of social advancement, its utilization in this sense is also rigidly controlled.

For marriage in the aristocracy, especially in the royal nobility, is to a very large extent endogamous—'family marriage' as the Nupe call it. As the Nupe-Fulani regard themselves all as related, and as most families of the nobility are more or less closely related by marriage, practically all 'family marriages' of this kind are at the same time marriages within the ruling class. The Fulani in Nupe, moreover, following Mohammedan practice, encourage parallel cousin marriage (which is forbidden by the traditional marriage rules of the country) as well as cross-cousin marriage, and thus widen enormously the scope of 'family marriages', especially between descendants in the male line. Family marriage in Nupe, finally, is characterized by a much lower bride-price than that paid in ordinary exogamous marriage. This leads to the rather paradoxical situation, on which my informants invariably commented, that the wealthiest and proudest classes of the country favour 'cheap' marriage, while the humble commoners and peasants are committed mostly to a very high bride-price. The explanation is that the low bride-price in this case supplies an additional incentive for endogamous marriage—'class endogamous' marriage, as it were—and thus for the preservation of the social identity of the ruling classes (as well as, incidentally, a strengthening of their group solidarity).[1]

Indeed the counterpart of the incentive of a low bride-price in 'class endogamous' marriages is the 'deterrent' of an exceptionally high bride-price demanded in the case of marriages between the classes, i.e. between men of the *tálaka* class and girls or women of the nobility. Such cases are accordingly rare. Yet we may note that if a chance of such marriage exists, if the girl loved the man sufficiently to overlook the difference in social status, the high bride-price alone proves no obstacle. For friends and relations would join forces to find the money and to enable the ambitious suitor to make his luck by this advantageous marriage. The benefits of his new position would be considered sufficient promise of an eventual ample gratification. One of my Bida servants was an example: the son of a commoner, he had succeeded in winning the love of the daughter of a very high *saraki* and eventually, after considerable difficulties, in marrying her with money borrowed from friends and relations.

The endogamous marriage rules only ensure that the women of the ruling classes should marry within the class; they do not attempt to exclude the less dangerous form of dilution implied in the marriages of the men to women from other classes and strata. Indeed, the polygamous nature of marriage in Nupe, which forces the men to seek wives

[1] One of my informants who belonged to the *saraki* class even went so far as to explain the whole principle of having a different bride-price for 'family' and 'outside' marriages as a political measure taken by the *saraki* and Fulani nobility with the purpose of preventing commoners from marrying into their class. Though incorrect as regards the facts, this interpretation is significant as an expression of the dominant class sentiments.

from outside their social group, precludes an application of 'class endogamy' in this sense. Marriage of this kind between the strata has reached enormous dimensions. And this shows, incidentally, that the rule of 'class endogamy' serves, even in the case of the Fulani rulers, the interest only of a social identity and solidarity and not, as one might perhaps assume, of racial purity.

POLYGAMY AND SEX MORALITY

In Nupe as in most polygamous societies in which marriage is by bride-price (and by high bride-price at that) the number of wives a man possesses becomes an infallible index of wealth and status. In the peasant districts, where we find comparatively little inequality of wealth, the range of polygamy also varies in narrow limits. Genealogies which I collected in the two Nupe villages Doko and Kutigi show the following range of polygamy (the figures refer to middle-aged or old men, both of the living and previous generation):

| | Number of wives | | | | | | |
	1	2	3	4	5	Over 5	Total
Number of cases	68	96	20	11	1	1	179

The average is thus 2.1 wives per man.[1] To quote a similar average for Bida would be meaningless: the great inequality of wealth and status is reflected in the widely varying range of polygamy. In the houses of the *talakaži*, the 'poor ones', monogamy is the rule; in the 'middle class' the conditions are much the same as in the peasant districts; but as regards the men of substance and rank, though it would be correct to say that they have rarely less than four wives, the upper limits of their polygamy are very fluid, and cannot even be ascertained with any accuracy. Popular notions attribute to certain royal princes and, above all, to the kings of Nupe, numbers of wives varying between 100 and 200. Even the late *Etsu* Saidu is reported to have had sixty wives. Discretion forbade any direct inquiries. Besides, the vagueness in the legal definition of 'wife' and 'marriage' in these cases would have detracted from the value of the information. According to Mohammedan law a man may have four wives only. But this rule is easily circumvented by limiting the number of legal wives whom one marries with religious rites to four (or four at a time), and relegating the rest to the position of mere concubines. In the houses of the higher as well as of lesser nobility I found

[1] The range of polygamy varies to some extent locally. In Mokwa, for example, I obtained the following figures:

| | Number of wives | | | | | | |
	1	2	3	4	5	Over 5	Total
Number of cases	44	28	3	3	..	..	60

The average is, again, 2 wives per man.

the practice of divorcing ageing wives and replacing them with more attractive girls. The ex-wife, especially if she had borne children, would be allowed to stay on in the house and would continue to be supported by the husband, or ex-husband—a wife on pension, as it were. The late *Etsu* of Agaie was partial to a different method: he used to marry off his 'pensioned' wives, at very low bride-price, to *talakaši* and peasants, who were either glad to find a 'cheap' wife or else afraid to refuse so exalted a gift. Among the upper classes of Bida old men, long past marrying age, would still add young girls to the number of their 'wives'. Aphrodisiacs (which one can buy from the barber-doctors in Bida) and stimulants (above all, kola-nuts) keep alive their sexual appetite. Old S., who died in 1935, 70 years old, had married a new young wife only the previous year, and a son was born to him ('to him' at least in the legal sense) posthumously.

This classbound polygamy deeply affects the sex morality of the women and, indirectly, of the society at large. Respect for chastity and the sanctity of matrimonial ties dominates the traditional moral concepts of Nupe. But this 'double morality' of a social system which legitimizes unrestricted sexual desire of the men in one privileged stratum, but would force similar desires in other strata into the realm of illegitimate and indictable action, is in danger of defeating itself. In Bida it has clearly provided a strong stimulus to extra-marital sex relations in all classes. Moreover, the starved sexuality of the women in the large polygamous households strives to find an outlet.[1] The insecurity of their legal position tends to remove the barriers of conventional matrimonial morality. Thus many of the younger wives or concubines seek satisfaction in illegitimate relationships and even semi-professional prostitution.

Adultery, including adultery in this extreme form of semi-professional prostitution, is extremely widespread among women of every status. Prostitution in the strict sense (practised as a profession and in brothels) does not occur in Bida. But we have heard that the kola-nut vendors on Bida night-market, all married women, are prostitutes at the same time.[2] We shall learn later of the close association between women's trade and prostitution (and the large majority of Bida women are traders of one kind or another). 'Every woman', an informant told me, 'whom you see beautifully dressed in the streets of Bida after dark, is a "bad" woman.' Informants, themselves married men, were all agreed that there were hardly any 'good' women left in Bida. But when I asked them what the husbands were doing about this they said: 'Nothing; what could we do?' Indeed, they can do little but shut their eyes. The obvious alternative, divorce, is impossible in most cases. Poor men cannot afford to divorce their wives, for this would mean forfeiting part of the bride-price and thus their only chance of finding another wife; moreover, the economic dependence of many husbands on their wives (of which we shall hear more in a later chapter) forbids such a course.

---

[1] In the royal 'harems' homosexual practices—called *madigo* or *lutu* (the Arabic word for homosexuality)—are, in fact, said to occur.

[2] Their 'tariff' is commonly known: it varies between 6d. and 1s.

Men who have to uphold their prestige and social position would never risk the publicity and ridicule of divorce proceedings in which they would have to appear in the role of the wronged husband.[1] The amorous affairs of Bida noblemen supply, in fact, an ever-welcome topic for the town gossips. When some years ago two popular noblemen quarrelled, everyone knew that it was about a girl and had the details at their finger-tips. Only the men of very great wealth and highest status are in a position to restrain or threaten their unfaithful wives. For one thing, they can afford to forfeit more than one bride-price, and can thus divorce their wives (according to Nupe Mohammedan law) without invoking elaborate public proceedings. Besides, wives and paramours would hesitate to provoke the enmity of these powerful personages. It is not unnatural, then, that (as my informants said) the wives of these men supply the only example of unimpaired marital fidelity in Bida—another no less striking instance of 'double morality'.

If the older married men are either resigned or complacent, the younger men see in illegitimate adventures only an exciting and tempting aspect of Bida life. We shall meet later with their ideal, the dashing young man 'about town' who can 'have' all the women he wants and can boast of his conquests. The women who avails herself of the loosened marriage ties may be talked about and called (behind her back) a 'bad woman'—*nyizagi banza*, a 'worthless woman'. But in their ordinary behaviour towards these women, when meeting them in the street or in the house of a mutual friend, the men will never fail in their respect towards them or betray by a sign their moral prejudices. This ambiguous attitude is symptomatic of a society which, though still conscious of its traditional dogmatic appreciation of chastity, is yet adapting itself to a spreading laxity of morals.

There is indeed evidence to show that sexual licence has been greatly increasing in the last generation or two. But there is also evidence of the fact that sexual licence on a smaller scale and within strictly defined limits enjoyed a legitimate existence in traditional Nupe society. The anomaly of public morals which would condemn sexual licence yet at the same time sanction it in a certain well-defined social domain is familiar to the student of society. In Nupe as in all other societies this qualified admission of sexual licence is due to various social causes. A first cause lies in the nature of sex itself, namely, in the reaction to the restraint on all pre-marital and extra-marital sexual relations which characterizes the traditional sex morality of the people. Another cause is the large floating population in Bida, composed of traders, warriors (formerly), labourers (to-day), that is, men who come to Bida without their wives and depend on prostitution for the satisfaction of their sexual appetite. A third cause is embodied in the institution of female trade. We shall see later that women's trade involves a loosening of matrimonial and family ties and tends to become identified with licentious living. In female trade Nupe society thus has grasped a ready occupational framework for that domain of sanctioned

[1] Clear evidence of this is the scarcity of divorce cases, which form two-thirds of all court cases in Bida, from the houses of the nobility.

sexual licence towards which the other social forces appear to be driving. The result is the close association between professional female trade and semi-professional licensed prostitution which we can observe to-day.

Yet admission into this 'domain' was in turn made dependent upon a certain qualification, namely childlessness. Here we can add a final, ideological motive to the social causes behind the moral development. It is embodied in the Nupe conception of barrenness as a state outside conventional morality, and its contribution is twofold: it helps to define more narrowly the group in which sexual licence shall be sanctioned, by making sterility of the women a criterion of admission; and it provides at the same time the spiritual framework for such social sanction, by linking it with certain religious or quasi-religious beliefs. To some extent the ideological association between barrenness and sexual licence can be reduced to certain obvious rational motives, which are, in fact, present in the minds of the people: childlessness is of great advantage in the life of the women traders whose profession involves constant travelling and long absence from home; moreover, the sexual indiscretions of sterile women are socially of less consequence than those of other women, being comparatively safe from discovery and precluding the more disturbing legal complications (i.e. birth of illegitimate children). But the social interpretation of barrenness also expresses certain more deeply rooted beliefs. To the Nupe marriage has no real meaning without progeny. Barrenness is regarded as a great curse and misfortune, and many cults and forms of magic are designed to secure fertility of the women or to cure barrenness. Traditional religious beliefs place barren women in a category apart and exclude them from participation in the most important annual cult of the country, the *gunnu*.[1] As the barren woman fails by the common standard of marriage and womanhood, she is also exempted from the standards of common morality. Adultery and unchastity count less in her than in other women. And although the stigma of immorality would still attach to the unchaste barren woman (she would still be called a 'worthless woman'), it would be, as it were, overshadowed by and fused with the other paramount stigma of barrenness itself.

The growth of sexual licence far beyond its traditionally sanctioned limits is again due to various causes, economic, political, and religious. The primary cause appears to be economic and will be discussed in that context. Its effectiveness, however, is greatly strengthened by the political and social factors which foster what I have termed the 'double morality' in Nupe society. We can also see that the Nupe conception of barrenness must itself indirectly aid these tendencies and defeat the limitations which it was meant to uphold. For in a country with spreading sterility and even birth restriction, a religion which withholds its sanctions of matrimonial morality in the case of childless women can prove but a weak bulwark against the tide of sexual licence. Mohammedanism in Nupe, committed as it is to that 'double morality', undermines rather than supplies forces of moral restraint.

[1] For a description of this aspect of barrenness see *J.R.A.I.* 1937, p. iii.

A comparison between sex morality in the town and in the villages will bring the final proof of our interpretation of the social causes of moral laxity and publicly condoned sexual licence. For in the villages, where the political and economic factors to which we have attributed this development are much less conspicuous than in Bida, sexual licence in this sense is absent also. The same informants who declared that there were no 'good women' left in Bida maintained that the opposite was true of the country. Within limits, this is correct. Semi-professional prostitution is absent and adultery is far less frequent than in Bida. Above all, it is not glossed over for fear of publicity and ridicule: it leads to quarrels and frequently to divorce. Nor are illegitimate amorous adventures applauded and bandied about. The more closely knit village life renders sexual promiscuity both more difficult and more risky, and the danger of provoking serious conflicts forces it into the sphere of clandestine and disreputable activities. The ideal of the Bida Lothario is absent in the Nupe village.

It is largely true to say that among the peasant women also the Bida ideal of the glamorous 'fast' woman finds no following. Or, more correctly, it finds no following among the peasant's wives and daughters who have chosen village life. For especially in the larger trading-places there is a certain (increasing) minority of women who leave the village to join the army of 'loose' women traders. However, they do not introduce their ways into village life itself. To quote again from my informants: 'Peasant women are on the whole better wives than our women in Bida. You see it when you come to a village: you will not find women with whom you can sleep. But who would want to sleep with them? They are badly dressed, they do not wash, use no scent, and smell of sweat. There are a few exceptions, though, for example the women in the house of the chief of K.'—referring to a village in which the chief's family was in many ways emulating the standards of Bida life. There is good sense in these cynical (though not cynically meant) remarks. Hard work, lack of leisure, the inability to afford nice dresses or the help of cosmetics, make the peasant woman comparatively unattractive; she ages more quickly than her more fortunate sister in town. It is not surprising that she should come short of the sophisticated urban standards of taste. If the peasant woman thus succumbs less to temptation, it is also true that less temptation comes her way. Having chosen peasant life she can but choose peasant morality also. The different sexual morality in town and village is thus essentially an expression of differences in economic conditions and of inequality of wealth and status.

It is tempting to dwell on this relation between economic and political factors and the attitude of the society towards the problems of sex and morality. There has been the tendency in recent anthropological writings to regard the elaboration of the sex theme in different cultures, the temperamental and personality traits which, in a society, appear associated with sex, as the expression of some ultimate quality in culture itself —the genius or *ethos* of a culture. That women in one society are 'gentle' and 'aggressive' in another, that one culture regards them as masculine workers and another as feminine mothers or partners in love, is all due to the mysterious workings of that genius of culture.[1] In a criticism of these views I have pointed out that the sex morality which a society makes its own and the whole *ethos* which its culture expresses are largely functions of the economic conditions prevailing in the society.[2] Of this the preceding discussion has, I think, provided conclusive evidence.

[1] M. Mead, *Sex and Temperament*, pp. 298, 310, and *passim*.
[2] 'The Typological Approach to Culture', in *Character and Personality*, 1937, p. 280 et seq.

CHAPTER X
GOVERNMENT IN MODERN NUPE

OFTEN in the foregoing description I have used the present tense as if the Nupe kingdom of pre-British days still existed. True, this was to a large extent an historical chapter; yet it described a development the results of which are still valid and still mould society to-day as they moulded it thirty, fifty, or even a hundred years ago. I was not merely reconstructing dead events and past phases. The Nupe kingdom and its society still exist, not only very vividly in the memory of the people but to a very large extent in concrete reality. This is not denying the force of social changes, but stressing the tenacity of a social structure that survives although its contents have changed materially. The recent economic and political changes have affected fundamentally the 'contents' of the social life of the country, the main interests and incentives round which it revolved. There are no more wars, raids, and conquests; slaves and feudal fiefs exist no longer. But ranks and titles and state offices linked with ranks and titles, still exist. Slaves have turned into *bara* or Native Administration officials; fiefs into administrative districts in the charge of royal princes. That the framework of the political organization could survive almost unchanged is in large measure due to the Administration of Nigeria under Indirect Rule and its tendency to utilize as far as possible the traditional social system. But a stronger proof of the tenacity of the Nupe social system is the fact that where the Administration had departed from it and tried to make way for a new development the old trend broke through, undeflected.

Two years ago the Administration built a new official residence for the *Etsu* Bida, with a brick wall, an imposing tower, a garage, and a flower garden—an emblem of modern Nigeria. Incidentally, for all its modernity the new house is but a replica of the hereditary palace of the Nupe kings, with special *katamba* for the *ena Ndeji* and *ena Maiyaki*, for *gitsúži* and *bara*, the *ena manži*, the men of the *Etsu Dogari*, and the commoners who come to wait on the *Etsu*. Now, this new house was built on 'neutral' ground, outside the town gates, as a symbol of the Government's intention to break with the division into three royal houses, which the Government considered harmful to the unity of the country.[1] The Administration believed itself to have overcome successfully the opposition of the late *Etsu*. An old and sick man, he was reported to have said—and his words were all over Bida—that he had agreed to the new site only because he knew he would not have to live in the new house. Which was true enough—he died before the building was finished. But the new *Etsu*, who willingly took up his residence in the splendid new house, one day surprised the District Officer by demanding that his 'proper house' in Bida, in his 'own' part of the town, should be put in repair at the expense of the Native

---

[1] See p. 93.

Administration. New house or old, in his mind the position of the Emir remained inseparable from that traditional personal link with the local town faction.

THE ADMINISTRATION OF THE EMIRATE

Let me describe the modern Government of Nupe Emirate, in official nomenclature, the Native Administration (N.A. for short) of Bida Division.[1] Out of the multitude of traditional ranks the modern Emirate has taken a certain number and embodied them in the N.A. as official posts, carrying a salary and to some extent also implying specific, new tasks. The salary is graded in accordance with the importance of the office, and the *Etsu* himself heads this new bureaucracy with a salary of £2,000.[2] The *Etsu* Nupe is still elected from the ranks of the royal princes by *gitsúži* and *sarakiži*, or more precisely by those *gitsúži* and *sarakiži* who hold appointments under the N.A. The *Etsu*, assisted by a council of four, looks after the affairs of the Emirate; he watches over law and order in the country, carries through measures of administration, tries certain legal cases, and controls appointments to offices and titles. Advised and guided by the District Officer in charge of the Division, the *Etsu* is the responsible head of his government. The agreement of both *Etsu* and District Officer is necessary for every administrative measure.[3] The appointment of a new *Etsu* is subject to confirmation by the Governor of Nigeria, and in extreme cases the Governor may depose the Emir on the advice of the District Officer and his superior officer, the Resident of the Province. The *Gabi Seidi*, formerly the head-slave of the *Etsu*, is to-day the official messenger between the Emir's residence and the Divisional Office.

The *Etsu's* council consists to-day of the following members: the *Ndeji*, *Maiyaki*, *Nágya*, and *Etsu Tafiẽ*. The *Ndeji*, the old 'Father of the Town', is the 'president' of the council. The *Maiyaki*, from a 'Minister of War', has become a 'Minister of Public Works' and a representative of the *Etsu* on tours of inspection. The *Nágya*, a royal prince, was formerly District Head of Mokwa, and was then co-opted into the council for the ability which he had shown in the administration of his district. The *Etsu Tafiẽ*, finally, was taken into the council in 1931, after the Bida disturbances, as an official representative of the *talakawa* (this is the Hausa form of *talakaži*, commoners), who formerly had no voice in the management of state affairs. I may say a few words about this appointment. Justified as was its aim, the appointment itself seems rather problematic. It was justified officially on the grounds that the

[1] The Administration of the other Provinces and Divisions where sections of the Nupe tribe are living is organized on identical lines; we may disregard them here.
[2] These were the salaries of the *Etsu* and the higher officials of the N.A. in 1934-6: *Etsu* £2,000; *Ndeji*, *Maiyaki* £180; *Nágya*, *Etsu Tafiẽ* £120; District Heads £150; Chief *Alkali* of Bida £180.
[3] No fixed rule can be laid down as regards the relative share of responsibility and initiative in this co-operation of District Officer and Emir. It varies considerably with the personalities of these two men, and also with the general trend of policy that might obtain in the Province at a given time.

Etsu Tafiẽ had been in pre-Fulani times the chief of the 'aboriginal population' of Nupe, the Beni tribe[1]—a justification which, as this chapter has shown, takes into account, out of the whole complex social structure of the kingdom, but one comparatively irrelevant fact: an external historical connexion with one isolated village community. Typical of what I have called the 'parochial outlook' of the village, the *Etsu Tafiẽ*, bearer of one of those 'petty village titles', having reached this new position through no acknowledged channel of 'social career', seems out of place in a council on which he could hardly hold his own against the traditional leaders of the country's fate, the highest ranks of the Nupe hierarchy. The insignificant role which I saw him play on the council seems to support my view.

Bida Emirate is divided for the purpose of administration into a number of districts; at the head of each is a District Head, appointed by the *Etsu* as a rule from the ranks of the higher royal nobility; he himself, as *Nágenu*, was formerly District Head of the Jima-Doko district (see table, p. 95). Some time ago the number of districts was reduced from ten to seven by amalgamating certain districts, making the area in charge of one District Head rather larger, and perhaps also more heterogeneous, than might seem advisable. Here is the list of districts and rank-holders appointed as District Heads.

List of District Heads

Former Districts	Present Districts	District Heads
Gbangba	Gbangba	Nakorji
Dakmon-Magwe	,,	,,
Badeggi	Badeggi	Ginya
Kacha	Kacha	Sheshi
Jima-Doko	Jima-Doko	Nágenu
Sakpe	Kutigi	Kpotũ
Egbako	,,	,,
Labovi	,,	,,.
Mokwa	Mokwa	Rani
Kyedye	Kyedye	Kuta

Two District Heads are not members of the royal nobility: the *Kuta* of the Kyedye, whose privileged position as a provincial chief directly under the *Etsu* had been recognized in the early days of British rule and had been renewed recently by the Administration, and the *Sheshi* of Kacha, who was appointed in 1934. He had been the hereditary village chief of Kacha, and his appointment to an office which had been held previously by the *Makũ*, a royal prince, was designed, like the appointment of the *Etsu Tafiẽ*, to open responsible state offices to the Nupe 'commoner'. Unfortunately this appointment was once more based on insufficient knowledge of the country. The territory over which the ancestors of the *Sheshi* used to exercise their rule as 'town-kings' of Kacha has been placed in the political rearrangement of the country mostly into a different Division, the Agaie Emirate. Also the town and

[1] See p. 25.

territory which he is called upon to rule to-day, the richest trade centre of the country, is inhabited to a very large extent by strangers, traders, craftsmen, and canoe-men from other parts of the country, many of them from Bida, that is, by people who reluctantly bow to the rule of a culturally 'inferior' peasant chief. It is not surprising, therefore, that his administration of the district proved unsatisfactory, and that the *Etsu* felt justified in urging the District Officer to reinstitute in this responsible office a member of his own class.

The District Heads live in their districts; they reside in the largest town and hold there their little court, an exact copy of a nobleman's household in the capital. They have to make frequent tours of inspection of their area, and at regular intervals they visit the capital to report to the *Etsu*, especially at the time of the great Mohammedan festivals when all officers of state assemble at the king's court. District Heads are sometimes transferred from one district to another, but the tendency to-day is to let them stay in one district as long as possible so as to become thoroughly familiar with the people and the local problems of administration. They are responsible to the *Etsu* for law and order in their districts, their main task being the supervision of tax collection; but they are also charged with such non-political tasks as finding pupils for the elementary schools of the Emirate. Their subordinates in the administrative machinery are the various Village Heads of the district, of whom we have heard already.[1] The District Heads are further assisted in their work by a staff of official and semi-official helpers— scribes, messengers, policemen, and the host of *bara* and henchmen who attach themselves to every man of rank.

TOWN ADMINISTRATION

The administration of Bida town has undergone many changes in the thirty or forty years of British Administration. The original system was based to some extent on the division of the town into a number of 'wards', each associated with an influential member of the Bida nobility. The town was divided into twenty *efu* (or, as they were known officially, *ungwa*—the Hausa word for town ward); five of these wards were grouped together as one large *ungwa*, and these four *ungwa* were placed under four men of high rank: *Ndeji*, *Maiyaki*, *Galadiman Gari*, and *Gabi Seidi*. The four *ungwa* bore no relation to the dynastic division of Bida into three *ekpã*; their arrangement simply followed the four main roads which cross the town from north to south and east to west. However, the four rank-holders in charge of the large *ungwa* as well as the other subordinate ward-heads in the small *ungwa* (or *efu*) were actually living in the part of the town over which they had been placed; the link of locality which is so relevant in Nupe life was thus recognized officially. Later, however, this system of ward-heads lent itself to certain abuses, bribery and extortion of tax-money; it was abolished by the Administration and replaced by a new system which now divides the town into four

[1] See p. 52.

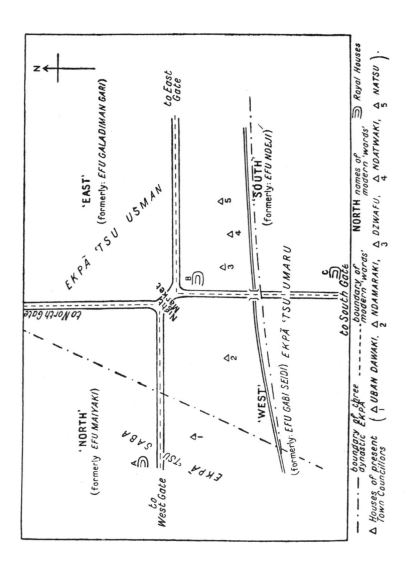

N

'EAST'
(formerly: EFU GALADIMAN GARI)

EKPĀ 'TSU USMAN

to East Gate

'NORTH'
(formerly EFU MAIYAKI)

to North Gate

EKPĀ 'TSU SABA

to West Gate

A

Night Market

B

'WEST'
(formerly: EFU GABI SEIDI) EKPĀ 'TSU UMARU

△ 1

△ 2

△ 3

△ 4

△ 5

'SOUTH'
(formerly: EFU NDEJI)

C

to South Gate

—·—·— boundary of three dynastic EKPĀ

— — — — boundary of modern 'words'

NORTH names of modern 'words'

⌒ Royal Houses

△ Houses of present Town Councillors (△ UBAN DAWAKI, △ NDAMARAKI, △ DZWAFU, △ NDATWAKI, △ NATSU).
　　　　　　　　　　　　　　　　1　　　　　　　　2　　　　　　　3　　　　　　4　　　　　5

ungwa (the same four *ungwa*), defined geographically as Bida North, South, East, and West. Four new officials were appointed who are no longer inhabitants of 'their' *ungwa* but are supposed to be jointly responsible for the whole town, irrespective of their personal connexions with one or the other locality. The Hausa and Yoruba communities of Bida, who live in *lálemi*, were placed under their own ward-heads. These six officials form the present Town Council. A royal prince, the *Natsu*, was appointed as its chairman, and at the same time as the representative of the *Etsu* on the Town Council. The attached sketch-map illustrates the changes in the town administration.

A certain inner weakness of this system becomes apparent at once. It lies in the disregard for the factor of locality and for those direct contacts and bonds of 'protection' and personal attachment which alone establish in Nupe a relationship of mutual confidence between the social classes, between ruler and ruled. It is not surprising therefore that the new division into four geographical areas 'did not work', and that in 1936, only three years after its introduction, a fundamental reorganization was contemplated.[1]

TAXATION

The taxation of the Emirate is fixed by the District Officer, who tours the country and, assisted by District Head and Village Head, assesses the income of the various villages and districts. The tax unit is the village area.[2] The distribution of the tax among the people of the village and its dependencies is left to the Village Head and his elders. Taxation varies partly from district to district and is also different in town and country. Complaints against too heavy taxation, or reports on defaulting, are forwarded through the District Head to the capital, that is, to the Emir's Council and the District Officer. Tax defaulters can be imprisoned.

Of the total tax revenue of the Emirate (to which are added fines, licence fees, &c.) 30 per cent. goes to the Central Government of Nigeria and 70 per cent. to the N.A. Treasury.[3] From the N.A. share in the revenue are paid the salaries of all (native) N.A. officials, the expenses of all Public Works for which the Emirate is responsible, the maintenance

---

[1] In a memorandum for the reorganization of the Bida Town Council, which I drew up on the request of the Administration, I have suggested (1) a town division based on the division into three *ekpã*, which is so eminently characteristic of the social life of the kingdom, and (2) a system of election of ward-heads by the people themselves. The latter would, in my view, utilize and render more valuable the channels of personal connexion between patron and client, trusted 'protector' and the ignorant, intimidated commoner who still feels that he could only benefit from the association with a man of rank and learning.—A paper on the same subject was published in abridged form in the *Summary of Lectures*, Oxford University Summer School on Colonial Administration, 1937, pp. 97–8. See also p. 123.

[2] Lord Lugard, Colonial Reports Misc., No. 40.

[3] This scale corresponds to the position of Bida Emirate as a First Class Emirate. In 1935–6 the scale was slightly altered in favour of the N.A. share, because the building of the *Etsu*'s new official residence—a typical item of N.A. expenditure—would not have been possible without this additional revenue.

of N.A. Hospital and dispensaries, schools, experimental farms, &c. Part of it is used to build up and maintain a substantial reserve fund to be used for unforeseen expenses, in the case of a famine, and suchlike. The apportionment of the tax revenue, above all the allotment of funds for new enterprises, is subject to the joint approval of *Etsu* and District Officer. It is, in fact, in matters of this nature that the harmonious collaboration of the two men is often put to its most severe test.

The far-reaching social change that the introduction of modern taxation has meant for Nupe kingdom cannot be easily exaggerated. The universal taxation under British rule has completely overthrown the former prerogative of tax exemption enjoyed by the nobility and the population of the town. It is not surprising therefore that these people should still strongly resent this abolition of their privileges. But those who resent it most strongly are not the men 'on the top', but rather the people of inferior status, such as guild-heads and Bida craftsmen, who had not been recompensed as many of the others had been in the share-out of new, well-paid official posts. The old guild-head of the Bida woodworkers once quite violently insulted and attacked me, and with me all White Men, for having robbed him of his former status and privileges. 'Formerly', he shouted at me, 'the other craftsmen would come humbly to my house prostrating themselves before me and would present me with gifts to show their loyalty. To-day I have to pay the same tax as they—can you wonder that they have become arrogant and simply ignore me?' One would expect, then, that peasants and small craftsmen and traders would appreciate the equalizing effect of the present system. This is not wholly so—partly for reasons to be explained presently, but partly also because the change had done away with the former system of voluntary gifts on which so much of their social security used to depend. By these gifts they established a personal link with the men of rank and influence, on whose assistance they could count in many situations when such assistance was of utmost importance. These situations have not and perhaps never will disappear completely. It is not surprising that the people cannot yet fully appreciate the 'impersonality' of the modern system, nor realize fully that in return for their tax-money, paid to an 'impersonal' Administration, they receive things no less valuable than the former personal link with powerful individuals: public security, law courts, roads, hospitals, schools.

Taxation is the most sensitive spot in any governmental system. It is perhaps not to be wondered at that the administration of taxes proved the most dangerous stumbling-block on the path of the young N.A. Native official after official, often in the highest position, has lost his post, and even gone to prison, for embezzling tax-money or levying illicit dues. However, there are two more serious weaknesses inherent in the taxation system—more serious because affecting more deeply the inner structure of the society.

The first concerns the (in my view) disproportionately high taxes in the Emirate. Bida Emirate as it exists to-day is not a rich country, the masses of the people are not well off; the discussion on the economic system will bring ample evidence of this. Nupe country is in this respect much less fortunate than, for example, the neighbouring Emirate of Ilorin, a much richer country, yet paying lower taxes. One at least of the reasons for the high taxation in Bida Emirate appears to be the high cost of the N.A.[1] To compare it again with Ilorin: there, with a much higher revenue, the expenditure on the Emir's court and the salaries of the higher N.A. officials are almost the same as in Bida.[2] To understand how such a situation could have come about we must envisage the historical frame of mind with which a Government committed to the policy of Indirect Rule is often tempted to approach the problem of administration. Historically, Nupe Emirate was one of the most important Emirates in the north of Nigeria. Culturally it still is so. Politically, however, it has shrunk to a small country, shorn of many of its former dependencies (e.g. the whole south-west bank of the Niger with the rich rice-growing district of Patigi and the large town of Eggã). Long wars and longer political unrest have impeded its economic recovery. Yet it could hardly be made anything else but a First Class Emirate, and its ruler had to be given the corresponding status, weighing heavily though it does on the country's revenue.

The second weakness lies in the method of assessment. The tax in the more advanced areas of Nigeria is—in theory—an income tax. But how, one is tempted to ask, can any native District Head and group of Village Heads acquit themselves satisfactorily of such a formidable task of assessment? In Bida town, where District Officers themselves have computed incomes and taxes, the taxes are sadly out of proportion with the income (at least to-day, after the economic depression of 1932–4). In certain cases where property and capital are easily assessable some sort of rough approach to an income tax on a sliding scale is possible, e.g. among the Kyedye canoe-men where the amount of tax can be assessed in accordance with the number of canoes owned by an individual. But among the large majority of the people whose taxable income consists exclusively of farm products such a method must fail. The result is a qualified poll-tax assessing the tax per head of the population but admitting two or three different grades: the higher tax is paid by able-bodied married men roughly between the ages of 22 and 50, the lower by men younger and older than this. Children, women (unless they are independent traders), and old men or invalids who can no longer work are free from tax. Now, whereas the traditional productive unit among the Nupe peasants is embodied in the family, taxation takes into account only the individuals. At the time of my stay in the country the last tax-receipts made out for the whole family, to be paid by the family head— as one can imagine very large receipts—were disappearing rapidly, giving

[1] A British trader who knew the economic situation of the country intimately framed his impression in the following words: 'The overhead expenses of the N.A. are too high.' Bluntly expressed though it is, the statement is far from unsound.

[2] In Ilorin, with a revenue of £28,885, the salary of the Emir is £2,250, and the salaries of 17 District Heads amount to a total of £2,539 (an average of £149 per head). In Bida, the revenue of which is £18,161, the Emir's salary is £2,000, and the salaries of 7 District Heads amount to £1,110 (an average of £159 per head). *Nigerian N.A. Estimates*, 1936–7.

way to the (much smaller) tax-receipts made out for individuals. It is, in fact, the present official policy of the Administration to encourage the issue and acceptance of individual tax-receipts throughout the country. Taxation thus ignores and even denies in its own powerful province the existence of the family unit—with what results we shall see later.

LAW

Let me try first to give a picture of the judicial system of Nupe kingdom as it existed in pre-European times. This is, naturally, an historical reconstruction. But the history to which it refers is not the history of a mythical past. It is a history well documented, and obtained from information which seems reliable and significant and which, collected from different sources, shows remarkable agreement on all main points. My chief informants were village elders and chiefs and the Mohammedan judges of Bida Emirate who, in charge of modern jurisdiction to-day, have witnessed and partly practised themselves the old system.

The theoretical difficulties with which the student of law in primitive cultures is faced are absent in our investigation. The problem, especially, whether to define the province of law on the narrow basis of systematic social control exercised by a politically organized society (Radcliffe-Brown) or, more comprehensively, as embracing all social sanctions that make for uniformity of conduct (Malinowski), is decided for us by the nature of the society which we are studying in the sense of the former essentially modern interpretation. Law in Nupe kingdom is quite conspicuously a concern of the political organization and forms part of the elaborate coercive machinery of the state. This does not mean that no sanctions or forms of redress exist which are applied outside the political framework and left to the more diffuse workings of public opinion and individual or group 'self-help'. But the scope of this non-political (or extra-political) law is extremely restricted. It comprises only two types of offences: religious offences—desecration of sacred objects or places, both Mohammedan and pagan—and kinship offences—litigation over inheritance, offences against traditional marriage rules (i.e. marriages in forbidden degrees), and also incest. I cannot describe here in detail the treatment which Nupe society meted out to individuals guilty of these offences. Suffice it to say that public ostracism which might force the culprit to self-exile or to confidence in his vindication by the deity was its main feature. The society thus exempted from its otherwise comprehensive scheme of formal political jurisdiction the two offences which were either of a nature transcending human justice (as in the case of religious offences, and also partly incest) or concerned only internal frictions in individual kinship groups. All offences that affected the relations between kinship groups or individuals from different kinship groups, and all crimes against human life, were regarded as a concern of the community at large.

But the comprehensiveness of political jurisdiction admitted of two degrees. Traditional Nupe law operated with a legal distinction which, corresponding in certain respects to the modern distinction between civil and criminal law, defined two classes of delicts: simpler delicts, which were settled by 'repairing' the damage that had been done, and here the Nupe did not speak of sentence or judgement but of *gyara*, reparation, or arbitration; and graver delicts, 'criminal' cases in the modern sense, which called for formal judgement and punishment—*sheri'a*. The following table summarizes the various crimes and offences according to this twofold classification. Let me emphasize that· these data are widely known, and that every village elder or older man in Bida is able to enumerate and explain the types of offences and the nature of the punishment. This wide-spread legal knowledge is clearly the psychological counterpart of the systematic co-ordination and centralization of Nupe jurisdiction.

Offences involving *gyara*	Offences involving *sheri'a*
Debts, small.	Debts, large.
Theft on a small scale and during the day; theft of fowls, sheep, and goats.	Theft on a large scale, theft of cattle or horses, and all theft committed during the night.
Adultery.	Adultery leading to fights and bloodshed.
Seduction of girl by unmarried man who is willing to marry her.	Seduction by married man who refuses to marry the girl.
	Murder and manslaughter.
	Highway robbery.
	Arson.
	High treason, i.e. rebellion of feudal lords against the king.
	Lèse-majesté (*gi tokó nyá tsu*, lit. abuse of the king).

The first type of offences was a matter for the local authority. In the royal domains it was dealt with by the chief and the elders, in the fief by the delegate of the feudal lord who resided in the village, in consultation with chief and elders. The sentences which this local tribunal could inflict were fines, flogging, and *shelá*, a practice closely akin to pillory: the culprit was marched through the village accompanied by drummers who proclaimed his offence.

The graver crimes, crimes which demanded *sheri'a*, were referred to the central authority—the court of the king and *Alkali* in Bida. They were, in fact, also called *leifi nyá tsu*, 'crimes of the king'. This highest court of Nupe could inflict sentences of every order, above all, the death penalty. The offences were brought to the notice of the central authority through the feudal lords and delegates. The villagers would report to their overlord in the town, or the feudal lord would have the news from his local delegate, and would then inform the supreme court of Nupe. The criminal was apprehended by the king's slave police and taken to the capital where the court was sitting. This system which made the feudal lords and delegates the 'recorders' of crimes and offences laid itself open to many abuses. The feudal lords could be influenced in favour of a better paying claimant, or prevented by bribes from reporting a particular case. The usual procedure as regards, for example, theft or debts was described to me thus: Up to the value of 10s. nothing would happen: 'you give the *egba* half this sum, he will quash the case, and you will still have a profit of 5*s*. Of course, if a larger sum is involved this is not so easy, for such an amount is difficult to hush up, and too many people would know about it.'

The judicial procedure in the capital followed, till recently, two different principles: the *sheri'a gboró*, 'straight judgement', for pagans, and the *sheri'a nya kurani*, 'judgement according to the Koran', for Mohammedans. The former represented the 'customary law' of the country, which would do justice to the local pagan customs; it also implied the oath on the sacred objects of pagan Nupe, especially the chain of Tsoede. The latter followed the written Mohammedan law and implied the oath on the Koran. Punishment of ordinary criminals was performed in the capital, on the open market—be it flogging, *shelá*, or capital punishment. In the case of political offences and in the case of men of rank, royal princes, or members of the high nobility, the execution took place under the cover of night and in the secrecy of their own houses. Whether this 'preferential' treatment expressed a last privilege granted to the ruling classes or whether such secrecy was thought to uphold the morale of the feudal kingdom I cannot say.[1]

All the various crimes and offences listed in our table became actionable only when there was a plaintiff. The state itself did not undertake to prosecute unless it was appealed to first by a person bringing a charge against some other person—with one exception: the crime *lèse-majesté*. The widespread knowledge with regard to this crime and its punishment in districts and groups which certainly never came into personal contact with the king precludes the assumption that in this case, too, the legal executive waited for a concrete charge being brought by the plaintiff in question, i.e. the king. Rather we must assume that the crime became actionable in an absolute sense, whenever and wherever it was committed, provided that witnesses of the act existed. Whether the information about the crime reached the central authority through private information or denunciation, or through the official channels of delegates and sub-delegates, I cannot say; but the important fact is that here the state took the initiative in prosecuting the offender. We have here the instance of an indictable offence in the modern sense of the word—a legal definition unparalleled in any known primitive system of law.

In this comprehensive and strongly centralized jurisdiction the political system of Nupe achieved its strongest hold over the peoples of the kingdom. Here the co-ordination of morality, the uniformity of cultures of which we have spoken, is secured by the most effective weapon, the coercive machinery of state jurisdiction. We possess certain evidence which shows that this comprehensive co-ordination was achieved gradually, and that the political system extended its judicial

---

[1] I have referred already to the ancient, pre-Fulani, judicial organization of the *ledu*, the 'King's Hangmen', who lived in villages on the Niger and there, far from the king's town, executed the criminals who were condemned to death (see p. 73). It is interesting to mention here certain stories current in Bida which record that the *ledu* organization was still used in the time of *Etsu* Usman against rebels of royal blood, who were imprisoned in Giragi, the *ledu* town closest to Bida.

control further and further in the course of time into domains of social life hitherto unaffected by state law. This extension proceeded on two planes: centralized control superseding local jurisdiction, i.e. moving the line of division between 'offences' and' crimes', and formal political law usurping domains that had been left originally to the informal workings of public opinion or self-help. An instance of the former is the treatment of witchcraft: we have heard of the secret anti-witchcraft society which the Nupe villagers could summon to detect and punish witches, and we have heard also that this secret society was brought later under the control of the Fulani rulers of Nupe. An instance of the second form of extension appears to be the treatment of adultery. Informants told me that formerly, at least in pagan communities, adultery was dealt with, not by legal measures but either by a religious sacrifice meant to safeguard matrimonial sanctity, or by self-help on the part of the husband, who was within his rights to beat up the paramour whom he caught *in flagrante*, strip him of his clothes, and drive him out into the street naked.

Now this strengthening of state jurisdiction is understandable from the viewpoint of the dynamic state endeavouring to extend its control over new groups and new aspects of social life. But here we note the rather surprising feature that there are indications of the subject groups themselves having welcomed and invited the extension of state jurisdiction. I was told in Mokwa that during the Fulani régime fathers of headstrong sons sometimes appealed to their feudal lord, and that the latter would lend his authority to the more severe forms of domestic punishment (i.e. flogging). This official cognizance of what is essentially a 'family affair' clearly represents an incipient stage of state jurisdiction. It is only one step from this appeal for moral support of the official organ of the state to a full acceptance of political jurisdiction in the sphere of kinship offences or litigations, for example litigation over inheritance or divorce, which has become reality to-day. How are we to explain this readiness on the part of the people to surrender the sanctions of custom and self-help to state jurisdiction?

The explanation lies in the evolution of the divided legal authority which had made this development inevitable. Two competing authorities of different range of power existing side by side and concerned with the same or closely similar domains of social life must be in danger of frustrating each other, as individuals dissatisfied with the decisions of one may be tempted to obtain help from the other. The elimination or (as in Nupe) surrender of the weaker authority is the result. Family heads could maintain their paternal authority only by appealing for support to that authority which had superseded their own in other social domains. We may formulate it almost as a social law that an expanding system of jurisdiction, once it begins to supersede another weaker system of jurisdiction, is bound to expand further; culture change in this sphere appears to be carried on by its own momentum.

But inevitable as is this development, so are the conflicts inherent in it. The surrender of new domains of social life to the judicial authority of the state means potentially surrender to an alien law. In our example the family heads invited the intervention of the political authority in the interest of preserving the existing code of conduct. But once this extraneous authority is admitted, it will have to be obeyed also should its decision run counter to the traditional code. Moreover, the rival authority may be appealed to equally by individuals or groups dissenting from the traditional conceptions of right and wrong. Ultimately, the issue will depend on whether the representatives of state jurisdiction are prepared to uphold customary practices and codes of conduct, or are committed to promote a uniform state law. The trend towards close political co-ordination and centralization must greatly limit the scope of such concessions as might be granted to the divergent legal conceptions in the various subject communities. The extension of state jurisdiction over new domains of social life may thus come to mean the substitution of existing traditional codes and doctrines by a new uniform state law.

I have stated this as a hypothetical case, being unable to produce concrete evidence to show that precisely this development occurred in the case of the various delicts and offences over which we found state jurisdiction already firmly established. I can only point to certain evidence of the reaction of group sections against what must have appeared to them as an excessive unification of the law, namely, certain attempts to change state jurisdiction back to independent local jurisdiction: thus the chief of the Kyedye is reported to have obtained from *Etsu* Abubakari the right to exercise full and independent jurisdiction in his tribal group; and the people of Sakpe and Kutigi claim to have been granted a similar legal franchise by *Etsu* Masaba in exchange for heavier taxation. However, the progressive extension of state jurisdiction and the trends underlying this development are still visible and effective in present-day jurisdiction, to which we shall turn presently. They appear, characteristically, in that domain of social life which was the last to be absorbed by state jurisdiction—kinship—and concern the relation between the spreading-modern state law of Nupe, Mohammedan law, and pagan customary practice.

Before we describe modern jurisdiction in detail we may examine for a moment the causes of the spreading of Mohammedan law in Nupe. It has no doubt been consciously fostered by the Mohammedan rulers of the country. But to some extent Fulani rule, still in British times, appears to have avoided excessive legal unification by allowing for customary pagan law—the 'straight judgement' in the case of pagans. Here, however, we find that the same effects that accompanied the 'divided authority' occur again in the case of the 'divided law'. The coexistence of two legal systems, one backed by the prestige and supreme power of the rulers of the country, the other reserved for the pagan subject groups, is again reduced to uniformity, the 'stronger law' ousting the 'weaker law'. We have concrete data to illustrate this process. The Mohammedan judges used to ask the parties appearing before them whether they were Mohammedans or pagans. The large majority proclaimed themselves Mohammedans, and desired to be tried according to Mohammedan law. Administrative Officers in areas where pagan and Mohammedan courts exist side by side also said that the people would generally prefer the Mohammedan court. They explain this attitude as due to the reluctance of the people to be classed with the more backward sections of the population. But there is also a more fundamental reason. Offences and litigation involve by their very nature dissension from established rules of conduct. It is thus often in the interest of offenders and litigants to dissociate themselves from traditional justice and to appeal to the rival law existing in the community. We shall see that in certain extreme cases the 'divided law' almost puts a premium on dissension from the traditional concepts of right and wrong.

In modern Nupe, then, Mohammedan law is paramount. The legal administration of the country is entrusted to *Alkalai*, judges trained in Mohammedan law, who reside in Bida and in the districts. The District Courts, of which there are seven in Bida Division, are courts of a lower grade—in official terminology, 'grade C courts'—that is, they are entitled to deal with civil cases involving fines up to £50 and criminal cases involving imprisonment up to six months, in case of theft up to twelve months. Bida town possesses a 'grade A court', the chief *Alkali*'s court, which combines the two different functions of a local court for the town and an appeal court for the districts. It has unlimited jurisdiction over all cases which under the Native Courts Ordinance are subject to the jurisdiction of Native Courts, i.e. excepting such cases as sedition, charges against Europeans, treason, trial by ordeal, and corruption of officials. The jurisdiction of the Bida Court also excludes homicide cases—an exceptional limitation which was imposed upon Bida after the disturbances of 1931. The *Etsu* with his councillors forms another 'grade A court' which deals with cases concerned with land, and constitutes at the same time a higher court of appeal for cases from the districts. The District Officer represents a final court of appeal for all cases. Cases excluded from native jurisdiction come before the High Court, which sits from time to time at the Headquarters of Niger Province, presided over by a professional British judge.

It is interesting to dwell for a moment on the description of a Native Court in action. Picture the court building: a spacious round house, with a gallery running round its outer wall. The *Alkali* has his place on a raised platform near the wall, books and papers spread out before him. On the floor, leaning against the platform, his assistant is sitting. In the Bida Court there are also scribes who take down the minutes of every case. Ushers, messengers, and sometimes policemen are standing at the doors. The Bida Court sits daily from 10 a.m. till 2 p.m., the District Courts whenever there are cases. The court procedure is very rigid. Plaintiffs and defendants are squatting in the centre of the court room, facing the judge, their hands folded in their laps; to rest one's hands on the ground means disrespect towards the *Alkali*. The place of witnesses is to the side and back of the plaintiffs and defendants. Women must sit in the outer gallery (at least in cases concerning divorce, adultery, and suchlike); they speak through a small window in the wall. You will recognize at once the peasant from the country: he sits there shy and frightened, often quite bewildered by the questions of the judge; often too, he has to be reminded to raise his voice, which is almost inaudible.

COURT HOUSE IN BIDA

THE *ALKALI* OF MOKWA

But in the Bida Court temper may run high, especially when people of standing and wealth are involved who not infrequently will argue and remonstrate with the judge. I have seen judges lose their patience with such unmanageable parties, shout at them and threaten them with punishment for this 'contempt of court'.

Before the pretentious Bida Court with its office hours and fixed rules of procedure, its crowd of subordinate officials, assistants, scribes, ushers, policemen, a multitude of cases are brought daily which fit well into its up-to-date routine: offences against the by-laws of a modern town (riding a bicycle without light, or riotous behaviour in the street or the market, &c.) and all the various disputes bound to occur where you have an intensive trade, complicated money transactions, and suchlike. But before the same court come the cases (and in this book we are only concerned with these) that are the expression of tensions and conflicts of the society in its old unchanged form—cases of inheritance, divorce, witchcraft. The extension of native jurisdiction over the problems and conflicts of a modern urban community, which is merely a question of applying jurisdiction and executive under the guidance of the British Administration, is of less interest to us than the progressive penetration of formal political jurisdiction into the domains of traditional native life, which is a problem of legislation that the native society must itself solve. In this, the modern Native Court is the legitimate heir of the pre-British system of law—heir both to its strength and its weakness.

We may say that the modern legal system is both more comprehensive (embracing, above all, the domain of kinship) and, viewed from the standpoint of the groups which submit to its jurisdiction, more alien than the old system. To explain this we must for a moment go back to a question discussed previously. I have said that every extension of a uniform jurisdiction and legislation over new social domains involves potentially the substitution of a new law for original codes and conceptions, and thus a certain disparity between the recognized law and the culture of which the old conceptions were an expression. This disparity is clearly a phenomenon of transition: every society will tend in the course of time to eliminate such a hiatus—either by reacting against the expanding judicial system and forcing it to adjust its too extravagant claims (we shall presently encounter instances of this)—or by completing that process of cultural assimilation of which the co-ordination of legal concepts represents only one aspect. We may assume that our table of jurisdiction in pre-British times, which shows a certain system of law firmly accepted throughout the society, refers to aspects of culture in which this process of mutual assimilation has been completed. Whether or not my hypothesis is historically correct, we must admit that where the process is still in motion, where the politically-backed law is only just extending its hold over new domains, the disparity of which I have spoken must be visible. This is indeed the case to-day, when Mohammedan law is being applied to kinship offences.

It would go beyond the scope of this book to study the relation between Mohammedan law as it is practised in Nupe and the traditional concepts of kinship conduct and kinship rights and duties. I may be allowed to reduce this relation to a simple formula: if the former is born of the social conditions of an urbanized stratified society and reflects the specific concepts of property and morality which have evolved there, the latter is typical of the peasant community, its economic pursuits, its values and interests. The Mohammedan law as it is applied in Nupe has undergone a number of significant changes in the comparatively short period of Fulani and later British rule. The knowledge of the more important changes (e.g. in the treatment of seduction and adultery) has spread throughout the country and the changes remain linked in the memory of the people with the names of the judges who were their originators. Some changes are regarded as good, others as bad, and accordingly judges have earned or forfeited the reputation of being 'wise men'. The lawgivers themselves have been aware of the necessity of bringing their extraneous legal machinery into at least partial harmony with existing conditions and conceptions.

Here a new aspect of the 'disparity' between law and culture reveals itself. The very fluidity of this evolution of a new legislation must remove the law from the orbit of the average citizen. He is no longer able to keep track of it as he could when the legal system could be reduced to the short list of 'civil offences' and 'crimes of the king'. I have encountered ample evidence of this kind—erroneous beliefs of individuals as to particular laws or forms of legal procedure. Some ten or fifteen years ago unscrupulous judges made use of the ignorance of the peasants and prosecuted, for 'neglect of their parental duties' the parents of girls and young men suspected of illegitimate sexual intercourse. The repercussions of this abuse are still felt, and many peasants dare not bring a case of seduction before the court for fear of being fined themselves. A conspicuous evidence of this gulf between the law and the people is the continued practice of peasants and commoners to seek out a Mallam or a person of standing and have him accompany them to the court when they are about to commit themselves to the vagaries of an unknown law.

The disparity between law and culture is naturally most marked in the slow-moving peasant communities, where social and economic conditions diverge most fundamentally from the social life of which Mohammedan law is an expression. Here the unfamiliarity of the judges, who come from the highest families of the kingdom and who are Bida born and bred, with the local situation and specific customary practices (e.g. marriage rules) may add yet another source of conflict.[1] Even the religious emblems upon which the Nupe were wont to take the oath are absent in the modern District Court which, instead, is using the Koran.[2] Pagans will always be ready to swear by the Koran if asked to do so by

---

[1] Some of the local *Alkalai* may be very reluctant to regard themselves as permanently attached to their station. They may be hoping for a speedy promotion, eventually to the court in Bida.

[2] In a court in the Nupe district of Ilorin Province a very enlightened *Alkali* used both Koran and the 'chain of Tsoede' to do justice to Mohammedans as well as pagans. In this as in similar respects much depends on the personality (and special training) of the individual judge.

the *Alkali*, said one of my informants, and will think nothing of perjuring themselves.

Let me quote a significant instance. An Ebe man had refused to let his daughter marry a Hausa whom she loved, having a different suitor from Ebe country in mind for her. The Hausa brought the case before the *Alkali* of Kutigi (some 50 miles away); the *Alkali* instructed the father to give his blessing to the marriage on the grounds that the Koran decreed that no father should stand between two young people who loved each other. The father swore an oath to that effect on the Koran and returned home. But after a month the Hausa came back, reporting that the girl's father had renewed his opposition to the marriage. Three times they were summoned to court, and three times the father agreed in the presence of the *Alkali*, only to revoke his agreement afterwards. At last I happened to be in the court and asked the man if perhaps the Ebe disliked letting their daughters marry outside the sub-tribe or tribe. Evidently relieved, the man said that this was indeed the case. Curiously enough, the girl, who had till then stubbornly maintained her desire to marry the Hausa, declared that she would obey her father as soon as the customary marriage rule was brought up in the court.

This example also illustrates the effects of what I have called above the 'divided law': the girl and her suitor, well knowing that if they submitted to the customary law as it was upheld by her father and most probably the village elders would not be able to marry, appealed to the Mohammedan court, whose decision, as they anticipated, was favourable to them. Here we see what I have mentioned above—that in districts in which the customary conceptions of law still obtain, modern legislation puts a premium on breaches of the traditional usage. This is shown most clearly in litigation over inheritance. According to Mohammedan law the property and land left by a family head should be divided equally among the sons; traditional rules of inheritance hold that land and property should be inherited by the younger brother, and that sons and brothers' sons should stay on the land working under the heir as under their sociological father. This rule expresses the interest of a farming community in maintaining landed property so far as possible intact, while the Mohammedan rule does justice primarily to owners of movable property, money, trade goods, or cattle. Now, for reasons which we shall examine in a later chapter modern economic developments have led increasingly to the adoption of the Mohammedan solution. But were individuals still to attempt to enforce the traditional rule, dissatisfied family members could easily obtain a reversal of this decision by appealing to the Mohammedan court.

Again we observe the effectiveness of the 'social law' which we have formulated above, that a stronger law ousts a weaker law. The existence of the divided authority which favours 'dissenters' from traditional law, must force chief and elders—the guardians of traditional usage—to surrender in ever larger measure the authority which they are still holding to the stronger authority of the state law, even to invite its intervention—as did the family heads who appealed to their feudal lord for support of their paternal authority. It is important to emphasize this, as

many Administrative Officers think it desirable that the village chiefs
and elders should continue to practise their informal arbitration side by
side with the existing official courts. Our data preclude the likelihood of
such a parallel development; they show that the tendency is rather
towards the virtual surrender of one to the other. We have heard that in
the present-day judicial arrangement the Village Head is expected to
send all legal cases which cannot be settled by arbitration to the District
Alkali's court. Now I have found the chiefs quite satisfied with this
state of affairs, which freed them of the responsibility in more serious
cases. Some seemed, in fact, quite frightened at the idea of taking over
this responsibility themselves, and were only too ready to leave a larger
and larger proportion of their judicial tasks to the professional judge.
'To-day', a chief said to me, 'people want written judgements in such
cases as divorce, inheritance, debts; *ama mi de takarda à*, but I have no
papers to give.' 'Papers' are only the modern symbols of the more
powerful and more permanent authority wielded by state jurisdiction;
in his own words the chief expressed the essence of that principle of
'divided authority'.

Shall we acquiesce with the chief in these results of an inevitable
process of change? I think not. Politically, the chief is divested already
of much of his former power. To divest him also of all judicial authority
is to deprive him of the last vestige of the most vital prerogative of his
office, which is the enforcement of a certain line of conduct upon his
community, and to sanction all deviations from it as acts detrimental to
the welfare of the community. It would amount to turning the chief
completely into a petty executive official, entitled only to carry out orders,
but with no right to voice public opinion. Besides, the disregard for
local customs by the professional Mohammedan judges is felt as a real
hardship by many. Even if more change is on the way, bound to promote
the final assimilation of Mohammedan law and customary practice, its
pace should be set by the people themselves, and not by an alien, un-
interested judge. In the nature of things the solution must lie in a compromise. In my view the best compromise would be to vest the Village
Head with the right (and, more important, the duty) to act as an assessor
in the court, with full consultative authority, whenever cases from his
community are brought before the *Alkali*.[1]

This does not contradict what I have said in a previous section about
the 'parochial outlook' of the village chief. The parochial outlook may
unfit him for responsible posts in the administration of the Emirate at
large, such as District Headship, which call for a wide view and an
appreciation of policy on, as it were, a national scale. But it is just this
parochial outlook which qualifies the village chief eminently for dealing
with legal cases, bound up as they are with local conditions. However,
there is a wider issue involved in this question—the most intricate
problem which modern administration has to solve, the problem of
centralization versus local autonomy.

[1] This solution is envisaged in the Native Courts Ordinance, which leaves it
to the discretion of the Native Court to appoint assessors from the ranks of
village chiefs and elders.

PROBLEMS OF ADAPTATION

The description of the political system of modern Bida has illustrated the relation between the social structure of Nupe society and the new Native Administration, the points of harmony as well as of divergence and conflict. I have just formulated one of the graver conflicts; we recognize it as one of the central problems of this analysis, the problem of cultural and social diversity versus political unification.

Modern conditions have re-designed the cultural map of Nupe country. Roads, railways, and river steamers demarcate new areas of communication and intercourse. The scope of economic co-operation has widened immensely, far beyond the political boundaries of Nupe. Important trade centres, nuclei of a new, cosmopolitan Nigeria, with their large colonies of strangers, have arisen on railway lines, motor-roads, near river ports or river bridges: Badeggi, on the railway, is such an example, or Baro on railway and river, and Jebba where the railway bridge crosses the Niger. New cultural centres are forming in the villages which are the seats of District Heads, Native Courts, schools, dispensaries, and trading-posts of the big merchant companies of Nigeria. But this development above all emphasizes anew the cultural and social gulf between Bida and the country. Bida is more than ever the seat of 'civilization' and learning, art, and fashion, the residence of the wealthiest traders and of the new ruling class—the salaried officials of the Native Administration. Bida harbours the highest school of the Province, a hospital, the workshops of the Public Works Department which give employment to many, the large 'canteens' of the European trading companies. It represents again, on a new plane, the 'core' of the kingdom, the area of social life close to the 'powers that be'. Modern Nupe has re-defined the old conflict between cultural diversity and political unification, it has not eliminated it. In the political sphere the Government is attempting to do justice to this vital problem by admitting commoners and peasants to responsible offices in the central administration. I have ventured to point out certain weaknesses inherent in this experiment. But the question of the success or lack of success which is likely to meet this administrative experiment is less significant than the fundamental question which of the two principles of social and cultural development these administrative reforms are envisaging, a strengthening of unification and centralization, or support and preservation of the social identity of village communities and cultures. The former tendency has been the trend of the historical development of the Nupe state (as of any state); it has also become almost an accomplished fact in the other spheres of present-day development, in economic progress and in the centralization which is part of educational and health policy. The choice is thus, I think, in reality taken out of the hands of the Government. But whatever policy is adopted, it can, for the present, mean little more than a preliminary arrangement. The final solution cannot be found in the realm of political organization; it will arise—and this our survey of the political history of Nupe kingdom has taught us—from cultural commonness itself. One of the main instruments for achieving this cultural commonness in modern Nupe is planned *education*. A twofold plan of education: an ever-increasing spread of general education, disseminating the elements of modern civilization which so far have remained a prerogative of the few, among town people and villagers, people of rank and commoners alike; and also a reformulation of the higher education in the capital, so as to make it less specialized and bring it more into harmony with the culture of the country at large, to make it less an expression of exclusive, class-conscious 'town culture', and more an instrument of understanding for Nupe, writ large. Only when this development is complete will the rigid, exclusive class boundaries be dissolved; only then will the *tálaka*, the Poor One, be able fully to stand on his own feet, to have his share in the administration of his country, and to dispense finally with those links of clientship and patronage which so far have been his only weapons to overcome the vulnerability of his position. On this new plane the question of centralization *versus* independent local administration may then be reopened, and with more prospect of a permanent successful settlement. A peasant once said to me: 'I send all my children to school, then they will be able to read and they will know what it says on tax-receipts and fine-tickets. No more cheating or extorting money then!' Put it in this crude and a little aggressive manner, or call it education as a 'means of cultural unification', it means the same thing.

In the town and its rigidly stratified society our problem takes a slightly different form. The question how to transform exclusively political domination into a system with more equal, more 'democratic' distribution of political influence and responsibility reappears as the problem of social mobility. The social mobility of the Nupe class system, restricted as it was under traditional conditions, has been restricted further and at the same time diverted into new channels by the modern development. Of the vast bureaucracy of the kingdom only comparatively few ranks and offices could find a place in the new society and could thus maintain together with the symbols of rank their social significance. True there are a number of newly-created offices and posts under the newly-created Native Administration: the post of *Ma'aji*, Treasurer, posts as teachers in Middle School and elementary schools, posts of clerks, scribes, N.A. 'Mallams', messengers attached to the various offices, and so forth. But the more important of these modern posts demand modern education, which at present has been enjoyed only by a small minority. It is a convincing proof of the fact that this minority is still to a large extent drawn from the classes of the nobility that almost all important N.A. offices, down to scribes and messengers, are in the hands of what have been for a century the privileged classes of Nupe.

War, the paramount factor of promotion and inter-class mobility, has disappeared; free competition, individual success, are almost excluded as channels of a social career. The system of offices is more exclusive to-day than it had been in feudal Nupe. The comprehensive scheme of promotion which used to embrace the whole scale of Nupe society is reduced to insignificance by the exigencies of specialized training and by the changed conception of office and responsibility. The Administration itself is undecided in its attitude to the question of promotion and career. Certain distinguished state offices were granted in accordance with the traditional conception of a social career, that is, to men who had attained a high position on the native rank scale. Such are the appointments of *Maiyaki*, *Ndeji*, and the Town Councillors of Bida. But other offices have been bestowed *ad personam*, for special ability, irrespective of the traditional rank or promotion. Thus, a former Head Teacher of Bida Middle School was raised to the position of something like a 'Chief Secretary' of the Emirate, and given the (Mallam-) title *Naïbi*. Or the *Nágya*, a member of the *gitsú* nobility, has been made a member of the Emir's council, although according to traditional practice membership of the *Etsu*'s council was reserved for the *sarakiži*, the military or civil ranks. The only promotion with universal application (and sure of universal appreciation) is promotion in salary. Fixed wages have become almost the only officially recognized symbols of social career. How then will class distinctions and inter-class movement re-establish themselves in modern Nupe? How will the native society adjust its conception of those paramount values in their cultural life, promotion, and status to the new situation?

The attitude of the people towards these questions is ambiguous and undecided—the typical attitude towards changing values. It is interesting to study the attitude of the young men of to-day, including those who have enjoyed the highest education the Emirate can supply, in Bida Middle School, towards the occupations which are open to them. It seems of little account to them whether they obtain the position of a clerk, an office messenger, or some other obscure post, or whether they are called to fill the post of a teacher or a responsible political official, as long as their appointment carries a salary. Again and again men of intelligence and high standing have said to me: 'All our native ranks and titles mean nothing to-day; what has meaning are only offices under the N.A., posts which carry real influence and wealth.' Yet it would be incorrect to infer from such statements as this that the traditional system of ranks and the whole concept of promotion and mobility are losing their vitality and significance. The class distinctions of Nupe are reduced to-day to distinctions of status devoid of their former economic and political significance; what seems to have remained intact is only the outer shell, a rigid empty structure. Yet I have often been surprised to see how little the meaning of this structure has been affected.

When I was in Bida a rich trader was just making all possible efforts to entrench himself in the position of a favourite of the king, and he was put down accordingly by 'those who knew' as the next candidate for promotion to a *saraki* rank. I have seen three vacancies occur among the higher ranks of the nobility; I have witnessed the ensuing party feuds, the passionate play of interests, the bartering for support and influence —all these signs of a charged social atmosphere which can be characteristic only of a system still intensely alive. And one of those enlightened, sophisticated informants who deprecated the traditional ranks and titles was the hero of the following story: I have just mentioned that the former Head Teacher of Bida Middle School, a very able (though un-scrupulous) man, had been attached for some time to the Administration in a very distinguished official position, with the title of *Naïbi*. When he was dismissed from his post for malversation the new Head Teacher definitely expected to be appointed *Naïbi* and even approached his superior officer officially to help him secure this post, to which, accord-ing to precedent, he felt entitled. This example is deeply characteristic. It shows that that fundamental trend in Nupe society is still alive: it reveals the anxious search for traces of a routine of promotion to which the people had adjusted their life, and the eagerness to rediscover in the new society in which they are living the paramount social value of their culture.

If the restriction of social mobility and the reduction in the number of official positions under modern rule have caused this moral uncertainty in the ruling classes, indirectly they threaten to unsettle the morale of the people at large. Not only because they render promotion from the lowest orders of the society so difficult, but because they have thrown out of gear the whole machinery of inter-class relationship. Many of the channels through which public opinion—the desires and grievances of the people—used to find its way to the ears of the rulers of the country have been rendered useless; clientship and similar forms of political attachment can no longer promise protection when the large majority of the men whom native society had endowed with status and rank can no longer claim any official standing. Or rather, the channels still exist and still continue to function in their way, but they have been forced under-ground, and they function in the subterranean sphere of intrigues and scheming. The Government, supporting those whom it has appointed, cannot stoop to recognize an authority resting only on the fluid, ill-defined loyalties involved in patronage and clientship. The former wide distribution of political influence, combined with the system of compre-hensive promotion, had secured a fairly efficient 'balance of power', and this 'balance of power' the powerless masses could turn to their advan-tage through the institution of clientship. The rigid present-day system ranges its authority exclusively behind the few men to whom it entrusts its offices; it must brand all other efforts at political influence as dis-turbing and even dangerous.

I have a concrete case in mind: a man of highest status in the native society, highly educated (in the Mohammedan sense), who was regarded by a large number of people, in the town as well as in the districts, as their patron and adviser in many questions. However, holding no official position, he was regarded by the *Etsu* and his entourage as an interloper, an unwelcome meddler in state affairs; and an over-cautious Administrator described him officially as a 'subversive element'. In a sense, he was that; he had been forced into this position, since the in-fluence which he attempted to exercise in favour of his clients and fol-lowers had to work outside, and not infrequently against, the established system. Yet had the rigidity of the present system not excluded him from an official position I have no doubt that he would have been able to use his influence over the people to the benefit of the country.

I need not enlarge upon the dangers of such subterranean activity—subterranean through no fault of the people themselves. The terrible flare-up in the witchcraft trial of 1931 is a lesson not easily to be forgotten. A remedy? I have suggested one above, couched modestly in a footnote: bring these channels into the open daylight; let the people themselves elect, periodically, at least in Bida town, their official representatives—Town Councillors in official nomenclature, People's Representatives in a wider sense.

That the people are equal to this task I need not elaborate further; nor would the group of likely candidates be too large and thus render an election difficult. The dangers involved in the solution which I suggest —the dangers of faction politics and intrigues—would be easily controlled once the whole network of relationships lies on the surface. However, one might object to my suggestion on the ground that it tends to keep alive the serf-like link of patronage which should rather be discouraged. To this I would reply, first: the personal link of patronage, little as it may appeal to the modern moral conscience, is for the present the only link of political representation that promises success. For the masses of the Nupe people as they are to-day, unenlightened, only too conscious of their weak position, economically and socially, it would be futile to attempt to find representatives in their own midst—they would be puppets in the hands of the experienced and infinitely better equipped ruling group. And second: a solution such as I have suggested would be most easily adapted to improved social conditions, that is, to a community with a universally higher level of enlightenment. Much more easily, in fact, than a system with carefully selected representatives whose position of confidence among the people is never put to a test. For the solution here suggested looks towards the future; it embodies one of the most vital elements on which the social achievements of the native peoples will finally depend, namely, political education—that training in political responsibility to the achievement of which the colonial policy of this country is irrevocably pledged.

CHAPTER XI
ECONOMICS: RESOURCES

ALFRED MARSHALL, discussing possible definitions of Economics, says: 'The less we trouble ourselves with scholastic inquiries as to whether a certain consideration comes within the scope of economics, the better.'[1] If any student of society is entitled to follow this practical advice it is the anthropologist. Clearly, his working definition of economics must be as wide and fluid as possible. In his field every fact referring to what Marshall would call the 'business side of life' must claim his attention; even apparently irrelevant details in the technique of production, exchange, or consumption may be significant because new and not hitherto examined under the aspect of economic problems. Such a wide definition of economics must do justice to three realms of facts: (1) the primary resources, in the sense of the physical substratum on which all productive activity ultimately depends; (2) the technical processes and forms of group organization which make up production in the narrow sense, i.e. which actuate and bring into existence the resources; and (3) the specific needs that exist in a society and on the satisfaction of which the efficiency of a productive system must prove itself.

This, then, will be our definition of the realm of economics: the utilization of resources for the satisfaction of culturally (or socially) standardized needs. The description of the needs themselves, elements of culture as they are, is part of the general description of the society. The relation between resources and the satisfaction of the needs will be examined under the heading of Economic Balance. In the description of the technical processes, however, we shall have to limit our field. In accordance with the general theme of this book we shall be concerned more with the group organization involved in production than with technology proper; we shall view productive labour under the aspect of human occupation rather than under the aspect of technical development. The description of the primary resources and their distribution will form the subject of this first section. It will examine above all that primary and ultimate resource of every productive system, savage or civilized, land.[2]

---

[1] A. Marshall, *Principles of Economics*, 1930, p. 27.

[2] For various reasons I have thought it better to omit from this book a discussion on hunting and fishing. Hunting is indeed of little importance in the present-day productive system of the country; it has been reduced everywhere to a secondary additional activity in the nature almost of a leisure-time occupation. In some parts of the country (e.g. in Bida and surroundings) hunting has disappeared altogether. Fishing stands in a different category. It is of paramount importance in the riverain area. But a description of the greatly varying fishing techniques in use in Nupe country, and of the very specific forms of labour organization involved in fishing, would lead too far. For the economic system of the country at large fishing becomes important in so far as it produces one of the most highly valued trading-goods of the country both in local and export trade. This aspect of fishing will best be discussed at a later stage, in the chapter on trade.

POSSESSION OF LAND

In the discussion of the rights to land obtaining in Nupe two facts must be borne in mind. First, the Fulani conquest, which resulted in the appropriation of part of the vacant tribal land; and second, the very low birth-rate and sparse population of the country. These two factors limit each other's effectiveness; moreover, they affect different parts of the country in different measure. We have seen that the appropriation of tribal land took place only in the area east of the Kaduna (Cis-Kaduna).[1] In the area west of the Kaduna (Trans-Kaduna),[2] land-tenure on the traditional tribal or village basis still obtains, and here the population factor shows itself effective in that it eliminates almost all pressure on the land and all more severe competition for landed possession. Owing to the political factors the opposite is true of Cis-Kaduna, and here a complex system of land ownership and land transfer, which in the extreme case amounts to outright purchase for money, reflects the attempts of the people to counteract the pressure on the land. That land disputes are extremely rare in Trans-Kaduna, but very frequent in the 'conquered' territory, is evidence of the same development. One exception may be mentioned at once: the especially valuable marsh-land groves and plots near river-courses, which the Nupe call *bata* (the Hausa *kurmi*). Disputes about this valuable kind of land occur now and again even in the land-rich Trans-Kaduna, and they are fought with special bitterness in Bida and the crowded 'conquered' territory. The following figures may be quoted in support of this statement: in the years 1934 and 1935 24 cases of land litigation came before the *Etsu*'s Court in Bida; 21 referred to Cis-Kaduna and 3 to Trans-Kaduna; of the latter none was a land case in the narrow sense of the word—one was a dispute about trees, and two were disputes over marsh-land plots.

The description of Nupe land-tenure may start most profitably with an enumeration of the various methods by which a man, stranger or native of Nupe, may acquire land or has been able to acquire land in the past. It must be said first of all that under traditional conditions only men can hold or claim possession of land. The dynastic policy of the Nupe kings has first led to women being invested with fiefs and landed property. Mohammedan law, besides, is inclined to confirm land holding by women in their own right. But the holding of land by women is still extremely rare, and limited to Bida and the surrounding districts I have come across one case only—a court case in which sons and brothers of a recently deceased woman contested the inheritance of her landed property. Needless to say, none of the parties concerned were peasants; the land had been acquired first through the channels of clientship, and the present claimants—Bida Mallams—wanted it only in order to sublet it for profit.

To return to traditional land-tenure. For a Nupe man who comes

[1] The territory between Kaduna and Gbako river, i.e. Beni country, and the districts east of the Gbako river, i.e. Badeggi and Kacha districts.
[2] Trans-Kaduna is the literal translation of the Nupe name for the area: *Lavunkpā* (*Lavun* being the Nupe name for the Kaduna river).

from farming stock, that is, whose family is holding land already, the usual way to acquire land is to exercise his claim to a parcel of the land that is held jointly by the family group, and which is administered and apportioned by the family head. This would be the procedure, for example, in the case of a young member of the family who had founded a family himself and now requests land for a farm of his own. More or less the same situation would arise in the case of a stranger, a native of Nupe though not of the particular village, or even a native of Nigeria (a Hausa or Yoruba) though an alien in Nupe, who, having been adopted into a household, may request land on which to settle. There is, however, the possibility that the family land available at the time is insufficient; or there might be a man desiring land whose family had not held land previously or had lost the claim to the land, e.g. through overlong absence. Here two main methods offer themselves: first, the man desiring land can exercise his right as a member, native or adopted, of the village community to request land (possibly additional land) from the chief, which may be either land that has been under cultivation previously but has fallen vacant, or virgin land within the village territory. Second, he can acquire new land through an arrangement with an individual landlord (using the term here in the widest sense); in other words, he can lease land temporarily for a rent in kind—a method known in Nupe as *aro*, 'borrowing'. In both these methods the land thus acquired is inalienable.

A third method closely related to borrowing is a lease for life or for an indefinite period, in most cases against a single payment in money to which is added a fixed rent in kind. This arrangement, which definitely recognizes the money value of land, may be tantamount to real purchase. Fourth, there exists hereditary tenantship, which gives the tenant absolute right over his land, including the right to dispose of it again or sublet it. This tenantship I shall call (for reasons which will become clear presently) *secondary* tenantship. It implies not a fixed rent but a share in the produce—a form of métayer system.[1] Finally, there exists a *primary* tenantship, in which a landlord who himself owns the land by the right of conquest or appropriation may cede complete and absolute rights over land to another person, Nupe or stranger, in recognition of (political) services rendered; here again a share in the produce is implied. The last two methods form part of the feudal organization of the Nupe state.[2]

We have thus five methods of land acquisition, which fall in two main categories: (1) Acquisition in virtue of membership of a group (kinship

---

[1] See A. Marshall, op. cit., p. 643.

[2] Different from these traditional methods of acquiring and transferring land is the method of land-tenure under the Native Land Ordinance Act, which, adjusted to modern requirements, involves the lease of native land to non-natives, i.e. non-Nigerians (a merchant who plans a trading-station, a missionary who intends to build a school or church, &c.). In such cases application for a lease of a parcel of the land that has been retained as Crown land must be made to the Administration. This method, and all questions entailed in it, will be disregarded in the following. It is, in fact, of very little significance in Nupe country where no commercial utilization of land and no settlement of non-natives exist.

ECONOMICS: RESOURCES

group or village community), holding 'corporate' rights to land. (2) Acquisition of land in virtue of a contract between individual landowners— a short-term contract such as the 'borrowing' of land, or a long-term, or indefinite, contract such as is embodied in tenantship and in the granting of land for services rendered. The methods summarized under the first category occur both in Trans- and Cis-Kaduna; of the methods summarized under the second category only 'borrowing' occurs in Trans-Kaduna; all acquisition and transfer of land for indefinite periods is restricted to the 'conquered' area east of the Kaduna.

Village Land

The village land is administered, that is, held in trust and apportioned —in Nupe terminology 'owned'—by the chief. Linguistically the specific character of his administrative right to the disposal of village land is not defined very clearly. The Nupe refer to the chief's control over land in exactly the same terms which they use for the direct utilization and ownership of land by a family head or any individual farmer. The Nupe would use the same term also when speaking of the territory belonging to a village, i.e. the land that is 'owned' by the people of the village collectively.[1] Understood in the widest sense of the word, this village land embraces a territory surrounding the village in a rough circle. It comprises three kinds of land, each called by a different name: (1) occupied land fallow or actually worked, in the hands of families or individuals—*latí*, 'farm'; (2) vacant land which has once been occupied but has fallen back to the common fund of land held in trust by the chief for future allotment—mostly referred to as *gonta*; and (3) a fringe of virgin land claimed by the village community as a land reserve—called *cikã*, 'bush', or, again, *gonta*. The second and third kind of land we will call 'village land' in the narrow sense, as against land of the first kind, 'family land'.

The border between the fringe of virgin land which is regarded as the land reserve of the village and the stretch of no-man's-land which separates it from the territory of the next village is fluid and never rigidly defined. There are no marks or boundary signs. But in the sparsely populated area of Trans-Kaduna this never leads to disputes between villages. The fluidity of this boundary is, in fact, an essential part of the elastic system of Nupe settlement, with its star-like expansion and founding of new 'colonies' which, step by step, extend the village territory. The area of village land rarely stretches beyond a radius of three miles: in other words, the Nupe farms are situated within an hour's walk from home. In some cases, where the farms are farther away, the farmers build small grass huts on the farms, in which they can find shelter in a rain or storm or spend the night if it is too late to walk home. Should the people of the village, in their search for new land, go beyond this easy reach, they would found new, permanent settlements, village

[1] The Nupe would say, for example: *Žitsu wũ kin kpátá*, the chief owns all the land; or *Dokociži wũ kin babó*, the people of Doko own the land round here; but also *Kolo-gá wũ latí-o*, it is Kolo who owns this farm.

'colonies' or *tunga*. The *tunga* thus possesses land in its own right, but at the same time pushes its territorial possessions further into no-man's-land.

Access to Village Land

There is no general rule for the distribution, within the area of village land, of the farms belonging to the various family groups and individuals. Roughly one may say that the small individual plots (called *bucá*—a term to be explained presently) are situated near the village and the larger family plots (*efakó* plots) farther afield. When old men own plots of their own they, too, are given plots near the village so that they should not have to walk too far. The different plots which belong to the group of people living together in the same house (as a rule, a single family group), whether the plots are worked jointly or independently by the various household members, do not necessarily lie together, but are frequently scattered. Nor have the people who live together in the same *efu* their land on adjoining sites, or in the neighbourhood of the part of the village where they live. We may add that, again, there exist no special signs or boundary marks to distinguish the property of different farmers. A narrow path, a border of shrubs, or a tree, serve as landmark.[1] But the different cultivation that may be practised on the different fields, or the different stage of cultivation which the different fields may represent (fallow land, land that has been worked for one year, or two years, &c.), make these boundaries more obvious to the eye.

This irregular distribution of farm-plots appears to be due to a variety of causes. To some extent it is entailed in the complex agricultural technique of the country, with its many different types of cultivation and its regular system of rotation of crops. Every farmer owns a certain number of fields—some under cultivation while others are lying fallow—which he tries to distribute over different sites so that he can utilize different types of soil, e.g. the marshy sites near watercourses for the cultivation of rice or sweet potatoes, dry sandy soil for ground-nuts, heavier soil for yam and cotton, and so forth. This arrangement also has the advantage of distributing more evenly the risks of failure. You often find farmers complaining that one site on which they have a farm is less good than another, or has perhaps suffered special injury that year through birds or through thieving baboons, or has been washed away by a flooded river. But the irregular distribution of farm-plots is also a result of the very method of Nupe settlement: it could not be otherwise with the farm-land lying in a circle round the large villages in which a numerous population is concentrated. There would not be room enough for all family groups in the village to have their lands arranged in compact blocks in equally favoured positions, both with regard to the distance from the village and to the quality of the soil. Moreover, some plots more heavily worked than others 'tire' sooner and must be replaced by virgin land lying farther afield; and growing families must provide more land for their

[1] A characteristic exception are a few marsh-land plots near Kacha, which are properly fenced in—'because of the many disputes' that arise over this kind of land.

adult members. All these factors have in the course of time contributed to make the map of Nupe village land the irregular patchwork it is to-day.

At the beginning of this section I have mentioned the possibility that a family head may have to request additional land from the chief for a junior family member for whom he cannot find sufficient land on his own property. To-day, this is rarely put into practice, usually only in the extreme case when a whole section of the family, finding the available land near the village insufficient or too poor in quality, sets out to colonize a piece of virgin land and eventually to settle there as founders of a new *tunga*. In the normal case—especially in Trans-Kaduna— when land has to be found for an individual family member, the family head is as a rule expected to possess sufficient land to effect this readjustment. The family head, owning three to four different fields, each of about 4 acres, can, in fact, well afford it in a society with so low a birthrate. The worst that may happen is that for a time the family head may have too much of his land lying fallow to be able to find additional land for the family member who desires a new farm. It is then that the method of 'borrowing' land is practised.

Let us consider now more closely the position of the chief with respect to the question of access to village land. Control over the land is part of his political authority. It is, as I called it, an administrative control only, and this is expressed in a balanced, twofold, limitation of the claims to land of chief and community, of the power of the chief to apportion or withhold land, and of the power of the family head to claim and keep land. As regards the former limitation, the chief cannot reasonably withhold land from any claimant of whom the other elders of the community approve. Nor is the chief's own farm-land out of proportion to that of any other family head with an equally large working-group at his command. As regards the latter limitation, the control which the chief retains over all reapportionment of village land is acknowledged whenever the main family land changes hands, that is, in the case of succession to the position and property of a family head.[1] The chief must be informed of all such changes, and in some parts of Nupe he summons at this occasion the family members with their new head and reminds them of their obligations towards each other: the family members, that they will now work on the land of the new family head, and the family head that he has now assumed the responsibility to feed and clothe his people and, some day, to supply them with land of their own. Sometimes a gift to the chief of one pail of whatever crop is just ripe seals the pact. The annual village tax in kind, *dzanká*, which, as we know, was formerly paid to the chief by every family head, is itself a land-tax, a recognition of the chief's control over the village land. It consisted in a gift of one to three bundles of millet or sorghum, the amount varying with the condition of the crop. A complete failure of the crop meant exemption from the *dzanká*. The *dzanká* was thus not regarded as a fixed tax, but rather as

---

[1] The succession to the position of family head being, in most cases, identical with the succession to a *nůsa* rank, the procedure described here holds good for both (see p. 50).

albárka (lit. blessing), a gift meant to express the 'blessing' that lay on the land which the family received from the chief.

Another expression of the chief's control over the reapportionment of land is that all land of families or branches of families which have died out, and similarly the land of families who have emigrated, falls back to the common fund of land reserve administered by the chief. The period within which the land of emigrants still remains theirs is fixed everywhere in Nupe as three years. After that time the chief is entitled to reapportion the land. Should an heir from the emigrated group return after a longer period, he could (like any other stranger) claim land in the village, but not as a rule the same land that his family had held previously. The dying-out of a family, or a branch of a family, seems a fact not easy to establish and always open to doubts in a social system in which small sections repeatedly split off the main body of the family. There is always the chance of an unexpected or belated claimant turning up, representing a distant branch which chief and elders may no longer have reckoned as likely to identify itself with the original family. But this is mainly a theoretical speculation; there occur few such cases in Nupe —none in Trans-Kaduna, where land is plentiful and vacated plots unlikely to be much competed for.

In Cis-Kaduna I witnessed an interesting case of this kind. A family head in Doko had died, leaving a small boy, who was then adopted by a childless brother of the deceased, living in a *tunga* on a farm of his own. The boy grew up on this farm and lived there contentedly until recently, after more than twenty years, the chief reapportioned the apparently unclaimed land that had belonged to the boy's father to two elders of high rank, the *Lile* and *Shaba* (both of the chief's family). Not until then did the young man return to Doko and make a formal claim for his ancestral land. But political motives rather than economic interest were behind this move; the parties in this case were, again, the chief of Doko and young Ndakó Gana, the 'dispossessed' descendant of the line of original chiefs. The chief had reapportioned the land in order to blot out the last visible connexion between the 'pretender's' family and the chieftainship of Doko; and the young man disputed the reapportionment on these very grounds. In the end he received back some of the original land and other new land in addition.

Here we discover a new significance in the apportionment of village land—its connexion with the bestowal of rank or office. This is not surprising in the communities (such as Doko) where the village ranks, like the land, remain in the possession of one 'house'. Later, we shall see more clearly, in the discussion of inheritance, that the Nupe kinship system tends indeed to couple attainment of family headship (which goes with rank) with inheritance of ancestral land. Considering, however, that the ordinary village land does not differ widely in quality and productive value, we can understand that this political aspect of land ownership is rather obscure—save in a case such as the one just quoted where political aspirations have attached to a specific property more than its proper share of symbolic significance. The political aspect becomes more prominent in connexion with a natural resource that shows this difference in quality and value to a much greater extent, namely, fruit-bearing trees.

In most districts the chief has a special title to certain economically valuable fruit trees wherever they grow, on vacant land or on people's farms. In Doko and Shebe this special chief's tree is the locust-bean, in Kutigi and Wuna the oil-palm. In Mokwa there exists another regulation, namely, that all shea-nut and locust-bean trees inside the town belong to the chief, while the trees outside are the full property of the man on whose ground they stand. Also there is in many places the general rule that no fruit tree on village land may be cut down without the special permission of the chief. Sometimes family heads exercise a restricted right to the 'chief's trees' growing on their land, i.e. they return two-fifths of the crop to the chief and keep the rest. But the chief may also grant the full possession of these trees as a separate right; thus he bestows the property of a certain number of valuable trees on an individual—young or old—as a recognition of higher civic status, together with the promotion to rank and title. The right to the trees, coupled with the rank, remains the property of the 'house', conditional upon the renewal of the appointment (to the same or a similar rank) after the death of each holder.[1] The shea-nut trees—to-day of considerable commercial importance—occupy everywhere in Nupe a special position. The trees on vacant land (virgin village land or no-man's-land) are common property. The women who collect the fruit go out in small parties and share the crop among them. The shea-nut trees on occupied farm-land belong to the owner of the farm.[2] In either case the exploitation of the crop is the exclusive prerogative of the women.

A few words may be given to a special variety of village land, the plots that are situated in the village itself, round the compounds and between the village efu. This land is owned by the people who live in the compounds adjoining the plots. Its inheritance and apportionment is ruled by the same regulations as the inheritance and apportionment of the houses themselves and will best be discussed in a later section. The land inside village and town differs only in one respect from the village land without: it is never left uncultivated. Manured as it is by the refuse from the houses it can be used continuously without the necessity of being left fallow for a period. If the owner of such plots leaves the village or the town and does not return for some time, leaving no one behind (which has happened frequently in Bida during the last twenty years), the neighbours will use the farm-plots; they are always ready,

---

[1] A certain complication arises when the modern official Village Head is not identical with the traditional chief, for the former may assume control over the land only, not over trees—he may indeed not possess any 'chief's trees' himself, at least not at the time of his appointment. There is no evidence as yet to show how this contradiction will be solved in the course of time—except an indirect evidence to be mentioned presently (see p. 189, n. 2), which tends to show that this separation of land- and tree-rights is allowed to last for several generations.

[2] The facts mentioned here will correct the statement made by some students of West African agriculture, that 'shea-nut trees are generally regarded as entirely common property' (O. T. Faulkner and J. R. Mackie, *West African Agriculture*, 1933, p. 27).

however, to give them up as soon as the former owner or his heir may return, even if he had been absent for a longer period than three years—the period of absence stipulated in the village. I have heard of no dispute that has ever arisen over these house-plots, either in the village or in Bida town.

Strangers as Settlers

From the land which the chief holds in trust he apportions land on request to strangers who come to settle in a Nupe village and equally, as we have seen, to natives of the village who, through long absence, have forfeited the claim to their family land. The procedure is the same for both. It is interesting to examine these regulations, especially because this form of granting land implies a previous adoption of the applicant into a local household. Generally speaking, the Nupe like strangers—respectable strangers—to settle in their villages. This fact reflects both the lack of pressure on the land and the attitude of a commercially highly developed country which is ready to welcome new citizens, very likely people who bring with them new techniques and new valuable knowledge.[1]

The stranger who decides to settle in a Nupe village will first stop for some time in the house of a family head, perhaps a friend, or friend of a relation, who is ready to accept him as a temporary member of the household. Be it a short or prolonged stay, strangers will never be expected to pay for their 'lodgings'. A small present of food or kola-nuts is the only compensation. The guest will keep his own *ménage*. But after a time he comes to be regarded as an adopted member of the house, and then it is time to make his request for land and a site for a house of his own. This request will always be done through the *emitsó*, the Owner of the House, who will bring the case of his guest to the notice of chief and elders. The *emitsó* will have to vouch for the character and reputation of the applicant—a bad reputation would invariably lead to a rejection of the application. The procedure (which varies slightly in different places) is this: a preliminary gift, called *emisa*, 'salute', consisting of ten to twenty kola-nuts, a fowl, a calabash of beer, or—more rarely—money, accompanies the formal request to the chief. Another gift of kola-nuts is made later to the chief's representative (one of the elders), who will go with the applicant to stake out the farm-plot and the site for the house, and who may become later an important witness if any dispute should arise. Now the new landowner sets to work. For two to three years he is exempted from tax. Then, when the crops have been good, he pays his first *dzanká*, not yet to the chief himself, but to the family head in whose

---

[1] We have mentioned evidence of this already, e.g. the Bornu settlers who have introduced onion-growing into Kutigi, or the Yoruba-Konú who introduced weaving and indigo dyeing in Yoruba fashion. At the hearing of a court case—it was a rather involved dispute over a house in Kacha that had been 'sold' by the late owner in order to obtain money for tax arrears (the only case of this kind that has ever come to my notice), as a result of which his widow had now no place to go to—the *Etsu*'s Court officially recommended that 'strangers should always be adopted into one's household and given a hut to live in'.

house he had been staying before, and the latter returns half of the gift to the chief. The next *dzanká* will be the ordinary land-tax of every member of the village community, presented to the chief directly. To-day the first part of the procedure has remained unchanged, except that the application (and sometimes the presents as well) may also be addressed to the District Head.[1] But the annual *dzanká* is now replaced by the Government tax.

The grant of land to strangers never includes the trees growing on the farm-land. They remain the property of the village chief or the other native inhabitants, and this makes the analogy between strangers and adopted household members full: for like the strangers junior family members cannot own trees, although they hold land of their own.[2]

Access to Family Land

This question will be examined in detail later, and no more than a short summary is needed here. Three methods regulate the access of the individual member of the family group to the family land held jointly by the group and administered by the family head. (1) Temp-orary and restricted access to this land is embodied in the right of every male member, boys as well as adults, to a small plot of his own, which he can work independently. Such plots are called *bucá*, and the individual work on the plots is called *bucá* work. (2) Adult male members of the family group, who have already founded a family of their own, may claim a large farm of the kind that is worked jointly by a number of family members. This farm and farm-work is called *efakó*. (3) The fullest access to family land is embodied in inheritance and in the succession to the position of family head. This position implies control over all family land that the family head holds in his hands. The first two forms of access are 'family affairs' arranged with-out any formality; the last transaction implies, as we have seen, a formal reference to the chief. The chief's control over the occupied village land is thus made conspicuous not with respect to land that is apportioned on a small scale to individuals for direct use, but with respect to the land that is to be held in trust for future distribution by the new family head. The chief, in other words, as he is bound himself to trusteeship, guarantees the trusteeship undertaken by others. The analogy in the position of chief and family head with respect to land is clearly recognized by the Nupe. Both are heads of corporate groups, and both administrators of the joint rights vested in the groups. Both, moreover, hold the same special, economically significant, right to trees.

---

[1] I am not sure if this is really prescribed by the regulations. I know that in Agaie Emirate all peasants thought it was. In any case it would save a lot of trouble, should disputes arise later, if one had the District Head for a witness of the original transaction.

[2] This rule also holds good with respect to large groups of alien settlers. In Kutigi, for example, it led to the anomalous position that the Benu settlers, although they had become the political rulers of the community and supplied the chief of 'Greater Kutigi', owned no trees at all in the beginning, and still own very much less than the family heads of the *kintsoži*, the Owners of the Land, that is, the original inhabitants.

No junior family member, even when already holding *efakó* land in his own right, may claim any share in the produce of the fruit-bearing trees. Only succession to the family head's position implies the usufructory right to the trees that stand on his or any other parcel of the family land.

Borrowing of Land

Land can be borrowed only for limited periods, as a rule for periods from two to five years, that is, in order to help a temporary shortage of land. The family heads or other 'landlords' arrange the transaction between themselves, not necessarily informing the chief, but always in the presence of witnesses who should be able later to testify to the nature of the transaction. Every landowner who has enough land is ready to 'lend' it in this way. In Trans-Kaduna the transaction is regarded as a friendly act, a 'helping out', quite natural between neighbours or fellow villagers. The borrower pays annually a fixed rent in kind, as a rule one bundle of millet or sorghum. In Cis-Kaduna the transaction gains a definite commercial significance: the borrower pays a small sum of money down, varying with the quality of the land (from 8*d.* for about one acre of ordinary land to 2*s.* for a much smaller plot on valuable marsh-land—the highest amount paid I found to be 6*s.*), and again the annual rent of one bundle or the equivalent in money.[1] In one case I found that regular farm-work for the owner of the land had taken the place of the annual rent in kind.

A landlord is free to cancel the lease before it has lapsed if the tenant is not working the land—as happens frequently; the court would confirm his right to do so, only ordering him to return the initial payment. But it may also happen that the landlord dies or emigrates while the lease is still running, or that for some other reason the lease is not recalled. In such cases the lessee often continues to work the land, although he has naturally ceased to pay the annual rent; he even comes to regard the land as his own whether he is working it or not, till one day it may be demanded back by the original owner or his heirs. In Trans-Kaduna, where no long-term transfer of land exists, any evidence as to the nature of the original transaction will at once settle the case. In the conquered areas of Cis-Kaduna, where land is let and sublet, and where short leases and leases for an indefinite period coexist, it is often difficult to establish clearly whether temporary or permanent lease had been arranged originally, specially when the witnesses of the original contract have died. What type of lease was originally intended is shown by the amount of the initial payment, whether it was high or low, that is, a 'real' payment, or only a *kyutá*, a gratuity. The latter, combined with a repeated rent in kind, establishes the nature of the temporary lease, the *jĩ aro*, 'borrowing'. But the continued working of the 'borrowed' land, and the failure of the original owner or his heirs to call in the lease, clearly alter the situation considerably. The attitude of the court in such

---

[1] Characteristically this annual rent is called in Bida—quite logically—*dzankã* 'tithe', but in the villages *kyutá*, 'present'.

disputes is this: if the original owner or his heirs had allowed the rent to
lapse without calling in the lease, and if the other party can prove that he
has worked the land for a long period, this is generally considered
sufficient evidence that the original owner has abandoned his claim to
the land, whether the new owner is at the time actually working the land
or keeping it as reserve. Long occupation is thus recognized as tantamount to ownership. In summing-up a land case in 1935 the *Etsu*
Nupe said: 'We do not agree that a man should be evicted from the
place which he has been working for a long time.' And in another case,
heard in 1934, the claim of the new 'borrower' to the land was confirmed
by the court 'because of the many years the farm had been in so-and-so's
hands'.

Litigation about 'borrowed' land comes up constantly before the
court in Bida. This is a typical case: A. suddenly demanded back two
farms which his grandfather and father had 'lent' to another man,
because A. was going to be married and needed the land for himself. He
based his claim on the fact that only *aro* had been intended, although the
rent had been allowed to lapse. Evidence of the original transaction was
difficult to obtain, so the court suggested the following compromise: the
transfer of the farm of A.'s grandfather was confirmed, but the farm
which A.'s father had 'lent' to the other man the latter was ordered to
return—a decision which is again based on the length of occupation.
The lack of precision in the concept of land-borrowing in Bida and Cis-
Kaduna is illustrated still better by the following case, not itself a court
case, but, as it were, a typical potential cause for such land-disputes.
A certain rich Mallam had 'borrowed' land from the *Cece*, a *bara* of L.,
a nobleman of high rank. He had paid 8*d*. down, and every year one
bundle of sorghum as rent, for five years. The *Cece* died in the meantime, and the present owner maintained in discussion with me that the
land was his and could be inherited by his sons after his death. When I
discussed the case later with the *Alkali* he confirmed my suspicion that
this was not so; the land could in theory be recalled any day after the five
years by the heirs of the *Cece*. But the *Alkali* admitted that this may not
be the case for ten or even twenty years; by then the rent would have
been allowed to lapse and the details of the original transaction would be
difficult to establish.

In the course of the Fulani conquest certain farms which were at the
time without a definite 'owner', the original owner having emigrated
before the lease had lapsed, and the lessees having ceased work on the
borrowed farms, were simply appropriated by the Fulani landlords
within whose territory this 'ownerless' land was lying.

Trees are included in this short-term lease or 'borrowing'. But the
strength of this regulation, in harmony though it is with the general
principles of Nupe land-rights, has been weakened under present-day
conditions. Economic stress has made fruit-bearing trees a very valuable
resource, and farmers have in a few cases ignored the traditional practice,
given away trees with the land, and even 'lent' trees independently of
the land they stand upon. This sort of temporary transfer of trees is a
simple means of obtaining money quickly (for example, for the payment

of tax): the owner of oil-palms or locust-bean trees would sell a year's yield of his trees to another person, who in return would pay the tax for him. The issue is still more confused where the transfer of the land with which the trees go appears to be in the nature of a lease for an indefinite period. In this case the original owner or his heirs could claim that the trees, at least, were essentially inalienable, and could be transferred only temporarily, that is, could only have been 'lent' and 'borrowed'. This is itself a compromise, and the attitude of the court in these disputes constitutes a further compromise. In 1934 a farmer had ceded a farm-plot with locust-bean trees on it to another party. After the death of the original owner his heirs reclaimed the trees (though not the land) on the plea that the transfer of the trees could in the nature of things have been meant only as a temporary transfer. The decision of the court was that the new owner should share the crop, fifty-fifty, with the former owners.

Long-term Lease and Purchase

We come now to forms of land-ownership which are typical of Bida and the conquered areas east of the Kaduna and which are almost completely absent in the Trans-Kaduna districts.[1] Among the people of Bida town who derive their livelihood from the land, a few descendants of the original Beni population still own land under tribal conditions, that is, under the conditions described under the heading of village land. Their farms are scattered over the land around Bida—the village land that used to belong to the old, pre-Fulani Bida. But most of this land had been expropriated early in the conquest, under one or other pretext, and the former owners and their descendants had left Bida and moved into the country to other villages or *tunga* settlements, where they found vacant land. Thus of the descendants of the Beni 'town-kings' of Bida only Ndakotsu, the eldest of a number of brothers, had remained in Bida and continued to work the small plots that he had been able to keep; the other brothers had left the town and settled in the country.

Long absence, or the dying out of a family branch, too, gain a totally different aspect here in Bida, as compared with conditions in the village. For the vacated plot is as a rule at once appropriated by one of the big landlords whose lands may surround it, or possibly by one of the three royal houses on whose territory the plot may lie. The latter procedure was, as we shall see, the practice in pre-British times and in the early days of British rule. A somewhat similar case happened during my stay in Bida: a Bida man had returned to the town after a long absence and, claiming his old land, found that it had gone to another man. According to Nupe customary law he had forfeited his right to the land, having been away for such a long period. However, the customary law is not adapted to cope with conditions as they obtain in the town and in 'conquered territory': for here no spare land exists that could be offered to

---

[1] The exceptions are a few *tunga* settlements which some Bida noblemen have founded outside the 'conquered territory', for example on the Wuya-Kutigi road. There are no *tunga* of this kind west of Kutigi.

the claimant in compensation for the land he had lost. Besides, the man's old land had changed hands several times in the meantime, and could not simply be taken away from the present owners who had spent work and money on it. The man was unwilling to move to a village, where he could find land, and unwilling, too, to take land in Bida for which he would have had to pay a small rent. He felt that he had been wronged, and being of a rather violent temper and a slightly unhinged mind he attacked the judge and threatened the *Etsu*, and his search for a new place where to live ended under lock and key.

The village ways of obtaining and securing land, rendered impossible by the social conditions obtaining in the capital and in what we have called the 'conquered territories', are replaced by a large variety of other, much more complicated—and costly—methods of land transfer. All land is in fixed hands; land cannot simply be claimed on the grounds of citizenship from the *Etsu* Nupe. Nor is land around Bida, especially the valuable marsh-land, often given away in short-term lease. But land can be acquired by the method of lease for life or of tenantship for an indefinite period. In Bida a large number of dependants of the royal household, fief-holders, former warriors, slaves, or Mallams who were attached to a noble house, possess land granted to them by the king or a powerful feudal lord. These landlords, usually not farmers themselves, are frequently prepared to let their land (or sometimes to sublet it if they themselves have obtained it by a similar arrangement) to men who are in need of land for their farms. If the landlord is of high rank the transaction is never carried out by him personally but always by an agent, who expects a small gratuity from the tenant for his services. The rent itself consists in a comparatively high initial payment in money —£1 to £2—and, again, the fixed annual rent in kind. M., a wealthy Bida man, for example, acquired two years ago a farm for his newly married son from a former slave of *Etsu* Mohamadu. He paid £1 in money, and undertook to pay an annual rent of one bundle of millet. The money was pocketed by the former slave himself, but the rent in kind went to the family of *Etsu* Mohamadu—a sign that the former owner was himself only a tenant (though a tenant of a different category). This transaction is definitely spoken of as sale and purchase of land. The lease itself is, in fact, 'sold' and 'bought'; for the original tenant has ceded all his rights, for a single payment, to the new tenant who takes over the lease from the (real) landlord. The concept of sale and purchase is emphasized further by the practice of the court rarely to bring up the matter of the annual *dzanká* in kind (although it is almost invariably implied in the transaction). The initial, single payment, and the nature of the right to the land which this payment entails, are the only points with which the court is concerned. The importance of the annual rent in kind, however, apart from the 'purchase' price, reveals itself in the practice of recalling the contract if the tenant leaves the land unworked (that is, is unable to pay the annual tithe). Also, if the tenant has for some other reason discontinued the tithe, the lease may be recalled (though here, as we shall see presently, modern court practice would not sustain the claims of the landlord).

The lease is only for a lifetime—at least in theory—and has to be renewed by another payment in money if the heirs of the tenant intend to keep the land. If tenants and landlord are on good terms, or are social equals, or if the landlord is under some obligation to his tenant, the renewal is a mere formality and may be granted for a small gratuity. Thus tenants often feel justified in regarding their right to the land as implying absolute ownership, ownership *har dbada*, 'for ever'. But the large number of disputes of this kind which come before the court prove that the arrangement is open to misinterpretation as well as misuse. Landlords who for any reason are dissatisfied with their tenants, or have found a higher bidder, may unexpectedly call in the lease, either at the death of a tenant or during his tenancy, or demand on the threat of eviction another, higher, payment from the tenant or his heirs. Here are two examples: A., a rich landlord, had 'sold' the same farm twice, first for 10*s*., and afterwards for 16*s*. E. transferred a farm-plot that had fallen vacant after the death of the tenant twice in two years, pocketing £3 altogether.

Like the practice itself the attitude of the court towards these cases of 'purchase' or indefinite lease is ambiguous and uncertain. Only in one respect the issue is certain: all evictions from planted land, between the times of sowing and reaping, is declared illegal on whatever grounds the eviction may be based. Every man is entitled to the fruits of his immediate work. As regards the wider issue the tendency of the court seems to be this: if the transfer of the lease has taken place fairly long ago, the fact of the long occupation (and actual working) of the disputed land is taken to entail permanent ownership; further payments of *dzanká* rent are discouraged, and thus the purchase of the land is recognized as an accomplished fact. (As already said, in cases of this kind an original short-term lease—'borrowing'—is often confused with transfer for an indefinite period or for lifetime.) In other cases, where the transfer took place more recently, the court suggested the alternative solution of a return either of the money or the land.[1] In one or two cases of this kind the *Etsu* even made it clear that he wished to discourage sale of land for money altogether. In summing up a land case that came before the court in 1934, he said that 'it was right to divide up land for the benefit of people who had insufficient land; but this should not be done for money'—a pronouncement which, though morally admirable, does not quite do justice to actual facts. For how, one might ask, can land be 'divided up' for the needy in an area where such strong pressure on land, and such multitude of vested rights in land, obtains, if no allowance is made for some sort of compensation? In the Nupe economic system, firmly based as it is on money, a monetary compensation, sale and purchase, seems the only solution, unless the Administration is prepared to repudiate the whole system of land ownership as it exists in the 'conquered territory' as well.[2]

[1] This decision, however, made no allowance for the diminished value of the land, in the sense that the man to whom it was returned might have to leave it lying fallow for a considerable period before being able to cultivate it again.
[2] In one dispute of similar nature, which came before the court in 1935, the

It will have been seen already that the land disputes which we have just described reflect more than merely disputable, equivocal land-contracts. The landlords who 'sell' the land are without exception men of the titled classes, courtiers, favourites, or former slaves of the king or of powerful noblemen, and the 'buyers' mostly commoners, peasants who have had no other chance of obtaining additional land. To-day they are coming to realize that their right to the land which they acquire is protected by the Native Court. But till very recently, in order to obtain their rights, they would have had to bribe their way through or to find a protector equal in rank and influence to the landlord who threatened to evict them—a typical source of the institution of clientship, which we discussed in a previous chapter.[1] A final example. A certain farmer had 'bought' land from D., a *bara* of the late *Etsu* Saidu. The *Etsu*, for reasons of his own, refused his confirmation of the deal—D., being a tenant of the *Etsu*, could not transfer the lease without the latter's per-mission—and the tenant had only one way open: he attached himself to another, more influential, *bara* of the *Etsu* and through him made various gifts to the *Etsu*, over £3 in money, a valuable civet cat, and promised besides an annual rent of two bundles of corn.

Hereditary Land: Secondary Tenantship

Clientship, combined with a métayer arrangement, becomes a factor in land-tenure also in another respect. A commoner who desired more land, or a new piece of land, could give himself into the service or 'patronage' of a landowning overlord and thus secure land as well as political protection. The conditions were: an initial gift in kind as in all pacts of clientship, occasional presents, visits and other expressions of homage, and finally a tithe (*dzanká* again) from his millet or sorghum crop. This submission to patronage was often the only means by which the peasants in Cis-Kaduna could hope to retain their property when threatened with expropriation, and also the only means by which they could secure new land, that is, access to what under tribal conditions would have been a reserve of village land. The necessity of obtaining land and enjoying its secure possession thus constitutes another of the main roots of clientship. The lease of land obtained by these methods is hereditary, and remains in the family, a comparatively safe possession—unless political factors interfere. The tenants are rarely allowed to for-get that the relationship between landlord and client implies more than merely a correct commercial relationship. Lack of respect, an apparent failure to render due homage, or behaviour suggestive of changed

Etsu himself suggested that the disputed piece of land (a river grove that was claimed by two neighbouring villages) should be bought for money by one of the parties. The purchase price fixed was 15s.

[1] Till very recently no peasant tenant would have dared to invoke the *Etsu's* or *Alkali's* help against his landlord; he would have been looked upon as somebody who had broken away from a firmly established tradition of loyalty, one-sided though it was. The tenant in the last example quoted above kept silent for fifteen years; not till 1934 did he venture to bring his case before the court and thus to obtain a final confirmation of his ownership.

allegiance, suffice to make the landlord refuse a renewal of the tenancy or even to cancel a running tenancy. Several cases of this kind have come to my knowledge; one even found its way to court: L., a nobleman of high rank, evicted his tenant (and this in the middle of the planting season!) because he had lacked in loyalty towards him and 'betrayed his confidence'.

Political changes have brought about an interesting development. To-day the initiative in this kind of tenantship has to some extent passed from the tenants to the landlords themselves. The landlords were, as we have seen, mostly warriors and courtiers who, living in the capital, never worked their land themselves, but settled their slaves on it, and had it worked by their labour. When slavery was abolished and wars came to an end, when the 'absentee' landlords no longer needed *bara* as soldiers for their private armies and could no longer support a large household of henchmen and hangers-on in the town, they offered their land to their *bara*, and so new settlers went out into the country, occupying the land and founding new farm settlements. Sometimes the noble landowners even settled some of their relations in this fashion on the land, nephews and younger brothers, for whom no place or job could be found in town.

All these farm settlements, whether they were for slaves or *bara*, for peasants turned client or clients turned peasant, are called *tunga*—the same name that is applied to the Nupe village 'colonies'. But the 'private' *tunga* has no name of the kind villages possess, but bears the name of the noble patron to whom it 'belongs'. These *tunga* settlements are scattered all over Cis-Kaduna, and surround Bida in a dense belt. There are innumerable hamlets called Sokyara, Maiyaki, Ndeji, or similar titles of nobility—the titles of the landlords under whose patronage the settlements were founded. To our description of the village *tunga* given in a previous chapter we will add here a few examples of the 'private' *tunga*.

Etsu-Kolo (about four miles south of Bida), consisting of two compounds, two families which are distantly related. Called after the founder of the *tunga*, the father of the present family head. This Etsu-Kolo had been, like his father before him, a *bara* of the *Cekpa* in Bida. Later, however, Etsu-Kolo transferred his allegiance to the then ruling Emir, *Etsu* Mohamadu. The change of allegiance proved good policy: *Etsu* Mohamadu procured for him the position of a Village Head for the whole district with its many *tunga* settlements. Since then the family had remained faithful to *Etsu* Mohamadu's house, even after the Village Headship had been abolished again; they are still paying their regular *dzanká* to his successors, at present to the *Shaba* in Bida.

Emi Bwori ('House of Bwori', one mile north of Bida), called after a certain Bwori, the head of the guild of Bida butchers, and a *bara* of *Etsu* Umaru. This Bwori settled his own slaves in this *tunga*. The present owners of it regard themselves as *bara* of the descendants of Bwori, but have abandoned paying *dzanká* to them; but they still go to 'salute' them whenever they come up to town.

Lumanen (four miles west of Bida), a group of very prosperous *tunga* settlements, founded at different times by relations and noblemen attached to the royal house of *Etsu* Masaba. One settlement has been built by the father of the present *Maiyaki* for his *bara*, and is accordingly called *Maiyaki*. A second settlement is called *Emi 'tsu Saba*, and was founded in the time of the father of the present family head, who was a slave in *Etsu* Masaba's house. A third settlement was built recently, by the present family head, who was a *bara* of the present *Etsu* Saidu (also of the Masaba dynasty). All three settlements still pay their regular *dzanká* to their patrons. This year's *dzanká* amounted to one bundle of corn and ten yams.[1]

Makū (one mile south of Bida), consisting of three compounds, called after the noble patron of a certain Ndatazi, a peasant who had had a farm somewhere else first and then moved to the present site, obtaining the land with the help of the *Makū*. He lives in one of the compounds; of the other two one belongs to his brother, and one to a distant relative by marriage, who left his old farm and came here, where the land is better, also becoming a *bara* of the *Makū*. Each of the three houses pays an annual *dzanká* to the present *Makū*. It amounted this year to three bundles of corn and ten yams per compound.

Saci (three miles east of Bida), called after the *Saci* of Bida (a nobility rank). It consists of five compounds; in one a son of the *Saci* is living—the other members of his family are living in Bida—in the other compounds *bara* of the *Saci*. They have discontinued paying their *dzanká*, but still pay regular visits to their patron in town.

One word about the economic arrangement obtaining in the *tunga*. The slaves had worked the land entirely for their masters; that is to say, they had no *efakó* (family) land of their own, but were fed and clothed by their masters, and were also allotted smaller, *bucá* plots, which they were free to work for themselves. The arrangement between the landlord and the *bara* whom he settles on his land is the same métayer system which also regulates the tenantship of the free peasant who accepts clientship in order to obtain land. To-day, the difference between former slaves and *bara* has disappeared; for to most of the freed slaves their change of status meant only a promotion from slave to (free) client. Both, in a good many cases, still acknowledge this form of dependence and, as we saw, still return the annual tithe from their crops to the patron, or at least still pay their respects dutifully. The *dzanká* is no longer a compulsory tribute, and would not be upheld by the court. It is a voluntary gift which confirms the relationship of patronage and protection—a relationship which is as real to-day as it was in former times: political protection for oneself and one's children is bought cheaply with a bundle or two of corn a year.

Hereditary Land: Primary Tenantship

The acquisition of land through clientship follows the general pattern of the Nupe feudal hierarchy. A man who obtains land as a *bara* obtains it from a man of higher rank, either a royal prince or nobleman who holds the land in his own right, or from a rank-holder or titled slave or a king's *bara* who has himself obtained the land from another landlord higher up on the hierarchical scale. These 'primary tenants', however, have acquired their land by a different method, namely, through certain

[1] This census was taken in 1934, when *Etsu* Saidu was still alive.

services which they have rendered to their overlords. Ultimately all land is derived from one source: the royal house, which again bestows land for services rendered. The title of the royal house to the possession of land is by the right of conquest. We must examine this more closely.

In the conquest of Nupe country the members of the royal family appropriated three categories of tribal land: all no-man's-land between villages, i.e. virgin land in the *cikā*, the uninhabited bush; also all village land which, once occupied, had been lying fallow for long, either because of the death of the owner or his emigration, or because a short-term lease (borrowing) had lapsed; finally, under certain conditions, the *Etsu* also seized the village land on the outskirts of the village territory, what we have called the 'land reserve' of the village. The first two kinds of land were divided up geographically between the three royal houses, as we have already seen, one receiving all land to the east of Bida, one all land to the west and north-west, and the third all land to the south of Bida. (See sketch-map, p. 81.) The last category of expropriated land (the village 'reserve') was sometimes appropriated by a ruling *Etsu* arbitrarily and irrespective of its geographical position in one of the three royal territories.[1] Of the land thus owned by the royal houses by the right of conquest the *Etsu* or royal princes of highest rank bestowed smaller or larger parcels on their followers, members of the nobility or slaves and *bara* 'for services rendered'; the land grant gave them complete and permanent rights to the land, in return for which they had to pay the usual annual *dzankā* in kind. The royal tenants—'primary tenants' as we have called them—then settled their own men in various ways on this land, either founding *tunga* settlements for them or subletting the land (or part of it) in any of the ways discussed above. Every landed property which we find in the 'conquered territory', excepting only the scattered islands of original village land, has thus been derived directly or indirectly, that is, through the hierarchy of feudal nobility, from one of the three royal houses of Nupe.

Apart from these possessions which were given away to rank-holders and henchmen the royal families have kept certain royal estates proper. This land is not transmitted in the ordinary way of inheritance to younger brothers or sons, nor is it alienable like the other lands appropriated by the royal houses, but can be claimed only by the three titled heads of the royal dynasties. Right to this special royal land is thus part of the promotion to rank and status within the dynasty and the political system at large. It implies absolute and permanent ownership; it implies more than merely the 'administrative' control over family land that is vested in the family head in the Nupe village. Yet it reflects the most essential element in Nupe peasant ownership of land—what I have called 'access' to the land in virtue of headship of the kinship group. This surprising analogy between feudal monarchy and peasant ownership is rooted in an analogy in the structure of the two groups as such, village

[1] Thus, for example, all the land in the district of Jima, south of Bida, belongs to the house of Umaru Majigi. But the village land of Kucigi, a village in this district, had been appropriated by *Etsu* Maliki (of the house of Usman Zaki) when he was *Etsu* Nupe and bestowed on one of his slaves, the *Cece*.

kinship group and royal 'house', different though they are in many other respects. The possession of land is only one instance of the joint, 'corporate', rights which characterize the two analogous groups. But of this we shall say more later.

Royal Estates

The three royal estates are situated immediately outside the town walls of Bida. On each of the estates we find a small hamlet, called *esoži*, where (former) royal slaves are living, who were appointed to work the land and look after the royal property.[1] Each of the three *esoži* is placed under the headship of a head slave, styled *Sokyara*—a titled overseer of the royal estates.

The first cultivation in the year—the clearing and first hoeing—was always done by large-scale communal labour in which over a hundred people used to join—slaves, *bara*, peasants from the neighbourhood—and which lasted for one or two days. The *Etsu* himself arranged for food and drink (sorghum beer) and for the customary band of drummers and flute-players to play during the work and at the dance afterwards. After this first cultivation the care of the land was left entirely to the slaves. Originally the whole yield of the royal estates went to the *Etsu* and to the other heads of the royal houses. The *esoži* used to supply over a hundred bundles of corn annually. The royal landlord gave his slaves in return food and clothing, and cared for their various needs. The married slaves (as everywhere in Nupe) were given fairly large individual farm-plots of their own which were not only sufficient to provide food for their families but as a rule also allowed some surplus for trade.

Under modern conditions the position of the royal slaves in the *esoži* has been assimilated to that of clients who only pay an annual tithe from the produce of their farms. But the different Emirs dealt differently with the question of adapting the management to modern conditions. *Etsu* Mohamadu, who was not very interested in farming, abandoned the communal work of the first cultivation; he also lost all personal touch with his *esoži*, and insisted only on the annual *dzanká*. *Etsu* Bello, on the other hand, maintained the communal work of the first cultivation; he demanded one-third of the total produce as 'tithe', leaving the rest to the people of the *esoži*. Under the late *Etsu* Saidu and under the present *Etsu* every family head in the *esoži* paid one to two bundles of sorghum or late millet to the royal landlord, the *Sokyara* acting as intermediary—the total tithe amounting to about ten to fifteen bundles a year. When the Government built the new residence for the present Emir a final change took place. The land outside the Wuya gate of Bida, which formerly belonged to the house of *Etsu* Masaba, was bought by the Government as a site for the new building, and turned into Crown land.[2] The

---

[1] During the dry season the three royal estates, being situated directly outside the town gates of Bida, are the natural camping-ground for the donkey and cattle caravans that pass through Bida. Now it is the customary practice that these camps—rather primitive grass-shelters erected by the people of the *Etsu*—are always pitched on the farm-land belonging to the ruling *Etsu*. His farms have thus the benefit of the well-manured soil.

[2] In accordance with Nupe practice the fruit-bearing trees were not included

present Emir, who comes from the royal house of Umaru Majigi, thus owns, unlike any of his predecessors, two royal estates: his own family estate near the Jima gate, south of Bida, and the new estate on the Crown land near the Wuya gate, which, like the residence itself, belongs to the modern accoutrements of his office. The *esoẓi* people on his family estate were prepared to work for him on the usual *dzanká* arrangement. But the *esoẓi* of *Etsu* Masaba—the *esoẓi* on the land that had now become his official estate—refused to work for their new landlord on the old terms, and demanded money wages. Finally, when the *Etsu* in 1936 started an experimental farm for mixed farming on his family estate, the *esoẓi* workers there also denounced the old agreement and demanded wages; for this was work of a new kind altogether, work carried out entirely for their landlord, no longer work after their own fashion, from which they could hand over the traditional share in the produce.

Non-agricultural Use of Land

A few words must be said in conclusion about rights to land that is used for other than agricultural purposes, such as clay-pits from which clay is obtained for pottery or for the sun-dried bricks used in house-building, the iron-ore deposits which are used by the native iron-ore smelters, or the space needed for the dye-pits of the indigo dyers. All these stretches of land, whether they are situated close to the house (like the dye-pits) or some distance away (like the clay-pits and the ferruginous hill-side) are accessible to all.

The thick strips of rain-forest near the rivers are specially valuable 'no-man's-land'. Here woodcarvers and carpenters find the timber they need for their work. The branches of certain palm-trees are used for rafters in roof building; a certain species of reed is used for the making of the curtain-like mats which the Nupe call *eshegi* (the Hausa *asabari*); other species of grass, and the leaves of the dum-palm, are used for mat-making and the making of straw hats. The fact that these materials are found only in certain places, far away from the town where the craftsmen who are using them are living, is turned to economic use, and the pro-curing of the raw material thus gains independent commercial signifi-cance: the big palm-branch rafters are sold on Bida market by the men who cut them; and men and women frequently use the time of com-parative leisure in the dry season to travel down to the river in order to collect dum-palm leaves and marsh-grass, which they sell later, for a little money, to mat- and straw hat makers.

The collecting and selling of firewood (which is done by women) and the cutting and selling of grass for roofing (done by men) belongs to a slightly different category. For in this case the non-agricultural use of land does not apply to 'no-man's-land'; the farmers and their families

in this transaction and remained the property of the original landlords, i.e. the head of the house of *Etsu* Masaba. Thus in January 1936, when the new official residence of the Emir had been standing already for almost a year, people from the house of *Etsu* Masaba were collecting the fruits of the trees on the new Crown land.

themselves make use of these secondary resources which they find on their land.

We may mention, finally, the various uses to which uncultivated land in the town—streets and open spaces in Bida or the larger villages—is put: women may put up little 'kitchens' by the roadside, where they cook food and sell it to passers-by; traders or craftsmen may build themselves a small hut to be used as workshop or booth; or neighbours may get together and build one of the little mosques on the open space between their houses, which you find scattered all over Bida town. No permission is necessary for these modest buildings. For larger enterprises, a big mosque, or a market, the *Etsu* in Bida or, in the village, the chief, would himself allot the necessary space. This practice includes modern requirements as well: thus *Etsu* Mohamadu, who had shown great sympathy for the work of the C.M.S. Mission, gave them a space for building a school and a compound inside Bida, in his own *ekpā* of the town, free of charge.

LIVE STOCK

Cattle-keeping plays a very secondary part in Nupe economics. This is shown most clearly in the very low *per capita* figures quoted in the statistical table at the end of this section. To-day cattle are owned only by the butchers who buy for the kill from the Bornu and Fulani cattle-traders who, with their huge herds, pass regularly through Nupe and Bida, on their way from the north and the south. I say 'to-day', because formerly many of the members of the Nupe aristocracy and the more wealthy among the Bida people used to own large herds of cattle.[1] Slaves taken from the Bororó-Fulani, the nomadic Fulani herdsmen, looked after the cattle. The cattle were always kept outside the town, frequently a long distance away; for they had to be moved from pasture to pasture according to the season, up north, away from the tsetse-infested area near the rivers, in the rains, and south again in the dry season. This meant, obviously, much trouble and cost, and this is mostly quoted as the reason which made the Nupe eventually abandon cattle-keeping altogether. *U de wahalla*, 'it is a great trouble', was the explanation given to me by the *Alkali* of Bida when I expressed my astonishment that it was so difficult nowadays to find people ready to buy a herd of cattle. I have known two cattle-owners—the last in Nupe; one was an ex-slave who died without heir in 1936 and left a herd of thirty-two head of cattle which at the time was tended for him by Fulani herdsmen who had their camp near Bida. It was at his death that the question arose where to find a buyer for the herd. The other cattle-owner was the late *Etsu* of Agaie, a Fulani by birth, who owned a large herd of very beautiful cattle, of over 200 head, which was tended by Nupe shepherds, the sons of ex-slaves of the *Etsu*.

I may, perhaps, add here an historical note: The cattle of the *Etsu* of Agaie were not, like the cattle to be seen at present in Nupe, of the

[1] Laird and Oldfield refer to the huge herds of cattle which they saw in the capital of Nupe kingdom, Rabá.

northern, humped, breed. They were humpless and of small build, evidently related to the dwarf cattle which exist to-day in certain areas in eastern and south-eastern Nigeria. These dwarf cattle are said to have been very widespread in eastern and northern Nupe country before the Fulani conquest; the Gbari, for example, maintain that they had owned, originally, large herds of these cattle which, to-day, have almost disappeared in this region. The traditions of Nupe speak of a magic connected with a bull or a cow with which the ancestor-king Tsoede endowed the first Beni chiefs. The *ketsá* ritual on the Niger river demanded the sacrifice of a bull, to be presented annually by the chief of the Kyedye. Evidently, these rites and sacrifices could only have referred to these dwarf, pre-Fulani cattle. Anyhow, there is no evidence that cattle have ever played any important part in the economy of the peasant areas, and possibly in the whole pre-Fulani kingdom.

The disappearance of cattle, however, from the Fulani-Nupe, and from the households of the rich, demands explanation. No doubt the 'great trouble' has played some part in this change. With the disappearance of slavery the problem of finding suitable and sufficiently cheap labour presented an additional difficulty. But the decision to abandon cattle-keeping was also due to a decided change in the attitude of the people towards this commodity. The herds of cattle were, in a word, capital. The Nupe do not live on the cattle, basing their diet on milk and butter, as the Fulani and other cattle people do. Nor are the cattle in Nupe linked to a whole system of religious beliefs, taboos, and ceremonial usages. The *Etsu* of Agaie (on whose herd I could examine these questions in detail) occasionally sold one or two head of cattle when he was in need of money—this was the only concrete use to which he or any of the Nupe cattle-owners would put their cattle. I cannot judge how far status and prestige may have formerly entered into this assessment of the value of cattle. I gathered that it could not have been of much significance; the possession of horses counted for much more. But the existing incentives to possess cattle must have been further weakened, and even reversed, by two changes in the present-day economic situation. First, by the enormous rise in the price of cattle, especially in the countries south of Nupe, which came with the increased (European and Europeanized) demand for meat and skins. Second, by the appearance of new means of economic enterprise, and the prospects of more profitable, large-scale trade, which necessitated a more liquid form of capital. It is a fact that a large number of rich cattle-owners soon sold their herds, attracted by the high price, and also realizing most probably the greater advantage that, under modern conditions, lay in transforming their stock into ready money.

This tendency to keep the capital 'liquid' is shown also in the readiness of the Nupe to experiment with different kinds of live stock. Thus we find here and there—and the same thing is reported from Nupe a hundred years ago—ostriches, which the Nupe buy from traders from the north, feed and tend and finally sell again with a profit. An enterprising chief had even taken to breeding horses; it was done on a very small scale, and was in Nupe an isolated case, but still characteristic of the general trend. The same trend is, finally, evident in the Nupe method of keeping sheep and goats.

Sheep and Goats

Very rarely do the Nupe farmers (or town people for that matter) breed sheep and goats. It is, once more, the principle of 'liquid' resources that counts. A great many farmers buy a sheep or goat when it is young, or when sheep and goats are cheap, and sell it again later on with profit, when they are in need of money. Certain regular fluctuations in the price of goats form the basis for this calculation. During the season of the great Mohammedan feasts, when rams are killed in almost every house, prices go up, to fall again during the rainy season, before the harvest, when there is little money coming in and accordingly little demand for animals.[1] This method of husbandry accounts for the very irregular distribution of sheep and goats at a given time, varying greatly with the individual need for money and the ability or inclination to invest money in animals. The general figures *per capita* of sheep and goats are surprisingly low (see the statistical table). The figure for Bida town is 0·12 and for the districts 0·71 per male adult. These figures reflect the very small money resources the Nupe have for engaging in this sort of seasonal trade. Throughout the year, and especially during the time of the Mohammedan festivals, a large number of sheep and goats have, in fact, to be imported from Hausa. But the figures also show that sheep- and goat-keeping is more frequent in the districts than in Bida. This bears out what I have said above about the influence of varied and expanding economic enterprise upon stock-keeping. Bida, though richer than the districts, is poorer in live stock; the centre of trade and of manifold economic interests keeps its capital more liquid than the country with its limited scope of economic prospects.

It is interesting to note in this connexion that in goat- or sheep-breeding the young animals always belong to the owner of the mother-goat or -sheep; the owner of the female animal may ask the owner of the male animal to let him have the animal for breeding, but this would be done without payment or return of any kind, merely as a personal favour. Female animals are accordingly more expensive than male animals, and the inducement to part with the mother-goat thus often overweighs the interest in the breeding itself.

Other Domestic Animals

The Nupe keep no pigs and eat no pork—an avoidance which is not, as far as I see, due only to Mohammedan influence. The few pigs one sees in the country belong to Yoruba.

[1] Prices for sheep and goats vary from 5s. to 15s., according to the season (see p. 316). The great seasonal changes are also shown in the figures for sheep and goats slaughtered in Bida in the different months of the year: January, 130; February, 150; March, 82; April, 151; May, 129; June, 68; July, 58; August, 114; September, 116; October, 119; November, 120; December, 122. The highest figures refer to January/February and April, the months of the Mohammedan festivals of *Ramadan* and *Muharram*; the lowest figures to June and July, in the middle of the rains, before the first harvest of the season.

There is little to be said about fowls. In every house chickens are kept; men and women, grown-ups and children, have their own chicken. Often one sees a young boy going to the market to sell 'his' chicken, given him by father or mother. The fowls are bought and sold regularly in the food-markets of every larger village. Fowls represent the most important sacrificial food of pagan (and to some extent Mohammedan) Nupe; almost every religious ceremony, communal as well as house-hold-rites, involves the killing of a fowl. Chickens are, besides, the most desirable food the Nupe know. Eggs are not marketed and in certain parts of Nupe not eaten. The Beni do not eat eggs because 'they make men sterile and women barren'. The Nupe also keep pigeons, for which they put up a bowl of water on a forked pole inside the house. Pigeons are not as a rule traded in the market, nor are they eaten regularly, but sometimes the eating of pigeons is ordered by diviners for ritual reasons.

Donkeys and Horses

About three-quarters of the donkeys which are found in Nupe belong to Bida town. They are transport animals owned mostly by traders, pack animals used in their caravans which carry palm-oil and salt from the river steamers up country, and bring natron down from Hausa and Bornu. In 1935 the only districts possessing no donkeys were those which have other means of transport: the riverain area, and the district of Mokwa through which the railway runs. Again, the largest number of horses is found in Bida. Horses, as I have said already, are a symbol of rank and status. The *Etsu* Nupe may, as a sign of his highest esteem, present a man with a horse. But every man who can afford it will buy one for himself or for his sons. A horse represents, if not the most profitable, the most noble expenditure or investment.

Yet, profitable in the narrow sense, or in the wider sense as implying enhancement of prestige—all these possibilities of investment of capital in live stock are determined by the amount of liquid capital available; in other words, by the volume of money in circulation. The economic stringency of the country which, starting from the decline in the market prices for native produce in 1934-5, as well as the subsequent recovery in 1936, is reflected clearly in the figures of the census of live stock for Bida Division for the last four years.

			Sheep	Goats	Horses	Donkeys
1933	.	.	5,788	28,856	1,196	111
1934	.	.	6,600	29,445	1,160	157
1935	.	.	5,010	25,876	917	137
1936	.	.	5,702	34,751	1,007	149

CHAPTER XII
AGRICULTURE: PRODUCTION
COUNTRY AND CROPS

BY far the largest proportion of the Nupe population work on the land. In the purely agricultural districts in Trans-Kaduna 9,000 out of a male population of 11,000 are farmers. Even in Bida town, the centre of crafts, industry, and trade, more than a quarter of the population earn their livelihood on the land.[1] This shows clearly the predominant position of agriculture in the productive system of the country. We have already spoken of the rich and complex character of Nupe agriculture, due both to the favourable configuration of the environment and to the advanced civilization of the people, who were always ready to adopt and introduce advantageous techniques of production from other groups. The wide scope and the complexity of Nupe agriculture enables the people to rely in their nutritive arrangements on a large variety of crops which, as we shall see, is well distributed over the year.

But these facts must be correlated with the facts of local distribution and specialization of agricultural techniques. The most important local specialization refers to marsh-land farming. The marsh-land comprises only perhaps one-tenth or less of the total land under cultivation. The intensive cultivation, however, and the concentration on certain specially valuable crops (above all rice) make it a most important factor in the productive system of the country. Other forms of specialization which, on a smaller scale, influence the productive and nutritive balance of Nupe, are due to differences in the quality of the soil and, indirectly, to population factors and conditions of landownership. Thus cotton and ground-nuts thrive specially in Trans-Kaduna, the most fertile region of Nupe. The comparatively poor selection of crops round Bida is due both to the more exhausted soil and the comparative scarcity of land in this most densely populated area. Less yam, for instance, is grown round Bida than elsewhere, as yam demands a new plot every year (see p. 209). Nor is bulrush-millet grown near Bida, although in this case the reasons put forward by the people are different: it is no good, I was told, to try planting this early crop near a large town; the multitude of birds would devour the crop as soon as it appeared. The difference in the quality of the land in Beni country and in Trans-Kaduna is also reflected in the varying length of the period during which a plot can be kept under continuous cultivation. In Mokwa a plot is generally worked for four to five years; round Kutigi for six to seven years; in Doko, in Beni country, only for three to four years. In this last district, with its heavy population and its restricted land-resources, a rudimentary system of animal manure, with horse- and goat-dung, is practised by the people. Asked to explain why it was that only this one section of Nupe was practising animal manuring, the people said: 'Look for yourself; you will see that

---

[1] Of a total of 7,714 Bida men 1,664 are farmers. The figures mentioned here are taken from a local census taken in Bida Division in 1930.

we have little land, much less than people in other parts of the country. We even have to make our farms up on the hill-side since there is no vacant land left in the valley.' This is true enough. When I visited Doko on my second expedition I saw that a few enterprising men had started farming on the steep stony hills at the back of the village—a thing nobody dreamed of doing when I stayed in Doko on my first expedition two years before.

The appreciation of manure has led in Beni country to an interesting co-operation between the population of a village, or a certain landlord, and the groups of nomadic Fulani herdsmen who come down regularly in the dry season to find pastures for their herds. The Nupe landowners invite the head of such a nomadic group, and sometimes induce him by presents of food or assistance in the building of the camp, to make his camp on their fallow land. This procedure is repeated every year with a new plot of fallow land. The year after the land has been thus manured it is taken under cultivation. I have myself seen the enormous difference in the growth of the crops between a plot on which the Fulani had made their camp and other, ordinary farm-plots.[1]

Cultivation is also to some extent carried on inside the villages and even inside Bida town. In the villages, where large open spaces separate the different *efu*, the cultivation inside the village is fairly extensive, and one grows there the main crops, millet, guinea-corn, ground-nuts, &c. In densely populated villages where there is little open space left, and in Bida town, the people still grow a few things. Something will be planted, in fact, wherever there is room, all along the town walls, round the compound wall, on any open space in front of the house and even inside the house. Here are grown chiefly greens and vegetables, beans, sorrel, red pepper, also sweet potatoes, cassava or maize, and hemp. As a rule the small plots in or near the house are planted with crops which are easy to tend, and this work is left to the old men who can no longer walk long distances and do heavy work. Even inside Bida there exists a certain specialization; on the small stretch of marsh-land that runs through the town, and in the thick groves on the banks of the two streams, typical marsh-land crops are grown: sugar-cane, rice, and bananas.

In this large variety of crops cultivated in Nupe not all are, of course, of equal importance from a nutritive or general economic point of view. Again, it is impossible to give a simple formula. The staple crops, the crops on which the food supply of the people primarily depends, are millet, sorghum, yam, and, to a lesser extent, rice. From the point of view of trade the most important crops are rice, ground-nuts, cotton, but also sorghum and yam and a few lesser crops. Cassava, maize, and sweet potatoes (grown inland) are of secondary importance only. This is shown clearly in the attitude of the Nupe farmer towards these crops. The pride of the farmer is always his millet, sorghum, and yam farm. Cassava and maize, the Nupe would say, grow anywhere, and anybody, farmer or no farmer, can grow them. A man who would rely on this

---

[1] Among the Bida landlords it is an accepted arrangement to place one's fallow land at the disposal of the Bororó previous to leasing it to a new tenant. The landlord can then obtain a much higher price for his land.

type of cultivation only would lay himself open at once to the criticism of his fellow farmers. As regards cassava, it is known to have little nutritive value—'only yam or millet or sorghum make a man strong'. Both crops may, however, provide a useful stopgap for the time between the harvest of the main crops.

We have said earlier in this book that the complexity of the agricultural system of the Nupe is due partly to the close contact they have had with other cultures, in particular with neighbouring groups. We realize here that this was more than an occasional contact, and more also than some obscure process of diffusion. It was to a large extent part of that assimilation and cultural 'learning' that goes hand in hand with intensive political unification of long standing and all that it entails— regular intercourse, a wide net of transport and traffic, and an everextending economic co-operation. As the kingdom brought together peoples from the marsh-land and from the inland forests, farmers from the 'yam countries' and farmers from the 'millet districts', it made them learn from each other and at the same time utilize each other's special resources. Assimilation and specialization are both features of an expanding economic area. We have, in fact, a threefold correlation; for these two features involve another, third, factor: a large-scale system of organized distribution, that is, trade and marketing.

FARMING TECHNIQUE

Like most African tribes the Nupe practise hoe-agriculture. They use two kinds of hoes, a large heavy type called *zuku*, and a small type called *dugba*. The *zuku* has a heavy handle, about 16 in. long, bent somewhat like a hook, into the angle of which the broad shovel-like blade (8 in. long) is fitted. The *dugba* has a straight handle, 20 in. long, with a less broad, slightly bent blade inserted at the end. The heavy hoe is used for throwing up mounds and ridges, the lighter hoe mainly for weeding and other less heavy work. The Nupe also use a long bushknife, *gada* (now mostly of European manufacture), for cutting grain stalks or digging out yam.

When using the heavy hoe the farmer stands across the ridge he is making, with legs wide apart, the body bent forward, and, gripping the handle of the hoe with both hands, he lifts it to the level of his head and shoulders and brings it down again between his legs, with one swing digging up the earth and throwing it behind him on to the mound or ridge he is preparing. When the mound or ridge has reached the proper height, he moves a few steps forward to repeat this action, until the ridge extends to the edge of the field. Having finished one ridge, the farmer turns round to throw up the next, parallel, ridge.

Nupe cultivation works both with large round mounds and low long ridges; the mounds are 2–3 ft. high and about 3 ft. in diameter, and are arranged in long rows; the mounds are spaced (measured from top to top) about 4–5 ft. in the same row and 6 ft. from row to row. The ridges are 1 ft. high and are drawn, more or less straight, right across the field in parallel lines about 3 ft. apart. The two types of cultivation are used for different kinds of crops. Ground-nuts, sweet potatoes, and certain vegetables are always planted in ridges, yam always in mounds. As regards the other crops, the rule is that in a first cultivation, that is, on a plot planted for the first time after having lain fallow, mounds are thrown up; in the subsequent year the mounds are turned into ridges, as a result of the practice of 'shifting' the ridges and interplanting in the second half of the planting season. The throwing up of mounds is by far the heavier and longer work. 'Lazy' farmers—in the eyes of the people—thus sometimes prefer the easier job of making ridges even in a first year's cultivation.[1] Big trees are always left standing on the farms and cultivation is carried out round them. The Nupe farmers appreciate the shade of big trees during the heat of the day. Small trees on the farm-land which do not bear fruit are lopped or cut about 4 ft. from the ground. This becomes important in the period of lying fallow; for the tree-stumps and undergrowth which the farmer leaves standing on his fields help to put the fallow land under a growth of 'bush' rather than grass, thus assisting and speeding up the regeneration of the soil.[2]

The cultivation on the marsh-land farms is adapted to the conditions of a natural annual irrigation by the flooded rivers and watercourses. The irrigated area is divided into square plots, approximately 6 ft. by 9 ft., each consisting of from four to six ridges running parallel and two ridges at right angles on the upper and lower end. The ridges are flat and narrow; they do not connect at the corners, but leave small channels open; by means of these ridges the water from the flooded river is distributed evenly on the cultivated plots, and at the same time kept standing there.

In the lay-out of the Nupe farms the aesthetic aspect is strongly pronounced. The farmers pay much attention to drawing their ridges nicely parallel and as straight as possible, and to distributing their mounds symmetrically over the field. The nice rounding-off of the border of a field is specially appreciated. Frequently one finds ridges and cross-ridges arranged in a symmetrical and even conspicuously ornamental pattern. Similarly, the skill and keenness of the farmer is judged by the clean look of his farm, with all weeds, leaves, and brushwood cleared away. An overgrown, untidy looking farm invariably elicits the comment: za-gá de kokari à, 'that man makes no effort'.

ROTATION OF CROPS

The Nupe system of agriculture is based on shifting cultivation combined with a well-worked-out rotation of crops. Plots are kept under cultivation for from four to seven years (see p. 205), i.e. till the land 'grows tired', and then abandoned temporarily. The individual farmer does not, however, always wait until failing crops have warned him of

[1] The mounds represent the more thorough cultivation, utilizing a deeper and, I believe, also heavier layer of the subsoil. This is shown in the fact that yam, which demands a heavy and more humid soil, is always grown on mounds, while ground-nuts, for which light sandy soil is best suitable, are invariably grown on the low ridges. (Cf. Faulkner and Mackie, op. cit., pp. 147–8.)
[2] See op. cit., p. 44.

the 'tiredness' of his farm-plot, but as a rule simply follows the general routine obtaining in his area, varying the standard period of cultivation occasionally by one year, in accordance with the special requirements of his farm-land. For the abandoned field a new plot is taken under cultivation, while the former is left to lie fallow, until eventually it will again be fit for cultivation. The period of lying fallow, dependent as it is on local conditions of land-tenure and individual land-holdings, varies much more widely than the period of cultivation—between four and fifteen years.

During the period of cultivation a strict rotation of crops is observed. There exists a comparatively large number of different types of rotation, of which I shall mention only the most important. The rotation depends on the crop which is planted first on a plot taken under cultivation. The following chart illustrates the most common types of rotation:

Table of Four-Year Rotation

	A	B	C	D
1	Yam	(Bulr.-mill.) late millet and sorghum	Ground-nuts (and cassava)	Cotton
2	Maize and sorghum or bulr.-mill.; late millet and sorghum	,, ,,	(i) bulr.-mill., (ii) maize, late millet, and sorghum	Bulr.-mill., late millet, sorghum
3	Bulr.-mill., late millet and sorghum	,, ,,	,, ,, ,,	,, ,,
4	,, ,,	,, ,, or fallow, or cassava, sweet potatoes, and beans	Cassava, sweet potatoes, and beans	Cassava, sweet potatoes, and beans

The main rules in this rotation are these: yam, cotton, and ground-nuts are 'one-year crops', i.e. they are invariably the first crops in the cycle of rotation and are not as a rule planted a second time on the same plot. On the contrary, it is well known that millet and sorghum do particularly well planted as a second year's crop after cotton, ground-nuts, or—in a less common rotation—red pepper. Where the rotation starts with millet and sorghum bulrush-millet is sometimes left out in the first year and added later, as it does not do very well as a first crop on a new field, especially if the rains happen to be late. Also it is sown mostly only where there are a number of neighbouring fields under cultivation; on isolated fields the danger of birds picking the crop is too great. On the other hand, land on which the two millet kinds and sorghum are planted in succession may 'tire' sooner than land planted with varying crops and thus have to be abandoned after only three years. The alternative choice, finally, after a first crop of ground-nuts (C (i) and (ii) in the table) depends mainly on the energy and keenness of the farmer; the crops listed under (i), i.e. the combination millet-sorghum, though more valuable, involve the heavier work, namely, a complete re-hoeing of the ridges.

Jebba Island, which is half marsh-land, is the only area where I found yam planted twice on the same plot. This type of cultivation necessitates a different system of cropping: between two yam crops sorghum alone is planted, without the additional two millet crops, which is said to exhaust the soil far less than does the mixed cropping. Even so, the field supports only three successive crops, and is left fallow after the three years. Before the second yam crop, i.e. after two years' cultivation, the operation of 'shifting the ridges' takes place, which we shall describe later in detail, and which, in the normal rotation, has to be carried out every year. As an alternative the people of Jebba Island practise a five or six years' rotation with four or five sorghum crops succeeding a first year's yam crop, the 'shifting of the ridges' being again inserted after two or three successive crops.[1]

The table shows further that certain crops are planted together on the same plot. This combined cultivation is much more extensive and much more varied than is shown in the table. The practice of 'interplanting' certain crops among others is one of the most characteristic features of the intensive and economical farm technique of the Nupe. The people speak, in fact, in connexion with this interplanting of *ewo banza*, 'useless ridge', meaning here the furrow between ridges or mounds; it is the 'useless ridge' that is utilized in the interplanting. This combined cultivation constitutes at the same time one of the most complicated aspects of Nupe farm technique because of the wide range of variations which it permits. These are the main combinations:

Simultaneous Interplanting. In the purely agricultural districts the two millet kinds and sorghum are planted together on the same mound, sorghum on the top and bulrush-millet and late millet on the flanks of the mound. The three crops are not planted quite simultaneously, bulrush-millet being sown a little before the other two crops (see chart, p. 213). The farmers near Bida practise various other combinations, e.g. late millet-sorghum, maize-sorghum, or late millet-sorghum with ground-nuts interplanted in the furrows.

Yam and okra are frequently planted together, yam on the top of the mound and okra at the foot.

Ground-nuts and cassava may also be planted together, ground-nuts on the top of the ridge and cassava in the furrow between the ridges. The same arrangement obtains with sweet potatoes and cassava.

Successive Interplanting. After the reaping of bulrush-millet or maize beans are sown in their place, i.e. on the same ridges or mounds, between the still growing late millet and sorghum plants.

Melons are frequently planted irregularly between various crops.

Cassava may be interplanted with any crop, e.g. yam or millet and sorghum, and at any time.

On the farm-plots close to the compounds, which are manured with the refuse from the house, no rotation is practised. Nor does such complicated rotation exist on the irrigated marsh-land farms. Here the same

---

[1] In Yoruba country, where the soil is much richer, three or four successive yam crops are said to be the rule.

plot can be cultivated for ten years or even longer. The cultivation follows every year the same pattern: two alternating root-crops, cassava and sweet potatoes, and, after they have been harvested, on the same plot, rice. On certain marsh-land farms in the Kaduna valley two successive crops of maize are grown. Other marsh-land farms again (on the rivers Gbako and Kaduna, and on a smaller scale near Kutigi) are devoted to the cultivation of onions and partly sugar-cane. Farmers in inland areas who possess a field close to a watercourse plant rice in addition to the usual inland crops.

To return to inland cultivation. Of the four types of rotation listed in our table (A B C D) the farmer selects a certain combination. Most farmers, as we shall see presently, cultivate two or three crops at the same time, the most frequent combination being ABC, ABD, and AAC (D), i.e. a rotation which includes the maximum proportion of staple food crops, millet, sorghum, and yam, together with one or two commercial crops. By a judicious overlapping arrangement, starting the different series of crops in successive years, the farmer secures an even distribution of these crops. This is an example from Mokwa, recorded in 1936.

	Plot 1	Plot 2	Plot 3	Plot 4	Plot 5	Plot 6
1935	..	Yam	Sorghum, millet	..	..	..
1936	Yam, ground-beans	Maize, sorghum, beans	Sorghum, millet	..	Ground-nuts	..
1937	Maize, sorghum	Sorghum, millet	Sorghum, millet	Yam	Cassava	Ground-nuts
1938	Sorghum, millet	Sorghum, millet	(?)	Maize, sorghum	Cassava	Cassava
1939	Sorghum, millet	..	..	Sorghum, millet	?	Cassava
1940	..	..	..	Sorghum, millet	..	Cassava

The main problem in determining a suitable system of rotation are the 'one-year crops'. It can be seen that, allowing for a minimum period of four years for lying fallow, a farmer must have at least four different plots under cultivation in order to obtain one of the one-year crops in every year of the rotation, or eight plots, in order to secure a continuous, uninterrupted, cultivation of these crops. Where such an extensive subdivision proves impossible, the number of one-year crops will vary from year to year, in accordance with the progressive stages of the rotation. In 1936 I found that of thirty-seven farms on which one or more of the three 'one-year crops' were grown only two farms combined all three, six combined the cultivation of yam and ground-nuts, seven of yam and cotton, and of the remaining twenty-two the cultivation was restricted to one of these three crops.

The selection of crops on which the farmer eventually decides and the cycle of rotation which he will accordingly adopt will thus depend primarily (ignoring here the question of the quality of the land) on the size of his farm-land and the possibility, or profit, of subdividing it into plots for different cultivation. Evidently, land cannot be subdivided indefinitely to make room for a large variety of crops. I have found that the farms under cultivation in Nupe varied in size from 2 to 10 acres, according to the number of men who are working together; the average size of farm corresponding to one able-bodied male adult is from 2 to 2½ acres. A farm of this size (i.e. a one-man farm) can still be subdivided into two or three plots, for the cultivation of different crops; larger farms can be subdivided into three or four different plots for cultivation. In addition to the field cultivated at a given time the farmer as a rule possesses from one to three fallow fields of the same size to which he turns when it becomes necessary to take a new field, or new plots on this field, into cultivation.[1] The following examples, which were collected in Lemu, a prosperous village north of Bida, may illustrate the relation between size of farm and selection of crops. These examples represent, of course, only stages in the four-year rotation, which explains the reason for the absence of certain one-year crops in the selection of crops which were grown that year.

1. Five men working together; total land under cultivation approx. 9½ acres. Grain (millet and sorghum), 6 acres (half of this plot was under yam cultivation the previous year); red pepper (formerly ground-nuts), 1½ acres; cotton, 2½ acres.

2. Three men working together; total land under cultivation 6 acres. Grain, 5½ acres; rice, ½ acre.

3. Two men working together; total land under cultivation over 4 acres. Grain, 2 acres; yam, 2 acres; ground-nuts, ¼ acre.

4. One man working; total land under cultivation under 2 acres. Grain, 1½ acres; rice, ¼ acre; red pepper, ¼ acre (½ acre under yam cultivation the previous year).

5. One man working; total land under cultivation over 2 acres. Grain, 1 acre; yam, 1 acre; rice, 200 sq. yds.

6. One man working (a young man, recently married); total land under cultivation 1 acre. Grain, ¾ acre; red pepper, ¼ acre.

These examples bring us to a further condition determining the selection of crops and type of rotation, namely, the size of the working group at the disposal of the farmer, and the efficiency of its organization; on its co-operation depends the carrying out of the complicated and at times overlapping schedule of planting, weeding, &c., without any of the crops being neglected. Finally, the selection of crops is also determined by the prospect of return, i.e. by the satisfaction of specific wants which the farmer may expect from the different forms of cultivation. We will for the present ignore this last point and concentrate on the second condition. In order to understand fully we must study more closely the agricultural calendar of the country. In the attached chart I have tabulated the schedule of Nupe agricultural activities. It will be best if I supplement it with a description of the more important agricultural activities as I have observed them in actual cases. First, however, a few comments are necessary.

[1] It can be calculated that for the continuous cultivation of two one-year crops, e.g. yam on 1 acre and ground-nuts on ¼ acre, in addition to an ordinary crop, e.g. grain on 1 acre, a total land possession, i.e. worked as well as fallow land, of 9–10 acres is necessary. The figures quoted above show that actual practice falls considerably short of this standard.

The Agricultural Calendar of Nupe

As mentioned elsewhere (see Appendix, p. 411) the Nupe peasant calendar counts 12 lunar months starting from the month which sees the beginning of the rainy season. It will be realized that the various dates given in this synoptic chart cannot be fixed exactly. To simplify the chart it is assumed that the rains start punctually on the 1st of April, and that the planting cycle thus begins with the first month in native counting. Needless to say that in practice the whole time-table will frequently be found to have moved forward or backward by as much as a fortnight or three weeks as the rains set in earlier or later than our key date. Besides, there occur certain other variations in the time sequence which are due to local conditions or the varying efforts of individual farmers; these variations have only partly been included in the chart.

Calendar		Planting operations		Trees	State of food stores
Europ.	Native	Inland farms (incl. irrigated plots)	Marsh-land farms		
April	1st month	Belated preparation of yam plots and planting of yams by farmers who have left it till the new season. Sowing of bulrush-millet and maize. Sowing of late millet and sorghum. Sowing of ground-nuts. Interplanting of okra, melon, and cassava.	Planting of cassava or sweet potatoes.	Fruit of locust-bean tree picked, also mango.	
May	2nd month	First weeding (takes 2–3 weeks). Short period of rest (5–7 days). Yam is sprouting leaves, bulrush-millet and maize 2 ft. high.		Locust-bean harvest finished.	
June	3rd month	Second weeding. Sowing of cotton. Planting of sweet potatoes, rice, and red pepper. Also of cassava grown on separate plots. Latest date for planting ground-nuts.		Shea-nuts picked and dried.	Yam and late millet begin to give out.
July	4th month	Harvesting of bulrush-millet and maize. Interplanting of ground-beans and late beans. First yam harvest. Picking of okra.	Harvesting of cassava and sweet potatoes; sowing of rice. Sowing of first maize crop.	Shea-nut harvest finished.	
	5th month	Third weeding, and 'shifting the ridges'. (This operation may be postponed by 2 months.)		Preparation of shea-butter.	Fresh sugar-cane. Scarcity of rice.
August		Beginning of first ground-nut harvest.			Fresh ground-nuts for food.
	6th month	Fourth weeding and transplanting of late millet and sorghum.			
September		Sweet potatoes and melons harvested.	Transplanting of rice.	Second mango crop.	Bulrush millet finished. Sorghum giving out in certain districts. New rice.
	7th month	Some farmers carry out the 'shifting of ridges' now instead of two months earlier. Harvest of early maturing rice.	Harvest of first maize crop.		

Calendar		Planting operations			
Europ.	Native	Inland farms (incl. irrigated plots)	Marsh-land farms	Trees	State of food stores
October	7th month	Second yam harvest. Harvest of ground-beans, sweet potatoes, and cassava grown on separate plots.			New yam, from second harvest, for storage. New sweet potatoes and cassava.
November	8th month	Preparation of new yamplots and planting of yam (may be postponed for 2 or 3 months). Second ground-nut harvest begins. Harvest of late millet.	Sowing of second maize crop.		Yam from first harvest finished. Sorghum giving out.
December	9th month	Harvest of sorghum. Picking of cotton and red pepper. Harvest of late beans.	Harvest of rice (late maturing crop).		Sorghum and late millet for storage.
January	10th month		Harvest of second maize crop.		
February	11th month	End of ground-nut harvest. Burning of farms. Some farmers prepare new yam plots now instead of 3 months earlier.		First mango crop begins, also harvest of locust-bean.	
March	12th month	Burning of farms goes on.			

Selection of Species and Varieties

Most of the crops enumerated in the chart occur in more than one variety. Yam is the only exception; although grown in a large number of different varieties in Southern Nigeria, it is known only in one variety among the Nupe, which is incidentally another proof that Nupe is not a 'real yam country'. Sorghum (*eyi*) was originally grown in Nupe in a number of varieties. I could collect names for three main sorghum varieties: *kúyi*, *dindórogi*, and *ekpā*. Of these three varieties *kúyi* has disappeared almost completely, and *dindórogi* is fast disappearing. The latter variety was formerly specially valued for the black and red dye that was obtained from the stalk. The importation of European dyes has reduced considerably its importance, so that to-day *ekpā* is grown almost exclusively. *Ekpā* is also agreed to be the finest and best tasting of the three varieties; its survival thus appears to reflect a certain growing fastidiousness with regard to food, which may well have influenced market prices and demands, and thus indirectly the policy of the sorghum growers.

Two varieties of rice are grown: the 'sweet' rice, a six-months' crop, in the river marshes, and a variety which matures in ninety days, on the less well irrigated inland farms. Till six years ago only the native variety of maize was cultivated. To-day the American variety (brought from Europe), which is sweeter and has a softer husk, is more and more widely adopted by the natives. This new variety is easily recognized since it is grown as a separate crop, in separate ridges, while the indigenous variety is interplanted through millet and sorghum or yam. The two millet varieties, finally, bulrush and late millet, have been mentioned already.

The proportion of maize and the various other millet and sorghum varieties in the productive scheme of one household is illustrated in the following typical example: on a farm which produced a total millet and sorghum crop of twenty bundles the different varieties were distributed as follows:

Bulrush-millet	.	.	2 bundles
Maize	. . .	.	2–3 ,,
Late millet	. .	.	8 ,,
Sorghum	. .	.	10 ,,

Sorghum and late millet are clearly shown to be the main staple crops as compared with bulrush-millet and maize, the importance of which, as we shall see later, lies in their subsidiary, 'stopgap', character.

Some enterprising farmers, and farmers in certain districts of Nupe, have added to this table of crops certain special, commercially valuable, plants or have given over a large portion of their farm-land to the cultivation of plants which normally would play only a secondary, unimportant, part. Thus we find henna (*lali*) cultivated in many parts; indigo (*eci*) is collected and prepared especially in the districts of Sakpe and Kutigi. Recently farmers in Lemu, north of Bida, have started the cultivation of red pepper (*yakã*) as a main crop, in the place of groundnuts. The first two kinds of produce have a considerable marketing value in the country, the last kind is meant for European export.

Clearing

The dry season is not completely a season of leisure. Many Nupe farmers will visit their fields more or less regularly even during that time, perhaps once a week, to 'look over the farm' as they say, to see that animals have not done damage to ridges and mounds, or to collect brushwood for fuel, or leaves for which there is always use in the Nupe household.

In the dry season comes also the first agricultural activity of the year, the *nwa tsaka*, the clearing and burning of the farms. On farms (fallow or virgin land) which are to be taken under cultivation for the first time, grass and shrubs are cut and afterwards the farms are burned. Old farms also are cleared summarily by burning the dead stalks, leaves, and undergrowth that have been left there from last year. Later the first rains will wash the ashes into the soil, thus completing the process of 'green manure', which the Nupe farmers consciously utilize (see p. 221). The burning of the farms takes place at any time between January and May; new plots, the clearing of which involves the heavier work, being as a rule burned earlier in the season, cultivated plots (on which the stalks and leaves are given ample time to dry and rot) towards the beginning of the rains. The heaviest and lengthiest work is the clearing of virgin land. If carried out early it will curtail seriously the short leisure season of the Nupe farmer, and if left till late will add to the work of an already very busy time of the year. Clearing virgin land is, in fact, considered so heavy and inconvenient work that the farmers, especially those who cannot count on the assistance of a large working group, make all efforts to avoid taking virgin land under cultivation.

This reluctance must be regarded as one of the main factors responsible for the growth of the institution of 'borrowing land', which we have described in the preceding chapter.

Sowing and Planting

The Nupe, possessing an elaborate calendar system which works with six seasons and twelve lunar months, have no difficulty in determining the coming of the rainy season. Besides, they regard the appearance (in April) of a small red insect, which is significantly called *gbama*, 'early rains', as a sign of the approaching rains. The first light showers, which as a rule are accompanied by thunderstorms, are ignored. After the first heavy rain, which may last for several hours or a whole night, has thoroughly softened the soil, village and town spring into activity. In the morning after the rain you will see the people wandering out to their fields. They walk in groups, neighbours or families together, fathers with their boys. Dogs trot behind their masters, and often a man or boy will lead a goat which will then feed on leaves and shrubs on the field. The men wear working dress: a loin-cloth and, if it is cold, a heavier cloth slung round the shoulders, and a straw hat as protection from the sun. They carry their hoe over the shoulder, and gourds with water, food and seeds, over the arm. In many parts farmers carry their bows and arrows with them when they go out to their fields as 'protection from wild beasts'—a habit which is dying out but slowly, although there is hardly any need for it to-day. I have never seen these weapons used.

The nature of the first farming activity depends on whether or not the farmer has done what 'good' farmers are expected to do, namely, planted his yams already in the rains, immediately after the harvest. If he has not done so he will now at once start preparing his yam field; if he has, he is free to turn his attention to the planting of bulrush-millet and maize. Of five farmers whose daily activities I was recording in Mokwa, three had planted yam in the rainy season and two (who both had to work single-handed) waited until the beginning of the new farming season. With the 'good' farmer, we will start with the planting of millet.

Again there are certain variations. Where millet and sorghum are planted as successive crops no hoeing or re-hoeing as a rule precedes the planting; as we shall see later the plots are normally prepared during the previous season. Where millet and sorghum are planted after other first-year crops or on a new plot, ridging, occupying the first few days of the new season, precedes the sowing. The technique of planting, moreover, varies slightly according to whether one plants on mounds or ridges, but is the same for both millet varieties and for sorghum. I will now describe the scene one will meet on the Nupe fields when planting is in progress. The farmer has divested himself of his superfluous clothing, his food and water gourds, and has placed his things out of the way, under a shady tree. Perhaps he has his small boys with him, whom he lets play by themselves in a corner of the field while he goes on with his work. Tied to his left arm the planter carries the seeds in a small gourd or his straw hat, keeping a ready supply in his left hand. In his right he carries the light hoe used for planting. With it he scratches the top or flank of the mound, while with his left, almost simultaneously, he throws the seeds into the newly made hole. The hole is then flattened out with the back of the hoe. Thus the farmer proceeds from mound to mound and row to row, working with amazing speed and ease: one man is able to sow about one acre in from five to six hours, with hardly any rest. This is the method used for sowing on mounds; sowing on ridges is even easier and quicker. No hoe is used, and the farmer can make use of both hands for the sowing, the seeds being pressed into the soft soil with the heel. The distance kept between two plants is a little over 2 feet. The sowing of one field with millet or sorghum is invariably done in a day or two, and is nearly always carried out single-handed. Where normally a larger group would be working together—brothers or a father and sons—the rest of the team would be occupied on another field, carrying out ridging, i.e. work for which co-operation is more urgently required. But when for one reason or another a farmer falls behindhand with his planting, ridging and sowing may have to be done at the same time. Once I saw a man and his two sons of 10 or 11 years carrying out this combined and hurried work: the boys were hoeing, preparing the ridges; the father followed in their tracks, sowing. After every ridge they had completed the boys waited for the man to catch up with the sowing. The ridges were crooked, irregular.

In these first days of the planting season the Nupe keep short days: they start comparatively late, about 8 a.m., and rarely return later than 2 or 3 o'clock. As the season wears on their working day extends. They start at daybreak and often do not return till 5 or 6 in the afternoon. They have their midday meal out on the farm, some bringing their own food, others having it brought out to them by their wives or daughters. At that time of the year, when fresh leaves and herbs are plentiful on the farms, the men rarely return home without a fair supply of various kinds: broad leaves which the Nupe women like for wrapping food in, or a special kind of aromatic leaf which the women use for their bath, or occasionally medicinal herbs used for various purposes. The men tie the leaves round their straw hats, and thus pleasantly and ornately attired wander home. A bath, a change of clothes, and afterwards the evening meal concludes their day.

To return to sowing. A day or two after bulrush-millet has been sown, maize is planted in very much the same fashion, again mostly in one day. Then one has to wait for another heavy rainfall before the next crops on the list, late millet and sorghum, can be sown. As a rule all four crops are sown within a week or ten days. These voluntary or involuntary waiting periods have their use: for often it becomes necessary to get one's tools repaired, perhaps a new blade fixed to the hoe, or to find new tools for the young boys who will, this year, join their fathers for the first time in the farm-work. By the time sorghum is planted the rains fall fairly regularly, and there is no need for further waiting.

The farmer turns directly to the planting of ground-nuts, which is reckoned to take from five to ten days. Ground-nuts must be planted on a new plot, and new ridges must therefore be prepared. The planting itself is also a slow process, the seeds are placed into the soil with the fingers and the earth then stamped down with the heel.

The planting of yams demands no less skill and patience. Yam is likewise planted on a fresh plot and involves the preparation of new mounds —the work of several days. The planting itself is also spread over a number of days, one man needing two or three days to plant one acre. Half a tuber is used as seed (called *ebu*). The planter carries the seed yams in a cloth tied round his waist; he inserts the tuber about 1 foot deep into the loose earth of the mound, and then pats the top of the mound back into shape either with his hands or with the light planting hoe. Having covered a section of the field, he goes over it again and places a grass cap over the top of each mound, weighting it down with earth; the grass cap protects the young plant from the sun and at the same time provides a convenient sign by which the planter can distinguish planted from unplanted mounds. About two months after planting stakes 4 feet high are put up on the side of the mounds, which will serve as support for the vine; sometimes a conveniently placed tree may be used for the same purpose.

Now, assuming that planting has started early in April, our time-table has taken us to the end of the month or the beginning of May. It is by then high time for the first weeding, which is to clear the ridges for the growing plant and to remove roots, leaves, and undergrowth which the burning of the farms has but imperfectly destroyed. Not until after this weeding, which takes the best part of three weeks, will the farmer be able to enjoy a short period of rest, between five days and a week. It reaches as a rule into June, and into the short break in the rains which is known as the 'little dry season'. The period of rest inaugurates a more leisurely period of work. In June many farmers work on their large farms only two days in succession, and rest on the third day, or devote it to the lighter work on the garden-plots round their houses. The 'second weeding', which takes from five to ten days, and is to clear the young millet plants of the high grass, is also a task allowing of comparative leisure, except when it coincides with the planting of cotton, a delicate and lengthy operation, which falls in the same time. Farmers who possess marsh-land plots are sowing rice in June; on inland farms cassava is planted—but cassava can be planted at any time, and needs little skill or attention: cuttings of the stem are simply put into the ground; one person can plant a half-acre field easily in a day. The beginning of July heralds a period of increased activity. It starts with the reaping of bulrush-millet, to be followed immediately by the sowing of beans and another, third, weeding. Let me illustrate the change from comparative leisure to renewed pressure of work by quoting a few entries from my diary for 1936.

Doko, 15 May.—Bulrush-millet 2–3 feet high. Yam vines fairly long. Yam stakes are being put up. Cassava and sweet potatoes are being planted.
Doko, 1 June.—The people have begun to sow cotton, and some farmers also rice. Grass on millet-sorghum farms very high. Weeding ('second weeding') in progress in many places.

Kutigi, 5 June.—Cotton is planted, weeding of millet-sorghum farms going on at the same time.
Kutigi, 15 June.—Weeding still in progress.
Kutigi, 5 July.—Harvesting of bulrush-millet and maize begins.
Kutigi, 12 July.—Bulrush-millet harvest finished; crop all dried and stored. 'Third weeding' in progress. Beans are sown.
Kutigi, 18 July.—First yams dug out.

Weeding and Transplanting

Let us for a moment interrupt our description and examine in more detail the technique of weeding and certain related farming operations. The Nupe practise four main weedings or hoeings, each of which is known by a special name. The first weeding, called *gongi* ('small grass'?), is carried out three or four weeks after the first planting and serves, as mentioned already, to clear the ridges from roots and undergrowth left on the farms from last year. At the same time the ridges which have not been newly made this year are re-done and put in proper shape. The second weeding, *nuvū*, follows about three weeks later, 'when the bulrush-millet is arm-high', and clears the millet plant of the newly grown grass. The third weeding or hoeing is called *sa wo gí*, 'making small ridges'; it combines a thorough cultivation with an operation best termed the 'shifting of the ridges'. Carried out shortly after the harvest of bulrush-millet, it consists in hoeing away the original mounds or ridges and throwing them up again on the side, in what used to be the furrows. Late millet and sorghum, which after the bulrush-millet harvest had been left growing from the flanks of mounds or ridges, are thus transferred to the new position, in the furrows between the new ridges. The *sa wo gí* is a delicate operation which may easily damage the growing plant. When it is carried out the original mounds are already much reduced in size by the rains, and when they have been shifted they have the appearance much more of long ridges than of separate mounds. The shifting of the ridges besides weeding the maturing plant provides fresh surface soil for the new ridges, which are then left, all prepared, for the next planting season.

The fourth weeding, called *mu ya* ('pulling out'), consists mainly in a thinning out and at the same time transplanting of late millet and sorghum. It is carried out four or five months after sowing, when sorghum is about 4 feet high. From the eight to ten shoots which grow from the seed about half are pulled out, their leaves are cut and the shoots transplanted either to a separate plot, if sufficient farm space is available, or to additional ridges thrown up along the edges of the original plot. Another method is to interplant the shoots through the original ridges or mounds, which in this case have been spaced specially wide apart. The transplanted shoots soon surpass the mother-plant in growth. The rice planters in the river marshes, I may add, who cultivate the late maturing variety, also practise thinning out and transplanting, three months after sowing.

An operation somewhat akin to the 'shifting of the ridges', which, in fact, is often referred to by the people as a 'fourth hoeing', is the *sa ci wo*, the 'making yam mounds'. Many farmers will try to prepare their new yam plots soon after the yam harvest, or at any rate before the beginning of the dry season.[1] They clear new plots, throw up the mounds, and plant the yams at once, thus having everything prepared for next year. In Nupe opinion one obtains bigger yams if one follows this practice, plants yam early, and leaves the seed yam in the ground through the whole dry season.[2]

The early preparation of ridges or mounds offers, on the other hand, two very concrete advantages: first, it means comparatively easy work, carried out as it is in the soft soil; second, it enables the farmer to start his planting without further delay as soon as the rains break. In the case of yam, particularly, this early planting removes one difficult crop from the already crowded time-table of sowing and planting.

Reaping and Harvesting

Our description of the agricultural activities of the year has taken us to the second phase in the farming cycle: harvesting. A fortnight after the harvest of bulrush-millet, following closely upon the third weeding, the first yam crop is dug up, and shortly afterwards the first ground-nut crop. There are two yam harvests. In July the farmers dig out yam for the first time, cutting one tuber from the plant and leaving the rest in the ground to sprout farther. This young yam is considered a delicacy; unlike the late yam it is eaten 'mashed'. Only a little of it is sold; most of it is consumed by the household. The fresh yam, however, lasts only a short time; the second yam harvest, in October–November, is the main harvest, at which the remaining tubers (three or four in each mound) are dug out.[3] Ground-nuts, too, are harvested twice. The first ground-nut crop is dug out between mid-July and the end of August, and used for food only; the second ground-nut crop, dug out between the end of December and the end of January—a much drier crop than the first—is used exclusively for sale to the European trading companies.

There is hardly any pause between the end of the first yam harvest and the fourth and last weeding. After this, however—it is by then the end of August or beginning of September—there is a certain lull in the farming activities, at least if the time-table has been kept fairly strictly. Till the next big item on the list, the second yam harvest, the farmer can enjoy a short respite of three or four weeks, during which he can take his work more leisurely. Even so, he remains fully occupied: he is still going regularly to the farm to clear away leaves and brushwood; those who have planted rice or sweet potatoes as additional crops harvest them now; the women pick the melons which have been interplanted with yam or corn. Certain farmers who were pressed for time earlier in the year have postponed the important third weeding until now. The lull continues to some extent after the second yam harvest. Now is the time

[1] In Bida this operation is often postponed till January or February.
[2] I cannot say how far this opinion is substantiated by fact. Agricultural officers whom I consulted on this question were unable either to confirm or to refute this native theory.
[3] In Leaba, in the extreme north of Nupe, i.e. close to the line which marks the northern boundary of yam cultivation, yam is harvested only once.

when 'keen' farmers prepare the yam plots for the next year, and re-hoe the yam mounds into ridges to be ready for next year's planting.

The harvest of late millet, which falls in November, is the signal that the last 'rush-period' of the year has begun. Let me first describe the harvesting of millet—the method is the same for both millet varieties and for sorghum. The millet and sorghum varieties cultivated in Nupe grow to a height of 6–8 feet. To reap the corn, the stalks are broken and cut close to the ground, and then laid in bundles in the furrows, where they are left for from five to seven days to dry in the sun (an exception is bulrush-millet, which may have to be dried artificially). Afterwards the heads of the plants are cut off with the bush-knife and carried home in large bundles, 50–60 lb. in weight, while the stalks are left on the fields. These bundles, called *epa*, are the Nupe unit of reckoning for calculating the yield, and also the standard 'load' (*kara*) used in the marketing of unthreshed grain.

The harvesting of late millet almost coincides with the beginning of the second ground-nut harvest. A fortnight or so later sorghum is brought in. Then follows in rapid succession, frequently overlapping, the picking of red pepper, cotton, and beans, while the ground-nut harvest is still going on. Lastly, grass on fallow farms is cut; when the last batches of ground-nuts are dug out, at the end of January, the agricultural cycle is completed.

Let us return for a moment to the harvesting of millet and sorghum. I have mentioned above that the dead stalks of millet and sorghum are left on the farms. Some of the stalks are retrieved after a fortnight, and used for mat-making (see p. 239). The rest, however, is left lying in the fields, till they are destroyed later in the 'burning of the farms'. The same applies to the stalks of maize, the cut-off vines of yam, and the leaves or stems of other plants. Thus the dead plants are allowed to rot on the fields, and fertilizing substance is washed into the soil by the rains which may fall in the weeks or months between the harvesting and the following dry season. This is the native system of 'green manuring' to which I have referred before. The Nupe are well aware of this effect, and say that these stalks and leaves *že taki*, 'become dung'.

The time-factor in reaping and harvesting is less sharply defined than in sowing and planting. Harvesting activities are spread more irregularly over a longer space of time. Certain crops, e.g. yam, cotton, sweet potatoes, and rice, are harvested in stages as the individual plants or batches of plants mature. During the (first) yam harvest, for example, I saw the farmer open two mounds only to close them again, having discovered that the fruit inside was not yet ripe. Again, the picking of certain crops, e.g. ground-nuts, cotton, red pepper, and beans, is a very long-drawn-out operation. But it may be speeded up—and a quick harvest of the 'cash crops' (cotton and ground-nuts) may be an urgent necessity in times of financial stringency—if outside help can be enlisted. The picking of beans, which involves no such motives, is often left till the very last, and carried out leisurely by the family after all the other crops have been brought in.

The harvesting that falls in the middle of the agricultural season, on the other hand, must be carefully fitted into this schedule of farm-work.

Q

For example, cassava and sweet potatoes grown on the marsh-land farms must be dug out quickly as rice is planted on the same plots almost immediately. The harvesting of bulrush-millet and the first yam harvest, if delayed, may interfere with the planting of cotton, and the third weeding. A quick harvest, for a different reason, is imperative also for late millet and sorghum; here it is the danger of monkeys and birds damaging the standing grain which forbids delay. The Nupe have various ways and means to combat this danger: they put up scarecrows and erect high platforms on the fields from the top of which boys try to scare off monkeys and birds, by shouting, throwing stones, brandishing long sticks, or swinging long ropes tied between the platform and a near-by tree. In districts where the danger is very great the farmers may have to spend the night on the farm shortly before the harvest to guard their fields from these unwelcome guests.

It is interesting to supplement this large-scale survey of the agricultural cycle with a view from closer range which could do justice to the varying individual arrangements. To illustrate this aspect of Nupe farming I have compiled the farming diaries of three Kutigi farmers for two typical weeks—one between the end of May and the beginning of June, when the work is temporarily easing off, and the second towards the end of June, when work is at its highest. These farming diaries show the scope of the individual variations of the general time-table. We shall see that they are fairly considerable—in details; but in general lines the activities of the three farmers conform closely to a common pattern. During the more leisurely season all farmers are ready to interrupt their work, and rest for two or three days in succession; but during the busy season only a very weighty reason will make them stay at home and leave their fields even for a day. Indeed at that time of the year you will find the Nupe villages deserted from early morning till about 3 or 4 in the afternoon, save for women, children, and old men. Another interesting fact emerging from the diaries is the disregard, under pressure of work, for the traditional day of rest, Friday. To work six days and rest on the seventh is a common practice in Nupe (in fact a practice said to have been common already in the times before the spreading of Mohammedanism). But a farmer who knows himself behindhand with his work will disregard the rule. Finally, we see that in labour groups consisting of several people the family head may sometimes enjoy a short rest while the young men carry on the work; or that if one of the workers is called away, for example, by some social obligation, the work of the group goes on unimpaired. An arrangement of this kind is evidently impossible in the case of the farmer *K.*, who works on his own.

N.	*M.*	*K.*
Labour group: father and three sons	*Labour group: father and one son*	*Labour group: one man*
31.5.1936		
Goes out to farm about 8 a.m. Eats midday meal on the farm, and returns about 4 p.m.	Goes out to farm together with *N.*, whose farm is close to his own. Also returns with him.	Is away from Kutigi; went to a neighbouring village for the funeral of his sister.

N.	*M.*	*K.*
Labour group: father and three sons	*Labour group: father and one son*	*Labour group: one man*

1.6.1936

| As previous day. | As previous day. | Returns in the evening. |

2.6.1936

| Stays at home, together with sons. | Stays at home, and visits *N.* in the evening. | Goes out to farm about 10 a.m., and returns at 4 p.m. |

3.6.1936

| Stays at home. Sons go out to farm in the morning, but are back at 2 p.m. in time to attend the market, which is held to-day. | Stays at home, works on garden-plots round the house. Son goes out to farm. | Stays at home; says he is tired from the journey. |

4.6.1936

| Goes out to farm at 8 a.m., returns for midday meal; sons stay longer. | Goes out to farm at 8 a.m., returns after midday meal. | Goes out to farm at 8 a.m., returns after midday meal. |

5.6.1936 (Friday)

| Stays at home, together with sons. Attends mosque in the afternoon. | Stays at home. Visits *N.* in the evening. | Stays at home. His brother, who lives in a hamlet, comes on a visit. |

6.6.1936

| Stays at home, says he is tired. Works on garden-plots, but will go to farm to-morrow. Sons go out to farm. | Goes out to farm at 8 a.m., returns for midday meal. | Goes out to farm at 8 a.m., returns for midday meal. |

22.6.1936

| Goes out to farm at 8 a.m., returns at 4 p.m. One son goes to Sakpe to attend wedding of a friend. | Goes out to farm at 7 a.m., returns after 4 p.m. | Goes out to farm at 8 a.m., returns after 4 p.m. |

23.6.1936

| Goes out to farm at 8 a.m., returns for midday meal. He hurt his hand and cannot work properly. His sons stay on; one son still in Sakpe. | Goes out to farm at 8 a.m., returns for midday meal. | Goes out to farm at 8 a.m., returns after 4 p.m. |

24.6.1936

| Goes out to farm at 8 a.m., but returns early as his hand hurts. Son who went to Sakpe returns in the evening. | Goes out to farm at 7 a.m., returns after 4 p.m. | Stays at home as he is tired and has stomach trouble. |

N.	*M.*	*K.*
Labour group: father and three sons	*Labour group: father and one son*	*Labour group: one man*

25.6.1936

| Stays at home, his hand not yet well. Sons go out to farm. | Goes out to farm at 7 a.m., returns after 4 p.m. | Goes out to farm at 7 a.m., returns after 5 p.m. |

26.6.1936 (Friday)

| Stays at home. | Stays at home. | Goes out to farm at 8 a.m., returns after 4 p.m. |

27.6.1936

| Goes out to farm at 8 a.m., returns at 5 p.m. | Goes out to farm at 8 a.m., returns after 4 p.m. | Goes out to farm at 7 a.m., returns for mid-day meal. |

28.6.1936

| Stays at home because tax clerk of chief had summoned all elders. Sons go out to farm. | Stays at home for same reason as *N.* Son goes out to farm. | Goes out to farm at 7 a.m., but returns early to meet the tax clerk. |

CONCLUSIONS

Throughout this chapter I have stressed the technical aspect of farming rather than its sociological context; I have laid particular emphasis on the time-factor. Nupe agriculture, complex and ambitious as is its scope, depends for its success on a very high degree of technical efficiency, both with regard to the organization of labour and individual skill and efficiency. The most conspicuous gauge of this efficiency lies in the successful use of the intricate and finely cut schedule of planting, weeding, and harvesting. This may not appear too easy: in Kutigi I learned—from the best farmers of the country—that the careful sowing of cotton may interfere with the second weeding, which is particularly important for late millet; this competition of two main crops for the attention of the farmer has often forced the planter to choose between them. Another complication in connexion with the growing of cotton is that the careful tending of cotton may hinder the yam harvest and the immediate preparation of the new yam-plots—an operation which appears preferable to many. But even the most rigid schedule of work must allow for a certain latitude. I have already given a few examples showing this. However, the essential point is that these deviations from the 'standard' times are recognized as such; there *is* a 'standard' schedule of farm-work and of its existence all farmers are equally aware, those who follow it as well as those who avail themselves of the latitude allowed in it. At every phase of farming operations a farmer will be able to tell whether or not he is 'on time'. The consciousness of the ideal time-table is clearly expressed in the common distinction between what 'good' and what 'bad' farmers do or are expected to do. The latitude which the ideal time-table allows carries its own corrective with it, be it merely moral or of a more concrete order. Ground-nuts, for example, may be planted at any time between the end of April and the end of May; but the late planter, as all agree, will be 'late for the tax money'. In Bida I watched farmers making new ridges for millet-sorghum in a field that had been already under cultivation the previous year rather late in the season; when I asked why they did not use the 'shifted' ridges, they explained that they had not performed the 'shifting of the ridges' the previous year, adding rather apologetically that they, the Bida people, were not as keen and efficient farmers as the country people, who as they well knew would rarely omit that operation.

Thus there is at least a moral premium put on the keeping of the delicate time-table and the overcoming of its various difficulties. Pride in farming achievements, publicly recognized and applauded, becomes a stimulus for attaining that high degree of efficiency on which Nupe agricultural production depends in so high a measure. Its final compensation lies, of course, in the concrete success of its ambitious scheme. Well carried out, it promises to satisfy the nutritive as well as the commercial demands of the community.

Here we are brought back to the third of the three conditions which appear to determine the Nupe farmer's agricultural planning and his choice between different crops and systems of rotation, namely, the consideration of the return—adequate return—which he may expect from his cultivation. If in his efforts to combine the cultivation of a certain number of crops the cultivator must take into consideration the efficiency of the labour at his disposal, he must, conversely, also consider how far the exercise of that highly efficient labour organization, or its direction to a particular task, is warranted by the prospects of an adequate return. The role played by considerations of this nature in Nupe agricultural economy is shown in the following examples. In 1934, the year of the 'slump', the majority of farmers in the ground-nut-growing districts declined to dig out the second ground-nut crop of this year as no sales were possible and it seemed hardly worth while to undertake the long and (since outside help would have to be called in) expensive task without the prospect of monetary compensation. Again, in 1936, a far better year, I learned that a number of Bida farmers who for various reasons had to carry out their farming single-handed were selling their harvest of ground-nuts together with the seed ground-nuts which they ought to have kept for the next planting season. The explanation was that one man alone could not grow any quantity worth selling. What they did therefore was to grow ground-nuts every second year only, and to buy seed ground-nuts in the intervening year, thus concentrating their modest 'labour-organization' on food crops and commercial crops alternately.[1]

[1] In figures this calculation works out as follows in the case of one of my informants: to have sold ground-nuts exclusive of the seeds would have brought him 1s. 6d.; instead of which he sold the lot for 4s., and bought back ground-nuts for seeds the next year, from profits made on mat-weaving, for 2s. 6d. This might not look a very convincing calculation to us, but one must realize that 4s. was almost half the tax money in his case (9s. 6d.), while a sum of 1s. 6d. would only have been a negligible contribution towards that most important expense.

It is natural, though from a certain point of view unfortunate, that to-day examples of this kind will almost invariably refer to modern commercial crops. The consideration of 'adequate returns' is thus given a narrower, and very specific, meaning. It cannot be denied that the extensive cultivation of these modern crops has accentuated the element of economic calculation in Nupe agricultural planning. Not only has the introduction of these crops considerably complicated the planting schedule, but it has also immensely emphasized the monetary aspect of the question of adequate returns. The 'all-or-nothing' viewpoint, or in the language of the economist, the 'marginal' considerations, which our examples have revealed, are no doubt due to its influence. I have said that these modern influences have 'accentuated' the element of economic calculation—they have not introduced it for the first time. To be satisfied with what the Nupe call, by a stereotyped formula, farming 'for the mouth only' is characteristic only of those sections which practise agriculture on the most modest scale, as a secondary occupation in addition to a craft, a trade, &c. We shall learn presently that even in its original form, before modern economic influences were brought to bear on it, Nupe agricultural production included a large measure of production for marketing and exchange.

DISPOSAL OF CROPS

Storage

We find both storage on the farm and in the house. Yam, sweet potatoes, cassava, and in some places the portion of millet and sorghum meant for sale are stored on the farm, either in the small huts (*evu*) which serve the farmers as temporary shelters, or in special store-huts (*kpyakpya*) built of sticks and branches put up, tent-like, against a tree and covered with leaves or grass. Inside, the fruits are heaped on a raised platform. The yam fruits are stored whole, and the fruits needed for food or marketing are collected from time to time, about twice a week, mostly by the men. The storing arrangement in this stick-and-branches structure is adapted to the need of the root crops for a drier and more airy storage than the clay granaries in the houses could provide. As regards the grain crops intended for sale, they are stored in these huts only for a short time, being disposed of very soon after the harvest. In the districts where little yam is grown, especially in the country round Bida, all crops, including yam, are stored in the house. Of cassava only small quantities are stored; as fresh cassava does not keep, it is first dried in the sun. But as the harvesting of cassava is not bound to any special season it is frequently dug out and used for food at odd times throughout the year; often in fact, dug out and eaten raw, it serves as a convenient 'quick lunch' to the farmers while they are working in the fields.

In the granaries in the house are stored millet, sorghum, maize (so far as this crop, grown in small quantities, involves any special storing), beans, ground-nuts, and all greens, each crop being kept in a separate granary. These granaries, called *edo*, are distributed between the living huts of the compound. Of egg-like shape, about 7 feet high and 4 feet in

A FAMILY HEAD REPAIRING HIS GRANARY

GRANARY AND COOKING PLACE IN A VILLAGE COMPOUND

diameter, they are built of clay, with strong, thick walls. Over the dome-like top a grass roof is placed as protection from sun and rain. The granary is raised above the ground, resting on stones or solid blocks of clay, to make it safe from termites. On one side, a little above the middle, is a rectangular opening which can be closed completely with a clay lid. At the beginning of the rainy season you will see the people everywhere busy repairing their granaries, or building new ones, which are to take the new crop. Later, when they have been filled, the lid is closed, and the granaries then left until their contents are required for food or sale.

Millet and sorghum are stored unthreshed, in whole heads. They keep remarkably well in these granaries. The method of storing un-threshed grain ensures a certain measure of ventilation and also prevents the grain from being packed too tightly in the granary, and thus becom-ing damp and mouldy.[1] As already mentioned, late millet and sorghum are left to dry on the fields for a few days before being taken home to be stored. Bulrush-millet, which is reaped during the rains, may have to be dried in special roast ovens before it is fit for storing. These ovens, *yaku*, which are used for various purposes besides the drying of millet—soap-making and the drying of shea-nuts—are built of clay, of roughly cylindrical shape, about 5 feet high and 3 feet wide, and are divided into half horizontally by a sieve-like grill. The bottom part of the oven takes the fuel (firewood), the upper half, which is open at the top, is the receptacle for the stuff to be dried or roasted. Frequently a small grass roof is put up over the oven to provide shade for the women working there. Every Nupe village possesses a large number of these ovens. They are placed outside the compounds, often on the outskirts of the village. They are not the property of individual households, but are built by the men of the village or village section in collective work, and used by the women—the drying and roasting being their work.

The seed plants are as a rule at once divided up from the crop. The seed yams are stored on the farm—unless yam is planted immediately after the harvest. The heads of millet, sorghum, and maize which are later to supply the seeds are stored, not in the granaries, but in the hut of the family head, where they are kept on a shelf of bamboo or wood underneath the roof.

The crops undergo no further treatment during the time of storage. As mentioned already, the Nupe do not dry yam.[2] Sorghum and millet are not threshed until the grain is being prepared for cooking or sale, although heads of unthreshed grain, packed in large bundles, are also offered for sale on the markets. The threshing is done in the courtyard

---

[1] This is actually the almost universal method of grain storage in Northern Nigeria. An indirect testimony to its efficacy I chanced to obtain from Hausa settlers in the Anglo-Egyptian Sudan whom I had occasion to visit in 1939. Chiefly for lack of proper building material for the construction of the Nigerian type of clay granary, these settlers have adopted the Sudan method of storage, i.e. storage of threshed grain. They all agreed that this method was inferior to the Nigerian, and preserved the grain much less satisfactorily.

[2] It is interesting to note that the Nupe colonies in Yoruba country and the Nupe communities which are living side by side with Yoruba communities in Ilorin Province have adopted the drying of yam.

of the compound or under a shady tree in front of the house. The grain
is either spread out on the floor and beaten with sticks or pounded in a
big wooden mortar. The former method can be used only in houses
which possess a hard, clean floor in front of the huts; where there is only
sandy ground (as is the case in many smaller villages) the second
method has to be adopted. The first method, besides, is only possible
when large quantities of grain are threshed. The small quantities normally needed for daily use are done more quickly by pounding. In either
case at least three people (women and girls) will be working together.
After threshing the grain is winnowed. This is done with the help of two
platters of basket-work, by repeatedly pouring the grain slowly from one
into the other; the woman who does the winnowing walks up and down
in front of the house, letting the breeze remove the chaff. Finally the
grain is milled, either on a grinding-stone or, again, in the mortar. The
latter is the heavier but quicker work, the former is slower but gives the
finer flour. The empty heads of grain left over after threshing are used
as fodder for horses; the chaff, collected after winnowing, as fodder for
sheep and goats.

Food Crops and Market Crops

The foregoing description of methods of storage and preparation does
not embrace all the crops grown in Nupe. Before we can make our list
complete we must consider another aspect of the question, namely,
whether the produce is used for household consumption or intended for
sale. No comprehensive simple distinction is possible: we can only mark
extremes—a few crops which are used exclusively for consumption or
for marketing, respectively, while the rest, the large majority of crops,
may be used for either purpose. The produce used for sale comprises
first of all the non-food crops: cotton (for European export), indigo, and
henna. Food crops grown almost exclusively for the market are: late
ground-nuts and red pepper (for European export), and rice and onions
(for internal markets or export to other countries in Nigeria). The
crops which are rarely sold and used primarily for household consumption are few: cassava, beans, a few vegetables, and sweet potatoes
and maize grown in small quantities on inland farms.

In the case of crops grown for export the question of storage does not
arise, at least not for the producer himself, for this produce is sold almost
immediately after harvesting (e.g. late ground-nuts, rice). Instead, we
have two new questions to consider. First, that of transport and pack-
ing. But this also is mostly a matter for the trader and middleman, not
for the producer. The native traders provide the big grass bags in which
the rice is packed and transported, the European trading-companies the
sacks for cotton; the other produce is transported in the ordinary
receptacles of the country, large baskets, gourds, or tin basins of
European manufacture.

Second, there is the question of the special preparation, an elementary
manufacturing process, which is frequently applied to the agricultural
produce intended for local trade before it is put on the market. In the
markets of Nupe agricultural produce is sold either as it is (e.g. yam,

rice, and partly ground-nuts) or after it has undergone a rudimentary 'refining' process (such as the threshing and milling of grain, the shelling of ground-nuts, &c.). Side by side with this trade there exists an extensive local trade in the 'finished' product, which means various kinds of prepared food. I cannot attempt a detailed description of the intricate and varied art of Nupe cooking. I will only enumerate the more important products of this native 'food-industry', which, like most food preparation, is in the hands of the women. It is of considerable import- ance for the economy of the Nupe household. There are three main kinds of such prepared food which are sold everywhere in the markets and streets of the towns and villages of Nupe: (1) a gruel of millet or sorghum, made with water, and called *ekwa* in the more jelly-like and *zambú* in the more solid form. It is eaten for breakfast or lunch, and nicely done up in banana leaves, bought by labourers, canoe-men, travellers, and some- times farmers going out to their fields—men who are unable to have their meals with their families or to have food brought out to them from home. (2) *Yisá* (Hausa, *fura*), bread-like balls made of late millet or sorghum and rolled in flour. Men and women attending markets are fond of buying this food and eating it with milk which they buy, there and then, from the Fulani women. (3) *Masa, kuli-kuli, bánkuru,* and *kara*— savouries of different kind, made of beans, sorghum- or millet-flour or ground-nuts, fried in shea-butter and prepared with various spices. They are eaten at any time of the day, practically by everybody who can spare an *anini* (a tenth of a penny).

To turn to the food crops proper. Our chart has established the even distribution of food crops over the year's cycle, a distribution which should, normally, leave every household well provided with food from harvest to harvest. Old yam should last till the new yam is dug out, sorghum and late millet till the new sorghum harvest—or at least till bulrush-millet— is reaped. I have found that June and July are the critical months: yam may begin to give out by the end of May or June, about six weeks or two months before the new yam harvest, and late millet and sorghum may become scarce by the middle of June. But bulrush-millet, which is harvested about that time, and maize, both from inland and marsh-land crops, make the transition easy.[1] So do also fresh ground-nuts, new potatoes, and partly the new rice, all harvested before the late main crops; I have mentioned already the 'stopgap' character of cassava.[2] A dry year, a late or failing harvest of early millet or first yam, may, of course, upset the balance temporarily in a district—till imports from the river area where yam matures earlier, or other districts, which have fared better, set it right again.[3] But the nutritive balance of the country must always remain dependent on the contribution of trade and markets:

[1] See p. 213.
[2] Cassava-flour as a substitute for grain-flour appears on the Nupe markets only for about two months, during July and August. Corn-gruel, a daily food in many Nupe households, can be made with rice-flour instead of sorghum- or millet-flour, if the latter has become scarce. This substitute is more expensive than ordinary corn-gruel, and is also said to be less pleasant to the taste.
[3] In 1936 the first yams appeared on the river markets on 6 July, while inland the first yams were dug out a fortnight later.

yam, maize, and early millet are not grown everywhere; special crops are cultivated on marsh-land and inland farms; and besides, there is the large population of Nupe which does not live on the land and can obtain its food only from the markets of the country. The Nupe agricultural system, as we have realized already, is adjusted essentially to a highly developed system of exchange and marketing. The surprisingly small number of crops grown exclusively for household consumption is perhaps the most striking proof.

The degree to which the individual farmer, and the farmer in the different districts of the country, adjusts his planting to the principle of exchange economy varies considerably. In the marshes of Niger and Kaduna almost the whole production of rice is intended for sale and export. But at the other end of the scale we find farmers who, able to cultivate a few crops only, have just enough to provide food for their families. We have already examined some of the conditions determining this changing balance between trade crops and food crops. Ultimately it only reflects that greater fundamental balance that underlies Nupe peasant economy: between the need of food for the group, and the need of commodities which are obtainable only by means of exchange, that is, money—which can itself be obtained only from the sale of farming produce.

TREE CULTIVATION AND FRUIT INDUSTRY

As stated in the first chapter, most of the fruit-bearing trees in Nupe are wild growing. Only two or three kinds are cultivated: the kola-nut tree, *ebi*, and to much lesser extent the banana, *yaba*; to these two indigenous plants we must add to-day the European imported mango tree, *mangoro*. In the case of trees the main productive activities refer therefore not so much to the planting and tending of the plants as to the collection of the fruits and the preliminary manufacturing process of the same order as that described in the preceding section. Only in a few cases can the fruits of the trees be utilized directly—for food, cooking, or marketing. Most fruits have to undergo a special 'refining' process before they become marketable or ready for use.

Banana

Only in Bida, Patigi, and Laboži did I see real banana plantations. They are small and of little importance, for bananas have little commercial value in Nupe; they are sold for an extremely low price (a bunch of about twenty for ½*d*. or less)—if they are sold at all. Bananas are eaten raw, and play in Nupe a part comparable to our occasional eating of fruit. In the banana plantations the plants are arranged in a circle of about 6 feet in diameter. The important thing is to plant them very deep in the ground (from 3 to 4 feet), and the whole circle has thus to be excavated to that depth. It is this heavy and slow work—unprofitable work from a commercial point of view—that, according to my informants, discourages the Nupe farmer from growing bananas. In Bida, where the soil is poor, the banana plot has to be manured with animal dung; in the bush plantations and in the forest groves where the banana grows wild the leaves are allowed to fall off and rot on the ground—an efficient system of natural fertilization, though not, apparently (unlike the 'green manuring' practised in agriculture), applied consciously.

Kola-nut

We have had occasion already to speak of the Kusopa, the kola-nut planters in the forest groves of Labozi. The Kusopa of Labozi and the neighbouring districts devote the larger part of their agricultural work to the cultivation of the kola-nut tree, growing little else besides—only a little millet and sorghum. The method of kola-nut cultivation is interesting. The trees are planted at the beginning of the rains. They flower for the first time after five years, about July, and after six years bear fruit, towards the end of October. The fruit is picked in February. From every harvest a gourdful of nuts is kept to be used as seeds, for nearly every year new trees are planted to replace old and barren ones. When planting a new tree the seed is buried hand-deep in the ground. To protect the seed the place where it was planted is covered with twigs; moreover, four banana plants are planted around it, in a square, about 6 feet by 6 feet. As the banana grows faster than the kola-nut the four banana plants provide shade for the tender young tree, and at the same time secure the necessary distance between newly planted trees. When the kola-nut tree reaches a certain height and no longer needs the shade of the banana plants, the latter are dug out and removed. The tending of the young kola-nut tree involves constant weeding—in which no hoe is used; only the 'bush-knife', so as not to hurt the delicate plant—and much watering. During the dry season the seedlings must be watered every four days. The need for humid soil explains the fact that the kola thrives only in the most humid part of Nupe, in the thick forest groves of Kusopa country.

This environmental factor is fully understood by the people. The failure of kola-nut cultivation in other districts of the Emirate (on which we shall have more to say presently) is partly attributed to the less favourable soil. But the traditional monopoly of kola-nut planting in Labozi is not, in their eyes, fully explained on such empirical grounds. A legend that has grown up round the cultivation of the kola-nut tree which tells about the discovery, by a Labozi woman, of the secret of kola-nut planting, supplies another explanation more convincing to their way of thinking. Let me quote this legend in full.

A woman was threshing grain for beer when a Hausa from Borgu, on his way back to his country, happened to pass. He crossed the threshing-ground and put down the load he was carrying. The woman went into the house to fetch water and to cook porridge for the guest. She brought the food and gave it to the Hausa. He ate the porridge and liked it very much. He opened his load, took out two kola-nuts, and gave them to the woman to thank her for the food. At that time there were no kola-nuts anywhere in Nupe country. The woman took the kola-nuts and put them on the threshing-ground. Later, when she took the grain into the house, she forgot the kola-nuts and left them lying there on the threshing-ground. One day, when she came out to the threshing-ground again, she saw these kola-nuts. She said: 'Look, the nuts which the Hausa gave me have come up.' She went and told the men of the house. They all came and looked. They cleared the ground around the young plants; they had two kola-nut trees then. After three years the trees bore fruit. The men picked the fruits and took them home. They broke the nuts open and ate them. They picked out the kernel, took it into the bush and planted it. When the kola-nut trees bore fruit again the men picked the fruits and took them to the king. This was the beginning of the kola-nut in Nupe. When they had taken the fruits to the king, he said: 'They are very nice indeed.' But the following year the trees did not bear fruit. So the men went to see the soothsayers. They said that the trees would not bear fruit again unless they sacrificed a human being. So the men went and told the king, and said: 'If we do not sacrifice a human being our trees will never bear fruit again.' Therefore the king gave them permission to take a human being and sacrifice it. They did so, and the trees bore fruit again. This was the beginning of human sacrifices in Nupe, with the permission of the king.

As the legend explains the origin of kola plantation in the country of the Kusopa, certain magic rites which are practised by that group—and by that group only—emphasize the unique position of the kola-nut planters. Only with the knowledge of that special magic can the success of the difficult and precarious cultivation be assured. The Laboži people practise two kinds of this professional magic. At the time when the kola trees are in bloom every planter will collect the dead leaves on his plantation, place them in a mortar, and pound and then burn them on the plantation. There is no spell or special ritual linked with this act, but by it, as by a magic act, the planter believes he will ensure a rich harvest. The second magic connected with kola-nut planting is performed for the whole group by the *Maji Tsuba*, the Master of Threshing (in the legend the first kola-nuts were growing from the threshing-ground), the village priest of Laboži. Annually, about two months before the picking of the kola-nuts, he performs a sacrifice in front of the hut in which, as the legend has it, the woman lies buried to whom the Kusopa owe the knowledge of kola-nut planting. To-day a white ram and cock are sacrificed, the blood together with some beer is poured on the threshold of the hut, and *Sokó*, God, is invoked that he may let the kola trees thrive. Formerly this sacrifice is said to have demanded a human victim. (See p. 90, n. 2.)

This connexion between planting technique and mythical and magic ideas, common all the world over, needs no special explanation. But in the case of the kola-nut planters it gains an additional significance. The special nature of the rite, its infrequent occurrence, correspond to the special monopolized technique. In the eyes of the people who, not kola-nut planters themselves, accept the existence of these special rites, it confirms and endorses the exceptional position of the Kusopa as the masters of a unique craft. About fifteen years ago the Administration planned to introduce the cultivation of kola-nuts into the other districts of Nupe. A few expert planters from Laboži were sent round to teach the farmers in places where the soil looked promising the almost secret art of kola planting. These efforts met with but meagre success. Local conditions were to a large extent responsible: the soil in the other districts seemed capable of producing only the inferior kind of kola, and frequently the trees bore no fruit at all. But to some extent the failure of the experiment was due to psychological factors. The lack of interest in their trees which these novices in kola-nut planting still display reveals the lack of incentive for the adoption of this new, difficult, and lengthy enterprise, officially encouraged though it was. The adoption of the new cultivation ran counter to a century-old specialization and monopoly, to an organization of production which, firmly rooted in legends and religious practice, has come to be accepted by the people as part and parcel of that inert, unalterable, entity: their culture—a point to which we shall return.

Locust-bean Tree

This is one of the most important trees in Nupe. It grows both inside the town and in the open bush. Every part of its fruit is utilized. The pods (*elo*) are sold, in large basketfuls in the markets of Bida. Both the whole fruits and the empty skins are marketed. The infusion of the skins, a black sticky liquid (*longoro* in Nupe, *mákuba* in Hausa), is used as dye for pottery, leather and woodwork, also as ink, and for staining and making ant-proof timber-rafters, walls, and floors; it gives them that neat polished appearance as if they had been treated with tar. A yellow powder found inside the pods (*elo nuwã*) is used to sweeten milk, water, and other drinks. The fermented seeds (*elo kosũ*), pounded and kneaded into small flat cakes (*kula*), are sold on the markets; strongly tasting, and even more strongly smelling, they form an indispensable ingredient of Nupe cooking, being used to flavour practically every dish. The fruits of the locust-bean tree are plucked by the women, with the help of long poles which have a forked piece of wood, almost like a pair of shears, tied to the top.

Shea-nut Tree

No less important than the locust-bean tree, the shea-nut tree grows wild everywhere in the thin bush country. The picking of the fruits is again women's work. Small groups of women go out together, help each other, and eventually divide the fruits which they have gathered. The women rarely stray very far from roads and paths, and never into the uninhabited bush. The fruit, *ekó*, is either sold to the trading-companies or manufactured by the women themselves into shea-butter, an important fat in Nupe cooking, and an important commodity in the markets of the country. The shea-nuts intended for export are first dried in the sun or in the roast-ovens described above. Shea-butter (*emikote*) is prepared in the following fashion:

After having been dried thoroughly, the nuts are shelled by hand. As a rule this lengthy work is left for one day, and next morning the inner, finer skin is peeled off and the nuts are pounded in a mortar to a coarse-grained flour. Plenty of water is added, and the dough is kneaded with hands and feet for a whole day. In the evening the preparation is covered and left standing overnight. On the next day the dough is transferred into a big clay pot. A little water is added and the pot put on the fire, where it is left boiling for the whole day. During the boiling the pure fat comes to the surface; it is skimmed and placed in another pot, where it hardens to shea-butter. The residue of the pure fat is used as a fuel for the Nupe clay lamps.

Oil-palm

This grows in the thick groves near watercourses and, covering a larger area, in the dense forest country round Yeti, in the north of Nupe, which is inhabited by the Kusopa, the Keepers of the Forest. The Kusopa of Yeti are accorded a position somewhat similar to that of the kola-nut planters of Laboži. They too are regarded as 'experts' from most ancient times, and their chief holds the title *Yikunu Dzuru*, 'Oil-palm', as a symbol of his tribe's close association with the tree.[1] But they are 'experts' on a much smaller scale and claim no monopoly with regard to the products of their trees. Moreover the palm-oil produced in Kusopa country plays an unimportant part in the economy of Nupe at large. It contributes only very little towards the needs of the country, and palm-oil has to be imported regularly—and has most probably been so imported for centuries—from the south, i.e. the great oil-producing countries in the forest belt. The export of palm-kernels from the Emirate is negligible. The fruits of the palm-tree are plucked by the men, who climb up the trees with the help of a hoop made of supple boughs, and throw the fruits on the ground. They are later collected by the women. The manufacture of oil from the palm-kernels is women's work.

The kernels of about twenty fruits are extracted and then boiled in water for one day. They are left to cool overnight. Next morning they are placed in a mortar, and the women knead the soft mass by treading on it. Later, cold water is poured over it, and a first oil comes to the surface. It is skimmed and boiled again, in another pot. The oil which now appears on the surface is the pure palm-oil, *emi dzuru* (lit. red oil). The residue is dried in the sun, later kneaded again in a mortar, and finally boiled. From this boiling a second, less pure, oil is extracted, called *edi*. Twenty palm-fruits give two small pots of pure palm-oil (about 4 gallons).

Palm-oil plays an important part in the Nupe household; the pure palm-oil is the chief ingredient in all soups and sauces which are eaten with the universal Nupe dish porridge-and-fish and porridge-and-meat. The less pure oil, which is gained as a second extract, is used for cooking yam, potatoes, and beans, but also serves—a rather indiscriminate ingredient— as a hair-lotion, ointment, laxative, and lamp-oil. On the Nupe markets only the pure 'red' oil, not the whole fruit nor the less pure second extract, is offered for sale.

As palm-oil is also used in the preparation of native soap we may add the description of this process; it is again women's work. Water is filtered through hot wood ashes, collected in a pot and boiled. In another pot a bowlful of palm-oil has been prepared. To this an equal amount of boiling ash-water is added. The mixture is again boiled, and is constantly stirred till it hardens. This mass is left to cool, and is afterwards kneaded into large balls. The quality of the soap depends on the purity of the oil used.

---

[1] The Kusopa of Yeti are also said to 'cultivate' the oil-palm. What this term implies in reality, and how far it refers to real tending of the trees, weeding, thinning out, &c., I cannot say, not having been to Yeti myself.

But as even the purest native-made soap can hardly compete with imported soap it is not surprising that soap-making is gradually disappearing, and has disappeared completely in Bida and the more progressive villages, such as Kutigi or Mokwa.

Indigo

Indigo, *eci*, is gained from two different plants, the indigo grass (*tsentse*) and the indigo tree (*eci* or *baba*). The grass grows wild in the thinned-out bush that surrounds most Nupe villages, but is also cultivated in some parts (e.g. Mokwa) and grown as a first crop before millet-sorghum.[1] The dye is gained from the decomposed grass which, after having been cut, is left lying in the open for from two to three months. The powder which is obtained by this method is mixed with ashes and placed in a sieve-like basket. Water is filtered through, and this gives the dye, which is allowed to drip directly into the deep clay-cemented dye-pits (called *marina*, as in Hausa). This technique of dyeing follows the Hausa fashion; and in Nupe as in Hausa the dyers, who also manufacture their own dye, are men.

The indigo tree is found scattered everywhere in the open bush, most densely in Trans-Kaduna. In the district between Kutigi and Sakpe we find even something like indigo-tree plantations which are tended by another group of 'tree-experts'. Here every village possesses large numbers of indigo trees, which are to some extent cultivated, i.e. cut and thinned out when necessary; they are not, however, planted or transplanted, but left to fertilize themselves. Among these indigo planters the making of indigo is men's work. But in the districts where indigo is gained from the scattered, wild-growing tree, the picking and preparing of indigo is done by women. The method of preparing the dye is in both cases the same; the leaves are pounded in a mortar, then left to ferment in water, mixed with ash, and finally rolled into balls. The finished product is used exclusively by the women dyers, that is, in a practice of dyeing in pots, and which appears to represent the original dyeing technique of Southern and Central Nigeria; according to Nupe tradition it was introduced into the country by the Konú weavers and dyers (see p. 188, n. 2).

Nupe country offers only a restricted market for indigo. The indigo manufactured by the wives of the Konú weavers, the total quantity of which is small, is either used by the women themselves or is sold in the markets—in the districts more than in Bida—where modern products have ousted almost completely the native technique of dyeing. The much larger output of indigo dye which is produced by the cultivators of the indigo tree is disposed of with the help of middlemen who trade it to Yoruba, the most favourable market for indigo, or is taken by the producers themselves to the nearest market of that country (Ilorin). This latter method secures the better price but may interfere with the normal agricultural activity. A family of farmers near Kutigi who

[1] This method of indigo cultivation is practised on a large scale by the Gbari.

owned twenty-five indigo trees had to take their produce to Ilorin market just at the time of the second yam harvest. However, they preferred to sell indigo first and to postpone the digging out of yam for a month or two, although this meant losing the always profitable market for the first yams of the season. The element of economic calculation, to which we have already assigned its place in the planning of Nupe agriculture, reveals its efficacy in this new context as well.

Not much need be said about the other fruit-bearing trees. The fruit of the mango tree is eaten when and wherever it can be picked or gathered up from the ground; it is not traded—like the banana it is 'just fruit'. The tender young leaves of the baobab (*muci*) are used as food; they are pounded and sold in the markets as a vegetable which is added to soup and meat. In order to obtain the tender leaves the owner of the tree lops the big branches so as to make them sprout new leaves. The cotton-wool-like kapok which is contained in the capsules of the silk-cotton tree (*lembubu*) is traded in one or two markets of the country; it is bought by the Bida cushion-makers and also by the canoe-men on the Niger, who use its fine fibres to stop leaks in their canoes. The commercial use of this tree and its fruits has not yet penetrated into the more remote districts: while in Kutigi, on the main road, natives were collecting kapok to sell it to the Bida cushion-makers, I found in Sakpe, only ten miles away but right in the bush, the cotton-wool left unused, lying on the ground to be carried away by the wind. When I asked a number of men why they did not collect it and take it to the market—I could call upon a boy from Bida whom I had with me to bear out my contention that this stuff possessed commercial value—they replied, not wholly convinced, that it would be too hard work. Another example of rudimentary 'economic calculation', with leisure weighed against money-profit.

INNOVATIONS IN PRODUCTION

From this discussion an interesting question arises: why have the Nupe, who have mastered the cultivation of kola-nut and banana, not taken to the cultivation of other trees as well, but left most of their fruit-bearing trees to the 'care of God'. If you ask a Nupe farmer he will give you one of two answers: either the vague theological excuse that God has planted the trees, and that God will look after them; or the more rationalistic but no less acquiescent explanation: 'If I planted a tree I should never see its fruit, only my grandchildren would profit by it. Our grandfathers have not planted trees for us, why then should we plant for our grandchildren?' The fact, well known to everyone, that the Kusopa plant and cultivate trees is yet easily dismissed. This is one of the cultural features typical of certain tribal sections which are simply taken for granted by the other groups. The myth that explains how it came about that just this and no other sub-tribe happened to become kola-nut planters, the special magic which the members of that sub-tribe are believed to own provide the spiritual background for this attitude. This acceptance of an existing productive specialization as if it were a final and unalterable fact was effective enough, as we have seen, to check the attempts to extend kola plantation in Nupe. Whether or not it will check other attempts at agricultural innovations one cannot say.[1]

Often in discussions of this kind the reluctance of a native group to adopt a certain innovation is summarily dismissed as being due to the inveterate, almost proverbial, 'conservatism' of the native races. Clearly, such an explanation does not meet the case. As regards the Nupe we should have to contrast their alleged 'conservatism' with respect to trees with the readiness with which they adopt new crops and agricultural techniques. Evidently, to adopt a new crop which shows results in a year's time, and which is easy to tend, often easier than the traditional crops (as in the case of maize or cassava), and to take up the difficult work of planting trees which may not bear fruit for six or seven years, is an entirely different thing. One can be easily fitted into the framework of established agricultural activities while the other involves a complete readjustment of the productive system. The Nupe are, within limits, extremely progressive people, and keen on trying out new things. These limits are determined by two factors: first, by the time that an ordinarily crowded working year could allow for additional tasks; other work, or precious leisure time might have to be given up for the sake of the innovation—a change that may or may not appear worth while to the Nupe farmer. The second factor is the measure of change which a readjustment of the native production would entail in this closely knit economic system, with its exact balance of specialization and exchange. Every radical change in the production, such as the adoption of tree-cultivation in a district, may upset this balance; it may, in other words, make the innovation less profitable. The fact that the Nupe farmer is go-ahead with respect to certain farm techniques and 'conservative' with respect to others is not due to any tribal or racial 'conservatism', but reveals itself as a clear instance of the working of free economic choice.

TECHNIQUE AND KNOWLEDGE

So advanced a technique and so conspicuous a standard of husbandry must involve a body of theoretical knowledge which goes far beyond the counsels of peasant lore, and could avouch statements of very nearly scientific authority. This is no doubt the case in Nupe farming. The understanding of the basic principle of manuring, the fixed rules with regard to rotation and lying fallow, the practice of thinning-out the growing plants, which is correctly explained as being intended to give the plant more space, they all confirm this.[2] Moreover, while in many African

[1] Rev. Ira W. Sherk, the head of the U.S. Mission at Mokwa, has been successful in making the people of a small neighbouring village adopt the cultivation of grapefruit. This innovation, carried out on a very small scale, and involving hardly any difficult readjustment of the native productive organization, bears out what is said later in the text about the limits that are set to all such innovations.

[2] I must record that one of my Bida informants, an experienced farmer, denied the value of ashes and the burning of fields as manure. He held that animal manure (with the regular use of which he as a Bida farmer was well acquainted) was the only effective manure. This critical attitude only emphasizes the element of empirical knowledge in Nupe farming technique.

R

communities rulings on agricultural technique and the organization of agricultural labour appear in the guise of magic devices and rituals, there is none of this in Nupe agriculture, which remains matter-of-fact and consciously based on empirical knowledge.[1]

In a productive organization of this kind special emphasis must be laid on the position of authority of the old and experienced farmer. It can be studied in action whenever groups comprising both older and younger men co-operate in farm-work. In family work as well as in non-family co-operation the older men always lead the work or supervise the work of the younger men; they point out mistakes to them and teach them the important rules of farm-work. I have frequently seen men scold boys for damaging a plant when weeding, or for planting seeds too close. Boys are made to work on the farms from the age of 6 or 7, first with toy-like light tools, later with the real heavy hoe, in order to learn through practice and under constant supervision. In Nupe farming very little is left to chance. I have, for example, never heard of anyone starting farm-work too early or too late in the season and thus wasting the seeds—a mistake not uncommon among more primitive agriculturalists. The quasi-scientific aspect of Nupe agriculture is made most evident in the 'theoretical' rulings which the people themselves are always ready to lay down. Thus informants formulated the following rule: there exist two kinds of rice, one taking 90 days, the other 180 days to mature; or this: the latest date for the planting of ground-nuts is the beginning of the third month (counted from the beginning of the planting season). Not all such rules are fully convincing to the European agriculturist—we remember the rule about planting yams before the dry season in order to make them grow bigger. But, on the other hand, there is plenty of evidence to show that the existing body of native farm-knowledge admits of experiment, and is constantly assimilating newly gained experiences. There is, for example, the new 'rule' about cotton and red pepper being excellent first crops before millet and sorghum. Experiment has besides been forced upon the native cultivator by the introduction of modern crops or varieties. Thus the people have tried with varying success to grow cotton on different kinds of soil; cotton-growing has also caused new difficulties with regard to the distribution of agricultural work, which can be solved ultimately only by experiment.[2]

Long experimenting, however, which does not lead to the incorporation of the new experiences into that solid body of farming-knowledge

[1] The one exception is the magic linked with the cultivation of kola-nut trees, which itself represents an exceptional form of cultivation. Apart from this magic there exist only the annual fertility cults which set the spiritual framework for farming activities in general, and certain varying, unsystematic forms of magic—charms applied to hoes, or a specific magic performed over a field—which are to ensure success in individual cases.

[2] In 1936 the Agricultural Officer of Bida Division travelled round the district to instruct personally the cotton-growers in the more important centres about the proper date for planting cotton—information which, coming many years after cotton-growing had been introduced in this area, only confirmed a point of technique which the people had already discovered for themselves.

easily turns into discouragement. In Kutigi and Sakpe I have spoken to many farmers who, discouraged by the increasing difficulties that appear to accompany cotton-growing, seemed determined to give it up altogether. We may, I think, draw a valuable lesson from this. If new agricultural schemes are to be introduced they must be brought in already well tried-out and fully adapted to the existing conditions. The adoption of a new crop or technique is to the native in itself a large-scale experiment; to make the people adopt a technique which has not been fully tried-out means to double this element of experimenting. It will prevent the new knowledge from being absorbed quickly in the 'body of Nupe farming-knowledge' on which the people feel they must be able to rely, and may eventually give them over to disappointment and discouragement.

BY-PRODUCTS OF AGRICULTURE

Agriculture and forest-cultivation produce as by-products certain raw materials which are used in Nupe home industries and handicrafts. Thus the grain-stalks which are left on the fields after the harvest are used for the making of fences, doors, and bedsteads: cut in fine strips, grain and maize stalks are used for mat-making; a vegetable dye, black and red, is gained from the stalk of a certain species of sorghum (*dindó-rogi*). Small trees which do not bear fruit are occasionally cut down by the owner of the field on which they stand and used as timber for house-repairs and suchlike. In all these cases it is the cultivator and his family themselves who use the plant or tree; the by-products of agriculture have no marketing value. This is different in the case of firewood and grass for thatching which, as I have mentioned already, is collected or cut by the Nupe women and marketed by the men (see p. 200).

It is frequently quoted as a characteristic feature of African agriculture that every part of a plant or tree that can be used in any way is actually utilized by the people. This is only partly true in Nupe. Only a small proportion, for example, of the grain-stalks is used in the various ways just described. A great many farmers are either unskilled in the craft which makes use of these by-products, or devote their spare time to other, to them more attractive or profitable, occupations. This comparative failure on the part of the Nupe farmer to utilize to the fullest possible extent the products of his land appears to be connected with the complexity and specialization of the productive system of the country. As we shall see later, only certain groups or individuals have specialized in mat-making, the making of bedsteads, or dyeing. The influence of specialization involving a clear-cut division between the agriculturist and the craftsman who utilizes the by-products of agriculture is most conspicuous in this case; big trees, when not fruit-bearing, may also be cut down and used as timber. But no farmer would ever attempt to cut a big tree himself for fear of bungling the job and being injured or even killed by the falling tree. He calls in the professional wood-cutter, who possesses both the necessary skill and experience and the special magic which alone can prevent the spirit of the tree from revenging himself on the person who is destroying his abode. These big trees have a money-value, and are sold to the wood-cutters and carpenters, who use the timber in their own industry. On the whole the Nupe are reluctant to cut down big trees, especially in the town, for they appreciate the shade which they give. But it happens occasionally that the owner of a barren tree, in need of money, has it cut down and sells the timber to wood-cutters or carpenters.

In the interest of forest-preservation the felling of certain trees has been made subject to the payment of a licence fee varying in amount from 5s. 6d. to £1 or more. This new rule involves an economic re-adjustment which the people—professional timber-workers as well as ordinary farmers—have not yet been able to achieve. The carpenters of Bida almost went on strike when the new licence was introduced, and refused to manufacture any more wooden stools and other products of their craft for fear of being unable to sell their goods for the higher price which the licence would necessitate. Another illustration is the case of an old man, a carpenter, who, unaware of the new rule, had bought a barren locust-bean tree in Bida for felling, for 7s. 6d. When he was requested to pay the licence fee of 5s. 6d. he was unable to do so. His case came before the Bida Court, but in consideration of his poverty and age the court reduced the licence fee for him to 1s. 4d. It is too early yet to say what effect this licence will have on the Nupe wood-working industry: whether it will lead to a technical readjustment and a change in the kind of timber used, or to a gradual deterioration and eventual dis-appearance of the indigenous wood-carving technique, which is already feeling the competition of the cheaper, and infinitely uglier, products in Western style: packing-case chairs and tables, deck-chairs, and the like.[1]

[1] It is to be feared that it will be this latter case with which Nupe wood-carving will meet. In other crafts these changes in material and partly style are already an accomplished fact: thus the Bida glass-workers have almost completely abandoned making their own glass, and make their bangles and beads of smelted down bottle glass of European manufacture; similarly the Nupe blacksmiths buy cheap sheet-iron at the trading stores, and no longer smelt their own iron ore.

CHAPTER XIII
AGRICULTURE: ORGANIZATION OF LABOUR

LABOUR organization in Nupe, in every field of economic activity, is characterized by a twofold principle: the distinction between individual work and family work or, in native terminology, between *bucá* and *efakó*. As the division of labour implied in this distinction also involves a corresponding division of income and property, our discussion of the organization of agricultural labour must at the same time be a discussion of the forms of property that obtain in relation to agricultural production. The terms *bucá* and *efakó* have, in fact, this wider meaning. Every kind of work done individually, its products and the income—individual income—derived from it, are *bucá*; and every work done jointly, in collective family work, producing output and income over which the family group or a section of the family group exercises joint rights, is *efakó*. Thus we find two different kinds of farm property: *efakó* farms which are owned and worked jointly by the family group, and *bucá* farms worked and owned by individuals. Similarly there are *efakó* granaries to hold the produce from the family farms, and *bucá* granaries to hold the produce which the individual members of the family group own and utilize. The family group or, more precisely, the section of the family group which forms the *efakó*-unit, owns from ten to twelve granaries which are as a rule placed close to the centre of the house. Every *bucá* owner has, besides, his own granary, which is usually found close to the wall of the compound. Obviously, in a system of labour based not on wages but on joint work and a share in the proceeds, the discussion of the labour organization cannot be treated separately from questions of ownership and land-tenure. On the other hand, a co-operative group consisting of a section of the kinship group cannot be described without constant reference to kinship organization. Frequent cross-references, and overlapping with other sections of the book, are thus unavoidable.

INDIVIDUAL AND FAMILY WORK

Let me begin with the *bucá*, which can be briefly described. Every male member of the family owns a *bucá*, with the exception of the family head who being the administrator of the *efakó* has no *bucá* himself. For his personal requirements he is entitled to draw on the *efakó* income. Young boys of 8 or 10 already possess *bucá* farms of their own. *Bucá* farms vary considerably in size, and grow with their occupants. The largest *bucá* farm which I found was about one acre, i.e. about half the size of the plot of land which on the family possessions is proportionate to every adult worker. The average *bucá* yield I found to be between one-third and one-half of the individual adult's share in the yield of the family farm. The *bucá* owner can work on his farm only 'out of business hours', when he is not needed for *efakó* work. Two different arrangements exist. The one found more frequently is this: every man works on the *efakó* farm from early morning till 3 or 4 in the afternoon; after that he is free to work his own individual plot. The second, less frequent, arrangement requires married men to work five days in the week, and bachelors six days in the week on the *efakó*, and allows them one or two days—including the weekly day of rest, Friday—on the *bucá*. The selection of crops which are grown on the *bucá* is of necessity very much simpler than that grown on the *efakó*; moreover, no collective work, not even occasional help, is possible for *bucá* work. Thus farmers grow mostly only the staple crops, sorghum, millet, or yam, on their *bucá* farms but sometimes, though rarely, also cotton or ground-nuts. The income from the *bucá* farm is used entirely for personal expenses, for clothes and additional food which are not provided by the family, such as savouries or kola-nuts, beer or palm-wine; for contributions to parties of friends, certain personal gifts, and so forth.

Bucá farm-work is not practised everywhere, and not even in every farming community. *Bucá* work and income of some kind, however, always exists. In certain areas where other forms of production (e.g. certain handicrafts) are practised besides agriculture—mostly forms of production involving less heavy work and higher money-return—these additional productive techniques supply the *bucá* work to which the men turn 'after hours'. Thus we find in Kutigi, the centre of Nupe mat-industry, mat-working adopted as *bucá*; in Mokwa, indigo-dyeing; while on Jebba Island, which is inhabited by the mixed farming and fishing community of the riverain Gbedegi, fishing with the drag-net (carried out in the evenings, i.e. after the day's farm-work) replacing the farming *bucá*.

The joint work on the *efakó* farm is carried out by a section of the household group, i.e. by a section of the family group which lives together in the same 'house' or compound. Only once have I found an *efakó* group comprising individuals who were living in different compounds. It was a transitional arrangement which had occurred in the course of the expansion of one household group, a section of which had split off and was preparing to take new land, farther afield, under cultivation. The 'emigrants' had already built a house in the new locality but were still, for the time being, working with the rest of the original household group on the old land. The whole household group, with its twenty-five to thirty male members, has most probably never formed a single *efakó* group, although informants, here as in so many cases only too ready to idealize the past, will often give exaggerated accounts of the size of the groups that formerly used to work together. Their estimates vary widely, between thirty and a hundred. However, even reliable informants put the size of the *efakó* group in pre-British days at a figure considerably higher than that observed to-day, namely, at from ten to fifteen. The average *efakó* group to-day numbers only two or three adult members. There is no doubt, then, and this is borne out by the evidence of genealogies, that the size of the *efakó* group has been steadily decreasing for some time. These are the figures relating to the size of the *efakó* working group in the case of fifty Nupe households which I have analysed (non-adult members of the working group are ignored in the table):

Number of men working together .	1	2	3	4	5	6	Over 6
Number of cases	17	13	11	6	2	1	. .[1]

The smallest *efakó* group, of one man, has obviously lost all the essential characteristics which distinguish it from the *bucá* group. In these extreme cases the *bucá* itself disappears, and we have single individual holdings, worked by one man, helped only perhaps by his boys who will stay with him until they are grown up, when they too will demand farms of their own.

The normal *efakó* group consists of a number of close relations—brothers and sons who are either unmarried or only recently married, and have one or two small children—working under the headship of the senior man, a father, father's brother, or eldest brother. Older men who are childless may also remain in the *efakó* group. In larger *efakó* groups and especially in groups the head of which is an old man, the family head may not himself join in the actual farm-work. He supervises it, he makes frequent tours of inspection to the farm, and he lays down the arrangement and order of the work for the day. As a family head he stands more aloof, and is free to use his leisure in his own way. The team-work which the *efakó* implies is of two kinds: actual working together, or co-ordinated working on different plots performing different tasks. Actual working together on the same plot is practised in the tilling of the soil and the preparation of ridges, in transplanting and harvesting. In this team-work a strong stimulus is embodied: the more experienced workers set the pace, and the others follow as well as they can, always conscious of the element of competition and display of efficiency embodied in the joint activity. The leader of the team is not, as we have seen, the head of the *efakó* group himself but the member next in seniority, in the traditional arrangement usually the younger brother or eldest son of the family head. Sowing, ordinary weeding, and the regular tending of the plants may be done by one or two workers of the group only, while the rest may be assigned tasks on other plots or sometimes a different kind of work altogether, such as the task of helping in the house, or taking farm-produce to a distant market.

Whatever the actual division of work, the consciousness of the individual share in the common labour is strongly pronounced, and with it the competitive element in the co-operation. Every co-worker in the team is aware of the number of ridges, for example, which stand to his credit in the common tilling; similarly everyone, at least among the adults, is able to describe precisely his share in the yield produced on the

[1] The proportion of *efakó* groups comprising more than four adults is in reality much smaller than is indicated in the table. A more superficial census of over 100 households, designed specially to ascertain the occurrence of large *efakó* groups, produced the same three instances of households with *efakó*-units of five or six adults.

common land. The system of individual *bucá* work which runs parallel to the family work no doubt fosters such reckoning; no doubt also that this form of reckoning, essentially competitive as it is, must enhance the energy devoted by the individual worker to the common task. But such an attitude must also foster the tendency to split up and eventually dissolve the working-unit. In a small hamlet near Bida I discovered an interesting form of transition between full co-operation, which yet recognizes the individual share in the common work, and complete dissolution of the working-unit into independent agents. In the case to which I am referring the *efakó* group was divided into two working-units, each being engaged permanently on different fields although the yield produced by the two sections was still collected as the common *efakó* yield. The *efakó* group was formed by a father—a man of over 50 —and his two married sons—of about 25 and 30. The father was working one group of plots and the two sons, together, another. The two groups of plots incidentally produced equally large crops, which was due to the fact that the old man could enlist outside labour on his farms and thus equalize the difference in working capacity between himself and his two sons.

MAINTENANCE OF LABOUR

The produce of the *efakó* is handed over *in toto* to the family head. It is stored in the *efakó* granaries, and only the family head has the right to dispose of it. We shall discuss later in detail the various uses to which he may put it. But let me describe here one aspect of the employment of the *efakó* income, namely its use for the benefit of the *efakó* members themselves who helped to produce it, speaking more generally, for the maintenance of the labour organization. The question of maintenance of labour has, first, a strictly material aspect, namely, the supply of the means of production—the agricultural tools. The main agricultural instruments used in Nupe farming, as we have seen, are two kinds of hoe, bush-knife, and axe. They all have to be bought from the blacksmiths or, in the case of the bush-knife, from the European store, and must be repaired periodically—expenses which are by no means negligible. A heavy hoe costs between 1s. and 1s. 6d., a light hoe between 6d. and 1s., axe and bush-knife between 1s. and 1s. 6d.; repairs may amount to between 3d. and 4d. each time, that is, perhaps 1s. a year. Now, as long as the individual worker remains in the *efakó* group, the head of the group supplies new tools and pays for repairs. A man who leaves the *efakó* group to work on his own may take away the tools which he has been using—they have become 'his' tools—but from now on he must himself pay the cost of all repairs or the purchase of new tools.

The second, human, aspect in the problem of maintenance of labour is the maintenance of the workers themselves. They are housed, clothed, and fed by the family head. The head of the *efakó* group is responsible for all expenses that occur in connexion with the repair of the house and the huts in which his co-workers live; he provides their clothing and food—the section of the family group which is regularly eating together and constitutes one *ménage* coincides in fact with the *efakó*-unit. The *efakó* head further pays the tax for his co-workers and is also expected to make himself responsible for establishing them socially when they have reached full adulthood, i.e. he will enable them to get married, by paying their bride-price. By allotting to the co-workers from earliest youth an individual plot for *bucá* work or allowing them the time for other *bucá* enterprises, he also puts them in the position of earning an independent income. They use it, as I have said, for their personal wants over and above those catered for by the family head—what we may call the small luxuries of life. When they desire to leave the *efakó* group and set up for themselves the family head finally provides the members of his group with the necessary 'capital' in the form of the tools which they may take with them, food for the first year while their new land does not yet bear crops, and, above all, in form of the parcel of family land which he allots to them as their own property. In order to do all this the family head must be able not only to draw on regular supplies of agricultural produce from the family land but also to avail himself of certain commodities of exchange and that universal medium of exchange, money. He must plan his money expenditure and accumulate reserves which can alone enable him to pay the large bride-price (which is always in money) when the time comes. The resources of the family working-unit thus gain the significance of capital proper, invested in the maintenance of labour; without it, without the prospect of fulfilling all these economic obligations towards the members of the working-unit, the *efakó* group cannot be maintained satisfactorily.

Here we come back to the decline or disintegration of the family working-unit under modern conditions which we have outlined in the beginning of this section. Now, every co-operative group must to some extent reckon with a periodical and temporary disintegration, that is, with the necessity of periodically readjusting its body of workers, replacing those who have died or are too old or who for other reasons desire to leave the group and to admit new, young members in their place. This is done through the twofold mechanism of inheritance and succession, and of release with regard to members who leave the group to work on their own. We shall examine inheritance and succession later; here it will suffice to say that in the Nupe system of inheritance the family farm goes to the relation next in seniority, younger brother or eldest son (in the classificatory sense). As regards the release of members from the group, the rule used to be that junior members remained in the *efakó* until they had more than two wives and more than two or three children. In the last five to ten years, however, many large *efakó* groups were dissolved after the death of the family head, and the family land, instead of being worked jointly by the remaining members of the family under the new head, was divided up among the various individuals who now work independently each on his own land. Moreover, nowadays young men who have just married frequently decline to stay in the *efakó*-unit and demand to be given a separate farm. I have noted many cases of this kind, in all parts of Nupe, in which the dissolution of the *efakó* group occurred between six and ten years ago.

How are we to explain this comparatively sudden change? Viewing it from the general economic point of view all the advantages seem to be on the side of a large labour-unit: our discussion of the agricultural technique of the country has taught us that a large labour group represents, in Nupe, the only means of cultivating a large variety of both useful and profitable crops. Moreover, a large *efakó*-unit assures a certain measure of leisure to the family head and the old men in general, by enabling them to leave a large proportion of the actual work to the younger generation. It assures also a better distribution of responsibility, counting more adults among its members than does the small working-unit. It utilizes more fully the important incentive of competition and is, finally, of great educational value; for only in large labour-units are the young boys likely to work regularly in the company of others of their own age.

But if from point of view of group efficiency and security the large working-unit appears superior to the small (say) one- or two-men 'group', it is not necessarily so when looked at from the viewpoint of the individual. Take the question of leisure and distribution of responsibility. In one of the instances in which I found a large *efakó*-unit having been dissolved recently (six years ago), after the death of the family head, I was given this as the reason of the change: the new family head, the eldest of five brothers, had availed himself liberally of the privilege of leisure which his position implied, and frequently went hunting while the others were working on the farm. Now, while they had accepted the same arrangement under the old family head, their father, they declined to accord this privilege to their eldest brother, and preferred to dissolve the whole unit and work each for himself. To-day, working on their own, the individual family members have a comparatively larger measure of freedom and leisure, which they are free to use as they like. They can use their own discretion in planning the farm-work: of the five brothers two have taken to spend their spare time in making mats, a leisure-time occupation which, they assured me, is financially very advantageous to them; one has left the village; and the family head himself can still spend part of his time in hunting. Against the considerations of group efficiency thus stand individual considerations of gain, which provide another, and in some respects very different, standard of appreciation by which to measure the value of the large labour-unit. The word 'gain' should not be understood in too narrow a sense. Freedom of movement, freedom to choose a different profession (we remember, for example, the openings which the political life of the capital offered to young men of adventurous spirit), even freedom to enjoy one's leisure independent of the dictates of family requirements—these spiritual values appear under certain circumstances as tempting to the younger generation as does the prospect of material gain.

The two standards of appreciation will coincide where the *efakó* group is in a position to guarantee the satisfaction of all needs and demands which the group-members might feel. Nupe family co-operation in farm-work, once apparently more satisfactorily adjusted, is now failing in this respect. This failure can be attributed to two different developments: to an increase in the needs and demands on the part of the individual members with which the system of family co-operation failed to cope; or to a decline in the efficiency of the group to maintain its former standards of maintenance. The Nupe *efakó* system has, in fact, failed on both accounts. As regards the first, a large variety of new needs and wants, temptations and values have spread, primarily from the town, and have begun to transform the original peasant culture; as regards the second, the family head is to-day frequently unable to meet out of the family income two financial demands which are regarded as essential to the *efakó* concept, the payment of the bride-price and the payment of tax for the individual members of the *efakó* group.

Certain of the influences which have thus led to the decline of the large working-unit are no doubt due to factors of modern culture change. Yet it would be wrong to regard the change in the structure of the working-unit merely as a result of the outside influence of culture contact. The structural change forms part of a much wider phenomenon; it is the result of an intrinsic economic development, namely, the readjustment between productive organization and needs existing in the society. If the change were due exclusively to culture contact we should expect to find the larger working-unit preserved only in backward, 'unsophisticated', districts. This is not the case. The table on p. 243 showed that three households out of fifty had working-units composed of more than four adults. Of these three households only one belongs to a backward area—the household of the chief of Doko. The two other examples come both from one of the most progressive places in Nupe, Lemu, and from a group of farmers who, as mentioned before, have but recently undertaken the cultivation of a new commercial crop, red pepper, to replace another commercial crop, ground-nuts, which had not proved an economic success. A large working group is essential to the cultivation of this new crop. In these two households the young men have remained in the *efakó*, content with their position, while the family head, in turn, is able to provide bride-price and tax-money. Here, then, culture contact so far from being responsible for the dissolution of the large working-unit has on the contrary supplied a type of production which enables the large working-unit to maintain itself; paradoxically, culture contact has placed the *efakó*-unit in a position to satisfy those very demands and needs which culture contact has newly imposed upon the society. However, these instances from Lemu are exceptional: neither in Mokwa, the centre of ground-nut cultivation, nor in Kutigi, where cotton is grown on a comparatively large scale, has the large *efakó* group survived. The exceptional cases which I have discovered are too few to warrant a more far-reaching, systematic explanation. Moreover, whereas in this case attractions and temptations appealing to the younger generation are partly responsible for the social change, individual differences must play a considerable part. We can only tentatively point to a certain negative evidence: the absence of some of these 'temptations' in Lemu which have made the younger generation in Mokwa and Kutigi claim an early economic independence. Lemu is neither a centre of native trade, nor does a profitable alternative occupation to farm-work (e.g. a handicraft, carried out in one's leisure-time) exist there, nor, finally, has its connexion with the political life of the town ever been as strong as in those other places.

COLLECTIVE LABOUR

The co-operation of the *efakó* group is more or less regularly supplemented by a system of mutual assistance and large-scale collective labour among the villagers, an institution which the Nupe have in common with all other Nigerian tribes. Its help is enlisted in all cases in which the *efakó* group by itself would be insufficient to secure efficient cultivation —be it because of its smallness, or an unforeseen obstacle such as illness among its members, or irregular rains,[1] or simply because its ambitious programme demands larger co-operation than is at its disposal. The Nupe have two systems of collective labour devised to operate in different situations: *egbe* (the Hausa *gaya*) and *dzolo*.

The *egbe* is the more general type of collective labour. It is not limited to farm-work, but is organized for every kind of work which demands large-scale co-operation and specially for work done, not for one household alone, but for the community at large. Thus the building or roofing of a big house, for example the chief's house, repairs of a bush-bridge or a stretch of road which is maintained by the village, are carried out in *egbe* work; repairs of the town wall, formerly, and repairs of the building of a Native Administration rest-house, to-day, are equally typical occasions for the *egbe*. However, in Bida and in many larger places a large proportion of work of this kind has now been taken over by professional labour. But in Bida as well as in the hinterland farm *egbe* is still practised regularly.

The help of *egbe* for farming is enlisted mostly for tilling and the first and second weeding, more rarely for the third weeding and the clearing of new yam-plots. A few days before the *egbe* is to take place the young men of the family go round to their friends and neighbours and invite them to the *egbe* on such and such a day. *Egbe* work is on the whole work for the younger people. A ready frame for their co-operation exists in the age-grade associations of which all the young men of a district are members. As they arrange throughout the year meetings and feasts in which they all join, they now organize the collective farm-work for one of their fellow member's family. The family head sends out a special invitation to drummers and musicians to play at the *egbe*. The accompaniment of music plays a very important part. Finally, the host prepares food and beer for the feast with which the *egbe* invariably ends.

Early in the morning drummers and flute-players walk out to the farm on which the *egbe* is to take place. They play and sing while they walk, beating on their drums the characteristic rhythm of *egbe* music, and everyone who meets them knows at once their destination. Some of the

[1] I once witnessed a third weeding carried out by collective labour in September, after an unexpected dry spell. The farmer explained to me that if the rains had been normal and ordinary farm-work not delayed, he would have carried out the third weeding in ordinary family work.

EFAKÓ WORK ON A FARM NEAR BIDA

FARMING *EGBE*

working party follow the musicians, the rest meet later out on the farm. When all have assembled the young men start work. They work in a group of ten or twelve, starting on the same side of the field, leaving plenty of space between each other. Everyone is working his own ridge and, having finished one, he turns to the next with hardly any pause. The drummers and flute-players walk alongside the field abreast of the workers. Older men stand at the side, watching, criticizing, commenting. Often you can hear them call one of the workers by name, exhorting him to ever greater efforts, or shouting impatiently: 'Quicker, quicker!' When one field is finished some of the young men, the captains of the age-grade association among them, will execute a short dance, balancing their heavy hoes in the air and heavily stamping on the tilled field, while the drummers are arrayed behind them, beating the rhythm of the age-grade *take*.[1] Then workers and audience—and every *egbe* attracts a large audience—move on to another field, while some of the older men may stay behind to sow the newly tilled plot. On another occasion I saw the young men working in two groups of about equal strength, each under its own leader—one of the captains of the age-grade association. The groups started on opposite ends of the field, working towards each other. Now and again a worker would get up, survey with one glance the work which his group had been doing, and cry out in a long high-pitched yell; others were shouting with deep hoarse voices at every stroke of their hoe. The speed with which they worked, the whole atmosphere of the *egbe*—the constant drumming, the shouts from the audience—had something deeply exciting, almost feverish. I have seen a team of fifteen young men, the oldest between 19 and 20, the youngest 14, clear and till a farm-plot of one acre in two and a half hours.[2] The *egbe* work still more than *efakó* work is animated by an intense spirit of competition. The worker who has quickly finished his ridges will stand up and look round, proudly showing off his splendid work; he will chaff his fellow workers about their clumsy progress, their crooked ridges; he executes a little dance, singing, and shaking his hoe to show how leisurely he can work and still beat the others. When all the work is finished the whole party, musicians, workers, and onlookers, repair to the house of the owner of the farm. Here the feast which concludes the *egbe* is celebrated with plenty of food, corn-beer, and dancing, and much boasting and prancing of the young men, who are the heroes of the occasion. Nor is their boasting and prancing without significance. In the village communities where the traditional age-grade system is still practised, one of the important side-issues of the *egbe* is that it represents a regular test in which the young men establish their qualification as farmers. From *egbe* to *egbe*, every year, their skill and their achievements are watched, compared, and judged by the older people. In the last *egbe* of the season, or some other outstanding *egbe* (e.g. on the farm of the chief),[3] the results of this competition are made known and the young

---

[1] See p. 395.
[2] In another case I saw six young men clearing a densely overgrown bush-plot for yam-cultivation of about a third of an acre in one hour.
[3] An *egbe* of this kind near Bida at which new titles were bestowed was

farmer who did best is given by his age-grade association the title *Sode*, the second highest title that can be bestowed on young men. A man who is once made *Sode* keeps his rank until some other claimant snatches the title from him, or if he had no competitors, until he joins the 'old men' and retires from the arena of the *egbe*. In the urbanized age-grade associations of Bida this title and the whole usage have disappeared. In other large places which follow Bida fashion, the title *Sode*, though still in existence, has become a title of minor importance, a long way down the list of age-grade ranks.

The primary advantage of collective farm-work lies evidently in the time-saving which it makes possible. The second weeding, for example, which normally takes from five to ten days, can be done by *egbe* in one day. But this valuable help must be paid for. The cost of an *egbe* of from fifteen to twenty workers—the cost of food and drink for the guests and the pay of drummers and musicians—is between 6s. and 8s. *Egbe* work, then, implies a calculation of investment and return, cost and profit. To-day, farmers try to lower the cost of *egbe*. In an *egbe* near Bida (the *egbe* just described, in which the workers were grouped in two teams) the owner of the farm contributed music and food for thirty people, but no beer or palm-wine. The fare was simple—no meat or fish—but plentiful: porridge cooked in palm-oil for the men, half a bowl per head (1 lb.), and corn-gruel for the women. This cheap *egbe* cost only 4s. yet proved still sufficiently attractive to make a large group of workers attend.

Yet there is one element of 'profit' in this calculation which cannot be put down in shillings and pence, and which is of utmost sociological significance. *Egbe* work is performed only on family farms, i.e. on the farms of family heads and old men in general. Younger people, whether they still work under the family head or have made themselves independent, are not entitled to the help of the *egbe*. Thus the *egbe* provides a twofold balance, in favour of the old men who cannot work as efficiently as the young, and in favour of the sociological head of the family group who, though perhaps no longer able to command the services of a large body of co-workers, can still command the assistance of collective farm-work.[1] How real this balance is was illustrated in the example given before (p. 244) of an old man, the family head, cultivating fields equal in size and yield to the fields worked by his two adult sons. With the splitting-up of families and the reduction of the *efakó* group, with the disappearance, that is, of the clear-cut distinction between family and individual farms, the significance of the *egbe*, too, must weaken. Information gained from a large number of independent witnesses testifies to the gradual loss of importance of *egbe* work in Nupe productive life. Once practised regularly on every farm it has now been

performed on the new experimental farm of the Agricultural Department which was tilled in collective work.

[1] Recognition of this privileged position of the sociological head of the group in a wider sense is expressed in the traditional rule, still valid in most peasant communities in Nupe, that the first *egbe* of the season is performed on the chief's land.

reduced to a system of merely occasional assistance. According to my informants the change is due primarily to the high cost of the *egbe*, which to-day few farmers can afford. This is no doubt true if we understand 'cost' in the relative and not in the absolute sense. In the very closely balanced budget with which most Nupe farmers must reckon to-day the comparatively large single outlay for the *egbe* may prove an insuperable difficulty. But this is not the whole picture. A cost is high only measured on the profit it can realize. And here we have seen that one of the most essential kinds of profit—moral profit—which the *egbe* can realize, namely, its assurance of the economic balance between the generations, has itself lost much of its significance in the life of the community.

The second type of collective work, the *dzolo*, is less important than the *egbe*. It is practised only for harvesting of those crops which demand a large working team (ground-nuts, cotton, and beans) and consists in the arrangement among a number of farmers to work in turn on each other's farms. The host provides the meal after the work. But there is no drumming or dancing, nor is any competition involved in the work of the *dzolo*. Neither is the mechanism of the age-grade associations utilized for this collective work, which is carried out on a much smaller scale than the *egbe*, and only between friends, i.e. families whose heads are friendly with one another. In the *dzolo* the tie of friendship evidently supplies that incentive to collective work which, in the *egbe*, is entrusted to the appeal of music and dance and the stimulus of competition.

WAGE-LABOUR

Assistance in farm-work by means of paid labour plays on the whole (we must add as yet) an insignificant part in Nupe production at large. It is called *kantsú* in Nupe but is often referred to by the Hausa name *lada*, i.e. wages. It is employed by the owners of farms who are not themselves farmers or who for other reasons cannot themselves look after their land. Paid farm-labour is a new thing in Nupe. It has no place in the traditional system of land-tenure and *efakó* work. Characteristically, it is almost completely absent in the rural districts; it is employed mostly in the large commercial centres in which a considerable proportion of the population belongs to the well-to-do 'professional classes', such as Kacha, Jebba, and, above all, Bida.[1] Let me give you a list of the cases I recorded in which wage farm-labour was employed. The employers were a number of traders in Kacha who had bought some land a few years ago but did not work it themselves; a number of traders in Bida; two Mallams in Bida; a Mallam in Jebba whose health did not allow him to work on the land (he was employing wage-labour for the first time); Native Administration officials in Bida—a few policemen, and teachers at the Bida Middle School; and lastly, the village chief of Kacha (who is at the same time District Head) whose time is taken up by official

---

[1] One of my Bida informants, himself a well-to-do member of the 'intelligentsia', estimated that six out of ten farmers in Bida employ wage-labour. Though I should regard this estimate as much too high it is significant for the outlook of the urban *bourgeoisie*.

work, and whose relations also assist him in this work as messengers and the like.

The labourers are all young men, mostly the sons of farmers, but occasionally also sons of impoverished *bourgeois* families (one of the labourers on my list was the son of a Mallam, another the son of a Bida *saraki*). Some labourers come from far away to the place where they expect to find employment: thus I found a young man from Lapai working in Jebba, and one from Bida working in Ilorin. Their working day is from early morning till about 4 o'clock in the afternoon, that is, the normal working day of the *efakó* worker. They get 2d. or 3d. a day and food; they work mostly for from four to ten days, some for a longer period, till they have collected a substantial sum of money. In no case has wage-labour in Nupe become a permanent, exclusive occupation. These young men seek only temporary employment and return after or in between their engagements to the family farm, where they carry on with the ordinary work of the season. Even a temporary absence of this kind may, of course, render the management of the family farm difficult and even precarious. For instance, the labourer from Lapai whom I have just mentioned, was working in Jebba as late as June, and could not return home before July when all the early planting and weeding would be completed. However, the need of money seems to outweigh all other objections. The main motive in undertaking wage-labour is invariably to obtain money for tax—either for oneself or as contribution to the parental household; next in importance is the motive to obtain money for bride-price.

It must be said in conclusion that though wage-labour represents a comparatively recent growth in Nupe society, the situation which created the need of wage-labour is not. Nor is the system of employed, i.e. non-family, labour the product of a recent development. Part of the social stratification of Nupe was, as we have seen, the creation of an upper class which owned land but did not work it. The labour which this class had to employ was of three kinds: slave labour, the labour of pawns, and, to a lesser extent, of clients. The first and the last kind of employed labour, both involving a social and political significance far beyond the aspect of labour, we have discussed already in a previous section. The second kind—labour of pawns—we will discuss later when analysing the concept of wealth.

DIVISION OF LABOUR BETWEEN THE SEXES (I)

The role which the women play in the agricultural production of the country lends itself to a simple formula. With very few exceptions the women do not perform any primary productive activity: they do no farm-work; they do not help in cultivation except occasionally when assisting the men in the harvesting of cotton or beans or the digging out of cassava—the easiest crop of all. Their sphere of work is, first, the 'refining' of agricultural produce to make it marketable, and secondly, the marketing itself. If the general formula is simple, the details of the division between 'primary' and 'secondary' productive activities, one assigned to the men and the other to the women, are involved and intricate. We will discuss them here only in so far as they refer to the household arrangements and leave the discussion of marketing proper for later.

The most elementary 'refining' process in this respect is the cooking for the household. In our general description we have reached the point when the various crops from the family farm have been harvested and stored. From these stores the family head will hand out regularly a certain amount to the wives for cooking. The arrangement varies with different crops: grain and beans, for example, are dispensed by the family head as a rule once a week or once in ten days; yams are brought in from the farm (where they are stored) about twice or three times a week, in the case of a family of three or four adults four to six yams each time, i.e. a supply sufficient for from two to three days; rice, the most expensive of all foodstuffs, is handed out only for the day when it is needed for cooking. The women plan the meals, but the men being in charge of the stores always know beforehand what they are going to have; occasionally they even order the 'menu' for the day. The amount of food which the men allow for cooking is adjusted to the exact require-ments: for example, if the men are having their midday meal on the farm, where they cook their own yam or cassava, they will hand out a proportionately smaller supply of yams, two or three, for the house, which must last for three days. In the town and among non-farmers the family head gives his wife or wives money for buying the necessary food about once in a week or ten days. The family head, however, does not provide for all meals, nor for every foodstuff needed in the household. He contributes food only for the main meals, midday and evening meal, and then only the bulk of the meal: grain, yams, rice, fish, and meat. Of other ingredients such as pepper, okra, or certain greens, he provides only those which he has grown himself. Other even most essential in-gredients the wife must invariably procure herself—even though they may have been obtained from trees growing on the land of the husband—namely, *kula* (made of locust-bean), *kuka* (made of the leaves of the baobab tree), palm-oil, shea-butter, and also salt. These things the wife has to buy in the market with her own money. Unless food has been left over from the night before, the morning meal consists mostly of corn-water or gruel, sometimes eaten with ground-nut or bean pastries, and is made of foodstuffs invariably supplied by the women. They will share the morning meal with their husbands, but will only sell it to the other members of the household, even including the children, for whose meal their father has to pay. Pastries and savouries are always made of foodstuffs which the women have to buy with their own money. They are then sold, and with considerable profit, in the markets or streets, except the titbits which a mother will always put aside for her children. If the husband feels he would like one of these delicacies he has to buy it, either from his wife or some other woman pastry-cook.

The Nupe women have also other, more important, sources of income which more than balance the financial obligations which they have to undertake in the household arrangement. The services of the women are indispensable, and are accordingly rewarded in the disposal of crops intended for marketing. There are various methods in the disposal of crops. One is the following: the family head hands the produce he intends to sell over to his wife, either the whole produce at once, immediately after the harvest, or small quantities at different times, according to whether he is in need of ready money or can wait for a better price later in the year. His wife will then sell the produce in the market and return the money she received for it to the husband. He gives her a little of this money, half as present, half as commission. His gift varies with the price which she has managed to obtain, and will express his appreciation of her more or less clever marketing. The woman may, of course, have to try a good many different markets if she wants to obtain the best price; and the men may not always be in a position to check the price which their wives quote to them after the sale. My information is that the women do not hesitate to take advantage of this lack of control; but the men, it seems, are as well aware of this and regard it as a legitimate way of making money. Another method, possible only if the women have sufficient money in hand, is this: the family head sells the whole produce directly to his wife after the harvest. She pays for it, stores the produce in her own granaries, and sells it later in the year when prices have gone up, possibly in small quantities at a time to obtain the best price. This method is as a rule applied in the disposal of palm-kernels and the fruits of the locust-bean tree. Another method in the disposal of crops does not enlist the help of the women of the house—although it may have to enlist the help of other women in the person of the traders. It is limited to a few kinds of produce only: rice, kola-nuts, and also palm-kernels in case one's own wife is not an expert in oil-making; these goods are sold by the family head directly to professional traders.

So far the role of the Nupe woman—more precisely the wife of the Nupe farmer—is that of a 'broker' and 'middleman'. In the disposal of the produce of certain fruit-bearing trees, however, the women are assigned direct and absolute property rights. The fruit of the locust-bean so far as it has to be plucked from the tree is disposed of in the way described above; but the fallen fruits of that tree belong entirely to the women of the house. They can do with them what they like, and the money which they obtain from the sale of the raw as well as the 'refined' produce belongs to them. Also, the whole produce of the shea-nut tree belongs to the women. The exploitation of the shea-nut tree, the fruit of which is of comparatively high commercial value, is regarded as a definite monopoly of the Nupe women, and as representing a direct compensation for their contribution to the expenses of the household.

The picking of the fruit of the shea-nut tree by small groups of women also furnishes an example of a co-operative organization among the women beyond the single household or family, somewhat similar to the system of collective labour organized by the men. There exists another form of collective female labour which is regarded by the people themselves as the exact counterpart to the men's *egbe*. As the men, in *egbe* work, build or repair houses and roofs, the women's collective work is employed in the beating of the floors of the huts or the platforms in front and between the huts. This work is done in the evenings, when the women have finished their own housework. It has all the elements of the *egbe*: the generous meal awaiting the workers, the singing and dancing— the beating itself is done rhythmically, to the accompaniment of songs (no musical instruments are employed in this or in any of the women's dances), and in its movements the motions of work and dance are attractively combined. The group of women fills the hut to overflowing. They are arranged in concentric circles, pressing closely against each other. Bent low over the floor they beat the ground three times with the heavy wooden flail which they hold in their right hand, then pull themselves up, lift both hands in the air, and take a measured dance step towards the centre and back again, and then bend down once more to resume the beating of the floor. Or they fill this rhythmical pause in the work with the verse of some interminable song, and while singing they move a few steps along in the circle; when the moving ring comes to a halt they bend down to their work, to interrupt it once more in the rhythmical motion of this 'ring-dance'. Nor is the incentive of competition absent in this *egbe* of the women. House-groups compete with house-groups; girls of different age are assigned different tasks: small girls of 6–7 are working slowly and silently on the outskirts of the group; girls of 12 or so are singing with the women and work towards the inside, trying to emulate the speed and ease of the grown-ups; and the adult women, leading in dance and work, spur their teams to almost breathless speed. As they work and dance, closely packed into the small dark hut, stripped to the waist, their bodies glistening with sweat and spattered with mud, beating, singing, stamping, and shouting, they seem to be actors in some exciting savage ritual rather than in ordinary work.

To return to the more prosaic aspects of the division of labour between the sexes, and to the question of the 'compensation' for her contributions to the household which the exploitation of shea-nut trees allows the Nupe woman. The clearly defined attitude of the people with regard to this question of 'compensation' and the economic rights of the women in general is illustrated in the following example. We remember that the roast-ovens in which the shea-nuts are dried before being marketed or manufactured into shea-butter are built by the men. Now, in Leaba I found that the women had to dry shea-nuts in the sun, a much slower and more laborious procedure, as all their ovens were dilapidated and sadly in need of repair. I inquired why the men did not build new ones. The men explained they had no time and money. I suggested, half jokingly, that the men might be given a share in the profits made on the shea-nuts and in return repair the roast-ovens. Whereupon the women, realizing that their own special interests were involved, joined in the discussion, which is interesting enough to be given here word for word.

Women: 'Why should we give the men part of our money? Do we not cook porridge for them?'

I: 'But he gives you the grain for making the porridge.'

Women: 'Yes, but *only* the grain. We have to contribute *kula, kuka,* salt, pepper and palm-oil.'

I: 'Surely you have locust-bean trees and red pepper in Leaba?'

Women: 'No, there are no locust-bean trees here, nor pepper.'

One woman: 'This is not true, we have pepper.'

Another woman (rather defiantly): 'Well, there still remains salt, *kula*, and palm-oil for which we, the women, have to pay.'[1]

---

[1] Another example of the clearly defined economic rights of the women is this: in the Nupe communities in the forest groves on the Niger, where there are no shea-nut trees, the banana is the property of the women and supplies them with fruits which they can dispose of in their own right.

CHAPTER XIV

INDUSTRIES
ORGANIZATION OF CRAFT-GUILDS

IN the Western world Nupe native industries would fall under the heading of 'home industries'. They are carried out in the home, or in workshops connected with the home, and their labour organization is to a large extent composed of members of one household or a number of related households and families. All the industries are carried out by men. But we find a certain differentiation with regard to the organization of labour, between industries carried out in individual work and industries based on co-operative group production or, in other words, between individual crafts and guild-organized crafts. For the co-operative organization is of a specific type. It represents a closed group, the membership of which is to a large extent hereditary in a number of families; outsiders can join it only through a formal adoption into the profession, after a period of apprenticeship. The group, moreover, is defined not only with regard to the productive pursuit but also socially and politically, as a specific social group, almost an artisan class, which enjoys official recognition and certain political privileges. Its internal organization, finally, is marked by a certain hierarchy of grades and ranks. These crafts thus present a picture closely resembling the organization of craft-guilds in Imperial Rome and the Middle Ages.

Of the native industries in Nupe the following are organized in craft-guilds: blacksmith work and the mining of iron ore; the craft of brass- and silversmiths; glass-making; weaving; bead-work; building; wood-work and carpentry; and, lastly, the profession of butchers. Tailoring and embroidery, leatherwork, indigo dyeing, straw-hat-making, mat-making, and basketwork are practised as individual crafts. The majority of Nupe crafts, especially guild-organized crafts, are concentrated in the town. But even where these crafts occur both in town and village (as in blacksmith work and weaving), they appear in their most typical form only in Bida, and are indeed symptomatic of the civilization which evolved in the capital of the kingdom. I cannot attempt here to describe in full all these native industries, neither from the technological point of view nor with regard to the details of their organization. I shall deal only with the most typical and, sociologically, most significant crafts.

It will be best, however, before entering into the description of the various crafts, to anticipate certain general features common to all of them. I have called their productive organization 'co-operative group production'. But co-operation in these crafts exists in two different forms and on two different levels: we have, first, co-operation of the group at large, i.e. the guild or guild section; and, second, co-operation in the narrow sense, i.e. the actual working together, of the individual labour-unit. We shall leave the description of the former to the sections dealing with the various specific industries and concentrate here on the latter, narrower, group co-operation. We shall see that it varies widely in scope and closeness, owing partly to the different nature of the productive technique and the varying demands upon co-operation which it entails, and partly also to extraneous factors, not involved in productive technique. The labour-unit in craft-work is called *efakó*, i.e. by the same name as the labour-unit in farm-work, to which, in fact, it corresponds in all essentials. Again we find a section of the family group working together under a senior relative who, as the common head, directs group co-operation, supplies the means of production (tools and raw material), and disposes of the proceeds from the group work. He also undertakes the other *efakó* obligations of paying tax for his co-workers, providing them with food, clothing, and bride-price. At the death of the *efakó* head the group member next in seniority takes his place. If old age disables the *efakó* head for active work he can retire from the labour-unit without giving up his position as the head of the group, i.e. without abandoning his control over the group income. Old men who have not reached the position of an *efakó* head when they are forced to retire will be supported by the labour-unit. The old men of the group are, moreover, often allotted a little farm-work close to the house, which allows them to make their contribution, even in old age, to the group income. We can see already that the ability of the group to 'pension off' their old men and late leaders depends essentially on the size of the labour-unit; a very small labour-unit is clearly incapable of making the necessary provisions, and we shall find that in the case of these labour-units the support of the old men is undertaken, rather irregularly in fact, by their family as a family obligation, and no longer forms part of the regular services of the labour-unit towards its members or ex-members.

With regard to the junior *efakó* members we find, again, the practice of releasing from the *efakó*-unit adult workers who desire to make themselves independent and to set up a separate labour-unit. The question always entailed in the release from the labour-unit, namely, of the acquisition of new means of production, is complicated in craft-work by the fact that here the means of production are to some extent immovable (e.g. the blacksmith's furnace and anvil, the glass-maker's furnace, the weaver's loom, &c.). It appears to be due to this difficulty that the release from the labour-unit in craft-work does not invariably involve withdrawal also from the workshop in which these means of production are fixed, but that, on the contrary, there is the tendency to stay on and share workshops, furnaces, and so forth, with the ex-fellow-workers. Only if the workshop is overcrowded will the worker or workers who are leaving the *efakó*-unit look round for another place, for example, a vacant furnace in another workshop, or the entrance hut of a compound, or (more rarely) build themselves a new workshop, with the assistance of family and fellow craftsmen. The withdrawing workers will be allowed to take with them the (movable) tools which they had been using, and will also be supplied as a rule, by the old *efakó* head, with raw material for the start. This setting-up of independent workers is in craft-work as in farm-work the last act of the functioning *efakó*.

The co-operative organization of *efakó* work also enables the group to train its adolescents and to bring them gradually into the system of co-operation. Young boys are employed first in easy auxiliary work, such as working the bellows in blacksmith and glass-work, or the spooling of cotton thread in weaving; sitting all day long in the workshop they learn a good deal from watching; when they are old enough they are given more serious work, which they carry out under the guidance and tuition of the *efakó* head till, eventually, they become fully fledged members of the labour-unit. In most cases the *efakó* work is supplemented by special individual, *bucá*, work. The relation between the two varies widely, with the specific nature of the craft and its productive technique.

BLACKSMITH WORK

The blacksmiths are called *tswata* in Nupe, or sometimes *tswata gbagba*, 'heavy smiths', to distinguish them from the *tswata muku*, the brass- and silversmiths. Nearly every village in Nupe possesses at least one or two blacksmith workshops. In Bida we find three groups of blacksmiths, whole blacksmith 'wards' in fact, each with its cluster of workshops, and each situated in a different *ekpã* of the town. According to tradition the three blacksmith groups are of different origin. One, in the old centre of Bida, *ba nîn*, claims descent from the original group of blacksmiths which was established in Bida when it was still a Beni village. At that time the head of this group, the *Majî Tswata*, the Master of the Blacksmiths, is said to have held authority over all the blacksmiths of Beni country. The blacksmiths living in the *Etsu* Masaba quarter, the smallest of the three groups, came to Bida comparatively late, from Trans-Kaduna. The largest blacksmith group in Bida, in the *Etsu* Umaru quarter, traces its descent to the blacksmiths of Rabá, the former capital of the kingdom. They came to Bida together with the king and court when Bida became the new capital of Fulani Nupe. As we shall see later, this last group has established itself as the supreme guild authority over the blacksmiths of Bida and all Nupe. The craftsmen of this group call themselves *dokodzaži*, after their head, who bears the title *Dokodza*.[1]

Technology

The blacksmith wards of Bida are of very different size; the smallest contains two workshops, the largest seven. In some cases the entrance-hall of the compound in which the families of the craftsmen are living serves also as workshop or forge. But usually the forge is in a separate hut which stands by itself a small distance from the compound; with its three or four wide doors, and the many small window-holes let into the wall to serve as passage for the smoke from the forge, the workshops can be easily identified. Inside are two furnaces, each screened in by an angular mud wall, about 3 feet high. On the inner side of the screen, facing the open fire, sits the blacksmith himself; on the other side of the

---

[1] It is interesting to note that the modern Emirate of Patigi, where the descendants of the old Nupe dynasty are reigning to-day, also possesses its group of 'royal blacksmiths', under another *Dokodza*. They came to Patigi together with the family of the present rulers, from Gbara, the ancient residence of this branch of the Nupe dynasty.

screen another man is sitting, who works the bellows. The bellows are
of the split-bag type common in Northern Nigeria; they are made of two
bags of goatskin which end in a clay tube and are worked with sticks fixed
on the top of each bag. The clay tube is buried in the ground and, passing underneath the screen, ends in the shallow furnace on the other side.
In this furnace charcoal is burned, which the blacksmiths make themselves. They also forge their own working tools (apart from a few
European tools, hammers and files, which have strayed into some of the
blacksmiths' huts): a club-shaped hammer, a long pair of tongs, and a
few chisels and pointed rods. The anvil, too, is of their own production;
it is a solid piece of iron, shaped like a toadstool, the foot of which is
buried in the ground. Of other working implements there is a bowl of
water in which the red-glowing iron is tempered, and a heap of fine
ashes in which the finished product is left to cool.

The technical process is simple. The bulk of crude iron is held over
the fire until it becomes red hot and pliable. It is then placed on the anvil
and gradually hammered into shape. The change from furnace to anvil is
repeated several times, until the object has been given its final shape.
Sometimes it is finished off with the help of files and chisels. The main
products of the Nupe blacksmiths to-day are blades for hoes, bush-
knives and crude axes, big nails and hooks for the big plank doors of
the Nupe houses, and small brackets used in canoe-building. Sometimes the blacksmiths also make the wooden handles for hoes and axes;
sometimes the customers prefer to buy only the blade and to make their
own handles. One man, I found, can produce two hoe-blades a day,
working from 9 a.m., with a pause for the midday meal, till 4 p.m., when
the Nupe working-day finishes.

Iron-work thus involves four subsidiary forms of production: the
manufacture of the bellows, of charcoal, of the tools, and finally of
the raw material used in blacksmith work, i.e. the mining of iron ore.
With the exception of the last all are undertaken by the blacksmiths
themselves. The blacksmith buys the goatskins on the market and sews
them together into the skin-bags used as bellows; he also produces the
mouthpiece of clay for the bellows. Ordinary tools, such as hammers
and tongs, are made by every worker individually; should it become
necessary, however, to replace the anvil, the whole group of blacksmiths
in the quarter (forty in all) would have to work together.

In charcoal-burning two or three men who share the same workshop
work together, and produce a store which is to last the whole workshop
for some time. Charcoal is burned in a clearing in the thick bush at
some distance from farms and habitations. Wood of two different kinds
may be used. Pieces of timber of about arm's length are piled 3 feet
high. A thick layer of grass is placed on the top, and the whole heap
is covered with sand, leaving only a small hole open. A dry piece of
wood is lit and pushed into the opening to kindle the fire inside, after
which the hole, too, is covered up, and the heap is left to burn for five
or six days.

The production of the raw material of blacksmith work deserves
special description. Formerly all iron used in blacksmith work was

mined and smelted in the country. The production of native iron ore
has been greatly reduced in recent years. To-day a large proportion of
the crude iron is bought from the European stores—the Nupe call it
kansana, 'dry iron', to distinguish it from the native mined *nyenkpa žiko*,
'black iron'. The competition of cheap European iron has made the upkeep of the large native foundries unprofitable; many have been
abandoned and allowed to fall in disuse, and even where they are still in
use only two or three out of perhaps six furnaces are still workable. But
in the busy season, shortly before the rains, when everybody needs hoes
and axes, the supply of European iron frequently runs out, and the
resulting shortage has to be relieved by calling on the supplies of native-
mined iron ore. Nupe iron-smelting can, in fact, no longer meet heavier
or more regular demands, although many Nupe farmers still prefer a
hoe made of native-mined iron—it is stronger, and lasts better, they say;
European iron is fit only for repairs, for patching hoe-blades, &c. The
tools of the blacksmiths and, above all, the anvil, are invariably made of
native-mined iron.

The iron-ore miners, called *edudaciži* (meaning 'workers in the deep'),
form a professional group distinct from the blacksmiths, although some
of them are blacksmiths as well as iron-ore miners. The mining is done
on the slopes of the low flat-topped ferriferous hills of the country. I have
heard of five different mining places: near Mokwa, near Shari, near
Patigi, near Kutigi, and near Pichi (about 8 miles from Bida). I have
seen only two; one in work, though on a reduced scale (near Pichi), and
one abandoned (near Shari). The iron-ore foundry near Pichi is the
largest in existence. Like the blacksmith groups in the districts round
Bida the iron-ore miners of Pichi submit to the authority of the guild-
head of the blacksmiths in Bida. His authority goes so far that, five
years ago, he could order two additional furnaces to be built in order to
increase the Bida supply of iron ore; these new furnaces, however, are
no longer in use.

The ore is scratched off the surface of the hill or dug out of shallow
pits. Close to the hill-side are the furnaces in which the iron ore is
smelted. Three furnaces are placed side by side under a large grass roof
which protects workers and 'machinery' from sun and rain. It will be
best to describe the very elaborate arrangement by means of two dia-
grams, the first of which represents a bird's-eye view of the furnaces, and
the second a vertical section through a furnace. We have first, a large
pit, 6 feet square and 6 feet deep. On one side a pot for water is let in
the ground; on the other the furnace proper is erected. It consists,
above ground, of a kind of chimney (*a*) made of thick clay, 5 feet high,
built over the mouth of an airshaft (*b*) which serves both as ventilator
and as opening for the fuel and the iron ore. On the other side of the
chimney are the two bellows (*c*), clay tubes formed somewhat like horns,
the wide mouth of which is covered with goatskin. The narrow bottom
ends of the bellows tubes are joined, under ground, with a long straight
clay tube (*d*), a little over 5 feet long, which is fixed in position by means
of wooden wedges. It opens into a cave-like space which forms an extension of the square pit. On the bottom of this space the iron ore is

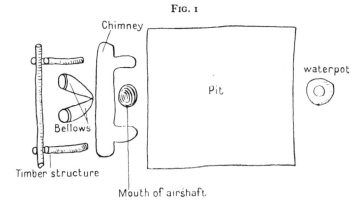

FIG. 1

Chimney

waterpot

Pit

Bellows

Timber structure

Mouth of airshaft.

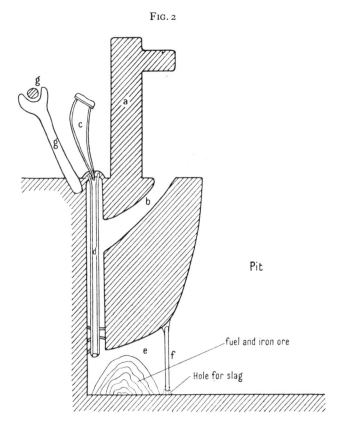

FIG. 2

Pit

fuel and iron ore

Hole for slag

placed, with charcoal piled over it. The 'cave' (e) is connected, by means of a narrow airshaft, with the mouth of the chimney (b). Cave and square pit are separated by a semi-circular clay plate (f), 1½ feet high, which is cemented into the opening so that it leaves only a small triangular hole open at the bottom. Through this hole the slag pours into the pit. One worker sits on a crude wooden bench which is supported by a timber structure (g), behind the bellows; he is relieved every hour. Other workers, two or three in number, act as stokers, feed the furnace with fuel and iron ore, and remove the slag by means of a long wooden stick with iron points, so that the small hole in the clay plate should be kept open. The iron ore is broken into small pieces by means of stones or hammers before it is placed in the furnace. The smelted ore remains behind the clay plate until the whole process is finished; then the clay plate is broken and the iron removed. The clay plate has to be made new and fixed in position every time the furnace is put to use. With the furnace all prepared, a lump of iron of the size of a large yam fruit can be produced in five to six hours' work.

We have already seen that the organization of blacksmith work and iron-ore mining (as of all guild-organized craft-work) involves two different types of co-operation, the actual working together of the labour or *efakó*-unit, and the wider co-operation in the framework of the occupational unit, the guild itself. We will examine first the composition of the labour-unit.

The men whom we find working in the same workshop are all related and belong to the same family group or section of the family group. The common workshop does not, however, invariably establish the labour-unit; the workshop group is the wider unit, for the men who occupy the same workshop are not necessarily also co-workers in the narrow sense. The labour-unit itself corresponds to the small individual family or section of the family—a father and his sons, or a number of brothers, who divide all work among themselves and in certain respects share the proceeds. All more important work is regarded as *efakó* work, i.e. the family head buys the raw material and receives the proceeds from the work carried out by his group. Less important work, mainly small repairs of hoes or axes, is regarded as *bucá*, and the money received for it belongs to the individual worker. Only adults, however, practise *bucá* work; small boys who are yet too young to carry out serious blacksmith work are assigned the work of blowing the bellows. In workshops where there are no young boys, the adult workers may take the bellows in turn; occasionally a woman, the wife of one of the blacksmiths, may help out.

The relation between these various units, workshop group, family group, and *efakó* group, is involved and variable. It will be best to illustrate it with actual examples. The first two are taken from the largest blacksmith group in Bida, the *Dokodza* people. In one of their workshops we find two adults and two boys working together—the boys blowing the bellows. They all belong to the same family and live in the same house. The two adults are brothers, and the two boys the sons of the elder brother. The four workers form a single labour-unit, under the elder of the two brothers, who is *efakó* and family head in one. His younger brother practises *bucá* work in addition to the family work. In another smithy (the smithy of the guild-head himself) we find five men sharing the workshop. They belong to the same family and live in the same house; their common family head is the *Dokodza*, the guild-head. The workshop group is divided into two labour-units. One, consisting of three men, is headed by the *Dokodza*'s younger brother, who works together with his two sons; the other, consisting of two men, the sons of the *Dokodza*, is headed—nominally—by the guild-head himself; being an old man he leaves the actual work to his sons. Each of the workers also has his own *bucá* work.

In the other blacksmith groups, especially in the villages, we find a more loosely knit co-operative organization with much smaller labour-units. In a workshop of the Beni blacksmiths in Bida I found four men working together, two adult brothers and the two young sons of one of the brothers. The kinship configuration is thus the same as in our first example; but here the workshop group is divided into two labour-units, one formed by the father and his sons, and the other, a 'one-man-unit', by the man's brother. Among the Kutigi blacksmiths one workshop numbered four men. They were two brothers and two more distant relations (a father's brother's son and a father's brother's grandson). The workshop was divided into four labour-units, each man working on his own. It will be seen that in these last two examples the division between *efakó* and *bucá* work has disappeared.

In addition to the craft the blacksmiths as a rule also practise a little agriculture on the farm-plots close to their houses, where they grow a few crops 'for the mouth'. These farm-plots are tended mostly by the old men of the family, who can no longer carry on the heavy work in the smithy. The crops belong to the family head, and are regarded as *efakó* property.

Blacksmith work, closely associated as it is with the requirements of agriculture for which it produces the main tools, is subject to the same market fluctuations. It has its busy season in the early rains, and is slack during the dry season. From December to February, the quietest season of the year, one smithy in Bida was producing four hoes a month; other workshops were doing only minor repairs. For two months, during the planting season (May and June), the same smithy turned out four hoes a day. At that time of the year the blacksmiths lay in a large store of hoe- and axe-blades, which is quickly disposed of in the village markets, while during the dry season they must often send their wives to the surrounding villages and hamlets to find customers for their products.

Let us examine the question of profits and cost of production. A blacksmith buys, for example, a lump of iron ore for 2s.; this quantity is sufficient for the making of six heavy or ten light hoes, which he sells at the price of 6d. and 1s. a-piece respectively, exclusive of the handle (which would be another 1½d.). On one hoe he makes a profit of between 2d. and 3d. In the busy season, when the blacksmiths have their hands full with work, the prices go up. A hoe which would be sold for 6d. in the dry season fetches 8d. in the rains, and one that would be sold for 1s.

SILVERSMITH

BLACKSMITH

in the dry season will sell for 1s. 4d. in the rains. In these two busiest
months of the year, then, the profits of the blacksmiths may be as much
as 7d. on every hoe, or over 1s. a day (one man can produce two hoes a
day). The blacksmiths of the *Dokodza* group in Bida seem very satisfied
with their economic situation. But the blacksmiths in the country, and
also the blacksmiths of the other, smaller, guild sections in Bida, are
bitterly complaining of the decline of native blacksmith trade. Some of
these country blacksmiths have turned farmers, or have at least taken up
farming on a larger scale than formerly, in order to balance the losses of
their industry. This retrograde movement is due to a variety of causes.
One which has affected all blacksmith groups in the country equally, is
the competition of European trade. Thus the Nupe blacksmiths have
lost almost their entire trade in bush-knives to the European trading-
stores; nor does the once very extensive trade in Bida hoes which the
Hausa caravans used to take north exist any more. The iron smelters
have suffered most severely under this competition. As we have seen,
their work has been almost completely disorganized under the pressure
of European competition. Other causes affect the blacksmiths in the
country more than in the town, and smaller groups more than larger.
The scarcity of money among the peasants has forced certain farmers in
Kutigi, for example, who were unable to pay in money for the hoes
which they needed, to offer a half-day's work on the farms of the blacksmiths in lieu of payment.[1] Closer intercourse and the increased facilities of transport between town and country have also deflected some of
the former custom of the village blacksmiths to Bida, where, owing to
the presence of the European trading-stores, there is less danger of a
shortage of raw iron occurring in the busiest time of the year. A final,
more subtle, cause of the decline in blacksmith trade, which attacks
smaller groups more severely than larger, lies in the failure of the
former to meet successfully the demands of what we have called 'maintenance of labour'. This influence will become clear when we examine
the second aspect of co-operation in native industries, namely, the co-
operative organization of the professional group at large.

Guild Organization

The term 'guild' is applied correctly only to the Bida blacksmiths,
whose organization shows the characteristic features of the guild system
—the closed profession, centralized control, the hierarchy of ranks and
grades. However, the individual blacksmith groups in Nupe, in Bida as
well as in the villages, are all modelled on very similar lines—although
the guild sections in Bida are organized on a larger scale, and also more
closely and efficiently. Moreover, the control of the Bida guild system
extends in certain respects over the whole country and the various independent local blacksmith groups. This widest professional unit is the
result of political rather than economic factors; it is expressed mainly in

[1] Prices in the country are higher than in Bida. In Kutigi a heavy hoe is sold
for 1s. to 1s. 6d. The difference in price seems chiefly due to the fact that the
Kutigi blacksmiths must obtain their iron through middlemen who bring it from
Bida, as there is no European store in the village.

the allegiance to a common head, the master of the *Dokodza* section in Bida. As this group of Bida blacksmiths is associated, historically, with Nupe kingship its head also holds his rank and position by appointment of the king of Nupe. The *Dokodza* claims that the blacksmiths in the whole of Nupe 'must obey him' in all matters concerning the profession. As an external expression of this allegiance he receives annually, at the occasion of the Great *Sallah*, a gift of crude iron ore from the various blacksmith groups of the country. Although this gift has now been abandoned the village blacksmiths still acknowledge (at least in theory) the supreme position of the guild-head in the capital, and never fail to pay their respects to him when they are in Bida. In return they count on his help and influence if they are in need of official intervention in the capital or at the court. The closeness of the co-operation under the guild-head, and the efficiency of his control over his fellow craftsmen, increases with the nearness to Bida, till, in the town, it takes the form of guild organization in the strict sense of the word.

The most effective unit, however, is not the guild at large, but the single guild section. The people of each group are of one *dengi*, one kinship group, related both by descent and frequent intermarriage. Every male born into the group is expected to become a blacksmith—'how can he become anything else', said my informants; 'we know no other job'. But, on the other hand, they would maintain that no man from outside could become a blacksmith. When I asked the *Dokodza* people why this should be so, they answered with a laugh: 'How can anyone who was not born a blacksmith become one?' Nevertheless, in another part of the town I discovered a man who, born of a family of traders, had adopted the profession of a blacksmith. He seemed to have been a rather more unruly youth than the rest of the family; for he had firmly declined to become a trader, like them; he had first studied the Koran and thought of becoming a Mallam, but later changed his mind, and decided to become a blacksmith: he 'liked it better' than either trading or studying. Certain maternal relations of his were Beni blacksmiths in a village near Bida. There he went, stayed with them for some years till he had learned the trade, and then returned to Bida, where he is now keeping a little workshop of his own in the entrance hut of the house of his paternal relations. Among the Beni blacksmiths in Bida I was told that formerly apprentices were taken regularly. The pupils came mostly from villages near Bida, and returned to their home as fully fledged craftsmen. The training took from three to five years, during which time the apprentice lived in the house of his master. No money was taken for the tuition, but after the completion of the apprenticeship the parents of the pupil sent a present of food and kola-nuts. Adoption into the profession went hand in hand with adoption into the guild, and the new craftsman would regard himself as a member of the guild section in which he was apprenticed. However, there have been no adoptions into the craft for many years now.

Each guild section has its own titled head and, besides, one or two other ranks which are bestowed on the family heads of the other large family groups in the section. The position of the head of the guild section is taken in rotation by these families, the 'second-in-command' succeeding to the position of the head at his death. Among the *Dokodza* people we find a threefold elaborate hierarchy which settles the succession even to the rank of the 'second-in-command': *Dokodza, Dokpa,* and *Shaba Dokpa* (lit. Successor of *Dokpa*). The smaller blacksmith section of the Bida Beni possesses two ranks: *Majï Tswata* and *Shaba Tswata.* The blacksmith groups in the villages, and also the groups of iron-ore miners, have similar rank systems.[1] The heads of the blacksmith groups, and to a lesser extent the other guild ranks, are respected, and their orders are obeyed by all co-workers. The main significance of their position lies in the fact that it is their task to organize all co-operative work within the group.

Co-operation and mutual assistance within the section takes many different forms. If the people of one workshop, for example, are unable to fulfil a certain order, they pass it on to another workshop; or if the occupants happen to be absent when a customer calls, their neighbours will always be ready to take the order on their behalf. When the workshops ran short of iron ore, the guild-head used to send messengers to the iron-ore miners to bring back a sufficient supply for the whole group; this form of co-operation, however, no longer exists, and to-day each workshop procures its own raw material. Co-operation of a more far-reaching order is concerned with the various tasks which we have placed under the heading of 'maintenance of labour'. We have already seen that these tasks involve co-operation and mutual assistance on a scale which transcends in varying degree the *efakó*-unit. Thus the division of labour in the preparation of charcoal implies co-operation of the whole workshop group. When it becomes necessary to forge and put up a new anvil an even larger group must co-operate in active work. We may add that the upkeep of the workshop itself, or the building of furnaces—especially the large furnaces used by the iron-ore miners— demands a co-operation much larger than that which the *efakó* group can provide. In none of these cases is the co-operation recompensed with a share in the profits (as is the case in *efakó* co-operation); nor is this co-operation organized on the basis of collective work of the *egbe* type; nor can it be explained, finally, by the fact that the co-workers may belong to the same family and household. Rather is it a co-operation based on membership of the same professional union—the guild or guild section—and mobilized by the appointed head of the group.

The head of the guild section is also responsible for maintenance of labour in a wider sense. His professional advice may be sought by all workers in the group if they have some difficult or unusual work in hand. He will also occasionally lend his people money if they need it for professional purposes (e.g. the purchase of crude iron ore), in other words, he provides them with the necessary working capital. Certain similar services towards the group are vested in the position of the *Dokodza* alone, that is, of the head of the guild at large. He arbitrates in all internal disputes among the blacksmiths of Bida, and is thus able to

[1] See chart of Village Ranks, p. 57.

prevent friction in his body of workers. He is also the agency through which important large orders reach the group. On a smaller scale this task also falls to the heads of the other blacksmith groups. But in the case of the guild-head it gains special significance; for these 'royal blacksmiths' worked for the largest customer of the country, the Nupe court. They could be certain of a constant large demand, e.g. for tools for the farm-hands working for the king, or various iron implements needed in the royal household, for horse bits and stirrups for the king's horses, or flint-locks for the guns of the bodyguard. These orders are given by the king or court officials to the *Dokodza*, who then distributes the work among the craftsmen of his group according to their capacity and skill, or, if the order proves too large, among the workers in other guild sections as well. The *Dokodza* also receives the payment for this work, and keeps the largest share; the rest of the money is divided equally among the whole guild section, whether they have been working on this particular job or not.[1] These royal orders have been greatly reduced recently, not only because many of the implements needed are obtained nowadays from the European stores, but also because many of the requirements of the royal household are now catered for by the Public Works Department in Bida. But when the present *Etsu* built his new house, in 1935, he ordered nails and brackets for all doors from the *Dokodza* people.

The part played by the guild-head (and to a lesser extent by the sectional heads) in providing labour and capital for his group explains the authority which he exercises over his fellow workers, and also his ability to act in certain circumstances as their 'financier'. On the other hand, the close co-operative organization of the guild section reveals itself as a device to meet these regular demands upon the production of the group. Here we can attempt to explain why the smaller guild sections in Bida (and similarly the village groups of blacksmiths) have suffered more severely under modern economic changes than did the *Dokodza* group. The size of the groups is itself significant. Only the privileged group of the 'royal blacksmiths' evolved a large-scale professional organization; the other groups, which did not have the same access to constant large-scale demands upon production, remained small, and more loosely organized. Now, we can assume that these smaller groups also obtained formerly a sufficient demand for their products from various sources. It may also be that their sources have failed sooner, and more completely, than the source with which the *Dokodza* people could reckon—the continued orders from the royal household are evidence of this. But these unequal changes are less significant in their direct effect upon production (which may be negligible)[2] than in their indirect effect,

[1] How, on the other hand, the authority of the guild-head can be adapted to new situations is illustrated in the following instance. When I went to inspect the furnaces of the iron-ore miners near Bida, I had to obtain a guide through the *Dokodza*. On our return to Bida the guide at once showed me the money which I had paid him to the guild-head; though he was allowed to keep it he could not have done so without first informing the guild-head, who could have deducted a part of the money.

[2] The order for nails and brackets for the royal house which we mentioned above brought in only 2s. and a gift of food.

through the medium of labour organization. The royal orders, though at present small and irregular, still mobilize the group organization of the *Dokodza* people in the traditional way. The general weakening of the guild organization brought about by recent economic and political changes, which is clearly visible in the decline of the authority of guild-head and sectional heads, has thus affected the largest and strongest group less than the smaller, and already weaker, guild sections. In their case the group organization has, in fact, been reduced beyond the margin of safety. We have seen that Nupe blacksmith work demands com-paratively large group co-operation for a successful maintenance of labour (in all its aspects). In a weakened organization, a markedly re-duced co-operative group, maintenance of labour becomes increasingly difficult. This is what happened in the case of the smaller blacksmith groups. And this difficulty, while not sufficient in itself to disrupt the labour organization, would yet weaken its resistance to the effects of economic change—a decline in trade, the competition of European goods—effects which (at least for the time being) have passed by the larger and more strongly organized section.

We can quote several instances of this: the division of labour which enables a workshop, say, of four men, to continue work while two of the men prepare charcoal is impossible in a small working unit, and a valu-able working day, possibly in the busiest time of the year, must be sacrificed. Or a workshop may have to interrupt its work when iron ore runs out and new raw material has to be fetched from the iron-ore miners—a task which, in large-scale co-operation, can be performed by one man for a number of workshops without deranging the work of the group. I have even witnessed cases in which work had been interrupted, or reduced to small repairs, because the workers had no money to buy raw materials; in a large co-operative group money would have been found more easily, especially with the help of the guild-head. In Kutigi I saw one of the two local blacksmith workshops left dilapidated for a whole year because the workers could not muster sufficient labour. The most conspicuous example of all is that of the iron-ore miners who had let their means of production, their furnaces, fall into disuse.

BRASS- AND SILVERSMITHS

The Nupe brass-smiths—*tswata muku*—reside almost exclusively in Bida. The only place outside Bida where brass-smiths have settled is Kacha, the rich trading-place, where these craftsmen from Bida hoped to find a profitable market. There are two groups of brass-smiths in Bida, one in the quarter of *Etsu* Masaba and one in the *Etsu* Usman quarter. The latter has lost its former importance. In technical skill both groups are equal, as I could test for myself; as regards work and design of the traditional type the group in the *Etsu* Usman quarter seems the more efficient. Yet its decline, unmerited though it was, is not difficult to understand. It was partly due to political factors. The group in the *Etsu* Usman quarter flourished during the régime of *Etsu* Bello, who was of the dynasty associated with this part of the town, and also under *Etsu*

T

Mohamadu before him, whose royal residence was not far from the brass-smiths' quarter. Here, as in many other instances, the invaluable royal patronage was extended primarily to the craftsmen living in the part of the town traditionally associated with the dynasty. With the change of the dynasty the royal patronage changed also, and under the late *Etsu* Saidu, of the house of Masaba, the brass-smiths in the Masaba quarter captured the largest and most lucrative trade. A contributory cause lies in the lay-out of modern Bida. The motor-road to the centre of Bida and the big market leads through the street of the brass-smiths in the Masaba quarter, while the other brass-smiths' group is situated in an obscure corner of Bida, away from roads and markets. Now, the brass- and silver-ware manufactured in Bida consists to a large extent of ornaments for men and women and other 'luxury' objects. A large proportion is intended for export, and certain goods are even made specially for tourists and European 'curio'-hunters. In either case the nearness of the big trading centre and the main thoroughfare of the town, with its opportunity for display and for attracting customers, must prove an advantage which is denied to the other, almost inaccessible, group of craftsmen.

The character of this luxury industry also explains its concentration in Bida. Its products find their way to villages and peasant districts as well. But a constant and large-scale demand exists only in the capital. Moreover, the concentration of this industry is, in sophisticated Nupe, a trade-mark of refinement and value, and a guarantee that its products express the latest fashions.

The technical equipment of the workshop of the brass-smiths differs in certain important details from that of the blacksmiths. The workshops of the brass-smiths, with their smaller and less smoky furnace, are more often housed in the compound itself, i.e. in the entrance hut. The tools are less heavy and adjusted to the finer technique. European hammers, chisels, and files are used to a much larger extent. The main products of the Nupe brass industry are sword-hilts and daggers,[1] horse-trappings, bowls, jugs, trays, ladles, and receptacles of various kinds, made mostly of beaten brass or copper; bangles and rings, which are cast in open clay moulds of bars of brass or silver or (nowadays) aluminium and then bent and twisted into shape; also hairpins and silver chains. Artistic decoration, especially ornamentation of the surface of these various objects, plays an important part. From old Nupe brass- and silver-work preserved in Bida and in European museums we learn the different styles in decoration which have succeeded each other in the course of the last hundred years. The style in fashion to-day is ornamentation in *pointillé* technique.[2]

The Nupe brass-smiths also practise soldering with tin, and one or

[1] The blades are old, mostly of German or Austrian manufacture, and have been traded for centuries to Nigeria and Nupe, across the desert, from North Africa.

[2] The oldest style appears to be a fluted design which I have seen on certain brass bowls; a later style which flourished at the end of last century, consisted in embossed ornaments which made special use of the flower motif. The *pointillé* style appears to have come in about 1910.

two have specialized in repairs of watches, sewing-machines, and such-like. They also practise a crude technique of *cire-perdue* casting. This technique is applied in the making of a kind of signet-ring, very popular both among men and women, and, by one expert, in the making of small brass figures of animals, which have become quite famous in Nigeria. These figures are traded by many of the itinerant Hausa traders and are bought by Europeans who take them for products of an interesting indigenous art. I cannot prove with certainty that these little figures— *zasâgiži*, as the Nupe call them, 'likenesses of man'—have never had a deeper significance. But I am inclined to think that they have not. They have no place in Nupe culture as it presents itself to us, either as re-ligious symbols or as symbols of wealth (in which form similar figures are used, for example, in Dahomey). I know, moreover, that in the case of the one expert who produces these figures to-day in Bida it was his own enterprising spirit that made him adopt and develop this (for a time at least very profitable) 'tourist industry'. To examine the cultural channels through which the suggestion of this production, the artistic *motif*, has reached Bida, is not part of my present task. I have, however, been able to trace two objects produced by this expert brass-worker to their original source. It is a case of what ethnographers call 'culture borrowing', and is sufficiently interesting to be quoted here. This brass-worker had for some time been producing 'dancing figures', little human figures which, by a clever utilization of stable equilibrium, were made to revolve and 'dance' on a small brass stand without falling off. He got the idea for these figures from a travelling Indian trader, who had shown him pictures of the model and explained the principle to him. He had paid the Indian 2*s.* for the 'lesson' and then proceeded to manu-facture similar figures himself. The same brass-worker also produced the figure of a cobra of typically Indian design, which he had copied from a figure he had seen in the house of a European.

The raw material used by the Bida brass-smiths is all imported. The Nupe, it appears, never mined copper, nor knew how to produce the alloy. In pre-European days, I was informed, brass and copper were brought up the Niger from Onitsa and Lagos. To-day copper is obtained from English pennies, and brass from rifle cartridges which Hausa traders buy up in the garrison towns of Nigeria and then sell to the brass-smiths of Bida and other towns. Silver is gained by smelting down silver coins which the brass-smiths procure from a Kaduna bank.

A few examples may illustrate the relation between cost of material and the profit made on the finished article. Brass ladles, an article for which there is great demand in Hausa country, are sold for 3*d.* apiece; for one ladle the brass from twelve cartridge-cases is used, costing 1½*d.*; the brass-smiths can produce two ladles a day, thus making a daily profit of 3*d.* Silver bangles are sold for 12*s.* a pair; the cost of the material is 10*s.*, and the working time from two to three days, allowing a daily profit of 9*d.* to 1*s.* Aluminium bangles, which are made to cater for the cheaper tastes, are sold in large quantities to traders and middlemen; half a dozen, which can be produced in one day, are sold for 2*s.*; the material (bought in sheets at the European store) costs 1*s.* 6*d.*, and the profit per day is thus 6*d*. The little brass animals, four of which can be done in from one to two days, are sold for 2*s*. to 3*s*. apiece; the material comes to only 8*d*. The highest profits are thus made on work that demands special skill, taste, or invention, such as the silver bangles or the brass figures.

Among the brass-workers as among the blacksmiths three or four men, often close relations, share the same workshop. But it happens not infrequently that people who are not relations work together in the same workshop, or that close relations work in different workshops. These are typical examples:

1. In this workshop three old men are working together, two of whom are brothers, and the third a distant relation who lives in a different household.
2. Here we find two distant (maternal) relations, who live in different houses, sharing the same workshop together with a young boy who is the pupil of one of the men.
3. This workshop is next door to 2. In it are working the two brothers of one of the men in workshop 2 together with another man, a distant relation, and a young pupil.
4. This is the largest brass-smith workshop in Bida. It belongs to the head of the guild section, and is shared by the guild-head himself, who, however, does not work there regularly, his two married sons, a married younger brother, and a stranger.

The labour-unit is much smaller than the workshop group, and also smaller than the labour-unit among the blacksmiths. Grown-up or married sons or brothers invariably work on their own, so that the working-unit consists as a rule only of a man and a boy, or frequently of one man only. Thus workshop 1 numbers three one-man labour-units, workshop 2 two labour-units consisting of one man and of one man and his pupil, respectively. In workshop 3 we have three labour-units, two consisting of one man and one of a man and a boy, and in workshop 4 five one-man labour-units. In these small labour-units the difference between *efakó* and *bucá* work must naturally disappear. The explanation for the smallness of the groups lies in the very nature of brass-smith work. It requires much less actual co-operation than the heavy work of the blacksmiths—in most cases, for example, the brass-smith blows the bellows himself. Brass-smith work, with its delicate technique and the large variety of objects which it produces, is also more highly specialized. Certain objects, such as bangles and ladles, are produced by all brass-smiths; but workshop 1 specializes in addition in sword-hilts and daggers; in workshop 2 one of the men produces the brass figures of which I have spoken; the men in workshop 3 are experts in the repair of sewing-machines, and so forth. A craft, finally, which follows fashion so closely and is always on the look-out for new attractive things must foster individual skill and inventiveness rather than collective enterprise.

The guild organization at large also differs in certain essentials from that of the blacksmiths. The training of apprentices plays a much greater part in this prosperous and up-to-date industry. The training is longer and may take up to ten years. After the completion of the period of training the new member of the profession joins one of the workshops in the quarter, while continuing to live in the house of his family. Large-scale co-operation is also of much less significance, since the furnaces are simple and easy to build, since no heavy anvils are used, and the forges mostly situated in the entrance hut of the house. The varied enterprises, and the spirit of 'individualism', render the advice or practical help of the guild-head less important. His organizing influence, however, is still an important factor. When, for example, the Bida brass-smiths first began to produce goods for Europeans, the guild-head took it upon himself to propagate this new profitable enterprise, and at the same time to assist the craftsmen in perfecting their technique. A District Officer who was a keen supporter of native arts and crafts had explained to him the kind of things that Europeans would buy—trays, ash-trays, finger-bowls, and suchlike. The guild-head himself led the way in the new production, and devised a system of guidance for his fellow workers. You can still see scratched into the mud wall of the guild-master's workshop circles, ovals, and squares of different size, which are the outlines of the objects the craftsmen were going to produce; they served as standard measures, and are indeed called by the Nupe *ema*, measure.

There are two ranks in the brass-smith guild, each presiding over one section: the guild-master, called *Muku*, and the 'Successor of the *Muku*', the *Shaba Muku*. They are the heads of the two large family groups which are said to have been the earliest representatives of the craft in Nupe and to which most of the brass-smith families trace (at least in theory) their descent. The two ranks are taken in turn by the two family groups. The present guild-master, a very old man, is living in the brass-smith group in the *Etsu* Usman quarter; the *Shaba Muku* is at the head of the more prosperous section in the Masaba quarter. With the growing prosperity of this guild section the authority and influence of the old guild-master have declined, and to-day the *Shaba Muku* is the more influential person. Even the most successful and most 'individualistic' young brass-smiths who have created their own special style treat the head of their guild section with the respect due to his position and experience.

Here, as in blacksmith work, the most important service which the guild-master renders his fellow workers is that of acting as an intermediary between the craftsmen and the court. Here, too, the king of Nupe places all his orders through the *Muku*, who then distributes them among the different workshops. The large orders of former days, for arms, sumptuous horse-trappings, ornaments of many kinds, have disappeared. The costly ornamented bowls, used formerly in every Nupe household of consequence as drinking-vessels or receptacles for food and kola-nuts, have been replaced by enamelled teapots of European or Japanese manufacture. But on a limited scale the court is still the most important customer of the Bida brass-smiths. To recall themselves to the king and to solicit his custom the brass-smiths make him an annual gift of products of their craft which is presented to him at the occasion of the Great *Sallah*. The present which the brass-smiths presented to the new *Etsu* at the first *Sallah* celebrated under his reign was, not unnaturally, especially costly. It was in form of a brass tray for kola-nuts which had been made in the workshop of the *Muku* himself and to the cost of which (6s.) every brass-worker had contributed his penny or halfpenny. The *Etsu* accepted the gift with thanks and sent a return gift of a large bowl of kola-nuts (worth 10s.), which was distributed among all the brass-smiths of the town. If here the organizing influence of the guild-master becomes again visible, the 'individualistic' element is present also. For, in addition to the collective gift, individual workers are free to send their own personal gifts and to attract the attention of the court to their own particular style and skill. Thus one of the Bida brass-smiths presented the *Etsu* at the Sallah with a covered brass bowl, worth 3s. He was rewarded shortly afterwards, when the *Etsu* placed an order for new horse-bits, in European style, with him.

GLASS-WORKERS

The glass-worker guild represents the most strongly organized and most conspicuously self-contained of the Nupe craft-guilds. In the whole of Nupe there exists only one group of glass-workers, the *masagá*, who live in Bida, in a separate quarter of the town which is named after them *masagá fu, efu* (quarter) of the glass-workers. They regard them-selves almost as a distinct tribal group. They have a tradition that they came originally from Egypt, and brought their art with them from the old home. Their tradition has also preserved the names of the various towns and countries through which they passed on their long journey which took them, eventually, to Gbara, the ancient capital of Nupe kingdom.[1] They had stopped at none of these many towns and villages as they could not find there the kind of earth necessary for the making of glass. They settled then in Gbara, where, as their tradition has it, they arrived at the time of Tsoede. Later, when the kings of Nupe moved their residence to other places, the glass-workers followed the court, to Jima, Lade, Rabá, and, finally, Bida.

The *masagá* obtain their raw material both by making their own glass and smelting down bottles of European manufacture. The latter kind of raw material, easy to obtain, and more attractive because of the variety of colours which it offers, has to a large extent replaced the original native-made glass.[2] Bida women, wives of the *masagá* as well as women from outside, regularly scour the town for empty bottles from European stores, households, offices, and dispensaries (where they can obtain the highly appreciated amber-coloured medicine bottles). Bottles of various kinds from other parts of Nigeria also find their way to the *masagá* quarter, bought up locally and transported to Bida, partly by railway, by the enterprising women traders.

The *masagá* nevertheless still produce their own glass as well. A

[1] My informants mentioned the following towns and countries: the 'land of the Arabs', the 'land of Bornu', Kano, and Zozo (Zaria).
[2] The actual cost of production is lower in the case of native-made glass. But this fact is balanced by the time-saving made possible by the use of bottle glass and also by the greater demand for coloured glass-ware.

certain type of glass, black in colour and of rather crude texture, which is bought widely in Nigeria, is made exclusively by the traditional method. I have had opportunity of studying this traditional technique of glass-making—a technique which is kept a secret by the glass-workers and which has never yet been recorded. Several writers on Nigeria, in fact, maintain that it has long since fallen into disuse and is even no longer remembered by the people. This native glass is called *bikini*, as against the glass gained from smelting down bottles, the name for which is *kallaba*, 'bottle'. The process of glass-making is long and complicated; it takes from three to five days according to the quantity of glass made. The glass can be made in the ordinary glass-maker's workshop, but the furnace must be re-dug especially for the purpose, since the furnaces used normally for glass-smelting are too wide and too shallow. The same men who ordinarily work in the workshop also carry out the making of glass. The glass-maker's workshop is built somewhat like the Nupe smithy, but has only one round furnace in the centre of the hut. For the purpose of glass-making the furnace is dug 5 feet deep and 2 feet wide. Throughout the process its mouth is covered with potsherds and broken calabashes which leave only a narrow passage for the smoke. As good Mohammedans, the *masagá* invariably start their glass-making on Friday afternoon, after their return from the mosque. The various ingredients have been collected and arranged inside the workshop: earth (the same earth that has been dug out of the furnace),[1] soda (*kanwa*) of the kind that is brought by Hausa caravans from Lake Chad, water in pots, and a vast quantity of firewood. The soda, which has been pounded to a fine powder, is mixed with sand and a little water till it gains a mud-like consistency. The mixture is placed on the bottom of the furnace, with firewood and a layer of grass for the lighting of the fire on top. The fire is lit, and the furnace is kept ablaze, day and night, till the process is finished. The men work in shifts so that there are always four workers tending the furnace; adding fuel, and occasionally probing the bottom of the furnace with long iron rods. The heat is so intense that the workers have to put up mat screens as protection. Six or seven hours after the lighting of the furnace large quantities of water are added, together with a handful of slag from a blacksmith's forge. After another twelve hours the substance in the furnace becomes liquid, *ke nuwā na*, 'like water', and after eight hours again the process is completed. The glass, a red-glowing semi-liquid mass, is fished out with long iron sticks and left to harden and cool on the sand outside. The cooling takes five to six hours, after which time the glass is ready for use in the other furnaces, where the finished products—bangles and beads—are manufactured. The colour of the raw glass is a deep glossy black. The *masagá*

---

[1] The sand is called *jikana*, which is the Nupe name for ordinary sand. The glass-workers informed me that the sand everywhere in the locality was suitable for glass-making. When I returned from Nigeria I brought with me samples both of the Nupe glass and the ingredients used in glass-making. Thanks to Professor Seligman the Courtauld Institute in London undertook to test the glass and the glass manufacture, by attempting to produce glass from these ingredients. The attempt was fully successful. For a fuller report on this experiment, and also on the technique of Nupe glass-making, see *Man*, 1940, 107.

have never possessed the art of colouring their glass. They have to do it indirectly, by mixing it with coloured bottle-glass. They also ornament their dark glass with dots, lines, and circles in various bright colours: the red colour is obtained by smelting down thin iron sticks, other colours by smelting down coloured glass or coloured glass beads (Venetian beads mostly).

Glass is, as a rule, made only in one workshop at a time, while the other workshops carry on the ordinary routine work. Men from other workshops who need new glass contribute soda and sometimes also firewood (or else pay in money for their share in firewood), and receive a proportionate quantity of raw glass. They pay the men who were tending the furnace in kind, returning to them a small quantity of the newly made glass.

The further treatment of the raw *bíkini* glass corresponds in every detail to the treatment of bottle-glass, except that the latter has to be crushed into small pieces before being used. It is smelted down, again, over the ordinary furnace, until it is semi-liquid and can be formed into beads and bangles of different shape and size. This finished glass is called *karuwa*. The furnace in which the raw glass was made is later rebuilt and adapted for this new work. It is made a little wider, banked up with a mud wall 1 foot high, and provided with bellows.

Nupe glass-making implies a strict organization of work and a well-planned distribution of the various tasks among the whole community of glass-makers. The assignment of tasks varies from day to day, according to when a particular workshop has completed the work in hand. The *masagá* quarter numbers thirteen workshops, and each workshop performs its assigned tasks. In one hut you may perhaps find the making of *bíkini* glass going on, while in another molten glass is formed into black bangles; in a third workshop coloured bangles are manufactured, or small black beads; another workshop, again, may specialize in blue and red beads that day, and so forth. The workers, four to six in number, sit round the furnace. One of them, as a rule a small boy, is blowing the bellows. The raw glass is thrown into the furnace, where it is left to liquefy. The glass-worker sticks small lumps of the semi-liquid glass upon the point of a long thin iron rod. Gripping the rod in his right hand, he holds it over the mouth of the furnace and, while the glass liquefies further in the heat, he rotates the rod rapidly, throwing the glass lump with quick, calculated movements into any shape he wants. A second rod, held in the left hand, helps in the process, and is used to produce the width of the bangle or to tap a bead into shape. In the single workshop the work is, again, carefully divided up: while one worker prepares the liquid glass, another shapes it into bangles or beads, and another adds the coloured ornaments.

The scheme of collaboration may change from day to day; every worker, frequently even including the man or boy at the bellows, is, in fact, a fully fledged all-round craftsman. The trained worker performs his tasks with ease and rapidity and, thanks to the smooth co-operation between the workers, the whole workshop equally maintains a very high speed of production. It takes one worker between three and four minutes to produce a medium-sized bangle; I estimated the total daily output of a single workshop at from fifty to sixty bangles.

The finished articles, the coloured and ornamented bangles and beads, are left to cool in a heap of ashes inside the hut to be collected later in large baskets and to be put aside for the traders who call regularly at the *masagá* quarter. The glass-workers have a small but busy market of their own in the centre of their quarter. To this market the traders in bottle-glass bring their goods, women from neighbouring hamlets and farms the daily supply of firewood, and other women traders grain and various food-stuffs for the households of the glass-workers. The traders in the finished article, however, buy the bangles and beads directly from the producers, i.e. the individual workshop. These traders are both men and women and, among the women, both wives of the glass-workers and women from outside. The *masagá* themselves never trade their glass-ware. Bida glass is bought and sold all over Nigeria—it is to be seen in every larger market of the country, in Lagos in the south, and in Kano in the north. There is a steady demand for it, and the *masagá* work regularly six days a week (resting only on Friday), all through the year, always certain of disposing easily of their output. They have neither time nor inclination for additional agricultural work, not even in the restricted form of farming 'for the mouth' which is common among all other Nupe craftsmen.

The people who work together in the same workshop are, as in the case of blacksmiths and brass-smiths, mostly close relations. But among the glass-workers the group which shares a common workshop also forms a single labour- or *efakó*-unit, working under a common head who organizes the group work, disposes of its output, and, in *efakó* manner, controls the income produced by the group. Even distant relations or strangers who have joined a workshop fall under the *efakó* rules. The labour organization of the *masagá*, then, does not allow for an individual *bucá* income in addition to the group income. Instead we find a new arrangement in the form of small regular 'wages' (at the rate of 2*d.* a day) which the *efakó* head pays his adult co-workers out of the income produced by the group. He keeps the rest and, with it, defrays the costs of production, i.e. the costs of fuel and raw glass or the occasional purchase of new tools from the blacksmiths, as well as the various family expenses entailed in his position as *efakó* head. This financial arrangement is clearly necessitated by the special conditions of labour: it would indeed be extremely difficult to calculate the share of the individual worker in this strongly co-operative form of production. The intensive co-operation itself is explained by the nature of this 'mass production' and by the demands of efficiency and economy: the use of a common furnace and a common store of fuel and raw material, the specialized tasks of the individual workshops and, in the single workshop, the elaborate division of labour, are all calculated to ensure a high degree of efficiency and economy. We note that the means of production are partly produced by joint labour (e.g. the building of the furnace), and partly purchased by the leader of the labour-unit out of his share in the group income (e.g. the iron tools, the fuel); and we note further that this method of production, which, in the interest of efficiency, has evolved centralized control of labour and means of production on a comparatively large scale, comes closer than any other Nupe craft to the principle of the modern factory system.

We have already seen that in the group at large, i.e. in the glass-workers' guild, a similar intensive co-operation obtains. Its organization falls to the guild-head, who assigns the different tasks to the various workshops and is responsible for the general planning of production. This planning must take into account the varying conditions of the market, and we find, in fact, that the guild-head, without interfering with the commercial transactions of the individual workshop, regularly consults traders and middlemen who visit the *masagá* quarter, and maps out accordingly the scheme of work for his community. On my many visits to the *masagá* I found that the guild-head could always tell me what kind of work was carried out in the various workshops, or when a particular workshop would start on a new task. The guild-head, who styles himself *Masagá*, has his own workshop, where his sons and brothers are working. He does not often work there himself, but certain difficult tasks, such as the making of very big, heavy bangles, which fetch the highest price, he alone can perform. The guild-head assists his co-workers with advice and practical help, also with small loans of money for the purchase of raw material or fuel; he arbitrates in internal quarrels, and he is, like all Nupe guild-heads, the accredited representative of his guild at the Nupe court.

The ever-expanding business of the Bida glass industry involves an almost permanent need of new labour. Formerly the glass-workers bought slaves and trained them in the craft in order to enlarge their machinery of production. To-day they are regularly accepting apprentices. In 1936 five young men were being trained as glass-workers. An apprentice applies to the guild-head, who will then place him in charge of a certain workshop. The training is calculated to take three years, during which time the apprentices continue to live in their own homes and come to the *masagá* quarter only to work. But when their apprenticeship is completed they not only move into the *masagá* quarter, but are expected to marry *masagá* women (as did also the slaves in former days). This adoption into the kinship group is considered essential and is as much a qualification for the practice of the craft as is the technical training itself. Thus the monopoly of the glass-workers is kept intact, and no new branches can be established outside their organization. Kinship interests and kinship co-operation are enlisted in the service of professional co-operation and solidarity and in maintaining the continuity of a highly specialized, monopolized and almost secret, technique of production. Economic interests, in turn, are seen to be sufficiently powerful to effect a radical adjustment in the kinship structure, and to create, in a patrilineal society, a matrilineal enclave.

WEAVERS

The weavers, called *edeluciži*, present another instance of the tripartite organization of Bida crafts. Each of the three *ekpā* of the town harbours one of the three guild sections of the weavers. However, according to Nupe tradition, weaving was not originally a guild-organized craft, but a free profession carried out individually, like mat-weaving, for example, to-day. It became a 'closed profession' and a guild-organized craft when the Nupe kings imported craftsmen from the south, who brought with them their own special technique and who, aliens in Nupe country, kept to themselves, neither intermarrying nor coming much in contact with the rest of the population. These imported groups of weavers were *konú*, freed slaves of war. They form two of the three groups of weavers which we find in Bida to-day. The first is composed of people from Salu, a town in Yagba country, who were settled in Bida by *Etsu* Masaba. The members of this group, which is the largest of the three weaver guilds, live scattered over the whole town; their guild-head, however, used to reside in the *Etsu* Masaba quarter. The second *konú* group is of Yoruba extraction, and is concentrated in the *Etsu* Usman quarter. This group has representatives also outside Bida, in a number of Nupe villages: Kutigi, Enagi, Sakpe, and Dabbā. The third group of weavers, in the *Etsu* Umaru quarter, is composed of Nupe proper. It is a very small group, consisting only of one compound. This Nupe group of weavers forms a section of a large kinship group which comprises farmers, who live outside Bida, as well. They trace their profession to a man who came to Bida from Rabá, as a *bara* of *Etsu* Umaru. Originally a warrior, this man later settled in the town and learned weaving from a *konú* craftsman. At that time, I was told, weaving was a lucrative and highly respected profession. Weaving has been the profession of his family for three generations now, and the family heads are received at the court and treated as official representatives of their group like all heads of guilds or guild sections. Small groups of weavers of Nupe extraction are also found in various villages in the Emirate. Their labour organization closely resembles that of this last group of weavers, but they remain outside the Bida guild system.

The technique of weaving is the same in all groups. Their loom is of the narrow upright type, worked with pedals, which is common all over Northern Nigeria. These looms produce narrow strips of cloth 5 inches wide. The looms are placed in a half-open shed, six to seven in one row, in the inner courtyard of the compound, each loom being worked by one man. The weavers have to buy a large proportion of their tools from other craftsmen: the shuttle and the wooden posts on which the loom rests, and which are frequently beautifully carved and painted, are made by the carpenters; the iron rods used as pedals and the iron bar upon which the finished strips of cloth are wound, are made by the blacksmiths. Only the weaver's reed is produced by the weavers themselves. A complete outfit for one man costs from 6s. to 12s., according to whether cheap plain or expensive carved wooden posts are used. The Bida weavers use mostly thread of European manufacture, both plain and coloured, and only very rarely native-ginned and -dyed cotton. The village weavers use mostly the latter kind.

The men who occupy a common workshed are members of the same family and household group. In one house, for example, I found thirteen looms, of which only ten were actually used, as the family numbered at that time only ten adult men. The individualistic nature of this work, however, in which no actual working together of several individuals is involved, is reflected in the restricted *efakó* arrangement, which comprises only a man and his young, as yet unmarried, sons. As soon as the sons are married, they work on their own, although they may continue to use the looms and tools which the family head had allotted to them when they were still working in the *efakó* group. The *efakó* head also supplies them with cotton thread for the start. When they are fairly launched on their new individual work they have to buy their own raw material from the proceeds of their work. Only the looms are still regarded as family property, and are kept in repair or replaced if necessary by the head of the household. In this case the individual worker pays the family head a regular 'rent' (called *lada*, lit. wages) of 2*d*. in every 3*s*. which he earns with his work—an arrangement which clearly takes into account the high cost of new looms. This arrangement, however, has been dropped; the young workers make themselves responsible for the cost of repairs or the purchase of their means of production, and the family head only receives occasional presents of food and clothing. In a number of cases I found the *efakó*-unit still further reduced, and even unmarried sons working on their own as soon as they reached the age when tax had to be paid for them. The difficulty which many family heads have to-day in providing tax money for a large family explains this disintegration of the labour-unit. The steadily declining demand for native woven cloth has been the main cause. In many houses looms stand unused, because weaving is no longer profitable, and young men, released from the *efakó*-unit, use their newly won leisure to turn at least temporarily to other, more lucrative, professions. In one weaver's family one of the three sons had given up weaving and become a messenger in the District Office; in another family, two of the six sons became servants in houses of Europeans, and only one of the two returned to his old profession after a number of years, having collected enough money for his bride-price and for a new start in his former profession.

The individual weaver is free to plan his work independently, and there are a number of different methods which he can adopt. The long narrow strips of cloth which the Nupe looms produce are always woven to a standard length of ten *kpere*, i.e. arm's lengths, the weaving of which takes five days. The most expensive, striped, cloth is then cut into five strips of two *kpere* each and sewn together, edge to edge, to form the complete *ede*, cloth, of the kind worn by women round the waist or as kerchiefs over the head. It is reckoned that one man can produce three to four lengths every month. The Nupe weavers work every day except Friday, but much time is taken up in getting the cloth sold. A weaver can entrust his goods to one of the brokers who have their shops on the Bida night market; but nowadays this means a long wait—even if one is lucky enough to get the cloth sold at all. Many younger men prefer therefore to do their own trading, and wander through the villages, often for three or five days, selling their cloth in village markets where there is less competition both in native-made and European goods. One piece of

cloth of this expensive kind is sold for 4s. 6d.; as the cost of the material
is 3s. 4d., the profit made in five days' work is 1s. 2d., or just under 3d.
a day. If cheaper, plain material is used the profit is slightly smaller; the
cost of the material for one piece of cloth is 1s. 6d., and the cloth is sold
for 2s. 6d., six pieces being again produced each month, which gives a
profit of 1s. per cloth, or 2d. a day. But instead of cutting up and sewing
together the cloth in form of the *ede*, the weaver can also sell the full-
length cloth as such to the cap-makers, or, better still, can make it into
caps himself. A weaver can produce one cap (made of one *kpere* of cloth)
each day, that is, twenty caps a month, allowing for two intervals of five
days each for the weaving of the cloth. The white cloth caps, called *fula*,
are very popular in Bida and are sold at prices from 9d. to 1s.; the cost of
the material being 6s. 8d. the profit on twenty caps is thus between 7s.
and 12s., or from 3d. to 5d. a day. It is interesting to note that this last
kind of work, although more profitable and also in much greater demand,
is nevertheless regarded as a slightly degrading occupation. *Fula* making,
my informants pointed out, is tailor's work, and not the proper work for
trained weavers; they undertake it, as they frankly admit, only in order
to obtain money for tax or bride-price. In this respect, then, the dissolution of the *efakó*-unit offers another benefit to the young members of the
group who are out for quick money: for, relieved of their duties towards
the head of the group, they are also relieved of their duties towards the
ethical standards of the profession, to which the older men still cling.

In the villages only cheaper qualities of cloth, mostly native-dyed
cloth, are produced; striped cloth which is sold for 1s. 3d., the material
costing 9d. and the dye 3d., and plain indigo-dyed cloth (a kind of cloth
that would find no buyers in Bida), sold for 1s. 9d., and produced at a
cost of 1s. 3d. But even when the village weavers produce the same
kind of cloth as the Bida craftsmen, they sell it cheaper, being content
with a smaller profit. Thus striped cloth of the kind sold in Bida for
2s. 6d. is produced by the village artisan for 2s., allowing a profit of 9d.
instead of 1s. 2d. On the other hand, the work and material of the village
weavers are known to be inferior to that of the Bida craftsmen. The
village weavers frankly admit it. They use the cruder indigenous dye
instead of European dyes, they gin their own cotton and work with this
inferior cotton-thread which breaks frequently during the weaving.
They take ten days for the weaving of a piece of cloth which the Bida
craftsmen finish in five. But just because they limit themselves to this
cheaper and cruder material and cater exclusively for the less wealthy
customers, they can stand the competition of European cloth better than
the Bida weavers, who have specialized in more ambitious and expensive
work. Here are the comparative prices: a striped cloth of European (or
Japanese) manufacture is sold in Bida for 5s., as against 4s. 6d. for Bida-
woven cloth and 1s. 3d. for cloth produced in the village.

Formerly, when the *efakó* system in weaving was still capable of supporting a whole family, the younger members of the *efakó* group practised a little farm-work as *bucá*. The family head did not join in this
additional work and often, if he was an old man, he did not even take
part in actual weaving. His income was supplemented by training

apprentices. This source of income, formerly quite considerable, disappeared when weaving became less profitable. Young boys of about 10 years, mostly sons of farmers, were the pupils; they stayed with the weaver for from four to five years, and the work which they produced during the time of their apprenticeship belonged to their master; when their training was completed the parents of the pupil would bring one bundle of corn as payment.

The loose organization of the labour-unit has its counterpart in the organization of the profession at large. Among the weavers no co-operation on a larger scale exists. We have even seen that individuals are quite ready to abandon the profession for other, more attractive, work—an attitude unprecedented among blacksmiths or glass-workers. Yet the symbols of guild organization, the guild ranks, are still preserved. Each group of weavers has its titled guild-head: the head of the Salu (Yagba) weavers is called *Majī*, and the head of the Yoruba weavers *Leshe*. He is also regarded as the head of all *konú* weavers in Nupe, and used to receive from them small annual gifts or tributes. But this common allegiance and co-operation reflects less the professional union than the tribal and cultural unity of these scattered Yoruba groups in Nupe country. The head of the Nupe group of weavers in Bida has no official title but is called simply *Ndakó*, Grandfather. The position of the group-head carries to-day none of the influence and authority which characterizes the guild-heads of other crafts; he neither receives gifts from the fellow craftsmen nor is he expected to advise or help them in their work. As in all other guild-organized crafts the official position of the guild-heads of the weavers was based originally on their role as intermediaries between the king and the craftsmen of Bida. But this role has lost very early all practical importance—earlier than it did in the other Nupe crafts. To quote the guild-head of the Yagba weavers: '*Etsu* Masaba still used to come to our workshops and order cloth personally from the *Majī*. But *Etsu* Umaru, who came after him, already bought what he needed on the market, and so did all the later kings of Nupe.'

BEADWORKERS

As a last example of guild-organized industries I will describe the organization of the beadworkers in Bida. Their craft shows certain specific features which make it specially interesting and distinguish it from the other crafts of Nupe. Beadworking represents, first of all, a typical refining industry, which involves a system of re-exportation comparable only to the most complex forms of economic enterprise found in Western civilization. It involves further the use of money capital and credit operations on a scale unparalleled in Nupe industry. It is, finally, a pure luxury industry, producing more expensive goods than either glass- or brass-work. These various factors have contributed to making the beadworking industry of Bida extremely vulnerable; it has suffered more than the other crafts from the economic stress of the recent years and, a significant result of this, presents the picture of a complete disintegration of co-operative production.

There are three groups of bead-makers, *lantana*, as they are called, in Bida, one in each part of the town. Their work consists in 'refining' the crude or plain beads which are brought into the country from the north by Hausa and Arab traders, that is to say, they polish and sometimes bore these beads and grind them to various new shapes. The grinding and polishing is done on large flat sandstones especially brought to Bida from the river Niger. The grindstones and a few small iron tools for boring represent all the utensils used by the beadworkers; they are comparatively cheap—the grindstones are sold for 1s. in Bida—and the full equipment of a worker costs not more than two or three shillings. The beads are finished in different styles according to the nature of the bead and also according to the prevailing fashion and the demands of the market. The following styles of beads are in fashion to-day: long slender round beads, used for the *egbogi*, the chains of beads which the Nupe women wear round the waist; small ball-like round beads, with highly polished surface; and small flat triangular beads, worn as necklaces. The Nupe dislike edged beads and beads with dull surface; beads of this kind are polished and ground down to the desired shape and appearance. The grinding and polishing of the beads is a long and delicate work. The average production per worker is three beads a day. The finished beads are strung on cotton thread and arranged in long chains in which beads of different kinds and styles are often mixed, and are then ready for the market.

The beadworkers have no special workshops, but carry out their craft in the entrance hut of the compound. Four or five men are working in one hut; each man works independently, sitting on the ground behind his grindstone. As in all other crafts, the men who share the workshop are usually close relations who live in the house of which the entrance hut serves as workshop. Occasionally there is a distant relation or a stranger amongst them who lives in another house and comes there only to work. More rarely an individual beadworker who has no relations practising the same profession would work alone in his own house. Traders and buyers, who bring beads to be polished or bored, or who collect the finished article, are constant visitors in the workshops of the *lantana*.

In the economic arrangement which obtains in the Bida beadworking industry the majority of workers are reduced to the position of mere labourers, working to order and paid at a piece-rate. One of the beadmakers in the workshop may act as contractor: he buys the crude beads from the Hausa or Arab trader and has them worked by his fellow workers. He divides the work among them and pays them ½d. per bead. The finished chain of beads is entrusted to the wife of the contractor; she will sell it in the market or to one of the traders in beads, who will then 're-export' these products of Bida fashion industry to the north. A chain of crude beads bought for 7s. will fetch 10s. as the finished article; 2d. to 3d. go to the woman 'middleman' as commission, and about 1s. 8d. (for a chain, say, of forty beads) goes to pay the wages of the labourers, so the contractor can make a net profit of 1s. 2d. on work that took three to four days to complete; the individual labourers make in the same time 5*d*. Evidently, only a man who possesses some capital can assume the role of contractor, and the ordinary beadworker can hardly hope, with his daily wages of 1½*d*., ever to attain this position. In a few cases I have found two contractors in the same workshop; but many other workshops numbered no 'capitalist' among their workers. In a situation of this kind two other methods are open to the beadworkers: either they buy the crude beads on credit from the traders and pay them back after they have sold the finished article; or they undertake the 'refining' work on a piece-contract for a trader in beads—the Hausa or Arab trader, or sometimes a 'capitalist' woman of the beadworker's family. In neither case does the work of the beadworkers include *efakó* work, even on the smallest scale. All work is done individually, and even unmarried young men are working on their own, being assigned by the contractor a task suitable to their skill and experience. The beadworkers, finally, do not practise farming in addition to the handicraft.

Formerly it was the family head and, on a larger scale, the guild-master who assumed regularly the role of contractor and financier. As in all other crafts the guild-head made himself responsible for 'maintenance of labour' in the group, which means that he undertook to provide the necessary working capital and credit and to distribute the work effectively among the craftsmen. The guild-head, called *Majï*, Master, also acted as the agent of the king in all matters concerning the trade in beads. When the foreign traders in precious stones arrived in Bida, they would not take their goods at once to the public market, but would show them first to the guild-head of the *lantana*, who would select what he needed, and what he thought suitable for the king and court. He would take the collection of newly arrived beads to the king and advise him on the purchase; then, receiving the order for the 'refining' of the beads, he would distribute the work among the workshops of the *lantana* paying the workers the usual piece-rate and keeping a large commission for himself. The constant demands of the court—the requirements of the fashionable ladies in the harems of Nupe royalty, bride-price and dowry (of which chains of beads form an essential part) which the king pays for innumerable relations and dependants—kept the beadworkers of Bida busy. Orders amounting to £5 and more at a time, which secured the *Majï* a commission of £1, were by no means rare. The profits made in this fashion enabled the guild-head to finance the ordinary work of his group and to offer them credit for the purchase of their 'raw material'. In these times of prosperity the individual worker who desired to act himself as contractor could without difficulty obtain large credits (up to £1 or £2) from the Hausa bead traders. The guild organization and the strong financial position of the guild-head were evidently regarded as sufficient security.

All this is a thing of the past. The court no longer buys beads from the beadworker guild. European beads, cheaper and much more attractive in shape and colouring,[1] have crushed the native industry. With the decline of the financial position of the guild-head, outside credit

[1] Some of the European beads which are sold in the markets of Nigeria are, in fact, specially manufactured as copies of the native style.

has also disappeared. The result is a complete disintegration of the guild system. The guild-head, no longer able to act as financier and contractor, has lost his position of authority; as his contribution to the productive organization of the group was concerned exclusively with these financial and credit operations, the very *raison d'être* of a guild-head has disappeared. This is evident in the manner in which the *Majī* is treated by the other craftsmen; no one pays the slightest attention to him. Since he is too old now to earn money, he is supported by his son —but this is entirely a family matter, and in no way concerns the professional group at large. He receives no gifts or shares in the profits, not so much as an occasional present of kola-nuts, which even in the greatly weakened guild organization of the weavers still marks the privileged position of the guild-head. If I have called this change in the productive organization of the beadworkers a decline and disintegration, it is also felt as such by the people themselves. To them, it appears as the sad decline of a once highly respected and well-organized craft: as one of them said, 'the beadworkers to-day live from hand to mouth; their *Majī* has no longer any authority; theirs is an unlucky trade' (*gwa ši*, lit. an unlucky hand).

CHAPTER XV

INDUSTRIES (continued)

INDIVIDUAL CRAFTS

THE guild-organized crafts represent, as we have seen, a specific social group or class—the class of skilled artisans—which only occasionally enlarges its membership by adopting individuals from other professional or social groups. The individual crafts, on the other hand, present a vaguely defined and ever fluid group which recruits itself from every stratum of Nupe society, the peasant class as well as the 'intelligentsia', slaves and clients as well as members of the nobility. We shall see presently that men of the titled classes who have lost their former sources of income frequently adopt an individual craft as a new means of livelihood. The technical conditions which contribute to make the guild-organized crafts into 'closed groups', organized on the lines of more or less intensive co-operation, are absent in the industries which are carried out as 'free professions'. Tailors, straw-hat makers, or mat-weavers need no workshops; they can work anywhere, in any part of the house, in sleeping-huts as well as in a corner of the *katamba*. Some craftsmen even wander from place to place and practise their work wherever there is a prospect of trade. Many Bida tailors, for example, have made a practice of visiting neighbouring villages on the market days or at the time of the annual ceremonies and festivals, when they can be sure of finding plenty of work. Nor does their work involve co-operation, or necessitate the use of expensive tools. Mat-weavers work with their hands, straw-hat makers use a block of clay or wood (called *ekugi*) over which they shape the crown of the head, a tool which they can easily make themselves. Tailors, embroiderers, or leather-workers need, in addition to the material, only needle and thread.

Although there exist, specially in Bida, experts in these crafts who practise them as their only profession, the technique itself is simple enough to be learned by anyone in a very short time. We remember the farmers who carry out a handicraft as *bucá* work in their spare time. People in the town similarly practise these handicrafts as leisure-time occupations, in addition to other work, or as a lucrative pastime. Many learned men and students of the Koran do a little tailoring beside. Embroidery, a more delicate work, involving taste and a certain skill, has become the pastime occupation of many members of the 'intelligentsia'. Of hat-making, on the other hand, the Nupe say that it is the ideal occupation for 'lazy people', who can do nothing else, meaning particularly those impoverished 'people of quality' who are neither skilled nor resourceful enough to find other means of livelihood.

The varied demands of the Nupe markets have also called into being various other, minor, handicrafts, some of which are so easy that young boys of 10 or 11 are encouraged to take them up as a first *bucá* occupa-

tion, for their pocket-money. For example, a father would give his boy
2d. to buy cotton-thread which the boy would then plait into trouser
strings and sell for 3d.; or boys work thin strips of leather into the
lacquered amulet strings which the Nupe wear round the neck, making
again a profit of 1d.

A few examples may illustrate the economic scope of these handicrafts. Straw hats are made of narrow strips of plaited grass, sewn together in spirals. The making of a good straw hat takes from three to
four days if the hat-maker buys the plaited strips of straw ready-made,
and five days if he plaits them himself. A plain hat is sold for 4d. to 6d.,
the material costing between 1d. and 2d. A more expensive type of hat,
in which part of the crown is covered with leather-work, is the product of
two craftsmen, straw-hat maker and leather-worker. A hat of this kind
sells for 1s. The Bida tailors produce a variety of goods: caps both plain
(machine-made) and embroidered; gowns, trousers, saddle-cloths. A
plain white cap is sold for 4d., the cost of the material being 2d.; a tailor
can produce four such caps a day. The embroidered caps are sold for 1s.,
the material costing 6d.; one cap is made in three days. Plain white
gowns, also machine-made, are sold for 7s. 6d., the cost of the material
being 5s.; it takes one or two days to make. A simple saddle-cloth takes
from three to five days to make; the cost of the material is 6d., and it is
sold for 1s. or 1s. 6d. A more elaborate cloth, embroidered and dyed in
various colours, takes twenty days to make; the cost of the material is 3s.,
and it is sold for 10s. An embroidered gown is made in fifteen to twenty
days. Embroidered Bida gowns are famous all over Nigeria; they are sold
for £3 to £5 in Bida, and for much more in the north. The cost of the
gown itself (which is made by the ordinary tailor) and of the material
used in the embroidery comes to between 15s. and 30s.; the profit of the
craftsman is thus between £2 and £3. But then, he may not be able to
sell a gown of this kind, or receive an order for an embroidered gown,
oftener than once a year.

We have already mentioned that certain villages, e.g. Kutigi, are
famous for their mat industry. Every man and boy in Kutigi works mats
in his spare time—and spare time here means just as much the leisure
season of the year as every hour that can be spared from farm-work.
When sitting in front of their houses in the evenings, even when walking
home from the farms, the people are working: they carry a supply of
dried grass dyed in different colours, in a kind of quiver under the arm
and, while they walk or talk, their fingers are busy plaiting the grass into
long, narrow strips. The strips are 3 or 4 inches wide, and up to 15
yards long. The Nupe make oval mats, in which the long strips are
sewn together in a multicoloured spiral pattern; or square mats, in
which the strips, cut to the same length, are sewn together edge to edge,
again in a multicoloured design. The Nupe also make square mats of
split sorghum and maize stalks, often dyed in red, yellow, and black,
which are harder of texture and have a glossy surface. The oval mats
take from five to seven days to make; the cost of the material—grass
brought from the river swamps (see p. 200)—and the dye is 5d.; the mat
is sold in Kutigi for 9d. or 10d., and in Bida, after it has passed through

the hands of a middleman, for 11d. or 1s. The square grass mats take ten days to make; the material costs 7d. or 8d., and the mat is sold for from 1s. 3d. to 2s. The mats made of stalks take a fortnight to make; the material costs nothing, as the stalks are found on the farm of the craftsman, and the dye is produced from the sorghum stalks; a plain mat of this kind is sold for 8d., a dyed mat for 1s.

If we reduce these various figures illustrating cost and profit to the average profit per day made by the individual craftsman (assuming that he is always working to full capacity) we obtain the following table:[1]

Commodity	Profit per day
Straw hats	1d.
Grass-mats, oval	1d.
Grass-mats, square . . .	1½d.
Mats made of stalk . . .	1½d.
Caps, embroidered . . .	2d.
Saddle-cloth, plain . . .	3d.
Saddle-cloth, embroidered . .	4d.
Caps, machine-made . . .	8d.
Gowns, machine-made . . .	1s. 10d.
Gowns, embroidered . . .	3s. 0d.

It will be seen that the Nupe price system is highly discriminative both with regard to the taste and skill needed in the production of a particular article and to the factor of risk involved in the production of more expensive and 'luxury' goods, the demand for which is less widespread. Hat-making, regarded commonly as the easiest craft of all, and at the same time a craft working for large constant demand, is remunerated most cheaply; the embroidering of gowns, which involves considerable taste and skill, and which can reckon only with a comparatively small and irregular demand, is remunerated most highly. This calculation of price and profit holds good similarly for the other products on our list. However, there are two conspicuous exceptions: machine-tailored gowns and machine-tailored caps command a price quite out of proportion with the other products of Bida handicrafts. We shall return later to this anomaly.

Even in these individual crafts we find whole families or household groups following the same profession. But just as often we find households in which three or four different professions are represented, and houses in which tailors, hat-makers, embroiderers, and, say, cushion-makers practise their craft at the same time, in the same *katamba*. In these crafts which involve no special training and in which the novice derives no special benefit from partnership with the more experienced older men, individual preferences have free play and outweigh possible tendencies to follow the example of one's family or one's elders. Bida

---

[1] At the time when these figures were recorded prices were lower than usual (see p. 292). The relation between the various prices, however, had remained unchanged. The profits quoted for mat-making in Kutigi supplement the statement made previously that mat-making represents a lucrative leisure-time occupation for the Nupe farmer. The demand for mats is, in fact, increasing, and latterly Kutigi mats have been exported to England through the United Africa Company.

men are always ready to try their hand at something new, and changes of profession are frequent. The record is held, perhaps, by a Bida man who started as a mat-maker (the occupation of his older brother), changed over to cushion-making, then to tailoring, and eventually to leather-work, which he found more lucrative and which he is practising at present. *Efakó* co-operation on the narrowest basis, between father and unmarried sons, occurs occasionally. Thus in a family of embroiderers a father and two sons worked together; working on the same gown, the father would execute the more elaborate designs, while his two sons carried out the simpler embroidery; the sons were maintained by the father, and all earnings went to him. With simpler kind of work, this co-operation is reduced further, and we find, for example, this arrangement between a father and his unmarried son, both straw-hat makers: the father took half of his son's earnings, and in return maintained him, and would in due course pay part of his bride-price (he would be unable to bear the full expense). But in the majority of cases this rudimentary co-operation, too, disappears, and even unmarried sons work entirely on their own.

One might wonder whether these 'individualistic' crafts have not, at some previous stage, shown a larger measure of co-operative organization. Remembering the weakening of guild-organized crafts under the pressure of modern conditions, we might, in fact, ask whether the individual crafts as we find them to-day do not represent merely a final stage of that incipient disintegration. This is indeed the case in one of the industries practised to-day as individual crafts—leather-work. Leather-work involves specialized technique and skill in much higher measure than do the other individual handicrafts. But it also used to involve comparatively large-scale co-operation of a group of workers, in the sense of an efficient division of labour, which was meant to ensure the execution of large and frequently urgent orders. A guild-head, called *Magajī*, organized and controlled group production; he also acted as the official intermediary between the craftsmen and the king, who was, again, their most important customer: for the Bida leather-workers supplied a large proportion of the military equipment of the Nupe army, such as saddlery and leather shields, sword-sheaths, and quivers for arrows.

The individual craft which is most a product of modern conditions is machine-tailoring. It introduces certain new features into the productive system of Nupe which are of special interest to the student of culture contact. Machine-tailoring does not demand long training or special skill—young men learn to use a sewing-machine in a week. The machine-tailor can reckon with a very constant demand for his services. The number of machine-tailors in Nupe has, in fact, greatly increased even during the periods which I spent in the country. In 1936, for example, I found six sewing-machines in Kutigi market, against three in 1934. Machine-tailors, like ordinary tailors, will regularly visit village markets (walking perhaps ten miles or more, carrying the sewing-machines on their heads), and appear in villages a fortnight or month before an annual festival, when their services will be greatly in demand.

They make as much as 1s. or 2s. on a market day; and shortly before the Great *Sallah*, for a week or ten days, they can reckon upon daily earnings up to 4s. Most machine-tailors do not buy their own material, but prefer to make up material brought by the customer, whom they charge a 'wage' (*lada*) of 2d. to 4d. a cloth. It is not surprising that the men who have taken up this most modern industry are mostly young men. They come partly from tailor families, but partly also—like many other 'free' craftsmen—from other professions and other social classes. The contribution of the 'gentry' is, again, considerable. Two of the five machine-tailors from Bida who are now working on the village market of Jebba Island are descendants of titled families.

You can buy a sewing-machine in Bida (second-hand or new) for £2 to £3. Some young men have themselves bought their own sewing-machines with money made in wage-labour. More often the sewing-machine is bought by the father of the young man (or occasionally his mother), who by this purchase sets up his son in an independent trade—as blacksmiths or weavers equip their sons with tools and looms to start them on their independent work. Unlike these craftsmen, however, the father of the machine-tailor may provide the machine before his son is married, and expect him then to find himself the money for his bride-price. The son who is yet unmarried may hand over a half or a third of his earnings to his father—but this is not a rigid rule. Married sons work invariably on their own; an occasional gift of five kola-nuts (never more) to the father is an act of filial piety rather than a recognition of 'business relations'.

The introduction of sewing-machines gives a new meaning to the question of maintenance of labour. Sewing-machines represent by far the most expensive means of production used in native crafts. They must occasionally be repaired, spare parts have to be bought, and eventually the whole machine will have to be replaced. The cost of maintaining these means of production seems more than balanced by the regular profits derived from the use of the sewing-machines. The question of obsolescence and replacement has not yet become acute. But already the problem of maintenance of labour in this new sense is felt. Blacksmiths and glass-workers, as we have seen, invest only a little money in their means of production—their main capital is labour. Weavers have to purchase looms and thus to invest a certain capital in tools; but specialized skill and training under experienced masters represent as much a 'working capital' as does loom or money. In machine-tailoring the money capital (the purchase money for the sewing-machine) represents the only investment of the craftsman; training and special skill are negligible factors. The money returns are, in fact, disproportionately high, measured by the traditional standards of skill or length of training. Here means of production and profit-bearing capital become one and the same thing. The machine must itself produce the profits out of which it will have to be replaced some day; and, through the medium of the machine, capital must reproduce itself, almost automatically. We discover, in a typical native home industry, the first traces of the modern industrial system.

MAT-WEAVERS ON THEIR WAY HOME FROM THE FARM

A MACHINE TAILOR

MEANING AND FUTURE OF GUILD ORGANIZATION

In examining the different industries of Nupe we have met with co-operative organizations of widely varying degrees of closeness and intensity. The individual crafts appear in this respect as one extreme, the zero point, as it were, of this scale of intensity of co-operation. What, then, are the conditions determining the degree of closeness in productive organization? Or, more specifically: Why are certain native industries guild-organized, and others left to independent individual enterprise? We can discover four conditions of the closeness of productive co-operation: (1) The nature of the productive technique and the measure of actual working together which it entails. In this respect the work of glass-makers and iron-ore miners must be placed at the top of the list, and the work of bead-makers or individual craftsmen at the bottom. (2) Special skill and experience involved in the productive technique. The glass makers, with their jealously guarded trade secret, again, top the list; the individual crafts represent the other extreme, of techniques which can be easily acquired by anyone. (3) The regularity of the demand for the goods produced by an industry, and thus, indirectly, its economic success. The work of glass-makers or brass-smiths presents one extreme, the work of bead-makers or weavers the other. (4) The comparative unimportance of originality and inventiveness on the part of the individual craftsman. In this respect brass-smith work shows the most 'individualistic', and blacksmith-work, the most closely integrated, form of production.[1]

The balance which, in the actual case, is achieved between these four factors determines the final structure of the productive organization. The issue is, however, complicated by the fact that different factors bring about similar results. Thus both a high degree of 'individualism' (as among brass-smiths) and a low measure of economic success (as among beadworkers) tend towards a dissolution of the co-operative organization. On the other hand, we find a certain closeness of organization visible in the tendency of craftsmen to work together in the same locality and perhaps in the same workshop, when most factors are pressing towards dissolution. Thus beadworkers of different families and households still tend to share a common workshop and to live together in the same quarter although their technique of production does not necessitate actual working together, nor the economic success o their craft favour co-operation. This qualified co-operation appears to be due to the advantage of keeping in close contact with one another for the purpose of profiting from each other's experience, and of keeping abreast of fashions and new styles.

Efficiency in group production appears, then, as the main motive for co-operation on a guild scale. But while the first and third condition refer to efficiency in the narrower, technical, sense of the word, i.e. ease, speed, and economy of production, the second condition reveals a more

---

[1] With the weavers we find an additional motive for closeness of co-operation in the tribal and cultural unity of these alien, 'Nupe-ized', groups. We can disregard this type of co-operation, which is not limited nor peculiar to labour organization.

specifically social and cultural aspect. Efficiency in this sense means
continuity of the craft and of craft knowledge; it means the ability to
raise, through the medium of an hereditary, imperceptibly changing
labour group, successive generations of craftsmen. If in these
respects production is planned for an unchanging future, the agency
of the third factor must expose it to the disruptive effects of time
and change. For it may appear as if modern economic changes
directed their most destructive attacks against this third condition
of closeness and co-operation, which is dependence upon regular
demand. This influence is especially visible in the gradual disappearance of orders from the main customer of the country, king and court.
The Great *Sallah*, once the occasion for numerous orders from the
court, which kept the workshops of Bida busy for weeks, is now an
occasion for making purchases at the stores that trade in European
goods. At the *Sallah* of 1935, the first *Sallah* of the newly installed *Etsu*,
the traditional royal gifts of kola-nuts were sent out, not in ornamental
brass bowls of native make, but in newly bought enamelled teapots; the
king's bodyguard, newly equipped, wore, not Bida gowns and turbans
or native-made straw hats, but red blankets and Trilby hats; and many
notables who would have appeared formerly on horses with costly
trappings and gorgeous saddle-cloths, rode in on new, shining bicycles.
Conspicuous though the competition of European goods appears, it is
not the only reason for the decline of Nupe craft-guilds. The very
organization of guild-organized crafts has contributed to lowering their
resistance to outside pressure. The inertia inherent in the rigid group-
organization with its traditional standards of production prevents the
craft-guild from readjusting itself to new demands with the same ease as
the individual craftsman, who is free to change his mode of production
and to gain success by new methods. The decision of the younger men
among the weavers to abandon the traditional production and to turn to
the more profitable production of cap-making, the success of the most
'individualistic' of all crafts, brass-work, are instances of this.

But readjustment involves in reality two different and independent
processes: adjustment to modern conditions may mean both adjustment
in price and cost of production, and adjustment with regard to the kind
of goods produced. A close examination of this question is of special
interest as attempts to preserve and help native arts and crafts are to-day
officially sponsored by the educational departments in many African
colonies. In these attempts the second type of adjustment is frequently
taken into account exclusively, the first being either ignored or artificially
eliminated by turning native crafts into tourist and 'curio' industries
which can command prices quite out of proportion to the native
economic system. That the Nupe crafts themselves have adjusted prices
to demands is clearly shown in the general fall in prices which has taken
place during the last five or ten years.[1] Thus mats of the best quality
were sold, nine to ten years ago, for 3s.; in 1934 for 9d. and 1s.; in 1936,

---

[1] In the two years I spent in Nupe country—two years which saw a partial
economic recovery—I witnessed a corresponding slight rise in prices of native
craft products.

after a slight recovery, for 1s. 3d. Straw hats ten years ago fetched 2s. 6d. and 5s.; in 1934 8d. and 1s.; in 1936 5½d. and 1s. 3d.; embroidered gowns sold ten years ago for £5 to £6; in 1934 they could be bought for 30s. or £2. But in the attempt to lower prices Nupe guild industries cannot go beyond cutting down profits; they cannot reduce the costs of production—or else they must weaken maintenance of labour and destroy the labour organization itself. One method of reducing what we might call in a broad sense costs of production was to discontinue the payments to family heads and guild-masters, as in the case of blacksmiths and weavers; another, to reorganize production on the basis of individual paid labour, as in the case of the bead-workers. Another, to save on the upkeep of the means of production: this was the case in native iron-mining. Native iron-mining is, in fact, the most convincing instance of the limits set to the reduction in costs of production. Native iron-ore mining was, as we have seen, not destroyed by the competition of a more satisfactory raw material; nor would the price of the native product alone have been responsible for its disappearance from the market. What was responsible was the relation between a low price and a 'high cost of production' which could not be reduced. In this primary industry in the strict sense of the word costs of production equal crude labour costs, i.e. time and human energy. When low prices made it impossible for the iron-ore miners to make enough money even to ensure sufficient food supplies, cost of production had to be reduced, i.e. time and energy taken away from craft-work and devoted to agriculture. We could study the effects of these elementary attempts at reducing 'labour costs', which were forced upon the craftsmen; only one way was open to them, and that was to work their furnaces wastefully, irrespective of gradual deterioration, even to the degree of allowing them to fall into complete disrepair.

Yet it would not be true to say that the economic system of Nupe has never evolved more satisfactory methods to meet these contingencies which every economy must reckon with. I have said that formerly the Nupe craftsmen employed slave-labour on a considerable scale. Now, slave-labour provided an important mechanism to safeguard the flexibility of the economic system with regard to labour costs and profits. Slave-labour represents an investment of capital almost in the modern sense; for by investing capital in slaves one invested surplus capital in a profit-bearing concern, and the surplus made in times of prosperity could thus be made to serve as means of reducing labour-costs in times of stringency. The craftsman who bought slaves could not only use them as cheaper labour in his workshop, but could also put them to agricultural labour, to produce food for himself and his family—food which otherwise would have to be bought out of the profits made in the craft. The Nupe industries have lost the primitive form of industrial capital, slave-labour, without having yet evolved the modern substitute, machinery. They must thus fall short of the most vital necessity in industrial productive organization, its adaptability to changing demands. These conclusions must not be ignored when planning the preservation or revival of African crafts and craft-guilds.

We can now place the two systems of industry side by side and compare their respective assets and defects. Against highly efficient co-operation and mutual assistance embodied in the guild organization we have to set the free play of competition allowed in individual crafts. Against the principle of continuity and planned training we have to set higher adaptability and larger scope for individual initiative and inventiveness. Broadly speaking, it cannot be doubted that uncontrolled, 'individualistic', industries stand a higher chance of developing production, possibly on new lines, and of achieving technical progress. Moreover, efficient training and continuity of craft knowledge can, to some extent, also be assured in the narrower form of co-operation vested in the small labour-unit; this is shown in the village groups of blacksmiths and weavers. The question which we have asked at the beginning of this section thus still stands: Why has Nupe society chosen, of these two possible methods of organizing industrial enterprise, the method that assured group efficiency and continuity on the largest scale, and group efficiency rather than progress and individual initiative?

The main reason lies in the political system of the country. The guilds are, as we have seen, built closely into the political framework. Let me recall the main facts: the guild-head is the agent of the king in all matters concerning the group; like the members of the nobility, he is the holder of an official rank, and is admitted to the *nkó*, the King's Council. The guilds themselves enjoy a privileged position in the Nupe state in that they were exempted from tax and were assigned a social position superior to that of other commoners, peasants, or traders. Yet they were, in other respects, very much controlled; they were bound to their profession and could not freely change it. They were even bound to the locality in which they practised their trade and could not move from it without permission of the guild-head. If a village chief desired to have a certain Bida craft represented in his village, he had to apply to the guild-head in the capital; this happened some years ago in Kutigi, when the chief requested the guild-head of the carpenters in Bida to send him a craftsman to settle and practise in his village. The craftsmen, then, are the king's craftsmen. Not only are they dependent on the king for their prosperity, but they are also controlled and supervised by him and his official agent, the guild-master. This organization of the craft-guilds amounts to a full control of the political system over all the more important industries of the country. We may even go further and say that this control was dictated by the needs of the state: based on constant warfare, committed to uphold the splendour of a huge court, the political system has to guarantee a dependable, uninterrupted supply of all that is needed—arms, tools, clothes, saddles, as well as the many symbols of wealth and status. Upon this dedication of the craft-guilds to the service of the state the seal is set by the discriminative social appreciation which the Nupe people extend to the different crafts.[1] The noblest craft is that of the brass- and sword-smiths, for they, as an informant put it, are 'the makers of arms'.

[1] See p. 103.

DIVISION OF LABOUR BETWEEN THE SEXES (II)

In none of the industrial activities described on the preceding pages women take any part, except, indirectly, in weaving. But there exist also certain special women's crafts—again, 'individual' crafts—the technique of which is known only to the women and the proceeds from which are women's property. We may note that the men are much more ignorant about women's crafts than they are about the special activities of the women in connexion with agriculture and housework, i.e. cooking, palm-oil manufacture, and so forth. I could always obtain very reliable information on cooking or shea-butter and palm-oil manufacture from men; but information obtained from men on, say, pottery, proved superficial and misleading. Often, in fact, the men refer you to the women rather than venture any information themselves. Woman's craftwork is thus much more specifically and exclusively a woman's concern. It is also more self-contained than cooking and similar activities, being hardly connected with the productive activities of the men. This is most clearly shown by the fact that in craftwork the women must produce their own means of production, unlike, for example, in shea-nut manufacture, in which the women use roast-ovens built by the men, and that, for this purpose, the women have evolved special forms of comparatively large-scale co-operation. At the same time women's crafts are much less widespread than women's other activities. The three crafts peculiar to women, indigo dyeing, pottery, and weaving (a special type of weaving), occur only in certain localities and social groups; there are large numbers of women in Nupe who do not practise any handicraft.

We have seen already that indigo dyeing by women is practised only in the few *konú* groups in Nupe country, where the men are the weavers and the women the dyers (see p. 235). The women's craftwork goes beyond this partnership; the women dye not only the cotton-thread which is used later by the men in weaving, but also any kind of ready-made cloth, old and new, that is brought to them by outside customers. For this work they charge 2*d.* to 3*d.* per cloth. Dyeing is done individually, every woman having her own dyeing-pot and making her own dye. But the women of one household often help each other in this work. Among the women dyers in Kutigi and Sakpe we even find a co-operation which goes beyond the single household. The pots in which the dyeing is done are arranged on a platform outside the compound or part of the village in which the dyers live. When building this platform and putting up the dye-pots all the women of the locality work together—it has been said already that the building and beating of platforms is women's work; the dyeing 'platform' itself thus represents a close analogy to the large workshed in which the weavers work. This co-operation among the *konú* women does not represent a specific and, as it were, additional productive organization, for it takes place within the existing framework of a closely integrated kindred, formed by these craftsmen and women of alien tribal origin. But here the interesting sociological question arises how this limitation of a woman's craft to a local and kinship group is achieved and maintained in a patrilineal and patrilocal society. The explanation is supplied by the endogamous organization of the *konú* groups, which marry mostly into other *konú* families of the same or a neighbouring village. In one or two cases in which intermarriage of a *konú* woman with a Nupe man has taken place, the wife took her craft with her and is practising it in her new home, but now as a completely individual craft, without the help and co-operation of her fellow craftswomen.

Pottery is widespread in Nupe, both in Bida and in the villages. Certain places are famous for their pottery, such as Jebba Island, Baro, Badeggi, and also Bida. The best clay for pottery is found near the river, and this may explain the superiority of the pottery produced in these localities, which are all situated on or near the river. But there exists also a regular trade in potter's clay; women from Badeggi take the excellent clay which is found in that district to Bida and sell it there to the local potters. Other inland places, even rich, busy villages such as Kutigi and Mokwa, have no pottery at all. But Mokwa is only ten miles from Jebba, the great pottery centre, and Kutigi market, on the main trade-route to the west and south, is amply supplied with pots from everywhere. Facilities for trade and communication thus make for specialization, and tend to eliminate inferior local production—a point to which we shall return in another context.

In Bida, too, we find a certain specialization in pottery. Clay lamps and the small pitchers which the Mohammedans use for their ablutions are made everywhere in Bida. Other kinds of pots are made in one *efu* only (the *efu* of the *masagá*, which is situated close to the river). These are large, wide pots used for cooking; tall pots, shaped somewhat like a column, which are in reality three round pots placed on top of each other and formed into one large receptacle—Nupe men and women store their clothes in these pots, which are called *etso*; and small round platters which, broken into small pieces, are used for making tessellated floors. We note that the women are here producing the 'raw material' for another typical woman's work, the making of floors. The making of these pots and platters is generally recognized to be much more difficult and to involve more special training than the manufacture of clay lamps and pitchers. The secret of the technique—for it is, in Nupe eyes, a secret—is only possessed by the women in three compounds in the glass-workers' quarter.[1] Mothers teach their daughters this technique, and we are, again, faced with the question how to account for the limitation of a technique which is transmitted in the female line to a local group formed according to the rule of patrilocal residence. The answer is more or less the same as in the case of the women dyers. The women potters from the *masagá fu* mostly marry into families of the same or a neighbouring *efu*. The girls who occasionally marry into the *masagá* quarter from outside are instructed in the art of pottery by their mothers-in-law. The daughters of the women potters, however, who marry outside (I recorded

---

[1] This technique involves the use of a crude potter's wheel—the only known case in Africa. Of the different groups of women potters in Nupe only those in Bida and Badeggi use this device. For the description of the technique I must refer to a future publication.

AN OLD POTTER WOMAN

THE WOMAN'S LOOM

three cases) abandon the craft altogether. Pottery also involves a certain co-operation between the women which goes beyond the single household. The pots are made in the house, individually, but the burning of the pots takes place in an open space outside, and in this the women from different compounds work together, building the fire of grass and firewood and using it jointly for the burning of their pots. This co-operation neither expresses kinship and tribal unity, as in the case of the *konú* women dyers, nor is it based on an organized occupational union as in the case of the handicrafts of the men. Rather is it an occasional, free co-operation for the sake of expediency which is suggested by the particular technique of this handicraft.

The question of the limitation of a woman's craft to a particular section of the population reappears, with a different meaning, in weaving. The women's weaving is done on the upright broad loom (21 in. wide), which, though produced to-day by the Bida carpenters, appears to have had its origin in the south, in Yoruba country, where I have also seen it used as a woman's loom. This technique of weaving is said to be comparatively new, and not traditionally Nupe, and may indeed have come to Nupe from Yoruba in the times of the Yoruba wars, through the medium of Yoruba wives and slaves of the Nupe nobility. For women's weaving is restricted to the womenfolk of the upper classes of Nupe society; only wives and daughters of the nobility or the 'intelligentsia' possess a loom and practise the craft. There is, in fact, no house of the upper classes in which you will not find several of these looms being used by girls and women. Conversely, looms and craft are completely absent in the poorer man's home. The technique is handed on from mother to daughter. In very few cases only was I informed that a wife had been taught weaving by her mother-in-law. The profit involved in this work corresponds to the average profit of the men's handicrafts. One big embroidered cloth, 2 yards long, is sold for 10s. to 15s., the material costing 5s.; the weaving takes thirty days (a cheaper, not embroidered, kind of cloth can be manufactured in half the time), and the profit per day is thus between 2d. and 3d. This gives us the explanation for the limitation of this craft to a specific social stratum. Only women who have servants (*bara* and formerly slaves) to help in the housework and to run errands for them can find the leisure for this long and delicate work. But the restriction of this woman's craft to one social stratum is only made possible through the existence of a unilateral endogamy—class endogamy—on the part of the women, who rarely marry beneath their station. If I am right, and these looms have been imported into Nupe from Yoruba, we have an interesting instance of class-restricted culture contact, that is, of cultural 'borrowing' which is at once fitted into, and made to subserve, the existing system of rigid social stratification.

CHAPTER XVI
FREE PROFESSIONS

IT is not surprising that a rich and complex culture like Nupe should possess its clearly defined *artes liberales*—its professional scholars, scientists, and artists, or, in a terminology more akin to the native conception, its Mallams, barber-doctors, and drummers and dancers. I will leave the discussion of the profession of Mohammedan scholars for the chapter on education, and deal here with the last two of these 'free professions'.

BARBER-DOCTORS

'Free professions' in the sense in which we are using the term here does not necessarily mean 'individualistic' professions or professions unattached to any organization or co-operative unit. If what I have said in the preceding chapter about the meaning of guild-organization is correct, we may expect to find it developed also in the field of these native *artes liberales*. In fact, we do find it, adjusted to the new field of activity, in the barber-doctors of Nupe. We can no longer speak here of home industry; nor is the element of co-operation and mutual assistance the same as in the industries. But the other factors that tend to call into being a closely co-operative organization are clearly visible: we find again the necessity of long, specialized training, even to the degree of adoption into a trade secret; we also find the existence of a constant 'market' for the products and services of the craft; and lastly, we find a close relation between the group of craftsmen and the political system of the country.

As in medieval Europe and the Orient, the barber of Nupe, *gozan*, is also doctor and surgeon. His activities are numerous: he cuts the hair of men, women, and children; he shaves the head and cuts the tribal marks of newborn babies at the name-giving ceremony. For a tenth of a penny he cuts finger- and toe-nails: a few barbers have specialized in tattooing. The barbers also dispense medicines (mostly worthless[1] infusions and charred powders made of herbs) for every known disease; they perform certain minor surgical operations—circumcision or blood-letting—and administer the *turare*, a potent inhalation of the smoke from certain medicinal herbs. Certain barbers know the secret of contraceptive medicines, others know cures against barrenness; others, again, are experts in the treatment of lunacy. This far-reaching competency is the most characteristic feature of the craft of Nupe barber-doctors. Leaving aside the ordinary routine work of the barber and certain simpler operations such as the cutting of tribal marks, we may say that every barber

---

[1] This judgement is based on an analysis in the Wellcome Research Laboratory in London, for which I am greatly indebted to this institution, of certain drugs made by the Nupe barber-doctors which I had brought home from Nigeria. The discussion of the more specifically medical questions I must leave for a future publication.

GROUP OF DRUMMERS

GUILD-HEAD OF BIDA BARBERS

has his own speciality, his own expert knowledge, his cures, and his special field. No wonder, then, that the Bida barbers are not of equal standing: there are famous 'celebrities', and there are also the smaller fry. The public is aware of these distinctions. It is well aware also of the special field of certain foreign barber-doctors who frequently come to Bida to practise. Thus, for example, it is generally known that the operation of removing the uvula of children—an operation said to help growth and secure better nourishment—is performed only by Hausa barbers. The more surprising, then, is the fact that this array of specialists and special cures is not equally accessible to every citizen of Bida or Nupe. For the barbers are organized in three independent guilds, one in each *ekpã* of the town. Neither doctors nor patients ever ignore these boundaries. Each guild, or guild section, is under its own titled head, who as a rule has also a 'second-in-command' (who is 'heir designate' to the guild-headship at the same time) to assist him in guild work. In the *Etsu* Umaru quarter guild-head and 'second-in-command' are called *Ndeji* and *Ndabaki*; in the *Etsu* Usman quarter *Tsadzo* and *Ndamaraki*; in the *Etsu* Masaba quarter we find only one guild rank, who is the present head of the guild at large, the *Sokyara*. This highest guild office is taken in rotation by the three guild sections.

The Bida barbers, busy and prosperous, do not practise farming in addition to their main occupation; nor do sons of barbers ever follow any other profession. On the contrary, men of other professions may become barbers. I have recorded three recent cases: two were adults, one a farmer and the other a (Fulani) herdsman; the third was a young man, the son of a straw-hat maker; the two adults settled later as barbers in villages; the young man, who came from Bida, remained there to practise his craft. To learn the barbers' craft proper does not take long: the apprentice works only a year under a master (without changing his habitation). The master, during this time, pockets the larger part of the apprentice's earnings. The apprentice himself buys the instruments of his new trade—a collection of old-fashioned razors, costing about 4*s.* to 5*s.* But to learn the medical side of the craft requires (I was told) a five-years' apprenticeship. One of the two men just mentioned had done this, and is to-day a practising 'doctor'. Let me add that neither the 'trade secrets' of the barber-doctors nor the training in the craft involve any magical or religious conception and form of procedure. It is purely a craft technique.[1]

The special cures and forms of treatment are secrets of individual barber families. They are handed on from generation to generation and are the common property of all adults in a family (though not of the

[1] Nupe society also possesses a certain group of 'doctors', or, more precisely, 'medicine-men'—*cigbeciži* (*cigbe* means 'medicine')—whose craft is based on magical ideas and is closely linked with divining and the religious system of the country. I cannot describe here their organization more fully. I will only say that they practise mostly in the pagan districts, and that they are united in a loose 'order', acknowledging a common head, the *Etsu Cigbeciži* in Bida. To-day the modern conception of the barber-doctor is gaining ground also in the pagan villages. I found a significant effect of this transition in two Nupe villages— 'medicine-men' and diviners who were practising barbers at the same time.

larger group, the guild section or guild). The work of the barbers is organized on the familiar lines of *efakó* and *bucá*. Although their work does not entail actually working together, a certain kind of work is regarded as a concern of the family group as such and as falling under the rules of *efakó*. The *efakó* principle itself is interpreted in an unusual sense. In the work of the barbers orders or summons do not usually reach the individual barber directly, but come to him via the head of the household, who allots the various tasks to the different family members. The proceeds from all work carried out on these lines are divided among the whole *efakó* group, in accordance with a certain schedule which takes into account the seniority of the different family members. The tasks which come under *efakó* rule are the most highly paid jobs: the shaving of the hair and the cutting of tribal marks at the name-giving ceremony, and the circumcision of boys. The first task is performed at the occasion of an important household feast, and the barber-doctors rarely fail to benefit from the generosity that goes with festal mood. These simpler operations are executed by the younger men of the family, but the family head and the older men will also be present, as guests quite as much as in their professional capacity—which latter may reveal itself in no more than an occasional hint thrown out to the young colleague. The barbers will all sit together, and in front of them there will be a bowl into which every visitor is expected to drop a coin, the largest contribution coming from the parents of the newborn child. Let us follow the fate of a shilling dropped into this bowl of the barbers at a name-giving ceremony in a Bida house: 2*d.* is retained by the grandmother, who held the infant during the operation; 1*d.* goes to each of the five junior members of the *efakó* group (including the young man who performed the operation); 1½*d.* each to two older men of the family, the family head and his younger brother; and 2*d.*, finally, to the head of the guild section.

All other work of the barbers is regarded as *bucá*: ordinary haircutting and shaving as well as medical treatment.[1] The latter, more lucrative, work is a prerogative of the older men, who alone know herbs and drugs and can perform the *turare*. The younger men will be taught these craft secrets when they reach a certain age. And thus another principle of family work is realized in the organization of the Nupe barber-doctors, namely, the balance in favour of senior family members which we have observed in the organization of farm-labour and native industries.

We have seen that in the distribution of *efakó* income a certain contribution goes to the head of the guild section. This, then, is a first instance of economic co-operation of the large professional unit. This co-operation is visible also in another, external, feature of this professional organization. In each of the three day-markets of Bida there is a special barbers' 'hall', a spacious open hut, where all the barbers (specially the family heads) meet in the afternoon, and sit and wait for clients and summons. This hut is built and kept up from a common fund. The existence of this common fund is itself evidence of a close co-operation in the financial field. Into this fund, which is called *dashí*, every barber

[1] The barbers are usually paid in money; but when the Bida barbers tour the country villages they often take firewood or food in lieu of payment.

ONE OF THE *ETSU*'S *KAKATI* PLAYERS

A PROFESSIONAL SINGER WITH HER BAND

pays a small amount of money at regular intervals; the fund is administered by the guild-head; he deducts from it money for possible common
expenses, and pays out the rest in full to every member of the guild
section in turn, after every pay-day. This financial arrangement is fairly
common in Nupe, specially among traders and labourers, and we shall
discuss it in more detail later. The barbers, however, are the only professional group which has embodied it in its professional organization
and utilizes it as a system of mutual financial assistance vested in the
craft-guild.

The guild organization is restricted to Bida town. In the villages, even
in the larger places, one or two barbers are sufficient to meet the normal
demand. Besides, the medicine-man of the pagan districts would constitute a serious competition to the Bida doctors. But so far as barbers
and barber-doctors are wanted in the country, the organization in the
capital supplies them, either permanently or temporarily. Certain Bida
barbers, for example, have settled in villages; others tour the country
regularly, stopping in this or that place for longer or shorter periods.
Even in these tours of the country districts round Bida, the barbers keep
to the territory of 'their' royal house, i.e. the royal house on whose land
in Bida their home stands. Although it clearly cannot be said of the
barber-doctors that they 'serve the state' in the same way as blacksmiths
or leather-workers, this arrangement is a striking evidence of the fact that
their association with the political structure of the country is as strongly
marked, and that they, again, are in certain respects the 'king's craftsmen'.

DRUMMERS AND DANCERS

The drummers in Bida, true to the more 'advanced' urban conception
of art, are individualists; in the village, where the art of drumming belongs not only to the recreational side of social life, but also forms part of
the organization of ritual and ceremony as well as production (we remember the part drumming plays in the farming *egbe*), it is less an 'art'
in the modern sense of the word than a 'craft', working for well-defined
institutionalized demands, and charged with responsibilities of a graver
order. Drumming in the village thus moves in the framework of a close
organization on guild lines. In every larger Nupe village we find a
special group of drummers and musicians who, though belonging to
different families and houses, yet recognize the authority of a common
head, the *Etsu Dzã*, the King of the Drummers. Certain other, subordinate titles, are distributed, in guild fashion, among the other
members of the craft. The art of drumming remains in the family and
is handed on from father to son. You may see small boys practising
drumming on little toy-like instruments under the eye of the father.
They will go with him wherever he is called to perform, watching him
and, when they are sufficiently advanced, accompanying him on their
own drums. Sometimes boys from other families desire to become
drummers. Their father will then get in touch with the head of the
drummers, and give him his son as apprentice. The young apprentice
will visit the drummer's house every day for his lesson. In the beginning

x

he will be allowed to use the drums in the house; later he will buy himself a drum of his own. No payment is taken for the tuition; but when the novice later performs at ceremonies or feasts, he will send his former teacher a small gift of money or food. The drums are made by the woodworkers on the river, who are alone in the position to obtain the suitable wood. One large drum costs 10s. The drummers themselves cover the drum and provide the goatskin for the diaphragm.

But all this is a thing of the past. To-day apprentices are hardly ever taken. The drummers, like so many other Nupe craftsmen, complain bitterly about the bad times. Formerly, they told me, they used to be paid 6s. to 8s. a night; to-day they receive 3s. for the night or, for one 'song' (played, for example, at a family feast), one kola-nut. This decline appears to be due to two factors: first, to the impact of Mohammedanism and the gradual disappearance of rituals and ceremonies in which drumming formerly played a prominent part and the songs of which were stored in the memory of the village drummers; and second, to the spreading of fashions from the capital, and the competition of the more 'refined', famous Bida drummers and musicians. The organization of the village drummers has survived only in the names of the guild ranks. The drummers, who once devoted only their spare time to farming, are to-day mainly farmers and carry on their old profession only as a sideline.

In Bida drumming and music were never tied to the narrow scope of limited traditional occasions; nor was the development of the artistic style rigidly hemmed in ritual. Both the profession and the style were allowed to develop freely, and the result is an impressive variety in artistic production and in its social counterpart, the organization of the craft. The Bida practice also introduces a completely novel element into the traditional craft, namely, music and dancing executed by professional women dancers and singers. A number of performers, drummers and women singers (who rarely come of one family or household) associate with one another, and form themselves into a 'band' or 'company'. In this form they become known, are invited to perform at feasts and similar occasions, and also tour the country, sometimes even going abroad to other large towns in Nigeria where Nupe music always finds an appreciative public.[1] In constant co-operation the 'company' builds up its special 'repertory' and evolves its individual style. There are several such 'companies' in Bida, each with its special repertory, style, and technique. They are known by the name of their leader, or by the name of the style in which they have specialized. Thus we find the group of the drummer Sogba, or the group of the woman singer Fati, or a group called *zawóro* (lit. 'new man'), so called because it performs in a style only developed since the days of the 'new men', i.e. the British. One or the other 'company' is known to be patronized by a certain noble family and will be summoned at every occasion when the services of drummers and dancers are required, a name-giving ceremony, a wedding, or an age-grade festivity. Certain drummers even enter a kind of *bara* relation with a nobleman

---

[1] I met a company of Bida drummers and women singers, whom I had known in Bida, in Lagos, where they were 'on tour'.

whose patronage they seek. Often the patron may order special com-
positions from 'his' drummers, for example, a personal drum signal,
called *take*, for a newly acquired nobility rank, or a song of praise on
himself, or a friend or relation.

Between these different groups there is no co-operation. Each group
is, economically, a closed unit. All earnings are divided equally among
the members. This division of the income has no bearing on factors of
family or household organization. Individual group-members may contribute to the expenses of their own families; but the 'company' is purely
a professional association, to which the categories *efakó* and *bucá* do not
apply. Professional and family concerns are, in fact, kept strictly separate, occasionally the two overlap, and we find a woman singer and
a drummer of the same 'company' who are man and wife; but just as
often a drummer has a wife, and the woman singer a husband, who
are not members of the 'company', nor even of the profession.

Drumming in Bida is a full-time occupation (sometimes a drummer
practises a little farming besides, but this is very infrequent). Each
company regularly adopts new members as old ones retire. The novices
serve their apprenticeship as minor performers of the 'company', until
they become fully fledged members of the craft. Sons of drummers
mostly follow the paternal profession; but many singers and dancers do
not come from families whose women have practised this profession
previously. Music and dancing in Bida is a vocation rather than a profession. The free competition of talent and individuality rather than
family tradition determines professional success, and thus the professional association in which the craft organizes itself. Indeed the profession of Bida musicians and drummers represents the only instance in the
economic organization of the country of a free association purely on
a business basis, and without the support of the framework of kinship
and hereditary tradition.

With regard to the profession of drummers and musicians town and
country have exchanged roles: we find the closed and hereditary professional group (though of much smaller scale than guild organization
proper) in the village, and the detached individual groups of craftsmen
in Bida. But the principle of hereditary craft organization has remained
essentially the same. We need only read village chief for king, and
village community for state, and we understand the new situation. For
the drummers, as we have seen, are as essential to the corporate life of
the village as are the craftsmen proper to the political life of the state. In
town-life, on the other side, drummers and musicians have no traditional
duties assigned to them which concern the common interests of the
group at large. Indeed the more varied social life of Bida, and the
appreciation of new fashions and special styles typical of the cosmopolitan town, foster that spirit of originality and inventiveness which
here as in all craft-work counteracts efforts at a closer co-operative
organization.

CHAPTER XVII

INDUSTRIAL LABOUR

THE influences of modern culture contact which we have seen at work in almost every field of Nupe production gain their fullest expression in this most recent native occupation. The employer is the Bida Native Administration; the employees are recruited from certain specific sections of the Nupe people, and the nature of this selection is deeply significant of the structure of the society.

We must distinguish two different categories of paid industrial labour: skilled permanent, and unskilled temporary, labour.[1] Skilled labour is employed in the workshops of the Native Administration Public Works Department, and comprises blacksmiths, mechanics, carpenters, and bricklayers, i.e. occupations which (with the exception of the brick-layers) are closely associated with the traditional native crafts of the country. Temporary unskilled labour is employed partly in addition to permanent labour in the N.A. Workshops, but mostly in occasional work demanding a large body of unskilled labourers such as construction work of various kinds. The term 'temporary' must be understood in a very loose sense; men who have been working as 'temporary' labourers, off and on, for ten or fifteen years figure prominently on my lists. Some move from place to place, wherever there is a chance of finding employment. As there are large numbers of alien, non-Nupe, labourers among those engaged in temporary work in Nupe country, so we also find Nupe workmen in other districts and provinces of Nigeria. A few of these labourers have never even had another, more or less permanent, profession, but have adopted their present occupation in earliest youth. None of them, however, are skilled and specially trained labourers. By far the largest proportion of temporary labourers go home and return to whatever their original profession was when their temporary employment comes to an end. In the sense, then, that their work as labourers constitutes an alternative to some other original occupation, they can all be classed under the heading of 'temporary labourers'.

The data on which are based the statistical tables which follow were compiled in and near Bida in 1936. It was a fortunate coincidence that at the time a large building programme was being carried out—the construction of new office buildings in Bida, and the rebuilding of a big bridge on the Badeggi road—in which a large body of labourers was employed. My census of temporary labour was taken among the workmen who were employed in this work. I have placed bricklayers in the same category with temporary labourers, although, technically, they represent a group of skilled, permanent, workmen; but the technique of

[1] To be quite precise we should distinguish four different classes of labour: permanent and non-permanent, and skilled and unskilled. As, however, all skilled labour is permanent, and all non-permanent labour unskilled, and as unskilled permanent labour represents only a small minority (8 individuals) it is simpler to deal with the two sub-divisions as one.

their work is in no way connected with a traditional trade or craft, which means, that they all had to abandon another, original, occupation (either of themselves or their families) and that their present work constitutes an alternative profession in the sense just explained.

TABLE I

Temporary Labour

Home	No alternative occupation	Alternative occupation	Seasonal labour	Length of employment as labourers				Totals
				Under 2 years	2–5 years	5–10 years	Over 10 years	
Bida	6 (3)	30	2	5	16	10	7	38
Country	1	3	15	10	5	3	1	19
Totals	7	33	17	15	21	13	8	57

Under 'No alternative occupation' I have listed in brackets the labourers who are studying the Koran in their spare time, but without intention of practising the profession of Koran teachers. The heading 'seasonal labour' refers to farmers who, for various reasons, seek work as labourers only in the dry season and return to their farm-work in the rains. It is natural that their number should be much larger among people from the country than among Bida men. All peasants, incidentally, who have become labourers during the last two years belong to this class of seasonal labour. Our figures further show that their number is greatly on the increase. Labourers pure and simple, as might be expected, come almost exclusively from Bida. The only exception is a man from Badeggi, the village on the urbanized railway, twelve miles from Bida; he is also the only country man who has been a labourer for over ten years. Under 'alternative occupations' I had to list a great many different occupations; Table III will show the various original, or 'alternative', occupations of temporary labourers. In Table II we shall examine the professional groups from which skilled permanent labour is recruited.

TABLE II

Permanent Labour

Occupation of the labourer	Occupation of the labourer's family							Total
	Guild crafts		Individual crafts	Farmers	Mallams	Traders	Nobility	
	Same	Different						
Carpenters	6	..	..	1	1	..	1	9
Blacksmiths	5	1	..	..	2	..	2	10
Total	11	1	..	1	3	..	3	19

The large majority of skilled workmen come, as we see, from families which have practised the same crafts on indigenous lines both in Bida and in the villages. The few 'outsiders' appearing in this group come mostly from families with no specific occupation, such as Mallams, and nobility.

The largest contingent of country people among the labourers is, naturally, composed of farmers and farmers' sons. Comparing Table III

TABLE III
Temporary Labour

	Home	Farmers	Guild craft	Indi-vidual craft	Mallams	Traders	Nobility	No altern. occupa-tion	Total
Occupation of father	Bida	4	1	13	9	1	11	..	39
	Country	10	..	..	6	..	2	..	18
	Total	14	1	13	15	1	13	..	57
Alternative occupation of labourer	Bida	4	1	20	8	..	..	5	38
	Country	16	..	..	2	..	..	1	19
	Total	20	1	20	10	..	..	6	57

with Table I we can see that of the 16 farmers who have sought work as labourers only 1 has abandoned farming permanently for labourer's work, while 15 remained seasonal labourers. Turning to the Bida contingent we see that among the different professions which contribute to temporary labour individual crafts come first and Mallams second—the most loosely organized occupational groups thus contribute most heavily to occasional labour. The occupations of the families of which these labourers come appear in a slightly different order of importance: individual crafts are, again, first, with 'nobility' second and Mallams third. 'Nobility' means here mostly the lower political ranks, above all 'household' and *bara* ranks. Their share in the contribution reflects the great political and economic changes that have deprived many members of this 'leisure class' of a livelihood mainly derived from warfare or political attachment.

But what are the incentives which led the men from the other occupational groups to give up their previous occupation or to undertake the work of labourers in addition to their ordinary profession? This question is answered by the data of the last table.

TABLE IV

		Married	Unmarried	Tax as reason
Permanent labour		9	12	..
Temporary labour {	Bida	9	13	4
	Country	6	9	5
Age 20–5		4	10	..
,, 25–30		3	8	..
,, 30–5		4	4	..
,, 35–40		4	..	..

The majority among permanent as well as temporary labourers is unmarried—although many of the men, as we can see, have reached, and partly passed, the age at which it is normal for the Nupe man to marry. The work as labourers in their case was undertaken with the intent to obtain money for the bride-price, a plan which did not always materialize as our figures show, especially in Bida. For there are many other uses for money, and some, as we shall see later, may interfere with the laudable intention of working for one's bride-price. In a number of cases the reason for becoming a labourer was to obtain money for tax, either for oneself or for one's family. One young labourer from the country gave his father 5s. out of his weekly wages of 7s. to put by for his bride-price; another kept 2s. to 3s. a month for himself, and gave the rest to his father. Many Bida labourers, on the other hand, used the whole money for themselves; some explained that they had become labourers because there was no money in their old profession, others because they wanted to be independent and because their fathers or elder brothers could not give them as much money as they liked to have.

To summarize: as one would expect, paid labour, especially temporary labour, does not represent a 'real' profession in the sense of an occupation involving special training and selection of workers. It is essentially a stopgap occupation chosen to supplement or replace a failing normal source of income. Owing to the specific composition of Nupe society the new profession is being adopted by certain social groups and strata more than by others. Yet in some respects paid industrial labour must be regarded almost as a modern continuation of forms of occupations which, in the traditional society, bore the same supplementary and stopgap character. As such it appeals strongly to the individual craftsman, to Mallams, and *bara*, who depend for their livelihood on similar forms of unskilled and partly temporary work. It differs from these other occupations, however, in that it is carried out on the road and in the workshop yard instead of in the home, and that it represents heavy manual labour, and not light work which it is easy to combine with a dignified social status. The labourers, unlike the individual craftsmen, can no longer pretend that they belong to the leisured class. If they receive better and more regular pay, they also lose caste. This explains why of the many hundreds of men who, once members of the privileged classes, are to-day men 'without occupation',[1] gaining a precarious livelihood from occasional work, only those coming from the lowest grade of the 'upper classes' have chosen the profession of labourers.

In the case of the peasants we can no longer speak of any inherent congruity between their work and the new temporary occupation. To them, especially to the peasants who do not practise a handicraft beside agriculture, paid labour in addition to farm-work, a form of labour, moreover, which keeps them for months from their homes, must appear as something quite new and unprecedented. If to-day paid labour is gradually attracting the peasant class as well, twenty or thirty years ago the (very prosperous) Nupe peasants had to be coaxed by all available means to undertake temporary paid labour, for example, in railway construction. The more 'sophisticated' Hausa and Yoruba were already then flocking in large numbers to work of this kind. Missionaries who knew Nupe country at that time told me that it was often impossible in the peasant districts to obtain even porters to carry loads; the promise of money did not attract them sufficiently to make them leave their homes even temporarily, to upset their whole routine of work or forgo their well-earned leisure. In certain backward and prosperous districts this

---

[1] An unofficial occupational census of Bida lists 1,130 men under the class 'no occupation'. They belong without exception to the titled leisured classes of the Emirate.

attitude has still survived: when I trekked through the country round Sakpe in 1936 I found myself in the same predicament, and although it was in the dry season and farming was at a standstill, I had eventually to agree to women carrying my loads as men were not available for this task. That the appeal of paid labour as a seasonal occupation for peasants is rapidly gaining ground cannot be doubted. The stopgap occupation can, in fact, be said to satisfy a definite want in present-day peasant economy.[1] The strength of its appeal still varies greatly locally. The large majority of the peasants whom I found employed as labourers in the construction of Badeggi bridge were local men or men from the neighbourhood of Bida. Of 19 labourers 14 came from Badeggi itself, 3 from hamlets near Bida, 1 from Kacha, 1 from a village farther afield (Jima), and none from Trans-Kaduna. The local selection does not merely reflect varying degrees of progressiveness or 'sophistication'; it also reflects the varying urgency of the wants for the relief of which paid labour is undertaken. The nature of these wants we shall discuss in detail later.

[1] To-day many Nupe peasants are ready to try any kind of paid labour, but will abandon it quickly if it falls short of their expectations of a regular and substantial income. Thus the Nupe of Leaba tried their luck in gold-washing, which is carried out on a considerable scale in that district. They had heard from Hausa labourers that one could make as much as 9d. or 1s. a day in this work. They had not realized, however, that the payment was not per day, but depended on the amount of gold which the individual worker can produce. As the Nupe were rather clumsy and slow, unlike the experienced Hausa labourers, their pay was small and irregular, and, gravely disappointed, they soon gave up gold-washing.

CHAPTER XVIII
WEALTH

THE examination of the problem of labour may be fittingly concluded with a discussion of the role played by wealth, free capital,
in Nupe economy. It is in keeping with Nupe production in general,
with its emphasis on individual property and money profits, that the
concept of wealth should be clearly pronounced. The principle of
accumulation of wealth as free capital pervades Nupe economics and, in
particular, serves to define the economic (and, indirectly, social) stratification of the society.

MONEY CAPITAL

The appreciation of wealth figures prominently in the educational
conceptions of the people. Young boys of 8 or 10, when they are given
a separate *bucá* plot to farm, are at the same time taught the value of
money income and money capital. Mothers will help them to market
their small produce for money, or will buy their produce directly from
them. And fathers and mothers, as we have seen, equip their children
with a first diminutive working capital, a penny or two, to start a profitable
trade (see pp. 286–7, 331). These profits enable boys and girls to defray
the expenses of the social obligations incumbent upon this tender age,
namely, contributions to the costs of the age-grade associations of which
they are members. Money expenses, partly involving the accumulation
of reserves, accompany Nupe men and women all through their lives:
money to meet the costs of kinship rituals—birth, weddings, and funerals
—money for the maintenance of labour, the purchase of tools, &c., or
for personal wants and the luxuries of life. Money also frequently forms
part of the inheritance left by men or women.

Farm produce or gifts in kind in general cannot fully replace money
expenditure. This is shown clearly in the nature of the universal gift in
Nupe—kola-nuts. Gifts of kola-nuts are more or less regularly exchanged between friends and relations; a gift of kola-nuts serves as the
traditional announcement, and invitation at the same time, extended to
kinsfolk at the occasion of forthcoming kinship ceremonies. Gifts of
kola-nuts also represent the traditional expression of political allegiance.
And, with the insignificant exception of the kola-nut growers, the donor
of the gift has to buy the kola-nuts on the market for money. The
largest single expenditure of Nupe economy, finally, bride-price, is paid
entirely in money (see the discussion of bride-price in Chap. XX). It
involves, moreover, accumulation of money reserve, or, if the bride-
price is paid in instalments, as it frequently is, careful planning of money
expenditure over a considerable period.

Although none of the larger forms of traditional money expenditure
were ever replaceable by gifts or contributions in kind, it is also true that
the practice of money expenditure has been increasing with the spreading of cultural influences from the town. It is natural that Bida society,

with its large population of non-farmers, should have developed the practice of money expenditure more extensively than the villages, and adopted money expenditure in certain instances in which, in the village, gifts and contributions in kind were the custom. The universal practice nowadays of giving and accepting presents of kola-nuts, for example, appears to have spread from the town, and to have replaced gifts of food or sorghum beer. Of similar changes in other fields we possess even more concrete evidence: thus the name-giving ceremony or funeral feast involves to-day contributions in money by guests and relations; in Mohammedan districts it is also customary to distribute alms (again in money) among the local Mallams. In the traditional form these kinship ceremonies implied gifts in kind, i.e. contributions of food and sorghum beer for the feast. Formerly, also, every household used to produce its own beer; to-day the manufacture of beer is limited to certain households so that the other families are obliged to buy it for money. Moreover, sorghum beer has been replaced in the town by palm-wine, which, as palm-kernels are largely imported from districts outside Nupe, must again be bought (see p. 234).

It is necessary to emphasize that this change represents a change of customs and fashion, and a change in the *form* of expenditure, rather than a change, or an increase, of expenditure itself. We shall, in fact, see later that the modern Mohammedan burial, for example, may come cheaper than the pagan ceremony, although in the latter contributions and gifts were largely in kind. In other words, the symbols of wealth are changing and becoming more unified, being adjusted to the symbols of wealth which have been adopted and standardized by the social and cultural *élite* of the country.

How, then, are money reserves and wealth in general accumulated? One method, which is widespread in Nupe, is to hoard money by burying it. Sometimes valuables, above all, precious beads, take the place of money, and are buried or concealed otherwise in a safe place. In a number of court cases over inheritance the question of discovering the hidden wealth (money or beads) of the testator played an important part. Another illustration of the practice of hoarding money came to my knowledge in connexion with inquiries into the continued use of cowrie-shell currency.[1] It is generally known in Nupe country that when cowrie-shells were finally replaced by English money and the former currency declared worthless many people buried their cowrie-shells in the hope that, some day, they might become legal tender again. Once I asked certain informants in Kutigi if they could show me any cowrie-shells. They said that they had none, and that cowrie-shells were no longer to be found in the country. I said that I was prepared to pay money for them, whereupon large baskets full of cowries suddenly turned up, and, the rumour having spread that the white man was buying cowries, I had to do my best not to be inundated with the suddenly rediscovered currency.

Another method of accumulating capital is the investment in interest-

[1] See 'A Ritual Currency in Nigeria—A Result of Culture Contact', in 'Notes and News', *Africa*, 1937, 3.

bearing enterprises ('interest' understood here in the widest sense). The nature of the enterprise varies with local conditions, and differs above all in town and country. Peasants mostly invest their money in live-stock (see Chap. XI). We have seen that Nupe inventiveness is always on the look-out for new opportunities promising a higher 'interest', even in the narrow field of stock-breeding as they know it: we have mentioned the buying and selling of ostriches, and the isolated experi-ment in horse-breeding of one village chief—incidentally the chief of a typical backwood village, Sakpe. In the town, and in the large trading-centres of the country, money is invested chiefly in trade, even by men and women who do not personally engage in trade. They would trust a certain sum to a trader of their acquaintance for a particular purpose, e.g. to help him finance a trading expedition to Kano or Bornu. The trader will use their capital together with his own, and will return it to them increased by the profits which it has brought when his business has been successfully concluded. The trader, of course, also derives a certain profit from these investments, as they enable him to enlarge the scope of his enterprise and to secure more favourable prices. Many most highly placed notables in Bida, not excluding the king himself, use this profitable method of investment.

Certain traditional and formerly highly important methods of invest-ment, above all war and slavery, have disappeared under the new political order. I have described in an earlier chapter the contributions of the houses of the Bida nobility to the wars and military exploits of their country and have also discussed slavery and slave trade. It remains to discuss the closely related traditional form of investment in 'human capital' which has become a thing of the past only quite recently, namely, money investment in human pledges (*sofa*, in Nupe).

PAWNING

Besides the pawning of human pledges, ordinary pawning—pawning of valuable goods—also occurs. My information is that beads, costly gowns, a sword, or saddle, all things of silver or gold, are frequently pawned as security for a loan. No interest is paid on the loan itself, and the transaction is regarded purely as an act of friendship. I have, how-ever, not discovered any actual instance of this practice. My impression is that it is not, and has never been, very widespread. Pawning of people, on the other hand, has grown to enormous dimensions. When pawning of human pledges was finally suppressed in Nigeria, in 1933–4, 3,000 pawns were released in Bida Emirate alone.

As slavery reflects the insecurity of the political rights of the con-quered subjects of Nupe kingdom, pawning reflects the economic in-security under which a large proportion of the population of the Emirate lives. The lack of flexibility, more particularly, in their economy tends to foster such radical means of escape from financial difficulties. Under the pressure of unexpected demands or certain imperative heavy ex-penses which cannot be matched by normal efforts—payment of bride-price; a heavy fine; money with which to bail a family member or bribe a judge—the people may have recourse to pawning one family member to procure money for another. Younger sons would be pawned to find the bride-price for the eldest son, whose marriage must be made possible. Or a father would pawn himself to provide money for his son, perhaps to save him from prison or a death sentence. Girls, too, are pawned, though as a rule for a smaller amount of money than boys or men. I have recorded an interesting case of 'multiple' pawning: a man of about 30 had pawned himself in order to be able to marry, but could not find the money to ransom himself. He continued to live in bondage till his son from this marriage was twelve years old, and thus fit to be pawned in turn. The boy took the place of his father as pawn in the same house, and the older man was released. I do not know when, or if, the boy was in turn released.

It is interesting to compare pawning with slavery. The first difference is that pawning is, at least in theory, regarded as a purely temporary arrangement. The father or elder brother of a pawn would always expect to release their relative from bondage in from five to ten years. The pawn works for his master, in his house or on his land, like all other household members, slaves, or junior family members. But unlike slaves, pawns are servants in the narrow sense of the word: they cannot expect friendly help from their master; they would not, for example, be married at the expense of their master—if they cannot afford the bride-price they must remain unmarried. On the other hand, the master may not beat or kill the pawn, as he may a slave: this would constitute a normal case of assault or homicide, actionable before the court. A pawn who is unwilling or unable to work satisfactorily, can, however, be exchanged for another more promising member of his family. Pawns and their whole family are held in general contempt. There is no shame in having become a slave—this is 'luck of war'; but pawns and their families are tainted with a disgrace not easily forgotten. In pawning poverty, itself a shameful state in the eyes of the Nupe, reaches its lowest ebb. Even house slaves look down upon pawns, and order them about as their inferiors.

Another difference between pawning and slavery is the amount of money involved. While the prices for slaves are firmly fixed, the loan for which the pawn is taken as security varies greatly, between £3 and £10. The work of the pawn during the time of bondage represents the 'interest' on the loan. The profit motive is expressed most clearly in the practice that girl pawns were accepted only for smaller amounts. For with girls one had to reckon with a shorter period of 'amortization' as they might get married early and be redeemed by the bride-price. However, the profit motive is not sufficient to explain the institution of pawning. A wealthy man could not, according to the Nupe code of morality, refuse a loan of this kind to a man who was badly in need of the money. Which means that the creditor might have to agree even to less tempting and profitable offers. Frequently he had to accept a young boy who, hardly yet an efficient labourer, would live in his house and learn farm-work or a craft only to be taken away again just as he had become a useful member of the household. For £5 one could buy outright a grown-up, well-trained, slave; for a pawn, with his restricted usefulness, one might have to pay more than twice the amount. There is no doubt, then, that the institution of pawning represented not only a profit-making, 'capitalist' investment, but also, to some extent, a 'humanitarian' duty linked with status and prestige, a crude attempt at alleviating the hardships involved in the unequal distribution of wealth. Well-educated Nupe men, themselves members of the wealthier classes, with whom I discussed pawning, even went so far as to explain pawning (at least on a moderate scale) as an institution of considerable educational value enabling the sons of the poor to study farm-work and husbandry in the houses of prosperous and enterprising men. They would admit drawbacks only in the excessive practice of pawning, which, they maintained, was a recent development, brought about by rising prices and rising cost of living. These drawbacks, as they saw them, were that with the increase in their numbers, the pawns, many of whom frequently worked together in the same household, grew lazy and irresponsible, and showed openly their resentment at having to work for strange masters. The complaints of my informants were thus that in the combination of material and moral rewards which the people of wealth and status expected from the institution of pawning, the material rewards had completely to give place to moral rewards.

A similar combination of material returns from invested wealth with benefits of a more abstract order—status and prestige—is also characteristic of the institution of clientship (already explained in Chap. VIII). The share of the 'abstract' benefits becomes larger the closer we approach forms of expenditure and investment bound up with social status: display of wealth in household arrangements, festivities, the equipment of one's retinue, and so forth. To this and similar questions we shall return later.

CHAPTER XIX
ECONOMIC BALANCE: EXCHANGE

IN the discussion of economic balance we approach a group of questions which modern economic theory regards as the principle subject-matter of economics, viz. the relation between means which exist in some degree of scarcity and their alternative uses for the satisfaction of needs and wants. We shall examine 'balance' under two aspects: first, the relation between means and their uses in a wider sense, as they exist and are balanced in the economic system of the society at large. In this sense economic balance can be equated with exchange and exchange-mechanisms. Secondly, economic balance can be approached from the angle of the economic unit, and understood in the sense of the relation existing between means and wants in the narrow compass of individual or group economy. Economic balance here can be equated with the relation between capacity to produce and the ability to satisfy existing wants, i.e. between income and expenditure.

Although the two aspects refer to the same phenomenon, and are thus clearly interdependent, it is necessary to point out that the relation between the two does not invariably lie on the surface. Certain wants which greatly influence individual economy do not enter openly into general exchange relations. I refer here to wants which flow from specifically social sources—the dictates of religious obligations, of etiquette, status and prestige, political interests, and so forth. Over and above the overt exchange-mechanisms which we study under the first aspect of economic balance we shall have to introduce, in the discussion of the second aspect, a certain 'invisible' exchange—exchange against such imponderables as moral values, or forms of social appreciation. We will examine these two aspects of economic balance in the order in which we have enumerated them.

CURRENCY, MEASURES, AND PRICES

The description of Nupe production has clearly established the nature of Nupe economy as a highly complex exchange-economy based on money. A discussion of exchange-mechanisms may thus profitably begin with the examination of the units of exchange, the currency, and certain fixed measures used in trade.

Before the adoption of British money cowrie-shells constituted the currency of the country. Its use still lingers—not in the currency that is actually used (although this, too, has been mentioned),[1] but in an abstract sense, in the native methods of reckoning money. Certain standardized amounts, e.g. bride-price, certain traditional gifts and payments, are expressed more often in cowrie-shells than in modern money. In the country figures in cowrie-shells are quoted commonly, and in connexion with every kind of payment, including food-prices and suchlike. Cowrie-

[1] See p. 310.

shells are a clumsy currency: you have to carry them about in bagfuls, and to count in thousands and tens of thousands. The numerical system of Nupe is fully equal to this task. Its elaboration and lucidity is not the least contribution to the efficiency of the exchange system of the country. Its scope is practically unlimited. A figure like 3,600,000 is expressed by this comparatively simple symbol: *gba kpotwani* (lit. two thousand times eighteen hundred, or, in more detail, two thousand times two hundred times nine). This facility in forming large numbers is due to the existence of a number of simple root words and multiples which are easy to handle. Omitting here the simpler figures 1–9, we find root words for 100, 200, and 2,000, multiples of 100 and 1,000 being formed by a simple multiplication of the root figures. For example, 400 is 200 . 2, i.e. *kpa gúba*, contracted to *kpoba*; 600 is 200 . 3, i.e. *kpa gúta*, contracted to *kpota*; 4,000 is 2,000 . 2, i.e. *gba gúba*, contracted to *gboba*; 6,000 is 2,000 . 3, i.e. *gba gúta*, contracted to *gbaotá*; 10,000 is 2,000 . 5, i.e. *gba gútsū*, contracted to *gbotsū*; and so on. A new unit is introduced as an alternative symbol for 20,000 cowries in the form of the *gura*, which is the name for the grass bags in which cowries were formerly packed. Thus 200,000 cowries (the traditional bride-price) make 10 *gura*; 400,000 20 *gura*, and so on.

The exchange rate between cowries and British money appears to have undergone some change. The original exchange rate, which I ascertained from the account of bride-price and tribute paid formerly, was 8d. for 2,000 cowries. Later the exchange value of cowries rose to 1s. for 2,000 cowries. This exchange rate is applied to-day when figures are quoted in cowries. Although cowrie-shells represented a currency in the strict sense of the word, they were used also for certain other purposes beside exchange, and had, above all, a certain value as ornaments. Gourds, bags, and musical instruments were formerly ornamented with cowries; but this practice has fallen into disuse.

To this elaborate system of units of exchange corresponds an almost as well-defined system of measures applied to commodities. We have spoken already of the *kpere*, the 'arm-length', a standard length used in measuring cloth; 10 *kpere* give, as we have seen, one full-length cloth. The measures used in selling agricultural produce are even more interesting, as quantities of these commodities do not lend themselves easily to simple forms of standardization. The unit for unthreshed grain is the bundle, *epa* (from *pa*, to tie up) or load, *kara*. It weighs very nearly 60 lb., but its size and weight vary a little according to the quality of the grain: of poorer grain there would be a larger quantity in the bundle, of better-class grain a proportionately smaller quantity, the main point being the equality in the value. Threshed grain is sold in large or small gourds, for which to-day tin bowls and basins are usually substituted. A large basinful of grain, *evo* (lit. gourd), contains twelve small bowls, *kpanu* (the latter taking a little over one pound). One bundle of unthreshed grain is reckoned to correspond to one *evo* of threshed grain. With maize five to six cobs are reckoned to give one small bowl of maize-flour. Rice is sold in large gourds (*evo*) or, more frequently, in small bowls, ten of which as a rule give one gourd. Beans are calculated in baskets (*kasa*); fruits and ground-nuts in *kasa* or *kara* (loads). The calculation is fairly precise, one 'load' of shea-nuts, for example, being reckoned to bring 2*s*., or one load of locust-beans 3*d*.

These examples suffice to illustrate the clear conception which the Nupe have of measures and marketable quantities. Combined with the universal use of money they result in a well-defined system of market prices. The calculation of market prices in Nupe corresponds closely to variations in supply and demand, above all, to seasonal fluctuations. We have already given instances. I will add here a few more which refer to the staple produce of the country.[1] In April and May 1936 one bundle of unthreshed sorghum was sold for 6*d*., in August and September for 9*d*. to 10*d*., and in certain places even for 1*s*. During the same time the price of bulrush-millet rose from 6*d*. to 1*s*. 6*d*. In April ten yams were sold for 6*d*.; at the beginning of June the price rose to 10*d*., and in July, shortly before the yam harvest, to 1*s*. 8*d*., to fall again in August to 6*d*. In the case of bulrush-millet and yam, the cultivation of which is restricted to certain districts, the fluctuations of price are markedly greater than in the case of the universal food-crop, sorghum. For rice, on the other hand, an expensive foodstuff for which there is only limited demand, and new supplies of which appear on the market three times a year, the price remained unchanged at 2*d*. for a small bowl.

These prices refer to village markets. Prices in Bida are always higher. When grain in the country sells for 6*d*. a bundle, the Bida price is 8*d*.; when the highest price in the country is 10*d*., it will reach in Bida 1*s*. and 2*s*. When yams are sold ten for 6*d*. in the country, the Bida price is ten for 9*d*., and so forth. Industrial products manufactured in Bida, on the other hand, are dearer in the districts, as the middlemen add a certain amount to the original price (between 1*d*. and 2*d*. in the shilling). Goods produced in the country which pass through the hands of the Bida trader on their way to Bida market or to markets abroad become markedly more expensive: thus Kutigi mats produced locally for 11*d*. are sold in Bida for 1*s*. or 1*s*. 2*d*., and abroad, for example in Lokoja, for 1*s*. 6*d*.

These regular variations and fluctuations in price must, to some extent at least, be based on a systematic common knowledge of the conditions which determine supply and demand in the country and which can thus sustain definite expectations of price developments at a given moment. Such a body of common knowledge indeed exists in Nupe. It is embodied in the universal experience that certain commodities are always plentiful in the dry season and get more and more scarce towards the close of the rains. It is also reflected in the generally accepted fact that prices are higher in the capital, which has to import a large proportion of its food-supplies, and which is also wealthier and possessed of a higher standard of living than the rest of the country. These considerations imply a further important fact viz. that distance between area of production and market, and the additional labour and loss of time involved in

[1] Certain fluctuations are determined by increased consumption during the festival season. Thus one sheep fetched 5*s*. in January and 10*s*. to 15*s*. in March, i.e. shortly before the Great Sallah, to fall again to 5*s*. during the rains (see p. 203, n. 1).

transport, enter into the calculation of price and profit.[1] Finally, the economic significance of 'waiting' is fully recognized, and goods sold are at a proportionately cheaper price when they can be disposed of in larger quantities. I found, for example, that a trader on the market would sell two bowls of grain for $1\frac{1}{2}d.$, but one bowl for $0.8d.$; a large *evo* (containing 12 small bowls) of the same grain could be had for $8d.$ One large *evo* of rice (containing 10 small bowls) is sold for $1s. 6d.$, while a small bowl would be priced at $2d.$ The factor of 'waiting' plays an important part also in the economy of the individual household. When money is urgently needed, or when for other reasons the whole crop is sold in one, the seller must be prepared to accept a less favourable price. A farmer in Lemu sold his whole crop of bulrush-millet and late millet for $4d.$ a bundle, in order to have sufficient money in hand for certain urgent household expenses (the marriage ceremony of one of his sons). With his sorghum crop he could afford to go more slowly, and obtained for it prices varying from $6d.$ to $9d.$ per bundle. Another farmer, near Bida, had to sell twelve bundles of late millet and sorghum for $1s.$ per bundle, as he was pressed for money for tax, well knowing that if he could afford to sell his grain in smaller quantities he could easily obtain $1s. 6d.$ a bundle.

This common knowledge of price-conditions seems also to explain the lack of haggling in Nupe marketing—to the student of African peoples a rather surprising feature. Cooked food, all victuals including grain, rice, palm-oil, &c., as also the common products of tailors, blacksmiths, mat-makers, and so forth, have 'fixed prices', and buyers will never try to bargain. They might, when buying yams or fish, a mat or a hoe, poke about in the goods displayed for sale till they find the biggest or nicest-looking specimen offered at the price they are willing to pay. Real haggling and bargaining is common only with expensive, more rarely sold, commodities, the price of which is always more or less fluid, and commodities the quality and perfection of which show many gradations: embroidered cloth, a woven gown, and all products of artistic value.

The common knowledge of price-conditions is limited by existing communications and forms of economic contact. Thus we find a uniform regulation of prices only within the area in which regular contacts of this kind exist; outside it the calculation of prices and profits, and productive planning in general, is determined by the varying local conditions of supply and demand. The most striking instance of this lack of co-ordination is perhaps the backward village of Sakpe to which I have referred in a previous chapter, where the people were unaware of the fact that the kapok from their silk-cotton trees had a money value in Bida. The following example, though referring to an exchange connexion going beyond Nupe country, is no less significant: in the same village, Sakpe, I met two men from Igbira country who had come to

---

[1] It is not unnecessary to mention especially this aspect of Nupe economic knowledge. For it is frequently found in more primitive societies that the economic value of time is not recognized and that native producers sell their goods at a distant market for the same price as they would locally.

Nupe to sell dogs, and were greatly disappointed to find that dogs had no market value in that country. It need not be stressed that modern development of communications has greatly enlarged the area in which common price-conditions obtain. Railways, steamers, and road transport have become regular factors in native marketing and in the planning of native production.[1] The stores of the European trading-companies, which are the centres for the marketing in commercial crops, have helped to expand further this framework of common economic conditions. But these last factors have at the same time introduced a new element of insecurity into the body of native economic knowledge. The new, wider, framework of reference includes conditions of supply and demand which go far beyond those embodied in the native productive system, and calculations of price which are no longer accessible to the experience of the native producer—the conditions of supply and demand, and the calculations of price, determined by the state of European or American markets. The erratic and, to the native, incomprehensible fluctuations in the price of ground-nuts or cotton are typical instances; we have seen how, in the extreme case, they may completely upset native agricultural planning. The price policy of the trading-companies may also place a certain native productive area in a more unfavourable position than others: thus the price for ground-nuts paid by the United Africa Company in Nupe (that is Niger Province) was 5s. 6d. per ton as against 11s., for an inferior quality, in Zaria or Kano. The conditions in cotton marketing were, till recently, similar.[2] Many enterprising native traders avail themselves to-day of the modern facilities of transport to visit these various towns and centres of trade: how can they be anything but bewildered by that unwarranted difference in price; or rather, they have learned to accept it as one more of the many incomprehensible arrangements brought in by 'the white man', and find a ready explanation for it in the fact that 'money is more plentiful in Zaria and Kano'.

We must consider here the relation between commodity prices and labour. The prices for the products of native industries given in an earlier chapter reflect, within limits, the varying amount of labour necessary for their production. The lowest daily profit with which the various Bida industries reckon is, as we have seen, between $1\frac{1}{2}d.$ and $2d.$ It is interesting to note that this amount corresponds to the lowest cost of living per day of an adult in Bida (see below, p. 342). The highest profits, on the other hand, may be determined not only by the amount of work, but also by the skill and artistic qualities which the work involves. We have seen that the artistic work of embroidery is paid more highly than ordinary tailor's work. If we compare, however, the average profits made in blacksmith work with the profits with which brass-smiths

[1] A Nupe trader known to me bought £5 worth of cheap kola-nuts in Lagos early in the season, stored them for 6 months, and then transported them by rail to Bida, where he sold his stock for £10.

[2] I was informed that this discrepancy in price was due mainly to the monopoly position of two large trading-companies in Niger Province, while in the north several companies have to compete with one another. The recently adopted control of the cotton markets by the Administration tends to maintain cotton prices at approximately the same level in the whole of Nigeria.

reckon, we make the somewhat surprising discovery that here the more refined work is not only not more highly paid but partly even worse paid than the cruder industry. Both as regards profits per day and profits per article produced the brass-smiths work on the whole with lower profits than the blacksmiths.[1] Why, then, does the calculation of price and profit allow for an appreciation of the specific artistic qualities of the work of tailors and embroiderers but not in the analogous instance of brass-smith work? But is it an analogous instance? In the case of tailors and embroiderers both the cruder and the more refined technique belong to the same class of production: they are both what we may loosely call luxury industries. In blacksmith and brass-smith work we have fundamentally different industries, one supplying necessities, and the other a typical fashion and luxury industry. The explanation thus seems to be that indispensability may equal aesthetic value; and that where these two diverse types of industry compete side by side the factor of necessity may balance or outweigh the appreciation of artistic qualities.

MARKET AND TRADE

We have had frequent opportunity to speak of the complexity of Nupe economics and of the far-reaching specialization of Nupe production, which must express itself most forcibly in the wide scope of trade and marketing. In a wider sense Nupe country itself is one big market. For Nupe is a country which exports and imports, and represents, besides, an important station on the route of transit-trade across Nigeria. The ancient trade-routes have to some extent been adjusted to-day to the new forms of communication, motor-roads, steamers, and railways. But to a large extent they have remained the same, for now as of old a large proportion of this transit-trade is carried to, and by, the water-way of the river Niger.

The following are the traditional trade-routes through Nupe. They run mostly roughly from north to south. One, coming from Sokoto and Birnin Kebbi, goes through Kontagora and reaches Nupe north of Mokwa; from here it goes either west, crossing the Niger at Jebba (formerly at Buka, five miles up the river) into Yoruba, or east through Laboži, Sakpe, to the Kaduna, which it crosses at Gbara, then south to Muregi and, after crossing the Niger, on to Yoruba and Kabba. A second route from Kontagora reaches Nupe Emirate north of Kuti-wengi, passes through Dabbã and Kutigi, and crosses the river Niger at Ogudu, on the way to Ilorin. An alternative to this route branches off at Dabbã, crosses the Kaduna at Wuya, and ends at Bida. A third trade-route passes through Birnin Gwari and Wushishi, and reaches Bida via Gbangba. There are three routes from Bida to the south and south-east: one through Jima and Dokomba, down the Kaduna by canoe to Muregi,

---

[1] The profits of blacksmiths per object are: 3d., 3½d., 6d.; per day, 6d., 7d., 1s. The profits of brass-smiths per object are: 1½d., 2d.; per day, 3d., 6d. Higher profits are only realized in the casting of bangles in precious metal, in the casting of brass figures for tourist trade, and also in the production of ladles in the modern cheap material, aluminium.

where the route crosses the Niger and goes on to Ilorin and Yoruba; a second, to Badeggi and Kacha, where it crosses the Niger to Eggã and Yagba country; the third route goes from Bida to Kacha, or Giddi, farther down the river, where the trade-goods are loaded on canoes on their way south to Lokoja, Idah, and Onitsa. In addition to these land routes we have also an 'all-water' route, the north terminus of which used to be at Rabá or Ogudu.[1]

Let me summarize the main facts concerning the 'international' commerce in Nupe. Nupe country exports a certain proportion of its agricultural produce, especially rice and Laboži kola-nuts, smoked fish, and a large variety of its industrial products. It imports various foodstuffs, especially palm-oil and European salt, cheap southern kola-nuts, potash, and live stock. It re-exports potash and beans from the north to the south, and palm-oil, European salt, and kola-nuts from the south to the north. This commerce follows certain interesting traditional patterns. A simple export trade from Nupe to another country is the exception: of this kind is the trade in smoked fish from the riverain districts of Nupe by rail to Ilorin and Ibadan, or the trade in Nupe glass, beads, brass, and silverware, which goes by canoe to Lokoja. In the majority of cases the import or export trade in a certain commodity is combined with a definite return trade in another commodity. Here we find the following regular 'patterns': donkey caravans from Hausa bring beans to Bida and return with kola-nuts (either the local Laboži nuts or the cheap southern variety). Other donkey caravans go north from Nupe; they are loaded in Kacha with palm-oil and salt, which arrive on the Niger Company steamers from the south, and return from the north with kanwa (potash) from Bornu. In Kacha the riverain Kakanda buy Nupe-grown rice, which comes down by canoe from Patigi and the Kaduna, and take it south to Onitsa, whence they return with palm-oil. Hausa traders from Kano bring horses and sheep and goats to Bida, to return to their country with Nupe straw hats. Another exchange pattern between Hausa and Nupe is the trade of potash against Bida embroidered gowns. In this trade the imported goods are invariably first sold for money, with which the goods for the return voyage are then purchased. All the variations that are theoretically possible in this threefold export and transit-trade are found to occur in practice. In other words, the Nupe merchant plays three different roles: he is either the local broker who arranges the sale of goods between importer and exporter; or he acts as wholesale trader and buys himself the imported goods to re-export them (himself supplying the transport) to their eventual destination; or he acts as retail trader and sells the imported goods either directly to the customer (on the Bida markets) or to other retail traders, who will dispose of them on the various village markets of the country.

We will begin our study of the marketing system of Nupe with the

[1] To-day the 'all-water' route goes to Jebba, the new railway and steamer station, and even farther north, the water-way north of Jebba having been made navigable for canoes. I have described this river-trade more fully in 'The Kede: A Riverain State in Northern Nigeria' (in *African Political Systems*, Oxford University Press, 1940, p. 165).

study of the village market. No Nupe town or village is without its market and its regular market-days. Larger places hold their markets once a week; smaller villages every fifth day (irrespective of the seven days' week). This arrangement, illogical though it may appear, is well adjusted to the needs of the country, where local transport is still to a large extent by porterage. It enables more people, and people from more distant places, to attend the markets in the bigger villages. I estimated the attendance of the big market at Kutigi, a village of 3,000 inhabitants, at from 400 to 500. The distance from which people come varies considerably. Kacha market, the largest market after Bida, attracts men and women traders from the capital, forty miles away. In Kutigi I met women traders from Lemu, which is thirty miles from Kutigi, who were selling pots made in Gbari country, another fifty miles north. Professional, full-time traders, men and women, regularly attend all the larger markets in the country, stopping in one village for five or six successive market-days, and then moving on to another place. The peasant women, on the other hand, who practise trade only as a 'side line' and whose marketing is concerned chiefly with the disposal of the produce from their houses and their husbands' farms, rarely attend markets which are more than six or ten miles from their home. These small circles of inter-village exchange form no less part of the comprehensive marketing scheme of the country than do the extensive journeys of the professional traders. For the system of local exchange areas is partly subordinated to the main axes of trade and traffic. We find an organization almost of relay stations, half-way houses of exchange, situated all along the main trade-routes of the country, above all on the roads leading to the capital.

On the western road to Bida from Wuya (which is 12 miles from Bida) there are three such 'relay stations', used for the different kinds of produce of which Bida is constantly in need. Duzko Wuya (lit. Market Wuya) on the right bank of the Kaduna is used by the women of Batati, a village fifteen miles inland, for trading their cotton to Bida traders whom they meet at this place. Zantica, six miles from Bida, and Lumanla, four miles from Bida, serve as exchange places for agricultural produce and firewood, which goods are brought to these places by the local women, and then bought and carried to Bida by traders from the town. A similar arrangement, with regard to yam and other farm-produce, obtains on the northern road to Bida from Lemu; the 'relay station' is a tiny village half-way between Lemu and Bida, the only importance of which lies in its use as an exchange market.

Similar relay systems which exist in the river area, following and branching out from the water-ways, serve as centres for the extensive trade in smoked fish. Here the local exchange circles are primarily determined by the varying conditions of transport. Thus the wives of fishermen on the lower Kaduna take their fish (already smoked) in their small canoes to the nearest riverside market, e.g. Jima or Muregi. Here a wholesale trader from Jebba buys up fish in large quantities, takes them, again by canoe (this time a large river-going canoe) to Jebba market, and sells them to another wholesale trader who will transport the fish (by rail or lorry) to the final destination—the inland markets of Bida,

Ilorin, Oshogbo, or Ibadan. Another method is that the wholesale trader who buys up the smoked fish at the local riverside markets also trades them directly to Bida, Ilorin, &c.; certain enterprising traders with plenty of capital may also charter canoes and, travelling from place to place, buy up the local produce before it comes to the riverside markets.[1]

I have emphasized on various occasions the close correlation between markets and specialization of production. Here is the place to state the case once more. Generally speaking, trade and transport which bring the products of one area within reach of another involve competition, and through competition the elimination of inferior forms of production. Trade and transport must thus tend to foster (as they are in turn fostered by) local specialization. Certain developments in the agricultural and industrial production of Nupe reveal the effectiveness of these influences also in that culture. The people of Jebba, for example, do not grow sugar-cane or onions on their land, although on a similar type of land in Rabá and Ogudu these crops are cultivated. They explain this situation as being due to the fact that they are farmers on a less extensive scale, spending much time on fishing and (formerly) hunting; they prefer to import onions and sugar-cane from these other places. For certain handicrafts our evidence is even more striking, for here competition owing to an expansion of trade has only comparatively recently replaced an indigenous craft by imports from another area. The women of Leaba formerly practised pottery; but when the regular canoe traffic, which used to stop farther down the river, was brought up to Leaba, and pots made in Jebba and Gbajibo reached Leaba market, the Leaba women gave up their craft; their own pots, they explained, were inferior in quality to the imported product, owing to the inferior potter's clay found locally.

In small villages no trade is done, and markets are deserted, on days other than market-days. In large villages the markets do a little trade—in food only—also on ordinary week-days. On the day after a market there is often quite considerable trade in goods which did not find a buyer the previous day. On market-day the people begin to arrive between 9 and 10 o'clock. The market is in full swing by noon, and from 1 to 3 is the busiest time. After 4 the attendance begins to scatter, and soon after that the traders remove their goods, and the market is left empty. Every kind of trade and craft is represented even in the smaller village markets. In the roofed booths which every market possesses the more valuable goods are displayed—products of native industries as well as European goods. Tailors and leather-workers work in open huts. In the open square framed by these booths and huts agricultural produce, food-stuffs of every kind, live stock, pots, and tools are offered for sale.

[1] Lately the wives of the fishermen have attempted to break down the 'relay system' and to dispense with the services of middlemen, having begun to market their fish directly in Ilorin and Ibadan. A place like Ogudu, on the road from the river to Ilorin, which formerly formed an important exchange place, has now lost this transit trade in fish. The chief of Ogudu, to whom I owe this information, remarked regretfully that the women have 'begun to understand' (lit. 'have seen light').

In one corner of the market barbers put up their open-air shop. In another corner butchers sell their goods, a drummer endlessly repeating the same rhythmical *motif*—the signal that the butchers have slaughtered that day—to attract the attention of the crowd.

SKETCH-MAP OF KUTIGI MARKET

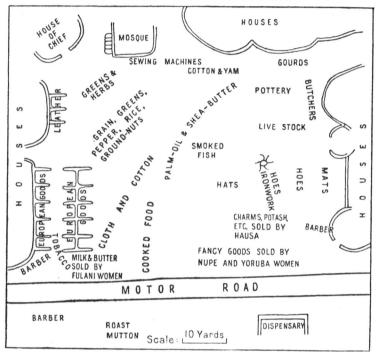

Markets in the wider sense of the word, places for exchange and trade, grow spontaneously with the needs of the country. But markets of the kind just described, with permanent buildings, booths, and stalls, have to be built and laid out specially. Moreover, provision must be made to guarantee the protection of the large attendance, especially of the traders from other districts and countries. The element of planning is clearly visible. The villages which decide to have a market of this kind will go to work methodically; formerly, they appealed first, through the royal delegate in their district, to the king, who would designate some of his private slave police to take charge of the supervision of the market. In the Mohammedan and semi-Mohammedan villages a well-known Mallam would be summoned to consecrate the market and thus ensure its prosperity. This practice is said to be still in use. Certain markets become, in fact, known by the name of the Mallam who dedicated them.

A sketch-map will best illustrate the well-planned arrangement of a typical village market—the market of Kutigi, to which I have referred above. A census of the same market will give quantitative data with regard to the attendance of the market and the goods which are offered for sale on an average market-day. The figures quoted, which are of necessity elastic, were compiled from a large number of regular observations during the months of February and March. The kind and quantity of goods traded on the Nupe markets reflect the seasonal fluctuations in supply and demand. It must be understood, therefore, that at other times of the year, especially in the rainy season, the composition of the market will be somewhat different. In a large centre like Kutigi, however, which can count throughout the year on imports from distant places, these changes remain within more narrow limits than in a small market which relies largely on local supplies. For the purpose of comparison I have also added the corresponding figures referring to ordinary week-days.

The chart shows that, in marketing, certain goods are regularly combined. The same women who sell grain also sell rice, red pepper, *kuka*, and partly palm-oil and shea-butter. The sale of yam is regularly combined with the sale of cotton, and sometimes of gourds; or cotton is sold by the traders in native cloth. Such goods as smoked fish, native tobacco, or cooked food, on the other hand, are always traded separately. The combination of goods offered for sale does not invariably betray the character of the seller, whether she is a farmer's wife, marketing his produce, or a professional trader or 'middleman'. The two categories, in fact, overlap to some extent. As a rule the women who sell grain, rice, *kuka*, red pepper, yam, and cooked food are only 'occasional' traders, i.e. are marketing produce from their husbands' farms. In the case of the women who combine the sale of grain, red pepper, rice, and palm-oil, grain and red pepper may well come from the farms of their husbands, while rice and palm-oil may have been bought by the woman from someone else. Or the woman who sells cloth and cotton may be selling her husband's cotton together with cloth which she purchased in Bida. The women, on the other hand, who sell tobacco, smoked fish, and various Bida goods are invariably professional traders or 'middlemen'.

The distinction between seller and buyer is no less difficult to elicit from the chart. The two roles are often combined in the same person. Many women who come to the market to sell agricultural produce or cooked food, or men who bring live stock or hoes, at the same time purchase various goods from other traders. But the market, in Africa as well as Europe, is more than merely a business institution. The people who attend it, whether they come to buy or to sell, also come for the sake of company and entertainment. In the market they meet friends and acquaintances with whom they can gossip and exchange news. There also the sexes meet, girls and their suitors. Rarely will there be a market-day on which drummers and musicians do not turn up also, and young men or girls join in a dance. This 'social' aspect of the village market must appeal more to the local people, than to the professional traders from Bida or other more distant places. It presupposes common interests, a familiarity and intimacy of long standing. The group of peasant men and women who are brought together regularly on market-

Census of Kutigi Market

Goods	Attendance and quantities of goods	
	On market-day	On ordinary days
Fulani butter and milk	4 Fulani women from camp in the neighbourhood, each with 1-2 gals. of milk and 1 lb. butter	2-3 Fulani women
Grain, rice, red pepper, *kuka*	30-40 women, each with 10-12 *kpanu* of grain and rice, 1 lb. of red pepper and a small bowl of *kuka*	2 women
Palm-oil, shea-butter, and salt	50-60 women, partly the same as those who sell grain and rice, each with 2-4 gals. of palm-oil (in old petrol tins)	2 women
Cotton and yam	10-12 women, each with 4-5 heaps of yam, each containing 6-8 yams. Quantity of cotton very variable	2-3 women
Smoked fish	30-40 women, each with one basket containing 15-20 fish	3 women
Various greens and herbs (partly used as medicine)	15 old women	..
Native tobacco	5 women	3 women
Live stock	Men with 4-5 sheep or goats	..
Pottery of different size	10-15 women, each with 10-15 smaller or 4-5 larger pots	..
Gourds	7-8 women, partly the same as those who sell cotton	..
Hoes	1-2 men, each with 4 hoes	..
Mats	Very variable, 2-10 mat sellers, mostly men	..
Cooked food (pastries, corn-gruel, corn-water, &c.)	20-30 women, the same as those who also sell grain or palm-oil, each with 2 pts. corn-water, 20-25 packets (in banana leaves) of corn-gruel, and 10-15 pastries	4-5 women
Meat	3 butchers, average 2 sheep or sometimes 1 bull or cow	They slaughter every second day
Straw hats	5 men	..
Cloth, various fancy goods	5 men in the booths, and 15 women (Nupe and Yoruba) in the square	..
Tailors	6 men, in the booths	..
Barbers	4 men	..
Leather-workers	4 men, in the booths	..
Charms, medicines, and potash	4 men, two of them Hausa	..
Roast meat	1 man, sitting on the road-side opposite the market	..

days indeed constitute a substratum of community life at large. The social life at the village markets utilizes, and creates or revives, at the same time the contacts and social relationships which characterize the 'area of common life'. It is no accident that this circle of five to ten miles radius from which the local attendance of village markets is recruited coincides with the area which is covered by local knowledge and interest in each other's affairs,[1] and within which intermarriage between different villages takes place.

[1] See p. 38.

I have described already at some length the markets of Bida so that there is little to add here. Bida possesses six markets, three main day markets close to the 3 royal houses, two small day markets—one near the west gate, one in the strangers' quarter—and one night market. In the distinction between day and night market the village distinction between the restricted trade on ordinary week-days and the extensive trade on market-days is in some respects repeated.[1] Multiply by ten the largest village market, and its attendance and the quantity and variety of goods displayed, and you have the Bida night market. Its average attendance has been estimated at 6,000, and as regards the goods which are bought and sold, I can only repeat that there is practically nothing that cannot be obtained there, from kola-nuts to beams for roofing, and from native-tanned goatskins to watches, scissors, or bicycle spare parts. Besides, there are scribes who will write letters for you, Yoruba money-changers (who charge a commission of one penny in the shilling), cooks who roast small pieces of mutton over the fire and sell the meat on wooden skewers to passers-by, drummers, barbers, tailors, loungers, not to forget the policeman who regulates the traffic and keeps watch (not always a sinecure) on disturbances of the peace.

In certain respects, however, marketing and trade in Bida differ essentially from their counterpart in the village. A first difference concerns the local distribution of marketing. Bida possesses, in addition to its four markets, also more or less regular shops which are open all day, such as the wayside shops in the street of the brass-smiths, where the womenfolk of brass- and silversmiths display the goods manufactured by the men, or the permanent shops in *lálemi*, the crowded strangers' quarter. Many traders, moreover, who will attend the night market keep during day-time little wayside stands on cross-roads or busy thoroughfares. The wide local distribution of shops corresponds to the typical demands of a large, decentralized town, in which the groups of potential customers are concentrated in widely scattered localities. At the same time it expresses a keener spirit of competition, and that doctrine of 'seeking out the customer' which is familiar to all more advanced systems of marketing. Two new stands which have only appeared during my stay in Bida will illustrate what I mean. One wayside shop established itself opposite the workshops of the Public Works Department, and its customers were the labourers, who would come out to buy food, sweets, and cigarettes; the other was installed close to the Bida Middle School, and catered for the occasional wants of schoolboys and teachers. In both cases two or three young women had joined forces and were keeping shop together. These wayside shops and stands do not pay rent; street corners and cross-roads are free to everyone; nor have any quarrels over claims to a particular spot arisen—as yet. But this is essentially a fluid process; and it is not unlikely that quarrels or litigation of this kind might arise in the future if competition becomes

[1] The day markets reflect the different needs of the large town as compared with the village markets. Firewood, for example, which is never seen on village markets as the women collect their own firewood on family farms, appears in large quantities on the day markets of Bida.

more severe and the advantageous positions secured by the enterprising first-comers are threatened by later recruits of the 'seeking-out-the-customer' movement.

Wayside shops also line the road leading from the north gate to the two large European stores—'canteens' in the popular idiom. Here the inventiveness of Bida traders has seized upon a new device to attract and 'seek out' the customer. Many peasants from backward villages who come to Bida to buy certain essential European articles, such as salt or sugar, either want to buy them in very small quantities—smaller quantities than they could obtain at the store—or are too shy and frightened to enter the stores themselves. These are the customers of the little stands outside the 'canteens': for here the peasants can buy the same articles in the smallest quantities and without having to undergo the ordeal of a purchase in the unfamiliar, forbidding, store.[1]

MODERN BUSINESS METHODS

The last example brings us to another essential difference between the marketing system in Bida and in the village. The large volume of native trade in European goods and the close business connexion between native traders in Bida and the stores of the trading-companies have introduced certain completely new factors into Nupe marketing. They are visible in local trade on the smallest scale as well as in the large-scale enterprises of wealthy Bida merchants. Trade in certain European goods allows a more rapid turnover and more certain profits than any branch of native economy. The native trader or middleman can, as we have just seen, turn to his profit the fact that he can make certain essential and highly valued goods accessible to the consumer by retailing them in such small quantities that their price (though relatively high) is low enough to be within the means of peasants and small craftsmen. It is, for example, a regular practice of Bida women traders to buy tins of 50 cigarettes at the 'canteen', and to sell them singly (or even cut in half); to buy boxes of matches, and sell them in little bundles of five; packets of sugar, and sell the sugar a piece or two at the time; or to buy 4-gallon tins of paraffin, and sell it in pint bottles. It is hardly surprising that the profits, though absolutely small, are relatively high, up to 100 per cent.[2]

---

[1] This fear is really a compound of shyness and suspicion—one is suspicious just because one is shy and unfamiliar with the ways of these modern institutions. A most characteristic instance, concerning a Bida man who, one would think, would hardly need to be shy or afraid, is the following: a Bida Mallam with whom I was very friendly came to see me one day and asked me if I would do him a favour and order spare tyres from the 'canteen' for a lorry belonging to a friend of his. His friend, he explained, disliked ordering them himself, for he knew he would be cheated and given the wrong kind of tyres. What had happened was that his friend had some time previously ordered tyres without, however, knowing that it was necessary to quote the exact size. He had been given tyres of the size most frequently found on the lorries running in the country, but unfortunately they did not fit his lorry.

[2] One tin of 50 cigarettes costs 1s.; one cigarette is sold for 0·3d., allowing a profit of 3d. in 1s. One box of matches, containing approximately 50 matches, costs 1d.; five matches sold for 0·2d. give a profit of 0·8d. in the penny. One

It is impossible to discuss in detail the business enterprises of the big merchants of Bida. Their business activities hardly differ in essentials from the business activities of Western civilization. They are the whole-sale traders who, working with large capital, buy goods from the European stores and supply the small retail trader with commodities which the latter sells in small quantities in the town market or peddles in villages and local markets. Some big merchants are contractors who run lorries for the transport of passengers and goods, others importers of goods from countries outside Nupe. Their business is to a large extent based on credit which they receive from the European trading-companies, and there are several Bida merchants who figure on the books of the trading-companies with debit accounts of £200 or more. I will only outline the effect which the introduction of commercial credit in the modern sense has had upon Nupe economy. The concept of credit itself is not alien to Nupe economy; but this new type of credit, which can be so readily obtained, opened to the Nupe trader a source, not only of working capital, but also of liquid capital as such. Native business men have learned to use this new economic device to the full, and in their own way—which is not always the orthodox way of credit operations. This is an actual and, I may add, typical instance: a Bida trader bought European cloth for £3 in the store, on a three months' credit. He then sold the cloth at a loss, for £2, to a retail trader who was not unnaturally very ready to pay in cash for these goods the normal price of which was well known to him. With the £2 our trader went round to the villages buying in advance the cotton crop of the year (this happened two months before the harvest was due). He paid an extremely low price—in certain cases only the annual tax-money of the farmer—and two months later sold the crop to the trading-company for an amount which was sufficient to pay his debt and to make a profit of £1 in addition.[1]

The increasing volume of European trade in Nigeria as well as in other parts of Africa is due to a large variety of causes. The cheapness and, generally, better quality of the European goods is often mentioned, and also the change of taste which is brought about by education and by the example of European standards of living. Our short survey of the influence of European trade upon the native economy in Nupe has revealed another aspect of the problem, the importance of which has hitherto been hardly realized. Trade in European goods, *qua* trade, is a highly lucrative enterprise which opens up a chance for business and profits unrivalled in purely native economy. It is to a considerable extent the native trader himself who is pushing trade in European goods. He is its keenest propagandist, for he is the one who benefits first and most.

4-gallon tin of paraffin costs 7s. 6d.; one bottle is sold for 6d., giving a profit of 8s. The higher the investment, the higher evidently the profit.

[1] The device as such, to sell goods at a loss for the sake of ready money, and to make the loss good on a subsequent sale, is not new. Hausa traders, for example, sometimes sell their (native) goods at a loss in Bida in order to obtain money, and with this money to buy certain Bida goods which they can sell in Hausa country at a profit large enough to cover their previous loss.

TRADE AS A PROFESSION

The majority of professional traders in Nupe are Bida men and women. For these professional traders the restriction to the small areas which are characteristic of inter-village trade does not apply. The whole country, and indeed the whole of Nigeria, is their field of activity. Trade, business, is independent of the boundaries of a community, a tribe, or language. Inside Nupe one of the results of this extensive trade is the regularization of hospitality towards traders in all larger villages of the country. Only a few traders may be able to find relations in the distant places to which their business takes them. The others are free to stop in every house. The rules with regard to the compensation for this form of hospitality which does not fall in the category of kinship duties vary locally. In Mokwa the guest maintains himself and is expected to give his host a parting gift of 10–15 kola-nuts (representing about 1s. 6d. in money). In Kacha, a much larger business centre, the population of which consists to a very large extent of traders, a stranger who has no relatives in the place may go to the chief, who will allot quarters to him. The guest receives lodging as well as food, but is not expected to make any gifts in return; he is expected only to return the hospitality in his own village should his host be taken there on his business trips.

Outside Nupe the Nupe traders are frequently more than merely birds of passage. They stay at a place for several months or even years at a time, and may possibly settle there permanently. We find such colonies of Nupe traders in every larger town of Nigeria, in the northern Emirates as well as in the Europeanized centres of trade in the south. In the north they speak Hausa; in the south they can mostly get on with Nupe (only a few Nupe men and women have learned Yoruba). Not the least convincing evidence of the century-old route of Nupe trade to the south, down the river Niger, is that Nupe language is understood all along this route. In places on the lower Niger where the lingua franca of the north, Hausa, is no longer understood I found that the people would speak and understand Nupe. Although in the life of the traders tribal and cultural affinities are subordinated to business interests, these links re-emerge in a new form. In these foreign parts where the Nupe live as aliens, they are drawn together by the link of their common language and common origin. They form small cultural enclaves, Nupe colonies, and tend to live together in the same part of the town. These colonies do not form social units or communities in the narrow sense of the word; rather, they are fluid, semi-temporary, groups brought together by the chance of common enterprise. They can hardly be homogeneous; they contain men and women from different sub-tribes and parts of Nupe country. Moreover, they spring up suddenly, and may disappear again as suddenly, owing to changes in the economic conditions. But while they exist they show a strong tendency to develop something like an organized community life. They all feel themselves as Nupe; they recognize the ranks and forms of status valid at home and elect a head or chief in Nupe fashion. Many men and women in these colonies are joined in the course of time by their family and relations; and many will, or hope that they will, some day return to their home country.[1]

In this description I have dealt with professional and non-professional traders as if they represented sharply distinct classes. There is, in fact, good sense in speaking in Nupe of *cewoce* or *koragba*, 'trader', as against other professions. The line of division, however, is fluid. It is more fluid among women than among men. Among the men we can at least define the extremes: the big trader is nothing but a trader, and the cultivator or guild craftsman is never a trader. But trade on a small scale goes hand in hand with the individual crafts and 'free professions', and an occasional business deal is welcome to everybody. But here a further distinction is necessary. The Nupe distinguish between traders proper and brokers, *dilali*. The brokers have as a rule their booths on the market, and undertake to sell goods for their clients for a small commission. It is interesting to note that while the Nupe traders are 'free' professions in every respect, the brokers are organized in a guild-like organization. They elect a guild-head, the *Etsu* or *Sarkin Dilali*, who is confirmed by the king and keeps in close contact with the court. As soon as a new trade caravan arrives at the *zongu* (the traders' camp outside the gates of Bida) he will go and see the traders and inspect their goods. It is his duty also to inform the king of caravans and goods that have arrived. He must ascertain the king's wishes with respect to these goods before he allows them to be placed on the open market. Here, then, we find again the element of political control which is so closely associated with guild organization. The *Etsu Dilali*, placed in control over all Bida brokers, levies a small fee from them, in return for which he guarantees them equal access to the valuable and profitable goods which arrive in Bida from abroad. He, and through him the whole organization of brokers, thus guarantee to clients and fellow members an efficient marketing organization, the avoidance of unsound competition, and business integrity. The organization of brokers differs in certain respects essentially from the guild organization proper. It does not utilize the principles of kinship (real or fictitious); nor does it attempt in any other way to ensure the solidarity and continuity of the professional group. It represents a 'free' association of 'free' business men, coming very close to the principle of the modern professional union.

DIVISION OF LABOUR BETWEEN THE SEXES (III)

The market census given above has shown that marketing and trade, too, are subject to the rules regulating division of labour between men and women. We can formulate certain general rules: all food-stuffs and agricultural produce, and of native industrial products manufactured by men those that are typical women's articles, are traded by women. To the first category must also be counted the native stimulants, tobacco for

[1] These remarks refer to a typical Nupe traders' colony in Ibadan which I have studied at some length. An instance of a trading-colony which has sprung up quite suddenly is Agege, a village ten miles north of Lagos, which, in 1936, had been in existence for five years only.

A WOMAN TRADER SELLING HER HUSBAND'S
SILVERWARE

A FOOD MARKET

snuff and smoking, its modern counterpart, cigarettes, and kola-nuts, although they are used mostly by men. To the second category belong the various products of Nupe fashion industry, rings, bracelets, chains, ladles, glass-ware, beads, and also the low carved stools, made by the carpenters, on which the Nupe women are wont to sit. The products of women's crafts are traded by women, irrespective of their use: thus the women sell cloth woven by women (used chiefly for women's dresses), indigo dye (which may be used by and for the men), native soap and pots, including the pitchers which the men use for ablutions. All goods produced by men and used by men are marketed by male traders: hoes, axes, arms, gowns, straw hats, books, leather-work, &c. Goods used by both sexes are traded by both men and women: for example, mats, and certain kinds of cloth of native or European make. Live stock is always marketed by men, only chickens are sometimes sold on the market by women.

Throughout this description the term 'woman' means married women as well as girls, mothers and wives as well as daughters. Small girls of 6 or 8 will already 'keep shop' in play, sitting behind a basket in which they have arranged a few pebbles, little rags of cloth or cigarette tins filled with sand, and silently display their 'goods', as they have seen their mothers and elder sisters do. Mothers always take their young girls to the market, letting them sit beside them and, if they are big enough, carry some of the loads on the way there and back. Girls of 12 or 13 will assist their mothers or deputize for them when they are called away; or they will take some of the cooked food which the women sell, and walk through the market and adjoining streets, crying out the wares, while the mother remains sitting behind her basket. This is, incidentally, an interesting division of labour between mother and daughter, and old and young trader in general. For it is against the dignity of grown-up women to cry out their wares—only young girls may do that. A girl of 14 or 16 is already fully initiated into the secrets of commerce, and will soon start to trade on her own, with a capital of a few pennies or a small store of grain or ground-nuts given her by her mother. By degrees the capital and the scope of her business will grow. I remember a court case in Bida in which two girls, between 14 and 15 years of age, had been summoned because they had fought on the market. The fight was about a piece of cloth which one girl had taken from the other, agreeing to buy it for a certain amount; but later she declared it to be too dear, and paid only half the agreed price. The price of the cloth was 6d., and the people in the court were very amused about this commercial transaction in (as the *Alkali* put it) 'little girl's rags'. However, 'little girl's rags' become real cloth, and even more valuable goods, in the course of time, and when the girl marries she is a fully fledged trader, and fully versed in the art of marketing which will be one of her duties as a married woman. Her earnings remain her own property and cannot during her lifetime be touched by her husband. Only when she dies will the husband be entitled to inherit her property.

This brings us to the question of the economic inequality of husband and wife. It is implied in this division of labour between the sexes which makes the women the main traders of the country that the women can as a rule command more liquid capital than the men. In this sense, referring to the liquid resources, it can be said that the Nupe women are on the whole wealthier than the men. This does not mean that their financial position is entirely unaffected by the limited resources of the husband. The wives of small farmers and craftsmen or, generally, impecunious husbands, have little scope for their commercial activities, and may be unable to derive from the household resources the necessary working capital for a profitable independent enterprise. Where there is little to sell there can be little profit; and this small profit may be swallowed up by the normal household expenditure. Even the utensils and goods which constitute the wife's dowry may disappear gradually in a household where there is no money with which to replace the stock of pots, clothes, and ornaments—the woman's initial 'capital' (see p. 351). The household of a diviner in Bida, whom I knew well, was a typical case. The man was of poor health, unable to do any serious work, and had to rely entirely on his income from divining, which was small and irregular. The wife maintained the household, poor and simple as it was. She was about 40 years old; she had nothing left of her dowry save the few rags which she wore, and a few damaged pots. Every day she bought grain for 6d. on the market, made corn-gruel and corn-water, and sold this food in the mornings in the street, with a total profit of 2d. With this money she kept herself and her husband and a small child.

But usually the wives even of men whom one would hardly call prosperous attain an impressive degree of solvency. Solvency in this connexion is a relative term, as the pecuniary demands which the wives have to meet are much smaller than those which devolve on the men as the heads of the household. Yet in many cases the women come to the succour of their men even in expenses of the latter kind. It is by no means rare, especially in Bida, to find families in which a mother undertakes to pay the bride-price for the sons. Much more widespread is the practice of wives lending their husbands money, for example, for the payment of tax. Of this practice we shall hear more later. Let me emphasize here the dependence of the husband on his wife with regard to these monetary obligations—a dependence which must increase as the independent economic enterprise of the women, commerce, is increasing in scope. This fact is essential for the understanding of certain moral issues involved in the expansion of women's trade in Nupe.

I have stated earlier that the line of distinction between professional and occasional traders is much more fluid among the women than among the men. Wives of farmers, craftsmen, Mallams, noblemen, traders, officials—they all are, or may be, traders. The enormous variety in the trade which is carried out by the Nupe women, and in the degree of their 'professionalization', cannot be reduced to a simple formula. The woman who sells every morning two or three dozen packets of home-made *kamu* (corn-gruel) for a tenth of a penny each, and the woman who buys £5 worth of rice, kola-nuts, or European cloth, do not really differ in anything except in the amount of capital they can lay their hands on. The difference in the distance which they cover when disposing of their goods—the peasant woman who walks eight to ten miles to the nearest local market, and the professional woman trader who travels to Lokoja or Ilorin by canoe or train—may seem but an external feature. Yet this factor of distance possesses a deeper significance. The essential difference between the professional and the occasional woman trader is embodied in the extent to which their trading and marketing becomes an independent, self-contained, and self-centred enterprise. Both the occasional and the professional trader are out for profit. But only the latter has adjusted her life fully to this aim. 'Proper' trade necessitates a freedom of movement, a full-time devotion to the task, which only women who have made themselves independent can afford. It means extensive journeys, and long absence from home. Obviously, the wife of a farmer or craftsman who must look after the house is less able to do this than the wife of a trader or a man of the leisured classes.

But the profession demands even more than comparative leisure. The long absence from home, the life on the road, in foreign villages and countries to which none of the normal contacts of the community stretch, means ultimately a dissolution of the bonds of marriage, household, and family. The disappearance of all moral control of the husband over his wife, or the local community over its women, expresses itself in the sexual licence claimed by these women. Female trade and immorality are in Nupe conception two things closely related. The women traders who go on these long expeditions and stay away from home for weeks, months, or even years, are commonly regarded as 'loose' women, as women who cannot help leading a 'loose' and 'immoral' life. The women traders prostitute themselves for money in the villages and towns where they stop on their trading expeditions. The money which they make is regarded by the people as legitimate a form of earnings as that gained from trade itself. When they return to their homes husband and family will receive them without question, and no blame would attach to them for the life which they had been leading while away. Public opinion, though outspoken in its general condemnation of moral laxity, yet countenances the sexual licence of women traders and accepts it almost as an institution. If people—men, as the spokesmen of public opinion—express their indignation at this danger to matrimonial morality, they attack, not the practice itself, but its disproportionate growth in recent times.

We have, in a previous chapter, discussed the social significance of this qualified admission of sexual licence in a certain limited social domain (see Chap. IX). Let me recall the salient facts: female trade, closely associated as it is with licentious living, provided the scope for that socially condoned sexual licence which other social forces seem to have made necessary. Thus female trade became in some respects a closed profession, the entrance into which was made dependent on the qualification of sterility. We may add here that, not unnaturally, women who were past child-bearing age could also legitimately join the profession of women traders. By means of these two qualifications an occupation which harboured some danger to common morality was limited to what were (to the society) the least dangerous groups. This limitation is no longer true. But the information which I collected on this point, from every part of the country, and every social stratum, leaves no doubt that the limitation did obtain, and that it is still regarded as the more adequate practice. Formerly, I was told, no peasant would have dreamed of letting his young wife go to distant markets the journey to which would involve spending the night on the road, away from home. Nor did women with children ever leave the home for these long expeditions to foreign parts. To-day, an ever-increasing number of Nupe women, young women and women with children, travel about the country, independent, and unrestricted by village morals. In the large trading-places in the south such as Baro, Lokoja, Ibadan, I have met many—they lived there, some with their children, as well-known traders and as equally well-known prostitutes.

We have learned that this development is due to a variety of social factors. We will discuss here the factors which are embodied in the economic changes, and which, in fact, appear to represent the main moving force. It is difficult to say for certain whether the floating population of wifeless men has considerably increased during the last generation. It seems to have done so. But speaking more generally, the rapid development of trade since the pacification of the country after the Fulani wars and specially after the British conquest cannot be doubted. It appears to have overtaken Nupe society unawares, as it were, without giving it the chance to readjust itself gradually to the new conditions. Trade, in the war-disturbed times of the past an occupation for men who could carry arms, fell now easily to the women. It called for new recruits, and seized upon the existing system of division of labour between the sexes—men as producers, and women as 'middlemen' and traders. Yet this organization, which was designed to fit into the narrow scope of village life, was adapted too readily to the purposes of the new widespread trade that developed in the Emirates. No other system of division of labour and specialization, it appears, could be evolved as quickly to take charge of the new tasks. It could not but disorganize social life. Family organization and the traditional concepts of morality fell victims to economic progress. The profit motive, here as in many other fields of Nupe economy, outstripped and overruled the interests of group cohesion and group stability.

CHAPTER XX
ECONOMIC BALANCE: MEANS AND WANTS
THE PROBLEM

IN the discussion of economic balance in this new sense we meet with certain methodological difficulties. The wants on which resources are expended form part of culture—they reflect customs, conventions, tastes, fashions. The ideal solution would obviously be to include here a description of the whole culture, political life, social organization, law, religion, education, recreation, and so forth, from the economic aspect. Yet even if this were possible the question would remain whether we could not produce an arrangement more adequate to the present problem than this enumeration based on the qualitative contents of the different domains of culture. As we are dealing here with questions of equilibrium, 'the more adequate' arrangement would clearly have to be in the nature of a weighted or graded order, i.e. a scale of economic values.

How are we to build up this graded order of values? Economists agree that economic incentives can be arranged in an order of intensity.[1] Yet economics can express the intensity of incentives only in terms of the concrete efforts expended on their satisfaction. Broadly speaking, the existence or intensity of wants is derived from the fact that they are satisfied, and that certain wants are satisfied rather than others.[2] This circular argument precludes the possibility of studying wants apart from their concrete satisfaction. As anthropologists, having defined economic relations as relations between means and the satisfaction of *culturally accepted* needs, we must presuppose that the scale of values has to some extent at least an existence *per se*, that is, is of some permanence, and is buttressed by cultural factors independently of actual demands. Without this theoretical separation of wants and their concrete satisfaction we could never attempt to frame such questions as why certain forms of satisfaction are highly in demand while others appear to be neglected although their 'value' is recognized by the society. We could never point out that certain needs may be highly valued in themselves, and may yet be disregarded because of an insufficiency of means. These are questions of the rationality of wants, of the motives behind wants, and of the efficiency of socio-economic systems in general (the main manifestation of which is the distribution of poverty and wealth). These questions, though admittedly beyond the scope of economics in the strict sense, deeply concern the student of society.[3]

We cannot demolish the circular argument of economics, which is, in

---

[1] L. Robbins, *An Essay on the Nature and Significance of Economic Science*, 1935, p. 86.

[2] D. M. Goodfellow, *Principles of Economic Sociology*, 1939, p. 28.

[3] The concept of poverty and wealth depends on the possibility of comparing the magnitude of incomes and forms of satisfaction secured by the income of different individuals. An inter-individual comparison of this kind is not admitted by theoretical economics. See L. Robbins, op. cit., pp. 137–40.

fact, intrinsic to all generalizations about human behaviour. But for the purpose of sociological analysis we must attempt to extend this circular argument over as wide a range of interconnected phenomena as possible. Wants are discovered in the way people behave; but in this discovery we are, unlike the economist, not bound by statistical evidence alone, but can with the help of our field methods study the actual behaviour of individuals in all its aspects. Behaviour comes to include also verbal behaviour and expression of beliefs, convictions, and ideals. Verbal behaviour may thus also supply us with evidence of the intensity of incentives. We are driven to admit the existence, side by side with 'concrete' evaluations as revealed in economic decisions, of diffuse 'theoretical' or 'moral' evaluations which may be at variance with the former.

We are, then, operating with a two-dimensional system of wants and values. It has, I admit, no validity in the economic universe of discourse.[1] Seen from the economic point of view the 'theoretical' evaluation merely represents the weaker incentive which, in the eventual economic decision, has been subordinated to the stronger and thus relegated to the sphere of ineffectual theoretical concepts. But the acceptance of the two-dimensional scheme is indispensable to the adequate description of human conduct. The reality which it defines is primarily of a psychological nature: it embraces the motivations and repressions behind the economic decision, and the significant attitudes and responses which accompany it—hope and regret, disdain or resentment, expectations of betterment or the consciousness of failure. Yet every one of these psychological reactions may become a concrete determinant of conduct and thus a potential drive for readjustment either in the narrow sphere of social mobility, i.e. in attempts of individuals to improve their position, or in the wider sphere of collective attempts to bring about (by force, if necessary) changes in the socio-economic system. We need say no more on this point: it is illustrated abundantly in the history of society.

We will make two further admissions: first, that the divergence between theoretical and actual evaluation is frequently the symptom of a merely temporary lack of adjustment, and thus of social change; and second, that the divergence is partly due to a certain ambiguity in the concept we are using of 'wants' or 'needs'. The first does no more than underline the significance of the phenomenon to the student of society. As regards the second, the following examination of the nature of the divergence will show that the ambiguity in the concept of 'wants' is due, not to inexact formulation, but to the nature of society. The divergence between actual and theoretical evaluation occurs in three different forms.

(1) The simplest and most familiar form of this divergence is that owing to time-lag. The actual evaluation frequently takes account of changed wants, while the theoretical evaluation still maintains pre-change standards.

[1] I suspect, though, that this dual definition of 'concrete' and 'theoretical' evaluation forms a parallel to a similar distinction made by economic theory, namely, between the 'real value' of commodities and their 'exchange value'.

(2) The divergence may be due to a differentiation within the structure of the group whose economic decisions we are studying. To put it schematically: individuals act always as members of groups; but every individual is at once member of different groups of progressive inclusiveness—family, kinship group, local group, tribe, state, &c. His conduct may thus be influenced by possibly conflicting standards of evaluation obtaining in the different groups. His economic decision may follow one standard of evaluation, while he relegates an alternative standard which he is either unable or unwilling to carry into action to the plane of 'theoretical' values. We may then find that the 'concrete' values adopted by individuals as members, for example, of the narrower group, appear as 'theoretical' values in the larger, comprehensive, group, and vice versa. Disregard of the alternative standards of evaluation owing to inability is typical of most forms of class stratification and, potentially, of class consciousness (in the economic sense). For here we see groups act according to evaluations derived from the sufficiency of means in their section, but yet remain conscious of wants and satisfactions obtaining in other, more fortunate, strata of the group at large. Disregard of alternative standards of evaluation owing to unwillingness, on the other hand, will mostly be found to indicate differences in social insight, which varies with position in the social group, with age, and experience. Thus the young labourers who preferred to purchase clothes and other temporary attractions rather than save money for marriage acted according to the ideals of the younger generation and disregarded the value which, as members of the kinship group, they should have recognized—values, moreover, which are upheld by the executive organs of the group, the elders and the family heads. We shall base our examination of the Nupe scale of values mainly on the widest range of social insight and (unless expressly stated) shall assess economic wants from the viewpoint of the family head.

(3) A final, most elusive, divergence is that between felt wants and abstract needs.[1] We must realize that the social significance of organized human conduct, shaped as it constantly is by convention and custom, is not exhausted in the attainment of a certain single satisfaction (which alone was aimed at), but normally implies the effectiveness of other wants and needs besides. Their satisfaction is attained, as it were, automatically, with the satisfaction of the conscious want, and may be embodied in the very conventional form which the satisfaction must take. Radcliffe-Brown has shown that the paramount ubiquitous need of this kind is that inherent in the structure of society itself, of integration and stability. Now, concrete evaluation may in certain cases run counter to that need, which would be relegated to the ideological validity of theoretical wants. These social needs are rarely present in the minds of individuals—except in those of far-sighted individuals acting as executive organs of their group. Rather the student of society hypothesizes their existence; for to him they reveal their existence and effective-

---

[1] Goodfellow assigns the study of 'wants' to economics proper, and the study of 'needs' to a separate discipline, which he calls Social Economics (op. cit., p. 275).

ness indirectly, through certain significant changes in the stability of social life.

With these methodological viewpoints in mind, we may now attempt to build up our scale of values. We cannot hope, of course, to make it exact in every grade or detail; but we can trace its outline which gives us the extremes of the scale—its maximum and minimum points—and, between them, certain well-defined marks. I propose to adopt a three-fold approach.

(1) We find the 'minimum point' of our scale in the demands upon resources which refer to the satisfaction of the physiological necessities of life—'primary needs', in Malinowski's terminology—above all, nutrition and shelter. With Malinowski, we realize that these needs never exist as such in society, that is, in the form of undisguised elementary impulses, but already appear in a certain conventionalized form, shaped and elaborated by culture.[1] Closely linked with these wants is another group which we may call, with Malinowski, 'derived' wants, in the sense that they refer to the maintenance of the productive organization by means of which the 'primary needs' are satisfied.[2]

(2) On this second stage we shall examine certain more or less fixed demands upon resources which are involved in institutions and customs and which are accepted with little variation, irrespective of status or wealth, throughout the society. Typical instances of these demands are bride-price and taxation.

(3) We study the wants and forms of satisfaction apparent in the conduct of the recognized *élite* of the society. They define the 'maximum point' of our scale, and we may take them to represent the ideals and generally desirable things—the things 'one ought to be able to afford'—in the opinion of the society at large.[3] I must add that this last assumption is justified only if we can prove that no rift runs across the ideological framework of the society separating the desires and tastes typical of the various social strata. We must reckon with the possibility of individuals of the lower social strata being well content with their 'station'; or of tastes and desires of higher social strata showing a caste-like exclusiveness. We shall see later that one of the main characteristics of Nupe society lies in the absence of a self-limitation of the former kind; the latter kind of rift, on the other hand, is negligible, and is restricted mainly to the prerogatives of royalty, for example, to the traditional insignia of rulership, the rules of dress and food of the Nupe kings, &c. In modern Nupe even these caste-like prerogatives have mostly disappeared.

[1] I cannot argue here the question whether or not sexual satisfaction should be included among these 'primary needs'; I have put sexual desires in the second group of wants mainly because they are subject to a much more complete cultural 'elaboration' and institutionalization.

[2] It will be seen that this definition is narrower than Malinowski's definition of 'derived needs', which can, in fact, be extended over the whole field of culture.

[3] In this assumption, which is justified by the stratified structure of Nupe society, we differ from Dr. R. W. Firth, who states that 'there is no final organization in primitive societies in the sense of a single individual or ruling group of individuals who are in a position to dictate all choices' (*Primitive Polynesian Economy*, p. 24).

But we must reckon also with another ideological rift in tastes and desires, which would affect all three stages of our investigation, namely a rift which might be involved in the complex and composite nature of Nupe culture. It would separate, not social strata, but different sections of the population, different cultural groups within Nupe society. A rift of this kind does, in fact, exist with respect to the different cultural standards valid in town and country, in the Mohammedanized capital and the pagan or semi-pagan districts.

STANDARDS OF LIVING: NECESSITIES OF LIFE

The extent to which the economy of an individual or a family group is able to incorporate into its 'balance' wants placed lower or higher on the scale of cultural values gives us what is generally called the 'standard of living'. We shall find that it is possible to arrange these varying standards in certain well-defined groups or grades, and to embody them in a comprehensive economic stratification of the society.

It will be best to begin with concrete illustrations of the economic balance achieved in Nupe households. Out of fifty household budgets which I have recorded I propose to select five representative examples, taken from different localities and differently organized household groups, in which we can study the main variations that occur. All these examples refer to peasant households. Unfortunately I found it impossible to work out budgets of this kind also for craftsmen and 'free professions' (with two exceptions to be quoted later). Their extremely fluid economy presented great difficulties: to reduce, in their case, income and expenditure to exact figures would have demanded much more time than I was able to devote to this task. However, just because these types of economy are more fluid and more easily adjustable to varying wants, they are of less interest to us than the more restricted and more rigid economy of the agriculturist.

Let me say a few words about the method by which I arrived at these records of Nupe household economy. I have examined households in Bida, Doko, Lemu, and Kutigi. The figures referring to the total farm-yield, and to the proportion of the produce kept for consumption or set aside for sale, were ascertained by inquiry. The nature of Nupe agriculture—the series of successive harvests, and the widely varying arrangements with regard to storage and sale of produce—precluded any more direct approach (e.g. by measuring the yield or the stores). However, there were important safeguards: first, as we have seen, the Nupe farmers are well acquainted with the use of standard measures, and indeed themselves use them to calculate their yield.[1] Moreover, after a number of preliminary inquiries (in which I was helped by reliable informants) I could already form an opinion as to likely averages and individual deviations. Finally, whenever any dubious figures emerged I could verify them by independent inquiries of other household members. In this respect the tendency of the Nupe farmers to keep track of the contributions of the various family members to the common store proved of considerable assistance.

[1] See p. 315. In the charts below the terms 'load' and 'bundle' are used as equivalents.

Household A

Tunga near Bida. Labour unit: one man. Family of four

Crops and trees	Total yield	Kept for household consumption	Sold	Additional income
Bulr.-millet	5 loads	All	..	Mat-weaving, for 9d. apiece. Total earnings 5s.
Late millet	3 ,,	,,	..	
Sorghum	8 ,,	5 loads	3 loads, for 2s.	
Beans	v. little	All	..	
Sw. potatoes	?	..	All, for 3s.	
Cassava	?	All	..	
Locust-beans	5 loads	..	All, for 1s. 3d.	

	s.	d.
Income from farm produce . . .	6	3
Total income	11	3
Money expenditure: Tax . . .	9	6

Household B

Bida. Labour unit: father and boy. Family of three

Crops and trees	Total yield	Kept for household consumption	Sold	Additional income
Bulr.-millet	Bad crop	No yield	..	Occasionally straw hat-making. Borrowed 1s. from relations for tax.
Late millet	6 loads	All	..	
Sorghum	6 ,,	,,	..	
Beans	?	..	All, for 2s.	
Yam	6 loads	All	..	
Rice	31 gourds	10 gourds	21 gourds for 3s. 6d.	
Locust-beans	..	..	Sold the whole tree for felling to the Bida brick-works, for 4s. 6d.	

	s.
Income from farm produce	10
Total income (incl. money loan) . . .	11
Money expenditure: Tax	11

Household C

Tunga near Bida. Labour unit: father (old) and married son (invalid). Family
of five

Crops and trees	Total yield	Kept for household consumption	Sold	Additional income
Bulr.-millet	Bad crop	No yield	..	Sold 2 young goats for 3s. each, in order to obtain the rest of the tax.
Late millet	10 loads	..	9 loads, for 9s.; 1 load given as *dzanká* to *Makũ*	
Sorghum	5 ,,	1 load	3 loads, for 3s.; 1 load given as *dzanká* to *Makũ*	
Beans	7 ,,	..	All, for 5½d.	
Locust-beans	9 ,,	..	All, for 3s.	

	s.	d.
Income from farm produce . . .	15	5½
Total income	21	5½
Money expenditure: Tax . . .	21	0

Household D

Kutigi. Labour unit: father and two sons, one of them married. Family of seven

Crops and trees	Total yield	Kept for household consumption	Sold	Additional income
Bulr.-millet	20 loads	All	..	Family head: occasional hunting.
Late millet	15 ,,	13 loads	2 loads, for 1s. 4d.	Hides sold for 2d. to 4d. apiece, total earnings 1s. 3d.
Sorghum	20 ,,	10 ,,	10 loads, for 7s. 6d.	
Yam	7 ,,	All	..	Sons: mat-weaving, for 6d. apiece; total earnings approx.
Cassava	?	,,	..	
Beans	2 loads	,,	..	10s. p.a. (i.e. *bucá* income). Each son contributes 3s. towards the family tax.
Ground-beans	1 load	,,	..	
Sw. potatoes	little	,,	..	
Ground-nuts	5 loads	Only seed	Rest, for 3s. 6d.	
Bananas	?	All	..	
Locust-beans	5 loads	..	All, for 1s. 3d.	
Palm-kernels	?	..	All, for £1 or 25s.	
Kola-nuts	5 loads	..	All, for 6s. 3d.	

	£	s.	d.
Income from farm produce	2	4	10
Total income (incl. contribution from sons)	2	12	1
Money expenditure: Tax	1	13	0
Egbe work		6	8
Final instalment of bride-price for younger son		10	0

Household E

Lemu. Labour unit: father and four sons, two of them married. Family of ten

Crops and trees	Total yield	Kept for household consumption	Sold	Additional income
Bulr.-millet	50 loads	20 loads	30 loads for 15s.	Family head: trade in rams and sheep.
Late millet	30 ,,	10 ,,	20 loads for 10s.	Total earnings approx. 10s. p.a.
Sorghum	40 ,,	20 ,,	20 loads for 13s. 6d.	Sons: *bucá* farmwork. Total earnings approx. 4s. p.a.
Beans	6 ,,	All	..	
Yam	?	A little	8 loads for 4s.	
Cassava	?	Eaten at once	..	
Sw. potatoes	?	,, ,,	..	
Cotton	10 loads	..	All, for 15s.	
Red pepper	4 ,,	..	All, for 8s.	
Locust-beans	6 ,,	..	All, for 4s.	

	£	s.	d.
Income from farm produce	3	9	6
Total income approx.	4	0	0
Money expenditure: Tax	2	7	0
Egbe work		6	6
Name-giving ceremony for grandchild		8	0
First instalment of bride-price for younger son		17	0

The construction of these household budgets is designed to show the main division of resources into those which are utilized in kind, i.e. for food consumption, and those utilized for exchange, i.e. for the acquisition of commodities and the satisfaction of other, non-nutritive, wants. We have said that the latitude in satisfying wants beyond the 'minimum level' gives us the standards of living and economic stratification.

Now, it is characteristic that Nupe society, which is so conscious of its class stratification, is equally conscious of its economic stratification and the varying standards of living. Even the principle of the 'minimum point' of the scale of values, the existence of a minimum cost of living, is clearly understood and, what is more important, generally accepted. I have worked out questionnaires referring to this minimum standard of living and collected answers from twenty men in Bida and the villages, of different classes and different degree of wealth. They all were in agreement on the essential points. Expressed in agricultural produce, i.e. staple food crops, calculated for a small family of four, the minimum annual cost of living amounts to 12 to 15 bundles of grain (of any variety) or 90 loads of yam, if the household relies on one of the two staple food crops; or, if both are combined, 6 to 8 bundles of grain and 40 to 50 loads of yam. Expressed in money, 1½d. per day is the lowest cost of living per adult. But this food, as my informants added, will hardly be nutritive, it would only 'make the belly swell'. With more nutritive food, the lowest cost of living is 3d. per day. Even this is not yet a high standard, for it excludes *na ma re na*, things 'that taste nice', e.g. sweetmeats, savouries, and suchlike. For a family of four or five I was given

the following daily 'menu' corresponding to a standard of living slightly
above the minimum:

Morning meal:	corn-water or gruel with 'bread' (*fura*) . . .	1½*d.*
Midday meal:	cassava, beans, or rice	3*d.*
Evening meal:	corn porridge	1½*d.*
Total cost	. . . .	6*d.*

If fats, shea-butter, or palm-oil are added in form of sauce, the bill increases by another 1½*d.*; meat or fish, the addition of which would raise
the meal to a much higher 'standard of living', cost 6*d.* a day extra. For
example:

Morning meal:	corn-gruel and ground-nut cakes . . .	1½*d.*–2*d.*
Midday meal:	corn porridge	1½*d.*
	palm-oil, greens, and spices	1–2*d.*
	fish	3*d.*
Evening meal:	rice	4*d.*
	palm-oil, &c. (partly left over from midday meal)	0·3*d.*
	meat or fish	2–3*d.*
Total cost	. . . .	1*s.* 1·3*d.*–1*s.* 3·8*d.*

Calculating the cost of food for a family of this size for a week and taking
into account that the morning meal often consists of food left over from
the previous day, and that meat, fish, and certain savouries are only
bought occasionally, we arrive at the sum of 8*s.* 9*d.* per week, or 1*s.* 3*d.*
per day.

These figures refer to the cost of living in Bida, where the majority of
the population have to buy their whole food. But in the village, food
other than the staple crops—including fats, fish, and meat—has also to
be bought for money. On the other hand, cost of living in the villages is
slightly cheaper, as is shown in the following example, which is again
calculated for four or five persons, and corresponds to a fairly high standard, comparable to the elaborate Bida 'menu' just quoted:

Morning meal:	corn-gruel and ground-nut cakes . . .	0·8*d.*
Midday meal:	corn-porridge and fish, with palm-oil, greens, and	
	spices	4*d.*
Evening meal:	the same	4*d.*
Total cost .	. . . .	approx. 9*d.*

The standards of living in the village are also lower than in Bida: an
average standard in the village would correspond to a low standard in
Bida. Dried fish rather than meat is the main item on the menu, meat
being eaten not more than once a week or, in poorer households, once in
several weeks. Rice, which appears fairly regularly on the Bida menu, is
rare in the village; sorghum-beer, on the other hand, which may replace
a regular meal in the village, does not figure on the menu of Bida households. But if the very high standard of living characteristic of the Bida
upper classes does not occur in the peasant households, the same is true
of the other extreme, the very low standard of living; for although I have
found many households in or near Bida which live on the very minimum
level, these very low standards seem absent in the village.

Let me give a few concrete examples to illustrate the food economy in typical Nupe households. They are taken from four households in Bida (Nos. 1 and 2) and in the country (Nos. 3 and 4). 'Menu' No. 1 is that of a wealthy noble household, No. 2 that of an average trader's household, No. 3 that of a prosperous peasant household in Kutigi (household D in the list of household budgets given above), and No. 4 that of an average peasant household in the same village. All four examples were obtained about the same time, the end of May and beginning of June. B = morning meal (i.e. 'breakfast'), M = midday meal, E = evening meal.

No. 1

19.5.1936.
  B. Corn-water and corn-cakes.
  M. Rice and fish.
  E. Rice and meat with palm-oil, greens, and spices.
20.5.1936.
  B. Corn-gruel.
  M. Rice and meat with shea-butter, onions, and spices.
  E. Corn-porridge and fish, with palm-oil, greens, and spices.
21.5.1936.
  B. Corn-gruel and bean-cakes.
  M. Rice and chicken.
  E. Corn-porridge and fish, with greens and spices.
22.5.1936.
  B. Corn-water and bean-cakes.
  M. Rice and fish.
  E. Rice and fish, with palm-oil, greens, and spices.
23.5.1936.
  B. Corn-water and bean-cakes.
  M. Rice and fish, with palm-oil, greens, and spices.
  E. Rice and meat, with palm-oil, greens, and spices.
24.5.1936.
  B. Corn-water and corn-cakes.
  M. Corn-porridge and fish, with palm-oil, greens, and spices.
  E. Rice and meat, with palm-oil.
25.5.1936.
  B. Corn-gruel.
  M. Corn-porridge and fish, with palm-oil, greens, and spices.
  E. Rice and meat, with palm-oil.

No. 2

18.5.1936.
  B. Corn-water and ground-nut cakes.
  M. Corn-porridge and fish, with palm-oil, greens, and spices.
  E. Rice and meat, with palm-oil.
19.5.1936.
  B. Corn-water and ground-nut cakes.
  M. Cassava with palm-oil.
  E. Corn-porridge and fish, with palm-oil, greens, and spices.
20.5.1936.
  B. Beans cooked in thick palm-oil, with salt and pepper.
  M. Boiled cassava, with palm-oil.
  E. Corn-porridge and fish, with shea-butter, greens, and spices.
21.5.1936.
  B. Bean-cakes.
  M. Corn-porridge and fish, with shea-butter, &c.—left over from previous day.
  E. Rice and meat, with palm-oil, greens, and spices.

22.5.1936.
  B. Corn-water and corn-cakes.
  M. Corn-porridge.
  E. Rice and meat, with palm-oil and spices.

23.5.1936.
  B. Corn-water and corn-cakes.
  M. Rice and fish, with palm-oil.
  E. Corn-porridge and fish, with palm-oil, greens, and spices.

24.5.1936.
  B. Hot corn-water and corn-cakes.
  M. Sweet potatoes and palm-oil.
  E. Corn porridge and fish, with palm-oil, greens, and spices.

Note that ground-nut cakes, though eaten repeatedly for the morning meal in this household, are absent in Menu No. 1. In the latter household it was explained to me that ground-nuts were 'out of season', and no longer good for making cakes—a culinary distinction which the less well-to-do (and less sophisticated) households do not follow.

No. 3

31.5.1936.
  B. Corn-gruel and beans.
  M. Yam and beans, with palm-oil, salt, and pepper.
  E. Corn-porridge and fish, with palm-oil, greens, and spices.

1.6.1936.
  B. Corn-gruel and beans.
  M. Yam and beans, with palm-oil.
  E. Corn-porridge and meat, with palm-oil, greens, and spices.

2.6.1936.
  B. Corn-gruel and beans.
  M. Corn-porridge and meat, from previous day.
  E. Rice and fish, with palm-oil, greens, and spices.

3.6.1936.
  B. Corn-gruel.
  M. Boiled yam with palm-oil.
  E. Corn-porridge and fish, with palm-oil, greens, and spices.

4.6.1936.
  B. Corn-gruel and beans.
  M. Beans with palm-oil, salt, and pepper.
  E. Corn-porridge and fish, with palm-oil, greens, and spices.

5.6.1936.
  B. Corn-gruel.
  M. Corn-porridge and fish, with palm-oil, greens, and spices.
  E. Rice and fish, with palm-oil, greens, and spices.

6.6.1936.
  B. Corn-gruel.
  M. Boiled yam, with palm-oil.
  E. Corn-porridge and fish, with palm-oil, greens, and spices.

No. 4

13.6.1936.
  B. Corn-water and ground-nut cakes.
  M. Cassava.
  E. Porridge and fish, with palm-oil (no greens).

14.6.1936.
  B. Corn-porridge, from previous day.
  M. Corn-porridge, left over from morning meal.
  E. Fresh corn-porridge with greens (no fish).

15.6.1936.
   B. Corn-porridge and very little fish (bought for 0·1d.), with palm-oil, greens, and spices.
   M. Sorghum beer.
   E. Corn-water and ground-nut cakes.
16.6.1936.
   B. Nothing.
   M. Raw cassava.
   E. Corn-porridge and fish, with palm-oil, greens, and spices.
17.6.1936.
   B. Corn-gruel.
   M. Corn-gruel and ground-nut cakes.
   E. Corn-porridge and fish, with palm-oil, greens, and spices.
18.6.1936.
   B. Hot corn-water and ground-nut cakes.
   M. Corn-porridge.
   E. Corn-porridge, left over from midday meal.
19.6.1936.
   B. Cold corn-water and corn-cakes.
   M. Cassava boiled in water.
   E. Corn-porridge and palm-oil (no fish).

In examining the budgets from the viewpoint of food economy, we find that in this one domain of wants they are already representative of widely varying standards of living. Measuring the produce available for food consumption in the various households against the standard of 12 to 15 bundles (loads) of grain per family of four, or 3 to 4 bundles of grain per head, we obtain the following relations:

Household A: family of four—13 loads, or over 3 loads per head.
Household B: family of three—12 loads (also yam), or over 4 loads per head.
Household C: family of four—1 load, or ¼ load per head.
Household D: family of seven—43 loads of grain (also yam), or over 6 loads per head.
Household E: family of ten—50 loads (also yam), or over 5 loads per head.

In other words, we find poverty, i.e. 'insufficiency of means', a certain marginal sufficiency, and also ample and prosperous, standards of living.

We can correlate the prosperity in this sense with certain other social factors.[1] The most prosperous households are found in Trans-Kaduna and in the country north of Bida (e.g. Lemu) where land is fertile and plentiful. Households with a large labour-unit are invariably more prosperous than households with a small labour-unit. The budget which expresses real poverty and insufficiency (C) comes from Bida, and from a small labour group whose efficiency was abnormally reduced: one of the two men who formed the labour unit was old and past work in age, and the other an invalid. I have spoken on different occasions of the detrimental effects upon production of the spreading dissolution of the large labour-unit. That a situation such as this could occur, that this prima facie inefficient productive arrangement which leads an old man and

[1] It will be understood that in this as in similar general statements I am referring not only to the selected examples, representative though they are, but to the whole material which I have examined.

an invalid to work on their own, could at all be tolerated, reveals most conspicuously the inherent weakness in present-day labour organization.

We turn now to the examination of the money surplus achieved in the various households. Here we find the same wide variations as in the examination of the output which was retained for food. But the two ranges of variation do not run parallel; which means that the Nupe peasant does not divide his above-minimum-output equally between nutritive wants and wants demanding money surplus. He may accumulate food-supplies up to what we may regard as the maximum at the cost of the money surplus (as in D); or he may go below the maximum in food-supplies in order to obtain a higher money surplus (as in E); or he may be forced to fall even below the minimum standard of food-supplies for the sake of a certain necessary money surplus (as in C). In order to understand the full significance of this we must anticipate here another demand upon resources which, though not expressing 'primary needs', possesses in native economy the same urgency and inevitability—tax. This demand was, in fact, already embodied in the budgets which we have drawn up. For when measuring 'sufficiency of means' with regard to the primary necessities of life we measured not ability to reach an adequate level of production, but ability to retain an adequate supply of produce after this other rigid demand had been met. Normally, every farmer would retain at least the necessary minimum supplies, which is easily achieved in the ample husbandry of prosperous households, but may prove impossible in the households which keep close to the margin. Here the free planning of the balance between essential food stores and produce for sale may be restricted by the necessity of providing the money 'surplus' for tax, even (as in C) to the degree of reducing food-supplies below the minimum level. Only after deducting the tax can we thus speak of 'real' surplus, in the sense of money resources that can be applied freely to wants, and only with respect to this final surplus can we speak strictly of sufficiency and prosperity.

With regard to surplus in this sense the correlation between large labour-units and high degree of 'sufficiency' is no longer true. In household D the family head could secure a money surplus only by claiming contributions from the *bucá* work of his sons—against the rules of *efakó* collaboration. In a great many cases (not recorded here) large labour-units, though able to produce a large surplus output, could not secure a corresponding money surplus. The explanation lies in the low market-price which ordinary agricultural produce commands. If large quantities have to be sold at once—as they must be where a large sum of money (e.g. for tax) has to be found by a single producer (i.e. the head of the labour-unit)—the price will be even more unfavourable. Only where the production comprises commercial crops, or generally crops commanding a high market-price, will it be possible to combine both aspects of surplus. We find, on the other hand, that households in which a handicraft is practised in addition to farm-work attain a higher measure of prosperity than households of farmers pure and simple. A profitable handicraft can procure ready money for certain urgent expenses, above all, tax, and thus free the household from the necessity of selling a too large proportion of the produce, or selling it in a hurry, at unfavourable prices.

From nutritive wants we proceed to the wants involved in the 'primary need' of shelter. The upkeep or building of houses represents a want which, occurring at much longer and more irregular intervals, does not figure conspicuously in the annual household budget. In the village, upkeep and building of houses is mainly a question of co-operative labour, involving little or no money outlay. Smaller house repairs, above all thatching, become necessary every three to five years; more complete repairs, such as rebuilding of huts or of the compound wall, are reckoned to occur every ten to twelve years. The small repairs are carried out by the household group, and take rarely more than two or three days. For larger repairs the help of neighbours and relations must be enlisted on *egbe* scale; they last much longer, according to the body of workers that can be mustered, and the work may often have to be interrupted for a day or two if the workers have other tasks in hand. Most building work in the village is left till the beginning of the rains, when the ground (from which the clay for building is dug) is soft, the grass for thatching not too dry (such grass is said to last less long), and when the people are still free from more exigent farm-work. We may add that the building of more elaborate houses of the kind that is found in the town and also in certain villages entails the employment of expert labour, and thus money expenditure, which varies widely with the style and scale of the work.

Finally, we add the 'derived wants' involved in agricultural production. Under this heading we include repairs and purchase of tools and the financing of *egbe* work. In the same category falls the payment of a fixed land rent in kind which obtains in the area round Bida (as in our example C). I have only partly been able to include these wants in the household budgets. However, the widespread efforts to economize, for example, on the cost of *egbe* work, or the neglected appearance of many of the sumptuous Bida houses, reveal the difficulties which many households find to-day in coping with these wants.

STANDARDS OF LIVING: CULTURAL REQUIREMENTS

The next step in our inquiry is to ascertain the demands embodied in cultural standards which the Nupe peasant has to meet out of the surplus (if surplus there be) derived from his production. We can group these demands under three headings. (1) Demands implied in kinship duties. In so far as the household or kinship group coincides with the labour-unit these demands overlap with those we listed under 'maintenance of labour'. (2) Demands implied in duties towards the community—religious, political, or social. (3) Certain personal requirements which are regarded, by convention, as essential, and even indispensable.

Under the first heading we list the expenses of kinship ceremonies and feasts—the name-giving ceremony for a new-born child, wedding feasts, and burial and funeral ceremonies. These expenses are borne primarily by the family head in whose house the ceremony is performed; but he can also count on contributions from the various relations and friends who attend the ceremony as guests of the house. We have noted the modern tendency among peasants to replace the traditional gifts in kind with contributions in money, which are customary in Bida. These expenses vary widely with wealth and status. The minimum costs—which interest us here—amount to about 3*s.* to 5*s.* in the name-giving ceremony and 8*s.* to 10*s.* in marriage and funeral ceremonies. In the case of junior family members this group of kinship expenses also includes certain occasional gifts in kind to elder relatives, especially the family head. In one Doko household (not quoted among our examples) a young farmer who worked on his own gave his whole produce of beans (worth 2*s.*) to his father and elder brother. In another household, in Bida, a man shared his crop of maize with his elder brother, who was the family head. Family heads, on the other hand, have to provide for the costs of education of their children or younger brothers (so far as it involves expenditure), e.g. the apprenticeship in the workshop of a craftsman, or the attendance at a Koran school or the Government school. They must bear the expenses that might be caused by illness—the purchase of medicines or of the services of diviner or barber-doctor. 'Pocket-money', finally, for children or junior family members is, as we have seen, supplied in the form of *bucá* work, which they are encouraged to take up.

Bride-price

The largest item under this heading is the payment of bride-price, which devolves, in traditional practice at least, on the head of the family section that is united in the labour-unit. I have pointed out already that the bride-price also involves the accumulation of wealth, and comparatively long-range planning and saving.

The bride-price is always reckoned in money, although it may be paid partly in kind; the gifts in kind, however, which may form part of the bride-price, such as cloth and beads, all have a definite money value, and must be bought for money. The Nupe bride-price, called *ewó yawó*, 'money of marriage', comprises a series of payments of varying amount, each of which is known by a special name: we have, first, the gift of the Greeting; we have further two gifts called Small Thanks and Great Thanks, respectively, the latter which represents bride-price proper, being sometimes referred to by the modern Hausa-Mohammedan term *sadeiki*; then there is the Money for Henna, to buy the henna with which the bride will adorn herself for the marriage ceremony, the Money for Pots, with which pots and cooking utensils will be bought, and finally a small gift to the bridesmaids who accompany the bride when she enters her husband's house for the first time. In the country these last two gifts are a comparatively recent introduction, having originated and spread from Bida. In addition to these various 'part payments' there is an annual gift of produce which is presented by the father of the bridegroom to the father of the bride during the period between the formal betrothal and the final marriage ceremony. The whole bride-price is

A a

rarely paid over at once; as a rule the various part-payments are made in the course of three to five years, in the order just given. The first gift, the Greeting, is meant to seal the betrothal and the agreement of the parents of bride and bridegroom. The various gifts listed after the Great Thanks are left till immediately before the marriage ceremony. Only the two largest 'instalments', Small Thanks and Great Thanks, can be paid partly in the form of gifts of cloth or beads; all other gifts must be in money. Let me give a concrete illustration. The bride-price of N., of Kutigi, who married in 1934, consisted of the following payments, all of which were in money:

	£	s.	d.
Greeting		1	6
Small Thanks		10	0
Great Thanks	3	0	0
Money for Henna		5	0
Money for Pots		10	0
Gifts to bridesmaids		2	6
Four annual gifts of food, to the total value of . .		10	0
Total	£4	19	0

Bride-price in Nupe has undergone great changes. From £3 in pre-British days it has risen later to £10, £15, and even £20. Recently it has fallen again to a more modest sum, between £5 and £10. The height of the bride-price has, in fact, caused the Administration to intervene in 1934, and to lay down a maximum amount of £7. On the whole, the people welcomed the reduction. But it has not been adopted uniformly; I have found a bride-price of £9 and £10 still being paid two years after the law was enacted. In very poor households, on the other hand, the reduction has merely academic significance, as these people may not be able to afford even that amount. My informations were that originally the bride-price represented a fixed sum—gba shita, 120,000 cowries (£3)—which did not vary with, nor depend on, prosperity or social status, as it does to-day. Similarly every item of the bride-price was fixed traditionally, the amounts in cowries being frequently used as alternative terms for some of these payments. This is the series of payments in the traditional Nupe bride-price:

	£	s.
Gba (lit. 2,000 cowries—a preliminary gift absorbed to-day in the Greeting)		1
Greeting, or gbaota (lit. 6,000 cowries)		3
Small Thanks		12
Great Thanks	2	10
Total	£3	6

With the rise, and subsequent fall, in the bride-price its amount was made dependent upon the varying standards of living. It is significant that the large items in the bride-price, Small and Great Thanks, have remained comparatively unchanged; the changes affected chiefly the smaller gifts, new ones being included, or increased or decreased in amount. Now a large bride-price, which comprises all these various gifts, is still the ideal. But certain new ways have been found to harmonize the ideal with lower standards of living. To-day a distinction which did not exist in former times is universally recognized, between bride-price entailed in ordinary marriage and bride-price paid in the case of *yawó dengi*, marriage in the family: the latter commands a lower bride-price, approximately £3, i.e. the original uniform bride-price. In every case in which I examined the relation of 'marriage in the family' to outside marriage my informants emphasized that there were more family marriages to-day than formerly because it had become so difficult to pay the high bride-price. We see, then, that the bride-price was not simply reduced in amount uniformly; rather a certain context was introduced—invented almost—in which a lower bride-price could be legitimately accepted. The lower bride-price, which would run counter to traditional cultural standards, was thus given a certain qualified sanction by the society. However, even the low bride-price cannot always be provided by the family head. And here we find another adjustment to the lower standards of living, namely, the spreading practice to pay bride-price only for the eldest son, while younger sons must either contribute to, or bear themselves, the cost of their bride-price. The traditional duty of the family head is expressed only in a symbolic transaction: the young man who has to contribute his own bride-price in many cases still hands over the amount to the family head, who will then take all the necessary steps and carry through all the negotiations.

To the bride-price we must add its counterpart, the dowry which the bride brings into marriage and which is paid by her father. Though paid over in one, immediately before the marriage ceremony, the dowry like the bride-price also implies accumulation of wealth over a long period. The amount of the dowry used to correspond exactly to the low, traditional bride-price. Although it fell short of the exorbitant bride-price of recent years, it has been adjusted to the level of a moderately high bride-price (as represented in our example), which proves clearly the underlying intention to balance it against the bride-price even to a degree of mathematical exactitude. Unlike the bride-price, the dowry does not consist in money payments, but in various gifts and contributions in kind. It is reckoned to provide the young bride with cooking utensils, pots, and clothes, sufficient to last her for the first four or five years of the marriage; it also provides food—very excellent food—for the newly wedded couple, so that for the first month or two they are independent of the earnings of the husband or contributions by his family. This is the dowry that corresponds to the example of bride-price quoted above:

	£	s.
10 large pots, costing 1s. each, representing a value of . . .		10
Beads, to wear round the waist, worth	1	15
5 pieces of cloth, worth between 5s. and 7s. each, representing a value of	1	10
Two months' food-supply, worth	1	10
Total	£5	5

Let us for the moment interrupt this description and examine the economic and sociological significance of the changes in bride-price. The question of the sociological significance or 'function' of bride-price has greatly engaged the attention of anthropologists. Yet the various answers which have been found, showing no little disagreement, mostly disregard the fact that institutions never subserve one single purpose, but rather combine ('amalgamate' as Malinowski puts it) a number of social purposes in their structure. The overt purpose of bride-price is clearly that of securing to a man the various legal rights over a woman which are embodied in marriage. Marriage marks the end of certain rights held over the woman by her own kin, above all, her parents, and their replacement by the new rights vested in the husband and his kin. Bride-price in this sense is adequately defined as 'an indemnification for . . . a . . . surrender of rights'.[1] However, as the bride-price is not supplied and received by bridegroom and bride themselves but by their parents or other senior family members, the transaction also has the two-fold social significance of actuating existing kinship bonds (between the bridegroom and his relations who provide the bride-price for him, and similarly between the bride and her family), and of confirming new kinship bonds which stretch, not between the two individuals, but between their families and kinship groups. The transaction of bride-price in this sense has the significance of a contract, to which the two families are the guarantors. The same applies to the parallel transaction of the dowry. Finally, a bride-price, or dowry, of considerable dimensions necessitates the accumulation of wealth and careful economic planning. Bride-price can thus also be said to provide a stimulus for production and economic enterprise in general—one of the motives which every society provides, and needs, to impel it to 'produce, to muster, to count, and publicize its wealth'.[2] This last aspect of the purposefulness of bride-price is, of course, not present in the conscious thought of the people themselves. It expresses a purpose or need read into the facts by the student of society. The first two purposes of bride-price, on the other hand, represent conscious motives of conduct, and the degree of their consciousness becomes evident in the changes which bride-price has undergone in Nupe.

Now, in the traditional Nupe bride-price the aspect of 'indemnification' is greatly overshadowed by the other two aspects. As we have seen, wealth was not 'given' but merely exchanged in the strict sense of the word, the bride-price being balanced exactly against the dowry. When bride-price increased disproportionately, far outstripping the dowry, the element of indemnification and payment as such came to the foreground. The people themselves link this surprising rise with the new economic and political development under British rule: 'Prices were high, and everyone had money.' To some extent this was no doubt due to an increased demand, the greater prosperity showing itself in a rising scale of polygamy. Partly also the motive of 'indemnification' gained a new, additional, significance, that of display for the sake of prestige. But the higher bride-price also showed the effectiveness of the third, economic, factor: for in the highly stimulated economic system the traditional stimulus embodied in the bride-price had to be increased in order to keep pace with the new, higher, level of production and expenditure.

[1] A. R. Radcliffe-Brown, in *Iowa Law Review*, xx, 1935, p. 295.
[2] D. M. Goodfellow, op. cit., p. 132.

This interdependence of bride-price and level of production also explains the limited success, among the more prosperous sections of the population, of the attempts of the Administration to fix the bride-price at a lower and, as it were, arbitrary figure.

Indeed the development of bride-price under the economic stress of the last decade shows how firmly the new 'want' of higher bride-price had struck root. The solution which the people themselves worked out left the 'indemnification' and the 'economic' aspect of the bride-price intact; it achieved the necessary adjustment by reassessing the 'sociological' or kinship aspect. The contribution of the family to the bride-price of its junior members was reduced to the symbolic transaction of the family head acting on behalf of the bridegroom who must himself provide the bride-price; above all, the new rules allowed a reduction in the bride-price in family marriages, i.e. marriages in which the marriage ties do not establish new, but utilize already existing kinship bonds.

We may mention here certain marriage rules customary among the upper classes of Nupe in which an outwardly similar result is achieved by a somewhat different process of reasoning. We have learned that bride-price is kept low in class endogamous marriages among the nobility; a man of status may also marry his daughter to one of his *bara*, and himself put up the bride-price, so that in effect no exchange of wealth takes place; and there is, finally, the custom among the upper classes to marry their daughters with a very low, nominal, bride-price to Mallams—the remission of the bride-price being regarded as a pious act. In these cases the bride-price is kept artificially low in order to ensure that the women of the aristocracy should all be married to men of the same class, or should marry certain men whom they would be unable to marry if the bride-price were high: the political and religious gain balances the material sacrifice.

The institution of bride-price in Nupe gives us an exceptionally clear picture of the multitudinous structure of institutions. It also illustrates the discriminating action of economic evaluation, which, out of the number of social purposes subserved in the institution, fastens upon certain specific purposes for transformation into concrete economic wants. Yet those that are not thus transformed need not be purposes which have lost their significance entirely, but may reveal it indirectly, in the form of 'theoretical values'. We recall the disintegration of the institution of bride-price in present-day Bida, in the case of those young labourers who spend their money among other things on 'women' instead of saving it for bride-price. Let us realize that in a society like Nupe, in which traditional morality forbids pre-marital sexual intercourse, the 'indemnification' aspect of bride-price also implies the purchase of legitimate sexual satisfaction. Now, these young labourers have discovered that to-day sexual satisfaction can be bought more cheaply, and without incurring the obligation of marriage. Short-sightedly, they perceive only this one need and disregard the other aspects of marriage and bride-price—the need of founding a family, of establishing new kinship bonds, and of ensuring continuity of the group. They admit these other needs—in theory; yet these needs are present, concretely, in the minds of the older generation (though it is unable to enforce its authority), and they will be present, we may assume, also in the minds of the young men themselves when they reach a more mature age and understanding.

The economic demands which we must list under the second heading—demands implied in duties towards the community—are comparatively light. In village economy they are embodied in the regular contributions to village rituals in money or kind, and in occasional gifts to the chief (mostly gifts of kola-nuts or produce, worth between 3*d.* and 6*d.*). To give an example of the former: the total cost of a village ritual of moderate dimensions comes to 10*s.*, which sum would be divided among, say, twenty households. But rituals may also be celebrated both more lavishly, and on a much smaller scale, with a cost between 3*s.* and 6*s.*[1] In Bida we have again certain expenses entailed in religious obligations—alms to Mallams, the traditional killing of a ram on the day of the *Sallah* or, occasionally, labour and money spent on the building of one of the small mosques in which neighbours and relatives worship.[2] Logically, tax should have been listed in this group of expenses.

The last group of 'cultural requirements'—personal wants—is the most fluid and the most difficult to outline. It follows most closely economic stratification and the varying standards of living. As we shall see later, almost every want in this group is seen against the standards set by the social *élite* of the country. In certain respects, however, we can attempt to define certain minimum wants even in this field. Thus every family head is expected to possess, in addition to his simple working clothes, at least one 'good' dress, a dark-blue or white gown, in which he would appear at meetings in the house of the chief and at various ceremonial occasions. Similarly he should own a white turban in addition to the straw hat or cap which he wears on the farm, ornamented sandals of leather, and a stick or carved staff to carry about; he should wear a heavy glass bangle round the arm, possibly a finger-ring and various charms of the kind that are sold by Hausa traders on the markets of the country.[3] A major failure to achieve these standards of personal requirements is regarded as a sign of poverty and disgrace. Often have I listened to old men complaining about the sad state of affairs which compelled them to be content with a shabby cloth or cap when gown and turban were more fitting to their age and status.

But here we must take into account that cultural 'rift' between urban and rural standards of which I have spoken earlier in this chapter. Many wants which either do not exist, or do not exist in the same urgency, in the village are considered essential in Bida. Here the closeness of the social *élite*, both in the literal sense of the word and in the sense of existing social contacts, raises the standards of living. In Bida, where one

---

[1] See my article on the *Gunnu*, p. 99, n. 2.
[2] The building itself is done by the people, the roofing and thatching by the professional builders of Bida. The costs were, in a concrete case, 10*s.*, and were divided among five households.
[3] These charms consist of a piece of paper supposed to be inscribed with a verse of the Koran or a Mohammedan formula of blessing, which is sewn in leather, and worn round the arm or neck.

can change one's profession and try new means of livelihood, these 'minimum' wants can be studied most profitably in the individuals who have abandoned their original occupation in order to better their standard of living. When discussing with labourers the reasons for their change of profession, I was given this as a typical reply: 'We are Bida people, not peasants; we are not satisfied to live as peasants do. We are not content with one gown and one cap; we want to go to the evening market and spend money; we want to make presents at the feasts in the houses of our friends, and we also want women.' Over half of these men were unmarried. Although their wages were comparatively high (7s. a week), they could not save enough for the bride-price—'our money disappears at once', they said.

The examples of household budgets from Bida which I have given above must then be interpreted with these viewpoints in mind. I will add here two more examples, of typically urban households, i.e. non-farming households, one of a weaver, and the other of a hat-maker, in Bida. The scope and money surplus of these budgets does not differ essentially from that of the peasant households. But even where the surplus seems larger, in figures, it is in effect more restricted. Note that the more prosperous of the two men, the weaver, is as yet unmarried. The less fortunate of the two, the hat-maker, had moreover given up hat-making this same year, and had become a labourer. It is not a paradox to say that the poor in Bida are poorer than the poor in the rural districts.

Household F

Bida. Profession: weaver, aged 30, unmarried

Output	Income	Additional income
48 pieces of cloth p.a., sold for 4s. to 4s. 6d.	Profit per cloth 8d. to 1s. 2d.	Farming on garden-plots close to the house, producing about a quarter of the annual food consumption.

	£	s.	d.
Total earnings . . £2. 8s. p.a.			
Money expenditure:			
own tax		11	0
contribution to tax of father (shared with brother) . . .		2	6
contribution to costs of food and clothing of father . . .		4	0
minimum cost of living for himself		8	0
Total	£1	5	6

Household G

Bida. Profession: hat-maker, aged 35, one wife

Output	Income	Additional income
Approx. 50 hats p.a., sold for 8d. each	Profit 5d. per hat.	Borrowed 2s. from wife

	£	s.	d.
Total earnings . . £1			
Money expenditure:			
tax		9	6
minimum cost of living . . .		12	0
Total	£1	1	6

It is impossible and unnecessary to reduce to £ s. d. the multitudinous forms of expenditure which fall under the heading of 'cultural requirements'. We have already seen that most often the surplus which can be derived from the main occupation is not large enough to cover them all. The various attempts to reduce or avoid expenditure, or to discover additional sources of income, are convincing evidence of this. To us, the most essential question is the selection and order of preference of expenses on which the hard-pressed household decides to economize. Individual differences play, of course, a certain part. In the quarter of the Bida beadworkers, for example, I saw among a number of dilapidated and neglected houses one whose excellent condition and nicely ornamented *katamba* spoke of the care which the inhabitants devoted to its upkeep. The financial position of the different families in the quarter was the same, yet one, to use the familiar Nupe expression, had 'made an effort' while the others had let things drift. Nevertheless, individual variations appear to be of little account in the general picture. The main differences occur, not between individuals, but between groups, that is, between the urban and rural population. I have just spoken of the young men of Bida who will forgo marriage (involving the bride-price) rather than the pleasures of town-life; they will spend money on dresses and feasts rather than contribute to the cost of the repairs of the family home. Perhaps the most striking illustration of this attitude was the utterly neglected state of the house of the guild-head of the carpenters and builders. Although the family numbered eight adult men apart from the old family head (two of whom had jobs in the workshops), and although house repairs were their profession, the men did not devote more than the absolutely necessary time and labour to the upkeep of the house, keeping the sleeping-huts in repair but letting compound wall and entrance hut go to rack and ruin. With a little money in hand, most Bida men will insist on a sumptuous marriage feast or naming ceremony for child or grandchild rather than save it for other expenses. I have twice attended such lavish feasts in neglected houses, in families whose income I knew to be small and precarious. But even the men with large and secure incomes will live above their means. Certain highly paid officials of the N.A. were heavily in debt to local traders and the European stores, having spent lavishly on dresses, luxuries, gifts to friends, and various forms of entertainment.

If in Bida expenditure on ostentatious display and on social obligations conforming to the standards of living which spread downward from the top of the social scale takes precedence of the more sober demands of bride-price, maintenance of the house, or saving in general, the villagers take the opposite view. In a small pagan village, for example, an annual ceremony had been postponed for three months for lack of money; in another case the same ceremony had been performed for three years in succession on a very small scale, owing to 'bad times'. Economies of this kind occur even in prosperous households: in the family whose budget I have quoted above under E the marriage feast of the eldest son had been postponed for one year so that it could be celebrated together with the naming ceremony of the first child, thus halving the costs of the festivity. In many essentially pagan villages Mohammedan burials are now becoming the fashion partly because, as I have reasons to believe, they are cheaper than the more elaborate pagan funeral feasts. Are then traditional customs such weak incentives, and regarded as of so little importance, that they are easily modified and even abandoned? Or shall we interpret this lack of appreciation as being due to an eminently reasonable attitude of the Nupe peasant? The answer is that the Nupe peasant or craftsman has little or no alternative choice. He is faced with two rigid, inescapable, demands which, between them, eliminate nearly all freedom of choice: one is maintenance of labour, involving food-supplies, clothing, and, to some extent at least, payment of bride-price for the labour-group on the co-operation of which the livelihood of the family depends; the other, even more rigid, demand is tax. The surrender of all these cultural wants is a result, not of 'reasonableness' or free choice, but essentially of external pressure.[1] That they still represent valid 'values', capable of determining social behaviour, is shown in that radical solution to secure their satisfaction individually if it proved impossible to secure them for the whole group, even at the risk of destroying the labour-unit.

The part played by tax in this failure of the Nupe household to adjust itself to the various cultural requirements was shown clearly in our analysis of the household budgets. We have seen that the balance could be maintained without difficulty only where a home industry (which, as we have seen, is carried out as individual work) could be relied on as a subsidiary means of the family income. Administrative Officers are well aware of this fact. Indeed, some are of the opinion that additional handicrafts or similar occupations, for example, work as temporary labourers, should be encouraged as a means of procuring money for tax without deranging the general scheme of household economy. Two Administrative Officers, of long experience, have pointed out to me that among the Hausa it is an established custom for young peasants to travel during the dry season and seek work of this kind, which would later enable them to pay their tax without difficulty. I am not qualified to discuss the fiscal implications of such a policy. But I may be allowed to point out its probable sociological and psychological effects, namely, that the encouragement of temporary labour of individuals must further, and indeed favour, that break-up of the labour- and family-unit the beginnings of which are already visible.

STANDARDS OF LIVING: STATUS AND PRESTIGE

We turn to the highest standard of living, that accepted by the upper classes of Nupe. Their needs and demands, the 'things they do' with their wealth, can again be grouped under the three headings which

[1] It must be said that certain Administrative Officers regard native festivities which fall in the time when tax is being collected as definitely conflicting with the prompt payment of tax. I have already mentioned (see p. 64) that in Bida Emirate all festivities (which, incidentally, happened to include certain harvest and fertility rites) were forbidden for a certain period until tax arrears had been paid.

characterize the standards of living of the lower social strata—with their meaning significantly altered. For 'maintenance of labour' read increase of capital and wealth; for 'demands of the community' dictates of status and prestige. The latter pervade the whole field of expenditure. Expenditure of wealth in any form, whatever its primary and avowed purpose, represents expenditure for the sake of status and prestige at the same time.

Investment of capital in human labour—slaves, pawns, or clients— also enhances the prestige of the man who can afford such investment and the life of leisure which it entails. The lavish scale of kinship feasts similarly reflects social status. Presents on a generous scale, to the king or influential noblemen, or liberal hospitality as befits the man of substance, are at the same time practical means of winning the favour of social superiors and securing a reliable political following. In the house of a Bida nobleman of moderately high standing, for example, six *bara* who lived with him, and five *bara* who lived outside, in their own houses, were daily guests at at least one meal—a hospitality which very nearly doubled household expenses.[1]

In a society in which marriage is by bride-price, and by high bride-price at that, the marriage arrangements must also become an index of wealth and status. Wealth and status are infallibly reflected in the number of wives a man possesses. We have seen that, while small peasants or small craftsmen and traders are content with one or two wives, no Bida man of standing would have less than four, and many even considerably more (whether legitimate wives or concubines). We will not exaggerate the share of prestige and status in this 'investment': the practice in the houses of the nobility to 'pension off' ageing wives and replace them by young attractive girls shows the contribution of more concrete motives also. On the other hand, wealthy Bida families will pride themselves in marrying off their sons at an early age, four to five years before they reach what is normally regarded as marriageable age. This is clearly done for the sake of prestige of the parents rather than for the benefit of the boy-husband, who, for example, may still be a pupil in the Government school (I have known of two such).

This twofold significance of economic incentives among the *élite* of Nupe society is no less clearly pronounced in expenditure of a more personal nature. 'Clothes make the man' in Nupe as elsewhere; in the possession of arms one sees not only fighting equipment, and in the possession of a horse not only a means of transport, but symbols of rank and status. I will conclude this list with the description of one cultural incentive which carries the concept of status and prestige into a rather remote domain of social life—travelling. Travelling forms indeed part of the life of the Nupe gentleman, and the young men of the higher nobility, especially the princes of the royal house, are sent, like their brothers in Victorian England, on a traditional Grand Tour. It takes them through the northern Emirates, to the cities and courts of famous

---

[1] The total consumption at the midday meal was approximately 5 lb. of porridge, made with fish and palm-oil sauce. The share of the family, including the family head, his wives, and his children, was 3 lb., that of the *bara* 2 lb.

rulers, with whom they stay as honoured guests, and whom they will repay, one day, by similar hospitality extended to their young relations. (I have mentioned, in a different context, how I met two princes from Sokoto whose Grand Tour had taken them to the court of the *Etsu* Nupe in Bida.) The noble tourists enjoy their travels and enjoy—as they put it—'seeing the world'. But this incentive of travelling for travelling's sake with which their education and cultural background inculcate them also serves, indirectly, the political purpose of fostering personal contacts and ties of friendship between the ruling families of Nigeria and, more specially, the widespread Fulani empire.

We must now ask ourselves to what extent these wants and incentives apply to the society at large and determine (more or less) the economic decisions of the people. We must ask, more particularly, whether there do not exist 'upper limits' by which the economic ambitions of the various classes are bounded—whether by choice or of necessity. Such limits exist in the form of objects and values which have come to be regarded as fixed symbols of political status and which, like status itself, are excluded from free economic choice, being attainable only by the ladder of social promotion. As fixed symbols of status, much as a uniform or decoration in our society, the glazed turban of the nobility, or the right to carry a silver sword, cannot be coveted as such. This limitation has also been accepted with respect to the recent innovation, the clock in the glass case carried by the body-servant of a noble master: the people outside the ranks of the nobility have not attempted—as well they might—to possess themselves of this new emblem of rank.

But though promotion to political status and acquisition of its paraphernalia represent things that 'cannot be bought' (we shall discuss certain exceptions later), most of the features characteristic of the social life on these more exalted planes are, in theory, of the nature of universal economic wants. Beautiful clothes, costly turbans, and the possession of a horse are widely desired and can be acquired by anyone who can afford the expense. Even wants which are so far beyond the means or labour which commoners and peasants can muster that for this reason alone they seem unlikely to become concrete ambitions outside the *élite* of the country, represent yet common wants and ideals. Thus we find the ornate high-gabled square or round entrance hut which is typical of the large houses of the Bida nobility also in certain villages, put up by chiefs or prosperous family heads. Beautifully ornamented houses of a more modest type, moreover, are found everywhere, in every section or stratum of the population. Now, one of the most convincing proofs of the universality of these economic wants is the absence of all unfavourable comments, especially in the form of ridicule, with respect to individuals reaching out for goals not normally attained in their station of life. This is a significant illustration: in the small village of Doko I observed one house built in an unusually sumptuous style—with coloured earthenware plates inlaid in the walls of the *katamba*. It belonged to a musician, an ordinary 'commoner', who had been very successful in his profession. The people who told me about the house and its owner admitted that he was neither a titled elder nor in any way a person of consequence, but did not find it at all out of place that he should have built himself such a pretentious house. We shall also hear later that in the Bida age-grade associations young men of low birth can even taste the thrill of having special drum-signals and songs composed for them like the members of the nobility.

Polygamy is another characteristic instance. The large-scale polygamy of the Nupe aristocracy remains beyond the reach of all other classes. Polygamy as it exists in the houses of the Nupe kings must even be regarded as a royal prerogative and thus as a fixed symbol of status. Yet polygamy on a more modest scale represents another universal want, the effectiveness of which can be studied in every stratum of society, and when peasants tell you of the 'good old times' when their chiefs and elders were able to marry large numbers of wives, they express the effectiveness of this incentive.[1]

We may also mention the demands of hospitality, which are recognized among the poor as well as the rich. Inability to fulfil these demands is regarded as a definite deprivation. Even in small peasant households will you find 'permanent' guests—persons who have been adopted into the household and may even be supported by their hosts when they are too old, or too ill, to gain their own living. Significantly, they were described to me as *ke bara na*, 'a kind of *bara*'.

One of the common ideals of the people of Nupe demands closer investigation. The reliance on employed labour by the privileged sections of the society establishes a separate leisured class, which lives by the labours of others and gains its livelihood to a large extent from the 'interest' borne by their human capital. Evidently, 'leisure' is a relative concept. In a society where the large majority works (say) ten hours a day, a group which can gain its livelihood by working only half the time represents already, comparatively speaking, a 'leisured class'. Thus for Nupe, as for every society, the definition of the leisured class must remain fluid. The well-to-do traders, the 'intelligentsia' of the Mallams, the rich landowners, and the well-paid N.A. officials, all are, in different measure, members of the leisured class compared with the hard-working farmers, craftsmen, or manual labourers. Let us understand the full import of this fact. Many forms of enjoyment depend upon leisure: recreation and aesthetic pleasures; among women, the possibility of keeping young and attractive. They all form part of the standard of living which is typical of the highest social stratum of Nupe. Again, they become, as such, also incentives for Nupe society at large, and affect the evaluation of specific occupations. We have studied their effectiveness in such reactions as the break-up of the family labour-unit under the influence of what we have called the 'new values and temptations' spreading from the town; we shall discover an even more conspicuous instance in the spreading of the Mallam profession.

---

[1] It is impossible to test the correctness of their sometimes rather extravagant claims. Yet the psychological reality of the incentive is unaffected by such questions of historical truth.

WANTS AND CULTURAL ASSIMILATION

Let me repeat that all these wants and incentives which are realized in the social *élite* also represent common incentives of the society at large, and of every social stratum, unattainable though they may appear in actuality. They remain 'ideals', and the inability to realize them is regarded as a failure, a shortcoming in the socio-economic system. There exist, however, certain exceptions: instances of that divergence, or rift, in the appreciation of certain wants and incentives which divides town and country. Though few in number, they occur in widely different domains of social life—nutrition, recreation, sex morality.

Certain instances concern the form of a want, the conventionalized taste in which it appears, rather than its essence. I have spoken in an earlier context of the different taste in intoxicants typical of town and country. The Bida people prefer palm-wine to the sorghum-beer which is drunk commonly in the village. Palm-wine is the native drink in the oil-palm countries of Southern Nigeria; we also find it, side by side with sorghum-beer, in certain riverain districts of Nupe where the oil-palm is cultivated. Bida itself imports palm-wine from these districts and the south. The adoption of this, as it were, alien drink by the people of Bida was explained to me as being due to the demands of Islam, which forbids fermented drinks like sorghum-beer, but permits palm-wine—at least in the eyes of the Nupe followers of the Prophet. I do not know how far this vindication of palm-wine will pass muster with Mohammedan scholars. But I think we may accept the negative feature of this interpretation, namely, the condemnation on religious grounds of sorghum-beer, which, as we shall see presently, represents a drink closely associated with pagan religious rites. Or I might quote the instance of the different styles of dance and music appreciated in Bida and in the peasant districts: in the town we find the dance of professional women-dancers who are watched by an appreciative audience; in the village the dance of peasant men and women who are performers and public in one.

In other tastes and wants town and country differ fundamentally. Let me quote two striking examples: the attitude towards sexual licence (about which I need say no more here),[1] and the attitude towards travelling. What I have said above about the appreciation of travelling in the social *élite* of the country could be extended to apply to the whole of Bida. To have travelled widely, to have 'seen the world', helps to establish the social standing of the townsman. The interest in travels even outweighs other, similar, interests. When I was collecting Nupe folk-lore I met with almost complete failure in Bida, although the villages had proved a most fruitful field. And this was the explanation which my Bida informants gave me: 'You must go to the villages to hear folk-tales. We Bida people have forgotten them all. No one wants them now. Why? Because when we tell stories, in the evenings, we like to hear about travels, and about other towns; we listen to the people who

[1] See Chaps. IX, XIX.

can tell us about Kano, Zaria, or Lagos.' The widespread familiarity with travelling, indeed the love of travelling, which characterizes the Bida people, has no counterpart among the peasants.[1] We have heard that even journeys to another district are rare and of little appeal to the villagers.

How are we to explain this negative form of culture contact? Why did cultural assimilation stop short of these few traits while so many other incentives and wants are spreading from the capital to the rural districts? When we examined, in a previous chapter, the different sex morality in town and country, we discovered its close functional interrelation with other social facts. Behind the divergent attitude we perceived the effectiveness of political and economic factors. This also points out the answer of the present problem. Sex morality can change only together with those other social determinants. Let me recall the main facts. Negative facts, such as the absence in the village of the 'double morality' of the capital, and also the absence of a large floating population which proved one of the incentives for the creation of semi-professional prostitution in the town. Positive facts, such as the more closely knit village life, which forbids the open and condoned matrimonial laxity characteristic of Bida; the efforts of peasant family heads to provide bride-price for an early marriage of the men, and thus to maintain the labour-unit; the conditions of labour in peasant households which tend to preclude sexual promiscuity among the women. The 'negative' culture contact which we are observing does not, then, represent a failure of assimilation in certain specific domains of culture, but the inertia of a cultural whole which cannot suffer changes in these domains without undergoing far-reaching changes itself.

The same is true of the incentive of travelling. In Bida, travelling serves the political interests of the ruling group; it is helpful to the productive enterprises of the town population; and it follows the political interests converging in the capital of the kingdom. None of these factors exists in the village. On the contrary, productive organization, political and religious life, move in a narrow compass beyond which the community affords no protection or promise of attachment.

In the case of the other, minor, instances of cultural divergence, which refer only to the form which a particular satisfaction takes, one might argue that the essential similarity of the wants themselves must tend to retard a more complete assimilation. But here again we must view the situation under the aspect of the cultural whole and the close integration within the whole even of apparently ephemeral traits. The appreciation of a certain kind of drink or a certain style of dance is indeed built firmly into the framework of village culture. Thus all religious rituals involve a libation of beer. The temptation to replace it with palm-wine would have to break down, not only an existing nutritive habit, but also, partly, the spiritual background against which the people (consciously or unconsciously) must regard their traditional beverage. The alternative solution of admitting palm-wine, and having different drinks for ritual and profane purposes, would involve an equally radical change in other

[1] See p. 39.

respects: not only in the productive arrangements which, in these circumstances, would no longer supply the ritual beverage as a matter of course,
but also in the psychological attitude, which would have to admit a ritual
beverage largely emptied of what Radcliffe-Brown calls 'social value', i.e.
which would be nothing but a ritual beverage, completely removed from
the habits of ordinary life. The village dance, again, is an expression of
group co-operation and coactivity in the recreational sphere. Like the
traditional occasions themselves on which it is performed—kinship
feasts, *egbe* work, religious ceremonies, and so forth—the dance mobilizes and intensifies group sentiments. We might even go so far as to say
that the unitary nature of the group which is thus mobilized forbids a
division into neutral performer and aloof lookers-on. The correlation
between professionalized performance and differentiation within the
group is indeed clearly visible in Bida. An aloof aesthetic appreciation
of professional dancers and musicians appears to represent the only form
of entertainment acceptable to a society in which class prejudices and
motives of status and prestige dominate all gatherings and festivities.
Class prejudice has fostered a conception of dignity set against public
exhibitions of this kind. The explanation is, I believe, that it would
obliterate, even though only temporarily, the demarcation of rank and
status. It is, in fact, quite inconceivable for a man of status to join in a
dance, even in his own house, for example, at a family feast—to dance,
that is, together with, and in front of, people who must invariably include persons of lesser station. Yet in the villages old men, even titled
elders, commonly join in the dances of the younger folk, without danger
to their dignity. To assimilate, then, the village dance to the performances which appeal to the 'sophisticated' people of Bida would mean
assimilating the complete social organization.

For the sake of the theoretical argument I have stated the case of this
negative form of culture contact a little more strongly than is warranted
by actual conditions. Throughout this book we have found evidence of
the gradual closing of the rift, and of the advancing assimilation even in
these domains of culture. But indeed our argument is supported by this
development. For the assimilation does not advance by the narrow
channels of confined, specific, cultural changes. Rather these changes
are carried by the tide of a far-reaching cultural adjustment which is
transforming the whole productive system and the organization of
labour as well as the social life at large in the Nupe village. The breaking
up of the family labour-unit, and the appearance, in the country, of
professional Bida musicians as spokesmen of what I have called the
'propaganda for the kingdom', are two convincing instances.

WEALTH AND STATUS

Hitherto we have been using the terms 'status' and 'prestige' as meaning one and the same thing. It becomes important now to distinguish
between them. By 'status' we understand a more or less fixed place on
the social ladder; 'prestige' represents a more fluid form of social recognition, gained by certain services or deeds in accordance with the

accepted code of society. Status in Nupe is determined by descent or formal promotion to rank and office. One of the accepted and most important means by which prestige can be gained is wealth. This raises the question of the closeness of the relation between status, and prestige gained through wealth. In other words, we must ask to what extent prestige gained through wealth tends to facilitate the attainment of status, and may even come to be regarded as its equivalent, or, conversely, to what extent high social status can be reached and maintained without adequate financial support.

Under traditional conditions social status and wealth could hardly become separated as political rank implied far-reaching economic privileges—the acquisition of fiefs and land, the chances of booty, profits from slave-trade, and so forth. Even assuming that considerable wealth could be accumulated also by groups outside the recognized social *élite*, such as traders and craftsmen, it is clear that their highest income could not rival the resources vested in a privileged political position. In present-day Nupe traditional political ranks and wealth are no longer inseparably linked. High social status does not invariably guarantee the demands of prestige also. The members of the *élite*, no longer in a position to combine the satisfaction of the more concrete wants with that of the demands of prestige, will have to choose between the different forms of expenditure. Yet here we find, rather surprisingly, that the expenses for the sake of prestige can be very considerably reduced without affecting the conception of status. The fixed symbols of status, the glazed turban and the silver sword, are either comparatively cheap or are heirlooms. The house, also inherited, may have to be left in disrepair; but its layout would still betray the status of its owner. Polygamy can be maintained to a certain extent thanks to the practice of marriage in the family, with low bride-price, which is customary among the *élite*. Horses, new dresses, ornaments, lavish hospitality—they all have to go. But travelling and leisure need not disappear. The former is satisfied by claiming hospitality from relatives or friends in distant parts, or even from social inferiors, who would not think of refusing such flattering requests. The latter manifests itself in the choice of profession of impecunious noblemen: very few have taken to farming or tried to learn a craft; theirs are mostly the unskilled 'free' professions of the leisured class. Thus even on the decline, the social *élite* secures the satisfaction of certain wants which to the lower orders of the society are permanently unattainable. Nupe society built up a strong defence of the prerogatives of status in the form of class-obligations and the utilization of inheritance. With its help the social *élite* of the country can hope to weather at least temporary difficulties and set-backs.

That this defence of class prerogatives has not yet lost its strength is evident in the hesitant attitude of the people towards accepting the new evaluation of wealth as independent of traditional status. The issue is by no means clear; it is confused by various concomitant factors, specially by the introduction of the new official ranks and positions under the N.A. some of which are vested in the old ruling class, while others have been bestowed on 'new men' from outside the traditional *élite*. But there is convincing evidence to show that high social status still attaches to traditional ranks, though they may no longer command their former financial reward, rather than to wealth alone. Evidently this is only a transitional solution. In a society in which high status is so closely identified with a definite standard of living the separation of the two cannot be maintained indefinitely, at least not without some radical change in the whole concept of the *élite*. Theoretically, had their ranks not been divided by the appointment of some of their members to modern official posts, the Nupe aristocracy could have chosen the diehard solution of reinterpreting the whole concept of status and making it independent of economic advantages. As it is, the old *élite* must either win back its economic supremacy (which is impossible, though the attempts have never been given up), or else admit the new nobility of wealth into its ranks. We can observe this new conception taking shape. The respect for the traditional values is only strong enough to maintain an external continuity—the continuity of the symbols of status. And the 'new men' are the first to submit to this rule which allows them to legitimatize their position: they buy the titles which are the only passports to acceptance among the social *élite*. Here then, we have a final, and most modern, use of capital investment, for the sake of social advancement in its purely abstract and symbolic form.

CHAPTER XXI

ECONOMICS AND SOCIAL STRUCTURE

ECONOMIC MOBILITY

THE lack of tangible data makes it impossible to formulate any theory about the extent to which economic mobility, i.e. movement between the strata, was a reality in pre-European days. We can only make a few statements based on social and historical facts the economic significance of which we can, with some certainty, assess. Economic betterment in every society depends on the possibility of increasing one's hold over resources and means of production. The Fulani conquest, and the exploitation of land which followed it, restricted, for one part of Nupe at least, mobility with regard to the main resource, land. The restriction could, however, be circumvented by means of political allegiance, i.e. by becoming the client of an influential landowner. There is also evidence that certain peasants and craftsmen have owned slaves and taken pawns, thus acquiring interest-bearing capital, and so rising above the average level of a peasant's or artisan's livelihood. In the ruling classes and among their dependants careers involving increased economic opportunities were the normal thing, whether they were expressed in a share in booty and slave-trade or in rewards to warriors and political followers 'for services rendered'. The reverse process, loss of economic opportunities, and in the extreme case the loss of all possessions, was no less marked. In the life of the peasant, such changes occurred in the course of wars and raids involving the destruction of homesteads, farms, and stores. The peasants in Nupe kingdom proper, though safe from slave-raids, were still exposed to similar attacks: punitive expeditions which, directed against a rebellious feudal lord, were fought on their land, or the visitation of armies which marched through and foraged from their farms. In the ruling group economic downfall could mean only one thing: political disgrace, often accompanied by confiscation of their property.

To-day the risks of war and raids have disappeared, together with the exploitation and one-sided source of income which they represented. Thus the new rule has to some extent levelled down the old economic inequalities. Clearly this levelling-down cannot have been equally welcome to every section of the population. Let me quote here the very frank and, in fact, typical statement of one of my most honest informants, an influential village elder of Mokwa. He admitted the great benefits of the present rule, thanks to which the *tálaka*, the poor man, enjoys safety from wars, raids, and political abuses. But then he added (rather heatedly in fact): 'But you have turned us all into *tálaka*.' This view, coming as it does not from a member of the ruling class but from a typical Nupe peasant, makes it necessary to review more closely the economic effects of the new order.[1] All our data tend to show that, although trade

---

[1] It incidentally supplies further evidence of the fact that a rise to superior economic position also occurred in the peasant classes.

and commerce have greatly benefited from the new development, the position of the peasants and craftsmen has not improved to the extent of enabling them to accumulate reserves and increase their resources to any considerable extent. The introduction of commercial crops, the cultivation of which is officially encouraged, represents a policy designed to open to the native cultivator the way to economic betterment. Yet the insecurity of these new resources may defeat their own ends. A more recent move to improve the economic position of the farmers was the launching of a policy to introduce mixed farming into Bida Emirate. Mixed farming, which had been adopted some years previously in certain northern Emirates, was started in Nupe towards the end of my second expedition. At that time only the demonstration farms of the N.A. and certain stretches of land belonging to the Emir, all worked by wage-labour, had been put under the new cultivation. While it is thus too early to describe actual results, it is possible to outline, from the study of the underlying principles, certain probable effects of this agricultural policy on the economic and social system of the country. They are sufficiently far-reaching to warrant here a more extensive examination.[1]

This policy envisages a gradual transformation of the whole of Northern Nigeria into arable country cultivated on Western lines, on the basis of individual landholdings. The working team should consist of one man and a boy. The 2 acres per head which have hitherto corresponded to an individual worker would be extended to 12, and eventually to 20 acres. The manure gained from the draught cattle would do away with the necessity of shifting cultivation and would allow practically unlimited cultivation of the same stretch of land. A four-field scheme of rotation is suggested, with one field manured, and the following crops grown on the different fields: sorghum and millet (on the manured field); cotton; ground-nuts; cassava and small crops. The most prosperous farmers in a district are to be persuaded to take up mixed farming first, thus giving an example which, it is hoped, many others will soon follow. The total cost of the draught cattle (two bullocks and one cow) and plough is £7 for an iron, and £5 for a wooden, plough. Farmers who are unable to buy the equipment outright will be given an advance on future profits of £1 to £1. 10s., or can pay an 'entrance fee' of approximately that amount, being expected to pay the rest, viz. repay the advance, in four yearly instalments which include a hiring charge of 5 per cent. The greatly increased yield should make these payments easy: it has been calculated that the farmer will be able to increase his production eightfold by the new method.

The scheme, admirable though its intentions are, may easily be wrecked if certain inherent dangers and difficulties are not carefully considered. Let us take the example of the most prosperous and progressive farmers of Lemu whose landholdings we have examined in an earlier chapter (see p. 212). We found that the total land under cultivation in the case of a working group of five and three men was 9½ and 6 acres,

---

[1] I am greatly indebted to the Superintendent of Agriculture in Bida for having allowed me access to the departmental files on mixed farming.

respectively. The larger group possessed one, the smaller two, fallow fields of the same size as the field under cultivation. Their total land-holdings, including both cultivated and fallow fields, thus amounted to 18 and 19 acres. Now, under the new scheme one individual would take under cultivation very nearly the whole landholdings of the family group. The other adult members of the family will have to obtain new land or (only too probably) they will give up farming. In Trans-Kaduna, with its large land supplies, new land might be found with no great difficulty from vacant or virgin village land. But even under these favourable conditions the fourfold increase of landholdings entailed in this development must lead, if not to actual land shortage, to serious competition for land. For one thing, farm-land for ploughing should lie closer together than it does now. The Nupe farmers will soon find it profitable to exchange their scattered ½ acre or 1 acre fields for larger and compact areas, an exchange which, involving a discriminative apprecia-tion of land, must invariably lead to land purchase and land sale. In Cis-Kaduna, with its limited land resources, land sales are, as we have seen, already practised on a small scale. Here, in the country of the big landowners, land purchase and land sale will increase rapidly under the new scheme.

The redistribution of land resources will go hand in hand with far-reaching changes in the economic stratification of the country. The prosperous peasant who was able to take advantage of the new scheme will in a few years' time command considerable resources. No doubt, the obvious way to invest the newly won capital will be in more ploughs and more land.[1] The more unfortunate farmers who, for reasons of poverty or lack of enterprise, are not able to avail themselves early of the new scheme will be hopelessly outdistanced by the rapid development. The increased agricultural production, of which a half will be for in-ternal consumption, must lower the price of food crops in the country. The small farmer, who relies on food crops more than on commercial crops, will be compelled to sell his produce at a price so low that he may be unable to pay his tax or to maintain his labour costs. Sooner or later he will succumb to the temptation to sell or let his land to those who, having benefited from the new scheme, will be anxious to acquire new land, and he will be forced eventually into the position of a landless labourer on the farms of the new landowning class. The Emir, on whose estate mixed farming has been established first, will be foremost among the new landlords of the country.

The levelling-down of economic inequality which accompanied the establishment of British rule in Nigeria will thus be replaced by a new, much more defined stratification. Poverty in the present productive system of the country is due, as we have seen, mainly to inadequate labour (disregarding here the factors of land shortage and tax), that is, to such factors as age, illness, misfortune, or ill-planned labour-

---

[1] This is not a mere hypothesis. The tendency to accumulate land is already noticeable in the northern Emirates where mixed farming was introduced earlier, and has led more than once to official attempts to keep landed property within certain limits.

organization, all of which—in theory at least—can easily be remedied. Poverty in the new scheme will be due to a fundamentally different inadequacy, the inability to secure the necessary means of production. It is a permanent, and even progressive, inadequacy, which must get worse with the continued process of production. For the same process that leads to accumulation of capital (in the modern sense of the word) in the hands of the owner of the adequate means of production will render more and more remote the chances of their acquisition by the people who are as yet without them. Economic inequality in its most extreme form, *latifundia* existing side by side with a landless proletariat, will be the final result.

These grave consequences can be avoided, and the valuable elements in the new policy saved, I think, by slowing-up the transformation of the agricultural system of the country until a corresponding transformation of the labour organization can be achieved. The increase in the cost of the means of production must be met by widening the basis of the co-operative unit which makes itself responsible for the maintenance of labour in this sense into co-operative societies. Co-operative societies, which could buy the new means of production from common funds, and would jointly own ploughs and cattle, would enable also the less prosperous farmer to profit from the technical improvements. A co-operative society which would include, for example, all the owners of adjacent fields would also be able to utilize ploughing to the fullest advantage without incurring the danger of large-scale land-exchange. The increase in the extent of cultivation would be gradual and well controlled, and the traditional labour-unit not rendered useless overnight; it would still be useful for supplementary farm-work (in the traditional fashion) at times when plough and cattle are employed on the field of a fellow member of the farm co-operative.[1]

RISK AND INSURANCE

Every productive organization must include in its calculations the factor of risk and insurance against risk. Certain risks are over and above the normal in that they are due to accidents outside the productive system itself, and beyond the range of foresight which the producers

---

[1] When I discussed this question in a lecture given at the Summer School for Colonial Studies in Oxford, in 1937 (see the *Summary of Lectures*), I was attacked by a member of the audience for attempting to 'boost poverty'. Now, this is a serious charge. However, I hope to have made it clear that my attempt was not towards fostering poverty or pampering backwardness, but towards avoiding a development which would create, and make permanent, the most dangerous form of poverty and economic dependence. To organize the less prosperous so that they should not be left behind in economic progress does in no way imply putting obstacles in the way of the more enterprising. 'The rich', as the chairman, who came to my assistance in the discussion, put it, 'will look after themselves.' It is interesting to note in this connexion that when mixed farming was discussed at the Residents' Conference in 1936 one Resident suggested that it might be feasible to utilize the Hausa *gaya* (collective farm-work) for the new agricultural organization. I presume that he, too, had in mind a co-operative organization of the kind suggested above.

can normally exercise. Such are wars, slave-raids, political abuses which might deprive a group of the fruits of its labour, the loss of a member of the working group through imprisonment, or—to-day—unexpected fluctuations in the market for export commodities. The insurance which the Nupe productive system can provide against risks of this kind is, of necessity, limited in scope and efficiency. I have spoken already of certain forms which this insurance took in the traditional society: client-ship and political allegiance. More interesting to us here are risks which are inherent in the productive organization itself, and which represent 'normal' risks in the sense that experience shows them to be ever pre-sent. Into this category come risks due, for example, to a failure of the crop, to marketing difficulties, a temporary economic stringency, or a temporary deficiency in the labour organization owing to illness or old age of individual members of the labour-unit. With risks of this kind the Nupe productive system is well equipped to deal, either through its normal labour organization or through certain mechanisms specially devised to provide 'insurance'.

The 'normal' risks in agriculture are insured against by means of the very constitution of the *efakó*, the co-operative labour-unit. A large co-operative group is capable of utilizing fully the highly diversified agri-cultural technique of the country, and of spreading cultivation, both locally and with regard to the crops grown, so as to eliminate the risk of a total failure. In a large working-unit it is also comparatively easy to make up for the temporary elimination of a worker. In a group of this kind invalid or aged group members can be assigned lighter work, or can even be supported by the rest of the group without doing any work. The smaller the group the more difficult it becomes to distribute tasks in this fashion, to spare a worker, and feed an 'extra mouth'. In the small, two-men or one-man labour-unit, the retirement of a member means the end of the working group, and his support places a heavy strain on the remaining organization. A new *ad hoc* arrangement may become necessary, in which independent small labour-units have to combine to maintain the retired member. Here is an instance which I noted in a *tunga* near Bida: a family of five was divided in two labour-units, one consisting of two adults, and the other of an old man, their father, who worked together with his two young grandsons. As his labour-unit could not produce enough for food and tax, the sons con-tributed ten bundles of grain a year towards the cost of their father's household.[1] That a situation of this kind may, in an extreme case, lead to a complete break-down of the 'insurance' scheme could be seen from household budget C quoted above, which showed an old man and an invalid still depending on their own greatly reduced working capacity. Another example is that of a farmer who had hurt his arm and, having been disabled for one year, became a temporary labourer the following year to make up for the losses he had sustained.

The group co-operation in the guild-organized crafts similarly pro-vides insurance against 'normal' risks. The guild organization, as we

---

[1] An analogous example from a family of craftsmen was quoted above, in household budget E.

have seen, not only supplies its members with efficient training, but also guarantees, to some extent, a steady market for their products. The guild-head, moreover, is enabled by the special resources involved in his position to act as the 'banker' of the group and come to the financial assistance of individual members.

Certain other economic arrangements designed to provide insurance operate outside the labour-unit, and are thus of special importance for the individual craftsmen and the free professions. The familiar recourse to clientship is a first instance. By sacrificing part of his personal freedom as well as his earnings, the *bara* buys the patronage of an influential person. Though this patronage will be appealed to specially against the 'extraneous' risks due to political factors, it plays a part also in more 'normal' circumstances. Thus I found that a barber had recently become the client of a certain nobleman in his quarter of the town in order to secure a regular and good clientele; it is significant that the father of the barber had not been a *bara*, i.e. had not felt the need to 'insure' his more prosperous business. A young hat-maker told me that he intended to attach himself as *bara* to an influential rank-holder, with whose help he hoped to start business as a trader. I have also spoken of the Mallams and drummers, to whom clientship means the guarantee of success in their profession.

A different method of insuring against risks is embodied in the practice of borrowing money. 'Pawning' represents the firmly institutionalized form of borrowing—an institution which provides against normal as well as abnormal risks, and in which a social relationship closely akin to that of patron and client forms the basis of the financial transaction. Other forms of borrowing occur irregularly, and with a narrow scope. No professional money-lenders exist; the individual in need of money borrows it mostly from close relations, more rarely from friends or 'patrons'. The most frequent form of borrowing is for a husband to borrow from his wife. An indirect form of borrowing money from one's wife, not uncommon in Bida, is the practice of wealthy women to contribute to the bride-price of their sons and to other expenses, which, in accordance with Nupe kinship ideas, should be borne by the father.

A final insurance arrangement is provided in a specific financial institution operating somewhat on the lines of a 'pooling club'. It is called *dashi* in Nupe (*adashi* in Hausa) and plays—or used to play—a very important part in Nupe economy. We must describe it here in detail.

The *dashi* is a pure business arrangement, a free association of a number of men and women who agree to enter this financial co-operation for a certain limited period. Each member undertakes to pay regularly (for example, every week, or five days, or every month) a certain amount of money into a common fund, as many times as the group numbers members. Each time when the contributions have been collected a different member is entitled to draw the total fund, until every member has had his share. Members may also contribute double subscriptions, and then be entitled to two 'draws' in the course of the *dashi*. The allotment of the fund does not follow a fixed rule, but is left to the head of the group to work out. A member who is urgently in need of money can request to be considered out of his turn. He can thus put his hands at once on a sum of money for which, normally, he would have had to save for weeks or months. In this, then, lies the benefit of the *dashi*. The administration of the *dashi* association is entrusted to a man of good reputation, for example, a well-known trader or the head of a craft-guild. People who decide to form a *dashi* request such a man to undertake its organization. He will summon the first, and only, general meeting of the group, at which all the important points are settled, and afterwards arrange all matters on his own. People who learn from neighbours or friends that a certain *dashi* is being formed are, up to the date of the first subscription, free to join it; after that, while the *dashi* is running, no new members are accepted. The 'chairman' of the association, the *Etsu Dashi* (King of the *dashi*) as the Nupe call him, is responsible for the collection of the subscriptions and the regular paying out of the fund. He does not himself pay into it, nor does he receive any money payment for his trouble. He is recompensed by being allowed to borrow from the fund occasionally for himself and his own business provided that the general arrangement on which the group had agreed, and the duration of the *dashi*, are not altered. Sometimes he also receives gifts from members who desire an early share without being able to show serious reasons for this request. When money is needed, for example, for a funeral, in the case of illness, or for the payment of bride-price, no gifts or bribes are necessary to secure immediate consideration. *Dashi* chairmen who have the reputation of being good organizers are in great demand, and may be continuously engaged in organizing and supervising *dashi* associations, often several at the same time. Women are regarded as specially able organizers: one of the most successful *dashi* 'chairmen' I met in Bida was a woman; she was actually living in Doko, where she had lived since her marriage, but organized a *dashi* in Bida, sending her messenger, a young girl, every Friday into Bida to collect the subscriptions.

Although the benefits of the *dashi* embrace every variety of risk and expense, its practice is limited to the professions which depend on regular money earnings and money investments. It is practised by traders and brokers, both men and women, by certain groups of craftsmen, the wives of farmers, canoe-men (who are enabled to buy their canoes with the help of the *dashi*), labourers, and officials. The schoolboys in Bida Middle School have a little 'pocket-money' *dashi* of their own, the subscription being 1d., paid every Friday. The farmers, although familiar with the *dashi*, do not practise it, nor have they apparently ever done so. Clearly their stores of produce are regarded as sufficient reserve, and their labour organization as sufficient 'insurance'.

The number of members and the amount of the subscription vary widely. The sharp distinctions of social and economic stratification are visible also in the organization of the *dashi*. A well-to-do trader or nobleman would never join one of the petty *dashi* associations of small craftsmen or tradesmen in which the contribution is a few pennies. They would form a small *dashi* of their own, with a high subscription, even if they have to be content with five members only. During my stay in Nupe I found the following *dashi* associations in practice: *dashi* associations formed by women, the wives of farmers in Doko, Kacha, and one or two other villages, in which the weekly subscription was 3*d.*: they numbered between twelve and thirty members; a *dashi* among the Bida barbers, with the subscription of 4*d.* weekly, numbering ten members (I was told, incidentally, that formerly their *dashi* was organized on a much larger scale). Another *dashi*, numbering twenty-four members, was formed by N.A. scribes; here the subscription was high, in accordance with their salary, 10*s.* per month. The teachers of Bida Middle School also formed a *dashi*, numbering twelve members, with a subscription of 7*s.* 6*d.* per month. Eight members of this group had formed a *dashi* with a subscription of £1 per month the previous year. Several *dashi* associations have disappeared owing to the economic stress. The labourers at the Bida workshops had practised the *dashi* till five years ago, but had given it up when their wages were lowered. The beadworkers, who had also practised the *dashi* formerly, had abandoned it owing to the decline of their business. I received the same information among carpenters, blacksmiths, and butchers. The canoe-men in Jebba, finally, who used to organize their *dashi* at irregular times, had not had a *dashi* for several years.

Returning to the general discussion of 'insurance': as the large co-operative unit in agriculture and home industry is disappearing, and, with it, the 'insurance' which it provided, one may wonder whether this must not bring the other, individual, insurance arrangements more to the foreground. It is thus rather surprising that the practice of the *dashi*, far from increasing, is disappearing. The people, as we have heard, explain this as being due to the general economic decline. The bead-workers said that they had no money to spare, and the barbers and labourers did not think it worth their while to organize a *dashi* with a small subscription. Borrowing, on the other hand, especially the borrowing by husbands from their wives, is markedly on the increase. Disputes over debts of this kind are frequent in divorce proceedings in Bida. The examination of household budgets also reveals a considerable number of instances (five out of fifty) in which husbands borrowed money, chiefly for tax, from their more prosperous wives; and even in remote places, such as fishing villages on islands in the Niger, where the women are by no means the enterprising traders they are in Bida or larger villages, husbands borrowed up to 8*s.* and 9*s.* from their wives. That under a continued economic stress borrowing may spread and increase further, and eventually lead to the introduction of professional money-lending, is not improbable. Borrowing in Nupe, which has once already reached a peak (in pawning), might well, in a different form, grow again to such dimensions.

It is clearly a sign of the growing instability of the native economic system that the solid and comprehensive insurance against risks which is vested in the co-operative labour-unit is disappearing, and that its place is taken by the most restricted, most temporary, form of insurance —borrowing. Once again, we encounter social and economic repercussions of the dissolution of the large labour-unit. If previously we have seen that this development has adversely affected certain aspects of production, the present case demonstrates forcibly that it affects the very stability of the economic system of the country. We cannot claim to be able to describe exactly how the labour-unit was working under traditional conditions, and to state categorically that the scheme of insurance entailed in it operated without difficulty or friction. But on the evidence which we possess it is reasonable to assume that under certain conditions, with a smaller taxation, and protected from severe, incalculable, market fluctuations, the large co-operative group represented—or would represent—an eminently stable and successful labour-unit. The process of transformation cannot be halted. Where the large labour-unit still exists, it may, given the conditions just mentioned, be preserved; where it has disappeared, it cannot be revived. Our conclusions point to one solution only: to the creation of new institutions and labour organizations which can be made to fulfil, under existing conditions, those tasks which fell formerly to the labour organization that has disappeared—above all, the task of insurance. Such institutions can be found in co-operative organization, saving societies, co-operative marketing, and suchlike—organizations which in other parts of Africa have amply proved their efficiency.[1]

ECONOMIC RELATIONS AND THE GROUP

Throughout this discussion we have dealt with family and kinship group purely in their economic aspect. We have interpreted the mechanisms which maintain the working-unit and thus the co-operation in its human substratum, the family group, in terms of economic relations only. Against this treatment of the problem one might argue that it sees only one side of it, and that the kinship and family structure must be taken into account also as an entity *sui generis*, which, within the framework of economic relations, exercises its own specific influences. One might argue, in particular, that as the Nupe *efakó*-unit is based on the family, kinship ties and kinship sentiments as such supply the binding forces of the labour group—'maintain labour', in our terminology— and that the binding forces which we have recognized, namely, commonness of material interests and benefits accruing from co-operation, are in reality mutual kinship obligations.

The double nature of economic obligations in a productive unit which happens to be a kinship-unit at the same time cannot be denied. The influence of kinship factors can, in fact, be made evident by comparing the labour-unit based on kinship, with similar labour-units in which kinship plays no part. While, in the former, co-operation is achieved by mutual obligations such as payment of bride-price, and supply of clothing, food, and shelter, labour of the latter order must be recompensed in the form of money wages. The effectiveness of kinship

---

[1] It has been said that our intention should always be to graft these new co-operative organizations on to existing, indigenous, organizations. The scope and the possibilities of such a scheme must not be exaggerated. Although the tasks with which the new organization is to be charged may have formed part of the traditional system, the organization itself may have to be newly created, and may, in fact (as in our case), have to replace a failing indigenous organization, rendered inadequate by modern conditions.

sentiments in co-operation was also implied in various statements made earlier in the discussion of economics. We have seen that the craft-guilds plan their labour organization on kinship lines, and reinforce the labour group by what we have called 'professional endogamy'. But let us realize that in doing this they do not appeal to abstract kinship ties or 'bonds of blood', but merely duplicate the common labour interests by corresponding family interests, namely, the concrete interests and forms of social interdependence entailed in intermarriage. Another instance of the influence of kinship ties became apparent in the fact that to-day sons would still agree to stay in the *efakó*, while brother's sons decline to do so. Yet we have also seen that even sons desire under certain conditions to be released from the *efakó*-unit. In the case of individual crafts and trade, kinship obligations, even of sons to fathers, are no longer recognized. The dissolution of the large labour-unit, moreover, has made it abundantly clear that its size and coherence is determined predominantly by economic interests and relations. Kinship bonds and sentiments are not strong enough to maintain a labour group once its economic usefulness is impaired. Generally speaking, then, kinship bonds, in order to supply a substratum for productive co-operation, must have the support of economic incentives—material benefits and forms of compensation. Where the latter fail, the kinship bonds themselves will fail in this task.

Though we cannot thus admit the effectiveness of kinship factors as such (at least not in a decisive measure) upon the labour organization, the reverse is no doubt true. The labour organization exercises a two-fold influence upon the structure of the family and kinship group: (1) through contributing to the co-operative mechanisms within the kinship group, and (2) through accepting the responsibility for certain tasks which are vital to the continuity and stability of the kinship group.

(1) The integration of the kinship group, that is, the 'internal adaptation' of the social unit (Radcliffe-Brown), is largely determined by the scope and closeness of contacts and forms of co-operation existing in the group. Co-operation in the same labour-unit thus represents one of the most important integrative factors in this sense. We remember also that the labour-unit coincides with the household-unit, and that the individuals who agree to work together also 'keep house', eat, and live together. The constant contacts and the lasting mutual adjustment entailed in this productive arrangement build up strongly coherent units. The reduction in size, and the splitting-up into small individual units, of the large labour-unit, must detract essentially from the integration of the family group.

(2) Speaking generally, the large labour group, led by old and experienced men, is more far-sighted in its economic planning than the small one-man or two-men unit. It allows for certain group interests which the individual worker will ignore, or discount as of lesser importance; it can assess necessities and wants more objectively, with a view to the fundamental needs of the group rather than immediate individual satisfaction. Thus the family head will place foremost the necessity of finding the bride-price for the junior family members in order to

establish them socially as full members of the community, i.e. as married men, and, indirectly, to assure the continuity of the family group. We have seen that even if the family head is unable to produce the necessary amount himself, and the young men have themselves to contribute, the family head would keep and save the money for them. The young men, left to themselves, are tempted to squander money on things which appear to them to be of greater urgency, and to disregard, to their own detriment as well as to the detriment of the group, the more distant necessity of marriage. As in the case of the Bida labourers, their money 'goes at once', and they remain unmarried even a considerable time after having reached marriageable age. In the extreme case a family head would even pawn the labour and liberty of a younger family member who is less essential to the group for the sake of keeping in freedom the elder, more important family member, or enabling him to found a family. We can go even farther than this. Older men, tending to uphold tradition, will plan labour and expenditure so that there should be money, food, as well as time available for family feasts or communal religious ceremonies. Their efforts thus serve (unconsciously) the interests of group integration at large, which the younger generation, not so fully steeped in traditional ways of thinking, may hesitate to put before more immediate attractions. Finally, by submitting to the authority of the older men in productive co-operation, the labour-unit also sustains their position of authority in a wider sense, as leaders of the community. We can say, then, that the large labour-unit is committed to the maintenance of the structure and the traditional values of the society, and that with its dissolution an important agency of social integration and continuity disappears.

The changes which the *gunnu* ritual has undergone recently are a convincing instance of this kind. In its traditional form the *gunnu* contained a certain most stirring scene which took place on the eve of the ritual, and which concerned the young men of the village especially. They were herded together in a certain place in the uninhabited bush, where they had to spend the night; they were to wait for a terrifying apparition, the spirit of the *ndakó gboyá*, who would question them about their moral conduct in the preceding year. If they were found guilty of having behaved disrespectfully towards their elders, they were flogged by their comrades at the command of the spirit. I have quoted already the article in which I described in detail the ritual and its effectiveness as a mechanism of social integration in the family group as well as the community.[1] But even from this short description we can gather the psychological importance of a ritual which uses such impressive stimuli to press home moral teaching, and to bind together periodically, in a common experience, the growing generation. Now, although the *gunnu* is still performed, the 'bush night' has been abandoned in many villages, and the explanation given was everywhere that the young men had refused to be subjected to the ordeal of this inquisition and punishment. The young men themselves were outspoken about the reasons of their refusal: 'We are now working as independently as the old men, we are paying tax for ourselves—why should we be flogged and threatened as if

[1] See pp. 25, 63.

we were small boys?' In their own words they confirm my argument that the weakening of productive co-operation entails a weakening also of other forms and bonds of group unity.

We may for the moment reflect on the fact that this progressive weakening of group integration occurs in a society with decreasing population. Partly this development underlines the strength and urgency of the forces which are working for the dissolution of the large labour-unit, and which here foster the tendency to split and reduce in size a working-unit which is already, as it were, automatically declining. But it also reveals the significant fact that a loosening integration and progressive subdivision of units is not invariably correlated with an increase in the size of groups, and the inherent difficulty of maintaining cohesion.[1]

The present discussion has transcended the domain of economics. Where previously we have attempted to demonstrate the effects of changes in the structure of the labour-unit within the range of economic relations, i.e. on productive organization and the stability of the economic system, we are now studying the significance of these changes for the organization and stability of the social group. We can trace the influence of the changing economic organization upon social structure through wider and wider circles. Take the institution of the Nupe market. We have seen that the peasant attendance of the local village markets coincides with a local group characterized by regular social contacts, intermarriage and 'common living' in general. The market meeting mobilizes the local community, adds to the common interests, and forms an important focus for these contacts and forms of intercourse. Like the labour-unit on a smaller scale, it contributes essentially to social integration. This is no longer true of professional trade, which is carried on across community boundaries, and remains independent of established group-ties. Like the modern labour-unit, professional trade accepts solely the dictate of the impersonal profit motive.

Expanding trade connexions of this kind are only possible in a social system which provides safety and protection outside the narrow boundaries of the local community. They depend, in other words, on the large-scale political organization of the state. Like the economic relations which take place within its confines, the integrative mechanism of the state is essentially impersonal, and based on abstract principles rather than forms of co-adaptation growing from 'common living'. The transformation in the group substratum of economic relations is thus determined by the same concepts which also determine the transformation of the largest group unit, from community to state. Technically, the expansion of trade and commerce, production and exchange, would have been impossible without the corresponding expansion of political control. It would, perhaps, be going too far to say that spiritually also the former would have been impossible without the latter—without the conceptual framework which the latter provided. But we are justified in saying that the two forms of expansion reflect, materially as well as spiritually, two aspects of the same social process.

[1] This latter view was expressed, in the form of a 'social law', by Professor Radcliffe-Brown.

CHAPTER XXII
EDUCATION FOR CITIZENSHIP

AS education in the widest sense must be described all efforts, organized or otherwise, which tend to impart to individuals habitual forms of acting and thinking. Understood in this sense, every social institution involves educational activities by means of which individuals are led to acquire the behaviour-patterns that make up the institution. Thus our description of economic life has involved the description of certain educational techniques—the training in productive methods, the imparting of economic knowledge, or of concepts of property and wealth. But most societies also operate with more formalized methods of education, specific educational institutions which make it their business to train the rising generation in forms of acting and thinking regarded as essential by the society. We shall deal in this chapter with these formalized educational institutions, of which there are two in Nupe: the institution of the Koran school, concerned with Mohammedan religious teaching, and the institution of age-grade associations. The shortest definition of an educational institution is by the 'type' which it is meant to produce. In this sense we can say that Mohammedan religious education produces the Mallam, the Mohammedan scholar, and the age-grade associations the *zoon politikon* as understood in Nupe. We shall see that in certain respects both types of education can be identified with motives and aims underlying the political system, and thus with institutions devoted to what I have called in the heading of this chapter 'Education for Citizenship'.

MALLAM SCHOOLS

There are many degrees and varieties of Mohammedan learning. The title 'Mallam'—*mân* in Nupe—which one encounters so often among the Nupe, is by no means a safe guide. For the man who has gone through a few years' study of the Koran, having learned by heart a few *sura*; the sand-diviner or charm-seller who writes out verses from the Koran and sells them as amulets; the man who has acquired real learning and scholarship, and who can read and write in Arabic and possibly in Hausa—they all are called Mallam. Though the title is used indiscriminately, no Nupe ignores the essential difference between scholarship and the thin veneer of semi-learning. The Nupe distinguish two grades of learning: the lower grade is the study of the Koran (*kurani*), which consists mostly in the memorizing of prayers and whole pages and chapters from the Koran; the higher grade is called *kpikpe*, knowledge, or *litafi* (Hausa), book, and consists in the study of Arabic and the careful reading of the Koran and the better-known commentaries. The most advanced scholars would study, in addition to these books, also the historical records of the Nigerian Emirates which have been compiled (in Hausa, written in Arabic script) by scholars of former days. Only a student of 'knowledge' can claim to be a 'real' Mallam. While there are hundreds of Mallams of the lower grade, there are few real scholars, and they are well known and highly esteemed. These scholars will occupy that most influential position which a Mohammedan culture accords to the men of learning.[1] Their advice will be sought by friends and strangers, in matters spiritual or profane.[2] The important political and religious offices of judge, scribe, and Imam at the town mosque are open to them. Some become attached to a noble household as 'private chaplain'. Royal princes and noblemen will seek their friendship, give them their daughters in marriage without bride-price, regarding marriage with a Mallam as *sádaka*, pious alms. Such is, the Nupe say, the *cinwa katū*, the Greatness of Learning. To some extent, however, the high reputation of the learned profession is reflected also in the persons of lesser erudition. Learning is, after all, relative. And a Mallam of very inferior scholarship judged by Bida standards, may be revered as a fount of knowledge in a small half-pagan village. These Mallams in the villages are frequently supported by the people and receive annual gifts of crops as *dzanká*, tithe.

The Mallams are, above all, teachers. They teach both children and adults, the former the Koran and the latter 'knowledge'. Every Mallam may, besides, be called in to perform a marriage ceremony or to officiate at a funeral—services for which they are remunerated according to their status and reputation. A few are well-to-do and own land, which is worked by their sons and pupils or, in some cases, by wage-labour. But most Mallams practise, in addition to teaching, some other occupation, which may or may not be associated with their scholarly profession, to supplement the meagre income of a Koran teacher. Some write out and illuminate pages of the Koran, or copy Arabic manuscripts, for sale. You can buy a sheet of this sort, very beautifully illuminated, for 5*d.* on the Bida market; more ambitious scribes would sell a whole copy of the Koran and receive for it—the work of five months—£1. Students of 'knowledge' eagerly buy these copies and use them in their studies. Other Mallams, again, embroider gowns, make straw hats or saddle-cloths, or do tailoring.

The size and standard of the Koran schools varies as widely as the status and standard of learning of the Mallams. You find 'schools' with two little boys for pupils, and these close relations of the teacher; and you find others—the schools of famous Bida scholars—the classrooms of which (as a rule the *katamba* in the Mallam's house) are crowded with pupils. The teachers are very jealous of the reputation of their school. When I was a regular visitor to Bida Koran schools the Mallam of one which I had not yet visited came to me complaining that I had left out his school, and quoted as reference a Bida Mallam of very high standing who was a special friend of mine. In the large Koran schools the Mallam himself teaches only the adult students of 'knowledge', while the elementary teaching is carried out by his sons or certain advanced pupils.

[1] Bida learning has a great reputation even outside Nupe; Mallams from Bida have been given important posts in other countries, and several Bida Koran teachers have established flourishing schools in Ilorin.

[2] One aspect of this spiritual advice is divining, which, as we have seen, plays an important part even in such political activities as the election of a high officer of state or the preparation for war.

Certain progressive Bida Mallams include the teaching of Hausa and elementary arithmetic in their syllabus, and many adults, traders and other native business men, attend their classes to acquire knowledge so invaluable to their trade.[1] In certain Bida schools you will find young girls being taught together with boys. They come from the families of the nobility, which, conscientious Mohammedans, insist on elementary religious instruction being extended also to women. Girls, however, are only taught the Koran, and do not study 'knowledge'.

Adult students, specially those who study the Koran or 'knowledge' for their edification, following another profession besides, visit the house of the teacher only for their lessons, which take place mostly in the evenings, once or twice a week, or even at longer intervals, according to the leisure which their occupation allows them.[2] Young pupils who live in the neighbourhood attend their classes daily while living with their family. Pupils whose family live some distance away will stay in the house of the teacher as members of his household.

The teacher of the Koran may not demand special payment for the tuition; according to Mohammedan principles religious instruction must be free—*ebo albarka*, 'for the sake of blessing'. The wealthy Mallam, in fact, scorns all such payments as contrary to the spirit of religion. The poorer Mallam depends on what the family of the pupil offers him as *sádaka*, alms: a penny or twopence every two months, or a bundle of grain (worth 9*d*. or 1*s*.) once a year. Even these small gifts are very irregular; in the school of a Bida Mallam of good reputation, whose pupils numbered thirteen, half of the parents had sent nothing for over a year. Sometimes it happens that a boy's father dies while the boy is still studying, and his relations are unwilling to pay for his education. In this case the Mallam will continue to teach the orphan, let him live in his house and give him food and clothing, again *ebo albarka* only. Koran teachers in the country are worse off than their colleagues in Bida. In Kacha a Mallam who taught Hausa and arithmetic in addition to the Koran and 'knowledge', and who had eight young and fifteen adult students, received no payment from his students except an occasional gift of kola-nuts. If he asked for money, the students would indignantly threaten to leave and to seek another teacher. But both poor and wealthy Mallams receive a final gift from the parents of the student who has completed his studies, either money (in Bida), between 5*s*. and 10*s*., or (in the village) grain or a goat. The teachers can also obtain a certain indirect remuneration by letting their pupils work for them. School-work does not take up the whole day, nor every day in the week. In their

[1] The Education Department in Bida has arranged special evening classes for these enterprising Koran school teachers, and gives them also certain practical assistance, for example, by supplying them with blackboards. This scheme of adult education is of considerable value in the spreading of elementary education among that section of the population which has not had the advantage of education in the Government schools.

[2] Students in a Koran school in Kacha, who were canoe-men by profession, attended the school whenever they returned to Kacha from their voyages, interrupting their classes for weeks and months at a time when they were out on a canoe expedition.

spare time the boys will help in the house or on the farm, or sometimes in the handicrafts which their teachers practise.

The students of 'knowledge' pay nothing for the tuition. But they have studied the Koran with the same Mallam under whom they are now studying 'knowledge'; and they will send their children again to his school, or to the school of his sons. Thus reputations are built up and firm links established between families of Koran teachers and families which patronize their school. There are Mallam families in Bida which have been teaching three generations of the same families. For the sons of famous Mallams will follow the profession of their father. Many also intermarry with other Mallam families. They carry on the reputation for scholarship won by their fathers and families, and thus help to build up the dynasties of Mallams, of which there are many in Bida and Nupe.

As teaching implies so meagre and irregular an income one might ask how it happens that certain Mallams become well-to-do, and even join the wealthy landowning class. These Mallams do not come from the families of the hereditary or office nobility. Although many men of this class study the Koran and 'knowledge', and proudly call themselves Mallams, they do not adopt the teaching profession, but remain amateurs, noble *dilettanti*. Sometimes a Mallam who in the past attained one of the official positions open to Mohammedan scholars has laid the foundation of the wealth of the family. Another has benefited from the close association as the 'guide, philosopher, and friend' of an influential personage—a clientship of more exalted order—and received land and wealth through the help of his patron. It is, for example, customary for all marriage services in the royal family—a most lucrative office—to be held by the Mallam who is attached to the house of the *Shaba*; or at all funeral services of the royal house the *Liman*, the head of the Mohammedan clergy, will officiate. However, wealthy Mallams are rare. Most Mohammedan scholars are poor, or at least unable to maintain themselves by their religious and educational work alone. But poverty is no impediment to scholarly reputation; nor does it detract from the honour of the profession. In fact, ordinary people will never call in a titled or even wealthy Mallam to perform a marriage or funeral service; they invariably prefer a Mallam of the *tálaka* class. A 'great Mallam is too weighty', they explain; they want a man whom they can offer a small *sádaka* as fee.

Among the Mallams of the town a certain loose economic co-operation exists, which comes into play at all such ceremonial occasions. At large marriage ceremonies or funerals several Mallams may be called in to assist the Mallam who is officiating. They will also divide part of the money which they receive for their services among their other colleagues in the same town quarter. Or the family which celebrates the ceremony will send *sádaka* to all the Mallams in the neighbourhood. This practice of communal benefits does not involve any closer or more formalized co-operation among the Mallams. The wide diversity between them with regard to social status, wealth, and standard of learning forbids any more strongly pronounced appreciation of their commonness beyond that fluid unity embodied in the fact that they all work with their brains, and represent, in a society of peasants, craftsmen, and traders, the intelligentsia. This will become even clearer when we examine the motley rising generation of Mallams.

Koran teaching begins as a rule in early youth, when the child is 6 or even 5 years old. The teaching of the Koran itself is reckoned to take five to ten years. Some pupils learn quicker than others, and in one school I found a boy of 13 already studying 'knowledge', while one of 17 was still worrying his way through the Koran. But on the whole this elementary stage is considered mere routine work which most students can master in the given time. The teaching of 'knowledge', on the other hand, depends entirely on talent and individual inclination. Pupils may be eager enough to try, but will give up later when they discover that 'they have no head for it' (a literal translation of the Nupe phrase). Nor can the time taken by these higher studies be fixed precisely. Ten to fifteen years is an average estimate—at least, after fifteen years' study one is reckoned to have become 'fully a Mallam'. But only prospective teachers will take this advanced course systematically, and continue their study year after year. The *dilettanti* pursue their studies much more irregularly and leisurely, and students of 35 or more may often be seen in the schools of the teachers of 'knowledge'.

The Mallam schools receive pupils from every class and every walk of life. I have compiled some figures to illustrate the social origin of the pupils of Bida Koran schools:

Father's profession	Mallams	Traders	Farmers	Guild-crafts-men	Indivi-dual crafts-men	Nobility	Clerks, messengers, &c.	Total
Studying: Koran	49	16	30	6	20	22	8	151
'Knowledge'	28	4	2	..	20	8	10	72

That the sons of Mallams are in a majority is not surprising, nor that individual craftsmen and members of the nobility should come next in number. Of the twenty-eight sons of Mallams who were studying 'knowledge' six were going to adopt a different profession (of messengers, clerks, labourers, or servants to Europeans). Of the forty-four other students of 'knowledge' sixteen were going to become Koran teachers either in Bida or in the villages. These sixteen prospective Mallams included, incidentally, the two farmers' sons. None of the sons of guild-craftsmen took up teaching as a profession: a proof of the strong organization of these 'closed professions'. The large number of farmers who send their boys to Bida Koran schools may appear surprising; and even more so that a certain number of them should take up the study of the Koran professionally (for among the boys who are at present studying the Koran a few are likely to become Koran teachers). One example may serve: a boy of 13, the only son of a farmer, was studying to become a Mallam. He was well aware that at the death of his father the land would be lost to his family. Nevertheless he would not return to farm-work. His father had made him a Mallam, and that was all there was to it. Again and again, in similar cases, I was told: 'We are no longer strong enough to work on the land', or 'After all, is the profession of a Mallam

A BIDA MALLAM AND ONE OF HIS PUPILS

AN AGE-GRADE ASSOCIATION DANCE

not as good as that of a farmer?' There is no evidence, incidentally, that physical disability, an ailment which might impair their working capacity, is a reason for sending boys to Mallam schools. The choice of the Mallam profession is, in the full sense of the word, a free choice of profession.[1]

The Mallam schools both in Bida and in the peasant districts are steadily increasing. The Nigerian Census mentions over 1,000 Koran schools in Niger Province, most of which are found in Nupe Emirate. I have estimated that Bida town possesses over 100 Koran schools, with over 1,000 pupils (out of a population of 24,000, with 5,000 male children). Kacha has fifteen Koran schools, Kutigi, a much more primitive and semi-pagan village, six, of which two already give higher instruction. This spreading of Mohammedan education leaves no doubt that parents increasingly desire their children to receive the benefits of Mohammedan learning. We have to accept this as a general trend in modern Nupe society, not so much towards true education—which few of the boys will ever attain—as towards the higher social status—the status of a leisured-class intelligentsia—which the position of a Mallam, rightly or wrongly, suggests.

Earlier in this book I have referred to the profession of Mallams as one of the mechanisms of social mobility. I have also called Mohammedan education, by means of which the religion and, indirectly, the whole spiritual background of the ruling classes is diffused throughout the country, one of the 'binding forces' of the Nupe state. Here we have found concrete evidence to support these statements. Let me summarize the main conclusions which we can draw from the present discussion. First, the profession of Mallams comprises contrasts of wealth and rank, which occur nowhere else in the framework of a single profession. The only common feature is that of a life without manual work, and of a certain social status raised above that of the ordinary commoner. Secondly, the Mallam profession is the only profession which we dis- covered in Nupe which is not ruled by the motive of material gains. On the contrary, people will sacrifice even the security of work on the land for the meagre and insecure income that goes with the rise in status and the attainment of the life of the leisured class.

AGE-GRADE ASSOCIATIONS

The Nupe name for age-grade association is *ena gbarúfuži*, lit. 'society' or 'association of the young men'.[2] Although nearly every Nupe boy or

---

[1] I had wondered whether there was any relation between the professional choice and the size of the family, whether perhaps in large families a son would be more likely to study for Mallam than in small families, where every member would be needed for farm-work. Then again, I thought it possible that in these days of the breaking-up of the family-unit orphans would be placed more readily in Mallam schools. Neither correlation, however, is true—as is shown in these figures: of 32 students of farming stock 9 were only sons, 10 were one of two sons, 9 had brothers who also studied the Koran, and 4 were orphans.

[2] Informants who have picked up a few words of pidgin-English translated *ena* as 'company'.

young man belongs to one or the other age-grade association, the age-grades are not a compulsory organization. No coercion is used to induce individuals to join the association, but failure to do so would be regarded as unusual, and under certain circumstances even suspicious. The constitution of the *ena gbarúfuži* is based essentially on the agreement of a group of individuals who, with clear knowledge of the purpose and the rules of the organization, form themselves into an age-grade association. Sociologically, then, our translation of *ena* as association is fully justified.

The description of the age-grade system of Nupe is complicated by the large number of variations that occur. There exist, above all, certain essential differences between the age-grade association in Bida and in the village; we shall, in fact, have to contrast the two throughout this discussion. The rules governing the internal organization of the age-grades are elastic: much more so in Bida than in the village. In the village association, too, minor differences occur, sometimes even between certain local associations in the same village. Thus, the age-factor itself is not rigidly defined, and the entrance age and age-limits of the different grades vary widely. Nor is the duration of the single age-grade fixed universally or permanently. In the village we find a more rigid arrangement: in Kutigi, for example, all age-grades last six years, in Jebba four years. In Bida the term of the age-grade association varies from four to ten years, and the duration may vary in different grades, in accordance with the wishes of the members.

In the village each grade is represented by one *ena* only, and age-grade associations ascend as a rule *en bloc* from grade to grade. Changes in the membership, so far as they occur, as the *ena* advances to higher grades, take the form of a slight decrease caused by death or emigration. In Bida each grade is represented by a number of associations, and prospective members have the choice of alternative associations. The rules of membership are more flexible in Bida. One may skip a grade—'rest', as the people say—one may start in a higher instead of the bottom grade, or one may leave the association before it advances to the highest grade, even before its term comes to an end. In two villages age-grade associations of which I examined the membership, which was 17 and 18 in the highest grade, had remained almost unchanged through the three grades of which the age-grade association is composed. In Bida there is much coming and going. In two *ena*, for example, the highest grade of which numbered 26 and 30 members, respectively, only 7 and 15, respectively, had gone through all three grades, 16 and 10 through two grades, and 3 and 5 had joined the highest grade without having passed through the lower grades.

The most common and, in the eyes of the people, normal type of age-grade association comprises three grades, which are numbered from the top downward: the senior grade is called First Grade, the middle grade, Second, and the junior grade, Third Grade or *ena dzakangíži*, Children's Grade. We shall deal, in what follows, with this most typical three-grade organization. The average age in the senior grade is 20 to 30, in the second 15 to 20, and in the junior grade 10 to 15. The age-limit for membership is about 30. It is interesting to note that the fact of marriage is of no significance—the highest grade comprises both married and unmarried men. The sign that a man is past the age of membership of 'young men societies' is the appearance of the external symptom of manhood, a beard—*za na de nŭkpayi na da ena be à*, 'a man who has a beard no longer joins the association'. In certain small communities the age-grade system may be limited to the two higher grades; in other communities a fourth, junior, grade is added, called *ena wawagĩži*, Association of the Small Children. This lowest grade is not taken seriously: it is regarded as mere *dzodzo*, play—of the children-playing-at-adults type—and shares with the other grades only their superficial external characteristics. The junior, third, grade is also in some measure regarded as less serious and significant than the higher grades, and as essentially a preparatory stage. Certain important activities of the higher grades are, as we shall see, of necessity excluded, or reduced to insignificant proportions, in associations which are composed of young boys. In one respect, however, the junior age-grade makes its own specific contribution to the age-grade system; it is the only one which has its counterpart also in the other sex. The highest age-grade, too, possesses certain specific features, in the form of certain age-grade ranks which are not bestowed on members of junior groups.

As *ena* membership is defined by age, and not by generation, it happens occasionally that, in large families, the young men of different generations but of approximately equal age belong to the same *ena*, and that young men of the same generation are members of different age-grade associations. The following genealogical diagram will illustrate a typical case. The letters S, M, and J indicate membership of the senior, middle, and junior age-grade, respectively; FH means family head, and a cross a deceased family member.

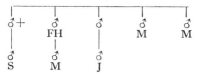

The separation from family and homelife is indeed one of the most characteristic features of the *ena gbarŭfuži*. The people attach considerable weight to the fact that the bonds and forms of obligation which are implied in the *ena* are of an entirely different, and specific, nature. Even small boys, the youngest members of the junior *ena*, will tell you with an air of importance that the *ena* has nothing to do with family, home, or parents. The father? 'Yes, we tell him, and we ask him sometimes to help out with money or food for a feast which we arrange. But he has no say in our *ena*.' Fathers will confirm this. In Kutigi parents were quite surprised, and laughed uproariously, when I told them about the titles which had just been distributed in a newly started junior grade; the boys had gone with the times and introduced titles which did not exist in the days of their fathers' *ena*. But for my information the parents would have remained unaware of these changes, which were regarded as a purely 'internal' matter of the age-grade association.

Let us now see how an age-grade association starts its life. We will begin with the Bida *ena*. Here the procedure is the same both in the foundation of a new *ena* and in its promotion to a higher grade. A number of boys or young men who have become well acquainted with one another in various walks of life, possibly when participating in a previous *ena*, decide to form themselves into an age-grade association. They meet in the house of one of them, a group of only six or seven members at first, and discuss how many more members they can muster. Each of the founders of the prospective *ena* then enlists other friends and acquaintances of the same age, till eventually the membership reaches the required number, twenty or twenty-five. The first thing now is to find a 'captain' and a 'president' for the new association, or, in native terminology, an *Etsu* and *Ndakotsu* (lit. Grandfather of the *Etsu*). The *Etsu* is a member of the age-group itself, as a rule one of the original founders, who is elected by the group.[1] The *Ndakotsu* must be of senior age: in the junior grades he will be a member of the next higher grade, and in the senior grade an adult who has 'passed', *go ga*, i.e. already gone through all the grades. Under their *Etsu* the members of the prospective *ena* approach a certain young man whom they regard as a suitable candidate, and request him to accept the position of president in the new association. Every member of the Nupe age-grades is assigned a certain rank which defines his place on the miniature social scale of the age-grade association for the duration of the *ena*. It is the first official duty of the newly elected *Ndakotsu* and *Etsu* to call a general meeting in the house of the *Ndakotsu* at which the distribution of these *ena* ranks is to take place. The elastic rules which govern duration and membership of the Bida *ena* imply also that no fixed rules can be laid down with regard to the time when associations usually start or 'change over' to higher grades. Moreover, in these associations in which only a small nucleus of members may remain faithful to the *ena* throughout its three grades long waits are likely to occur between the termination of one *ena* and the founding of a new association of a higher grade.

In the village the procedure governing the foundation and promotion of the *ena*, although the same in principle, differs in certain significant features from that obtaining in Bida. To begin with, the time when age-grade associations are started and promoted to higher grades is fixed permanently: it falls towards the end of the dry season, an arrangement which gives the new association time to be fairly launched when the agricultural season begins, and ready to undertake the tasks which, in a farming community, fall to the age-grade associations. The enrolment of members for the new *ena* is much less selective and arbitrary. In a small community where most boys of approximately the same age know each other, and normally meet in work or play, there is no need to canvass the new *ena* among friends and acquaintances. Nor is there any special search for captain and president of the new association. The village associations have, in fact, their *Ndakotsu* and *Etsu* appointed for

[1] Sometimes the captain of the second grade bears a different title, *Sokyara*.

them in advance. Shortly before the existing associations are dissolved previous to their reorganization on a higher grade, the outgoing presidents of the different grades appoint, as a last official act of their term of office, one of the members of their group as '*Ndakotsu*-elect' of the next junior group, i.e. the group which, in the new term, will take the place of the outgoing group. The *Ndakotsu*-elect will then take charge of the organization or reorganization of the new *ena*, and also of the appointment of a captain for the new association.

In these age-grade associations which rise *en bloc* to higher grades there is no gap between the termination of the old and the foundation of the new *ena*. The association which is about to be dissolved and promoted stages a last public appearance in a great feast, with music and dancing, to which all friends and relations are invited. A few days later the members of the *ena* meet again for the preliminary discussion in the house of the new *Ndakotsu*, for the distribution of the age-grade ranks which will be assigned to them in the new *ena*. When all ranks have been satisfactorily allotted the group arranges another large festivity, which is to announce publicly its reorganization and to inaugurate the new term. I had the good fortune to be in Kutigi in 1936, the year when the six years' term of the local *ena* came to an end and the general 'change-over' took place. It fell in the middle of March; the last public meeting of the old association was on the 7th of March, the session in the house of the *Ndakotsu* took place five days later, and the inaugurative meeting of the group in its new form as a senior grade on the 2nd of April.

Now, what are the qualifications for the position of a *Ndakotsu* and *Etsu*, and according to what principles are the *ena* ranks distributed? For the election of the *Ndakotsu* a well-established social position, good reputation, intelligence, and also a pleasant nature and, if possible, an open hand, are regarded as essential qualifications. A satisfactory financial position is essential because the *Ndakotsu* will be expected to entertain and to organize parties—and to do it in style. Most of these conditions also apply to the election of the group captain. The members of a newly founded Bida *ena* explained to me: 'We made Mohamadu our *Etsu* because he is a nice fellow. We all like him. He has good connexions; you see he is invited to the court; besides, he has plenty of money, and both his father and his mother are rich. He is also ready to spend it when we have a feast and want drummers and dancers.' On the other hand, a very ambitious young man who had been *Etsu* of an *ena* (of the second grade) and who hoped to be made *Etsu* again in a new, senior, association whose captain was resigning shortly, complained to me that his chances were slight, for he had not much money and could not afford the expenses which he would be expected to meet. It is implied in the nature of these qualifications that the *Etsu* is not always the oldest member in the group. In one *ena* which I analysed the *Etsu* was 20 when the *ena* started, and there were three members older than he. But as a rule he is of higher social position, and often better educated, than the rest of the members. Thus in a Bida *ena* which consisted almost entirely of tailors and embroiderers the captain was a weaver, the son of the Bida guild-head. In another group of a similar composition the captain was an expert cap-maker, who made the expensive, fashionable embroidered caps. And in a group the members of which came mostly from the classes of the nobility, the captain was the son of a late Emir. It has become the fashion for captains of Bida age-grade associations to adopt an additional, allegoric or symbolic, title, which would also give the *ena* its name. Bida associations compete with each other in the invention of high-sounding names, which should evince the refinement and selectness of the *ena*. Thus one *Etsu* was known as *Etsu Yimani*, 'King Faith', as the *ena* over which he presided prided itself of the piety of its members; another captain called himself *Etsu Hankuri*, 'King Forgiveness', for more or less the same reason; a third *Etsu Turu*, 'King of the Europeans', a title which was meant to bear witness to the fact that this *ena* was organized on 'European lines' (to be explained presently).

The financial qualifications and those of status are of less importance in the village, where inequality of wealth and status are much less strongly marked, although even in the village *ena* the captain may be of a somewhat higher social position than the rest of the members, e.g. the son or brother of a village elder of high rank. The symbolic names of age-grade associations are absent in the village, where age-grade associations are neither as numerous as in Bida nor as interested in advertising their refinement and selectness.

The allotment of ranks in a newly founded association of the youngest grade is largely a formality—although the popularity and influence of the young boys among their age-mates will to some extent be taken into account. We have seen that these junior age-grades are generally regarded as representing a preparatory stage rather than a fully fledged *ena*. In the higher grades the distribution of ranks becomes much more serious. Change of rank during the lifetime of the *ena* occurs only when a member dies or withdraws prematurely, especially if he was holding one of the higher *ena* ranks, which must be represented. But when the *ena* terminates and the members form themselves into a new group, a complete reshuffle takes place. As the different grades use largely the same rank-system this redistribution of ranks at the end of an *ena* makes conspicuous the promotion, non-promotion, or degradation—as the case may be. These changes in the holding of *ena* ranks reflect faithfully the success or failure of individual members in the previous association, the capability shown in the performance of group activities, and the popularity enjoyed among comrades and superiors. The eager competition notwithstanding, the task of distributing ranks justly and to everybody's satisfaction does not, as a rule, take very long. I have seen these discussions carried through in one or two afternoons. But then, the general discussion is only a last, formal, step. Mostly, the two leaders of the group have decided the distribution at least of the more important ranks long before the first general meeting. The *Ndakotsu* of a prospective village *ena*, for example, knew a few months before the group was actually called into being exactly whom he was going to invest with the three highest ranks. As a rule the authority of captain and president is sufficiently strong to carry the vote. But instances of disagreement and

long fruitless discussions also occur, both in town and village, and sometimes a compromise has to be effected by introducing a special title
(with the word *Tsowa* before any rank, equivalent to 'vice-' or 'sub-'),
which will satisfy a refractory member without upsetting the arrangement at large. Severe degradation, on the other hand, is rare, as it can
be easily circumvented in these associations which are not compulsory,
and cannot force members to accept their status. This is a typical instance: A very ambitious and vain young man of Bida who had held
high ranks in previous *ena*, but was given a very low rank in a senior
grade, resented this treatment as unjust; he could, however, do nothing
except to show his disdain by disinteresting himself in the association,
and staying away from all their meetings. Actually he never told me of
his shameful treatment when we discussed his association with the *ena*;
I learned of it only by chance when, examining a certain association, I
came across his name on the list of members.

The village *ena* comprises one rank which can be won only in strict
competition. We have spoken of this rank already (p. 250): it carries the
title *Sode*, and is bestowed on the best farmer of the group. Sometimes
there is also a second farmer's rank, won in the same way for which,
rather incongruously, the title *Maiyaki*, 'Minister of War', has been
chosen. These ranks are taken only in the highest and middle grade, and
are won in open competition at the first of the more important *egbe*
occasions of the season, frequently at the *egbe* performed on the farms
of the village chief. Traditionally, the title *Sode* ranked next to that of
group captain in importance and precedence. To-day it has been de-
graded to a lower place on the scale of ranks. Of course, neither the
title nor the particular qualification for which it is bestowed is recognized
in Bida. The rank of *Sode* is also the only rank that may change hands
(at least in theory) during the term of the *ena*. Although this happens
very rarely (I have not met with any actual instance), all people agree
that if at one of the occasions of collective farm-work an appointed *Sode*
proved himself to be inferior in skill to another member of the *ena*, he
would have to surrender his title.

Age-grade ranks are largely copied from the political rank-system
obtaining in the community to which the *ena* belongs. It is not a very
exact copy—although the *ena* tends to arrange its ranks according to the
order of precedence which they follow in the political hierarchy. In
Bida the distinctions between the different classes of political ranks are
not observed, and military and civil ranks, office titles and titles of the
royal nobility, are bestowed indiscriminately. The village *ena* remains
more faithful to the rank-system of the community, and would, for
example, adopt its typical, possibly uncommon, titles of elders. But as
the membership of the *ena*—especially of the junior grades—may be
considerably larger than the number of titled village elders, ranks from
outside the traditional rank-system may have to be introduced, prefer-
ably from the rank-system of the capital. The younger generation is
indeed always ready and eager to adopt such innovations. Rank-systems
of heterogeneous nature, and rather arbitrary precedence are the result.
However, we must not forget that the rank-systems of many villages ar

themselves similarly heterogeneous and arbitrary, including Bida titles among its traditional village ranks.

The system of precedence involved in *ena* ranks and grades is taken very seriously, and the rigid rules of etiquette which govern it are enacted with all solemnity. Much of the *ena* business takes place, as we shall see, within the single *ena*; but when members of different grades meet—for example, at family feasts in the house of a member, or at collective farm-work—submissive or condescending behaviour marks their relation towards each other. Members of a junior grade will never dance when members of senior grades are present, except with their special permission and at their request; in collective farm-work the junior grades work at the back of the team, at less important and less conspicuous tasks. Age-grade etiquette is even more emphatic within the individual association. At communal meals the 'subalterns' will wait till their superiors have eaten; at *ena* feasts subaltern and senior ranks will never dance at the same time; when greeting a superior, the age-grade member of lower rank will squat down and bend his head, exactly as prescribed for intercourse between superiors and inferiors in the social scale of 'real life'.

In the village *ena* it is only in general terms that the ranks indicate social position on the rank-scale of the association. In the town *ena* the ranks are sometimes chosen so as to indicate and do justice to the special gifts, or the special social position outside the *ena*, which characterize individual members. In this the organization of the town *ena* reflects the more highly differentiated social structure of urban society. Thus a Bida *ena*, composed largely of illiterate members, assigned to a young man who had been educated in the Government Middle School the title *Naïbi*, a rank of the Mohammedan clergy which can be held only by scholars. The rank-list of another *ena* included the rank *Boroti*, lit. Head of the Bororó, its holder being the son of the late Emir's 'regent-delegate' for the Bororó Fulani. Some Bida age-grade ranks indicate a certain official capacity held by a member in the *ena*. Thus I found a rank *Dzufã* (lit. pocket) bestowed on a young man who acted as 'purser' of the group. All purchases and payments for *ena* purposes were made through him; when, for example, a member decided to give a party for the group he would place his money contribution in the hands of the *Etsu*, who would then hand it over to the 'purser' as the member responsible for financial arrangements. In one *ena* I found the rather curious rank *Mataushe* (Hausa, lit. 'the man who rubs', i.e. 'masseur'), by which name a certain slave or body-servant of the Nupe king was known whose special duty it was to massage the feet of his master. In like manner it was the duty of this 'office holder' in the age-grade association to massage the feet of his *Etsu* at meetings of the group when his master felt tired.

One group of ranks typical of the Bida *ena* deserves special attention, namely the ranks which are organized on 'European lines' and copy, not ranks and offices of Nupe society, but ranks, offices, and even names of Europeans with whom the Nupe had come into contact. Such titles are often amusing and even puzzling. In one *ena* the head of the group was

not called *Etsu* but *Gomna Ture*, European Governor. Other ranks in
the same *ena* were *Kantoma* (Station Magistrate), *Joji* (District Officer),
Likita (Doctor); there was also the rank *Dupienne*, derived from the
name of Mr. Dupigny, a former Resident of Niger Province, a rank
Borti (Major Burton), *Mallam Smi* (Mr. Smith, a former Superintendent
of Education), and *Jamsi Dogo* (lit. Long James, a title which referred to
a former clerk in the Divisional Office); it was, not unnaturally, the
lowest title on the rank-list. Another *ena* organized on modern lines was
divided into two sections, a 'native' and a 'European' section, the former
consisting of Nupe titles, the latter of Europeanized names and ranks,
such as *Gomna, Joji, Likita, Rezdet* (Resident), *Kantoma, Misisi* (Mrs.),
Hafissa (Officer), and *Karamin Joji* (Assistant District Officer). In the
normal business of the *ena* these two sections behaved differently, and
were bound by different rules of etiquette, native and 'European', which
meant that the members of the 'European section' had to greet each
other in European fashion, by lifting their caps, and had to eat at a table
with fork and spoon. I could not help laughing when these rules were
explained to me; but the head of the group pointed out, rather indignantly, that this was the most natural thing in the world; after all, 'a
Governor does not eat with his hands'.

The seriousness with which these distinctions of ranks are observed,
the realism with which this playing at society *à la Européenne* is enacted,
forbids us to treat it merely as a childish and meaningless make-belief.
Psychologically, it has the significance of a substitute for thrills and
achievements which normal life cannot offer. The inclusion of titles and
forms of conduct copied from the British officials in the country is part
of that 'realism' which marks age-grade etiquette and precedence: it does
justice to the new political order of the society, and partly also to the fact
that high social position in present-day native society implies intimacy
with the Administration and high British officials. If it were asked why
the Bida *ena* chose as symbols for social gradation ranks and offices so
far removed from their ordinary life, I should point out that there is less
difference than one might assume between the two models which the *ena*
could choose—the model of European and the model of native society.
To the average Bida man the highest ranks and offices of his own society
are no less remote and inaccessible than the office of a District Officer or
Governor. We must add that the choice of a particular rank-system for
the *ena* is in no way determined by the social stratum from which it is
recruited. Bida age-grade associations of *tálaka* and *saraki* alike adopt
the highest ranks both of traditional and British society. Only for a small
minority—the few *ena* of the ruling class—may these ranks and offices,
and the whole exalted social life which they depict, one day become
reality. For the large majority they represent an infinitely remote,
imaginary social existence.

Here we are led to the wider problem of the relation between the world
of pretence built up in the age-grade association and the values of 'real',
that is, adult, social life. It can best be approached through a comparison
of village and town *ena*. In the village association the social life enacted in
the *ena*, and its prototype in adult life, stand in the relation of potentiality

and reality. The prototypes of *ena* ranks are all (at least theoretically) within the reach of the individual members. Every one of the young men who have gone through the *ena* may find when he reaches the suitable age that elimination by death or illness of senior relatives has singled him out for the position of a family head, and thus for a *nũsa* rank. Indeed, the promotion which accompanied his age-grade career will serve as an important qualification in the bestowal of the real rank by chiefs and elders. In certain respects all *ena* ranks of the senior grade retain their validity outside the *ena*, and after its expiry. The code of age-grade etiquette expires with the age-grade association. Not so the symbols of age-grade achievement: a man will be called by his rank rather than his name years after the *ena* has come to an end, often even for life—especially if he had held a very high rank. Men who have once been elected as *Etsu* or *Ndakotsu*, even when they are not, or not yet, appointed to a *nũsa* rank, will occupy a position of some distinction in their native village. Not only are they addressed and known by their *ena* titles, but village elders will pay attention to their opinion, and will entrust them with responsible tasks—in the organization of a ceremony, or of important collective work carried on outside the framework of the age-grade association. *Ena* ranks will never be confused with the political ranks of the village; they remain *tici nya ena*, ranks of the age-grade association. But although still only models of the 'real thing', they are 'real' in the sense that they indicate the varying qualification of individuals for access to the final social advancement. In the village *ena*, then, and similarly in the few age-grade associations in Bida which are recruited from the ruling classes, the *ena* rank-system anticipates a future social status; it introduces social concepts, and practises forms of conduct the effectiveness of which will be proved in adult life.

None of this is true of the average Bida association. Although here, again, the ranks attained in the senior grade accompany a man through life, they can claim no significance beyond that accorded to them by the rules of the game. A game indeed it is. These ranks let you enjoy fictitious contacts with a world of rank and power which you can never hope to enter in reality. Their upward trend, their incentive of competition, imply, not preparation or anticipation, but pretence, imitation—'substitution'.

Let us examine now the composition of the age-grade associations with regard to the social groups and strata which they absorb. In small villages a single age-grade association includes the youths of the whole village, and may even go beyond it, including the 'dependencies' of the village, the small *tunga* settlements, or linking a number of *tunga* settlements with one another. In the scattered hamlets round Bida the boys and young men of three to four hamlets join in a common *ena*. In very large villages (e.g. Kutigi) the age-grade is subdivided into a number of associations, each embracing one large, or two or three small, neighbouring, village *efu*. The age-grade itself, however, stretches across the whole village community, and the different associations conform to the same pattern with regard to the length of the term, and the time and year of the 'change-over' from grade to grade. In Bida the subdivision goes much farther, and we find a large number of disconnected associations, which are no longer co-ordinated or conform to a common pattern. I estimate the number of age-grade associations in Bida at 200. The individual *ena* is, again, bound up with locality, and includes boys and young men from the same part of the town. But here two new factors enter: social differentiation, and divided political allegiance. The very fact that the Bida *ena* finds its members among friends and close acquaintances already expresses the tendency to make it socially homogeneous, and to limit its membership to individuals from the same social stratum, or the same professional group. *Sarakiži* and *talakaži* never mix in the same *ena*. Nor do prosperous traders or Mallams join the same *ena* as peasants or small craftsmen; nor does, finally, the youth of the craft-guilds intermingle—glass-workers, blacksmiths, weavers, all have their separate age-grade associations. The limitation with regard to locality and close acquaintances is less rigid in the highest grades than in the junior grades. For as in the course of years the membership decreases, some members having died, others having left the *ena* or perhaps the town, it sometimes becomes necessary to open the membership of the higest grade to people from other parts of the town. Yet no *ena* would accept members from beyond the boundary of the town *ekpā*. The political solidarity of the three dynastic divisions of the town is thus reflected in, and even, as we shall see, actively supported by, the age-grade associations of the capital.

Here once more we gain insight into the social significance of the Nupe age-grade association: it underlines and fosters the solidarity of the existing social groupings. This means something different in the village and in the town. In the former it refers to the village community at large, and we find the age-grade associations stretching across it, and across the large kinship units and 'houses' into which the village society is divided. We can liken the age-grade system to a horizontal plane cutting across the separate structures of the extended families, with their wide base, tapering off to the apex of the one official representative of the family group, the titled elder. The age-grade association must thus counteract all possible separatist tendencies of individual kinship groups and sustain the large-scale integration on which the existence of the village as a social unit depends. In large villages this integrative scheme is in some measure narrowed down, owing to the size of the groups that can be absorbed effectively in a single age-grade association. It assumes, in fact, a somewhat different aspect, in uniting the extended kinship units within themselves—in the form of the large *efu* group—that is, in holding together the widely expanded structure which is to support the apex of a common official representative.

In the town the existing social grouping is created and held together by political and class interests. Here again, the age-grade association fosters the unity of a group which is to submit, in 'real' life, to a common head. But he no longer represents the 'apex' of an organically grown structure; as the *ena* is largely the product of a free, voluntary association, the group loyalty which it fosters is towards the freely chosen leader of a local political faction.

The integrative tendencies in the *ena* are expressed in every one of the typical age-grade activities. In the village they revolve round the three centres of social life: work, recreation, religion. In the Bida *ena* the first is reduced to insignificant dimensions; the second is raised to almost paramount importance; the third remains on the whole unchanged, being only transferred to a different plane—Mohammedan religion.

I have already spoken of the role which the *ena* plays in organizing collective farm-work in the village. We need only add that these activities concern the higher age-grades more than the junior groups, the members of which are not yet skilled farmers. It is commonly agreed that every young man who has gone through the three grades leaves the *ena* a fully trained farmer. Not everyone can become a *Sode*; but the success of the team counts for much. Here the *Ndakotsu* will prove his capability as organizer. He will put his pride into making his team the most efficient—all means being counted as fair. An old man, still known as *Ndakotsu*, told me how he used to help his group of workers to defeat all the other teams by means of a charm which 'made their hoes go twice as fast'.

Under recreational aims we must understand both recreation in the narrow sense—age-grade feasts and 'parties'—and the conventional festivities with which the Nupe celebrate kinship events: naming ceremonies, weddings, and funerals. The recreational activities in the narrow sense concern the individual association; in the celebration of kinship events to which all young men who are related to the family are invited, members of different grades frequently join. The *Ndakotsu*, *Etsu*, and also the members of higher rank are expected to entertain the group in their houses at fairly regular intervals. There will be food, drinks, kola-nuts, and often drummers and dancers. In Bida the members of the *ena* meet at least once a month at such parties. Smaller festivities are attended only by the *ena* members themselves; to the larger meetings, especially those which mark the beginning and end of the *ena* term, friends and relations of both sexes are also invited. At one of the festivities with which the inauguration of the new age-grade term was celebrated in Kutigi I counted well over a hundred guests.

Let me take you to such an age-grade feast in Bida. It is held in the courtyard of the house. It starts in the afternoon or evening and lasts far into the night. The guests sit and squat in a closely packed circle, leaving a small space in the centre for drummers and dancers. On one side the host is sitting together with *Etsu* and *Ndakotsu*; as a rule they only sit and watch the performance; but the guests are ready at every moment to exchange the role of spectators for that of performers. There exist special *ena gbarúfuži* dances, performed at these occasions: they consist of a slow, graceful forward-and-backward movement of a row of dancers, five or six young men, who dance side by side, the arms stretched out and the body bent slightly forward, setting their feet in small, measured, steps. Group follows group in the dancing arena. Individual dancers leap into the 'arena', and perform a short solo or *pas de deux* of leaps and cart-wheels which, when executed skilfully, will be greeted with applause or, when less successful, with good-natured laughter and banter. There are special drum-signals for every higher *ena* rank which are sounded when the young men take the scene and join in the dance. Rich age-grade associations, or certain high rank-holders in the association, even have special dances and songs composed for them, which are played, not only at these meetings of the *ena*, but also whenever the *ena* members appear elsewhere at a public gathering. Drummers and woman dancer would walk up to the young man, and the dancer would recite the song which she composed in his honour.

> Moonlight makes all things good to look at.
> The *maba* bids the townsfolk farewell for the night.
> Give us of thy knowledge,
> Ibrahim Ganleyi,
> Thou grandson of wealth.[1]

Drum-signals and songs are not the only symbols of age-grade status. At every such festivity one of the drummers or some self-appointed 'master of ceremonies' will assume the role of an announcer. He is called *maba*; announcer and jester in one, he must be witty and have the gift of the gab. He collects the small gifts of money which guests make to drummers and dancers; he announces the name and rank of the donor and recites the virtues of his ancestors and famous relations (impressiveness counting more than truthfulness), adding such praises or witticisms as seem appropriate to the rank of the donor and the amount of the gift. We see again how closely Bida age-grade etiquette follows its model—the Nupe nobility; it copies every detail of its symbols of status and wealth, even such features as the specific interpretation of dignity forbidding persons of high rank to join in the common dance.

It is easily understood that in the village, along with the model, the copy must be absent also. At the gatherings of the village *ena* professional dancers and musicians are rarely summoned. There is no *maba* and no extolling the feats and virtues of celebrated ancestors. Age-grades and age-grade ranks 'own' their special drum-signals and dances; but they are associated with the group, and not with certain individuals who can afford to pay for the distinction.

The religious events in which age-grade associations participate concern all grades. In the pagan ceremony especially the different grades are allotted different tasks, which imply in varying measure admission to the esoteric ritual activities. The main religious ceremony of pagan Nupe, the *gunnu*, makes the *ena* members the protagonists of its ritual drama and dances. Another ceremony, which occurs only in the Benu

---

[1] This song, which was composed by the *zaworo* group of dancers (see p. 302), in the honour of the young man called Ibrahim Ganleyi, was recorded at an age-grade feast in the house of a well-known Bida Mallam. It begins in the fashion of all Nupe songs with the quotation of a well-known proverb. The term *maba* which occurs in the second line is explained in the description that follows.

sub-tribe of Kutigi, Enagi, and Dabbã, the *gani* even dramatizes the age-grade structure itself, its system of ranks, and the promotion from grade to grade. The *gani* assigns different ceremonial duties to the different grades, and involves certain symbolic tests of manhood of progressive severity which the different age-grades, one after the other, must undergo. The ceremony can, in fact, be regarded as a ritual of age-grade initiation. However, I must leave the description of this ceremony, closely associated though it is with the conception of age-grades, for a future occasion.

Let us turn to the Mohammedan religious ceremonies. At the celebration of the *Sallah* the age-grade associations play a much less specific role. They arrange a small festivity in the house of their group captains on the eve of the *Sallah*, at which—as in all houses of Bida and Mohammedan Nupe on that evening—a ram is killed and eaten. On the following morning the various *ena* of the town meet in the market to join the thousands of people who will follow the royal procession to the mosque and round the town walls, and gather later in front of the Emir's house, listening to drummers and musicians, and watching the display of the horsemen and the coming and going of the royal guests.

The celebration of the Mohammedan New Year, on the other hand, called *navũ* in Nupe (lit. torches), represents the climax of the public appearances of the Bida *ena*. The *navũ* is essentially a festival of youth. Its ritual acts, which appear to express, symbolically, the death and renewal of the year, are carried out by the young folk of Bida. On the eve of the New Year, at sunset, all the age-grade associations meet in the houses of their captains, and then march to the market of their town quarter, where all the associations of the *ekpã* forgather. They carry burning torches of grass in their hands, and are clad in simple, scanty garments. Three long processions, one in each *ekpã*, move slowly through the streets of Bida, down to the arm of the river flowing through that part of the town. The boys sing and dance while they walk, and throw their torches high up in the air, catching them as they fall. Arrived at the river, they take off their garments, and, clad only in a loincloth, wade into the water. There is no atmosphere of ritual or ceremony about it; they splash and play in the water, dance, wrestle, sing, and laugh at the clumsiness of those who drop and extinguish their torches. All the time the torch-play goes on; they play with the torches like balls, throwing and catching them. It is a dangerous game: I saw many lucky escapes, and quite a few incidents not so lucky.

Girls and young women, too, go to the river to bathe on the *navũ*, and the sexual attraction adds its stimulus to the general excitement. The *navũ* is, in fact, the only occasion on which I have seen the Nupe indulge in open, undisguised, sexual play. Torches are thrown into the water to light up the spot where girls are bathing almost naked; boys accost girls in the water, and couples disappear in the dark of the river-banks. But the *navũ* is in more than one respect a period of licence. Indeed, more important than this amorous play is the licence which was extended till about fifteen years ago to all acts of violence and assault that might occur on *navũ* night. And such liberty of action was not

limited to acts of violence committed unwittingly, in the course of the
torch throwing and playful fighting. The torch processions invariably
led to serious organized fights between the three *ena* groups from the
three divisions of the town. On their way back from the river one
ena would ambush another, and try to invade its 'territory'. A fierce fight
would ensue, lasting the whole night, fought with torches, sticks, stones,
and even formerly (as my older informants maintained) with swords and
guns. Serious wounds and loss of eyesight were a common feature of these
'battles of youth', which were fought with all the violence of heated
party feuds. For party feuds they were—inspired by the political rivalry
that is embodied in the threefold dynastic division of the kingdom. Let
us reflect that the *navŭ* provides the only occasion at which all the
scattered age-grade groups of Bida are united in common action. The
unity which they achieve is typical of Bida society—a unity based on
partisanship and political factions. The acts of violence committed in
the *navŭ* fights led the Administration to intervene, and the fights were
forbidden under *Etsu* Bello. Yet the memory is still vividly alive.
Younger and older men who have once participated in a fight still
proudly recount their feats which helped their side to win. But even
young boys, novices at the *navŭ*, are aware of the traditional significance
of the ceremony. At the *navŭ* of 1936 schoolboys from the Middle
School had been encouraged by their teachers to send, for the first time,
an official contingent to the *navŭ* procession and to take their place
among the age-grade groups. The boys did not anticipate a 'proper'
navŭ; for, as they explained to the director of the school, if they were to
behave according to traditional standards, 'the *yan doka* (police) would
get nasty'.

Certain important activities and obligations embodied in the age-
grade association outlive the lifetime of the *ena* and accompany the individual through his whole adult life. The celebration of kinship events
with the co-operation of age-grade associations is a first instance. All
members of an *ena* are required to appear at the kinship feasts celebrated
in the house of one of the *ena* members, and this duty applies both to
comrades and ex-comrades. When a man celebrates the naming ceremony of a new-born child, or the wedding of himself or a close relative,
or when he buries his father or elder brother, he will expect all his old
comrades to come, to bring their congratulations or condolences, and to
join the family guests. The Nupe greatly appreciate kinship festivities
on an imposing scale, with a large—and generous—attendance. Age-
grade loyalty is thus enlisted to make the festivities a success and to add
to the prestige of the host. The readiness of the ex-members of an *ena* to
fulfil these social obligations towards an old comrade depends, however, on the rank which he had held in the *ena*, and on the popularity
which he enjoyed among his fellow members. If the age-grade association is thus designed to contribute to the social prestige of its ex-
members in adult life, this dependence on the goodwill of one's
comrades must, in anticipation, act as an important controlling influence
upon behaviour in the age-grade association itself.

There exists also a certain clearly formulated code of conduct which lays down the rules of behaviour for *ena* members, and which is again valid for life. These rules demand friendliness towards one another, and avoidance of all quarrels; mutual assistance in work (though not with regard to loans); respect towards one's superiors in the group; and respect also for the sanctity of marriage among all fellow members. The significance of this last rule, which applies to brides as well as wives, in age-grade associations the lifetime of which comprises the years when the adolescents first awake to the reality of sex, when they court and finally marry, need not be emphasized especially. Yet only in the village can the rule be regarded as tending to eliminate quarrels and feuds which must disrupt the community. In Bida it is in effect abetting matrimonial laxity outside the small group to which this code applies. The narrow political and class loyalty of the Bida *ena* has thus its counterpart in the no less narrow *esprit de corps* with its qualified respect for matrimonial rights.

In the case of a breach of the age-grade code the culprit is summoned before the *Etsu* and *Ndakotsu*, who have the right to punish him. A first, light offence may entail only a warning. Repeated offences will be punished more severely. If a young man shows himself lazy in *egbe* work or reluctant to fulfil the obligations of collective farm-work, it is regarded as sufficient punishment to order him to work in the back row, among the youngest and most inexperienced *ena* members. In the case of more serious offences the penalty may take the form of social ostracism: the *Etsu* and *Ndakotsu* would rule that no member of the *ena* must attend festivities in the house of the offender. This sentence, I was told, soon brings the culprit to heel; he will kneel down in front of the *Etsu* and ask him for forgiveness, protesting that he would henceforth mend his ways. In certain age-grade associations, especially in Bida, fines are inflicted in the case of graver offences against the *ena* code. Expulsion is never practised, not even as a penalty of the gravest of all age-grade offences—misconduct with the bride or wife of a comrade. However, my inquiries into the occurrence of this offence were invariably answered with a blunt denial. Whether or not it was founded on fact I have no means of deciding. Quite possibly the *esprit de corps* of the *ena* forbade admission of so shameful a charge. The rather too sweeping denial with which my questions were met makes it appear not unlikely: 'We are like brothers,' many of my informants said, 'who would steal a brother's wife?'

In one respect, at least, this statement is undoubtedly an exaggeration. Age-grade comrades are not 'like brothers'. The intimate relation between age-grade comrades which this simile suggests is not true to facts. The relationship existing between friends, on the other hand, is often likened to the relationship between brothers, and does in certain respects resemble it. But age-grade comradeship as all informants agreed, is sharply distinguished from friendship, and the mutual obligations of friendship in no way coincide with those implied in *ena* membership. The subject is worth pursuing.

A man (or woman) will never have more than one friend. The friend may come from a different locality, a different profession, even a different tribe. I have seen friendship between a Nupe and a Yoruba in Jebba, and between a Kutigi farmer and a *konú* weaver, between a Bida tailor and a peasant from Patigi. Only social class remains an effective barrier even in friendship. Unlike age-grade comrades, friends will help each other with money. Friends may also exchange their children, that is, adopt each other's children, and marry them to their own children—as is also done by men who stand to each other in the relationship of classificatory brothers. This practice has the aim, as the people say, 'to increase friendship'. The essential difference between age-grade fellowship and friendship is thus clear: if the former fashions sentiments of 'belonging together' on the basis of similarities in outlook and interest, i.e. similarities involved in common locality, tribal origin, common occupation, the latter unites individuals *qua* individuals, in a union which is essentially new, and initiates rather than follows existing bonds and sentiments.

It remains to discuss the *ena nyentsugìži*, the age-grade associations of the girls, and the relation between the parallel age-grades of the sexes. I have said already that the girl's *ena* is limited to the youngest age-grade. As explanation of this different organization among the girls the people argue there can be no senior grades among girls, since the approximate age limit of the junior grade, 15 to 16 years, coincides with marriageable age. Unlike boys, the girls can no longer carry on in the *ena* once they are betrothed or married; their duties towards husband and family cannot be reconciled with age-grade activities. This explanation is borne out by the characteristic relations that unite the parallel *ena* of boys and girls. They both take exactly the same titles; and a boy and a girl who bear the same title enter a special, close, relationship: the boy calls the girl *nna*, mother, and the girl the boy *nda*, father. Girls' and boys' groups meet at the various feasts which age-grade associations arrange. It is the duty of the girls to prepare food and beer, the money being contributed by the boys, and to serve it at the *ena* feast. The *Etsu* of the boy's *ena* presents the girls with kola-nuts. The girls will sing and dance, and the boys will watch, and then, in their turn, the boys will perform before the audience of the girls. They all behave with utmost dignity, and even severity: the *ena* is quite obviously not the place for flirts and amorous play of the kind one can observe between boys and girls who meet in the street or market. The symbolism of the names by which girls and boys address each other—names which are never used by lovers or by husband and wife—emphasizes the 'respectable', non-sexual, nature of this relationship, even to the extent of excluding any reference to legitimate sex relations— marriage. It is supposed to happen occasionally that boys and girls who were brought together in the *ena* marry afterwards. I have not come across an actual case. The relationship between them, while the *ena* lasts, is definitely meant to be in the nature of comradeship, and must never lead to sexual relations. Yet once the girl is married, it may be difficult to maintain this aloofness. The danger of jealousy on the part of the husband, and possibly the temptation of carrying comradeship with the other sex to a more intimate relationship, forbid a continuation of the girls' *ena*. So much for the interpretation of the *ena nyentsugīži* on the lines of the Nupe argument.

But if for women the age-grade career comes to an end with marriage, while for men marriage represents neither a limit nor even a conspicuous grade in the age-grade career, this reflects also the different sociological significance that marriage has for women and men. For women, it is the end of one life and the beginning of another. It means change of home and family bonds, and initiation into new aims and duties. For men, marriage—a first marriage—does not even coincide with the periodical readjustments in the labour-unit, i.e. the release from the *efakó* group which, as we have seen, takes place as a rule when a man has two wives or grown-up children. The social career of the men—achievement of economic independence, promotion to office, and responsible position in the community—only begins to fulfil itself long after their first marriage; that of the women is meant to enter its last phase in marriage. Indeed we have seen that when the woman claims the right of an independent, continued, social career, she must buy it with the sacrifice of the marriage union.

As regards the institution of the parallel age-grades its practical value seems to be that it prepares the ground for the first experiences of sex relations. Or rather, it aims at circumventing, and dulling, this unsettling first experience. Enabling the sexes to meet in the critical age, between 13 and 16, as it were on neutral ground, openly and respectably, it tends to remove some of the secrecy and unhealthy curiosity that is part of the mental transition from the self-contained existence of early youth to the new awareness of the polarity of sex. Our study of adult sex morality has left no doubt about the restricted effectiveness of this native 'co-educational' scheme. It must fail because it is, like all faulty education, in the nature of a palliative. It breaks the adolescent, we might say, gently, to the moral code of adulthood, but it adopts this code in all its dangerous narrowness and its rigid exclusion of amorous experiments and pre-marital sex relations. If age-grade discipline paves the way for adult sex morality, it does so also with respect to its repressions and inhibitions, and that final sweeping reaction against conventional morality which we could study in the adult life of the Nupe people.

To summarize. The age-grade associations include the adolescent male (and to lesser extent female) population of Nupe from early youth up to the threshold of adulthood. The most vital years in individual development are thus brought under the influence of this institution. We have studied the decisive part which it plays in moulding the personality of its members and in defining their attitude towards tasks and problems which they are to face in adult life. The essence of the institution of age-grades is, then, preparation—a twofold preparation. Its first aspect is the fashioning in the framework of the age-grades of sentiments of solidarity which are to bind the group at large.

This involves an important theoretical problem which has greatly engaged the attention of modern sociologists and social psychologists, namely, the possibility of transferring co-operation and solidarity

achieved in one context of social life to other social contexts.[1] Our data
allow us to make the following observation on this point: co-operation
and solidarity fashioned in the age-grades appear capable of being
transferred to other social contexts because of two conditions which they
satisfy. Co-operation and solidarity are not left to grow at random and,
as it were, unconsciously; rather they are of a specific, *ad hoc*, type; they
clearly formulate their purpose and operate in the sphere of distinct
awareness. Moreover, age-grade co-operation is actuated in circumstances of psychologically impressive nature, i.e. in the context of
religious experiences. But age-grade integration also admits its own
limitation in that it avoids attempting to bridge over the deepest existing
social gulfs, of local community and social class.

The second aspect of the preparation embodied in the age-grade
system is the training of the adolescent, through discipline and certain
concrete activities, in the tasks and duties which await him in adult life,
and in the values and incentives which he will have to make his own. In
the village this preparation represents a first step towards a final social
career; in Bida it mostly implants in the mind of the adolescent values
and incentives, as it were, *in abstracto*, without promising equally their
fulfilment in later life. It teaches people who will never share in direct-
ing the fate of their country to appreciate, and make their own, the
motives and values which govern the conduct of those who do. It im-
parts, if not claims to responsible citizenship, yet its spirit.

THE MEANING OF NUPE LIFE

If we compare Nupe religious teaching with the teaching implied in
the age-grade system we find that the two educational institutions supplement each other in many respects and that, between them, they take
in the whole field of 'education for citizenship'. The Mallam school
offers promotion to one social plane; the age-grade association practises
promotion in the framework of a complex scale of steps and grades. The
promotion afforded by religious education is 'real', in the sense that it
involves social privileges in adult life; that practised in the age-grades is
fictitious, even vicarious, and concerns mental readiness rather than
concrete achievements. Religious education, finally, creates a loosely
organized professional group and at the same time fosters a much wider
psychological unity, which embraces the whole of Nupe society, across
tribal and class boundaries. The age-grades create an intensive solidarity,
but only in a very narrow framework, and give tribal and class boundaries a wide berth. Common to both religious education and the age-
grades is the social upward trend, the motive of rise and promotion.
This upward trend appears indeed as the paramount motive in Nupe
cultural life. If it is possible to reduce a whole culture to a single
formula, to a fundamental unitary *ethos*, we find it in this *leitmotif* of

---

[1] Cf. F. C. Bartlett, in *The Study of Society*, 1939, p. 43: 'A specially interesting question is: if cooperation is established in one respect, when and how far
does this help individual members of the groups concerned to cooperate in
other respects?'

Nupe education. No aspect of culture affords closer access to the paramount cultural motives and values. For education not only teaches openly the specific aims and conceptions of life accepted by the society, but reveals them also indirectly, in the motives and conceptions which it utilizes to call forth the desired response.

Is, then, the reverse equally true? is behaviour that does not conform to this conception of life met with public disapproval? One might indeed ask if Nupe culture did not reserve some legitimate place within its framework for individuals to whom its dominant trend was uncongenial, and who represent what some anthropologists have called 'deviants' from the type of personality which the society regards as so highly desirable.[1] I must admit that I have found no conspicuous instances of such 'deviant' types. But we can guess the public response towards such social or cultural 'failures' from certain occasional incidents: for an attitude that belies the upward trend, and this dynamic aspect of self-advancement, is indeed regarded as a 'failure'; such individuals would be dismissed by the people with a mental shrug—'u de kokari à', 'he makes no effort'. As the Nupe state undertakes to govern the moral life of the people and to co-ordinate rigidly their conceptions of right and wrong, so its education attempts a complete unification of types of personality.

Yet successful suppression in normal life may only mean that the 'deviant' type is forced into abnormality and will reveal itself in psychopathological cases. I have admitted in the first chapter the scantiness of data concerning mental disorders among the Nupe. But so far as they exist they seem to bear out the view that mental disorders in Nupe are largely symptoms of the failure of individuals to adjust themselves to the demands of the social environment. I have mentioned that the large majority of psycho-pathological cases that came to my notice presented the clinical picture of paranoid schizophrenia, with marked delusions and persecution-mania. Now modern psychiatry has shown that schizophrenia is essentially the result of inadequacy to a social environment. Indeed, in the few cases which I could examine more closely features of the social environment conspicuously entered the clinical picture. One man was under the delusion that he had been persecuted by a person of very high rank and robbed, through his intrigues, of his home and family; another maintained that intrigues against him at the court had cost him his land; a third case was that of an old man who was under the delusion that his younger brother (whom he admitted to be the more clever and successful of the two) was out to kill him. In creating these very specific delusions the psycho-pathological individual escapes from the consciousness of his own inadequacy. Though distorted and purely negative, the fears and anxieties which make up the delusion are the same fears and anxieties that accompany the successful mental adjustment to the *ethos* of Nupe life—the anxiety to 'get on' in the world, not to be left behind in the race for rank and position, or the fear to lose the support of the 'powers that be', on whose influence one's career and safety depend. The border-line between normality and abnormality is that between

[1] Ruth Benedict, *Patterns of Culture*, and Margaret Mead, *Sex and Temperament*.

anxiety and unceasing efforts to master reality or, conversely, the open admission of inability to live up to the exigent standards of the social *ethos*, and that complete withdrawal from reality and surrender to subjective emotional and thought-life which we classify as pathological.

Have we, as sociologists, to leave off here, and to regard the *leitmotif* of Nupe culture as an ultimate, irreducible, fact—as would be the view of certain modern schools of anthropology—or can we hope to trace it farther, and to correlate it, as we could most cultural traits, with other, more fundamental, social facts?

Not having examined in this book the whole field of culture, we can only venture on a tentative answer. But I believe that such a correlation is possible. The upward trend in social life is entailed in the class structure of the Nupe state; in the existence of a social *élite* which must both renew and widen its ranks by admission of selected groups from outside its sphere, and build its strength on a population whose motives and ways of thought are in conformity with its own aims. The particular form which the upward trend takes, that complex social ladder of many steps and grades, is part of the 'admission of selected groups'; it is explained by the necessity of controlling and canalizing the upward trend, lest it should endanger the position of the ruling group itself. The *ethos* of Nupe society does thus not represent a unique, irrational, and, as it were, autonomous cultural trend, but the product of an interdependence of phenomena which is open to rational interpretation. Behind it we perceive the public approval of forms of behaviour which are essential to the integrity of the class-organized state.

In reducing the *ethos* of Nupe culture to necessities involved in the social structure we have not merely reduced one unknown quantity to another. The class-state built upon, and expanding by, conquest is not a unique phenomenon, but a typical and regular occurrence in the history of society which we have learned to correlate with specific environmental and historical happenings. These themselves fall outside our range of vision: the environmental factors which made the river Niger the hotbed of powerful military states; environmental changes which have most probably started the tribal movements resulting eventually in conquests and the formation of states with an alien ruling class; political developments in the north of Nigeria which resulted in the Fulani conquests of the central kingdoms; or the historical changes in civilization which gradually led up to greater political concentration and the evolution of centralized states. I do not mean to defend an absolute determinism of this kind. I will not deny that Nupe culture may have added specific features of its own to this general development; it may well be that certain autonomous psychological determinants, not entailed in these external conditions, have played an important part in moulding the structure of the Nupe state and the psychological traits and motives which it has made its own. I have worked out elsewhere the principle of 'alternative solutions' of which a cultural adjustment to environmental and historical demands may admit.[1] In these alternative solutions we

[1] 'The Typological Approach to Culture', *Character and Personality*, v, No. 4, The Duke University Press, 1937.

discover the effectiveness of such autonomous psychological tendencies.
The specific *ethos* of Nupe culture may indeed embody such an 'alternative solution'. But the extent to which this is true, the extent
to which the autonomous psychological forces limit or qualify the
effectiveness of historical and environmental factors (which we must
regard as sufficient to explain the evolution of the social structure as
such), can only be ascertained on the basis of comparative studies of
similar, class-organized, societies. This is, once more, outside the scope
of the present investigation.

APPENDIX I

BIBLIOGRAPHY

THE following list comprises the works of early travellers and writers on
Nigeria and Nupe, arranged in chronological order, some of whose data
were invaluable for the historical descriptions and reconstructions of this
book.

IBN BATUTA (1353), describing the various countries on the Niger
(which he knew as the Nile), mentions one called *Youfi* or *Noufi*, south of
Mouli (Muri?), as 'one of the most important countries of the Sudan', and
its 'sovereign as one of the greatest kings of the area'. 'No white man
[Arab?] enters *Youfi*, for the negroes there would kill him as soon as he
arrived.' These remarks have been interpreted by some authors as referring to Nupe, or Nouffie as it was called by certain early travellers. But
it is very doubtful whether this can be true. Ibn Batuta gives the same
name *Noufi* also to a certain tribe in East Africa, some 'six weeks' march'
from the sea. Moreover, *Leo Africanus* (1520) makes no mention of Nupe.

Commander CLAPPERTON, *Second Expedition into the Interior of Africa*,
1829.

RICHARD and JOHN LANDER, *Journal of an Expedition to explore the
Course and Termination of the Niger*, 1832.

MACGREGOR LAIRD and A. K. R. OLDFIELD, *Narrative of an Expedition
into the Interior of Africa*, 1837.

Rev. J. F. SCHOEN and SAMUEL CROWTHER, *Journals of an Expedition up
the Niger*, 1842.

HENRY BARTH, *Travels in North and Central Africa*, vols. ii and v,
1849–50.

A. C. G. HASTINGS, *The Voyage of the Dayspring*, 1857.

Dr. W. B. BAIKIE, R.N., *Notes on a Journey from Bida in Nupe to
Kano in Haussa*, 1862. Journal Royal Geographical Society, 1867.

A. F. MOCKLER-FERRYMAN, *Up the Niger*, 1892.

Canon C. G. ROBINSON, *Nigeria, our latest Protectorate*, 1900.

Lady LUGARD, *A Tropical Dependency*, 1906.

APPENDIX II
TRIBAL MARKS OF NUPE SUB-TRIBES

BENI sub-tribe:
  Traditional marks:

Modern marks
(i.e. Bida marks):   and

BENU sub-tribe:
  Traditional marks:

Modern marks:

'NUPE ZAM' of Kutigi:
  Traditional marks: and

Modern marks:

KUSOPA sub-tribe:
  Traditional marks:

Modern marks: identical with Bida marks.

DIBO sub-tribe: and

GBEDEGI sub-tribe:

KYEDYE sub-tribe:

EBAGI sub-tribe:
Traditional marks:

Modern marks: very mixed. Have adopted Bida and Kutigi marks.

BASSA NGE sub-tribe:
Traditional marks:

Modern marks: 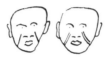 and also Bida marks.

KAKANDA tribe:
Modern marks: identical with Bida marks.

APPENDIX III

HISTORICAL CHART OF NUPE RULERS

A.D.
1463?   Birth of Tsoede.
1493   Tsoede taken as slave to Iddah.
1523   Tsoede's flight from Iddah.
1531   Tsoede established himself as king of Nupe in Nupeko.
1591   Tsoede's death.
1591–1600 *Etsu* Shaba.
1600–25 *Etsu* Zavunla.
1625–70 *Etsu* Jigba.
1670–9 *Etsu* Mamma Wari.
1679–1700 *Etsu* Abdu Waliyi, foundation of the capital Jima.
1700–9 *Etsu* Alyu.
1710–13 *Etsu* Ganamace or Saci.
1713–17 *Etsu* Ibrahim.
1717–21 *Etsu* Idirisu.
1721–42 *Etsu* Tsado.
1742–6 *Etsu* Abubakari Kolo.
1746–59 *Etsu* Jibiri, the first Mohammedan king of Nupe. He was driven from his kingdom after thirteen years' reign. Died in exile in Kutigi, where his grave can still be seen.
1759–67 *Etsu* Ma'azū's first reign. Power of Jima at its height. He resigned the throne and left Nupe to live in Yauri.
1767–77 *Etsu* Majiya I.

1777–8	*Etsu* Ilyasu. He is said to have disappeared suddenly.
1778–95	*Etsu* Ma'azū's second reign, after having been requested by the people to return to Nupe. Mallam Dendo (Manko), the Fulani emissary, appeared in Nupe.
1795	*Etsu* Alikolo Tankari. Reigned only for eight months, and was deposed by the people.
1795–6	*Etsu* Mamma. Foundation of the capital Rabá. Division of the kingdom.
1796–1805	*Etsu* Jimada, reigning at Jima. War with Majiya II. Jimada was killed in battle at Jengi (Ragada?).
1796–1810	*Etsu* Majiya II, reigning at Rabá.
1806	Majiya's war against the Fulani. Siege of Ilorin and defeat of Nupe armies.
1810?	The Fulani, supported by Idirisu, son of Jimada, conquered Rabá. Majiya fled to Zuguma. Idirisu (Yisa) installed as shadow-king of Nupe in Adama Lelu, near Eggã, by Fulani.
1810(13)–30	*Etsu* Idirisu (Yisa), reigning at Adama Lelu.
1830	Idirisu's rebellion against the Fulani. He was killed in the battle. Mallam Dendo recalled Majiya from his exile and made him shadow-king of Nupe in Zuguma.
1830–4	*Etsu* Majiya's second reign, in Zuguma.
1831	Death of Mallam Dendo.
1836	Rebellion and death of Tsado, Majiya's son. Usman Zaki, son of Mallam Dendo, was crowned first Fulani *Etsu* of Nupe.
1838	First rebellion of Masaba, Mallam Dendo's youngest son, against his brother. Established himself as rival king of Nupe in Lade.
1841	Masaba's second rebellion. Usman Zaki resigned the throne.
1847	Rebellion of the Hausa general Umar Bahaushe against his overlords. Masaba fled to Ilorin.
1850	Fall of Bida and defeat of Umar Bahaushe by Fulani armies under Umaru Majigi. Usman Zaki's second reign.

GENEALOGY OF THE FULANI EMIRS OF NUPE

Mallam Dendo ⟨ Adama, Fulani of Gwandu.
Fatima, Nupe of Dabbā.

Majigi	Abdu Gboya	USMAN ZAKI (1)	Mustafa	Ibrahim	Mamudu	MASABA (2)	
UMARU MAJIGI (3)		MALIKI (4)	Descendants held the ranks *Shaba* and *Kpotū* in this generation	Descendants held the rank *Makū* in this generation	Descendants held the ranks *Shaba* and *Kpotū* in this generation	Mamudu	ABUBAKARI (5)
MOHAMADU (6)		BELLO (7)	Descendants held no high ranks in this generation	Descendants held the rank *Makū* in this generation	Descendants held no high ranks in this generation	SAÏDU (8)	
NDAYAKO (9)							

EMIRS' names in capital letters. The numbers in brackets after their names indicate the order of succession.

APPENDIX V

NOTES ON THE NUPE CALENDAR

THE calendar of the Nupe peasant is an agricultural calendar. It is based on lunar months, and starts with the first rains, i.e. roughly in April. From the beginning of the rains the people count twelve, thirteen, and sometimes fourteen months until the new rains break. The last month of the old year (i.e. the 13th or 14th month) is then identified with the first month of the new year. The year is divided into six seasons, each comprising two months, as follows:

> *gbama* first rains
> *zuzūkd* rainy season
> *malikd* (cf. the Hausa *marka*)—heavy rains
> *sabakd* time of growth
> *gbāfere* cold season
> *banagū* hot season, or small-pox season.

Frequently, however, the Nupe peasant refers to the different months of the year by their number only, speaking of 'first month', or 'second month', and so on. The name *zuzūkd* is also used to denote the whole rainy season, and the whole dry season is called *yikére*, which means, literally, harvest.

This calendar is the pre-Islamic, original, Nupe calendar, which is rapidly going out of use, specially in Bida and the larger, semi-Mohammedan, villages, being superseded by a Nupe adaptation of the Mohammedan calendar. The latter, also operating with twelve lunar months, may coincide with the Nupe peasant calendar in the years when the Mohammedan New Year falls in the neighbourhood of April. But when the two do not coincide, and differ by a month or more, the time reckoning of the peasants in the semi-Mohammedan districts is thrown into serious confusion.[1] The Mohammedans, incidentally, unlike the pagan peasants, use the names of the months rather than the numbers. The Nupe-Mohammedan names of the months are as below. It will be seen that the idea of the original Nupe calendar, with its twin months grouped in six seasons, has been preserved in the new nomenclature:

1. *Etswa navŭ*—month of the torches (so called after the custom of throwing fire-brands during the celebration of the Mohammedan New Year).
2. *Etswa bawa gani*—month preceding the *gani* (a Nupe ceremony).
3. *Etswa gani*—month of the *gani*.
4. *Etswa togaya*—'twin month' (taken over from Hausa).
5. *Etswa togaya guba*—second twin month. These two months are believed to be unlucky, and no important events, such as a wedding or naming-ceremony, will be celebrated during them.
6. *Etswa bawa azŭ za gbakó*—month preceding the fast of the old men (i.e. first part of Ramadan).

[1] In June 1936, travelling from Kutigi to Jebba, I found that the Mohammedanized people of Kutigi were counting the second month, while the pagan Jebba Islanders maintained that it was the fourth.

7. *Etswa azŭ za gbakó*—month of the fast of the old men.
8. *Etswa bawa azŭ*—month preceding the (general) fast (i.e. Ramadan).
9. *Etswa azŭ*—month of the (general) fast.
10. *Etswa Salagí*—month of the small 'Sallah' (the first Mohammedan *Id* festival).
11. *Etswa bawa Salakó*—month preceding the great 'Sallah'.
12 *Etswa Salakó*—month of the great 'Sallah' (the second *Id* festival).

INDEX

Administration, British: and Bida town, 160; economic and political development under, 352, 368; and land-tenure, 192; and *Etsu* Mohamadu, 84; and Mohammedan law, 172; officials, 391; and village chiefs, 64; and ward-heads, 160.

— Native: vi, 52, 55, 58, 60, 64–5; and bride-price, 350, 353; and cotton-growing, 318; and crown-land, 182; and expenses, 162, 164; and mixed farming, 367; and *ndakó gboyá*, 142; officials, 52, 148, 157, 163–4, 175–8, 251, 356, 373, 391; Public Works Department, 43, 175, 268, 304, 326; and tax-revenue, 162, and the *Shaba*, 93–5; and women ranks, 148.

Administrative Officer, 357, and the courts, 174, 176; and village chiefs, 52, 64, 176.

Adultery, 56, 152, 154–5, 168.

Agaie, ix, and Bida, 89, 115; birth rate, 6; and Emir of Gwandu, 89, 115; Emirate of, 13, 79, 159, 189; *Etsu* of, 115, 152, 201–2; Mallam Baba and, 78–9; Masaba and, 82; population, 8, 11, 13.

Age-grade associations, 16, 37, 50, 248–51, 309, 360, 383–401.

Agricultural calendar, 213–16, 225, 252, 386, 411; — department, 238, 249, 367.

Agriculture: organization of labour, 241–56; production, 205–40; *see* Crops, Farming, Farm-land, Manure.

ajele, 115–16, 119.

Alkali, as *bara*, 125; at Court, 92, 129, 331; in court, 101, 117, 126–7, 166, 170, 172, 174–7, 191, 199; hereditary office, 99–102; office purchased, 98; his rank, 97, 124–5; *Etsu* Saidu and, 95; training, 171; and village chief, 57; *see also Liman*.

Ancestors, 32–3, 36, 44, 53, 66, 75, 130; *see also* Tsoede.

Anthropology, iii, vii, 72, 155, 335, 352, 403.

Apprenticeship, 257, 266, 272, 278, 282, 299–302, 349.

Arabic, 23, 59, 115, 132, 378–9.

Armies, private, 40, 105, 123.

Army, Nupe, 77, 80, 84, 98–9, 109–11, 130.

aro, 182, 191; *see also* 'Borrowing' of land.

asiri, 78; *see* Dendo, Magic.
Atta of Idah (Eda), 75.

Baboons and monkeys, 184, 222.

Badeggi, and Bida, 43, 81; District Head, 95, 159, 181; labourers, 308; motor road and, 81, 140, 178; population, 11; pottery, 296; and railway, 175, 178, 305; and tribal land, 185.

Baikie, W. B., 82.

bara, 123–7, 358–60, 371; and District Heads, 160; drummers, 302; and land, 204; and Shaba Usman, 120; ex-slaves, 155; soldiers, 105–7, 110, 112, 118, 196; *see also* Clientship.

Barber-doctors, 10, 42, 103, 298–301, 325, 349, 371–3.

Baro, 1, 43, 138, 175, 296, 334.

Barrenness, *see gunnu*.

Basa Kom, 16.

Bassa Nge, viii, 12–14, 82–3.

Bataci, 19, 22–5, 79, 109.

Bead-workers, 41, 103, 257, 282–5, 291, 373.

'Beating the ground', 140, 148, 255.

Bello, *Etsu*, 42, 84, 96, 147; and communal farm-work, 199; genealogy, 410; his motor car, 139–41; and *ndakó gboyá*, 90; sold titles, 98, 108.

Beni, and Bida, 25, 40, 44, 78, 84, 109, 114, 116, 135, 139; blacksmiths, 259, 264–8; confederacy, 25–6, 69, 73, 82, 119, 121; country, 21–2, 37, 181, 205, 212–13; core of the Nupe kingdom, 76, 115, 159, 192, 259; and eggs, 204; emigrants from, 21; and private fiefs, 113–14; and the number four, 47; and Gbari, 21; land, 89, 212; *Etsu* Masaba and, 118–19; as a royal domain, 115–16, 119; sub-tribe, 19, 22–4, 65, 407; tribal marks, 407; 'town-king' of Bida, 25, 44, 111, 135, 139; and Tsoede, 74; villages, 21, 39, 53, 116; and war, 104.

Benin, 74–5.

Benu sub-tribe, 19, 20, 23, 63, 83, 100, 108, 189, 407.

Benue river, 12.

Bicycles, 292, 326.

Bida, birth rate in, 6; dispensaries in, 5; Division, 5, 11, 83, 158, 170, 204, 238; dynastic divisions in (*ekpā*), 43, 89, 100, 102, 119–21, 126, 160–2, 201, 259, 269, 278, 283, 299, 393; Emirate, 4, 8–13, 40, 52, 59, 92,

Gana-Gana, 10, 19.
gani, 20, 23, 396.
Gara, 16, 40, 73.
Gbagede, 76, 83, 85.
Gbajibo, 79, 149, 322.
Gbako river, xii, 181, 211.
Gbanga, 11, 36, 81, 96, 159, 319.
Gbara, 20, 74-7, 259, 274, 319.
Gbari, viii, ix; and cattle, 202; and *gunnu* cult, 16; and indigo, 235; and Lemu, 71; and Masaba, 80, 82; as 'Outside People', 115.
'Gbari Slaves', 21-2, 70, 76, 85.
Gbedegi, and fishing, 242; and Kusopa, 109; and Kyedye, 24; language, 23; and *mamma* cult, 23; Masaba and, 82; pagans, 25; sub-tribe, 19; tribal marks, 407.
Gbira, 13, 82-3, 115.
Gebba, 44, 51, 65.
Gifts, 60, 61, 129, 163, 190. *See also* Kola-nuts.
gitsúzi, 93-7, 113, 147, 158. *See also* Nobility, Royal Nobility.
Glass-making, 1, 43, 102-3, 140, 240, 257-8, 274-8, 291, 296.
Gold-washing, 308.
Government, British, *see* Administration.
Gowns, 62, 67, 91-2, 116; embroidered, 61, 120, 287-8, 379. *See also* Sandals, Turban.
Grave-digging, Master of, 46.
Group-behaviour, 132; -consciousness, 131, 150.
Guild-head, of beadworkers, 284-5; of blacksmiths, 261, 264, 266, 293; of brokers, 102, 330; of carpenters, 356; and *dashi*, 301, 371; of glassworkers, 278; and the king, 92, 294; as rank-holders, 102, 294; and taxation, 163; of traders, 92; of weavers, 279, 282, 293.
gunnu cult, 5, 16, 23-5, 39, 45, 54, 63, 141, 154, 298, 354, 376, 395.
Gwandu, 77, 80-1, 89, 91, 109, 115.

Hausa, ix; customs adopted from, 132; mports from, 2-3; ranks and titles, 99; as settlers, 40, 43; traders, 275, 283-4, 328, 354; words and expressions, 2, 23, 59, 71-2, 97, 106, 125-6, 132, 140-1, 147, 160, 181, 229, 233, 235, 248, 251, 329, 349, 371, 378, 380, 390.
Hereditary succession: Alkali, 99; chieftainship, 51-6; Mallams, 381; nobility, 98; in priestly ranks, 47, 99, 381; in lowest professional ranks, 47; rank-system, 55; titles, 101, 108.

Homosexuality, 152.
Horses, as booty, 99; breeding, 311; census of, 204; Hausa traders and, 320; markets, 42, 120; in Rabá, 85; as royal presents, 91, 204; as symbols of rank, 61, 128, 130, 143, 202, 204, 359; Tsoede's, 74.
Horse-trappings, 270, 273.
Hospitality, 13, 56, 329, 358-60, 364.
Hospitals, 4, 5, 7, 43, 163.
House-building, repair of, 348.
Human sacrifices, 90, 232.
Hunting, 14, 46-7, 56, 59, 180, 247, 341.
Husband and wife. *See* Marriage.

Ibadan, ix, 10, 11, 16, 320-2, 330, 334.
Idah, 73-5, 320.
Idirisu, 78-80, 83.
Ilorin, ix, and Mallam Dendo, 78-9; Emir of, 13, 83, 113, 164; Koran teachers from Bida in, 379; *Etsu* Majiya and, 78-9; and Masaba, 81; and population movement, 10-11; taxes, 10-11; trade-routes and, 319, 322.
Immigration, 34-6, 75-84.
Incest, 165.
Income, of chiefs and elders, 60-2; *Etsu*, 90-1, 142; of family head, 281; group, 258, 277, 340-2; individual, 241, 245; women's, 253.
Income-tax, 164.
Indigo, 2, 188, 200, 228, 235-6. *See also* Dyeing.
Indirect Rule, vi, 157, 164.
Inheritance, 169, 171-3, 181, 187, 245.
Intermarriage, 24, 63, 71, 136, 266, 325, 375.
Investiture, 94.
Iron-ore workers, 2, 200, 240, 257, 260-7, 291-3.
Irrigation, 3, 208-10, 213-14.
Islam. *See* Mohammedanism.

Japanese manufactures, 273, 281.
Jebba Island, ix; and age-grade associations, 384; and agriculture, 210, 252, 322; and Chain of Tsoede, 49, 73; chieftainship in, 51, 65; and fishing, 22, 24-5, 56, 321-2; Kyedye and, 24-5; and Nupe calendar, 411; *nūsa* ranks, 48, 51; pottery, 296; and the railway, 175, 320; and sacrifices, 25; trade-routes and, 319-20; wage-labour in, 251.
Jibiri, 76.
Jima, 81; once the capital, 36, 76, 274; its population, 11; present *Etsu* former District Head of, 159; and Umaru Majigi, 198, 200.
Jimada, 77-8.